ORIGINS OF NEW MEXICO FAMILIES

ORIGINS OF NEW MEXICO FAMILIES

A Genealogy of the Spanish Colonial Period

Revised Edition
by Fray Angélico Chávez

New Foreword by Thomas E. Chávez

Museum of New Mexico Press, Santa Fe

Revised edition copyright © 1992 Museum of New Mexico Press. *All rights reserved.* No part of this book may be reproduced in any form or by any means without the expressed written consent of the publishers. Protected under international and pan-American copyright conventions.

The Museum of New Mexico Press is a unit of the state of New Mexico's Office of Cultural Affairs.

New material herein constitutes a Revised Edition of the original 1954 book entitled *Origins of New Mexico Families,* reissued in facsimile edition in 1975 under the imprint of William Gannon, Publisher, Santa Fe, New Mexico.

Cover design by Linda Seals
Cover calligraphy by Mary Lou Cook
Illustrations by José Cisneros
Manufactured in the United States of America
10 9 8

LIBRARY OF CONGRESS CATALOGING-IN-PUBLICATION DATA

Chávez, Angélico, 1910–
    Origins of New Mexico families : a genealogy of the Spanish colonial period / by Angélico Chávez. — Rev. ed. with a new foreword / by Thomas E. Chávez.
      p. cm.
    Rev. ed. of: Origins of New Mexico families in the Spanish colonial period.
    Includes bibliographical references (p.).
    ISBN 0–89013–239–9
    1. Hispanic Americans—New Mexico—Genealogy. 2. Spaniards—New Mexico—Genealogy. 3. Mexican Americans—New Mexico—Genealogy. 4. New Mexico—Genealogy. I. Chávez, Angélico, 1910– Origins of New Mexico families in the Spanish colonial period. II. Title.
F805.S75C47 1992
929´.3789´08968—dc20
                                                                                  92–29024
                                                                                       CIP

Museum of New Mexico Press
P.O. Box 2087
Santa Fe, NM 87504–2087

To My True Father
SAINT FRANCIS OF ASSISI

Failing to find a Maecenas or a Lord Chesterfield to finance this venture, even among those who ought to care, I dedicate it to thee, so lacking in funds, like myself.

CONTENTS

Foreword to Revised Edition	ix
Introduction	xiii
Oñate Entrada by *José Cisneros*	xxii

PART ONE: THE SEVENTEENTH CENTURY

Families Alphabetically: *Abendaño* to *Zamorano*	1–114
Demonstration Chart (*Chávez*)	18
Page from Inquisition Records, 1626	67
Demonstration Chart (*Robledo-Romero*)	96

PART TWO: THE EIGHTEENTH CENTURY

Vargas Entrada by *José Cisneros*	116
Families Alphabetically: *Abeyta* to *Zamora*	119–314
Page from Matrimonial Investigation, 1716	130
Demonstration Charts I and II (*Baca*)	142–143
Page from Santa Fe Marriage Register, 1734	210
Page from Spanish Archives of New Mexico, 1712	237
Demonstration Chart (*Españoles-Mexicanos*)	248
Demonstration Chart (*French and North-South Spanish*)	274

APPENDIX

Additional Family Couples in Charts and Other Persons	315
Demonstration Chart (*Ortiz Clerical*)	330

ADDENDA TO ORIGINAL 1954 EDITION

Families Alphabetically: *Abeyta* to *Zárate*	339
New Names in New Mexico, 1820–1850	403
Families Alphabetically: *Abilucia* to *Zepeda*	404
Bibliography	439

FOREWORD TO REVISED EDITION

EVERYONE SUSPECTED, some even claimed to know, that they were descended from the first Spanish settlers. They were the stock of founders, perhaps of one of the famous governors. No thought was given to any basis in fact nor speculation as to how this could be. Between the first Hispanic settlement in New Mexico, in 1598, and the genealogy of New Mexico's original families, published originally in 1954, almost four centuries had passed with some thirteen generations intervening, yet the steps from the sixteenth century almost to the present were made, we discover, with regularity.

Significantly, from Juan de Oñate's initial settlement in 1598, through the Pueblo Revolt (from 1680 into 1693), to the eighteenth century and the chaotic events of the nineteenth century, little attention had been paid to the details of familial relationships, that is until Fray Angélico Chávez assumed the monumental task whose results are now before you. The question of which members of the original families had returned after the exodus of the revolt embodied the obvious realization that only descendants from those returning families could lay claim to any connection with New Mexico's original Spanish people. As time passed, population increased and new generations of immigrants moved from the south into New Mexico. Who were these new people, and how quickly did they mix into the already-existent families?

In some respects, the interrelationships of these generations of people settling in New Mexico, among themselves as well as with the indigenous populations, is a story that could only be extracted through piecing together genealogical relationships. Such relationships become human only when details about the person become known. Together, these fleshed-out individuals and the genealogy they spring from go a long way toward illuminating the historical picture. En route, the scholar invariably is led to some unexpected surprises.

New Mexico is fortunate that the Catholic church has retained records from the first Spanish settlements. These records include nuptial investigations and testimonies (*diligencias matrimoniales*) and baptismal, burial, and marriage books and records. While poor care, deterioration, loss, and theft over the years have left the records incomplete, enough documentation has survived to form, when combined with evidence available in other collections, a fairly clear picture.

Genealogical research requires a special kind of person with a particular aptitude and talent. Obviously, for New Mexico, a command of seventeenth- and eighteenth-century Spanish as well as a comprehension of the ecclesiastical resources are integral requirements for such research. Once gathered, the information must be meticulously organized.

New Mexico's native son, Fray Angélico Chávez, was perfectly fitted to construct such an historical/genealogical tome of New Mexico's Hispanic families. While working on other projects, he noted and compiled the interrelations of individuals and families, the sum of which became, upon its 1954 publication, a landmark in New Mexican historiography.

The first edition, and its subsequent facsimile reissue (1975) of *Origins of New Mexico Families,* is limited to the seventeenth- and eighteenth-century period that Fray Angélico was studying in the early 1950s. After the release of his genealogy, however, he continued to delve into the archives, publishing additional findings between 1956 and 1957 in *El Palacio,* the magazine of the Museum of New Mexico. This later research extended the book's range into the nineteenth century.

Unfortunately, subsequent reissues of this seminal book did not include the additional information. So, as the book continued to sell out, readers had to look elsewhere for the nineteenth-century story. They had to go to libraries or find a copy of the particular issue of the magazine. Some individuals are known to have photocopied the articles, which they stuffed in back of the book.

With the Museum of New Mexico Press's publication of this long-awaited Revised Edition, the readership for this always-popular work will be rewarded with a record that faithfully follows New Mexico's families into the nineteenth century, from where the final chapter can be gleaned in current parish records and living memory.

This new edition should enjoy the fine reception of its forebear. There is no reason to think otherwise, for the book is timeless, the research solid, and the information invaluable. Here is a story of a people who survived not to the tune of blaring trumpets, triumphant parades, and grandiose banners but through the daily toil necessary for survival. *Origins of New Mexico Families* will continue to reach out to people who heretofore have had little interest in history or cultural heritage. They will spot their own surname, or learn of a friend's ancestor, or notice some common threads that will enliven what they see and know of New Mexico's modern world—and want to learn more.

Thomas E. Chávez,
The Palace of the Governors,
Museum of New Mexico

INTRODUCTION

THIS WORK is a sort of by-product. While going through countless old manuscripts for data on the Franciscan Missions of New Mexico, more particularly in an effort to further clarify the history of the venerable statue of La Conquistadora in Santa Fe, I began collecting bits of information on people appearing in these ancient documents. After several years of digging, Mission facts were still relatively scanty, while notes on the lay pioneers had piled up considerably. It was like the case of a miner who sifted a hill of ore for gold, setting aside any silver he encountered; in the end the silver far outweighed the gold. The only thing to do was to render the silver useful.

After much cross-filing and comparing, and some additional research, the present work took shape. As I had hoped, it aided me greatly in reconstructing the beautiful story of La Conquistadora in intimate detail. But, to my surprise, it also turned out to be a comprehensive, if incomplete, record of the original Spanish families of New Mexico. The full stories behind each name and note, too lengthy to include here, have furnished me with a knowledge of Spanish times that could not have been acquired in any other way. This knowledge will serve me in good stead in various fields of endeavor.

This printed compilation will also prove useful to others, I am sure, who are working in any field of research having to do with the first two centuries of New Mexico's existence as a Spanish colony. New Mexicans interested in their remote forebears will find it intriguing as well as revealing. If I restricted myself to this particular period, it was because my original project on the Missions covered the same time and territory. It might as well be also emphasized here that this survey is possible because, in these first two centuries, the population was a homogeneous whole and relatively small, due to the region's almost complete isolation during all that time.

(The story changes in the Nineteenth and Twentieth Centuries. Even before the American Occupation of 1846, there was a great influx of French-Canadians and Anglo-Americans who married New Mexico women. After 1846, besides Americans from the "States," there were also Englishmen, Irishmen, Scots—Danes, Germans, and Jews, too. When Fort Marcy and Fort Union were in their heyday, such intermarrying was more pronounced, and to a degree not generally known or realized. The result was not merely an addition of non-Spanish names and the infusion of non-Latin blood in the roster of New Mexico families, for a goodly number of these outsiders later took their half-Spanish families to the Pacific coast, while many went "back East," so that even then "Coronado's Children"—or better still, "Oñate's Orphans" — began contributing substantially to the American melting-pot. What two major wars have done in this present century is beyond imagining.)

The Two Colonizations

The Spanish Franciscan Missions and the Spanish Colony of New Mexico began together with the OÑATE CONQUEST, or the arrival of his colony in 1598. Both the Mission and the Colony suffered defeat and exile in the Pueblo Revolt of 1680, and both returned as one in a second act of colonization and conquest in 1693, the VARGAS RECONQUEST. Since the surviving refugee colonists of the Oñate period were greatly augmented by new colonists brought by Vargas, the Reconquest of 1693 was really a new and distinct colonization of New Mexico. Hence the major division made here of New Mexico Families into the Seventeenth and the Eighteenth Centuries.

While the pioneer Oñate colonists actually were sixteenth-century people, their activities in New Mexico, and those of their children and grandchildren, covered practically all of the Seventeenth Century, from 1598 to 1693. Likewise, the remnants of these people who returned with Vargas, as also his new colonists, were seventeenth-century folk who, with their descendants, made civil and church history in New Mexico throughout the Eighteenth Century, and two decades of the Nineteenth, until the end of Spanish Rule in 1821.

Families of the Seventeenth Century, 1598-1693
The Oñate Conquest

Don Juan de Oñate, first colonizer of New Mexico, arrived at San Juan de los Caballeros in the summer of 1598 with about a hundred and thirty Spanish soldiers, many of these with their families, as well as some Indian servants from New Spain. About eighty additional soldiers arrived in 1600, some of these with their families. However, mutinies, battle casualties, and a major desertion from the colony, reduced the number of original pioneers considerably. Of more than two hundred names found in the Oñate lists, less than forty established themselves permanently in the new land.

From 1610 to 1680 other officers and soldiers came, singly or in very small groups, and these married the daughters and grand-daughters of the first colonists. In 1677, three years before the Rebellion, the Viceroy sent up fifty convicts to serve as soldiers for some years; of these fifty, not more than two remained to found a family.

Geographically, the "Kingdom of New Mexico" reached from Taos Pueblo down the Rio del Norte to Guadalupe del Paso (now Ciudad Juárez). Outside the Rio del Norte Valley, the Missions as far west as the Moqui (Hopi) Pueblos were considered part of the Kingdom; in the same way, those east of the valley at Picuris, Pecos, the Galisteo Basin, and the Tigua and Piros Pueblos east of the Manzano range. There was only one Spanish town, Santa Fe. The rest of the settlers lived in what they then called "estancias" up and down the river from Taos to Socorro. Some families resided at short-lived Tajique east of the Manzanos, while others, at least that of the "Alcalde Mayor" of a Pueblo, lived near the Pueblos west of the valley. Guadalupe del Paso also belonged to the

Kingdom; it was founded as one of the New Mexico Missions, its first white settlers and officials were New Mexicans, and its inhabitants considered themselves natives of New Mexico throughout this early period.

In 1680 the northern Pueblos banded together in one big effort to drive out the Spaniards, killing a score of missionaries and some families, and taking some women and children captive. The rest of the colony fled south to the region around Guadalupe del Paso, where they founded the towns of El Real de San Lorenzo, Ysleta, Senecú, Socorro, and others. Here they stayed for thirteen years, during which time ineffectual attempts were made to reconquer the Kingdom. During this exile, too, some of the best and most numerous families abandoned their fellow-refugees and went south into New Spain.

Families of the Eighteenth Century, 1693-1821
The Vargas Reconquest

Don Diego de Vargas, second colonizer of New Mexico, was appointed to lead the refugee colonists back to their homeland. In 1692 he made his first "Entrada" into New Mexico, in which he peacefully received the submission of the Pueblos, now weakened by wars among themselves. But he had already noted that the original New Mexicans, considerably reduced by the 1680 massacre and by the subsequent desertion of families that left for New Spain, were too few for an effective attempt at re-colonization. So he recruited soldiers in Spain and New Spain, as well as civilian colonists with their families in the Valley of Mexico and the country around Zacatecas. Hence his Reconquest colony consisted of various distinct groups.

1. **The Native New Mexicans.** Here were the faithful Archuletas, Bacas, Chávez, Luceros, Montoyas, etc., whose families had increased during the thirteen-year exile at Guadalupe del Paso.

2. **The Soldiers from Spain.** How many of Vargas' "hundred gentlemen soldiers from Spain" actually came is not known, but only a few remained to found families, like Páez Hurtado, Fernández de la Pedrera, Roybal, and others.

3. **The "Españoles Mexicanos."** The Viceroy himself had selected these "sixty-seven" Spanish families living in the City and Valley of Mexico. They were assembled by Cristóbal de Velasco, but came under the supervision of Fray Francisco Farfán, their number decreasing somewhat during the long journey.

Here came the names of Aragón, Medina, Ortiz, Quintana, and many others. While some individuals seem to have hurried up to join the expedition as soldiers for the Reconquest in December, 1693, the bulk of these people did not arrive in Santa Fe until June, 1694.

4. **The Families from Zacatecas.** These people were recruited at Zacatecas and the Mines of Sombrerete by Juan Páez Hurtado. There is no known list of them extant, so that families belonging to this group are known from references in scattered sources. Here came such names as Armijo, Vigil, Vargas, etc. These people did not arrive in Santa Fe until May, 1695.

5. **New Mexicans of Guadalupe del Paso.** Some people who had lived, or were even born, at Guadalupe del Paso, and considered themselves New Mexicans, decided to move north, like the Padillas and Pereas. Similarly, several northern New Mexicans were allowed to remain in the new settlements they had founded in 1680, where their descendants are found to this day. By this time, however, the Crown had decided that this southern district did not belong to the Kingdom of New Mexico, but to the Province of Nueva Vizcaya.

Geographically, the Kingdom was smaller in extent than before the Rebellion. For Guadalupe del Paso had been separated, the Moqui Missions were not re-founded, the Manzano or Salinas district lay uninhabited, as also the area around Socorro. However, new settlements sprang up along the Rio del Norte from Taos Valley down to Tomé. Two new "Villas," besides Santa Fe, were Santa Cruz de la Cañada and Alburquerque. On the sites of former "estancias" the increasing number of settlers formed into hamlets on either side of the river. In the second half of the century, people ventured away from the main valley, as at Abiquiu and Ojo Caliente, then Santa Barbara, Truchas, and Trampas on the mountains northeast of Santa Cruz; there were also some small outposts in the Jémez and Cabezón area. It was not until shortly after the turn of the century that settlers ventured further south to Socorro, or west to the Cebolleta country; to the east, some families went to live at San Miguel del Vado when a military outpost was established there. Otherwise, people had stuck close to the Rio del Norte because the roving tribes of Indians had made life precarious away from it; in fact, raids by them into the valley settlements were severe and frequent.

New settlers came sporadically between 1700 and 1800, bachelors who married local women and left many descendants. There were two Frenchmen already in Vargas' time, Archevéque and Grolet, and two others who came later,

Alaríe and Labadíe. Other newcomers were officers and soldiers sent to the Santa Fe Presidio who decided to stay permanently, like Delgado, de la O, Miera, and Villanueva. Some others were merchants travelling between Mexico City, Chihuahua, and the "Kingdom," like Pino, Clemente Gutiérrez, and Durán Bachicha. Still others were nephews or brothers of the missionaries, like Gabaldón, Mariño, and Sánchez Vergara. Occasionally, descendants of old New Mexicans who had stayed at Guadalupe del Paso in 1693, like Telles, Bernal, and Tapia, returned to their ancestors' land of birth. New blood was also introduced, though rarely, when some New Mexican returned from a business trip in Mexico City with a bride.

A mixture of all these closely inter-related people, hemmed inside a short stretch of the Rio del Norte Valley for more than two centuries, was what made up the Spanish population in 1821, when New Spain broke away from the Crown and became the Republic of Mexico, automatically including the ancient Kingdom of New Mexico within its borders. It was the same population found by the American Army of Occupation twenty-five years later, in 1846.[1]

Genealogical Note

Many people will naturally be interested in the origin and development of their own particular ancestry and family name. Here they will meet each family as found "in the record." Some initial Aztec admixture, which has to be mentioned here for having already appeared in print, was admitted by individuals in some cases, but often as not was cast as a false aspersion on a par with immorality or a lack of culture. In brief, it was small enough to be absorbed by the general preponderance of Spanish blood. The main fact is that these New Mexico pioneers, the great majority of them, were people of whom we can be justly proud.

However, many of us New Mexicans have dreamed of our Conquistador forefathers as some sort of knighted gentry—to the secret, and sometimes undisguised, mirth of our non-Spanish neighbors, who wrongly believe them to have been nothing but peons and convicts. This present work, I trust, will temper both extreme opinions to the benefit of all.

---

1. Another element of the population were the *genízaros*, who were descended from diverse Plains Indians and other nomadic Indian captives. They now had Spanish surnames, many had Spanish blood, and all knew only the Spanish language. Generally, these were the "poor ignorant Mexicans" described by American writers and travellers of those times.

As will be noticed, some of the Conquistadores appear to have had noble antecedents in the dim past, but all were now ordinary military and pastoral people, good folks in the main, who were neither peons nor convicts. True, the misdeeds of some have come down to us, while the good deeds of most were interred with their bones, since court records do not concern themselves with men's virtues. But enough material exists to picture their fortitude and piety, their constant courage, and a marked innate sense of idealism. As I have elsewhere tried to bring out, these pioneer New Mexicans did not come seeking religious and civil liberty for their own group, like the New England colonists. Nor were they looking primarily for mere material benefits and a new home, like those of New France. Rather, in the truly characteristic fashion of southern Castile (La Mancha and Extremadura), they risked life and limb chiefly because they had been promised the title of "hidalgo" if they came and stayed. An empty incentive, this, to any other people, but not to these whose names and blood went back ultimately to that stark land of central Spain where Cervantes had his Don Quijote and Sancho Panza seeking for "islands" to rule.

Their penchant for adding ancestral names to their own immediate ones, ridiculous as it may seem to our modern democratic brevity, was one external feature of this Castilian spirit of the times. Another was that of attaching whatever titles they could lay claim to. Thus a third-generation López became López Sambrano de Grijalva. Or some individual strung out his titles of "Capitán, Alcalde Mayor, Regidor que fué, Hermano de la Tercera Orden, Alguacil del Santo Oficio"—ad infinitum. (The author's name and appendages on the second title-page of this book are in playful reference to this practice.)

The most important feature brought out here is the inter-relation of all New Mexicans in one big family, at least as far as the first two centuries are concerned. To this purpose, I have appended genealogical footnotes, as well as intricate diagrams, showing lines of ancestry running down from every direction, and from the most diverse sources, to my own father and mother. This looks, I know, like the height of presumption on my part, to intrude into a work of such general scope with strictly personal particulars that should interest no one else. But there was need for a graphic unifying medium to hold these thousands of loose facts together, to lend direction to their compilation. I would much have preferred to use the family trees of noted historical figures, and also of leaders of our times. However, these were not available (some of them I sought in vain), while I did happen to have a wealth of personal material perfectly suited to this end; its rich complexity, which only a dedicated researcher might garner in no less than a decade, made possible the various combinations shown on the charts. This use of one and the same family in all the diagrams does bring out the points discussed much more graphically than if various separate groups had been treated.

This, of course, brings out no noble pedigrees, and none were sought, but does forcefully illustrate the thesis by indicating the many-faceted relationship that exists among Hispanic New Mexicans. Many as these lines of descent may seem, they are but a fraction of a possible total, since, for example, an adult living today would have to find over five hundred contemporary grandparents in Vargas' time. Yet, this fraction is a good indication of what the total would be —a more widespread inter-relation.

The method adhered to in this work is one of definite proof in linking parent and child at each generation. Where enough material is not available, especially in the more remote Seventeenth Century, reasonable assumptions are made, but the assumptions are stated as such. For the links in a chain of ancestry cannot be merely guessed at from a similarity in names—each link of parent-child relationship must be forged with definite proof, or at least a plurality of circumstantial indications. And if the skipping of one such little link is so vitally important, and disastrous, it can readily be seen how a long jump to Queen Isabella or William the Conqueror can be so silly.[2]

✦ ✦ ✦ ✦ ✦ ✦ ✦ ✦ ✦

This is the time to thank those in charge of the institutions named in the Bibliography where the material used is preserved, for their unfailing helpfulness and courtesy. Personal thanks are due in particular to Dr. Arturo J. O. Anderson, who is actually the Historical Department of the Museum of New Mexico, for his constant help and interest in making documents available and

---

2. There are professional hawks who prey on the gullibility of people by connecting them with a noble or famous ancestor at a price. Last year a New Mexican living in Arizona showed me a beautifully hand-printed and crest-illuminated volume which he obtained for several hundred dollars. The clever compiler of it furnished the heraldic history of some noble house of that particular name in Spain, and also of a member of the family who came to Mexico City in the Sixteenth Century—all presumably correct. But then he had the cheek to make up a long string of fake ancestors down to this poor man's grandfather in New Mexico. The victim now wanted me to check these names with local records, and I had to disillusion him. Still, I could see that he thought I was all wrong, and the "expert" who made such a beautiful volume must be right. It all began with his answering an ad of a Chicago firm which, because his name was Spanish, referred him to a similar establishment in Mexico City.

in the tedious work of preparing the manuscript for the printer. In this connection his secretary, Rosita Roybal, and my sister, Nora Chávez, share in this appreciation.

No less grateful am I for the exquisite drawings, to me the best part of this otherwise drab study, from the pen of my friend, José Cisneros, of Mexico City and El Paso, whose talents as an illustrator are already known in the world of fine books.

To those ladies, young and younger, who worked so hard at gathering pre-publication subscriptions, my heartfelt thanks. For although published under the imprint of the Historical Society of New Mexico, this book had to be launched on a subscription basis because the Museum and Historical Society lacked funds from the State Legislature and other sources for this purpose. And here the highest thanks must go to the printer himself who, in the face of a woefully inadequate inflow of needed subscriptions in these days of high printing costs, offered to bring forth the work at his own financial risk, and in no less a superb example of book-making than you see here.

Fr. A. C., o.f.m.

PART ONE
THE SEVENTEENTH CENTURY

Las Cinco Chagas de mi Senhor,
cual Cinco Chavez de azul en or . . .

ABENDAÑO

SIMÓN DE ABENDAÑO, or *Avendaño,* was the son (or son-in-law) of Juan López Holguín and Catalina de Villanueva. He was born in Ciudad Rodrígo,¹ and was already dead by 1622, when he is mentioned as having been married to *María Ortiz* in Santa Fe; she was also dead at this time.²

His wife appears to have been a daughter of Cristóbal Baca (Vaca) and Ana Ortiz who came with her parents in the same group of the year 1600, where she is listed as María de Villanueva.³

Their daughter, *María de Abendaño,* married Diego de Vera in 1622, and later became the wife of Antonio de Salas. It seems as though there were no other Abendaño children, the parents having died early. That Simón had this surname, and his wife had other ones than that of "Baca," shows how people in those times often harked back to grandparents for their surnames. This practice often creates a difficulty in establishing relationships. María is mentioned as a sister-in-law of María de Albizu.⁴

---

1. **AGN, Mex., Inq.,** t.495 ff., 89-103; see **BACA,** this section, for difficulties regarding this particular relationship.
2. **Loc. cit.**
3. **Oñate,** p. 209; see note 1.
4. B-H, III, p. 183.

AGUILAR

NICOLÁS DE AGUILAR was a native of Yurirapundaro, Michoacán. He was the son of Pedro de Aguilar, deceased, and of Isabel de Villagómez, a native of the same village. His maternal grandparents were Fernando de Villagómez, an original Conquistador of Michoacán Province, and Luisa Pérez, also born in the same village. When eighteen years old, Nicolás left his widowed mother and went to the northern frontier settlement of Parral, where he worked as a miner and soldier for six years. From here he fled to New Mexico after committing a murder.¹

Aguilar lived in New Mexico for some time prior to 1660, serving as an unscrupulous lackey of Governor López Mendizábal. As *Alcalde Mayor* of the Salinas district he persecuted the missionaries with devilish fury and humor. The friars referred to him as "Attila."² Finally he was summoned before the Inquisition in Mexico City, where he had to answer for his crimes; found guilty, he was banished from New Mexico for ten years and deprived forever of holding any office.³

On coming to New Mexico he had married *Catalina Márquez,* daughter of Francisco Márquez and María Núñez of Santa Fe. At the time of his trial, between 1660 and 1665, they had four children: *Gerónima, María, Isabel,* and *Nicolás.*⁴ An Ynez de Gracia, living in the Salinas country near Cuarac, was mentioned as being his sister-in-law.⁵ After this, no more is heard of Aguilar. The family either followed him to New Spain, or stayed in New Mexico under their mother's name, and with good reason.

* * * * * * * *

Francisco de Aguilar, *Sargento,* married but without children, was among the New Mexico people when the Indians rebelled in 1680.⁶ He was one of the fifty convicts brought to New Mexico in 1677, sentenced to serve as soldiers. Then he is described as thirty-eight

[1]

years old, the son of Francisco Aguilar and a native of Puebla, sentenced to two years of service without pay.[7] He was gone from the exiled colony at Guadalupe del Paso by 1681, probably back to Puebla, since he had stayed longer than his term called for and was under no obligation to remain with the real New Mexico colonists.

1. AGN, Mex., Inq., t. 512, ff. 85-90.
2. Ibid., f. 113.
3. Cf. Troublous Times for his brief but telling stay in New Mexico.
4. AGN, loc. cit.
5. B-H, III, p. 169.
6. Revolt, I, pp. 143, 176.
7. B-H, III, pp. 317-324.

ALBIZU

TOMÁS DE ALBIZU (*Alvizu* or *Arvizu*) is mentioned as early as 1623, when he went to the City of Mexico with a message for the Viceroy. Returning with the 1625 wagon-train escort to New Mexico, he was referred to as a captain.[1] In 1632, already an *encomendero*, he led the soldiers sent to Zuñi to avenge the death of Father Letrado.[2] Religious-hating Governor Eulate reprehended him and another officer in 1626 for singing in the Santa Fe church choir.[3] By 1636, he had risen to the rank of *sargento mayor*, when he gave his age as forty-two.[4] His origin, however, is not known.

His wife was *Beatriz de Pedraza*.[5] The oldest Albizus mentioned in the 1680 Indian Rebellion, to all appearances their sons, were *Felipe* and *Antonio*.

Felipe de Albizu, *Sargento Mayor*, was married, having two grown sons and six small sons and daughters in 1680.[6] In 1681 he declared that he was fifty-two years old and suffering from a stomach ailment. He signed his statement.[7] The name of his wife is not known.

Antonio de Albizu was a captain, and a resident of the Rio Abajo district, when he escaped the 1680 Indian massacre.[8] He was forty-three or forty-five years old in 1681, when he signed a declaration that he was a native of New Mexico and married; he was described as having a good stature, a thick and partly gray beard, chestnut hair, and a lame finger on the right hand.[9]

Antonio's wife was *Gregoria Baca*, a daughter of Antonio Baca. They had a son, *Juan*, and also a daughter, *María*, who married Francisco Pérez Granillo in 1681.[10] The wife and son are ascertained from charts of the Baca and Jorge de Vera families.

Juan de Albizu was described in 1681 as a native of New Mexico, single, and as having a good build, a plump face, no beard, and fine, chestnut hair.[11]

* * * * * * * *

Two other Albizus described in 1681 were:

Mateo (Matías) de Albizu, seventeen years old and single,[12] and

José de Albizu, twenty-eight years old and married.[13] Both were born in New Mexico, and looked alike with their good features and chestnut hair. They could well have been the sons of Antonio de Albizu.

Two other young Albizus were:

Tomás de Albizu, born in New Mexico, twenty-nine years old and married, but dark complexioned,[14] and another

Tomás de Albizu, also a native of New Mexico, eighteen years old, single, of good and slender build, with an aquiline face, no beard, and straight hair.[15] How these two and the preceding pair were related is hard to say. All might have been the children, except the younger Tomás, of Felipe de Albizu.

Other people of this name living in this century were:

María de Albizu, forty years old in 1661,[16] and most likely a daughter of old Tomás; and, in the same period,

Felipe de Albizu,[17] perhaps the man of this name previously treated;

Juana de Arvizu, wife of Felis de Carvajal, 1664,[18] perhaps the same woman who was a granddaughter of Francisco Gómez;[19] and

Luisa de Alvizu, wife of Gabriel de Soto, resident of Guadalupe del Paso in 1715.[20]

No people of this name returned to New Mexico with Vargas in 1693.

1. **AGI, Contad.,** legs. 725, 726, 729, **Data;** Benavides, 1634, p. 110.
2. Benavides, 1634, p. 301.
3. **AGN, Mex., Inq.,** t. 356, f. 285.
4. **BNM,** leg. 1, pp. 470-504.
5. **AGN,** loc. cit., t. 372, f. 14.
6. **Revolt,** I, p. 141.
7. Ibid., II, p. 57.
8. Ibid., I, pp. 69, 79.
9. Ibid., II, pp. 52, 114.
10. **DM,** 1681, No. 3.
11. **Revolt,** II, p. 138.
12. Ibid., pp. 65, 114.
13. Ibid., pp. 47, 114.
14. Ibid., pp. 59, 111.
15. Ibid., pp. 63, 138.
16. **AGN,** loc. cit., t. 587, pp. 362, 375, 386.
17. Ibid.
18. Ibid., t. 507, p. 281.
19. B-H, III, p. 253.
20. **DM,** 1715, No. 5.

ALISO

TOMÁS DE ALISO, twenty years old, the son of Juan Manso and born in Valle de San Miguel in New Spain, came to New Mexico with the convicts of 1677. He had a good physique, a dark, long face, a large forehead, and thick eyebrows, and was sentenced to serve with pay for as long as he wished![1] He was still in New Mexico when the Pueblos rebelled; he was described in 1681 as twenty-seven or twenty-nine years of age, a native of San Miguel el Grande, and married in New Mexico.[2] Not being bound to return to New Mexico proper, he either stayed at Guadalupe del Paso or returned further south to his place of origin.

1. B-H, III, pp. 317, 324.
2. **Revolt,** I, p. 69; II, p. 123.

ANAYA ALMAZÁN

FRANCISCO DE ANAYA ALMAZÁN was already in New Mexico in 1626 and married to *Juana López,* daughter of the late Francisco López and María de Villafuerte.[1] He was born in Mexico City, the son of Pedro de Almazán, who came from Salamanca to the capital city of New Spain. There he was in charge of metals at the royal mint until his death. His mother was Ynez de Anaya, also a native of Salamanca. One brother, Agustín, was an *encomendero* at the Alóndiga in the Valley of Mexico; another was an Augustinian priest who died in the Amilpas district of Mexico City; while a third had gone to the Philippines and had not been heard of since. Two sisters of his were María de Anaya, married and residing in Mexico City, and Ana María de Guzmán, wife of Baltasar de Viana of Mexico City and mother of Fray Pedro de Viana, a Dominican.[2]

In 1642, Francisco and his Rodríguez son-in-law were in jail when Governor Rosas was murdered.

Francisco served as a prominent captain in New Mexico until his death in 1662 while *Alcalde Ordinario* of Santa Fe. He was buried in the Santa Fe Parroquia.[3] His death was attributed to sorrow when his son, Cristóbal, was arrested by the Inquisition and taken to Mexico City for trial. Following his death, Governor Peñalosa confiscated the tributes of his *encomienda* at Cuarac, Picurís, and Cienega.⁴ His wife was Juana López *de Villafuerte,* daughter of Francisco López of Jerez and María de Villafuerte, a native of Quatitlán. She was twenty-three in 1626, and survived her husband.⁴ᵃ

Their four children were *Cristóbal, Francisco, Ynez,* and *Ana María de Guzmán.*⁵ Ynez married Alonso Rodríguez, and Ana María became the wife of Andrés López Sambrano.

Cristóbal de Anaya was born around the years 1626-1629, having been baptized and confirmed by Fray Alonso Benavides.⁶ Very much involved in Church-State politics of his time, he was arrested by the Holy Office in 1661 for supposedly heretical remarks. After almost four years in prison, during which he stood trial various times, he was lightly punished by taking part in a ceremonial procession in Mexico City and in others at Sandía on his return. But still he had the boldness to come back home on a white horse and wearing a red burnoose to prove, as he said, that the Holy Office had dismissed him with honor.⁷ Unintimidated by all these experiences, he continued in his old mocking ways, for as late as 1669 complaints were being made against him by Fray Juan Bernal, a future martyr.⁸ Although only thirty-eight in 1663, when he stated that he was a native of Santa Fe but a resident of the Sandía jurisdiction, he had served as Royal Standard bearer (*Alférez Real*), Inspector, and Captain of Militia. He had started soldiering at the age of eleven.⁹

His wife was *Leonor Domínguez de Mendoza,* daughter of Captain Tomé Domínguez and Elena Ramírez de Mendoza; they had these four children in 1663: *Cristóbal II,* eleven years old; *Catalina,* eight; *Francisco,* five; and *María,* two.¹⁰

In 1680 death fell suddenly on Cristóbal, his wife, six children, and four others of his household, when the Santo Domingo Indians pounced on his *estancia* at Angostura, leaving their naked bodies across the threshold.¹¹ Two of his adult sons are mentioned as being soldiers. When Vargas' forces came in 1692, a youth was brought to the general who claimed to be a son of Cristóbal, having been a captive since 1680; he was placed in the care of his uncle, the Armorer Francisco Lucero de Godoy.¹² This youth was most likely the Adjutant *Francisco de Anaya Almazán* who drowned when crossing the Río del Norte in June, 1694.¹³ A curse, it appears, had decreed that this entire family should perish.

Francisco de Anaya II, Captain and *Alcalde Mayor* of the Tanos pueblos, was married to *Gerónima Pérez de Bustillo,* daughter of Hernando de Hinojos and Beatriz Pérez de Bustillo. They had two children in 1663: *Juana,* nine years old, and a boy, five.¹⁴ After his wife's death, he married *Francisca Domínguez,* a sister of his brother's wife.

In 1680 he was in command of a squad which was attacked by the Santa Clara Indians on August 9 or 10. He and five soldiers escaped and subsequently took part in the defense of Santa Fe.¹⁵ Meanwhile, his wife and children were reported killed, and his son, *Francisco,* "el mozo," was slain at Galisteo.¹⁶ Two years later a captured Indian deposed that he had seen Francisca Domínguez' nude body out on a field, her head bashed in, and a very small infant dead at her feet.¹⁷

Francisco passed muster in 1680, declaring that the enemy had killed his entire family

---

1. **AGN, Mex., Inq.,** t. 356, ff. 310-314; t. 372, f. 18.
2. **Ibid.,** t. 582, pp. 80-84.
3. **Ibid.,** p. 80; **Ortiz Trial,** ff. 21v, sqq.
4. **Ibid.,** t. 507, pp. 276, 327-328.
4a. **Ibid.,** t. 356, f. 310-314; t. 372, f. 18; t. 582, pp. 80-84; t. 507, p. 276.
5. **Ibid.,** t. 582, pp. 80-84.
6. **Ibid.,** p. 85.
7. **Ibid.,** t. 582, exp. 2, containing entire trial.
8. **Ibid.,** t. 666, ff. 532 sqq.
9. **Ibid.,** t. 582, pp. 80-84.
10. **Ibid.;** also **DM,** 1680, No. 1.
11. **Revolt,** I, pp. 23, 66.
12. **First Expedition,** pp. 130, 134.
13. **Bancroft, NMO,** fragment, Vargas Journal.
14. **AGN, loc. cit.,** t. 582, pp. 80-84, 1303-1304; t. 596, Pt. 2, f. 161; t. 507, pp. 28, 348.
15. **Revolt,** I, pp. 9, 16.
16. **Ibid.,** pp. 16, 96-97.
17. **DM,** 1682, No. 6.

and that he had nothing left.[18] In 1681 he said that he was forty-eight years old, a widower; he was described as having a medium build, protruding eyes, a thick and partly gray beard, and wavy chestnut hair.[19] During the Otermín Campaign of 1681, he declared that he had served His Majesty for thirty-eight years.[20] In 1691 he was *Mayordomo* of the Conquistadora Confraternity,[21] and in 1693 he returned to New Mexico with a third wife.

18. **Revolt**, I, p. 151.
19. **Ibid.**, II, pp. 42, 115.
20. **Ibid.**, pp. 319, 334.
21. **OLC**, pp. 8, 69.

APODACA

DIEGO GONZÁLEZ DE APODACA, an *Alférez*, is mentioned in New Mexico as being in prison in October, 1661, and at least until May, 1662, condemned to death for incest with his step-daughters. Their mother was a sister of Captain Andrés López de Gracia.[1] His place of origin is not known. He resided with his wife and family in the Salinas district,[2] probably at Tajique. From the marriage of his son, *José*, we learn that his wife's name was *Sebastiana López de Gracia*.[3]

Diego was not executed, for he was reported two years later as staying with his family at a brother-in-law's house on the Río del Norte.[4] After this period he is not heard of again, having died or left New Mexico prior to 1680, for he does not appear in the Revolt lists.

His wife's antecedents are difficult to unravel. Apparently, she had been first married to a Montaño; at least this was the surname of her three daughters, *Magdalena, Catalina,* and *María Montaño*, the probable principals in the incest case.[5]

José González de Apodaca, legitimate son of the foregoing couple, and widower of *Antonia Martín* (who died in 1683) married *Isabel Gutiérrez* on August 12, 1686. He was thirty at the time.[6] In 1681 he signed the muster-roll at Guadalupe del Paso, stating that he was twenty-eight years old and married.[7] He was described as a native of New Mexico, of medium build, with a pock-marked, aquiline face, and straight hair.[8] Like other people of the Salinas country, he was proficient in the Indian tongues, and so rendered valuable service as an interpreter during the Otermín Campaign of 1681.[9] He and his family returned to New Mexico with the Reconquest.

Francisco de Apodaca was a brother of José.[10] He was married to *María Martín*, and both returned with their family with Vargas in 1693.

Cristóbal de Apodaca passed muster with his wife and two children in 1680,[11] but there is no mention of him in 1681. His wife's name was *Regina Peralta*.[12] He, if not also his wife, returned with the Reconquest. What relation he was to the other Apodacas cannot be established. Most likely he was their brother.

* * * * * * * *

Juana de Apodaca, alias *Arzate* and *Maese*, was the natural daughter of Catalina Montaño by a Spanish-born father, Domingo [de Arzate]. She was taken captive as a girl in 1680 and was rescued twelve years later with a small daughter. Her colorful life and connections help in establishing several relationships.[13]

1. **AGN, Mex., Tierras**, t. 3268, f. 448; **ibid., Inq.**, t. 507, Pt. 1, f. 23.
2. **Ibid.**
3. **DM**, 1686, No. 1.
4. **AGN, Mex., Inq.**, t. 507, Pt. 1, f. 23.
5. Cf. **López de Gracia** and **Montaño**.
6. **DM**, loc. cit.
7. **Revolt**, II, pp. 76, 192.
8. **Ibid.**, pp. 98-99; his age here is forty-eight, apparently a mistake.
9. **Ibid.**, p. 359.
10. Relationships established from **DM**, 1691, No. 1, and Montaño, Maese charts.
11. **Revolt**, I, p. 159.
12. **DM**, 1707, No. 2.
13. Cf. **Montaño, Maese, López de Gracia; Rodríguez, Sebastián**.

ARAGÓN
(See *López de Aragón*)

ARCHULETA

ASENCIO DE ARECHULETA was one of the Oñate soldiers who came in 1598. He was twenty-six years old, the son of Juan de Arechuleta and a native of Eibar in Guipúzcoa. He is described as having a medium build, black beard, and a slight wound on the forehead.[1] At the famous battle of Ácoma, January 23, 1599, he accidentally shot his bosom partner-in-arms, Lorenzo Salado de Ribadeneira.[2] In 1603 he escorted four friars from Mexico City to San Gabriel.[3] During Governor Peralta's term, 1610-1614, he acted as an ecclesiastical notary and was thus involved in many a fracas which resulted in a strong anti-Peralta faction composed of Archuleta's relatives, "of whom there were many."[4] Asencio was dead by 1626, when he was cited as living three or four years previously, and when he was the Syndic of the Franciscans.[5]

His wife was *Ana Pérez de Bustillo*, daughter of Juan Pérez de Bustillo, and they had a son, *Juan*. One daughter, *María*, was the wife of Captain Juan Márquez; another, *Lucía*, married Diego de la Serna; a third, unnamed, was the wife of Matías López del Castillo; a fourth, *Gregoria*, married Diego de Santa Cruz.[6]

Juan de Archuleta was an outstanding citizen like his father. (The family dropped the first *e* of the name at this early stage.) He, too, was most active as a captain in the political life of the times, especially in the drawn-out affair which ended in the assassination of Governor Rosas in 1642. As *Regidor* of New Mexico at the time, he belonged to the anti-Rosas faction; on July 21, 1643, he was beheaded with some of his political associates and in-laws by Governor Pacheco.[7] I have not encountered his wife's name or identity. Juan's name, as a *Sargento Mayor* and captain, is on Inscription Rock, dated 1632, and also in 1636.[8]

Juan de Archuleta II, presumably the son of the preceding Juan, was thirty-eight years old in 1664 and a resident of La Cañada. His wife was *María Luján*, a daughter of Juan Luján.[9] As a Rio Arriba leader, he was a sort of lackey to Governor Peñalosa.[10] Before this, in 1661, he had acted in the same capacity to Governor Mendizábal.[11] Around this time, or later, he was sent to the bison plains to bring back the Taos Indians, who had fled from their pueblo.[12]

Melchor de Archuleta, mentioned in these connections, seems to be the man of this name who had an *estancia* at La Cañada in pre-Revolt times.[13] Hence, he and Juan can be considered as, most probably, the sons and heirs of the first Juan de Archuleta.

Considering their respective ages and the time in which they lived, other brothers and sisters of Juan and Melchor were the following:

Francisco de Archuleta, who married Bernardina Baca at Guadalupe del Paso, on November 29, 1678;[14]

Josefa de Archuleta, wife of Bartolomé Romero III of Santa Fe;[15] and

Ana de Archuleta, wife of a certain Durán.[16]

In the Revolt lists of 1680-1681, only two male Archuletas appear, and both named "*Juan de Archuleta*." One is twenty or twenty-six years old and married, born in New Mexico, of medium height, with large eyes and long thick hair.[17] The other is nineteen or twenty, born in New Mexico, but single; he is accompanied by a family of twelve—mother, brothers and sisters, uncles and aunts, nephews and nieces. His height runs from tallish to medium, thickset, and he, too, has large eyes and long black hair.[18]

Apparently, these two are first cousins, the older one a son of Juan de Archuleta II, the younger a son of Melchor. They will be discussed with other Archuletas who returned with the Vargas Reconquest in 1693.

1. Oñate, pp. 187-8.
2. Villagrá, Canto XXVII; Doc. Ined., Vol. XVI, pp. 270-76.
3. AGI, Contad., leg. 704, Data.
4. Cf. Church and State, pp. 27-40.
5. AGN, Mex., Inq., t. 356, f. 260.
6. Ibid., t. 372, ff. 7, 9, 11; t. 356, f. 266; t. 587, pp. 317-8.
7. Cf. Church and State, pp. 127-175; Ortiz Trial, f. 9.
8. Art and Archaeology, Vol. 34, p. 147.
9. AGN, loc. cit., t. 507, pp. 291-8, 1686.
10. Ibid., p. 457.
11. AGN, Mex., Tierras, t. 3268, ff. 637, 660.
12. Doc., Hist. de Mex., p. 125; statement of Fr. Vélez Escalante, 1778.
13. Sp. Arch., I, No. 2.
14. First M-Book, Guad. del Paso, f. 22, Bandelier Notes. This is the very first Spanish wedding at that Mission.
15. AGN, Mex., Inq., t. 666, ff. 561-2.
16. Sp. Arch., loc. cit.
17. Revolt, I, p. 157; II, pp. 71, 116.
18. Ibid., p. 149; II, pp. 61, 106-7, 129.

ARRATIA

GASPAR DE ARRATIA was a twenty-year-old *Alférez*, married and living in Santa Fe in 1628.[1] By 1631 he was dead, his young widow being *María de los Angeles Martín*. She was the daughter of Captain Alonso Martín Barba.[2]

Francisco de Arratia lived in the following generation. He was one of the Governor's henchmen who violated the honored right of sanctuary by arresting one of the Chaves men in the Santo Domingo Pueblo church in 1663.[3] Very likely he was the son of Gaspar.

Felipe de Arratia is the only one of this name mentioned in the Revolt lists of 1681. He was twenty years old and a native of New Mexico, single, having a tall figure, broad nose, ruddy, beardless face, and large eyes.[4] Perhaps he was the son of Francisco. He returned to New Mexico in 1693.

* * * * * * *

A different Arratia clan was brought from Parral sometime before 1664 by Governor Peñalosa. He took María Barrios, daughter of *Catalina de Arratia,* as his public concubine. She and her relatives who came with her made the Palace of the Governors resound with their wild merrymaking. She bore Peñalosa at least one daughter.[5] It is not known if any of these people mixed with the colonists.

1. AGN, Mex., Inq., t. 363, f. 6.
2. Ibid., t. 372, exp. 19, f. 10.
3. Ibid., t. 507, Pt. 3, f. 346; Pt. 4, f. 479.
4. Revolt, II, p. 118.
5. AGN, loc. cit., t. 507, pp. 232, 250, 591.

ARTEAGA

PEDRO DE ARTEAGA was in the wagon-train escort to New Mexico in 1658.[1] He and his wife, *Josefa de Sandoval,* came as settlers during Governor López Mendizábal's term. He was a native of Mexico City and twenty-six years old in 1661; Josefa was twenty.[2] Nothing more is known about them, nor were there any Arteagas left in New Mexico when the Indians rebelled in 1680.

A *María de Sandoval,* wife of Cristóbal Trujillo,[3] might have been a daughter of Arteaga. But, more likely, she was related to Ana Manzanares y Sandoval (*q.v.*).

1. AGI, Contad., leg. 749, Data.
2. AGN, Mex., Inq., t. 587, pp. 361, 375, 387; t. 594, p. 313.
3. DM, 1687, No. 1.

ÁVALOS

ANTONIO DE ÁVALOS (*Ábalos*) first appears as superintendent of the Salinas salt mines in 1660.[1] Although born in New Mexico around the year 1630, as he later deposed, he has no antecedents of this name, unless there is a connection with *Cristóbal de Aviles,* of Oñate's troops.[2] In 1680 he is mentioned as being married, with eight children.[3] The following year he is described as being fifty years old, a native of New Mexico, of good stature, tall and slender, dark, with an aquiline face and crooked nose, and coarse hair.[4] In all these depositions he is mentioned as a captain, and able to sign his name. His wife was the daughter of an Isabel Baca, who was the Padre's cook at Tajique in 1662.[5] From his son's marriages we learn that her name was *Juana Ruiz Cáceres.* These sons were as follows.

Pedro de Avalos, residing with his parents at the Real de San Lorenzo in 1681, married *Francisca de Torres* on October 12.[6] He was described in September, 1681, as twenty-four or twenty-five years old, single, with a good build, long, straight face, scant beard, and bushy eyebrows.[7] While a soldier at Guadalupe del Paso he signed as a matrimonial witness in 1694 and 1695, giving his age as thirty-nine and forty.[8] In 1685, Pedro registered a mine in the Fray Cristóbal Range, saying that he had discovered it during an *entrada* into New Mexico (Otermín's 1681 Campaign). Part of the stakes he gave to his brother Antonio.[9]

Antonio de Avalos, fifteen or nineteen years old, was mentioned as the son of the elder Antonio in 1682.[10] He and a *Gerónima de Herrera* were wedding sponsors together in 1694 at Guadalupe del Paso.[11] She was most probably his wife, as a brother of his married an Herrera.

Juan de Avalos, thirty years old in 1705, is then mentioned as Pedro's brother[12] and as a soldier of the Presidio of Guadalupe del Paso.[13] His wife was *Josefa de Herrera,* and their daughter *Isabel* married an Antonio de la Peña at Guadalupe del Paso in 1711.[14]

Leonardo de Ávalos, twenty-two years old and a native of New Mexico, the son of Captain Antonio de Ávalos, deceased, and Juana Ruiz, married *Francisca de Valencia,* on August 25, 1699. He was a soldier of Guadalupe del Paso at the time.[15]

Salvador de Ávalos married *Lugarda Torres* at Guadalupe del Paso in 1718.[16] Perhaps he was a brother to Pedro, who had also married a Torres.

María de Ávalos, wife of Antonio de Padilla, and both dead by 1718, might well have been a sister of the foregoing men.[17]

The Ávalos family did not return to New Mexico with the Vargas Reconquest.

---

1. AGN, Mex., Inq., t. 587, p. 171.
2. Oñate, p. 193.
3. Revolt, I, p. 43.
4. Ibid., II, pp. 76, 98, 110.
5. AGN, loc. cit., t. 512, f. 156.
6. DM, 1681, No. 1.
7. Revolt, II, pp. 79, 138.
8. DM, 1694, No. 11; 1695, No. 15.
9. Sp. Arch., I, No. 1.
10. BNM, leg. 2, Pt. 3, f. 364.
11. DM, 1694, No. 12.
12. Ibid., 1705, No. 10.
13. Ibid., 1695, No. 9.
14. Ibid., 1711, No. 6.
15. Ibid., 1699, No. 7.
16. Ibid., 1718, No. 12.
17. Ibid., 1718, No. 2.

ÁVILA

NICOLÁS DE ÁVILA was one of twelve soldiers recruited at Zacatecas for New Mexico in 1633.[1]

A *Luisa de Ávila* and her mother, Juana de Bohórquez, were in the prison of the Holy Office in Mexico City when some New Mexicans were on trial in 1662-1663.[2] If New Mexicans, they were very likely the wife and daughter of Nicolás. At any rate, neither they nor their name are heard of again for the remainder of the century.

1. AGI, Contad., leg. 845A, **Data**.
2. AGN, Mex., Inq., t. 512, f. 180.

AYALA

LUIS DE AYALA came to New Mexico in 1677 as a volunteer guard of the prisoners sent in that year. He was seventeen years old, the son of Luis de Ayala and a native of Mexico City at San Lorenzo. He had a good physique, a fair and ruddy complexion, blue eyes, and a large forehead.[1] He was still in New Mexico when the Indians rebelled in 1680. From Guadalupe del Paso he fled to Casas Grandes in 1681, but returned at the Governor's call.[2]

ANTONIO DE AYALA was one of the convicts of 1677, the son of the same, twenty-one years of age and born in Mexico City at San Lorenzo.[3] His description is so much like that of Luis that they might well have been first cousins. He, too, was in New Mexico in 1680. The following year he signed the muster-roll, and was described as being twenty-one years old, married in New Mexico, but without children; a native of Mexico City, he was tall and slim, with a scant beard, long and wavy hair, and a small scar on his right eyebrow. He acted as notary in several proceedings.[4] Neither Ayala returned to New Mexico with the Reconquest.

1. B-H, III, p. 317.
2. **Revolt**, I, p. 69; II, pp. 155, 187.
3. B-H, loc. cit.
4. **Revolt** I, pp. 16, 119; II, pp. 38, 106, 144, 146 sqq.

BACA

CRISTÓBAL BACA (*Vaca*) was one of the captains who came to reinforce the Oñate colony in 1600. He was the son of Juan de Vaca, born in Mexico City, of good stature, dark complexioned, well-featured, and thirty-three years of age.[1] He brought his wife, three grown daughters, and a small son. His wife was *Doña Ana Ortiz*, daughter of Francisco Pacheco, also born in Mexico City.

The children were *Juana de Zamora*, *Isabel [de Bohórquez]*, *María de Villanueva*, and the boy, *Antonio*, all of them born in Mexico City. With them came a female servant, Ana Verdugo.[2]

Baca's family was among the few who remained at San Gabriel when the rest of the colonists deserted; Cristóbal himself was very critical of some friars who led the desertion.[3] In 1603 he commanded the escort which brought four new Franciscans from Mexico City.[4] In 1613 he was acting as Syndic for the friars.[5] After this he disappears from the records, but his descendants begin to fill the annals of New Mexico.

Of the three daughters, *Juana* became the wife of Simón Pérez de Bustillo, *Isabel* married Don Pedro Durán y Chaves, and *María* was the wife of Simón de Abendaño. The family name was passed on down by *Antonio* and a younger brother, *Alonso*, born in New Mexico. (For further speculation on Juana de Zamora, see *Montoya*, note 4.)

Antonio Baca was a captain by 1628 and twenty-eight years old, he said, married and living in Santa Fe.[6] He was the main ringleader in the anti-Rosas faction which caused this Governor's death.[7] He also was the leader of the people who defied the Governor by barricading themselves with the friars at Santo Domingo Pueblo. His turbulent career ended on July 21, 1643, when he was beheaded with others in Santa Fe.[8]

His wife was *Yumar Pérez de Bustillo*, forty years old in 1631.[9] She, too, had come to New Mexico as a child with her parents. Of their three known daughters, *Gertrudis* married Antonio Jorge, *Ana* was the wife of Francisco López de Aragón, and *Gregoria* married Antonio de Albizu. What later Bacas were their sons, if any, cannot as yet be ascertained.

Alonso Baca, a contemporary of Antonio, was to all appearances Antonio's younger brother. As a young captain he led a small exploratory expedition three hundred leagues into the eastern plains in 1634. He gave his age as fifty-five in 1644, but must have been a year or two younger.[10] In the middle of the century, he uncovered a serious Indian plot.[11] He was one of fourteen conspirators ordered executed by Governor Pacheco in 1643 (when Antonio died),[12] but all these fourteen escaped death; Alonso was still living at his place in the Río Abajo district as late as 1662.[13] Nothing more is known about him, not even his wife's name. *Cristóbal Baca*, mentioned in 1663 as *sobrino carnal* of Antonio Baca, was apparently his son.[14]

* * * * * * * *

When the Pueblos rebelled in 1680, there were only four adult male Bacas listed: *Cristóbal, Ignacio, Manuel,* and *José*.

Cristóbal Baca, just referred to as a nephew of Antonio Baca, signed the muster-roll as a captain, married, with three grown sons and three daughters.[15] He was the son-in-law of Diego de Trujillo, both of whom were persecuted by the ill-famed Governor, López Mendizábal.[16]

His wife was *Ana Moreno de Lara*, and it seems as though Cristóbal was dead by 1687, when she and some of their children are mentioned. These were the girls: *Catalina, Juana,* and *Luisa;* and the sons, *José, Manuel,*[17] and *Ignacio,* who must have been the third son mentioned by his father in the muster-roll. José and Manuel were mentioned with their father in 1682.[18] Of the daughters, *Catalina* married Antonio Gallegos, *Juana* became the wife of Francisco Xavier II, and *Luisa* appears to be the woman of this name who was the second wife of Ignacio de Aragón.

José Baca was described in 1681 as being seventeen years old, single, and having a medium thick-set stature, a beardless face, large eyes, and chestnut hair.[19] At Guadalupe del Paso he married *Josefa Pacheco*. On July 3, 1687, he got into a fight with his brother-in-law, Silvestre Pacheco, who killed him.[20] He had a daughter, *Juana,* who became the wife of Nicolás Ortiz III, after the Reconquest.

Manuel Baca was described in 1681 as twenty-five years of age, married, with a good, thick-set build, a ruddy face, thick beard, and wavy hair.[21] He was a soldier with Ignacio Baca at Guadalupe del Paso in 1684 under Captain Roque Madrid.[22] His wife was *María de Salazar* (Hurtado), who returned with him and many children in 1693.

Ignacio Baca was twenty-four years old in 1681 when he signed up as a captain, married, with four small children and twenty servants; he was tall and slim, with an aquiline face, fair complexion, wavy red hair, no beard.[23] By 1684 he was a *Sargento Mayor* at the Presidio of Guadalupe del Paso.[24] As Assistant *Alcalde* of the Real de San Lorenzo he arrested Silvestre Pacheco for killing José Baca in 1687, but by October, 1689, he had died.²⁵

His family was an ill-fated one. His widow, *Juana de Anaya Almazán,* returned to New Mexico in 1693 with her two sons, *Alonso* and *Andrés,* and five daughters. When the Indians rebelled again in 1696, she was killed at San Ildefonso with Fathers Corvera and Moreno. With her died Alonso, while Andrés was massacred at Nambé, thus ending the male line of this family. Two daughters were also killed, *Leonor,* married to Pedro Sánchez, with a daughter and son of her own, and *Rosa,* who was still single.²⁶

Of the three surviving girls, *María* had married Tomás Gutiérrez; *Gerónima* and *Margarita,* probably living with relatives since childhood, later married Francisco Rodríguez Calero and Diego Lucero de Godoy, respectively.

* * * * * * * *

The correct spelling of this family name is "Vaca," but already in the Seventeenth Century "Baca" had come into common usage, and was the accepted spelling after the Reconquest. Although it is derived from "Cabeza de Vaca," a title and name received by a Spanish hero in the year 1212,²⁷ the full name was never once used by this New Mexico family for over two centuries.

Several Vacas came to the New World shortly after its discovery. Among those in Cortés' time were Diego de Vaca, a native of Mancilla in León, and Luis Vaca, a native of Toledo.²⁸ Either of these could have been the father of Juan Vaca, the father of our Cristóbal Baca.

---

1. Oñate, p. 206. — Here Hammond has "María de Villarubia," but to me the manuscript reads more like **Villanueva** (AGI **Patronato**, leg. 22, Ramo 4, f. 511). This, and the fact that the same source gives Juan López Holguín two daughters, **María Ortiz** and **Ana Ortiz**, and his wife as Catalina de **Villanueva** (Ibid., f. 490), poses an unresolved problem. It mixes up this family with that of Captain Cristóbal Baca, whose wife was Ana Ortiz, while one of their grown daughters was María de Villanueva. The two other Baca girls are Juana de Zamora and Isabel, who turns out to be Isabel de Bohórquez. Were the Holguín girls the same women named as the wife and one daughter of Cristóbal Baca? (Holguín, by the way, was Captain Baca's sergeant major.) It would seem so from other sources, and from relationships in this book. Yet, what the actual relationships were in this Holguín-Baca group remains a mystery. For this reason, the relationship between Simón de Abendaño and Holguín is left unsolved, and that of Simón's wife, María Ortiz, as Baca's daughter, assumed for the present as a working hypothesis.
2. Ibid., p. 209.
3. Ibid., pp. 148 sqq.
4. AGI, **Contad.**, leg. 707, **Data.**
5. AGN, Mex. Inq., t. 316, f. 164.
6. Ibid., t. 356, f. 302; t. 363, ff. 4, 12; t. 372, ff. 3, 4.
7. Cf. **Troublous Times**, pp. 127-176; his wife's niece was a principal in the affair, **Ortiz Trial**, ff. 1-80.
8. Ibid., p. 175; AGN, loc. cit., pp. 594, 263.
9. AGN, loc. cit., t. 372, f. 18; t. 380, ff. 253-254.
10. Doc. Hist. de Mex., p. 218; AGI, **Patronato**, leg. 244, Ramo 7, Doc. 16, p. 119.
11. Revolt, II, p. 299.
12. Twit. Coll., No. 280, copy.
13. AGN, loc. cit., t. 512, f. 130.
14. Ibid., t. 372, p. 263.
15. Revolt, I, p. 157; II, p. 197.
16. AGN, loc. cit., t. 594, p. 263; ibid., Mex. Tierras, t. 3268.
17. Sp. Arch., II, No. 45, murder of José.
18. BNM, leg. 2, Pt. 3.
19. Revolt, II, pp. 66, 129-130.
20. Sp. Arch., loc. cit.
21. Revolt, II, pp. 123, 186.
22. HSNM, No. 2845.
23. Revolt, I, p. 139; II, pp. 46, 107.
24. HSNM, loc. cit.
25. Sp. Arch., loc. cit.
26. Old Santa Fe, III, pp. 332-373.
27. Hodge, **Spanish Explorers**, etc., p. 3.
28. AGI, Mex. Aud., leg. 1064, Pt. 1.

BARRIOS

Alvaro de Barrios, son of Luis González, twenty-six years old and born in Coímbra, Portugal, was in Oñate's forces of 1598.¹

Francisco de Barrios was a soldier in the 1608 wagon-train coming to New Mexico; the name appears again in another escort of the year 1655.² There is no known connection between these two men.

Nicolás de Barrios, a native of Tocotitlan, was among the convicts of 1677. He escaped from his guards on the way to New Mexico,³ but might have been recaptured, for a man of this name, twenty years old, was a witness at Guadalupe del Paso in 1683.⁴

Then there is the Barrios woman and her relatives brought up from Parral by Governor Peñalosa.⁵ These disconnected facts are here recorded in an effort to shed light on this name as it appears after the Reconquest.

---

1. Oñate, p. 188.
2. AGI, **Contad.**, legs. 748, 850, **Data.**
3. B-H, III, pp. 317-324.
4. DM, 1683, No. 1.
5. See **Arratia**.

BERNAL

FRANCISCO BERNAL came to New Mexico as a boy in 1598, or else was born at San Gabriel sometime after. He was a brother of *Catalina* and *María Bernal,* and of Juan Griego the younger, all children of Juan Griego and Catalina Bernal.

His wife was *Bernardina Morán,* who was twenty years old in 1631, the last time either of the two are mentioned.[1] Who their children were cannot be ascertained. Why Francisco took his mother's name, while Juan took his father's, is not known, unless they were half-brothers. There is a *Juan Bernal* in the soldier escort of 1608 who very likely was the younger Juan Griego.[2]

Isabel Bernal, another sister of Francisco, married Sebastián González; these were the progenitors of the numerous clan that went under the name of González Bernal. *María* married Juan Gómez Barragán, *Catalina* married Juan Durán, and *Juana* was the wife of Diego de Moraga.

The Bernal individuals living at the time of the 1680 Indian Rebellion were descendants either of Francisco Bernal or of the Bernal sisters, choosing this appellation instead of their father's. Catalina Bernal, a widow, extremely poor, who passed muster in 1680 with a family of nine persons, children and grandchildren, was in all likelihood the widow of Juan Durán.[3]

A *Francisco Bernal,* single and twenty-two years old, is the only male Bernal listed. He had a family of eight, mother, brothers and sisters, nephews and nieces. He was described as a native of New Mexico, of medium, thick-set build, very swarthy, with curly hair, and somewhat bow-legged.[4] Most likely he was a son of the first Francisco Bernal and Bernardina Morán.

Several Bernal folks, mostly women, returned with the Reconquest.

1. **AGN, Mex., Inq.,** t. 304, ff. 187-188; t. 356, f. 312; t. 372, f. 14.
2. **AGI, Contad.,** legs. 707, 850, **Data.**
3. **Revolt,** I, p. 157.
4. **Ibid.,** I, p. 151; II, pp. 60, 134.

BOHÓRQUEZ

Cristóbal Romero de Bohórquez was mentioned in 1625 as residing in New Mexico but holding no *encomienda*.[1] Nothing more is known about him; perhaps he resided in Nueva Vizcaya.

Francisco de Bohórquez was in the escort of the wagon-train of 1640.[2]

For *Juana de Bohórquez,* see *Ávila.*

None of these were related to Isabel de Bohórquez, wife of Don Pedro Durán y Chaves.

1. **AGI, Contad.** leg. 729, **Data.**

2. **Ibid.,** leg. 736, **Data.**

BRITO

Cristóbal Brito, a sixty-five-year-old Canary Islander, and *Juan de León,* a thirty-year-old native of Cádiz, were with Oñate's early troops,[1] but no connection can be found between them and certain people of low estate who were natives of New Mexico in 1680 and 1693. Perhaps they were descendants of the Indian slaves which Brito brought along.

Juan Brito and his wife, *Antonia Ursula Durán*, had lived in Santa Fe before the Rebellion.² Also,

Antonio Brito and his wife, *Magdalena de Dios*.³ The 1680 Revolt lists carry no male Britos; hence those who returned to New Mexico in 1693 were minor children at that time.

---

1. **Oñate**, pp. 202, 193.
2. **DM**, 1692, No. 3; 1694, No. 12.
3. **Ibid.**, 1706, No. 2.

CABINILLAS

Juan Velásquez de Cabinillas (or *Cabanillas*) was the son of Cristóbal de Hidalgo de Cabanillas, a native of Zalamea la Serena, and twenty-four years old when he came in Oñate's army of 1598. He was small in stature and had a chestnut beard.¹ He was one of the soldiers who leaped down from the cliff of Ácoma and lived to tell the tale.²

José Velásquez was a soldier who sought the right of sanctuary in the Santa Fe church in 1613.³

Isabel de Cabinillas, mentioned in 1631, was the sister-in-law of María de los Ángeles, daughter of Alonso Martín Barba.⁴ Her husband was Diego Martín Barba.⁵ The name does not appear again after this date. Perhaps there is some connection with the Hidalgo family.

---

1. **Oñate**, p. 189.
2. **Ibid.**, p. 114.
3. **AGN, Mex., Inq.**, t. 316, f. 153.
4. **Ibid.**, t. 372, exp. 19, f. 10.
5. **Ibid.**, f. 7.

CADIMO

FRANCISCO CADIMO was also an Oñate soldier of 1598, thirty-six years old, the son of Pedro Cadimo, and a native of Salaíces de los Gallegos, having a good stature, black beard, and a freckled face.¹

Two women mentioned in 1631 could well have been his daughters: *Francisca Cadimo*, twenty, who was the wife of Gerónimo Pacheco, and *Ana Cadimo*, wife of Alonso Gutiérrez.²

The name appears again, and for the last time, in 1667. *Alonso Cadimo*, known mostly as Alonso *Romero*, and nicknamed "Jola," lived with his wife at the *estancia* of Felipe Romero near the Pueblo of Sevilleta. He was a native of Santa Fe, and married to *María de Tapia*.³ Alonso apparently died prior to 1680; but his widow, married to Mateo Trujillo, did return to New Mexico in 1693 with two children: *Ana María Romero*, who married Juan de Villalpando, and *Diego Romero*, who married María de San José and thus founded a distinct Romero family.

---

1. **Oñate**, p. 189.
2. **AGN, Mex., Inq.**, t. 372, exp. 19, ff. 13-15.
3. **Ibid.**, t. 608, f. 427.

CAMPUSANO

Francisco Campusano does not appear in the 1680-1681 lists, but he was living in the Guadalupe del Paso area in 1682 with his wife, *Ana de Aragón*, a daughter of Captain Francisco López de Aragón and Ana Baca.[1] He gave his age as nineteen in that year.[2] He does not appear with the Reconquest soldiers and settlers.

But two female Campusanos did come up to New Mexico in 1693. These were *Micaela Campusano* and her sister *Magdalena de Ogama*, mother-in-law of a Felipe Padilla of Santa Fe.[3] Magdalena cooked the meals for the workmen while they were restoring the ancient chapel of San Miguel in 1710.[4] She was living in Santa Cruz three years later when she gave her age as sixty.[5]

1. AGN, Mex., Inq., t. 1551, ff. 375-378.
2. DM, 1682, No. 5.
3. Sp. Arch., I, No. 1071.
4. Kubler, pp. 11, 18.
5. Sp. Arch., II, No. 187.

CANDELARIA

BLAS DE LA CANDELARIA does not appear in any records of the 1680 Indian Rebellion or those prior to it. But among the native New Mexicans in dire need at Corpus Christi de Ysleta in 1684 appears "the widow of Blas de la Candelaria."[1] She was *Ana de Sandoval y Manzanares*, who returned with her children after the Reconquest.[2] This shows that Blas had died before 1680, and that his sons were minors at that time and, therefore, were not listed among the exiled colonists.

1. AGN, Prov. Int., t. 37, pp. 100-104.
2. Cf. Sp. Arch., I, p. 141.

CARVAJAL
(Vitoria Carvajal)

JUAN DE VITORIA CARVAJAL (*Carbajal*) came as an *Alférez* under Oñate in 1598. He was thirty-seven years old, the son of Juan de Carvajal, and a native of the town of Ayotepel in the Marquisate of the Valley, having a medium stature and a chestnut beard.[1] Oñate sent him back to New Spain to bring back the reinforcements of 1600. At this time he was a captain, and was described again as before, with the added observation that he was well-featured and had a mark on the right side of the face above the left eye. He was now returning to New Mexico as a member of Oñate's war council.[2] As *Alcalde Ordinario* in 1614 he was accused of illegally assuming authority in ordering the execution of an Indian assassin while Governor Peralta was in prison.[3] He is mentioned in 1622 as being the Syndic of the Franciscans.[4] He then referred to himself as a married man and a "first founder of this land."[5] As Standard-bearer for the Holy Office he accompanied Father Perea, head of the church in New Mexico, in a memorable procession which went out from Santa Fe to meet an incoming Governor, Don Francisco Nieto de Silva.[6]

Carvajal's wife was *Isabel Holguín*, daughter of Juan López Holguín and Catalina de Villanueva. She was accused of trafficking in "magic roots" in 1626.[7] Their three known sons were, in all likelihood, *Agustín, Gerónimo,* and *Felis.* A daughter, whose name is not known, was the wife of Don Fernando Durán y Chaves. Most likely another daughter was *Magdalena,* wife of Domingo González.

Agustín de Carvajal was one of the fourteen men ordered executed for sedition by Governor Pacheco in 1643, but he escaped the sentence[8] with his Chaves brother-in-law and the others. He is mentioned in 1660 as being thirty years old and residing in the jurisdiction of Galisteo. He had lost his first wife, *María Márquez,* and was now accused of having married a close relative, *Estefania Enriquez,* nineteen years old.[9] Agustín was mentioned as a brother-in-law of Don Fernando Durán y Chaves and a brother of Gerónimo de Carvajal.[10] The two brothers had married two Márquez sisters.

Widowed again, Agustín had taken a third wife prior to 1680. She was *Damiana Domínguez de Mendoza,* widow of Álvaro de Paredes and daughter of old Tomé Domínguez. He was sixty in April of that year, and Damiana was fifty. With them was Doña *Ana de Carvajal,* fifty-six years old, perhaps the widow of Don Fernando Durán y Chaves.[11] That following August both Agustín and Damiana, with a grown daughter and "another woman" (Ana?), were massacred by the Santo Domingo Indians at their Angostura home. Two weeks later their bodies were found by the fleeing refugees of Santa Fe, who found no signs of his sons or the rest of the family.[12] Who these surviving sons were is impossible to say.

Gerónimo de Carvajal was a brother of Agustín, as just noted. In 1661 he was referred to as being thirty-one years old and the husband of *Margarita Márquez.*[13] At this time he was also *Alcalde Mayor* and Captain of the Tanos in the Galisteo Basin, and also claimed half of the Awátobi *encomienda.*[14] His hacienda was located at "Nuestra Señora de los Remedios de los Cerrillos," in the jurisdiction of San Marcos Pueblo. At this time, 1669, he claimed the Sandía jurisdiction as his birthplace.[15] In this connection, his wife was referred to as being twenty-six years of age, a native of Santa Fe, and a daughter of Doña Bernardina Márquez. In 1656 she figured in a scandalous but colorful incident involving Governor Manso, together with the fake baptism of one infant and the fake burial of another, so that her child by Manso could be spirited to Mexico City to be reared by his natural father.[16] Yet by 1669, when Fray Juan Bernal recommended Gerónimo as a virtuous and honorable man, he also spoke highly of Margarita.[17]

Gerónimo must have been dead when the Indians rebelled in 1680, for he does not appear in the Revolt lists. But Margarita was still living in 1682, when her daughter, *Ana Márquez Carvajal,* wife of Don José de Chaves, attempted to poison her husband with a designedly non-fatal dose.[18] Another daughter seems to have been a *Josefa de Carvajal,* wife of Cristóbal de Velasco at this time; also, a "Doña María Márquez."[19] Their two sons could well have been *Antonio* and *Ambrosio,* described further on.

Felis de Carvajal is mentioned in 1661-1664 as being twenty-six years old, born in the Estancia of San Nicolás in the Sandía district, and married to *Juana de Arvizu.*[20] He had part of the Senecú *encomienda,* and was referred to as a "noble man, the son of Captain Juan de Victoria Carvajal." His wife might well be the woman of this name who was referred to as a grandchild of Francisco Gómez, the Portuguese.

No mention of Felis is found in the 1680 Revolt lists; hence he can be presumed dead by then. However, the journals mention the hacienda of "Luis" de Carvajal on the Río del Norte;[21] undoubtedly, the refugees (or the transcribers) meant to write "Felis."

Other early Carvajal persons were:
Alonso de Carvajal, mentioned in 1663 as

"*fulano* de Carvajal," brother-in-law of Pedro Varela.[22] He was a brother or son of the preceding man. He and his wife, *Ana Varela*, had a son, *Juan Antonio*, who married a Josefa Martín in 1701; both his parents were referred to as deceased.[23]

Magdalena de Carvajal, forty years old in 1631, and wife of Captain Domingo González,[24] was most likely the eldest child of Juan de Vitoria Carvajal.

Juana de Carvajal, the second wife of Juan Lucero de Godoy, could have been Magdalena's sister. She died at El Real de San Lorenzo in 1683.[25]

The Carvajals mentioned in the 1680 Revolt rolls are all relatively young men.

Antonio de Carvajal, a native of the Sandía district,[26] signed his declaration in 1680 as being married and accompanied by his wife, mother, and four younger brothers and sisters.[27] In 1681 he declared himself to be twenty-three years old and married. He was very sick at the time as a result of falling off a horse. His family, including his mother and other relatives, consisted of thirty-three persons in all, and was accused by fellow-refugees of taking more than their share of relief rations. Antonio himself was indicted for profiteering with the Pedro de Chaves clan.[28] In the same year he left the exile colony without permission, and is mentioned in this connection with Pedro Márquez as being a son-in-law of Pedro de Chaves.[29] Hence, Antonio was not a son of Agustín, but of Gerónimo de Carvajal; and it appears as if his family cast their lot with the Pedro de Chaves group and never returned to New Mexico.

Ambrosio de Carvajal distinguished himself in the flight south from Santa Fe by capturing a Tewa Indian for interrogation, August 23, 1680.[30] In 1681 he signed the muster-roll as a bachelor accompanied by his mother and three grown sisters.[31] This would tie him in with Antonio, just treated. The fact of his knowing the San Marcos Pueblo area so well also suggests his being a son of Gerónimo de Carvajal. Ambrosio was twenty-five years old in 1681, having a medium stature, a large face, black hair and beard.[32]

Luis de Carvajal, a minor in 1680, was described in 1682 as a bachelor, twenty-one or twenty-two years of age, a native of New Mexico, of good build and features, with black hair and beard, and a long nose.[33] He followed Antonio in the muster-roll, whose younger brother he might have been, or else a son of Felis (Luis) de Carvajal.

Nicolás de Carvajal was mentioned merely as a bachelor, twenty-one years old, in 1681.[34] That his Christian name derived from the estancia of San Nicolás suggests his being a son of Felis de Carvajal.

Few Carvajal people returned with the Reconquest in 1693 and, except for Juan Antonio, son of Alonso, none can be connected with their ancestors. Nor do they play a major role in later times as did the Carvajals of the Seventeenth Century.

* * * * * * * *

There was another *Juan de Vitoria Carvajal* with Oñate's forces. He is generally referred to as "Juan de Vitoria," and was entered in the Casco muster-roll, on February 17, 1597, as a native of Mexico City and the son of Alonso Ruiz,[35] but does not appear in the 1598 or 1600 Oñate lists. However, he did arrive in New Mexico, for in 1609 he was in Governor Peralta's escort,[36] and again in 1613, identified once more as the son of Alonso Ruiz de Gusmán.[37] He is last mentioned in 1617 as an *Alférez* thirty-six years old, and in the company of Captain Juan de Vitoria Carvajal, fifty-five years of age.[38] These two men were most probably closely related, but what part the younger man played as a colonist and progenitor cannot be ascertained.

The Carvajal individuals who first came to the New World were above the average in estate. The genealogy of a Luis María de Carvajal in New Spain was linked with that of Oñate. Among the Cortés *Conquistadores* was an Antonio de Carvajal, a native of Zamora, who could have been the grandfather of Juan de Vitoria Carvajal.[39]

1. **Oñate**, p. 189.
2. **Ibid.**, p. 205.
3. **Church and State**, p. 36.
4. **AGN, Mex., Inq.**, t. 485, f. 61.
5. **Ibid.**, t. 356, f. 302.
6. **Ibid.**, t. 372, exp. 19, ff. 3-14.
7. **Ibid.**, t. 356, f. 310.
8. **Twit. Coll.**, No. 280.
9. **AGN, loc. cit.**, t. 587, pp. 305, 321-322, 386-388, 457-459.
10. **Ibid.**, p. 316; t. 507, pp. 39-42; t. 608, f. 433.
11. **DM**, 1680, No. 1.
12. **Revolt**, I, pp. 23, 66.
13. **AGN, loc. cit.**, t. 587, pp. 247, 361-362, 375-386.
14. **Ibid., Tierras**, t. 3268, p. 307.
15. **Ibid., Mex., Inq.**, t. 666, ff. 559-563; t. 507, pp. 409-415.
16. **Ibid.**, t. 507, pp. 39-42.
17. **Ibid.**, t. 666, ff. 532-533.
18. **Ibid.**, t. 1551, f. 382.
19. **BNM**, leg. 2, Pt. 3, ff. 290-291.
20. **AGN, loc. cit.**, t. 507, p. 281.
21. **Revolt**, II, p. 285.
22. **AGN, loc. cit.**, t. 507, Pt. 5, f. 575.
23. **DM**, 1701, No. 1.
24. **AGN, loc. cit.**, t. 372, f. 8.
25. **DM**, 1688, No. 1.
26. **AGN, loc. cit.**, t. 587, f. 51.
27. **Revolt**, I, pp. 37, 148.
28. **Ibid.**, II, pp. 53, 150, 162, 180.
29. **BNM**, leg. 2, Pt. 3, ff. 354-357.
30. **Revolt**, I, p. 20.
31. **Ibid.**, II, pp. 54, 150.
32. **Ibid.**, p. 118.
33. **Ibid.**, p. 139.
34. **Ibid.**, p. 78.
35. **AGI, Mex., Aud.**, leg. 25, Pt. 1.
36. **Ibid., Contad.**, leg. 711, **Data.**
37. **Ibid., loc. cit.**, leg. 716, **Data.**
38. **AGN, Mex., Inq.**, t. 316, f. 175; t. 318.
39. **AGI, Mex., Aud.**, leg. 72, list-title 148a; leg. 227; leg. 1064, Pt. 1.

CASAUS

DON ROQUE DE CASAUS first came north from Mexico City as a soldier in the wagon-train escort of 1625. He brought his wife and children with the intention of residing in the new settlement of "N. S. de Piedad de Cerralbo,"[1] which was not in New Mexico proper. However, in 1629 he was the leader of another escort that reached Santa Fe; here his name was given as Don Roque Medón de Casaus.[2]

By 1626 he was a resident of Santa Fe and a captain. His wife's name was *Doña Isabel de Luján*.[3] He was an evil counselor of Governor Rosas.[4] The last mention of Casaus was made in February, 1639, when he was a member of the Santa Fe council.[5] No other Casaus persons are mentioned in the Seventeenth Century, nor are there any descendants found in the 1680 lists or after.

The name is not to be confused with that of the *Casados* family of the Reconquest.

1. **AGI, Contad.**, leg. 729, **Data.**
2. **Ibid.**, leg. 731, **Data.**
3. **BNM**, leg. 1, Pt. 1, pp. 470-504.
4. **AGI, Patronato**, leg. 244, Ramo 7, doc. 22, p. 161.
5. **B-H**, III, p. 57.

CASTILLO
(See *López del Castillo*)

CEDILLO
(See *Sedillo*)

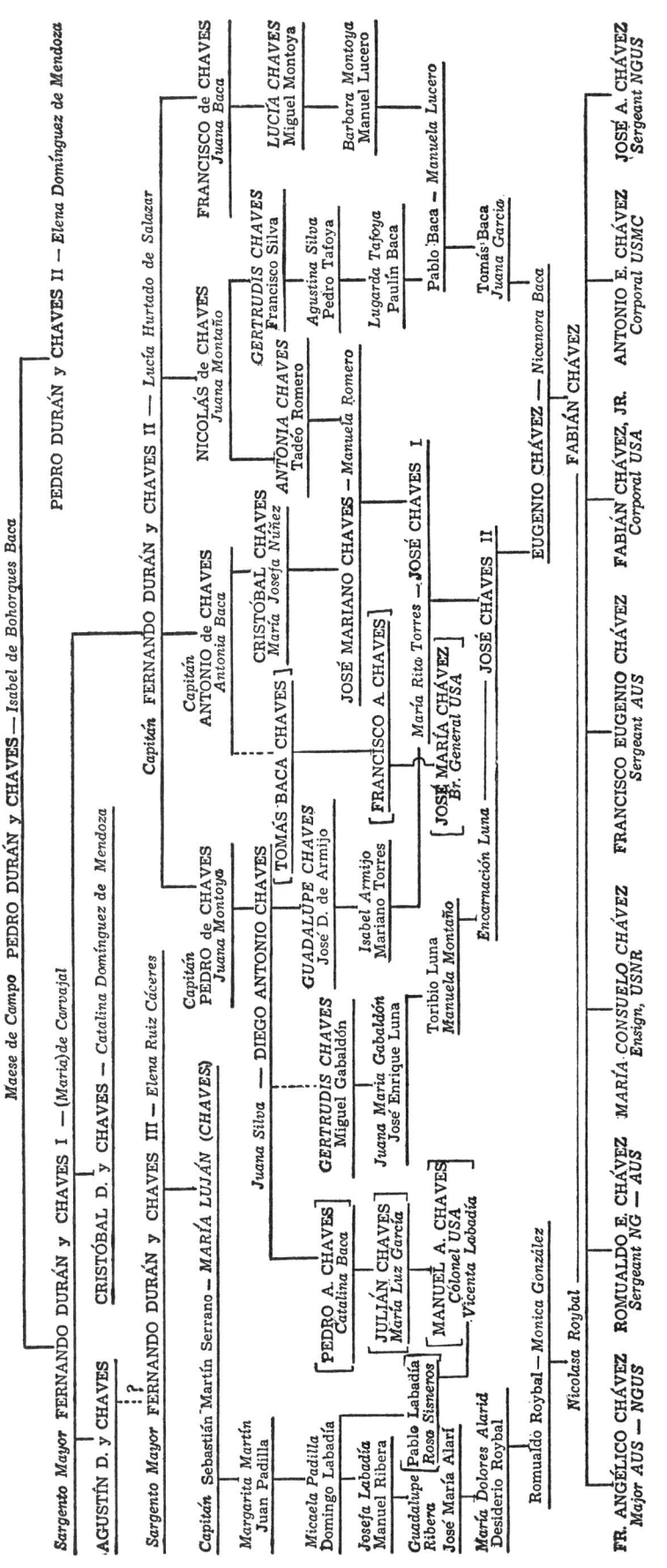

CHAVEZ CHART—This and succeeding diagrams, built around one and the same family, for which facts were at hand, are designed to demonstrate different aspects of New Mexican descent and inter-relationship. They are applicable to any old New Mexico family, though in an infinite variety of combinations. This is a plural name-ancestor chart, in which at least six Chávez lines descend to a single family, over and above the one transmitting the name. For curiosity's sake a military twist is added, to include known military figures who descend from the first known resident "Field Commander" of all colonial troops in New Mexico. The bottom line shows, too, how one single family, typical of so many large families in New Mexico, has contributed to the national defense in our time.

CHÁVEZ
(*Durán y Chaves*)

DON PEDRO (GÓMEZ) DURÁN Y CHAVES, progenitor of the numerous Chávez family of New Mexico, finds first mention under this name in 1613 when as a captain he was sent to Taos Pueblo to collect the Governor's tribute.[1] By 1626 he was *Maese de Campo,* or Commanding General, of all royal troops in New Mexico, when he testified that he was sixty years old, a native of Llerena, and one of the founders of the Villa of Santa Fe.[2] In February, 1610, the year Santa Fe is believed to have been founded by Governor Peralta, he was down at the Port of Acapulco, taxing the cargo of a ship being fitted for a Philippine voyage; the ship's Admiral, Zevallos, did not make the voyage, but succeeded Peralta as Governor in 1614.[3] Hence, Chaves must have reached New Mexico later in that year, 1610, for the founding of Santa Fe. This, apparently, was not his first trip to New Mexico, for other data identify him as the *Sargento,* Pedro Gómez Durán, of Oñate's troops of 1600.[4] Here he was described as a well-built man of good features, "fifty" years old, the legitimate son of Hernán Sánchez Rico, and born in Valverde in the jurisdiction of the Grand Master of Santiago.[5] In 1602 he signed a petition to the Viceroy, asking that the infant colony be made a full *"República"* with a *"Capital,"* and that large grants be made to the supplicants.[6]

(Valverde de Llerena is a village some ten miles east of the city of Llerena in Estremadura, once famous as the headquarters of the Grand Master of the Order of Santiago. In June, 1952, I visited these places and examined the parish books. The sixteenth-century registers have been lost, but the seventeenth-century volume was full of the names, *Chaves, Sánchez, Gómez, Durán,* and *Rico,* in various combinations. Half of the population of Valverde is still named *Chaves* (and *Chávez*), and practically all of the folks in the neighboring hamlet of Verlanga.—Llerena's famous citizen is *Don Luis Zapata de Chaves* (1526-1594), a Knight of Santiago who was once imprisoned as unworthy of his knighthood for being a Don Juan; he wrote a famous historical poem, *Don Carlos Famoso,* on the deeds of Charles V, which Cervantes did not consider very highly as literature.[7] Part of this poem, describing the origin of the Chaves name and crest, together with a gold signet bearing the family coat-of-arms, was inherited by Colonel Manuel A. Chaves, but everything has been lost.[8] Since the first New Mexico Chaves was always addressed as a "Don," and he brought along a quotation of *Don Carlos Famoso,* what was he to the noble poet, a close relative?)

The wife of Don Pedro Durán y Chaves was *Doña Isabel de Bohórquez,* who was forty years old "more or less" in 1626, and knew how to write. She had a sister, Juana.[9] She owned an hacienda at a place called Arroyo del Tunque in the vicinity of San Felipe Pueblo, where a mulatto servant of Chaves had married a San Felipe woman.[10] Don Pedro was a brother-in-law of Antonio Baca;[11] hence Isabel was really a Baca, one of the three girls mentioned with their parents in 1600. She was, perhaps, a second wife of his, but his first in New Mexico, since she was some twenty years younger.

A *Sargento* in 1600, a *Capitán* by 1613, a *Sargento Mayor* (major) by 1623 "during the Jémez Campaign,"[12] Don Pedro had become over-all commander by 1626. How long he lived after this is not known. As a faithful executor of Governor Eulate's orders, he incurred the enmity of the Mission friars, several of whom berated him in writing, in 1621 and 1626, for impeding the Mission program.[13]

His known children were *Fernando, Pedro II*, and, most likely, a daughter *Isabel,* wife of Juan Domínguez de Mendoza.

Don Fernando Durán y Chaves, the "eldest son of his father," and named presumably after his grandfather, Hernán, inherited Don Pedro's *encomienda* and lost it later during a political fracas,[14] during the term of Governor Pacheco. He is first mentioned in contemporary documents of 1638 when, as Lieutenant Governor of the Sandía or Río Abajo jurisdiction, he testified that he had accompanied Governor Rosas in an expedition to the Apotlapihuas.[15] Testifying many years later, in 1660, he gave his age as forty-three,[16] so that, if born in 1617, he was the son of Isabel de Bohórquez; nevertheless, he was older than his brother Pedro II. In 1644, August 17, he had testified that he was born in New Mexico and was thirty-five years old. His brother Pedro was thirty-three.[16a]

Don Fernando was embroiled in two major political crises, the first around the year 1640, and the second around 1660. The first was the Governor Rosas affair when he testified against him in favor of the friars, being a captain at the time.[17] He got into Governor Pacheco's good graces by attending the execution of eight conspirators in Santa Fe, July 21, 1643, and was appointed an *Alcalde* by him; but when Pacheco turned against the friars, he took the friars' part.[18] Pacheco then condemned him and thirteen others to be executed for sedition. It seems that he escaped execution by fleeing from New Mexico, thus losing his *encomienda*.[19] For in 1646, he and his son, Don Agustín de Chaves, were in the soldier-escort that brought a new governor, Don Luis de Guzmán, from Mexico City to Santa Fe.[20] The next major issue, in 1660 and after, and for the same reasons, took place under the tenures of Governors López Mendizábal and Peñalosa. At this time he was a *Sargento Mayor*.[21] The crowning incident took place in August, 1663, when Peñalosa violated the right of sanctuary by removing Fernando's brother Pedro from the Mission at Santo Domingo Pueblo, and subsequently imprisoned him in the Palace of the Governors with Fernando and the latter's son Cristóbal.[22] He died some years after, for in April, 1669, he is referred to as recently deceased.[23] He might have died in an Indian expedition he led in 1668.[24]

His land holdings, as can be inferred from those of his heirs, were those inherited from his father in the Sandía jurisdiction, from the boundaries of San Felipe Pueblo down through Bernalillo to Atrisco. His wife was a *Carvajal*, a sister of Agustín de Carvajal. Their known children were *Agustín*, *Cristóbal*, and *Fernando II*.

Don Agustín Durán y Chaves is first mentioned when he accompanied Don Fernando in escorting Governor Guzmán from Mexico City to Santa Fe.[25] For reasons unknown he went to Parral in 1665 and never returned.[26] A later Fernando, of Taos, seems to have been his son.

Don Cristóbal Durán y Chaves was imprisoned with his father and his uncle Pedro in 1663. Still single in that year, he gave his age as twenty-four, stating that he was a resident of the Sandía district.[27] In the following year he said that he was twenty-five, still at Sandía, and married to *Catalina Domínguez de Mendoza*,[28] who was a daughter of Tomé Domínguez II and Catalina López Mederos.[29] In 1667 he pulled out a dagger on a friar for writing satires on certain New Mexicans.[30] As he does not appear in the 1680 lists, it is presumed that he was dead or had left New Mexico.

The two later men called *Fernando Durán y Chaves*, the *Sargento Mayor* and the *Capitán*, were too old in 1680 to have been his sons.

Don Fernando Durán y Chaves II, *the Capitán*, was, to all appearances, the third son of Don Fernando and his heir in New Mexico.[30a] He was mentioned as an *Alférez* and "youth of good repute" by Father Bernal in 1670.[31] A captain by 1680, he fled the Indian Rebellion with the Río Abajo people, but was the only one among the leaders who voted to turn back and help the Santa Fe colonists.[32] Unlike the rest of the Chaves family, his uncle Pedro's family, and his first cousin Fernando, the *Sargento Mayor* of Taos, he did not try to impede the resettlement of New Mexico, nor did he ask to return to New Spain.[33] He passed muster in September, 1680, as a married man with four small children and two servants, and was described in 1681 as a settler willing to return, thirty years old, married, and having a good stature with a fair and ruddy complexion.[34] He must have been somewhat older than this, for he later testified at Guadalupe del Paso that he had witnessed the beheading of eight men in 1643.[35] Or else, chary of signing a paper against the Governor, he was referring to his father's experience in that year.

His wife, as learned from post-Reconquest sources, was *Lucía Hurtado de Salas,* who fled with him and their four little children in 1680. They returned with a much increased family in 1693. This is the most important Chaves family, being the only one to return with Vargas, and is thus the parent stem of succeeding generations in New Mexico.

* * * * * * * *

Don Pedro Durán y Chaves II was the second son of the original Chaves and younger brother of Don Fernando I. Still much alive in 1680, he gave his age as seventy. Those who testified against him at Guadalupe del Paso for taking an undue share of the refugees' rations deposed that in 1637 he was still a boy in his mother's care, which also shows that his father was dead by this time.[36] But by 1642 he was already married. As a youth he went on three campaigns, one of them with his uncle, Antonio Baca.[37] In the Governor Rosas affair, he was one of the four masked men who accompanied the assassin, Nicolás Ortiz,[38] and for this complicity he was later banished from New Mexico by Governor Guzmán.[39] His arrest, not a political one but over a question of livestock, in the Santo Domingo Church, has just been cited, at which time he held the rank of *Sargento Mayor.*[40]

His *estancia* lay four leagues north of Isleta Pueblo on the Río del Norte.[41] In 1667 he gave his age as forty, giving Santa Fe as his birthplace. His wife was *Elena Domínguez de Mendoza,* the daughter of Captain Tomé Domínguez.[42] In 1680, his family joined the Rio Abajo settlers in their flight to Guadalupe del Paso. He gave his age as seventy, declaring a son already bearing arms, ten minor children, and thirty servants.[43] In 1681 he complained of his poverty, the fact of having served the King without salary or an *encomienda,* boasting that his grandparents [the Bacas] had been among "the first conquistadores and pacifiers" of the Kingdom, and that his father [Don Pedro I] and "those others ended their lives there in the royal service."[44] But the other refugees contradicted him by proving that he had not only deprived some families of their rations by taking an undue share, but was also profiteering in stock and textiles; they agreed that his forebears had done great things, but that he himself had been a military slacker as well as a commercial profiteer all his life.[45] In the years following, he secretly did his best to impede the return of the colonists for the reconquest and resettlement of New Mexico[46], and finally the intermarried families of Pedro de Chaves and Tomé Domínguez were allowed to leave the Guadalupe del Paso district and move south into New Spain.[47] This is how the greater portion of the Chaves family failed to repopulate New Mexico after the Reconquest; however, they are the progenitors of old families of this name in what is now northern Mexico.

* * * * * * * *

Don Fernando Durán y Chaves, *Sargento Mayor,* has been confused by historians in the past with the Captain of the same name, who was, to all appearances, a first cousin. This one resided in Taos valley in 1680, when the Indians massacred his wife and three children. He and a grown son, *Cristóbal,* were away from home on that fateful day; on returning that evening to find everything lost, they made their way to Santa Fe and found that city besieged by the Indians, so they continued on south and caught up with the Rio Abajo refugees, to bring the first news of Santa Fe's resistance to the rebel Pueblos.[48]

Fernando was described in 1681 as a widower, thirty-four years old, tall, thin, of good features, and having a thick black beard. His son *Cristóbal* was entered on the muster-roll with him.⁴⁹ Down in Guadalupe del Paso he sided with his uncle Pedro and the Domínguez de Mendoza clan. He even fled to Mexico City with his son to make a complaint before the Viceroy in their name.⁵⁰ He had a sister, María de Chaves, who was the wife of Bernabé Márquez.⁵¹ His wife, murdered at Taos, was *Elena Ruiz Cáceres,* as we learn from two daughters of his who as little girls escaped the massacre of 1680; possibly, they were captured by the Taos Indians and were rescued in 1692, or else they were with their mother's relatives who escaped. One of these was *María* who became the wife of Sebastian Martín Serrano, and the other was *Josefa,* who married Antonio de Cisneros. But Fernando and young Cristóbal never returned to New Mexico; yet his name remained in the valley of Taos in the "Rio de Don Fernando," and the lands which "Don Fernando de Chaves" owned at present Ranchos de Taos before 1680.⁵² By elimination, he can be presumed to be the son of Agustín de Chaves.

Cristóbal de Chaves, son of the above Fernando, was mentioned in 1680-81 as having escaped from Taos with his father; he was sixteen or seventeen years old, single, tall and swarthy, with a mole on the right cheek.⁵³ Three years after the Reconquest, in 1695, he was stationed at Cuquiasachi in the frontier of Sonora.⁵⁴

Other Chaves people of the younger generation who appear in the 1680-81 Revolt lists, were members of the Pedro de Chaves clan and faction who did not return to New Mexico with the Reconquest.

Don José Durán y Chaves had his wife, a child, and ten servants. He was described as being twenty-six years of age, married, and having a good stature, a thin aquiline face, a thick beard, and half-closed eyes.⁵⁵ His wife was *Ana Márquez Carvajal,* daughter of Margarita Márquez. His wife tried to poison him at El Real de San Lorenzo in 1682, but another Chaves by the name of Juan took the non-fatal potion by mistake and became ill.⁵⁶ He was a first cousin of Pedro Varela. He was perhaps a son of Don Pedro II, siding with him and the Domínguez clan against returning to New Mexico.

Don Juan Durán y Chaves was eighteen years old in 1681, described as having a good body, fair complexion, a ruddy pockmarked face, with red and curly hair.⁵⁷ He was the one who drank the poison meant for José de Chaves, and was a brother of María de Chaves,⁵⁸ and therefore also of Fernando, the *Sargento Mayor* of Taos. In 1682 Juan killed a certain Diego Domínguez,⁵⁹ and this is the last we hear of him.

Don Tomás Durán y Chaves, nineteen years old in 1681, and married in this year, declared that he could not take part in the Otermín Expedition because he had no one with whom to leave his wife and livestock; yet at the same time he was trafficking in cattle and other trade with old Don Pedro de Chaves and others.⁶⁰ His excuses and actions show him to be the "son bearing arms" which Don Pedro mentioned in 1680.

These are all the Chaves men listed in the 1680-81 muster-rolls. As previously stated, they moved to what are now the northern States of Mexico, some of them perhaps further south.

* * * * * * * *

Others of the name who figured in the initial years of New Mexico's colonial history, but who left no trace, were *Diego Núñez de Chaves* and *Alonso de Chaves*. The first was an *Alférez*, native of Guadalcanal (in Estremadura near Llerena), who came in 1598 and was killed at the famous battle of Acoma.⁶¹ He could have been related to Don Pedro de Chaves. His wife was a daughter of the *Contador* Sánchez of the same Expedition, all of whom returned to New Spain. — *Alonso de Chaves* was one of the loyal soldiers who did not desert the colony in 1601, but he is not heard of again. He is most probably Alonso Sánchez, Oñate's treasurer and father-in-law of Diego Núñez de Chaves.⁶²

The name of *Chaves* (Latin, *clavis*: plural, *claves*) is the old Spanish and Portuguese word for "Keys." As related by the poet Zapata de Chaves, it was first given to two Ruiz brothers who were knighted for wresting the Portuguese town of Chaves from the Moors in the year 1160; its coat-of-arms of five keys was also bestowed on them. The origin and development of the name, as well as of the family of New Mexico, was treated by me in an article, "Don Fernando Durán y Chávez." Some suppositions made in it are confirmed or corrected in this present writing.[63]

The correct spelling of the name is *"Chaves,"* for it is not a patronym to merit the final "z" like most Spanish names of this ending. But all of Latin America, Portugal, and in some instances in Spain, the "z" ending is used. On a couple of occasions others inverted the name as "Chaves y Durán," but this was their error; nor was this family related to the one known simply as "Durán."

A curious fact regarding the New Mexico family is that the title of "Don" was used for all of them during the seventeenth century, when the prefix was otherwise applied only to the Governor. Not even the more prominent Gómez Robledo and Domínguez de Mendoza men were accorded this title of nobility. The signatures of Don Pedro and the two succeeding Don Fernandos also bear the prefix.[64]

After the Reconquest the title of Don was applied to all landholders and magistrates and, by the Nineteenth Century, to almost any man reaching old age.

1. AGN, Mex., Inq., t. 316, f. 152.
2. Ibid, t. 356, f. 268.
3. AGI, Contad., legs. 713, 720, Data.
4. See Don Fernando D. y Chaves, 18th-century section, and youngest son, Pedro Gómez Durán.
5. Oñate, p. 202; AGI, Patronato, t. 22, pt. 5, doc. 3, f. 503.
6. AGI, Mex., Aud., leg. 121, No. 165.
7. Cejador, Julio, Historia de la Lengua y Literatura Castellana, t. III, p. 90; Ferias y Fiestas en Llerena, Llerena (Badajoz), 1947, pp. 2, 3.
8. NMHR, Vol. VI, No. 1, pp. 101-4.
9. AGN, Mex., Inq., t. 356, f. 301.
10. Ibid., t. 372, exp. 19, f. 17.
11. Ibid., t. 356, f. 302.
12. Ibid., f. 266.
13. Ibid., ff. 266, 285-7, 290.
14. Revolt, II, p. 166.
15. AGN, loc. cit., t. 385, ff. 8-9.
16. Ibid., t. 666, f. 533.
16a. AGI, Patronato, leg. 244, Ramo 7, pp. 86, 92, 102.
17. AGN, Mex., Inq., t. 385, ff. 8-9; t. 425, f. 641.
18. Cf. Ch. and State, pp. 175-85.
19. Twit. Coll., No. 280; Revolt II, pp. 148, 166.
20. AGI, Contad., leg. 740, Data.
21. AGN, loc. cit., t. 507, pp. 45-6, 85-6, 126, 744.
22. Ibid., t. 507, pt. 2, f. 361v.
23. Ibid., t. 666, f. 533.
24. B-H, III, p. 279.
25. AGI, loc. cit.
26. AGN, loc. cit., t. 608, f. 420; t. 666, f. 552.
27. Ibid., t. 507, pt. 2, ff. 134, 232, 271-2, 784.
28. Ibid., p. 239.
29. Domínguez-Chaves charts.
30. AGN, Mex., Inq., t. 610, ff. 123-4.
30a. Chaves charts and fact of inheriting Sandia lands.
31. B-H, III, pp. 278-9.
32. Revolt, I, p. 79.
33. Ibid., II, pp. 25-6, 391.
34. Ibid., p. 141; Sp. Arch., II, No. 5.
35. AASF, Sp. Period, No. 5, f. 2.
36. Revolt, II, p. 166.
37. Ibid.
38. Ch. and State, p. 162.
39. Revolt, loc. cit.
40. AGN, loc. cit., t. 507, pt. 4, ff. 361, 479.
41. Ibid., t. 595, f. 272; t. 529, f. 558.
42. Ibid., t. 608, ff. 384, 379; t. 507, pt. 5, f. 576.
43. Revolt, I, pp. 67-8, 75, 169, 142.
44. Ibid., II, pp. 22, 52, 148.
45. Ibid., pp. 162-80.
46. Ibid., p. 399.
47. BNM, leg. 2, pt. 3, ff. 354-7.
48. Revolt, I, p. 152.
49. Ibid., II, p. 108.
50. BNM, leg. 2, pt. 3, ff. 267, 275, 283, 290, 357-8.
51. Ibid., f. 290.
52. Sp. Arch., I, No. 240; Cf. Sebastián Martín Serrano and Carlos Fernández, next century.
53. Revolt, I, p. 152; II, pp. 71, 108.
54. AGI, Guadalajara, leg. 151, pt. 6, f. 1.
55. Revolt, I, pp. 140, 176; II, pp. 40, 130, 318.
56. AGN, Mex., Inq., t. 1551, ff. 379-83.
57. Revolt, II, p. 139.
58. AGN, loc. cit., ff. 379-81.
59. Ibid., f. 382.
60. Revolt, II, pp. 53, 150, 162-6, 176.
61. Oñate, pp. 114, 190.
62. Ibid., pp. 147n, 117, 145-6, 150.
63. El Palacio, Vol. 55, No. 4, pp. 103-21.
64. AGN, Mex., Inq., t. 356, f. 268; t. 385, exp. 15, f. 9; Ibid., Tierras, t. 511, series No. 4486; BNM, leg. 2, pt. 3, f. 397; Sp. Arch., II, No. 120.

CRUZ

(Cruz Catalán)

JUAN de la CRUZ, also known as Juan Catalán because he was from Cataluña, came with the Oñate forces in 1598. He is described then as being thirty-two years old, a native of Barcelona, the son of Antonio de la Cruz, having a bright reddish beard and a wounded right arm.[1] He was in the wagon-train escort of 1613 between Mexico City and Santa Fe,[2] and by 1631 he held the rank of *Alférez*, his wife being a *Beatriz de los Angeles*,[3] a native of the valley of Mexico who figured in several instances concerning witchcraft.[4] She appears to be the woman of this name who came in 1700 as a servant of Cristóbal de Brito.[5]

Their two known children were *Pedro* and *Juana,* who married Juan Griego II.

Pedro de la Cruz was twenty-four years of age in 1632 and serving as a soldier.[6] In 1660 he stated that he was fifty years old; his wife was *Bernardina Morán.* The fact that he was an uncle of Maria de la Cruz Alemán, daughter of Juan Griego II and Juana de la Cruz, shows that he was the son of Juan de la Cruz.[7] His residence was at La Cañada, still standing after the Reconquest,[8] but he was already dead by 1680 as his name does not appear on the Revolt lists.

There are no individuals of this name in the 1680-81 muster-rolls, hence any male descendants of this family were minors at the time. Post-Reconquest records, however, show that there were several women, and also some male minors, who escaped the Indian massacre.

One individual of this name who acted as town-crier or herald for the Governor was a *Nicolás* (or *Sebastian*) *de la Cruz,*[9] but there is no way of linking him with the above family. He could well have been Sebastian *Rodríguez.* (q.v.)

1. Oñate, p. 190.
2. AGI, Contad., leg. 718, Data.
3. AGN, Mex., Inq., t. 304, f. 189.
4. Ibid., t. 304, f. 186 et seq.

6. AGN, loc. cit., t. 304, f. 195.
7. Ibid., t. 587, pp. 315-6.
8. Sp. Arch., I, No. 818.
9. Revolt, I, p. 116; II, p. 157.
5. Oñate, p. 210.

CUÉLLAR

PEDRO de CUÉLLAR CORSADO, thirty years old, son of Juan de la Cruz and born in the Kingdom of Guatemala, came to New Mexico as a convict in 1677, to serve as a soldier for four years.[1] He must have married in New Mexico after his arrival, for the Indians killed his wife and daughter in 1680 while he was with the Leyva party that had gone down to Guadalupe del Paso to meet the Mexico City wagon-train. His *estancia* near San Felipe Pueblo was sacked and destroyed.[2] He does not appear in the 1681 lists, but in 1683 he is mentioned as having run away from the refugee colony.[3]

Andrés de Cuéllar, eighteen and a native of Mexico City, was also in the 1677 convict group, sentenced to two years.[4] He must have left on finishing his term before 1680.

1. B-H, III, pp. 317-22.
2. Revolt, I, pp. 23, 37, 143.

3. BNM, leg. 2, pt. 3, ff. 267-83.
4. B-H, loc. cit.

DOMÍNGUEZ de MENDOZA

TOMÉ DOMÍNGUEZ (without "Mendoza") came to New Mexico with his grown family around the middle of the century.[1] His sons testified that he had died around the year 1656 at the age of ninety-six.[2] His family had settled in the Sandia jurisdiction where they intermarried with the Chaves clan.

Elena Ramírez de Mendoza, wife of Tomé "el Viejo," and who gave the "Mendoza" ending to this family, was already dead by 1661, as was also her husband.³ She had a sister, Juana de la Cruz y Mendoza, who was Governor Peñalosa's housekeeper; her son, Luis de Ulloa, was the Governor's page.⁴ The Domínguez de Mendoza children, born in Mexico City, played important roles in seventeenth-century New Mexico history.

The sons were *Tomé the Younger, Juan,* and *Francisco.* Of the daughters, *Damiana* married Álvaro de Paredes in 1660, and later, Agustín de Carvajal; *Leonor* was the wife of Cristóbal de Anaya; *Francisca* became the wife of Antonio Márquez, and then of Francisco de Anaya; *Elena* married Don Pedro Durán y Chaves.

In April, 1680, Tomé II was fifty-four years old, Damiana was fifty, Juan was forty-six, and Leonor was forty, all living on their lands south of Sandia Pueblo.⁵

Tomé Domínguez de Mendoza II, *"el Mozo,"* had a flourishing *estancia* below Isleta Pueblo as early as 1662.⁶ It was he who obtained the release of Don Pedro Durán y Chaves after the famous "right of sanctuary" case. His wife was *Catalina Lopéz Mederos,* sister of one Pedro López.⁷ In 1666 he was named interim Governor when Gov. Villanueva returned to New Spain for eye-treatment.⁸

In August, 1680, Tomé and his family fled south with the rest of the Rio Abajo people.⁹ He passed muster as a *Maese de Campo* with a full complement of arms, four soldier sons and thirty horses, declaring that he himself was married, as also three of his sons, with eight children among them—the entire family consisting of fifty-five persons, including servants. He also claimed that thirty-eight relatives had been killed by the Indians.¹⁰ The following year he claimed to be sixty-one years old with gout and stomach disorders, and boasted of having served the King in New Mexico since he had "reached years of discretion." Since last year, one of his sons, *Tomé III,* had died in battle; two others, *Juan* and *Diego,* had been seriously wounded by poison arrows; and the fourth, *Francisco,* had taken part in the latest Indian conflicts. In the 1680 outbreak, said he, the Indians had killed many of his sons, daughters, grandsons, a grand-daughter, two sons-in-law, his brothers, nephews, and two *callados.*¹¹ Others, however, thought otherwise of his conduct, accusing him of moving all his hacienda goods out of New Mexico, burying ploughshares and other implements on the way to lighten the wagons, when he well knew that the Santa Fe people were besieged and in need of help; now, in 1681, the entire family was profiteering on the misery of the exile colony.¹² The next year, 1682, Tomé and Don Pedro de Chaves got permission to depart with their families for New Spain, and so they never returned to New Mexico.

This particular Tomé's name has been perpetuated in the village on the site of his *estancia* which now bears his name.¹³

His children were *Tomé III, Juan, Diego, Francisco,* and *Antonio,* who are treated further on. Probably his daughter was *Juana,* wife of Cristóbal Durán y Chaves.

Juan Domínguez de Mendoza was already an adult taking an active part in New Mexico political life in 1662, having come from Mexico City "a few years ago."¹⁴ In the spring of 1680 he gave his age as forty-six,¹⁵ but in 1681 he said he was fifty-two, a native of Mexico City, married and accompanied by his wife, children, and a son-in-law.¹⁶ An able commander, he was placed in charge of Guadalupe del Paso in that year by Gov. Otermín, and as Lt. General of Cavalry was also entrusted with a campaign against the New Mexico Pueblos. This latter turned into a fiasco due to his own machinations contrary to the Governor's policy.¹⁷ Still with the exile colony after his brother Tomé had left, Juan led a memorable Expedition into the Texas interior in 1684,¹⁸ but in the following year he was the leader of a desertion plot involving others of his family, including his son *Baltasar.*¹⁹ Juan must have fled around this time, for in March, 1689, his son Baltasar obtained permission to leave for New Spain with his mother, *Isabel Durán y Chaves,* and her servants.²⁰ Coming together sometime afterwards, Juan and his son made a voyage to

Spain, undoubtedly to seek royal favors. They lost all but their lives in a shipwreck, and Juan died shortly after in a Madrid hospital after forty-four years of Indian fighting in New Mexico.[21]

Baltasar Domínguez de Mendoza, the only known son of Juan, returned from Spain and in October, 1692, was asking for the Governorship of New Mexico, or at least some other important post in Sonora. (See preceding note.) Juan's only known daughter was *Maria*, wife of Diego Lucero de Godoy, who also got permission to leave for New Spain in 1689.[22]

———

Francisco Domínguez de Mendoza, forty-seven years old in 1664 when Captain of the jurisdiction of Zia and Cochití, was also born in Mexico City. His wife was *Juana de Rueda*, who most probably came to New Mexico with her husband.[23] Old and blind in 1680, he survived the Indian Rebellion with his family of five.[24] His name appears no longer after that date, having perhaps died before the fall of 1681. Their son, *Antonio Domínguez de Rueda*, asked for permission to leave for New Spain in 1684.[25] A sister of Antonio, *Petrona*, seems to be the woman who married a Bartolomé Trujillo at Guadalupe del Paso in February, 1681, and later married a Simón Martín in New Mexico after the Reconquest.[26]

* * * * * * * *

The following are other members of this large family mentioned at the time of the Indian Rebellion of 1680 and succeeding years.

Tomé Domínguez de Mendoza III, eldest of the four sons of Tomé II, was killed as a *Sargento Mayor* in a battle with the Indians in 1681.[27] His wife, to all appearances, was *Catalina Varela de Losada,* native of Santa Fe and residing in Chihuahua as late as December, 1737, with a son, *Julian;* another, *Cristóbal,* had moved up to Santa Fe and died there around this time.[28]

Juan Domínguez de Mendoza, Captain and second son of Tomé II, was thirty-five years old and married in 1681. He was seriously wounded in battle shortly after,[29] but nothing more is known about him.

Diego Domínguez de Mendoza, thirty-seven and married in 1680, was the third son of Tomé II. He was also wounded in battle in 1681 and claimed to be suffering from poisoned arrow wounds in the leg and arm when he passed muster.[30] He survived, however, for he was active in black market dealings shortly after between Guadalupe del Paso, Parral, Sonora, and Casas Grandes.[31] He appears to be the Diego Domínguez killed by Juan de Chaves in 1682.[32]

Francisco Domínguez de Mendoza, the fourth adult son of Tomé II, was twenty-five years of age and married in 1681, and also took part in the Otermín Campaign. He, too, engaged in profiteering with his brothers.[33]

Antonio Domínguez de Mendoza, a fifth son of Tomé II, was a minor in 1680, and therefore not on the muster-rolls. He is without doubt the one unmarried son, age twenty, who was still in his father's care in 1681.[34] In that year Antonio, son of the *Maese de Campo* Tomé D. de Mendoza and Catalina López Mederos, married *Juana Romero*.[35] The next year he fled from Guadalupe del Paso with his wife.[36]

Presumably, all the surviving sons of Tomé II, including the families of the two deceased sons, left south for New Spain, with or without permission.

———

Antonio Domínguez de Mendoza (or *de Rueda*) was the son of Francisco D. de Mendoza and Juana de Rueda. A Captain in 1680-81, he was described as married, thirty-two years old, a native of New Mexico, tall and slender, having good features and long red hair. He also took part in the Otermín Campaign of 1681.[37] He was mentioned in 1682 as being the son-in-law of Alonso García, the Lt. General of the Rio Abajo, and father-in-law of Don Juan Severino.[38] His wife was *Juana García de Noriega*. Antonio asked to leave Guadalupe del Paso in August, 1684,[39] but was apparently turned down, for by 1689 he had died and his widow was still with the exile colony.[40]

This family is important because the children, all daughters, returned to New Mexico with the Vargas Reconquest. These girls were: *Antonia*, who first married Andrés Hurtado and then Tomás Jirón de Tejeda; *María*, wife of Antonio Godines; *Teresa*, married to Diego González de la Rosa; *Leonor*, wife of Miguel Martín; and one whose name is not known, the wife of Juan Severino Rodríguez de Zeballos.

José Domínguez de Mendoza was a soldier with the Leyva party which had gone to meet the Mexico City wagon-train at Guadalupe del Paso when the Indians struck the northern colony in 1680; in this recorded instance he signed his name without "Mendoza."[41] But in the following year he used the full name, and was described as a bachelor, newly arrived from a trip to Parral, twenty-four years old, swarthy, with an aquiline face, coarse hair and beard.[42] In 1682 he was mentioned as a native of New Mexico, the natural son of Ana Velásquez, when he asked to marry a Juana López.[43] In that same year he ran away from the refugee colony,[44] but must have returned or was apprehended, for he came to New Mexico with the Reconquest. In 1692 he rescued his sister *Juana* and her four daughters and one son from Indian captivity.[45] He and *Juana* were some of the *callados*, or illegitimate children, of the Tomé Domínguez family.

---

1. **AGN, Mex., Inq.**, t. 507, pt. 6, f. 785.
2. **DM, 1680,** No. 1.
3. **AGN,** loc. cit., t. 582, p. 36.
4. **Ibid.,** t. 507, pp. 415, 1231, 1303-4.
5. **DM,** loc. cit.
6. **AGN,** loc. cit., t. 595, f. 272.
7. **Ibid.,** t. 507, pp. 49, 239.
8. **AGI, Contad.,** leg. 768-A. **Data.**
9. **Revolt,** I, pp. 39, 55-60, 89-90, 106.
10. **Ibid.,** p. 138.
11. **Ibid.,** pp. 35, 145, 151.
12. **Ibid.,** pp. 162, 172.
13. **AGN,** loc. cit., t. 595, f. 272; **Bancroft, Mex. Mss.,** No. 232, ff. 123-52.
14. **Ibid.,** t. 507, pt. 6, f. 785.
15. **DM,** loc. cit.
16. **Revolt,** II, p. 95.
17. **Ibid.,** pp. 69, 183, 215-17 et seq.
18. Cf. **AGN,** loc. cit., t. 37.
19. **Sp. Arch.** II, No. 35.
20. **Ibid.,** No. 48.
21. **AGI, Guadalajara,** leg. 151, pt. 6, series No. 8949 et seq.; leg. 73, f. 158.
22. **Sp. Arch.,** II, No. 49.
23. **AGN,** loc. cit., t. 610, f. 990.
24. **Revolt,** I, p. 151.
25. **HSNM,** No. 2844.
26. **DM, 1681,** No. 6; **Sp. Arch.,** II, No. 137b.
27. **Revolt,** I, p. 138; II, pp. 145-51.
28. **Sp. Arch.,** I, No. 422.
29. **Revolt,** I, p. 67; II, pp. 35, 145-51.
30. **Ibid.,** I, pp. 79, 119, 138; II, pp. 37, 145-51.
31. **Ibid.,** II, pp. 165-6, 176.
32. **AGN,** loc. cit., t. 1551, ff. 379-81.
33. **Revolt,** II, pp. 36, 145, 151, 165-6, 176.
34. **Ibid.,** p. 35.
35. **DM, 1681,** No. 2.
36. **BNM,** leg. 2, pt. 3, f. 356.
37. **Revolt,** I, p. 176; II, pp. 80, 100.
38. **BNM,** loc. cit., f. 320.
39. **HSNM,** No. 2844.
40. **DM, 1689,** No. 2.
41. **Revolt,** I, pp. 37-151.
42. **Ibid.,** pp. 71, 142.
43. **DM, 1682,** No. 5; also, 1680, No. 1, for sister **Juana.**
44. **BNM,** loc. cit., f. 274.
45. **First Expedition,** p. 184.

DURÁN

JUAN DURÁN is mentioned as early as x1628 as the husband of *Catalina Bernal*, daughter of Juan Griego.[1] He was also called "Juan *de la Cruz*" when involved in a case concerning pagan Indian rites.[2] Most likely he is the Juan de la Cruz, nineteen years old, who came with Oñate in 1598, the son of Juan Rodríguez and a native of the Valley of Toluca; he was described as somewhat swarthy, beardless, and tall.[3] Possibly he began using the name *Durán* to distinguish himself from another Juan de la Cruz, the Catalán. In 1632, Juan Durán and his wife were involved in a hex trial; here mention was made of a son, *Nicolás Durán*.[4] A daughter, *Catalina*, was the wife of Juan Morán.

Nicolás Durán was sheriff of the Council in 1642. He was mentioned in 1663 as being an "aide" to Governor Peñalosa, and having a wife and children in Santa Fe.[5] To all appearances, he was the Nicolás mentioned above. He was not alive by 1680, but from the marriage of a daughter, *Catalina*, we learn that his widow's name was *Antonia Trujillo*.[6]

Juan Durán II, thirty-five years old in 1657 and a native of Santa Fe, was a soldier who accompanied wagon-trains to and from Mexico City in 1657, 1658, and 1661.[7] He seems to have been a grandson of the first Juan Durán through his daughter Catalina, wife of Juan Morán.[8] In 1680, Juan Durán and his family of eleven persons, including his brothers and sisters, escaped the Indian massacre.[9] But he himself is not mentioned in the following year, having died or run away from the exile colony.

Other Durán persons in the 1680-81 lists were as follows:

Salvador Durán, Adjutant, thirty-one (or forty-one) years old, escaped with his family of twelve, including daughters and servants. He was a native of New Mexico, married, of good stature, with a swarthy complexion, straight coarse hair and long, and a scant beard.[10] His wife's name was *Ana Márquez* (or *Luján*), as we learn from the marriages of their children: *Miguel, Diego, Lázaro,* and *Juana,* wife of Tomás Núñez.[11] Another daughter, very likely, was *Josefa,* married to Agustín Griego.[12] Salvador was most likely the son of Nicolás Duran since both, more advanced in the social scale than the other Durán people, consecutively held the same position of "*Ayudante.*"

Luis Durán, thirty years old and married in 1681, was described as being of medium height, slender, swarthy, with eyes having much white showing.[13] Nothing more is known about him.

This family was altogether distinct from the Durán y Chaves group.

1. **AGN, Mex., Inq.**, t. 304, f. 188; t. 372, exp. 19, f. 13.
2. **Ibid.**, t. 363, f. 12.
3. **Oñate**, p. 191.
4. **AGN, loc. cit.**, ff. 187-8.
5. **Ibid.**, t. 596, pt. 2, f. 157; **Ortiz Trial**, ff. 20, 21v, 36-39.
6. **DM**, 1693, No. 5; 1693, No. 5; 1695, No. 13.
7. **AGN, loc. cit.**, t. 571, exp. 8, ff. 226, 232; **AGI, Contad.**, legs. 749, 754, 755, **Data**.
8. **AGN, loc. cit.**, t. 596, pt. 2, f. 157; t. 608, f. 431.
9. **Revolt**, I, p. 151.
10. **Ibid.**, I, p. 148; II, pp. 49, 142.
11. **DM**, 1705, No. 10; 1694, No. 29; 1697, No. 1; 1698, No. 10.
12. **Sp. Arch.**, II, No. 187.
13. **Revolt** II, p. 133.

DURÁN y CHAVES
(See *Chávez*)

ENRÍQUEZ

CRISTÓBAL ENRIQUEZ was a thirty-year old *Alférez* in 1636.[1] Apparently a native of New Mexico, and, considering a custom of reaching back to a grandparent's name, he could well have been the son of Juan Rangel, an *Alférez* who came in 1600 to join Oñate's forces; he was described as tall and well featured, twenty-five years old, a native of Mexico City and the son of "*Cristóbal Gaspar Anrríquez.*"[2]

Cristóbal Enríquez was a first cousin of Agustín de Carvajal, hence their respective mothers must have been sisters. In 1660, Carvajal was accused of having married a close relative, *Estefania Enríquez,* Cristobal's daughter. This girl was, moreover, a second cousin of Carvajal's first wife, María Márquez; hence, Cristóbal's wife and María Márquez had mothers who were first cousins. Cristóbal was beheaded with eight other men in 1643 by Governor Pacheco.[3]

Cristóbal Enríquez II was forty years old in 1680-81, married, and with a family of seven small children and nine servants. In the latter year he claimed to be in poor health and unwilling to join Otermin's Expedition back into New Mexico, unless the government took care of his family and unusually large stock in the poverty-stricken exile colony at Guadalupe del Paso.⁴ He was also accused of taking an undue share of the King's relief sent to the refugees.⁵ This Enríquez could well have been the son of the previous man of this name. He is the only Enríquez among the refugees, and he did not return to New Mexico with the Reconquest.

1. AGN, Mex., Inq., t. 595, f. 407.
2. Oñate, p. 206.
3. Ch. and State, p. 175.
4. Revolt, I, pp. 68, 76, 147-8; II, p. 149.
5. Ibid., p. 162.

ESCALLADA

JUAN de la ESCALLADA is first noted as a soldier escorting the wagon-trains in 1652 and 1658.¹ He died before the Indian Rebellion in 1680. His widow, *Ynez Lucero* (or *González*) escaped the massacre with two widowed daughters and four small children.² Her name is given as González in 1682 when identified as the mother of *María de la Escallada*, twenty-five years old, widow of Andrés de Peralta, and her sister *Juana*, widow of Manuel de Peralta.³ In that same year, María gave Juan de la Escallada and Ynez Lucero de Godoy as her parents when she married Sebastián de Herrera.⁴ There were no male children to pass on the name.

Escallada's origin is not known, unless his name was a corruption of "Escarramad."

1. AGI, Contad., legs. 747, 749, Data.
2. Revolt, I, p. 151.
3. AGN, Mex., Inq., t. 1551, ff. 375-8.
4. DM, 1682, No. 4.

ESCARRAMAD

DON JUAN de ESCARRAMAD was another single individual who carried the title of "Don" before his name. As such he appears in the Oñate lists of 1598, a soldier twenty-six years old, the son of Don Juan Escarramad and a native of the City of Múrcia. He was short of stature, having a chestnut beard and "changeable eyes."¹ His signature in 1617, when he declared himself forty-eight years old, carries the title. In that year he was living in Santa Fe with his wife and children.² Between the years 1613-17 he was a key-figure in serious disputes between Gov. Peralta and the friars. It began with his wounding of a certain Simón Pérez, followed by the entry of the latter's many relatives, then the friars, into the controversy. He then went to Mexico City in 1614, "on business," where he made depositions against the Franciscans. On his return he was imprisoned for scurrilous remarks against the friars which he would not retract.³

* * * * * * * *

In 1636, a certain *Alférez* Francisco de Ribera of Santa Fe, widower of *Melchora de Escarramán*, asked to marry again.⁴ And in 1640, a Polonia Varela, widow of *Julian Escarramán,* asked that her marriage to a subsequent husband be annulled.⁵

Were these two people children of old Juan de Escarramad? They might have been servants of his, as they seemed to be of low estate. The name was not passed on, not even by Juan de la Escallada, if he was his son or grandson.

1. Oñate, p. 121.
2. AGN, Mex., Inq., t. 316, ff. 176-8.
3. Cf. Ch. and State, pp. 29-45.
4. AGN, loc. cit., t. 595, f. 407.
5. Ibid., t. 425, ff. 633-44.

FERNÁNDEZ de la FUENTE
(See *Fuente*)

FONTE

Cristóbal Fonte lived in New Mexico around the year 1663. His wife was *María Ramos,* alias *Varela,* twenty-two years old and a native of New Mexico.[1] It could be that his name was a misspelling of "Fuente."

---
1. AGN, Mex., Inq., t. 507, pt. 2, f. 136.

FRESQUI

JUAN FRESCO first came to New Mexico about the year 1617 with two other Flemish men. They were residents of Mexico City on a tour of mineral exploration. They went back to New Spain for mining equipment; on their return to Santa Fe, the people destroyed their equipment out of envy and resentment.[1] This return of Juan Fresco, or *Frescos,* took place in 1625, in the wagon-train that brought Fray Alonso Benavides. Juan deposed at this time that he was Flemish, fifty-five years old, and a miner by trade. His signature appears to spell out the name "Frishz."[2] Having stayed and married in New Mexico, he became *Juan Fresqui,* unless the individual of this name was his son—or an altogether different person.

By the end of the following century this family name was further hispanicized into "Frésquez."

Juan Fresqui, a Captain already dead by 1667, had been *Alcalde Mayor* of Isleta.[3] Although there were no adult male Fresquis in the 1680-81 Revolt lists, several people of this name after the Reconquest give proof that some minor children or grandchildren of his escaped the massacre.

A *Juana Fresqui,* wife of José de Leyva, was killed by the Indians in 1680.[4] Her two daughters were rescued from captivity in 1692 by a relative, Juan Holguín.[5] The latter's mother was *Magdalena Fresqui,* already dead by 1695.[6] These two women were apparently daughters of Juan Fresqui.

---
1. Doc. Hist. de Mex., p. 25.
2. AGN, Mex., Inq., t. 356, f. 266.
3. Ibid., t. 608, ff. 379-88.
4. DM, 1682, No. 3.
5. First Expedition, p. 184.
6. DM, 1695, No. 8.

FUENTE, de la

Bernardo de la Fuente was one of the convicts of 1677 sent to serve as soldiers in New Mexico. He was forty-eight years old, the son of Francisco and a native of Mexico City at La Merced, condemned to four years without pay. He had a good build, dark complexion, a large forehead and short nose.[1]

* * * * * * * *

Juan Fernández de la Fuente was a Captain stationed at Casas Grandes in 1681-84, in the company of New Mexicans from Guadalupe del Paso, like Francisco Ramírez de Salazar and Alonso Garcia de Noriega.²

Another *"Juan de Fuentes"* died at Casas Grandes in 1682.³

―――

This surname appears after the Reconquest in the Guadalupe del Paso district, very likely the children and other descendants of Juan Fernández de la Fuente. One of these, *Josefa de la Fuente,* married a New Mexico refugee, Diego Hurtado.

―――

1. B-H, III, pp. 317-24.
2. **HSNM**, No. 2843.
3. **BNM**, leg. 2, pt. 3, ff. 354-7.

GALLEGOS

JOSÉ and ANTONIO GALLEGOS were brothers who came to New Mexico sometime prior to the 1680 Rebellion. José was married and had three children by 1680, the family escaping the massacre while he was with the Leyva escort party at Guadalupe del Paso.¹ He does not appear in the 1681 lists because he had fled the refugee colony.² Having returned or been brought back, he and his family came to New Mexico with the Reconquest. In 1694 he declared that he was forty-one years old and a native of Parral.³ From post-Reconquest marriages we learn that his wife was *Catalina Hurtado,* and their children: *Diego, Nicolás, Juan,* and *María.*

―――

Antonio Gallegos was a brother of José.⁴ He escaped in 1680 with the rest of the Rio Abajo people, probably taking his absent brother's family with him. He himself was married and had two very small children.⁵ He was present at Guadalupe del Paso the following year and signed up for the Otermín Campaign.⁶ He is undoubtedly the Antonio *Laces* [?] who was twenty-six years old in 1681 and a native of New Vizcaya [Parral] married in New Mexico; he was then described as tall and slim, having a long face, large eyes, blond hair and beard.⁷ In 1683 he was declared a deserter, like his brother.⁸

His wife was *Catalina Baca.* Both appear to have died before the Vargas Reconquest; however, their children returned to New Mexico, probably with their uncle José's family. They were: *Antonio II, Elena,* and *Felipe.*

―――

1. **Revolt,** I, pp. 37, 144, 173.
2. **BNM,** leg. 2, pt. 3, ff. 267-83, 356.
3. DM, 1694, No. 20.
4. **BNM,** loc. cit., f. 356.
5. **Revolt.** I, pp. 140, 173.
6. **Ibid.,** II, p. 151.
7. **Ibid.,** pp. 54, 119.

GAMBOA

JUAN de GAMBOA figured in 1661 as the father of *Petronila* de Gamboa, a girl of low estate who was supposedly raped or seduced by Gov. López Mendizábal. Her mother's name was *María Pacheco.*¹ The child of this affair was Juan de Gamboa II who figured in a marriage squabble in the following century.² The first Juan seems to have had another wife, *Luisa* (or *Lucía*) Martin, by whom he had a daughter, *Felipa,* who later married Agustín de Salazar. Petrona had married an Andrés Ramírez del Prado, the latter having died before 1680. Their identities are deduced from eighteenth-century marriages of their children.

―――

Only three adult male Gamboas are found in the 1680-81 lists.

Lucas de Gamboa was killed by the Indians

when Gov. Otermín sent him with a message to Alonso Garcia in the Rio Abajo district.[3] His widow, *Isabel de Archuleta,* passed muster with their six small children.[4] Lucas was most likely a son of Juan de Gamboa.

Juan de Gamboa II, eighteen years old and single, passed muster in 1681 with his widowed mother [Maria Pacheco], and his brothers and sisters. He was small of stature, beardless, with long straight hair.[5]

Antonio de Gamboa was also eighteen and single in 1681, but was not described further.[6] He was, no doubt, the Antonio Ramírez de Gamboa, son of Andrés Ramírez del Prado and Petrona Gamboa, both deceased and natives of New Mexico, who married *Luisa de Tapia* four years later.[7]

1. **AGN, Mex., Tierras,** t. 3268, pp. 182-5.
2. **DM,** 1705, No. 10.
3. **Revolt,** I, p. 12.
4. Ibid., p. 158.
5. Ibid., II, p. 100.
6. Ibid., p. 80.
7. **DM,** 1685, No. 1.

GARCÍA

GARCIA is one of the most common Spanish surnames. Among the Oñate soldiers of 1598 was *Marcos García,* thirty-eight years old, the son of Tomé Garcia and a native of Sanlucar de Barrameda; he was greyish and dark with a good physique.[1] By 1608 he was a Captain, when he led a soldier-escort back to New Mexico.[2] Nothing more is known about him, or who his descendants were, if any.

Alonso García was in the wagon-train escorts of 1636 and 1643.[3] He was in New Mexico too early to be Alonso Garcia de Noriega, treated further on. Some unidentified Garcias of later generations, and not of the Garcia *Holgado* group, might derive from either of these two men.

1. **Oñate,** p. 192.
2. **AGI, Contad.,** legs. 707, 712, **Data.**
3. Ibid., legs. 736, 738, **Data.**

GARCÍA HOLGADO

ÁLVARO GARCÍA HOLGADO and a *Simón García* were mentioned as soldiers of the Oñate troops that came in 1600, but were not described.[1] In 1609 Álvaro was an *Alférez* escorting the wagon-train that brought Gov. Peralta to New Mexico.[2] By 1625 he was a Captain, forty-eight years old, and living in Santa Fe. He gave a Captain Juan Gómez, "the interpreter," as his brother-in-law.[3]

His wife was *Juana de los Reyes,* forty or fifty in 1631, and a sister of Juana Sánchez, thirty-five [wife of Gómez]. These two women were accused of using bizarre remedies to hold their husbands' affections.[4] Their children were *Diego, Juan,*[5] and, possibly, *Francisco.* A daughter (or grand-daughter), *Lucía López de Gracia,* was the wife of José Nieto.

Álvaro appears to be the progenitor, either by a second wife, or else through one of his sons or daughters, of the López de Gracia family group.

———

Diego García Holgado, son of Álvaro, was mentioned as a soldier of Santa Fe, twenty-seven years old in 1632 and thirty-two in 1636. His wife was a daughter of the *Alférez* Sebastián González. Diego was killed sometime prior to 1644 in an Indian campaign.[6]

———

Juan García Holgado, brother of Diego, was living at the Isleta district in 1638.[7] He held the office of *Alcalde* of Alameda Pueblo around the year 1650.[8] He was still living in the Rio Abajo country as late as 1667 with the rank of Captain, his wife being *Ana Pacheco.*[9]

Francisco García (Holgado) is first mentioned in 1632 as being twenty-two years of age and a soldier of Santa Fe.[10] He later established his residence in the Rio Abajo area near Isleta, having also lived in the Salinas region of Tajique and Cuarác when those Missions were in existence. He was a brother-in-law of José Nieto and Pedro de Leyva.[11] A weaver by trade, he was once forbidden by Gov. López Mendizábal to make cloth for the Franciscans' habits.[12] In 1665 he declared himself to be a captain fifty-seven years old and a native of San Gabriel del Yunque. A resident of Isleta and a widower at this time, he said that he had two daughters living with him.[13] After the Indian Rebellion, though dead prior to 1680, he was still remembered as a good "Protector of the Indians."[14]

Diego García Holgado, twenty-six or twenty-eight years of age in 1681, is the only adult male of this surname mentioned during the Revolt period. He was described as a native of New Mexico, married, with a good slender build, swarthy, and having thick black hair and beard.[15] In the first Vargas Entry in 1692, he rescued a relative of his [Juana de Apodaca] with her two children.[16] He was the son of any of the above three men.

A *Magdalena García* who passed muster in 1680 with eight persons in her family was most likely Magdalena *Montaño.*[17]

1. **Oñate**, p. 209; "Holgado" name not given here.
2. **AGI, Contad.**, leg. 711, **Data.**
3. **AGN, Mex., Inq.**, t. 356, f. 316.
4. **Ibid.**, t. 732, f. 14.
5. **Ibid.**, t. 304, ff. 190-1; **BNM**, leg. 1, pt. 1, ff. 470-504.
6. **AGN**, loc. cit.; **AGI, Patronato**, leg. 244, Ramo 7, doc. 22, p. 161.
7. **Ibid.**, t. 304, f. 190; t. 385, f. 12.
8. **Revolt**, II, p. 299.
9. **AGN**, loc. cit., t. 608, ff. 419-37.
10. **Ibid.**, t. 304, f. 196.
11. **Ibid.**, t. 512, ff. 7, 8, 156; t. 587, pp. 81-129.
12. **Ibid.**
13. **Ibid.**, t. 507, pp. 732-3; **Tierras**, t. 3268.
14. **Revolt**, II, pp. 290, 301.
15. **Ibid.**, pp. 72, 124.
16. **First Expedition**, p. 184.
17. **Revolt**, I, p. 149.

GARCIÁ MUERTE

Francisco Garciá Muerte, forty-two years old and a native of Cádiz, where he still had a wife, was among the refugees at Guadalupe del Paso where he enlisted as a soldier in 1681.[1] He came with the convicts of 1677, when he was listed as the son of Antonio, twenty [?] years old and a native of Cádiz, having a good physique, a broad face, thick eyebrows, and sunken eyes. He was sentenced to eight years.[2] The description of his features suggests the possibility of his having received the "Muerte" as a nickname. He did not return to New Mexico, apparently.

1. **Revolt**, II, p. 136.
2. **B-H**, III, pp. 317-22.

GARCÍA de NORIEGA

ALONSO GARCÍA (without "Noriega") came to New Mexico in the middle of the century from the City of Zacatecas, his birthplace. In 1660 he gave his age as thirty-three; he owned the Estancia de San Antonio in the Rio Abajo, twenty leagues from Santa Fe.[1] By 1667 he was a Captain; his wife was *Teresa Varela.*[2]

He was the Lieutenant General of the Rio Abajo area, and holding the rank of *Maese de Campo,* when the Indians rebelled in 1680, and as such was held responsible for the flight of the Rio Abajo people without going to the aid of the colonists in Santa Fe. For this reason he underwent a court-martial by Gov. Otermín.[3] He was also *Alcalde* of Sandía at this period.[4] In the following year he still held his old titles, showing that he had exonerated himself. Ill in bed in September, 1681, he was ready to return for the reconquest of New Mexico; he was described then as being fifty-four years old and a native of Zacatecas, having a good physique, partly grey hair, protruding eyes, and an aquiline face. A married man, he had a large family of children and sons-in-law.[5] In 1682 he deposed that he had three sons and two sons-in-law bearing arms.[6]

One of his sons, *Lázaro*, had been killed by the Indians in 1680.[7] The others were: *Alonso II, Juan,* and, most likely, *Tomás*. Of his two known daughters, *Juana* was married to Antonio Domínguez de Mendoza, and *Josefa* later became the wife of Alonso Rael de Aguilar. These children added "de Noriega" to their family name, derived most likely from their father's parents or grandparents.

Juan García de Noriega, also known simply as Juan de Noriega, or de Noriega García, lived with Alonso García before and after 1680.[8] He passed muster in 1681 as a native of New Mexico, married, twenty-three years old, of medium build with a long face and chestnut hair.[9] A later matrimonial investigation of his daughter states that he was born in Zacatecas, but this looks like a mistake of the informants. Juan took part in the Otermín Campaign of 1681, and in the first Entry of Vargas in 1692.[10] He was a member of the Confraternity of La Conquistadora.[11]

His first wife was *Margarita Márquez*, dead prior to 1690 when a daughter, *María Ana*, married Miguel de Herrera. By his second wife, *Francisca Sánchez de Yñigo*, he had a son, *Francisco*, and two daughters, *María* and *Juana*. This family did not return with the Reconquest, remaining at Guadalupe del Paso where the following generations rose to prominence; some intermarried with Santa Fe people in the following century.

Alonso García de Noriega II, "*el Mozo*," passed muster in 1681 as a native of New Mexico, married, and thirty years old; he was swarthy and pockmarked, with a large nose and long straight hair.[12] He took part in the Otermín Campaign as a very useful *Alférez*, and is not to be confused with the youth Alonso García [de Gracia] who also figured in it.[13]

Alonso took part in the Reconquest of New Mexico by Vargas in 1692 and 1693. From other documents of the period we learn that his wife was *Ana Jorge de Vera*, by whom he had these sons: *Luis, Alonso III, Tomás,* and *Vicente*. Alonso's second wife was *María Luisa Godines,* whom he married sometime after the Reconquest, and whom he left a widow when he was wounded by an Apache arrow, sometime before or during 1696, on the road from Guadalupe del Paso to Santa Fe at the Paraje del Agua Escondida; he died at Sevilleta.[14]

Tomás García (without "Noriega") passed muster in 1680, extremely poor, with a family of six, wife, children, and grandchildren.[15] He is not listed in 1681, having perhaps died. Nor is it known if he belonged to the Noriega family group, the third living son of old Alonso García. Perhaps he was a García Holgado, as he seemed to be too old to be a son of Alonso.

---

1. **AGN**, Mex., Inq., t. 587, f. 97.
2. Ibid., t. 608, ff. 379-84.
3. **Revolt**, I, pp. 62 et seq.
4. **DM**, 1680, No. 1.
5. **Revolt**, II, pp. 82, 95.
6. **BNM**, leg. 2, pt. 3, f. 310.
7. **Revolt**, I, p. 55.
8. **BNM**, loc. cit.; **DM**, 1680, No. 1.
9. **Revolt**, II, pp. 883-4; 102-3.
10. Ibid., pp. 221-3, 378; **First Expedition**, p. 253.
11. **OLC**, p. 69.
12. **Revolt**, II, pp. 80, 100, 192.
13. Ibid., pp. 265, 359.
14. **DM**, 1696, No. 23.
15. **Revolt**, I, p. 149.

GÓMEZ BARRAGÁN

JUAN GÓMEZ BARRAGÁN was already dead in 1631 when his widow, *María Bernal,* is mentioned.[1] He seems to be the Juan Gómez, deceased by 1626, who had come in the soldier-escort of 1613-16, and acted as a Tewa interpreter in 1621.[2]

He had a daughter, *María Barragán,* who was the first wife of Diego López del Castillo.[3]

Cristóbal Gómez Parraga was a Captain who in 1661-2 was appointed the leader of the soldiers and wagon-train to Mexico City.[4] He might have been a son of the preceding man, having corrupted the name as so often happened; or he might have been altogether unrelated.

Andrés Gómez Parra was a *Sargento Mayor* in Santa Fe at the time of the 1680 Rebellion. By some error he was reported killed during the siege of Santa Fe, whereas it was a different officer, Andrés Gómez Robledo. Gómez Parra was active in the Otermín Campaign the following year when he hanged an apostate Indian at Jémez.[5] Perhaps he was a son of Gómez *Parraga*. He is the only man of this name in the Revolt lists, there being no others with the last name of *Parraga* or *Barragán*. The other Parra people mentioned belonged to the *Cobos de la Parra* group.

1. **AGN, Mex., Inq.,** t. 372, f. 10.
2. **Ibid.,** t. 356, ff. 265v, 282v; **AGI, Contad.,** leg. 718, **Data.**
3. Ibid., t. 587, pp. 315-6.
4. Ibid., t. 585, f. 511.
5. **Revolt,** I, p. 59; II, p. 300.

GÓMEZ ROBLEDO

FRANCISCO GÓMEZ, born in "Coina," five leagues from Lisbon, was the son of Manuel Gómez and Ana Vicente, both of whom died when he was a child. Reared at first by his elder brother, Fray Álvaro Gómez, a Franciscan of Lisbon and Commissary of the Holy Office, he passed on into the household of Don Alonso de Oñate at the Court of Madrid. Oñate brought him to Mexico City, and from there Francisco came to New Mexico to join the young colony of Don Alonso's brother, Don Juan de Oñate.[1] 1604 is probably the year in which Don Alonso sailed for the New World.[2] Francisco Gómez became the most outstanding military official in New Mexico during his life-time, occupying every office of importance, including that of High Sheriff of the Holy Office.[3] In 1641, Governor Flores on his deathbed appointed him as interim Governor, but he was not accepted by the hostile council of native New Mexicans. He was fifty-four at the time.[4] Gómez died at the ripe old age of eighty and was buried in the Santa Fe parish church, sometime around the years 1656-7.[5]

His name appears often. In 1616 and 1625 he was the leader of the Mexico City wagon-train escort; in the latter year he conducted Gov. Sotelo and Fray Alonso Benavides, and a statue of the Virgin which, as *La Conquistadora,* became forever famous in New Mexico through the initial efforts of his wife and children.[6] Father Benavides showered him with praise and favors in the beginning, but later suspected him of too much attachment to an anti-religious Governor, Don Juan de Eulate.[7] Gómez had always been a critic of certain friars in power, thus incurring their enmity and that of a local political faction. His Portuguese origin did not help, so that even after his death he was accused of being a Jew, not only by birth, but in secret practice. It is very possible that he was of Jewish extraction.[8]

Gómez had married *Ana Robledo,* a native of San Gabriel del Yunque, and daughter of Bartolomé Romero and Luisa Robledo.⁹ A woman of spirit, she stood up for her husband and family. The precious dresses of La Conquistadora were in her care. She was still living in 1664 when she stated that she was sixty years old and a native of San Gabriel.¹⁰

They had seven children who were known under the compound name of *Gómez Robledo.* They were named as follows in 1663: *Francisco,* on trial by the Holy Office in Mexico City; *Bartolomé,* single, Regent and High Sheriff in Santa Fe; *Juan,* a young soldier, single, in Santa Fe; *Andrés,* twenty years old, a soldier of Santa Fe, still single; *José,* eighteen, and serving as an aide to a major official; *Francisca,* married to Pedro Lucero de Godoy; and *Ana María,* maiden, living with her mother in Santa Fe.¹¹

Francisco Gómez Robledo was most active in the civil and military life of his day, especially after his father's death. Family enemies accused him and his brothers, as also his deceased father, of Judaical tendencies, so that he had to undergo trial in Mexico City, where he cleared himself and the family name. Thanks to this trial, we know the family's story in great detail. Francisco declared that he had been baptized by Fray Pedro de Ortega in Santa Fe, with Governor Sotelo and Doña Isabel de Bohórquez, wife of Don Pedro D. y Chaves, as sponsors; the same Governor was his godfather in confirmation, administered by Fray Alonso Benavides. (Part of the Judaical evidence in the eyes of ignorant accusers was an abnormal coccyx or "little tail" that Francisco and a brother had!) ¹²

Francisco was most devoted to the Confraternity and devotion of La Conquistadora, of which he was *Mayordomo* at the time of his trial, and perhaps continually after that until 1684, when he was still mentioned in this capacity.¹³ Together with his brothers, Bartolomé and Andrés, he served as member of the *Cabildo* of the Kingdom.¹⁴ At the time of the 1680 Rebellion he held the rank of *Maese de Campo* and played an important part before and during the siege of Santa Fe.¹⁵ He fled south with Governor Otermín and the Santa Fe colonists; he passed muster in 1680 as Lieutenant to the Governor, married, with one grown son besides two small ones and five daughters, an unmarried sister, a sister-in-law with seven small children, and twenty servants.¹⁶ In 1681 he was described as being fifty-three years old, a native of New Mexico, married, of good stature and features, with red hair and mustache, and partly gray.¹⁷

The grown son mentioned was a natural son, *Antonio,* twenty-eight years of age, single, having a robust body, plump beardless face and thick black hair.¹⁸ In 1663, his father had declared him, then five years old, and a sister *María,* five or six, as his natural children.¹⁹

Francisco remained with the exile colony, but is mentioned as deceased by December, 1693,²⁰ hence did not return to his pre-Revolt lands north of Santa Fe.²¹ Nor is it known who his wife was, or his minor children, or if any of them returned with the Reconquest. A *María Gómez* who appears in the following century could well be his natural daughter. (As for *Antonio,* a guess of mine is that he was the son of a López del Castillo woman; that he had certain natural children by Juana Luján at Guadalupe del Paso, 1681-1693, and these came to New Mexico as "*Gómez del Castillo.*" Moreover, they were very close to the Roybal-Gómez Robledo clan in the Pojoaque area.)

Bartolomé Gómez Robledo was an *Alférez* and single in 1663. While his brother Francisco was on trial in Mexico City he had fled to New Spain with all of Francisco's horses and mules, as well as the tribute from Acoma Pueblo, probably to aid him in his need.²² Later he appears holding high posts with Francisco and Andrés. He was still mentioned as being single in 1681, a *Sargento Mayor* forty-one or forty-two years of age. He was a native of New Mexico, tall and slender, with red hair, beard partly gray, and a wound-mark on the forehead. With him was a natural son, twenty years old.[23]

This son, *Bartolomé II*, was tall and thin, with a ruddy beardless face, pleasing features, and long straight hair.[24] (This man might well be the culprit of my "Gómez del Castillo" guess, instead of his cousin Antonio.) Neither he nor his father appear in New Mexico after the Reconquest.

Juan Gómez Robledo was mentioned as a young soldier in 1765, when he and his brother Andrés set aside a large quantity of piñón, from Pueblo tributes, for Governor Peñalosa.[25] He was supposed to have a "little tail," like Francisco, which others had seen while bathing in a stream during an Apache Campaign; hence the nickname of *"Los Colitas"* for all the brothers.[26] Juan does not appear in the 1680-81 Revolt lists, having either died or left New Mexico before this period.

Andrés Gómez Robledo, twenty years old and single in 1663, said he was twenty-four, a native of Santa Fe, and still single in 1665, when he and his brother Juan helped Gov. Peñalosa cheat on sacks of piñón kept at the Gómez *estancia* of Las Barrancas in the Rio Abajo.[27] Andrés served with two of his elder brothers in the General Council of the Kingdom prior to 1680. When the Indians struck he was a *Maese de Campo*, most active in the defense of Santa Fe in which he lost his life, the only officer killed.[28]

Andrés had married Juana Ortiz, a daughter of María Ortiz de Vera, or Baca, by Diego de Montoya or a previous husband. Juana escaped with the Santa Fe refugees; with her went her orphaned children, all girls, most of whom figured after the Reconquest as the wives of prominent leaders. Their names were: *Margarita*, wife of Jacinto Peláez; *María*, who married Alonso Romero and then Diego Arias de Quirós; *Francisca*, wife of Ignacio de Roybal; *Lucía*, married to Miguel de Dios Sandoval; and *Rosa*, who died single. Perhaps a *Juana*, who married Domingo Roybal, was a sister of theirs.

José Gómez Robledo, mentioned in 1663 as being eighteen years old, is not heard of again. Like his brother Juan, he either was dead by 1680 or had left New Mexico.

Apparently, not a single male of the famous Gómez Robledo family returned to New Mexico with Vargas, for the name is not met with again, except in connection with the daughters of Andrés who made much of it.

---

1. **AGN, Mex., Inq.**, t. 583, ff. 341-6; B-H, III, p. 253; **El Palacio**, Vol. 55, No. 8, pp. 235-7.
2. B-H, I, p. 212.
3. AGN, loc. cit.
4. Ch. and State, p. 175; **Ortiz Trial**, ff. 43, 44, 57, 58, 61v.
5. AGN, loc. cit., f. 275.
6. AGI, Contad., legs. 718, 726, **Data**; Benavides, 1634, p. 110; OLC, pp. 34-6; El Palacio, Vol. 57, No. 10, pp. 299-301.
7. Ch. and State, pp. 101-2; AGN, loc. cit., t. 356, ff. 270-1.
8. Ch. and State, pp. 85-184; **Troublous Times**, pp. 190-5; B-H, III, p. 253; AGN, loc. cit., t. 507, p. 318.
9. AGN, loc. cit., t. 583, ff. 341-6.
10. Ibid., t. 507, f. 306; pp. 186, 312, 318, 327, 336, 405.
11. Ibid., t. 583, ff. 341-6.
12. Ibid., t. 583, ff. 278, 341-6.
13. OLC, pp. 5, 16, 55, 68; El Palacio, Vol. 57, No. 10, pp. 299-301.
14. B-H, III, p. 294.
15. **Revolt**, I, pp. 4, 9, 96, 100.
16. Ibid., pp. 137-8.
17. Ibid., II, pp. 36, 109.
18. Ibid., I, pp. 137-8; II, pp. 36, 137; not to be confused with Antonio Gómez, Tigua Indian in same narratives.
19. AGN, loc. cit.
20. Ritch Coll., Box 2, No. 25.
21. Sp. Arch., I, No. 818.
22. B-H, III, p. 138.
23. **Revolt**, II, pp. 36, 137.
24. **Ibid**.
25. AGN, loc. cit., t. 507, pp. 726-7.
26. Ibid., t. 585, f. 511.
27. Ibid., t. 507, pp. 726-7; has Andrés' only known signature.
28. AGI, Guadalajara, leg. 138, pt. 2, No. 3690; **Revolt**, I, p. 16; El Palacio, Vol. 55, No. 8, pp. 234-5.

GÓMEZ de LUNA
(See *Luna*)

GÓMEZ PARRA
(See *Gómez Barragán*)

GÓMEZ de TORRES
(See *Torres*)

GONZÁLEZ

DOMINGO GONZÁLEZ, *"El Gallego,"* (The Galician) was a native of the Spanish province of Galicia and forty years of age in 1664. He was living in Santa Fe with his wife, *Francisca Martín*.[1] Three years later he was dead when his wife related an incident as to how her husband, a native of Spain, had been entrusted with some valuables by Gov. López Mendizábal and his wife prior to their imprisonment by Gov. Peñalosa.[2] Nothing more is known about him.

Antonio González de Escalante is known to have lived in New Mexico prior to 1680. He was, perhaps, the "Antonio Torivio Gonzales," a bachelor, seventeen years of age, who signed the muster-roll in 1681.[3] And he might have been a son of the preceding Domingo González, since he distinguished himself from the numerous other González people. All that is known for certain is that he did not return to New Mexico with the Reconquest, and that two children of his, by his wife *Luisa Lucero de Godoy*, married in Guadalupe del Paso long after the Reconquest. Their mother had died by 1715, but their father was still living in 1718.

These children were: *Dionisio*, twenty-five, who married his first cousin, Geronima Romero, at Guadalupe del Paso, September 30, 1715; and *Antonio*, born in Guadalupe del Paso, who there married Beatriz Suazo in 1718.[4]

1. **AGN, Mex., Inq.**, t. 507, pp. 370, 382, 644; t. 596, pt. 2, f. 218.
2. **Ibid.**, t. 608, ff. 412-14.
3. **Revolt**, II, p. 66.
4. **DM**, 1715, No. 4; 1718, No. 3.

GONZÁLEZ LOBÓN

DOMINGO GONZÁLEZ was a native of Portugal, the brother of another soldier in New Mexico, Sebastián González.

Domingo is first mentioned in 1617 as an *Alférez* forty-five years old who knew Geronimo Márquez for seventeen years,[1] hence had been in the New World since 1600. In 1625 he was mentioned as a Captain, with his son Domingo, as escorts of the wagon-train to Mexico City.[2] He must have brought his whole family back to New Spain with the intention of not returning to New Mexico, for in 1627 he was ordered to return with his wife and children or else incur heavy penalties.[3] Later, in 1660, his children mentioned this trip when they testified that, after having been confirmed by Fr. Perea in New Mexico, the entire family, including the parents, had been re-confirmed by a Bishop in New Spain.[4] In 1631, Domingo declared that he was sixty years old and a brother of the *Alférez* Sebastián González. His wife was *Magdelena de Carvajal*.[5]

His wife was most likely a daughter of Juan de Vitoria Carvajal. Their known children were *Juan, Diego,* and *Domingo,* and their sisters, who came to be known as the "*González Lobón*" family,[6] probably harking back to a Lobón grandparent; as such they were distinguished from their first cousins, the *"González Bernal"* family group.

Juan González Lobón, eldest of the family, was forty years of age in 1660 and, as a henchman of Gov. López Mendizábal, a baiter of the friars who was described by them as a buffoon.[7] Diego and Domingo González Lobón were his brothers, and they had sisters, all living in Santa Fe.[8]

Diego González Lobón was a resident of Santa Fe in 1661 when his wife, *Margarita Pérez*, was unjustly imprisoned by Gov. López Mendizábal.[9] It was told that Diego had stolen something from this Governor and had fled to New Spain,[10] while others reported (in 1663) that the Governor had sent him into exile.[11] Anyway, he was on the good side of the next Governor, Peñalosa, who sent him to Mexico with the proceedings of his predecessor's *residencia* and trial.[12]

Domingo González Lobón, except when mentioned with his two brothers, cannot be distinguished elsewhere because the "Lobón" name is not used.

Antonia González de Vitoria was a sister of Diego González Lobón and an aunt of a Pedro de Montoya.[13] Her full name also links her with her mother's Carvajal family. A native of Santa Fe, she was an important witness concerning gubernatorial scandals in 1664, when she was forty-eight years old and a widow.[14] Again she was an important witness late in 1705, when she was too old to recall her years.[15] Perhaps she is the Doña Antonia González mentioned in 1682 as the widow of Esteban Maese.[16]

González people who passed muster in 1680-81, and are not positively identified as González *Bernal,* might belong to the *Lobón* group.

Domingo González, single, passed muster in 1680 with a family of seven, which consisted of his mother, brothers, and sisters.[17] He does not appear in 1681, unless he is a *"Pedro"* González, native of New Mexico, twenty-one and married; he had a robust medium build, with a plump face, large eyes, thick black hair, beard, and eyebrows.[18]

Sebastián González, Adjutant, signed his name every time he was required. He was married in 1680 and had eight children.[19] In 1681 he gave his age as twenty-six, and was described as married, of medium height, with a swarthy aquiline face, thick beard, and partly gray black hair.[20] He had owned lands near Santa Cruz which were asked for by others in 1700, since he had not returned to New Mexico with the Reconquest but had stayed at San Lorenzo del Paso.[21] There he signed two testimonies at this period.[22] He might be he same man who married a Maria del Rio at Guadalupe del Paso in 1714.[23]

---

1. **AGN, Mex., Inq.,** t. 318.
2. **AGI, Contad.,** legs. 726, 729, **Data**; Benavides, 1634, p. 110.
3. **Ibid.,** leg. 728, **Data.**
4. **AGN,** loc. cit., t. 587, pp. 309-10.
5. **Ibid.,** t. 372, f. 14; **Ibid.,** exp. 19, f. 18.
6. **Ibid.,** t. 587, p. 307.
7. **Ibid.,** pp. 17, 215, 309-10; t. 594, pp. 192, 358-60.
8. **Ibid.,** t. 587, p. 307.
9. **Ibid., Tierras,** t. 3268.
10. **Ibid., Mex., Inq.,** t. 594, p. 280.
11. **Ibid.,** p. 314; since **Lobón** is omitted here, it might refer to Diego González **Bernal.**
12. **Ibid.,** t. 507, pt. 1, f. 123.
13. **Ibid.,** t. 596, pt. 2, f. 157.
14. **Ibid.,** t. 507, pp. 405-6.
15. **DM,** 1705, No. 10.
16. **AGN,** loc. cit., t. 1551, f. 382.
17. **Revolt,** I, p. 150.
18. **Ibid.,** II, pp. 51, 130.
19. **Ibid.,** I, pp. 119, 152-3, 176.
20. **Ibid.,** II, pp. 52, 123.
21. **Sp. Arch.,** I, No. 400.
22. **DM,** 1699, No. 9; 1705, No. 10.
23. **Ibid.,** 1714, No. 2.

GONZÁLEZ BERNAL

SEBASTIÁN GONZÁLEZ is first mentioned in 1626 as an *Alférez* of Portuguese birth.[1] He said he was forty years old in 1632, a resident of Santa Fe, and father-in-law of Diego García, brother of Juan García [Holgado].[2] He was one of the four Regents of New Mexico in 1642, when he gave his age as forty-five. His wife was *Isabel Bernal*, daughter of Juan Griego and Pascuala Bernal.[3] She and her family did not get along very well with her brother-in-law Domingo González,[4] founder of the Lobón group.

To all appearances, the children of this family were *Diego, Antonio,* and *Juan*, all known as *"González Bernal";* and also their sister, name not known, who was married to Diego García. Though first cousins to the González Lobón family, they formed a distinct clan, identified for generations with that of *"los Griegos."*

Diego González Bernal was *Alcalde Mayor* of San Marcos Pueblo in 1661, *"Provincial de la Hermandad,"* as well as Regent and Procurator General of the Kingdom.[5] In 1663, as *Alcalde Mayor* of the large Pueblo of Galisteo, he wrote to Governor Mendizábal against the friars,[6] and so might be the Diego González (if not the Apodaca one) who with Nicolás de Aguilar tried to debase the poor, aged Padre of Tajique.[7] In that year he fled to New Spain.[8] He and his brother Antonio are often mentioned together.[9]

Diego's wife was *Felipa Jiménez García,* still living as a widow in 1687;[10] she was the daughter of a certain Juan Jiménez.[11] Which of the González Bernal individuals of the next generation were their children is hard to say.

Antonio González Bernal was twenty-six to thirty years old in 1661 when he was acting as secretary of the *Cabildo*. He gave Santa Fe as his birthplace.[12]

Juan González Bernal and his wife, *Apolonia*, are mentioned in 1663 as belonging to the "Griegos." A daughter of theirs was involved in an affair with a Pedro de Arteaga.[13] As late as 1703, two daughters of Juan González Bernal, *Melchora* and *Antonia González Bas*, were claiming Santa Fe property that had once belonged to Isabel Bernal [their grandmother].[14]

* * * * * * * *

Francisco González Bernal was the only one who registered with the full name in 1680. He signed as a widower, accompanied by his mother, a widowed sister-in-law, and five nieces.[15] This mother was most likely Felipa Jiménez García, widow of Diego González Bernal, while the widowed sister-in-law was the widow of Juan González Bernal, with her daughters Antonia, Melchora, and three younger ones.

A *Francisco Bernal* who passed muster in 1681, and a Francisco González, married and twenty-three years old,[16] might be this same Francisco González Bernal, since they are not mentioned in 1680.

Sebastián González (without "Bernal") passed muster in 1680, married and with four children.[17] He registered in 1681 as a native of New Mexico and married, and was described as slender with a long face, scant beard, and having thick, black hair.[18] His home before the 1680 Rebellion was in the Cañada district.[19] Unlike the other man of the same name who stayed in Guadalupe del Paso, he returned with the Reconquest, later identified as a González *Bas*, but coming somehow under the Bernal classification.

Domingo and *Sebastián González*, the Portuguese brothers, might have been the sons of *Diego Blandín,* one of Oñate's soldiers. He was forty years of age in 1598, a native of Coimbra in Portugal, and the son of Diego González.²⁰

1. AGN, Mex., Inq., t. 356, ff. 277-316.
2. Ibid., t. 304, ff. 190, 193-194; Ortiz Trial, ff. 44-46; AGI, Patronato, leg. 244, Ramo 7, doc. 16, p. 90.
3. Ibid., t. 372, f. 10.
4. Ibid., f. 14.
5. Ibid., Tierras, t. 3268, pp. 353, 384-448; he can easily be confused with Diego González **Lobón** and Diego González **de Apodaca.**
6. Ibid., Mex., Inq., t. 594, f. 6.
7. Ibid., f. 46.
8. B-H, III, p. 138.
9. AGN, loc. cit., t. 587, pp. 361, 375, 386; t. 507, p. 1665.
10. DM, 1687, No. 1.
11. AGN, loc. cit., t. 594, exp. 1, f. 7.
12. See Note 9.
13. AGN, loc. cit., t. 596, Pt. 2, f. 161.
14. Sp. Arch., I, No. 929.
15. Revolt, I, p. 146.
16. Ibid., II, pp. 44, 197.
17. Ibid., I, pp. 146, 177.
18. Ibid., II, pp. 198, 132.
19. Sp. Arch., I, No. 818.
20. Oñate, p. 188.

GONZÁLEZ de APODACA
(See *Apodaca*)

GRIEGO

JUAN GRIEGO answered the Oñate muster-roll at Casco in 1597, declaring that he was accompanied by his wife, and that he was a native of the City of Candia in Greece, the son of Lázaro Griego.¹ On another occasion, the same year, he gave "Negroponte" as his birthplace,² and this is the place he also gave in 1598, when he was entered as the son of Lázaro Griego, thirty-two years old, a native of Greece in "Negropote," of good stature, gray-bearded, with a big wound on the forehead.³ If born in or near Candia, in Crete, he was not only a contemporary but also a fellow-townsman of the great painter in Spain, Domenico Theotocopuli, otherwise known by his Italo-Spanish nickname of "El Greco." Was Juan Griego's family name also so hard to pronounce that even his father was known as "the Greek"?

Still living, and an *Alférez,* in 1631, Juan gave his age as sixty.⁴ His wife, *Pascuala Bernal,* was dead by 1626.⁵ Their known sons were: *Juan II, Lázaro,* and *Francisco* (this latter went by the name of Bernal). Their daughters were *Catalina Bernal,* wife of Juan Durán,⁶ *María Bernal,* married to Juan Gómez Barragán, *Isabel Bernal,* wife of Sebastián González, and *Juana Bernal,* married to Diego de Moraga.⁷

Juan Griego II was already married to *Juana de la Cruz* in 1626; she was the daughter of Juan de la Cruz, *"el Catalán,"* and Beatriz de los Ángeles.⁸ In 1661 he declared that he was born in Santa Fe, and was a captain fifty-six years old at the time.⁹ In this same year he was referred to as being of the same age and having recently returned from a prolonged stay outside New Mexico.¹⁰ Although dead before 1680, he was still remembered after the Reconquest in connection with his old homestead at La Cañada.¹¹

His known children, all Griegos, were *Nicolás, Blas,*¹² *María de la Cruz Alemán,* wife of Diego López del Castillo,¹³ *Graciana,* married to Francisco Xavier,¹⁴ and *Juana,* nicknamed *"La Clériga."*¹⁵

Lázaro Griego is mentioned briefly in 1628 as the son of Juan Griego. Nothing more is known about him, except that he is mentioned in 1642 with his brother, the Captain Juan Griego (II).¹⁶

For *Francisco (Griego) Bernal,* see *Bernal.*

Nicolás Griego, son of Juan Griego II, was dead before 1680, since he does not appear in the Revolt lists. His wife was *Antonia Martín,* by whom he had three daughters, *Catalina, Juana,* and *María,* who were claiming their father's land in Santa Fe years after the Reconquest. Catalina was married to Diego Trujillo.[16a]

Blas Griego escaped the 1680 massacre with seventeen persons in his family, made up of wife, children, and servants.[17] In 1681 he was described as a native of New Mexico, thirty-four to thirty-seven years old, married, tall and thin, swarthy, with black hair and beard.[18] As late as 1703, he and his sister Juana, *"La Clériga,"* had not returned to Santa Fe from Guadalupe del Paso.[19] He was an officer of the Confraternity of La Conquistadora in 1685.[20]

* * * * * * * *

Other Griegos listed in the 1680-81 Revolt documents are the following:

Juan Griego, extremely poor, with wife and child. He was twenty-nine, born in New Mexico, with a good stature, slender and swarthy, having an emaciated face, black hair and beard.[21] In 1682 he was bedridden and unable to answer a muster-roll call.[22] He was perhaps a son of Juan Griego II, or perhaps of Lázaro, if the latter ever had a family.

Juan Griego, a contemporary of the same name, was not married when he passed muster in 1680 with seven persons, his mother, brothers and/or sisters, "and another boy." He was nineteen or twenty, a native of New Mexico, possessing a good physique, large eyes, a pointed, beardless chin, and long hair.[23] He very probably was the son of the late Nicolás Griego, and was accompanied by the widowed Antonia Martín and his three sisters.

Bartolomé Griego was a youth killed by the Santa Clara Indians in August, 1680.[24]

Agustín Griego, single, passed muster with his mother, brothers and/or sisters, and was proficient, and very useful to the Governor, as an interpreter in the Tewa language.[25] In 1681 he was described as a bachelor twenty-four years old, born in New Mexico, tall and slender, swarthy, having a long, beardless face, a long nose, and black hair.[26] He was still living in 1690,[27] but it is not known if he actually returned with the Reconquest. His widow, *Josefa Luján,* and their son, *Miguel Ángel,* were living in the Río Arriba area in 1713.[28]

---

1. AGI, Mex., Aud., leg. 25, Pt. 1.
2. Ibid., Pt. 2.
3. Oñate, p. 192.
4. AGN, Mex., Inq., t. 372, Exp. 19, f. 13.
5. Ibid., t. 356, f. 312.
6. Ibid., ff. 312-313; t. 372, Exp. 19, f. 13.
7. Ibid., t. 372, f. 9.
8. Ibid., t. 304, ff. 186, 312-313.
9. Ibid., t. 596, Pt. 1, f. 30.
10. Ibid., t. 587, pp. 362, 375, 386.
11. Sp. Arch., I, No. 818.
12. Ibid., Nos. 294, 337, 929.
13. AGN, loc. cit., t. 587, pp. 315-316.
14. Ibid., t. 596, Pt. 2, f. 212.
15. Sp. Arch., loc. cit.
16. AGN, loc. cit., t. 304, f. 190; Ortiz Trial, ff. 14v, 18.
16a. Sp. Arch., loc. cit.
17. Revolt, I, pp. 16, 119, 145.
18. Ibid., II, pp. 45, 127.
19. Sp. Arch., I, No. 294.
20. OLC, p. 55.
21. Revolt, I, p. 150; II, p. 121.
22. BNM, leg. 2, Pt. 3, ff. 338-340.
23. Revolt, I, p. 148; II, p. 140.
24. Ibid., I, p. 10.
25. Ibid., pp. 4, 150.
26. Ibid., II, pp. 140-141, 195.
27. DM, 1690, No. 1.
28. Sp. Arch., II, No. 187.

GUADALAJARA

DON DIEGO DE GUADALAJARA was in Santa Fe as early as 1636.[1] He was a member of the *Cabildo* in 1639.[2] In 1643 he accompanied the Mexico City wagon train as an escort.[3] By 1660 he had a flourishing *estancia* on the Río del Norte six leagues from the Pueblo of Alamillo.[4] Don Diego was a native of Oaxaca, and "married in New Mexico," although there is no record of his wife's name or relationships. By 1665 a grown son of his, *Francisco,* had left New Mexico and was residing in Chalco.⁵ As *encomendero* of the Pueblo of Sevilleta, Diego employed Indians for his personal profit, making them haul salt from the Salinas district.⁶ In 1654 he had led an expedition to the Río de las Nueces country in present Texas.⁷

A daughter of his, *Jacinta Bernardo y Quirós*, was the wife of Felipe Romero, who had his homestead in the same Río Abajo area. She gave her age as twenty-seven in 1667.⁸ No male children were left in New Mexico to pass on the family name.

1. **BNM**, leg. 1, Pt. 1, pp. 470-504.
2. **B-H**, III, p. 57.
3. **AGI, Contad.**, leg. 738, **Data.**
4. **AGN, Mex., Inq.**, t. 587, p. 17.
5. **Ibid.**, t. 507, Pt. 4, f. 450.
6. **Ibid.**, t. 594, f. 112.
7. **BNM**, leg. 2, Pt. 3, pp. 410-411.
8. **AGN**, loc. cit., t. 610, Exp. 7, f. 63; t. 608, ff. 417-427.

GUILLÉN

Francisco Hernández Guillén was entered in the Oñate lists of 1597, accompanied by his wife, two daughters (one of them married), his son-in-law, and a granddaughter.¹ Another source states that both girls were over fifteen years old.² Fifty years of age in 1598, Francisco was a native of Sevilla, the son of Hernán Pérez; he had a good stature, grayish hair, and a red beard.³

Cristóbal Guillén, twenty, the son of Diego Guillén and born in Mexico City, also came in 1598; he was of medium height and beardless.⁴

Juan Guillén was in the guard escorting the wagon-train in 1608.⁵

Which of these three passed down the name through 1600 to 1680, without its being mentioned in between, remains to be discovered. Only one Guillén appears in 1681.

Salvador Guillén, thirty-three, married, and born in New Mexico, had a good stature, swarthy complexion, no beard, black and thick hair, and scars like those of a burn on his neck.⁶ No connection has been found between this man and some individuals of this name in New Mexico shortly after the Reconquest.

1. **AGI, Patronato**, 22, Pt. 5, p. 771.
2. **Ibid., Mex., Aud.**, Pt. 2.
3. **Oñate**, p. 192.
4. **Ibid.**
5. **AGI, Contad.**, leg. 850, **Data.**
6. **Revolt**, II, p. 140.

GUTIÉRREZ

ALONSO GUTIÉRREZ is first mentioned in 1626 as a forty-year-old married soldier of Santa Fe.¹ By 1641 he was an *Alférez*, fifty-five years of age, according to his testimony, and residing in Santa Fe.² His wife was *Ana Cadimo*, thirty years old in 1631,³ most probably the daughter of Francisco Cadimo, and sister to Francisca Cadimo, wife of Gerónimo Pacheco.

Alonso's origin is not known. In 1600 there came a *Domingo Gutiérrez*, thirty years old and a native of La Palma in the Canary Islands; he was short, round-faced, well-bearded.⁴ Then there was Captain *Juan Gutiérrez Bocanegra*, forty-four, son of Alonso de Cuenca and a native of Villanueva de los Infantes. He was tall and black-bearded.⁵ No connection has been found between either of these two and Alonso.

Roque Gutiérrez was a native of New Mexico who lived in the middle of the century and had died before 1680. He was present at the dedication of the Guadalupe del Paso Mission in 1668,[6] probably stationed there as a soldier. What relation he bore to the preceding Alonso Gutiérrez is not ascertainable either; nor is there further direct mention of him. We know of him and his wife, *María de Tapia*, through marriages of their children in the years following the Indian Rebellion.

These children, minors in 1680-1681, were: *Alejo*, who married María Naranjo; *María*, wife of Juan Cedillo; *Lucía*, who married Baltasar Francisco de la Peña; *Isabel*, wife of José Gonzalez de Apodaca; and, perhaps, a *Juan Roque* associated with them.

Felipe Gutiérrez was twenty-five years old when the Indians rebelled, but was away in 1680, perhaps with the Leyva party waiting for the wagon-train at Guadalupe del Paso. In 1681 he passed muster as a native of New Mexico, married, twenty-six years old; he was tall and slender, beardless, and pockmarked.[7] From post-Reconquest data we know that his wife was *Isabel de Salazar* and that they had a son, *Francisco*.

Felipe was most likely a younger brother of Roque.

Lorenzo Gutiérrez passed muster in 1680 with his wife and one small child.[8] But he is not heard of in 1681 or after, having died or left the exile colony.

* * * * * * * *

Antonio Gutiérrez de Figueroa was not related to the preceding family. A native of Zacatecas, he first appears in the muster-roll of 1681 as a nineteen-year-old bachelor, described as tall and slim, with a fair complexion, red hair, and no beard.[9] He joined the Vargas colonists in their return to New Mexico in 1693.

---

1. **AGN, Mex., Inq.,** t. 356, f. 299.
2. **Ibid.,** t. 425, f. 638; **Ortiz Trial,** ff. 39, 49v.
3. **AGN, Mex., Inq.,** t. 372, f. 12.
4. **Oñate,** p. 202.
5. **Ibid.,** p. 188.
6. **Ocaranza,** p. 69.
7. **Revolt,** II, pp. 86, 104.
8. **Ibid.,** I, p. 147.
9. **Ibid.,** II, pp. 63-64, 140.

HERAS, de las

MARCOS DE LAS HERAS came to New Mexico as a volunteer guard of the convicts sent up in 1677. He was twenty-two years old, a native of Santander, the son of Martín de las Heras. He was described as having a good physique, small forehead, and thick eyebrows, his face marked by smallpox.[1] Three years later, in 1680, he was *Alcalde Mayor* of Taos.[2] Mentioned in April of that year as a sort of official,[3] he does not appear in the Revolt annals of the following August or afterwards.

An incomplete matrimonial investigation in 1694 concerns the marriage of Manuel Fernández de Vargas and *Luisa Pascuala*, daughter of a Marcos Sánchez de la Cruz and Bernardina *de las Heras*, both deceased. Since this man's name occurs nowhere else, it could be, as sometimes happened, that the parents' names were transposed, and the girl was the young daughter of Marcos de las Heras and Bernardina Sánchez de la Cruz, both of whom had died before August, 1680.[4]

---

1. **B-H,** III, p. 317.
2. **Doc. Hist. de Mex.,** p. 117.
3. **DM,** 1680, No. 1.
4. **Ibid.,** 1694, No. 18.

HERNÁNDEZ

There were several *Hernández* individuals in the Oñate troops of 1598 and 1600. Besides *Francisco Hernández Guillen* (see *Guillen*), there were the following:

Francisco Hernández Cordero, twenty-two, a native of Guadalajara in New Galicia, the son of Rodrigo Fernández Cordero, of good stature and beardless.¹

Gonzalo Hernández, fifty, a native of Coimbra and the son of Pedro Alonso Falcón, having a good stature and gray hair.²

Antonio Hernández, thirty-three years of age, the son of Francisco Simón, and likewise a Portuguese soldier of Braga; he was tall and chestnut-bearded.³ This same man appears also in the 1600 lists, having gone down to New Spain to bring back new troops.⁴

Diego Hernández Barriga, twenty-five, a native of Moguer, was well-built and well-bearded.⁵

Francisco Hernández (Guillen?) was in the wagon-train escort of 1617.⁶

Bartolomé Hernández was in the Peralta escort of 1609.⁷

Rodrigo Hernández, Sargento Mayor, accompanied Juan de Mondragón back to New Mexico in 1653.⁸

Diego Hernández was killed by the Jémez Indians in 1626.⁹

There were no adult male Hernández people among the refugees of 1680. A widow, *María Hernández,* appeared with her four children.¹⁰ Who her husband was, or her parents, is not known so far; any of her children who might be boys would most likely bear their father's name.

1. **Oñate**, p. 190.
2. Ibid., p. 192.
3. Ibid.
4. Ibid., p. 202.
5. Ibid., p. 207.
6. **AGI, Contad.,** leg. 723, **Data.**
7. Ibid., leg. 711, **Data.**
8. Ibid., leg. 747, **Data.**
9. **AGN, Mex., Inq.,** t. 356, f. 299.
10. **Revolt,** I, p. 159.

HERRERA

JUAN DE HERRERA, according to his children and grandchildren, was a "first Conquistador," that is, he had come with Oñate's troops or in the first years of the New Mexico colony.¹ However, it is impossible to identify him with several of the same name in that period.

A **Juan de Herrera,** twenty years old, came in 1600; he was the son of Francisco de Herrera and a native of Mexico City, of medium height, round-faced, with a beard starting to grow.² Another **Juan de Herrera,** also a native of Mexico City, the son of Cristóbal de Ávila, came with the wagon-train escort guard of 1613.³ This was perhaps the man married in 1626 to a *Leonor Hernández* of Querétaro,⁴ whose likely son was another "Juan de Herrera," of the same social scale, who was in the guard that took Governor Mendizábal back to New Spain in 1661.⁵

Our Juan de Herrera, therefore, was most likely the twenty-year-old soldier described in 1600. He held the *encomienda* of Santa Clara and Jémez throughout his lifetime, and was a member of the Council in 1642.⁶ He donated some of his land before 1680 to the Franciscan Mission of San Juan.⁷ Other lands of his in the Cañada area were inherited after the Reconquest by an Isabel González.⁸ His old *estancia* there was still remembered in 1696.⁹ He had died well before 1680, but we know that the same man is meant in the foregoing citations because some of his children appear in the documents cited. From the marriage of two of his children, Miguel and Isabel, we know that his wife was *Ana López del Castillo,* who had also died before 1680.

Their known children were as follows: *Juan* II, *Antonio, Miguel, Ana María, Eugenia,* who married Antonio de Córdoba, *Isabel,* wife of Cristóbal Tafoya, and, possibly, *Josefa,* wife of Domingo Martín Serrano.

Juan de Herrera II was already married prior to 1680,[10] but he must have been away from New Mexico at the time the Pueblos rebelled. However, he passed muster in 1681 as a native of New Mexico, twenty-three years old, married, having a good and slender build, a long face, and good features.[11] His wife's name is not known, nor those of his children, if any. He and his brother Antonio were stationed as soldiers at Guadalupe del Paso as late as 1715, when he gave his age as forty-nine;[12] however, both were back in New Mexico when the estate of their brother-in-law Cristóbal Tafoya was probated.[13]

Antonio de Herrera was twenty-eight in 1681, single, and holding the position of adjutant. He was then described as a native of New Mexico, having a good stature, and black hair and beard.[14] Following the Reconquest the family kept on living in Guadalupe del Paso, but in 1705, his sister Eugenia returned to New Mexico with the rest of the family.[15] Two children of his married at Guadalupe del Paso; *Antonia* with José de Padilla in 1711, and *Victoria* with Ignacio Padilla in 1718. Their mother was *Agustina* (or *Francisca*) *Gómez*.[16]

The story of *Miguel de Herrera* and the rest of the family belongs in the next century.

* * * * * * * *

MARCOS DE HERRERA may or may not have belonged to the preceding family group. He had died or was gone from New Mexico before 1680. His wife was *Francisca Gutiérrez;* their son, *Domingo,* was thirty-three years old in 1683;[17] hence Marcos was an adult already in the first half of the century.

Domingo de Herrera, son of Marcos, was residing at Taos when the Indians struck in 1680. They killed his wife, seven children, his mother-in-law, and two brothers-in-law.[18] He was spared because at the time he was with the Leyva escort guard at Guadalupe del Paso. This he mentioned when he applied to marry again in 1683. Here he said that he was thirty-three years old, born at La Cañada, and a resident of Taos when the Indians killed his first wife, *María Ramos.* The woman he now married was *María Martín,* widow of Antonio Luján.[19] Very likely he returned with the Reconquest. His widow was living in Santa Cruz in 1710 with her sons, *Juan* and *Francisco*.[20] *Leonor* de Herrera, wife of Agustín Sáez, might have been her daughter.

* * * * * * * *

Other Herreras mentioned in 1680-1681 Revolt annals were the following:

Cristóbal de Herrera was a youth killed at Tesuque in August, 1680, on the day Father Sánchez de Pro was slain.[21]

Nicolás de Herrera, twenty-four and a native of New Mexico, single, passed muster in 1681. He was of medium height with broad shoulders, very swarthy, with black, curly hair and beard, and large eyes with much of the white showing. With him were his widowed mother and several brothers and/or sisters.[22]

Francisca de Abrega escaped with eight children and grandchildren.[23] She might well have been the Francisca *de Herrera* Abrigo who in 1634 was the twenty-year-old second wife of Alonso Martín Barba.

---

1. Bancroft MSS, SWO, 1784.
2. Oñate, p. 205.
3. AGI, Contad., leg. 716, Data.
4. AGN, Mex., Inq., t. 356, f. 310.
5. Ibid., t. 587, p. 404.
6. Sp. Arch., I, No. 311; Ortiz Trial, f. 12 sqq.
7. Ibid., No. 823.
8. Ibid., No. 311.
9. Ibid., No. 818.
10. Ibid., No. 311.
11. Revolt, II, pp. 60, 126. Twenty-three seems too young an age.
12. Sp. Arch., loc. cit.
13. Bancroft, loc. cit.
14. Revolt, II, pp. 81, 101, 124.
15. Sp. Arch., II, No. 108.
16. DM, 1711, No. 4; 1718, No. 2.
17. Ibid., 1683, No. 1.
18. Revolt, I, pp. 147, 176.
19. DM, loc. cit.
20. Sp. Arch., II, No. 160.
21. Revolt, I, pp. 7-10.
22. Ibid., II, pp. 81, 101, 131.
23. Ibid., I, pp. 151-152.

HERRERA CORRALES

SEBASTIÁN DE HERRERA CORRALES was not related to the foregoing Herreras. He was in New Mexico already in 1661, when he was twenty-six years old.[1] He was also the Royal Standard Bearer in that year when he declared that he had been born in Conil in Lower Andalucía.[2] Having deserted his post at the Presidio of Cerro Gordo, or Parral, he had fled north to Santa Fe and married there.[3] In 1663 he made a complaint against Governor Mendizábal for sending him to Taos right after his wife had given birth to their child.[4]

In 1680, by then a *Sargento Mayor,* he chanced to be in Taos on a visit, together with his wife, mother-in-law, and a brother-in-law. On the August days that the Indian Rebellion broke out he happened to be in the Ute country with the *Sargento Mayor,* Don Fernando D. y Chaves (his host, probably). Finding their families massacred on their return, they slipped past the Taos rebels, as also those of La Cañada, and Santa Fe, and caught up with the fleeing Río Abajo people, to whom they gave the first news about the situation in the north.[5] He passed muster shortly after with one son of military age, two other younger sons, and two small daughters, declaring that the enemy had killed his wife, mother-in-law, and brother-in-law.[6] In the following year he gave his age as forty-two.[7]

In 1682 Sebastián asked to marry *María de la Escallada,* widow of Andrés Peralta. Here we learn that his parents were Juan de Herrera Corrales and Juana García Yngenia, both natives of Conil. His first wife, slain in Taos, was *Juana de Aragón.*[8]

The children by this first marriage were: *Sebastián,* "el mozo," the young son of military age, sixteen years old in 1681, and described as a native of New Mexico, tall, with a beardless, aquiline face and long red hair;[9] *María,* already married to Nicolás Lucero de Godoy;[10] *Juana,* who married Pedro Varela de Losada;[11] *Josefa Gertrudis,* seventeen and single at San Lorenzo in 1682,[12] who might be the Josefa de Herrera who married Juan de Ávalos. It cannot be ascertained if any males of these Herreras returned to New Mexico.

1. **AGN, Mex., Inq.,** t. 587, pp. 361, 375, 386.
2. **Ibid.,** t. 596, Pt. 1, f. 16.
3. **Ibid.,** t. 594, p. 278; **Tierras,** t. 3268, pp. 300-302.
4. **AGN,** loc. cit., t. 594, p. 59.
5. **Revolt,** I, pp. 57-59, 175.
6. **Ibid.,** p. 139.
7. **Ibid.,** II, pp. 38-39.
8. **DM,** 1682, No. 4.
9. **Revolt,** I, p. 139; II, p. 136.
10. **AGN,** loc. cit., t. 1551, f. 385.
11. **Ibid.,** loc. cit.; **Sp. Arch.,** I, No. 728.
12. **AGN,** loc. cit., ff. 375-385.

HIDALGO
(See *Cabinillas*)

PEDRO HIDALGO is first heard of when he escaped the Tesuque Indians, August 10, 1680, after he saw them kill Father Sánchez de Pro.[1] He passed muster with a family of eight persons, and was described as being thirty-four years old, a native of New Mexico, of good stature, swarthy, with a thick beard and short, curly hair; he also had the scar of a burn on his neck. (See *Guillen.*)[2] At Guadalupe del Paso he was an officer of the Conquistadora Confraternity.[3]

From later sources we know that his wife, and mother of his son *Alfonso,* was *Ana Griego Montoya,*[4] also referred to as Ana *Martín* Griego in 1705, residing as a widow in Guadalupe del Paso.[5] A literate man, Hidalgo had acted as a notary for the friars, as may be seen in *diligencias matrimoniales* between 1682 and 1694. He also acted as interpreter for the Pecos when Vargas made his first Entry in 1692.⁶ Neither he nor any of his family returned to New Mexico in 1693 or after.

Alfonso Hidalgo married *Ana María Maese* at El Real de San Lorenzo in 1701.⁷

1. **Revolt**, I, pp. 5-7, 96.
2. **Ibid.**, I, p. 149; II, pp. 43, 128.
3. **OLC**, pp. 55, 63.
4. **DM**, 1701, No. 5.
5. **Ibid.**, 1705, No. 10.
6. **First Expedition**, p. 169.
7. **DM**, 1701, No. 5.

HINOJOS

HERNANDO DE HINOJOS (*Ynojos*) and his brother SEBASTIÁN appear in the 1597 Casco roll of Oñate's forces as natives of Cartaya, Condado de Niebla, the sons of Juan Ruiz.¹ Hernando was thirty-six years old in 1598, when he was described as having a good stature and a chestnut beard; here again he was mentioned as a native of Cartaya, the son of Juan Ruiz, and brother of Sebastián Rodríguez.² He might be the Hernando "Yñíguez" who escorted Father Jiménez to New Mexico in 1608.³ As a captain, then also Procurator General for the Kingdom, he accompanied the wagon-trains in 1613 and 1617.⁴ His brother Sebastian was killed at Acoma in 1598.

Hernando's wife was *Beatriz Pérez de Bustillos*, who was mentioned as his widow by 1632.⁵ A known son of theirs was *Miguel*, and a daughter, *Gerónima*, was the wife of Francisco de Anaya;⁶ also, it seems, another Hinojos by the name of *Juan*.

Miguel de Hinojos, son of Fernando, held the *Alcaldía* of Jémez until Governor Mendizábal took it from him prior to 1663. He acted as bondsman for Nicolás Ortiz in 1642.⁷ In 1661 he claimed the *encomienda* of Humanos Pueblo by reason of his being the son of "one of the Conquistadores, Hernando de Hinojos." He also said that he had a brother [Juan?], whose name he did not mention.⁸ Miguel also owned lands on the Santa Fe River about a league south of the Villa.⁹

It is not known if he was married or, if so, who his wife was. A daughter of his, *María*, wife of a certain Juan de Vega, seems to have had an Apache mother.¹⁰

Juan Ruiz de Hinojos was one of the eight soldiers of the anti-Rosas faction beheaded by Governor Pacheco in 1643.¹¹ He could well have been the brother mentioned by Miguel.

Other people of this name mentioned briefly in the early part of the century were as follows:

Agustín de Hinojos and *Catalina de Hinojos* acted together as wedding sponsors in 1639.¹³ Agustín was a member of the Santa Fe *Cabildo* in 1639.¹⁴ In 1646 he was in the guard that escorted Governor Guzmán.¹⁵ He carved his name on Inscription Rock in 1636.

Matías de Hinojos was in the escort guard of 1640.¹⁶

Cristóbal de Hinojos was present in 1668 at the dedication of Mission Guadalupe del Paso.¹⁷

The adult male Hinojos living at the time of the 1680 Indian Revolt were the following:

Hernando de Hinojos, Adjutant, who with a family of five persons escaped the massacre.¹⁸ In 1681 he was described as a native of New Mexico, thirty-six years old, married, with a good stature, a thick and partly gray beard, and thick, black hair.¹⁹ The following year, giving his age as thirty-eight, he testified concerning some persons who had run away from the exile colony.²⁰

Diego de Hinojos passed muster in 1681 as a bachelor twenty-three or twenty-four years of age, and all alone. He was a native of New Mexico, having a good slender build, wavy hair, curly mustache and beard, and small, black eyes.[21]

Juan Ruiz de Hinojos, twenty-three, passed muster in 1681 without further description, and is not heard of again.[22]

These men were descendants of either Hinojos brother of Oñate's times, as also some women married or single who appear in New Mexico in Reconquest times. But it seems as though no male member returned.[23]

1. AGI, Mex., Aud., leg. 25, Pt. 1.
2. Oñate, p. 200.
3. AGI, Contad., leg. 707, **Data**.
4. Ibid., leg. 716, **Data**; AGN, Mex., Inq., t. 318.
5. AGN, loc. cit., t. 372, f. 8.
6. Ibid., t. 596, Pt. 2, f. 161.
7. Ibid., f. 156; Ortiz Trial, ff. 39 sqq.
8. AGN, Tierras, t. 3268, pp. 262-263.
9. Sp. Arch., I, No. 488.
10. AGN, Mex., Inq., t. 596, Pt. 1, f. 66; this Vega, not a New Mexican, was Peñalosa's barber and back in Mexico City by 1663 (ibid., t. 594, Pt. 2, f. 594).
11. Ch. and State, p. 175; Ortiz Trial, f. 6v.
13. AGN, loc. cit., t. 571, esp. 8, f. 230.
14. B-H, III, p. 57.
15. AGI, Contad., leg. 740, **Data**.
16. Ibid., leg. 736, **Data**.
17. Ocaranza, p. 69.
18. Revolt, I, p. 150.
19. Ibid., II, pp. 42, 113, 352.
20. BNM, leg. 2, Pt. 3, p. 279.
21. Revolt, II, pp. 64, 134, 195.
22. Ibid., p. 68.
23. Cf. El Palacio, Vol. 56, No. 4, pp. 99-101.

HOLGUÍN
(See *Olguín*)

HURTADO

The *Hurtado* soldiers in the Oñate lists seem to be identical with individuals later referred to as "Jiménez." The large Hurtado family of this century stemmed from a different person who came much later.

ANDRÉS HURTADO is first mentioned in 1661 as a captain thirty-three years old.[1] He was born in the city of Zacatecas and was then living in the Sandía district. In 1664 he was a captain of cavalry and also Syndic of the Franciscans. His wife was *Bernardina de Salas y Orozco*.[2] Andrés also held the *encomiendas* of Santa Ana and neighboring pueblos; in this capacity he was cruelly persecuted by Governor López Mendizábal for his friendship with the friars. Though a regent and a procurator-general of the Kingdom, he was made to take his entire family from Sandía to Santa Fe in the dead of winter, in 1661.[3] He was dead when fateful 1680 came around, but his widow and several of her children not only escaped the massacre but returned with the Reconquest in 1693.

His wife, known also as Bernardina *de Salas*, simply, or *de Salas y Trujillo* (or *Osorio*), was a grand-daughter of María de Vera, one of whose daughters had married Francisco de Trujillo. The Hurtado children were numerous: *Lucía de Salazar* (*Salas*, or *Hurtado*), wife of Captain Don Fernando D. y Chaves; *Isabel de Salazar*, third wife of Juan Lucero de Godoy; *María de Salazar*, later married to Manuel Baca;[4] and their Hurtado brethren, *Andrés, Diego, Francisco, Martín, Mariana*, who later married Manuel Vallejo; *Catalina*, later the wife of José Gallegos; and *Juana*, captured by the Indians in 1680 and rescued by her brother Martín in 1692.

In the muster-rolls following the Indian Revolt, the Hurtados appear as follows:

Diego Hurtado, married, declared a daughter and his mother, with five young sisters and two servants.[5] These were undoubtedly Doña Bernardina and the as yet unmarried sisters, Isabel, Catalina, María, Mariana, and a fifth whose name has not been encountered. In 1681 Diego was described as being twenty-three or twenty-four years of age, married, tall and slim with good features, wavy hair and no beard. He passed muster with his brother Andrés.[6] Diego and his wife, *Josefa de la Fuente*, were dead by 1694 when their daughter, *Juana*, married Cristóbal de Cuéllar.[7]

Andrés Hurtado II, mentioned as Diego's brother, was a bachelor twenty or twenty-two years of age in 1681; he was described as a native of New Mexico, swarthy and beardless, of good stature, with an aquiline face and curly hair.[8] He was a soldier at the Presidio of Guadalupe del Paso in 1689 when he married *Antonia Domínguez*.[9]

Francisco Hurtado enlisted in 1681 with Andrés. He was sixteen, single, a native of New Mexico, with an aquiline nose, no beard, and short, curly hair.[10]

Martín Hurtado, too young to pass muster in 1680-81, was a soldier in Vargas' Expedition of 1692, when he rescued his captive sister and her children.[11]

---

1. **AGN, Mex., Inq.**, t. 587, pp. 361, 375-386.
2. **Ibid.**, t. 507, pp. 276, 548, 1327, 1680.
3. **AGN, Tierras**, t. 3268, p. 97; B-H, III, pp. 186-193; cf. **El Palacio**, Vol. 55, No. 4, p. 117.
4. This use of the maternal surname by the three eldest girls suggests the possibility of their being half-sisters to the younger children who used the Hurtado name.
5. **Revolt**, I, p. 144.
6. **Ibid.**, II, pp. 60, 111-112, 186, 199.
7. **DM**, 1694, No. 30.
8. **Revolt**, II, p. 138.
9. **DM**, 1689, No. 2.
10. **Revolt**, II, loc. cit.
11. **First Expedition**, p. 237.

JIMÉNEZ

JUAN JIMÉNEZ HURTADO, *Alférez*, and his brother, ALONSO, were in Oñate's muster-roll of 1597. They were the sons of Fernando Jiménez Hurtado and natives of Medina Sidonia in Spain.[1] Nothing more is heard about them under this full name; a *Juan Hurtado*, however, is listed among Oñate's troops of 1600 without being described.[2] But in the 1598 lists there is a Juan Jiménez, thirty years of age, the son of Francisco (Fernando?) Jiménez, black-bearded and of medium height, who says he is a native of Trujillo.[3] Perhaps this Juan was an altogether distinct individual.

Juan Jiménez, "the younger," was living in New Mexico in 1665 with his wife *Catalina Durán*.[4] He was, therefore, the son of an "elder" Juan Jiménez in New Mexico, any of the men previously listed. He was also referred to in 1663 as the father-in-law of a certain Diego Velásquez,[5] and also of Diego González Bernal.[6] It could be that Velásquez and Bernal were one and the same man. Anyway, we learn many years later that González Bernal's wife was *Felipa Jiménez García*.[7]

Francisco Jiménez was referred to in 1663 as belonging to the Griego clan.[8] Hence he was either a son or a nephew of Felipa Jiménez. He seems to be the Captain Francisco Jiménez who was massacred at Pojoaque with his wife and entire family in 1680.[9] No other Jiménez is given in the Revolt rolls. The house of Francisco Jiménez was still remembered at La Cañada after the Reconquest.[10]

---

1. **AGI, Mex., Aud.**, leg. 25, Pt. 1.
2. **Oñate**, pp. 128, 209.
3. **Ibid.**, p. 200.
4. **AGN, Mex., Inq.**, t. 608, f. 431.
5. **Ibid.**, t. 594, f. 6.
6. **Ibid.**, f. 7v.
7. **DM**, 1687, No. 1.
8. **AGN**, loc. cit., t. 596, Pt. 2, f. 161.
9. **Revolt**, I, pp. 10, 96.
10. **Sp. Arch.**, I, No. 818.

JORGE

JUAN JORGE, the son of Juan Jorge *Griego* [the Greek?], was a native of the town of Los Lagos and thirty-five years old when he came with Oñate's troops in 1600. He was tall and dark.[1]

Manuel Jorge is mentioned as the armorer or blacksmith imprisoned by Governor Mendizábal in 1661.[2] He was married at the time.[3] In 1658 he received pay as official Armorer of New Mexico, having been appointed in 1655 to succeed Gaspar Pérez.[4] Apparently, Manuel was the son of the Greek (or half-Greek) Juan Jorge. His trade as a worker in metals confirms this supposition. If the following Jorge is his son, his wife might have belonged to the family of Diego de Vera and María Ortiz Baca.[5]

Antonio Jorge de Vera was a resident of the Rio Abajo in 1661; he is mentioned posthumously as a captain who had died before the Indian Revolt of 1680. His wife was *Gertrudis Baca*[6] and their known children were *Antonio, Ana,* wife of Alonso García de Noriega, and *Isabel,* wife of Antonio Montaño de Sotomayor.

Antonio Jorge, the only adult male of this name in the Revolt lists, escaped the Indian massacre with a family consisting of his mother and two sisters,[7] as given above. He was described in 1681 as a bachelor twenty or thirty years old, a native of New Mexico, having a fair complexion, good physique, and a broad face.[8] A captain by 1692, he took part in the Vargas Expedition of that year; he accompanied the Royal Standard-Bearer, Don Fernando D. y Chaves, in leading the ceremonial parade in the Conquest of Santa Fe.[9]

A *Sargento Mayor* in 1694, Antonio married *Catalina de Espínola* in Santa Fe on December 28; here he gave his parents' names as Antonio Jorge de Vera and Gertrudis Baca, both natives of New Mexico and deceased; he also declared that he was forty years old, single so far, and a native of El Alamo, five leagues from Santa Fe.[10] The following year, less than eight months after the wedding, he was dead. From a subsequent marriage document of his widow we know that he was buried at Santa Cruz.

Isabel Jorge de Vera, Antonio's sister, and wife of Antonio Montaño, is important because facts known about her shed light on many relationships concerning her family and some early Bacas. She was a granddaughter of Captain Antonio Baca and first cousin to Juan de Albizu.[11] She was seventy years old in 1733, a very poor widow living in Albuquerque,[12] where she died, on November 25, 1736.[13]

Bernabé Jorge is mentioned in 1701 as having received the first grant of the old Pueblo of La Ciénega from Vargas.[14] He is not heard of again, but there is a strong possibility that he is none other than *Bernabé Baca* of the early Eighteenth Century. The name of Jorge died here; if other male Jorges returned with the Reconquest, they might have become Bacas also.

---

1. **Oñate**, p. 208.
2. **AGN**, Mex., Inq., t. 507, p. 1319.
3. **Ibid.**, t. 596, Pt. 2, f. 156v.
4. **AGI**, Contad., legs. 748, 759, **Data**.
5. Cf. **Vera** and **Abendaño**.
6. **DM**, 1694, No. 28; B-H, III, p. 145.
7. **Revolt**, I, p. 157.
8. **Ibid.**, II, pp. 83, 102.
9. **BNM**, leg. 4, No. 1.
10. **DM**, loc. cit.
11. **Sp. Arch.**, I, No. 411a.
12. **Ibid.**, II, No. 379.
13. **Bur-2**, Albuquerque.
14. **Sp. Arch.**, I, No. 732.

JURADO de GRACIA

PEDRO JURADO DE GRACIA, Captain, and his wife *Brianda de Salazar* are mentioned as living in New Mexico in 1654.[1] It appears as though he moved south permanently to the new post of Guadalupe del Paso.

Francisco Jurado de Gracia and his wife *Lucía Varela de Losada* were mentioned in 1695 as natives and residents of the Real de San Lorenzo, when their daughter, *María*, married Juan Fernández de la Pedrera.[2] María, however, declared that she had been born at El Bosque in the jurisdiction of Sandía.[3] From this it appears as though her father, a son of Pedro Jurado de Gracia, had come to New Mexico where he married a Varela girl, then returned to Guadalupe del Paso after María's birth. He is most likely the Francisco Jurado de Gracia, married, who signed up with the New Mexico soldiers at Guadalupe del Paso in 1681.[4] Both he and Lucía were members of the Confraternity of La Conquistadora.[5]

An *Isabel Jurado de Gracia* had been the wife of Diego Romero de Pedraza, according to the marriage of a daughter, Gerónima, at Guadalupe del Paso in 1715.[6] There were no people of this name living in New Mexico proper when the Indians rebelled in 1680.

1. **AGN, Mex., Inq.,** Exp. 8, f. 231.
2. **DM,** 1695, No. 3.
3. **Ibid.**
4. **Revolt,** II, p. 37; **BNM,** leg. 2, Pt. 3, f. 335.
5. **OLC,** pp. 63, 69.
6. **DM,** 1715, No. 4.

LEDESMA

FRANCISCO DE LEDESMA, twenty-five years old, a native of Talavera de la Reina and the son of Juan Fernández de Ledesma, came with Oñate in 1598. He was described briefly as black-bearded and of medium height.[1] What he was to the following man cannot be ascertained.

Bartolomé de Ledesma resided in the Spanish settlements near the Salinas Pueblos during the middle part of the century. His name appears in connection with the itinerant German, Bernardo Gruber. He was dead by 1667, his widow being *María Martín*, perhaps a daughter of Hernando Martín Serrano, for the latter was the executor of Ledesma's estate.[2] It seems as though Ledesma was the same person as the captain, *Bartolomé de Salazar*, who died as *Alcalde Mayor* of Zuñi and Moqui. In 1662 his widow, María, was accused of scandalous conduct.[3] The existence and lives after the Reconquest of some Ledesmas and Salazar people tend to confirm this suspicion.

An *Ynez de Ledesma*, dead before 1693, had been the wife of Antonio Martín Serrano,[4] both most likely members of the Ledesma and Martín Serrano family group of Las Salinas.

1. **Oñate,** p. 193.
2. **AGN, Mex., Inq.,** t. 666, ff. 393-400.
3. **Ibid.,** t. 595, ff. 121-127.
4. **DM,** 1698, No. 11.

LEÓN
(See *Brito*)

LEYVA

PEDRO DE LEYVA first appears in New Mexico in 1661, a man forty-two years old.[1] By 1664, when he gave his age as fifty, and his birthplace as El Valle de San Bartolomé in New Spain, he was a Captain and Lieutenant Governor for the Salinas Pueblo district. His wife was *Catalina García*.[2] He was a *compadre* of Diego González Lobón, whom he helped to escape from Governor Mendizábal's wrath to New Spain.[3] In 1669, as *Alcalde Mayor* of the Salinas, Leyva exiled Alonso Martín Barba because of concubinage.[4]

His wife, Catalina, belonged to the García Holgado family.[5] Their children were: *Pedro II, José, Juan, Nicolás,* and *Dorotea*. The last three were massacred with their mother at Galisteo in 1680.[6] Pedro himself was away from home at the time, in command of twenty-seven men who went to Guadalupe del Paso to escort the Mexico City wagon-train to Santa Fe. There he and his companions learned about the Pueblo Rebellion in New Mexico. Under the presumption that the Governor and the northern refugees were dead, he was elected and installed as temporary Governor for a short-lived term, until he met Governor Otermín and the Santa Fe refugees at El Alamillo; there he learned about his family's fate. At this time, also, he held the high military rank of *Maese de Campo*, and was well thought of by all, having been a resident of New Mexico since 1637.[7] He signed the muster-roll in 1681 as a *Maese de Campo* sixty-eight years old, a widower without children; he then took part in the Otermín Campaign against the Pueblos.[8] Not all of his sons were lost, as will be seen.

Pedro de Leyva II was not home at the time of the Revolt, perhaps with his father's escort party. In 1681 he signed up as a captain, *"el Mozo,"* thirty-four or thirty-six years old, a native of New Mexico, and married. He was described as having a good stature, red-bearded, and with curly, chestnut hair; the left thumb was missing, and the other injured. He also took part in the Otermín Campaign.[9] As late as October, 1694, he appeared as a marriage witness,[10] but was dead by March, 1696, when his daughter *Ángela* married Sebastián Fernández de Vargas. She was sixteen then, having been born in the Río Abajo area. Her mother's name was *María de Nava*.[11]

José de Leyva, who for some reason added *"de Nevares"* to his name, also was away from home when the Indians struck. In 1681 he signed up as a captain, thirty-two years of age, and the son of the *Maese de Campo* Pedro de Leyva, both widowers.[12] He was described as a native of New Mexico, of good stature, having a long face, thick hair and beard.[13] He served as a Tigua interpreter during the Otermín Campaign,[14] a linguistic gift acquired, no doubt, in the Tigua pueblos of the Manzano range. José's wife, *Juana Fresqui*, had been killed by the Indians in 1680, and he remarried in 1682, at the Real de San Pedro de Alcantara. The new wife was *Estefania Márquez Domínguez*.[15]

When his first wife died, his two daughters were taken captive, most likely by the Tanos of Galisteo. These two were found in 1692 when a certain Juan Olguín claimed the two daughters of José Nevares, soldier of Janos, as his relatives.¹⁶ The elder sister, single, and daughter of Nevares, then a soldier at Janos, was found at San Juan Pueblo,¹⁷ and seems to be the same Ángela de Leyva, wife of Cristóbal Torres, at whose daughter's wedding, her first cousin of the same name appears as sponsor with her husband, Sebastián de Vargas.¹⁸

Some of these Leyvas returned with the Reconquest, as will be seen.

* * * * * * * *

A new settler by the name of *Francisco de Leiva* appears among the new settlers of the 1693 colonists from Mexico City. He was a native of Villafranca and a miner by trade, but ran away before the colony reached New Mexico.¹⁹

1. AGN, Mex., Inq., t. 587, pp. 361-362, 375-386.
2. Ibid., t. 507, p. 728; ibid., Tierras, t. 3268.
3. Ibid., Mex., Inq., t. 594, p. 280.
4. Ibid., t. 666, f. 555.
5. Ibid., t. 512, ff. 7, 8, 156; t. 587, pp. 81-129.
6. Revolt, I, pp. 11, 25, 97.
7. Ibid., II, pp. 163-166.
8. Ibid., pp. 95, 157-342.
9. Ibid., pp. 122 sqq.
10. DM, 1694, No. 6.
11. Ibid., 1696, No. 10.
12. Revolt, II, p. 55.
13. Ibid., p. 119.
14. Ibid., p. 342.
15. DM, 1682, No. 3.
16. First Expedition, p. 184.
17. Ibid., p. 144.
18. DM, 1708, No. 1.
19. BNM, leg. 1, Pt. 1, p 790.

LÓPEZ

FRANCISCO LÓPEZ, a native of Jerez, was already dead in 1626 when his family was involved in some dark doings in Santa Fe. His widow was *María de Villafuerte*, forty years of age and a native of Quatitlan. They had a grown daughter, *Juana*, married to Francisco de Anaya Almazán.¹ Father Benavides made some uncomplimentary remarks about her and her sons, whose names we do not know.² Perhaps this family is the origin of the *López de Gracia* group.

Francisco, early in the century, fired his arquebus at Governor Argüello,³ and this might be the cause for his early demise.

* * * * * * * *

JUAN LÓPEZ, a native of Cartagena de Levante, came to New Mexico with the twelve soldiers recruited at Zacatecas in 1633,⁴ and was married in Santa Fe, February 17, 1634, to *Ynez de Zamora*, daughter of Diego Montoya and Ana Martín Barba.⁵ This Juan López ran into difficulties with the friars at Cuarac,⁶ and Governor Zevallos testified in March, 1634, that López already had a mulatto-*mestiza* wife in Habana.⁷ It is not known if this charge of bigamy was proved.

1. AGN, Mex., Inq., t. 356, f. 310.
2. Ibid., ff. 314, 293.
3. Ibid., t. 507, f. 1229.
4. AGI, Contad., leg. 845A, Data.
5. AGN, loc. cit., t. 380, ff. 233-247.
6. B-H, III, p. 129.
7. AGN, loc. cit.

LÓPEZ de ARAGÓN

FRANCISCO LÓPEZ DE ARAGÓN, or simply *de Aragón*, is mentioned among the soldiers escorting the wagon-train from Mexico City in 1640 and 1646. In 1642 he acted as attorney for Nicolás Ortiz.¹ By 1661 he is referred to as dead. His widow, *Ana Baca*, a sister of Antonio Jorge's wife, lived in her "estancia del Álamo" about four leagues from Santa Fe. Governor Mendizábal berated her for being devoted to the Franciscans, also claiming that she owed him money borrowed for her daughter's wedding.² A daughter, *Juana*, married to Sebastián de Herrera Corrales, was massacred at Taos together with her mother and, it seems, a brother.³ Another daughter, *Ana,* was the wife of a Francisco Campusano, both still living in 1682.⁴ No male Aragóns are mentioned in the Revolt lists or later. This was the end of this family, entirely distinct from the one which came from Mexico City in 1693.

1. AGI, Contad., legs. 735, 736, 740, Data; Ortiz Trial, ff. 27, 39-43, 50-52.
2. AGN, Mex., Tierras, t. 3268, pp. 105-108.
3. DM, 1682, No. 4; Revolt, I, pp. 57, 175.
4. AGN, Mex., Inq., t. 1551, ff. 375-378.

LÓPEZ del CASTILLO

DIEGO LÓPEZ DEL CASTILLO had been in New Mexico twenty-six years around the year 1660. He had first married *María Barragán* in Santa Fe, and after her death got a dispensation to wed her first cousin, *María Griego,* also known as *María de la Cruz Alemán,* daughter of Juan Griego II.¹ Diego, who gave his age as sixty-four in 1664, was a native of Sevilla, and residing in Santa Fe.²

When the Indians rebelled in 1680 he was a *Sargento Mayor* more than eighty years old, according to his testimony; he was married and had two daughters with him.³ The following year he said he was ninety-six and a native of the "Kingdoms of Castile," and was described as "a very old man" with a family of daughters. The scribe noted that he was slender and healthy in spite of his many years.⁴ In marriage investigations of this period he gave his age as ninety-six and ninety-seven.⁵

1. AGN, Mex., Inq., t. 587, pp. 305-316.
2. Ibid., t. 507, p. 351.
3. Revolt, I, p. 143.
4. Ibid., II, pp. 34, 106.

MATÍAS LÓPEZ DEL CASTILLO was thirty-five years old in 1626; hence he could not have been Diego's son or father, but a brother, very likely. He was married to a daughter of Ana de Bustillos and living in Santa Fe.⁶ His wife was therefore an *Archuleta,* daughter of Asencio. Matías was also in the soldier-escort of 1628.⁷ One daughter of his seems to have been *Ana* López del Castillo, the wife of Juan de Herrera. After the Reconquest there were more family matches between this Herrera family and that of Pedro López del Castillo. (Cf. *González Bas.*)

Pedro López, married, escaped the 1680 massacre with his wife and infant daughter. He was thirty-one, tall, and slender, with a long face.⁸ He returned to New Mexico in 1693, and from data of this period we know that he belonged to this family group.

5. DM, 1681, No. 1; 1682, No. 4.
6. AGN, loc. cit., t. 356, f. 266v.
7. AGI, Contad., leg. 728, Data.
8. Revolt, I, p. 143; II, p. 99.

LÓPEZ de GRACIA

ANDRÉS LÓPEZ DE GRACIA was an *Alférez,* residing at San Antonio de Isleta in 1638, when he also acted as Royal Standard-Bearer in an expedition.¹ He had wagons running the route between Santa Fe and Mexico City in 1662.² In 1663-1664 he is mentioned as the father-in-law of a certain Ramírez and the brother-in-law of Diego González de Apodaca.³ *María* López de Gracia, wife of Francisco Ramírez, was therefore his daughter.⁴ *Sebastiana* López de Gracia, wife of Diego de Apodaca, turns out to be his sister.⁵

By 1661 Andrés was a captain and the first *Alcalde Mayor* of the new settlement of

Guadalupe del Paso.[7] In this capacity he was present at the dedication of the Mission in January, 1668.[8] In 1680-1681 he held this post at Casas Grandes when he was instructed to prevent New Mexican refugee colonists from going south into New Spain.[9] A *José López de Gracia* was his assistant *Alcalde* at Casas Grandes and was most likely his son. The name of his wife is not known, nor his origin.

Governor López Mendizábal, among other wild statements against the friars, once mockingly declared that Andrés was the son of a friar of Isleta, who, in the dim past, had appropriated Indian land and there founded the settlement of Pajarito for his mistress and their seven or eight children, called *"los Gracias."*[9] The charge is absurd, as it does not fit in with other facts. Andrés and his sisters might well have been the children of an Esteban López stationed in Santa Fe in early times.[10] Yet Mendizábal's canard could have some innocent basis, and what follows is a bit of conjecture.

On February 10, 1605, a *Fray Antonio de Gracia* entered the Franciscan Order in Mexico City. He was a native of Sevilla, the son of Juan *López* and Gerónima *Millán*.[11] Now, *no such friar ever came to New Mexico*. But he could have lawfully left the Order after investiture and before ordination, and come to New Mexico as a soldier; or a brother of his. Anyway, this could account for the surname of Andrés and his sister Sebastiana; also, for the unique name of a member of this family, *María López Millán,* wife of Francisco de Valencia, apparently Andrés' sister.[12] Even if this conjecture is not correct, the circumstantial similarity of names is most interesting.

* * * * * * * *

Other persons of this name who cannot be classified within the family were as follows:

Pedro Ventura de Gracia, who, with Andrés, escorted Governor Guzmán in 1646.[13] Nothing more is known about him.

Isabel López de Gracia, wife of Pedro de Cedillo, very likely a daughter of Andrés.[14]

Lucía López de Gracia, wife of José Nieto of the Salinas district,[15] perhaps a sister of Andrés.

Esteban López de Gracia, Captain, passed muster in 1680 with two sons-in-law of military age and two daughters.[16] He might be the "Esteban de Gracia" who fled the exile colony at Guadalupe del Paso sometime later.[17] Among other fugitives mentioned with him was an "Esteban López" who is elsewhere mentioned as escaping with his family in 1680.[18] What relation these men bore to the other López de Gracias cannot be ascertained.

---

1. **AGN, Mex., Inq.,** t. 385, f. 10.
2. **Ibid.,** t. 512, f. 88.
3. **Ibid.,** t. 594, p. 340; t. 507, p. 39.
4. **Ibid.,** t. 587, p. 454.
5. **DM,** 1686, No. 1.
6. **AGN, loc. cit.,** p. 284; **ibid., Prov. Int.,** t. 37, p. 352.
7. **Ocaranza,** p. 69.
8. **Revolt,** I, pp. 87, 156-158, 185.
9. **AGN, loc. cit.,** t. 594, p. 340.
10. **Ibid.,** t. 582, p. 85.
11. **Bancroft Coll., Mex. MSS,** No. 218, t. III, f. 17v.
12. **AGN, loc. cit.,** t. 666, f. 406; t. 512, f. 102.
13. **AGI, Contad.,** leg. 740, **Data.**
14. **DM,** 1695, No. 16.
15. **AGN, loc. cit.,** t. 507, p. 732.
16. **Revolt,** I, p. 152.
17. **BNM,** leg. 2, Pt. 3, ff. 283, 356.
18. **Revolt,** I, p. 148; II, pp. 51, 108.

LÓPEZ HOLGUÍN
(See *Olguín*)

LÓPEZ MEDEROS

JUAN LÓPEZ MEDEROS, a captain, resided with his wife at Isleta in 1626.¹ He appears to be the Oñate soldier of 1600, Juan López *Medel*, thirty-six years old, tall and black-bearded, the son of Pedro López Medel and a native of the Isle of La Palma.² He brought along three female Indian servants, two of them single with a daughter each, and the third with her husband,³ which leaves much room for conjecture. Nothing more is known about him.

1. AGN, Mex., Inq., t. 356, f. 260.
2. Oñate, p. 203.
3. Ibid., p. 210.

Pedro López Mederos lived in 1664 at the *estancia* of Tomé Domínguez de Mendoza in the Río Abajo. The latter was his brother-in-law.⁴ From other sources we learn that Domínguez' wife was *Catalina* López Mederos.⁵ Pedro and Catalina must have been children of Juan López Mederos.

He was a captain fifty-five, or sixty-five, years old in 1681, when he was described as being married, of medium height, robust, and swarthy.⁶

4. AGN, loc. cit., t. 507, p. 49.
5. DM, 1681, No. 2.
6. Revolt, I, p. 143.

LÓPEZ de OCANTO

JUAN LÓPEZ DEL CANTO, twenty-five years of age, the son of Pedro del Canto and born in Mexico City, came with Oñate in 1598. He was described as having a good stature, a black beard, and a cross on his forehead.¹

Juan López de Ocanto, a captain thirty-five years of age in 1642,² was in all likelihood the father of the next man.

Domingo López de Ocanto, twenty-seven in 1661, was clerk of the *Cabildo* of Santa Fe in 1661, holding the rank of *Alférez*. His wife was *Juana de Mondragón*.³ In this year he complained that Governor Mendizábal had taken from him the *encomienda* of Nambé and Jémez which had belonged to his Conquistador father, Juan López *de Ocanto*. Mendizábal retorted that Nambé had been given to Domingo's elder sister, since he was but a child when his father died.⁴ Father Bernal referred to him in 1669 as a man of virtue.⁵

Domingo was a *Sargento Mayor*, forty-two years old, in 1680. He claimed to be ill at the time, declaring that he was married and had six children.⁶ The following year he was in good health and took part in the Otermín Campaign.⁷ In 1682 he is mentioned as having died en route to New Mexico.⁸

José López de Ocanto was nineteen years old and single in 1681; he was described as a native of New Mexico, of medium height, with a round, beardless face and black, wavy hair. He also went on the Otermín Campaign.⁹ He is numbered in 1682 among those who ran away from Guadalupe del Paso.¹⁰ Apparently he was a son of Domingo.

María López de Ocanto, wife of Salvador Romero, and *Luisa López de Ocanto*, wife of Juan de Ribera, were most likely sisters of José.¹¹

1. Oñate, p. 189.
2. Ortiz Trial, ff. 27, 46.
3. AGN, Mex., Inq., t. 582, pp. 250-252.
4. Ibid., Tierras, t. 3268, p. 207.
5. Ibid., Mex., Inq., t. 666, f. 530.
6. Revolt, I, p. 141.
7. Ibid., I, p. 171; II, p. 39.
8. BNM, leg. 2, Pt. 3, f. 354.
9. Revolt, II, pp. 136, 264.
10. BNM, loc. cit., p. 292.
11. DM, 1702, No. 3; 1710, No. 10.

LÓPEZ SAMBRANO

ANDRÉS LÓPEZ SAMBRANO first appears in 1642 at Parral, testifying against the Baca faction. He was back in 1661-1664 as a forty-three-year-old captain acting as Lieutenant General of the Zuñi-Moqui district. He was a native of San Miguel in Culiacán. His wife was *Ana María de Anaya*.[1] Fray Juan Bernal thought little of his character.[2] His wife was a daughter of Francisco de Anaya Almazán and Juana López de Villafuerte,[3] and they had a son, *Diego*.[4] A daughter, *Josefa*, was the first wife of Francisco Lucero de Godoy.

Another **López Sambrano (Hernán?)**, husband of an *Elena Gómez*, who had had the *encomienda* of Awatobi, was a brother of Andrés.[5] An *Hernán Sambrano, Alférez*, mentioned in the soldier-escort in 1625,[6] might well be this man. He and Elena had a son *Francisco López*,[7] and perhaps another, named *Diego López*.[8]

Diego López Sambrano was a thirty-year-old captain, born and residing in Santa Fe in 1669, with his wife *María Suazo*. Father Bernal thought little of him.[9] In 1680, by then a *Sargento Mayor* and forty-two years of age, he escaped the Indian massacre with his wife, six small children, and seven servants.[10] He was described in 1681 as a native of New Mexico, thirty-eight years old, married, and tall with red hair and small eyes.[11] His daughter, *Juana*, married José Domínguez de Mendoza.[12]

Lands that once belonged to him were recalled as late as the year 1705.[13] It was this individual who, along with Luis de Quintana and Francisco Xavier, was not wanted back in New Mexico by the Indians parleying with Vargas in 1692.[14]

1. AGN, Mex., Inq., t. 507, pp. 245, 259; t. 585, f. 511; Ortiz Trial, f. 2.
2. AGN, loc. cit., t. 666, f. 533; t. 594. pp. 386-388.
3. Ibid., t. 507, pp. 257, 276.
4. Ibid., t. 594, p. 378.
5. Ibid., t. 507, p. 248.
6. Benavides, 1634, p. 110.
7. AGN, Tierras, t. 3268, p. 252.
8. Ibid., Mex., Inq., t. 507, p. 1300.
9. Ibid., t. 666, f. 564.
10. Revolt, I, p. 141; II, p. 39.
11. Ibid., II, p. 96.
12. DM, 1682, No. 5.
13. Sp. Arch., I, No. 932.
14. First Expedition, p. 83.

LÓPEZ
(*Unclassified*)

Several López persons living in New Mexico at the end of the century, who did not add another surname, could have belonged to any of the foregoing family groups.

Luis López was an illiterate captain living in Senecú as *Alcalde Mayor* of the Piros in 1667.[1] His *estancia* lay between the old Pueblos of Socorro and Qualacú and was referred to under his full name.[2] As late as 1769, Bishop Tamarón was told that the site was called "Luis López" after its original owner prior to the Indian Uprising of 1680.[3]

Nicolás López was killed at Santo Domingo in 1680.[4] Children of his by his wife, *Ana Luján*, find mention after the Reconquest.

Francisco López, a captain, escaped the massacre in 1680 with his wife.[5] He was described the following year as a native of New Mexico, forty-two years of age, tall and slim, having a swarthy complexion, black, curly hair, and the last joint of the little finger on the left hand broken.[6] He was, perhaps, the son of Elena Gómez and her López Sambrano husband.

Diego López, a bachelor, was twenty-six or twenty-seven in 1681; he was described as a native of New Mexico, having a good stature, a fair and ruddy complexion, and large eyes.[7] His description compares well with that of Diego López Sambrano, who might have been his father.

A *Diego López, "the Younger,"* is mentioned briefly in 1681,[8] and might be the same man.

Also mentioned in passing was a *José López*, sixteen years old and single.[9]

Cristóbal López, forty years old and married, appears in 1681, described as a native of New Mexico, tall and slender, with a very dark complexion and long, coarse hair.[10]

* * * * * * * *

Felipe López (García), twenty years old, the son of Juan and born in Mexico City at San Pablo, came to New Mexico in 1677 as a convict.[11] He seems to be the soldier, Felipe López, reported killed at Santa Clara Pueblo in 1680.[12]

José López was another convict of 1677. He was then twenty-five, the son of Francisco Ybarra Salazar, and also born in Mexico City at San Pablo,[13] and hence very likely a cousin of the preceding man. He might have gone back before 1680, since he is not mentioned again.

* * * * * * * *

Bernardo López de Peñuela, single, and a native of Agreda in Spain, appears in the muster-rolls of 1681. He had a good physique, an aquiline, pock-marked face, and a scant beard.[14]

1. AGN, Mex., Inq., t. 608.
2. Revolt, II, p. 364.
3. Tamarón, f. 132.
4. Revolt, I, p. 66.
5. Ibid., p. 151.
6. Ibid., II, pp. 78, 116-117.
7. Ibid., pp. 51, 140.
8. Ibid., pp. 187-188.
9. Ibid., p. 44.
10. Ibid., pp. 84, 103.
11. B-H, III, pp. 317-322.
12. Revolt, I, pp. 9-10.
13. B-H, loc. cit.
14. Revolt, II, pp. 63, 139.

LUCERO de GODOY

PEDRO LUCERO was the name of two distinct persons, both captains, who were cousins. One was forty years old in 1628, referred to as *"El Viejo."* The other was twenty-eight, and known as *"El Mozo."*[1] Together they had gone in the military escort of the wagon-trains in 1616-1617, 1621, and 1631.[2] Since the "Godoy" surname was applied only to the younger Pedro, and since the latter was already married in Santa Fe in 1628, plus other contributing facts, it can be assumed that he is the founder of this New Mexico family. The other Pedro disappears from the scene in those early years.

PEDRO LUCERO DE GODOY was a native of Mexico City, where he had a brother, Francisco. Another, Diego, was a secular priest there. Pedro was involved in most of the church and political intrigues of his time, although he managed to steer clear of unpleasant consequences experienced by others. By 1663, when he gave his age as sixty-three, he had attained the rank of *Maese de Campo*.[3] In this same year he was Lieutenant Governor of the Kingdom as well as Syndic of the Franciscans.[4]

His first wife was *Petronila de Zamora*, who married him, she later claimed, when but eleven years old.[5] To all appearances, she was the Petronila listed as the youngest child of Bartolomé Montoya and María de Zamora when they came to New Mexico in 1600.[6] They had a daughter, *Catalina*, who married Diego Romero, son of Gaspar Pérez,[7] and also a son, *Juan*, also prominent in public affairs. Another son, *Pedro*, *Alcalde* of Santa Fe at this time (1663), might have been a child by Petronila, or else by his second wife.

Pedro's second wife was *Francisca Gómez*

Robledo, who was also active in affairs connected with the Palace of the Governors in Santa Fe.[8] In 1663 they had five daughters "of marriageable age," and the young *Pedro,* just mentioned.[9] Another son, *Francisco,* figured in later historical events. One of the daughters, *María,* who was perhaps the youngest, became the wife of Lázaro de Misquia.

Two other Lucero women, *Ynez,* wife of Juan de la Escallada, and *Luisa,* married to Pedro Montoya de Esparza, were most likely his daughters. Lucero also had a stepson, *Antonio de Salas* (q. v.).

Pedro died well before the Rebellion of 1680. His second wife appears to be among the colonists who were massacred, from a statement of Diego Lucero de Godoy.

Juan Lucero de Godoy, Pedro's eldest son, was Secretary of Government and War in 1663.[10] Up until 1693, he claimed to have served the King for fifty-two years, from the time that he was seventeen until his present age of sixty-nine. He had resided in Santa Fe for forty years; his property there was at the "Pueblo Quemado."[11] Juan was a *Sargento Mayor* and the *Alcalde Mayor* of Santa Fe when he escaped the Indian siege of 1680 with his wife, four grown sons bearing arms, and four grown daughters.[12] The next year he was described as having a good stature with a large, pock-marked aquiline face, crooked nose, and fifty-nine years old.[13]

His sister, *Catalina de Zamora,* escaped with four grown nieces and five servants. The Indians had killed two of her nephews and more than thirty other relatives.[14]

Juan's first wife was a *Luisa Romero.* The second was *Juana de Carvajal,* who escaped with him in 1680 and died at San Lorenzo three years later; on January 14, 1689, he married *Isabel de Salazar,* daughter of Andrés Hurtado and Bernardina de Salas.[15] They returned with the Reconquest.

His four sons by either or both of the first two wives were *Juan* II, *Antonio, Nicolás,* and *Pedro.*

Pedro Lucero de Godoy II, mentioned by his father as being *Alcalde* of Santa Fe in 1663, is not heard of again.

Diego Lucero de Godoy, a young *Alférez* in 1663, was a *Sargento Mayor* residing in Taos in 1680. A widower, he had applied to marry a supposed daughter of Tomé Domínguez de Mendoza in April of that year, but no marriage took place.[16] He was with the Leyva escort party when the Indians struck in August, and later he declared that thirty-two persons of his household had been massacred, including his brothers and sisters, sons, and servants.[17]

On February 16, 1681, he married *María Domínguez de Mendoza,*[18] and in September he passed muster as a married man, thirty-eight years old and a native of New Mexico, of tall and slender height, with a fair, ruddy complexion and long, red hair.[19] In 1685 he was involved in the Juan Domínguez plot to abandon the colony,[20] but in 1689 he received permission to move south to New Spain with his wife María Domínguez.[21] Since his entire pre-Revolt family was killed, Diego left no descendants to re-settle New Mexico.

Francisco Lucero de Godoy, *Alférez* and Armorer, escaped in 1680 with a family of twenty-two, including wife, children, and servants. He was tall and erect with a thick beard, a wound-scar on his mustache and another on the right side of his nose.[22] His lands in Santa Fe, which formerly belonged to Andrés López, were on the Ciénega road.[23] In 1692 he took part in the Vargas Entry as a captain of artillery and armorer.[24]

His first wife was *Josefa López de Grijalva,* daughter of Andrés López Sambrano.[25] Her daughter testified years later that it was she who took out the venerated statue of La Conquistadora when the besieged people of Santa Fe withdrew to Guadalupe del Paso in 1680; she also personally brought it back, and was still living in Santa Fe in March, 1695.[26] Josefa died shortly after, and Francisco then married *Catalina de Espínola*, the young widow of Antonio Jorge de Vera.[27] He also was devoted to La Conquistadora.[28]

The children by his first wife were: *Francisco Mateo, Beatriz, Josefa, María*, wife of Juan de Alderete, and *Lucía*, wife of Francisco del Río.

Nicolás Lucero de Godoy, Adjutant of the Kingdom and twenty-seven years old in 1680, seems to have been a brother, the youngest, of the preceding Luceros. He was married, tall and slim of stature, with a reddish beard, long and straight chestnut hair, and large, blue eyes.[29] His wife's identity is not known, but he was a brother-in-law of Pedro Varela.[30] It is not known if he or any children of his returned with the Reconquest.

* * * * * * * *

Other members of this vast Lucero family mentioned in the 1680-1681 Revolt lists are as follows:

Nicolás Lucero de Godoy, distinct from the preceding Adjutant, is first mentioned in 1681 as a married native of New Mexico, thirty-four or thirty-six years old, of medium height, with good features, a thick beard, and long, wavy hair.[31] He was most likely a son of Juan Lucero de Godoy and Juana de Carvajal.

Antonio Lucero de Godoy, *Alférez*, passed muster in 1680, declaring that the Indians had killed his wife, two children, and four servants.[32] In the following year, still a widower, he enlisted as a colonist for a return to New Mexico.[33] He had a brother, Juan de Dios Lucero.[34] From a general view of various relations he seems to have been a son of Juan Lucero de Godoy.

His first wife had been a blood-niece of Juan Domínguez de Mendoza.[35] By 1685 he was married to *Antonia Varela de Losada*, or *de Perea*, with whom he returned to New Mexico in 1693.

Juan de Dios Lucero de Godoy passed muster in 1681 as a bachelor twenty-five years of age; he was of robust, medium height, having good features, a thick, black beard, and wavy hair.[36] Between September 23 and 26, when he passed muster again, he had taken a wife. This was *María Varela*, as we learn from a son's marriage later on,[37] probably a sister of his brother Antonio's second wife. In 1705 he was assistant *Alcalde* at Guadalupe del Paso, and still living there in 1718. His son, *Tomás*, was married there to María Madrid.[38]

Juan Lucero de Godoy passed muster on September 12, 1681, as a married man twenty-six years of age.[39] He is hard to place, yet seems to be the man of this name who returned with the Reconquest.

Francisco Mateo López de Godoy thus signed an *auto* of Otermín in 1680,[40] and again some minutes of the Confraternity of La Conquistadora in 1685.[41] His name points to his possibly being a son of Francisco and Josefa *López* Sambrano. He is met with again after the Reconquest.

Pedro Lucero de Godoy passed muster on September 26, 1681, and was described as a bachelor of twenty-two, with a medium stature, broad shoulders, good features, long and black wavy hair, and a black beard.[42]

A *Pedro Lucero* passed muster on September 30; he was nineteen years old and single, described as having a medium, thickset stature, with a beardless face, black hair, and large eyes.[43] If not the same man, one of these seems to be the youngest son of Juan Lucero de Godoy, whom the latter mentioned as being eighteen years old the previous year.

Matías Lucero, thirty-six or forty, and a native of New Mexico, signed two testimonies at Guadalupe del Paso in 1689.[44]

1. AGN, Mex., Inq., t. 363, ff. 2-12.
2. Ibid., t. 316, f. 176; AGI, Contad., legs. 718, 723, 732, Data.
3. AGN, Tierras, t. 3268, ff. 548-557.
4. Ibid., Mex., Inq., t. 507, pp. 295, 1693.
5. Ibid., t. 372, ff. 9-12.
6. Oñate, p. 209.
7. AGN, Tierras, loc. cit.
8. Ibid., Mex., Inq., t. 507, pp. 300-330.
9. Ibid., Tierras, loc. cit.
10. Ibid.
11. Sp. Arch., I, No. 422.
12. Revolt, I, p. 137.
13. Ibid., II, pp. 45, 107, 177-181.
14. Ibid., I, p. 151.
15. DM, 1689, No. 1; 1st M-Book, Guad. del Paso.
16. DM, 1680, No. 1.
17. Revolt, I, pp. 28, 140-141.
18. 1st M-Book, Guad. del Paso.
19. Revolt, II, p. 101.
20. Sp. Arch., II, No. 35.
21. Ibid., No. 49.
22. Revolt, I, p. 148; II, pp. 19, 135, 197.
23. Twit. Coll., no number.
24. First Expedition, p. 134.
25. López-Anaya charts.
26. AGN, Mex., Inq., t. 701, f. 322; El Palacio, Vol. 57, No. 10, p. 301.
27. DM, 1695, No. 6.
28. OLC, p. 62.
29. Revolt, I, p. 139; II, pp. 42, 117, 139.
30. Sp. Arch., I, No. 728.
31. Revolt, II, p. 113.
32. Ibid., I, p. 45.
33. Ibid., II, pp. 48, 112.
34. BNM, leg. 2, pt. 3, f. 338.
35. Sp. Arch., II, No. 35.
36. Revolt, II, pp. 37, 110, 113, 200.
37. DM, 1711, No. 3.
38. Ibid., 1705, No. 10; 1711, No. 3; 1718, No. 2.
39. Revolt, II, p. 59.
40. Ibid., I, p. 119.
41. OLC, pp. 55, 59; my error here in transcribing "Lucero" for "López."
42. Revolt, II, p. 113.
43. Ibid., pp. 141-142.
44. DM, 1689, Nos. 2, 9.

LUIS

JUAN LUIS, *"El Viejo,"* passed muster in 1680 with his wife, one grown son, and three small children.[1] In 1681 he said that he was sixty to sixty-six years old, a native of New Mexico, and was described as having a good and robust stature, a long face, and gray hair.[2] Later, in 1689, Captain Juan Luis, with his wife and children, is mentioned among the refugees at Guadalupe del Paso who are related in some way to José Baca, recently murdered by Silvestre Pacheco.[3]

The name "Luis" is heretofore unknown in New Mexico. A clue as to its origin comes later when this individual appears as a witness under the names, "Juan Luis *Luján*" and "Juan *Ruiz* Luján." He is, moreover, a native of Santa Fe, from seventy to eighty years of age at the time.[4] In other words, this Luis family belonged to the Ruiz Cáceres-Luján clans, the name having become corrupted as in other instances. Apparently, Juan Luis' wife was a Baca, perhaps the *Isabel Baca* who was the mother of Juana Ruiz Cáceres, wife of Antonio de Ávalos.

Juan Luis, "the Younger," passed muster in 1680 with his wife and one child.[5] He was described in 1680 as being forty-one years of age, a native of New Mexico, tall, with good features and large eyes.[6] Among those who fled to New Spain in 1682 were a son of Juan Luis and his son-in-law.[7]

A **Pedro Luján** is mentioned in 1695 as the son of Juan *Luis* Luján.[8] He could have been one of the three small children of 1680; also, perhaps, *Estela Luján*, wife of Francisco Márquez in the following century.

1. Revolt, I, p. 140.
2. Ibid., II, pp. 74-75, 96-97.
3. Sp. Arch., II, No. 45.
4. DM, 1689, No. 2; 1693, No. 1; 1694, Nos. 8, 27; 1695, No. 19.
5. Revolt, I, p. 140.
6. Ibid., II, pp. 74-75, 97.
7. BNM, leg. 2, Pt. 3, p. 284.
8. Sp. Arch., II, No. 198.

LUJÁN

Among the soldiers sent to Oñate at San Gabriel in 1600, there were three from the same place of origin, and with parents of identical surnames, all of whom must be considered in dealing with the large *Luján* family of New Mexico.

JUAN LUJÁN was twenty-seven years old and short of stature, born on the Isle of La Palma, the son of Francisco Rodríguez.[1]

JUAN RUIZ CÁCERES, thirty, was also a native of La Palma in the Canaries, the son of Pedro *Ruiz* [or Rodríguez].[3]

PEDRO RODRÍGUEZ, thirty years old and short of stature, no father given, was also a Canary Islander of La Palma.[4]

All more or less of the same age, and most probably related in some way, were perhaps first cousins. The descendants of the first two became confused already at the end of the century, when the word "Luján" is used indiscriminately. The *Luis Luján* family just treated is an example; also, *María Luján* (Ruiz Cáceres), wife of Sebastián Martín Serrano in the next century.

JUAN LUJÁN, the Canary Islander cited above, arrived in 1600 with a female Indian servant, single, Francisca Jiménez by name.[4] Many things in the records point to the probability of his having married this servant, or someone else like her. His known children were *Juan* II, *Francisco,* and, perhaps, a *Mariana* Luján who was the wife of Juan de Perramos, or Ramos.[5] His name, or else the younger Juan's, is found on El Morro with the date "1632."

Juan Luján II finds mention as an active participant in the political intrigues of Governor Rosa's times and after. He was a captain and *Alcalde Mayor* of the Taos-Picurís district.[6] He was a brother-in-law of Francisco Gómez [de Torres or Robledo?] and a kinsman of Pedro Lucero.[7] In 1661 he had an *estancia* in Taos Valley, and was then known as "El Viejo" in relation to a younger Juan Luján, who was most likely his son.[8] A daughter, *María,* was the wife of Juan de Archuleta. Juan died on November 15, 1663.[9]

Francisco Luján, apparently Juan's brother, was an *Alférez* in 1641 and thirty years old.[10] As early as 1631 he was married to a *Lucía Rodríguez,* aged twenty.[11] With Juan he was involved in the Rosas murder affair, and with him escaped the capital fate of their less fortunate compatriots. His sphere of action was in the Queres territory of Santo Domingo and Cochití.[12] He died before 1663.

His second wife was *María Ramos,* the daughter of his "sister," María Luján. Enemies of the friars later accused them of granting Francisco a dispensation to marry his blood-niece.[13] But Mariana, wife of Juan Ramos, was not necessarily his blood-sister; she appears to have been the bastard child of María, Indian servant of Juan López.[14]

* * * * * * * *

The Luján people listed in the refugee rolls of 1680-1681 are as follows:

Matías Luján, soldier, passed muster with a family of eight, including wife, children, and brothers-in-law.[16] In 1681 he was described as a native of New Mexico, twenty-five to twenty-nine years old, married, having a good stature, slender, with a dark complexion, thick, black hair and beard.[17] He had been born in the Cañada area, at the place called San Cristóbal after the Reconquest, and there he had his residence before the Rebellion.[18] He might have been a son of Juan Luján II, if not a member of the Ruiz Cáceres group. His wife, *Francisca Romero,* and their family returned to New Mexico with the Reconquest.

Domingo Luján was twenty-six and married in 1681. He was described as a native of New Mexico, of good stature, swarthy, with black hair and a thick beard. He had been stationed outside New Mexico proper, perhaps at Guadalupe del Paso, when the Rebellion came; hence he was not among the refugees of 1680.[19] Apparently he is the man of this name who, against strict orders, gave some gunpowder to a Cochití [half-] brother of his during the Otermín Campaign in 1681,[20] as well as the soldier of this name who was killed in 1693 when chasing a cow on horseback.[21] Meanwhile, between 1680 and 1692, his wife and children had been held captives in the Pueblos, as will be seen later. His Cochití connections make him a possible son of Francisco Luján.

Antonio Luján escaped the 1680 massacre with his wife and children. He was described in 1681 as a native of New Mexico, forty-two years of age, married, of slender medium height, with a thick beard and straight, partly gray hair. He had a son, eighteen years old.[22] Antonio died the following year, after six years of marriage, and was buried in the Socorro del Paso church; his widow, *María Martín*, married Domingo de Herrera in 1683,[23] and returned to New Mexico with her family in 1693.

Agustín Luján escaped in 1680 with his wife, two children, and three sisters-in-law. He was described in 1681 as a native of New Mexico, twenty-six years of age, with a good, robust stature, aquiline face, and good features, black hair and beard.[24] Perhaps he is the individual who married a *Luisa Varela* in Santa Fe after the Reconquest.

Miguel Luján is mentioned briefly as a recruit in 1681,[25] and is very likely the same man, a brother or brother-in-law of Juan Ruiz Cáceres, who was left by Vargas to guard the tower-chapel in the Governors' Palace in December, 1693; he barely escaped from it with his family when the Indians decided to keep the city. At this time he had a young son who is called both *Agustín* and *Cristóbal* in the same incident.[26]

Diego Luján also escaped in 1680 with his wife and two small children. A native of New Mexico, twenty-four years old and married, he was further described as having a good stature and features, with large eyes and long, straight hair.[27] His wife was *Juana de Salazar*, a *coyota* of Zuñi.[28] Both ran away from the Real of San Lorenzo to Parral in 1682. Their son, *Sebastián*, returned to New Mexico with the new colonists of 1693, but they remained at El Real de San Juan in Nueva Vizcaya.[29]

Juan Luján, twenty years old and single, registered as "Juan *Barba*" in 1681, having escaped the previous year's massacre with his widowed mother and his brothers and sisters. He had a long face, straight hair and noticeable smallpox scars.[30] His father was the *Alférez* Esteban Barba who was killed at Santo Domingo Pueblo in August, 1680.[31] In 1682 he fled to New Spain (Parral),[32] where he married and later joined the 1693 colonists as *Juan Luján*.[33]

1. **Oñate**, p. 203.
2. Ibid., p. 202.
3. Ibid., p. 204.
4. Ibid., p. 210.
5. AGN, Mex., Inq., t. 372, exp. 19, f. 8.
6. Ch. and State, pp. 138, 173; Troub. Times, pp. 7, 73-74, 86.
7. AGN, loc. cit., t. 596, Pt. 2, f. 160.
8. Ibid., Tierras, t. 3268.
9. Ibid., Mex., Inq., t. 507, pp. 291-298, 564.
10. Ibid., t. 425, f. 638.
11. Ibid., t. 372, exp. 19, f. 8.
12. Ibid., t. 507, p. 59; Ch. and State, pp. 173-184; Ortiz Trial, f. 3.
13. AGN, loc. cit., t. 587, pp. 305-311.
14. Oñate, p. 210.
15. AGN, Tierras, t. 3268, p. 320.
16. Revolt, I, p. 158.
17. Ibid., II, pp. 62, 124.
18. Sp. Arch., I, No. 818; II, No. 89.
19. Revolt, II, pp. 38, 137.
20. Ibid., p. 263.
21. AGI, Guadalajara, leg. 140, f. 68.
22. Revolt, I, p. 138; II, pp. 64, 125-126.
23. DM, 1683, No. 1.
24. Revolt, I, p. 145; II, p. 126.
25. Ibid., II, p. 195.
26. Ritch Coll., Box 1, No. 225.
27. Revolt, I, pp. 144-145; II, p. 125.
28. DM, 1705, No. 6.
29. Ibid.; Sp. Arch., II, No. 109.
30. Revolt, II, pp. 99-100, 78-79.
31. Ibid., I, p. 66.
32. BNM, leg. 2, Pt. 3, ff. 354-357.
33. Sp. Arch., II, No. 54c.

LUNA

JUAN GÓMEZ DE LUNA was a captain and interpreter in the Indian languages whose wife was *Juana Sánchez,* forty to fifty years of age in 1631, sister of Juana de los Reyes, who was married to Álvaro García Holgado.[1] In 1621 he had traveled down to Zacatecas and there visited an uncle, Mateo de Luna, who was a secular priest.[2] All this and other passing mention were in connection with certain unorthodox remarks attributed to him, one of these by the wife of Pedro D. y Chaves.[3] Still, he was the Syndic of the Franciscans in 1636. As a captain in 1664 he was accused, with Matías Romero, of trading illicitly and capturing slaves for Governor Rosas.[4]

There was a *Melchor de Luna* in Oñate's 1597 list who was a native of Puerto de Santa María, and the son of Baltasar de Morales.[5] He seems to be identical with a Melchor *Gómez* and a Melchor de *Torres*. Hence there seems to have been a very close relationship between this Melchor, Juan Gómez de Luna, and Francisco Gómez de Torres (*q.v.*).

Diego de Luna is mentioned, in passing, in 1654 as being nineteen years old.[6] He was the only adult male Luna at the time of the 1680 Rebellion, reporting with his family of three children and thirty other persons, including his mother-in-law, brothers- (or sisters-) in-law, and servants.[7] He was an *Alférez* forty-eight years old, a native of New Mexico, tall, with a long face and long straight hair.[8] He and his wife were mentioned as kinfolk of the Francisco de Torres family, all natives of New Mexico.[9] In this year, 1687, the family of Captain Diego de Luna, consisting of twenty-nine persons, was numbered among those in dire need at the exile settlement of Corpus Christi de Ysleta.[10] In 1692 he was ordered to assemble his men for the first Entry of Vargas into New Mexico.[11] He was a witness on August 31, 1693, at a wedding in Ysleta, when he gave his age as more than sixty.[12]

Presumably, he returned with the Reconquest in the following months of 1693, but is not heard of again. He was listed as a member of the Conquistadora Confraternity in 1689.[13] Several Lunas re-settled the Río Abajo district.

---
1. AGN, Mex., Inq., t. 372, f. 18; t. 356, f. 316v.
2. Ibid., t. 356, f. 260v.
3. Ibid., ff. 285, 301.
4. BNM, leg. 1, Pt. 1, ff. 370-504; AGI, Patronato, leg. 244, Ramo 7, doc. 22, p. 161.
5. AGI, Mex., Aud., leg. 25.
6. AGN, loc. cit., exp. 8, f. 227v.
7. Revolt, I, p. 150.
8. Ibid., II, pp. 76, 98.
9. DM, 1687, No. 1.
10. AGN, Prov. Int., t. 37, pp. 100-104.
11. First Expedition, p. 51.
12. DM, 1693, No. 5.
13. OLC, p. 70.

MADRID

FRANCISCO DE MADRID came to New Mexico in 1603 as a *chirrionero de los carros,* bringing ten new soldiers and four friars.[1] In 1626 he said that he was thirty-two years old and married, boasting that he was one of the "ancient settlers." (Hence he must have been several years older.) At this time he was mentioned as a brother-in-law of Pedro Márquez. He signed his name "Madril."[2] His wife was *María de la Vega Márquez,* or simply without the "Vega" name.[3] By 1639 he was a captain, when he gave his age as forty-six,[4] and two years later he was a member of the Santa Fe *Cabildo*.[5]

His children, to all appearances, were: *Francisco* II, *Francisca,* wife of Juan Varela de Losada;[6] and *María,* nicknamed "*Mariaca.*"[7] An *Alférez, Cristóbal de Madrid,* who escorted some colonists to New Mexico in 1641, might have been another son,[8] or perhaps the elder Francisco was meant since Cristóbal is not heard of again.

Francisco de Madrid II was despised by Governor López Mendizábal for "his pretension."[9] His wife was a daughter of Juan Ruiz Cáceres.[10] His sons were *Lorenzo, Roque,* and, perhaps, *Francisco* III, *Pedro,* and *Juan,* treated further on.

Lorenzo de Madrid, an elder brother of Roque de Madrid and son of Francisco de Madrid II, boasted in 1698 that he was the oldest Conquistador and settler in the Kingdom.[11] He was at Guadalupe del Paso when the Indians rebelled, and there he passed muster in 1680 as a *Sargento Mayor* with his wife, a son of military age, and three servants.[12] He was described as a native of New Mexico, married, forty-seven years old, tall and swarthy, with black hair and beard; he was also lame in one arm.[13]

His first wife was an *Antonia Ortiz [Baca?]*, who bore him these sons: *Nicolás, José, Jacinto,* and *Francisco Tomás Simón*.[14] Of these, José seemed to be the only one living and with him in 1680. His second wife, the one with him at this time, was *Ana de Almazán,* widow of Andrés López de Sambrano, by whom he had no children; but they did have six adopted ones, the eldest of whom might be the *Lucía* who was made captive in 1680 and rescued by her "brother" José in 1692.[15] The rest of Lorenzo's life is told in the next century.

Roque de Madrid, son of Francisco de Madrid II and grandson of Juan Ruiz Cáceres, was the husband of *Juana de Arvid (López)*, daughter of María Pacheco and grand-daughter of Gerónimo Pacheco.[16] He escaped the 1680 massacre with his wife and two small children, and was described in 1681 as a native of New Mexico, a captain, married, thirty-seven years old, tall and slim in stature, swarthy, with a gray beard and thick, black hair.[17] In the Vargas Entry of 1692, Roque rescued from captivity a certain Petrona, wife of Cristóbal Nieto, and her children, all of whom were related to his wife.[18] The annals of subsequent campaigns are filled with his activities as a military leader. These, and his descendants, are treated in the following century.

* * * * * * * *

Other Madrid men who appear in the 1680-1681 muster-rolls are the following:

Juan de Madrid escaped with his wife and six small children, and was described in 1681 as a native of New Mexico, forty years old, of thickset, medium build, dark, with curly, gray beard and thick, black hair; also, a cataract over the left eye.[19] He had three successive wives: *Micaela Martín, María de Mondragón,* and *Ana Holguín*. His family stayed at Guadalupe del Paso where a son, *Francisco,* married María de Salazar at Socorro del Paso, in 1703; a daughter, *Manuela,* became the wife of Antonio Valencia in 1710; and another, *María,* married Alonso Cisneros in 1690.[20]

Francisco de Madrid III appears to have been an older brother of Roque; also, the preceding Juan, for that matter. Francisco escaped in 1680 with his wife and four small children, and in the following year was described as a captain forty-two years old, a native of New Mexico, married, of medium height, swarthy and gray-haired.[21] He seems to have died by 1705, when a Juan de Ávalos testified that he (Francisco) was the father of two now adult illegitimates, and that he had heard this from both Francisco and Roque de Madrid; Roque wrote back indignantly denying the charge.[22]

Pedro de Madrid also appears to be a brother of the foregoing men. He passed muster in 1680 with his wife and five small children. In 1681 he held the post of adjutant and was from forty to fifty years of age. He was described as a native of New Mexico, of good stature, with very thick and partly gray beard and long, wavy hair.[23] His wife was *Yumar Varela Jaramillo*. Pedro and his family must

Sample page from *AGN, Inquisición*, tomo 356, foja 268, dated January 30, 1626. Signed attestations by Don Pedro Durán y Chaves and Francisco de Madrid.

have stayed permanently at Guadalupe del Paso. One son, *José,* born there after the Rebellion, married a Josefa de Contreras at Senecú del Paso.²⁴ A daughter, *Lucía,* also born there, married Pedro Meusnier.²⁵

José de Madrid, not mentioned in 1680, passed muster in 1681 as a native of New Mexico, married, and twenty-two to twenty-five years old. He had a good, robust stature, dark complexion, thick, black hair and beard.²⁶ He was the son of military age mentioned by Lorenzo de Madrid the previous year. An adjutant in 1692, José found his "sister," Lucía de Madrid, a captive at Zuñi; single when captured in 1680, she had two children, one about twelve.²⁷

José's wife was *María Trujillo,* with whom he was a sponsor in 1686.²⁸ He might be the man of this name who was on trial in 1693 for living in concubinage and for trying to kill his wife.²⁹ He was dead by 1711 when a daughter, *María,* married Tomás Lucero at Guadalupe del Paso in 1711.³⁰

---

1. **AGI, Contad.,** leg. 842A, **Data.**
2. **AGN, Mex., Inq.,** t. 356, f. 268.
3. **Ibid.,** t. 372, ff. 11, 17.
4. **Ibid.,** t. 369, f. 4v.
5. **B-H,** III, p. 57.
6. **AGN, loc. cit.,** t. 507, p. 1646.
7. **Ibid.,** t. 596, Pt. 2, f. 156v.
8. **AGI, Contad.,** leg. 736, **Data.**
9. **AGN, loc. cit.,** t. 596, Pt. 2, f. 156v; t. 587, pp. 386-388.
10. **Sp. Arch.,** I, No. 486.
11. **DM,** 1697, No. 17, b.
12. **Revolt,** I, pp. 35, 143.
13. **Ibid.,** II, pp. 66, 129.
14. **Sp. Arch.,** I, No. 502.
15. **Ibid.; DM,** 1694, No. 34; **AGI, Guadalajara,** leg. 139.
16. **Sp. Arch.,** I, No. 486.
17. **Revolt,** I, p. 142; II, p. 122.
18. **First Expedition,** p. 184.
19. **Revolt,** I, p. 145; II, pp. 56, 122.
20. **DM,** 1690, No. 2; 1703, No. 1; 1710, No. 13.
21. **Revolt,** I, p. 141; II, pp. 75, 98, 331.
22. **DM,** 1705, No. 10.
23. **Revolt,** I, p. 151; II, pp. 44, 112.
24. **DM,** 1709, No. 13.
25. **Ibid.,** 1699, No. 9.
26. **Revolt,** II, pp. 85, 103-104, 142.
27. **First Expedition,** p. 237.
28. **DM,** 1686, No. 1.
29. **Ibid.,** 1693, No. 2.
30. **Ibid.,** 1711, No. 3.

MAESE

JUAN MAESE, a *Sargento* twenty-eight years old in 1632, had an *estancia* somewhere in New Mexico. He is mentioned in passing and is not heard of again.¹

Esteban Maese lived in the middle of the century; his widow, *Antonia González,* was still alive and quite old in 1682.²

Among the refugees of the 1680 Indian Rebellion, only two male adults of this name can be found, *Alonso* and *Luis.*

Alonso Maese, married, escaped with fifteen persons in his family, including his mother [Antonia González?] and children, all very poor.³ In 1681 he stated that he was forty years old, and had a son who was twenty. Alonso was briefly described as being of medium height and having thick hair.⁴ Elsewhere, this son of his is referred to as *Juan Maese.*⁵

Alonso's wife was *Catalina Montaño.* They did not return with the Reconquest but remained at El Real de San Lorenzo, as may be seen from their children's marriages. *Juan* had married an Estefánia González, whose daughter, María, married a Juan de Varela there in 1709;⁶ *Gabriel* applied to marry Beatriz Lucero de Godoy in 1691, but it is not known if the marriage took place;⁷ *Francisco* married Juliana del Río at Guadalupe del Paso in 1701; and *Ana María* became the wife of Alfonso Hidalgo in the same year.⁸

Luis Maese was most likely Alonso's brother. In 1681 he was described as a native of New Mexico, thirty years old, married, of medium build, having good features, black hair and beard.⁹ His wife was *Josefa de Archuleta,* and both returned to Santa Fe in 1693.

---

1. **AGN, Mex., Inq.,** t. 372, f. 15; t. 304, f. 187v.
2. **Ibid.,** t. 1551, f. 382.
3. **Revolt,** I, p. 147.
4. **Ibid.,** II, pp. 58, 125.
5. **BNM,** leg. 2, Pt. 3, f. 225.
6. **DM,** 1709, No. 3.
7. **Ibid.,** 1691, No. 1.
8. **Ibid.,** 1701, Nos. 2, 5.
9. **Revolt,** II, pp. 43, 126.

MÁRQUEZ
(*Márquez Sambrano*)

GERÓNIMO MÁRQUEZ was the *Maese de Campo* of the troops which joined Oñate in 1600. He was forty years old, a native of Sanlucar de Barrameda, the son of Hernán Muñoz Zamorano. He was described as swarthy and black-bearded.[1] In the Puana muster-roll of 1597 he had the rank of Captain of Artillery, when his father's name was written as Hernán Martín Sambrano, and his birthplace as San Lucar la Mayor.[2] With him came his wife and five grown sons.[3] His name runs through all the Oñate annals as an adventurous leader. He was exiled from New Mexico,[4] but he returned—if ever the sentence was carried out. As late as 1631 he was living at his *estancia* at Acomilla in the Río Abajo district.[5]

His wife's name is not known, but an ambiguous statement makes her seem to be a *Doña Ana de Mendoza*, daughter and granddaughter of leading Conquistadores of New Spain. She had three sisters who were nuns, and was a niece of Don Fernando de Oñate as well as a first cousin of Francisco de Zaldívar.[6] Their five sons were: *Francisco, Pedro, Juan, Hernando,* and *Diego*. A daughter, *María*, became the wife of Francisco de Madrid.

Francisco Márquez was forty-three in 1631 when he was mentioned as the brother of the late Hernando Sambrano, and the husband of *María Núñez*, sister of Diego Bellido.[7] His wife was from Socorro de los Piros.[8] They had a daughter, *Catalina*, who married Nicolás de Aguilar.

Pedro Márquez was an *Alférez* thirty-five years old, married, and living in Santa Fe in 1626, the brother-in-law of Francisco de Madrid, and brother of Hernán Márquez Sambrano.[10] He died shortly after, for his widow, *Catalina Pérez de Bustillo*, nineteen, was living at her *estancia* at La Cañada in 1631.[11]

Juan Márquez is mentioned as the son of Captain Gerónimo Márquez as early as 1613.[12] He, too, died early, for his wife, *María de Archuleta*, was a widow, thirty years old, in 1631.[13]

There was another *Juan Márquez*, thirty-six years old in 1639-1641, who was an *Alférez* and Treasurer of the Holy Crusade, and is said to have been murdered by order of Governor Rosas.[14] He was a son, no doubt, of any of the Márquez brothers, perhaps of Juan.

Hernando Márquez was an *Alférez* in 1625.[15] He was dead by October, 1628, when his brother Pedro accused a Mexican Indian woman, Beatriz by name, of causing Hernando's death through witchcraft.[16] Hernando had been living in concubinage with a Juana de la Cruz, also accused of hexing him after he spurned her.[17]

Diego Márquez was accused as a major accomplice in the death of Governor Rosas, and was beheaded in Santa Fe with seven other captains in 1643.[18] His widow, *Doña Bernardina Vásquez*, was still living at the *estancia* of Los Cerrillos in 1660 with her daughter *Margarita*.[19] Their children were: *Cristóbal, Pedro, Bernabé, Margarita*, wife of Gerónimo Carvajal, and, perhaps, *Catalina*. Diego also had a natural half-breed son, who lived as an Indian at Santo Domingo by the name of *Alonso Catiti*.

* * * * * * * *

Members of this family living in 1680 and after were the following:

Pedro Márquez escaped the Indian massacre with one son. The enemy had carried off his wife and daughter.[20] In 1681 he gave his age as forty, saying he was a native of New Mexico and a widower. He was described as thickset, with a plump face pitted by smallpox.[21]

In 1672, Francisco Márquez rescued his aunt, Lucía——, wife of Pedro Márquez residing at Casas Grandes, and her daughter.[22] This Pedro was from Nambé.[23] He was a cousin of the namesake who follows. This family probably never returned to New Mexico.

Pedro Márquez, a captain, escaped with his wife, two children, and six servants.[24] He gave his age as thirty in 1681, saying he was married and ill in bed. He was accused of profiteering with the Chaves - Domínguez clans at the expense of the refugee colony at Guadalupe del Paso.[25] This was natural, as his wife was a daughter of Don Pedro de Chaves, with whom he left the colony in 1682.[26] As a brother of Bernabé Márquez,[27] he was a son of Diego Márquez and Bernardina Vázquez. Alonso Catiti, a *coyote* Indian leader of Santo Domingo Pueblo, was referred to as a brother of Pedro.[28] This family, with its kindred Chaves and Domínguez families, did not return with the Reconquest.

Bernabé Márquez was besieged by the Indians at his ancestral place of Los Cerrillos, and was rescued on the night of August 12, 1680, by a force sent by Governor Otermín from Santa Fe. With him were his wife and six half-grown children, seven servants, and a brother-in-law [a Chaves] of military age.[29] He was described in 1681 as thirty-eight or thirty-nine years old and married, a native of New Mexico, having a good, slender build, a thick beard, and chestnut hair.[30] He was a brother of Diego Márquez. His wife was *Doña María de Chaves*, sister of the *Sargento Mayor*, Don Fernando D. y Chaves, who had escaped from Taos in 1680.[31] Bernabé fled to Mexico City in 1683 with this brother-in-law, to get permission to abandon New Mexico for good, but turned back.[32]

The name of his eldest son was *Diego Márquez*.[33] This entire family did not return to New Mexico, presumably leaving for New Spain with the Domínguez and Pedro de Chaves clans.

Antonio Márquez, Captain, escaped in 1680 with his wife, five children, and eight servants.[34] He was thirty-eight in 1681, described as a native of New Mexico, with a good stature and features, black hair and beard. He went on the Otermín Campaign of that year.[35] The Antonio Márquez mentioned in 1668 as having three oxen that belonged to the German trader, Bernardo Gruber, was most likely this man, and so a resident of the Río Abajo area.[36] His wife was *Francisca Domínguez*. Their daughter, *Estefánia*, married José de Levya in 1682.[37]

Francisco Márquez, not listed in 1680, is mentioned as married and twenty-two years of age in 1681.[38] He is the one who in 1692 rescued his aunt Lucía and her daughter from Indian captivity.[39] He ran away from the exile colony with a Domingo Luján in 1682, but both came back or were caught.[40] He and his family returned with the Reconquest.

---

1. Oñate, p. 203.
2. AGI, Guadalajara, leg. 25, Pt. 1.
3. Ibid., Patronato, leg. 22, Pt. 5, f. 719.
4. Oñate, pp. 104-150.
5. AGN, Mex., Inq., t. 304, f. 189.
6. AGI, Mex., Aud., leg. 72, Title 1489.
7. AGN, loc. cit., t. 372, Exp. 19, ff. 18-19.
8. Ibid., f. 20.
9. Ibid., t. 512, f. 90.
10. Ibid., t. 304, f. 186; t. 356, ff. 267-303.
11. Ibid., t. 356, Exp. 19, f. 7.
12. AGI, Contad., leg. 716, Data.
13. AGN, loc. cit., t. 372, ff. 11-17.
14. Ibid., t. 425, f. 640; B-H, III, p. 49; AGI, Patronato, leg. 244, Ramo 7, doc. 22, p. 167.
15. AGI, Contad., leg. 726, Data.
16. AGN, loc. cit., t. 304, f. 186; t. 372, Exp. 19, ff. 18-19.
17. Ibid., t. 304, f. 189.
18. Ch. and State, pp. 127, 162, 175-176.
19. AGN, loc. cit., t. 581, p. 69; t. 507, f. 24.
20. Revolt, I, p. 145.
21. Ibid., II, pp. 133, 145.
22. First Expedition, p. 184.
23. BNM, leg. 2, Pt. 3, ff. 354-347.
24. Revolt, I, p. 148.
25. Ibid., II, pp. 55, 162-165.
26. BNM, loc. cit.
27. Ibid., f. 364.
28. Revolt, II, pp. 261, 279, 295, 386.
29. Ibid., I, pp. 11, 20, 97, 119, 152.
30. Ibid., II, pp. 40, 109.
31. BNM, loc. cit., f. 290.
32. Ibid., ff. 275-283.
33. Revolt, II, p. 115; Bartolomé is very likely an error.
34. Ibid., I, p. 145.
35. Ibid., II, pp. 125, 319, 391.
36. AGN, loc. cit., t. 608.
37. DM, 1682, No. 3.
38. Revolt, II, p. 72.
39. First Expedition, loc. cit.
40. BNM, loc. cit., f. 290.

MARTÍN BARBA

ALONSO MARTÍN BARBA was a fifty-year-old captain living in Santa Fe in 1632.¹ His wife was *María Martín*, allegedly poisoned by a María Bernal with whom Alonso was having relations. A daughter of his, *María de los Ángeles*, twenty-two, was the widow of Gaspar de Arratia, and a son, *Diego*, was married to Isabel de Cabinillas.² In 1634 his grand-daughter, Ynez de Zamora, child of *Alférez* Diego de Montoya and *Ana Martín*, married a *Sargento* Juan López. Alonso himself, fifty-three at the time, and his second wife, *Francisca de Herrera Abrego*, were the wedding sponsors.³ This Francisca de *Abrega* escaped the Indian massacre of 1680 with eight children and grandchildren, all very poor.⁴

Alonso's children were: *Diego, Alonso, María de los Ángeles, Ana,* and another daughter [*María*?] who as early as 1613 was married to a Francisco [de Salazar? Montoya?] whose last name is illegible.⁵

Diego Martín Barba, son of Alonso, was a captain living in Santa Fe in 1637 with his wife, *Isabel de Cabinillas*.⁶ In 1642 he gave his age as thirty. He was one of the eight captains ordered beheaded in 1643 for complicity in the death of Governor Rosas.⁷ His name is carved on Inscription Rock with the date "1636."

Alonso Martín Barba II was mentioned in 1660 as a son of Alonso Martín Barba of La Cañada. He was an *Alférez* living in Chililí.⁸ Sometime later he was exiled from the Salinas country for concubinage with his *comadre Ynez*. He was dead by 1669.⁹

Alonso had a younger brother, referred to once in 1663 as "*Fulano*" Barba,¹⁰ who might be either the *Domingo* or *Esteban* mentioned in the Rebellion records.

The three Martín Barbas found listed in 1680-1681 are the following:

Domingo Martín Barba, forty-two or forty-four years of age, escaped with his wife and five children. He was described as a native of New Mexico, of good, slender stature, swarthy, with a thick, black beard, and some upper teeth missing.¹¹

Esteban Barba was an *Alférez* killed at Santo Domingo with the friars and two other soldiers.¹²

Juan Barba, twenty years old and single, escaped with his widowed mother and young brethren; he was described as having a long face, straight hair, and smallpox scars.¹³ He was the son of Esteban Barba. Years later he returned to New Mexico as Juan *Luján*. His sister *Josefa*, daughter of Esteban Barba and *María Luján*, appeared as a marriage witness in 1687.¹⁴

1. **AGN, Mex., Inq.,** t. 304, ff. 191-195.
2. **Ibid.,** t. 372, Exp. 19, ff. 7-10.
3. **Ibid.,** t. 380, ff. 233-247.
4. **Revolt,** I, pp. 151-152.
5. **AGN, loc. cit.,** t. 316, f. 172.
6. **Ibid.,** t. 304, f. 7; t. 372, Exp. 19, ff. 7-10.
7. **Ch. and State,** p. 175; **Ortiz Trial,** ff. 6v, 30-32.
8. **AGN, loc. cit.,** t. 587, pp. 45, 80.
9. **Ibid.,** t. 666, f. 555.
10. **Ibid.,** t. 594, Exp. 1, f. 7v.
11. **Revolt,** I, p. 68; II, pp. 105, 123, 146.
12. **Ibid.,** I, p. 66.
13. **Ibid.,** II, pp. 99-100.
14. **DM,** 1687, No. 1.

MARTÍN SERRANO

HERNÁN MARTÍN SERRANO came with the original Oñate colony of 1598. He was then forty years old, the son of Hernán Martín Serrano and a native of Zacatecas, tall of stature, sparse-bearded and pockmarked.¹ He is designated in the 1597 muster-roll as the

Sargento of the Expedition. His wife, *Juana Rodríguez,* and family are with him; he has cattle, horses, utensils, and even a millstone.[2]

In 1626, Captain Hernán Martín Serrano, seventy years of age, was considered an ancient settler and resident of Santa Fe.[3] He had two sons, *Hernán* II and *Luis. María Martín,* first wife of Alonso Martín Barba, was very likely his daughter.

Hernán Martin Serrano II gave his age as twenty-five in 1632, when he was known as Hernán Martín "*el Mozo.*" He was involved at this time with a woman of low estate in Santa Fe although his residence was at La Cañada.[4] In 1635 he gave his age as twenty-seven, and in 1641 as forty, and in 1642 as over thirty-eight.[5] He declared himself to be fifty-eight in 1664, an *encomendero* and a captain, and a widower at this time. He also said that he had been born at El Yunque.[6] By 1660 he was living in Santa Fe, while his brother Luis lived in the paternal lands at La Cañada.[7] Some years later, 1667-1669, he appears to have been living in the Salinas district, along with José and Juan Martín Serrano and a María Martín, widow of Bartolomé de Ledesma.[8] These three were his children, apparently. *Juan* died prior to 1680, for he is not mentioned then, and his widow was living with in-laws at Corpus Christi de Ysleta in 1684;[9] *José,* also, who is not mentioned again.

Hernán, or Hernando, appears to have had at least three successive wives: *María Montaño,* mother of Pascuala Martín who married Diego Durán;[10] *Catalina Griego,* mother of another Cristóbal Martín who married Juana de la Cruz;[11] and *Josefa de la Asención González,* several of whose children were living in Santa Fe after the Reconquest.

Hernán's activities at the time of the Indian Rebellion testify to his vigor. He passed muster in 1680, in the company of the Salinas-Socorro area, as a captain more than eighty years old. With him was a family of nine—wife, children, and grandchildren.[12] In the following year he gave his age as seventy-six or seventy-seven, and was ready to serve as a soldier. He was described as a native of New Mexico, married, of good stature, robust, with gray beard and partly gray hair, and a film on his left eye.[13] He had become proficient in the Indian tongues, so that he served as an officer and interpreter of the Jumana language during the Domínguez Expedition into Texas in 1683-1684.[14] Born around the year 1604, he would have been close to ninety if he was alive to return with the Reconquest; anyway, his vast and diverse progeny did come back to New Mexico in 1693.

Luis Martín Serrano, brother of Hernán, was disliked by Governor Mendizábal for his friendship with the friars; he also accused Luis of being the man who broke down the door when Governor Rosas was assassinated.[15] He lived at La Cañada, where he allegedly hid an illegitimate child of Governor Manso before it was spirited off to Mexico City.[16]

His wife was *Catalina de Salazar,* who was a widow by 1663. At this time we learn that Luis had been the *Alcalde Mayor* and Captain of the Tewa jurisdiction.[17] Catalina was very likely a daughter of Captain Sebastián Rodríguez de Salazar. Luis' descendants can be distinguished from those of his brother Hernán because they sometimes appended her Salazar name to that of their father.

Luis Martín Serrano II was, in all likelihood, their son, as also a *Pedro Martín Serrano de Salazar.*

Luis Martín Serrano II escaped the 1680 massacre with his wife and twelve children, four of these being sons of military age. Luis held the rank of captain.[18] The next year he gave his age as forty-eight or fifty, and declared that a son of his, eighteen years old, was ready to bear arms. He himself was described as a native of New Mexico, married, having a good, slender physique, dark complexion, black hair and beard, and a mole on the left cheek.[19] Two sons who were described as his were *Antonio,* twenty-six, and *Luis,* "the

Younger," thirty-four; both were married.[20]

His wife was *Antonia de Miranda,* as we learn from later sources. Their children were, besides *Luis* III and *Antonio,* another who has been identified as *Francisco.* Two daughters are also known: *María,* wife of Antonio Luján, and *María Rosa,* who married Nicolás López. Since this family returned to New Mexico in 1693, they will be fully treated in the next century.

Cristóbal Martín Serrano appears in 1681 as a married man of twenty-six, having a good stature, but slender, with black eyes, thick, black hair and beard.[21] To all appearances, he was a son of Hernán Martín II. He and his wife, *Antonia de Moraga,* are met again after the Reconquest with their children, *Cristóbal* II, *Diego, María,* wife of Manuel Antonio Domínguez, and *Josefa.*

Domingo Martín Serrano escaped in 1680 with his wife and two children. He said that he was thirty-two in 1681, and was described as a man of good stature with a long face, thick beard, and long, black hair.[22] He and his family returned with the Reconquest and settled in Santa Cruz; hence he can be presumed to be the fourth son mentioned by Luis Martín II.

His wife was *Josefa de Herrera,* and their children: *Diego, Blas, Matías, María,* wife of Juan Luján, and, perhaps, another daughter who married Pedro Sánchez de Yñigo.

Apolinar Martín (without "Serrano") passed muster in 1680 with his wife, two children, and three servants. He was described as a native of New Mexico, thirty-three to thirty-seven years of age, of medium, robust size, swarthy, much pitted by smallpox, and having thick, black hair and beard.[23] Nothing more is heard of him after 1684, when he was residing at Ysleta del Paso with four Martín Serrano families, those of Juan Martín's widow, and of Antonio, Cristóbal, and Domingo Martín.[24]

---

1. **Oñate,** p. 193.
2. **AGI, Patronato,** t. 22, Pt. 5; **AGI, Mex., Aud.,** leg. 25, Pt. 1.
3. **AGN, Mex., Inq.,** t. 356, f. 267.
4. **Ibid.,** t. 304, ff. 184-185; t. 372, Exp. 19, ff. 5, 9.
5. **Ibid.,** t. 425, f. 639; t. 380, f. 250; his signature appears in several of these references; **Ortiz Trial,** ff. 47v, 48v.
6. **AGN, loc. cit.,** t. 507, pp. 1758-1768, 388-674.
7. **Ibid.,** t. 587, pp. 87-88; t. 594, p. 267.
8. **Ibid.,** t. 666, ff. 393-400.
9. **Ibid., Prov. Int.,** t. 37, pp. 100-104.
10. **DM,** 1694, No. 20.
11. **Ibid.,** 1697, No. 5.
12. **Revolt,** I, p. 157.
13. **Ibid.,** II, pp. 48, 128.
14. **AGN, Mex., Inq.,** t. 37; **NMHS,** No. 2854.
15. **AGN, loc. cit.,** t. 594, pp. 261-267; **Ortiz Trial,** f. 6v.
16. **Ibid.,** pp. 39-42.
17. **AGN, Tierras,** t. 3268, pp. 265-268.
18. **Revolt,** I, pp. 143, 173.
19. **Ibid.,** II, pp. 55, 131.
20. **Ibid.,** pp. 67, 120, 185, 194, 197.
21. **Ibid.,** p. 120.
22. **Ibid.,** I, p. 142; II, pp. 65-66, 128-129.
23. **Ibid.,** I, p. 145; II, pp. 68, 121.
24. **AGN, Prov. Int.,** t. 37, pp. 100-104.

MESTAS

JUAN DE MESTAS, or de *Mesta,* was an Asturian (*Montañés*) who lived briefly in New Mexico between the years 1655 and 1660; he probably belonged to Governor Manso's personal retinue. Some brothers of his were with him, and these also returned with him to Mexico City, where he was living in 1661.[1] From his association with the infamous Nicolás de Aguilar we can presume that he spent much of his time in the Salinas district, from whence, legitimately or otherwise, came two Mestas individuals.

Tomás de Mestas (here also de *Amestas*) and his brother *Juan* escaped the 1680 massacre with only a horse and sword between them. They had a family of seven persons— their mother, brothers, and nephews. Both passed muster together in the following year.[2]

Tomás was described as a native of New Mexico, twenty-two or twenty-three years old and a widower, having a medium stature and broad shoulders, with a long face, very small eyes, wavy, chestnut hair, and no beard —or rather, a very scanty red beard. With him were his mother and brothers.³ He is not heard of again.

Juan de Mestas was described as a native of New Mexico, single, twenty years old, having a good stature, a fair complexion, a long face, and chestnut hair and beard.⁴ Juan returned to New Mexico with the Vargas Reconquest, having married during the 1680-1693 exile. At his second marriage in Santa Fe he said that his parents were unknown and called himself "Juan de Mestas *Peralta*." The description of the two Mestas brothers shows the blood of the northern Spaniard who came with Governor Manso; the Peralta name suggests their mother's family origin, or else they were reared by a person of this name, perhaps the *Sargento Mayor* Andrés de Peralta who was killed at Santo Domingo Pueblo in 1680.

Anyway, Juan de Mestas, through his seven sons and numerous daughters, is the founder of a vast family of the next century which in modern times corrupted the name to "Maestas."

1. **AGN, Mex., Inq.**, t. 512, f. 116; t. 587, p. 416; **AGI, Contad.**, leg. 748, **Data.**
2. **Revolt**, I, pp. 148, 176; II, p. 50.
3. **Ibid.**, II, pp. 105, 130-131.
4. **Ibid.**, p. 131.

MIRANDA

ANDRÉS DE MIRANDA is mentioned briefly in 1617.¹ It could be that *Blas de Miranda* was meant, or he could have been the latter's father, if related at all.

Blas de Miranda was among the fourteen soldiers escorting the wagon-train to New Mexico in 1636.² However, he had been living in New Mexico prior to this time. His wife, in 1631, was *Juliana Pérez de Bustillo*, niece of María de Archuleta.³ He went with another soldier-escort in 1658.⁴ His lands were in the valley of Taos, referred to by Vargas in 1692 as *"lo de Miranda."*⁵ The name did not exist in 1680 or after, except for *Antonia de Miranda,* wife of Luis Martín Serrano II, who was perhaps his daughter.

1. **AGN, Mex., Inq.**, t. 316, f. 183.
2. **AGI, Contad.**, leg. 736, **Data.**
3. **AGN**, loc. cit., t. 372, Exp. 19, f. 9.
4. **AGI**, loc. cit., leg. 749, **Data.**
5. **Doc. Hist. de Mex.**, p. 128.

MIZQUIA

LÁZARO DE MIZQUIA was the officer in charge of the convicts sent to New Mexico in 1677. He was twenty-four, the son of Domingo, and a native of Villa de Motrico in Guipuzcoa. He was tall and fair, with a broad face, large forehead, and thick eyebrows.¹ He stayed in New Mexico and married *María Lucero de Godoy*, daughter of Pedro Lucero and Francisca Gómez Robledo.²

In 1680 he took an active part in the defense of Santa Fe, and from there went with the refugees to Guadalupe del Paso, with his wife and two children.³ In 1681 he said he was twenty-nine, a native of Motrico, and married in New Mexico. He was described as having a good stature and features, a fair and ruddy complexion, with a thick, reddish beard and long, reddish, straight hair.⁴ He and his family remained at Guadalupe del Paso after the Reconquest, where he was Procurator of the Kingdom for that area in 1695.⁵

His daughter, *Francisca,* married Bernardo

de Chaves on January 7, 1699,⁶ and later Juan de Ulibarrí. In her last will she left her three small Chaves children in the care of her brother *Domingo de Mizquia.*

1. B-H, III, pp. 317-322.
2. DM, 1694, No. 34, Del Río-Lucero Case.
3. Revolt, I, pp. 16, 146.
4. Ibid., II, pp. 37, 109-110, 150 sqq.
5. DM, 1695, No. 9.
6. Ibid., 1699, No. 4.

MOHEDANO

Juan Mohedano, a native of Mexico City, came in the escort of the wagon-train in 1641.¹ Nothing more is known about him.

In 1660, Diego Romero, son of Gaspar Pérez of Flanders and María Romero, was accused of having had a child by his first cousin, *"La Mohedana,"* wife of a certain *"Mohedano."*² This means that a grand-daughter of Bartolomé Romero and Luisa Robledo had married this Juan Mohedano. But if they had any male children, they must have changed their name, for it does not appear again.

1. AGI, Contad., leg. 926, Data.
2. AGN, Mex., Inq., t. 587, p. 93; t. 512, ff. 179-181.

MONDRAGÓN

JUAN DE MONDRAGÓN was an *Alférez*, thirty-four years of age, who was a Regent of Santa Fe in 1637.¹ The house of *Juana Sánchez* and Juan de Mondragón is mentioned in 1641;² this woman was most likely his wife, from the name "Sánchez de Monroy" used by a descendant. It could be that she was the same "Juana Sánchez" who had been married to Juan Gómez. In 1642, as a captain, Mondragon acted as a witness.³

A Juan *Alonso* Mondragón is mentioned in the matter of train-escorts from Mexico City in 1629; and Juan, already a captain, did go with the escorts of 1639, 1643, and 1653.⁴ He held the *encomienda* of Senecú in 1660, and in 1664 was also High Sheriff of Santa Fe.⁵ He was more than eighty years old and very poor, when he passed muster in 1680 with twenty-four members in his refugee family.⁶ He died two years later in Guadalupe del Paso.⁷

Juana de Mondragón, wife of Domingo López de Ocanto in 1669, was most likely his daughter.⁸ Two others, *Melchora de los Reyes* and *Sebastiana*, were living in Santa Fe after the Reconquest and claiming land owned by their father before the "uprising of the Indians." ⁹

Sebastián Sánchez de Mondragón, also known as *Sánchez de Monroy*, was the only Mondragón, besides old Juan, who passed muster in 1680-1681. He was reported as being married and very poor, with a family of three (not necessarily his children).¹⁰ In 1681 he gave his age as twenty-three or twenty-five, and was described as a native of New Mexico, married, having a medium build, swarthy complexion, with black and very curly hair, a black mustache and scant beard.¹¹ In 1692 he acted as an interpreter during the first Vargas Campaign.¹² He returned with the Reconquest.

1. AGN, Mex., Inq., t. 369, f. 6.
2. Ibid., t. 425, f. 644.
3. Ortiz Trial, ff. 27, 46-48.
4. AGI, Contad., legs. 730, 747, Data; B-H, III, p. 52.
5. AGN, loc. cit., t. 587, p. 133; t. 507, p. 456.
6. Revolt, I, p. 147.
7. BNM, leg. 2, Pt. 3, f. 354.
8. AGN, loc. cit., t. 582, pp. 250-251.
9. Sp. Arch., I, No. 289.
10. Revolt, I, p. 152.
11. Ibid., II, pp. 63, 130.
12. First Expedition, p. 80.

MONTAÑO

Isidro Xuares, twenty years old, the son of Pedro Xuares MONTAÑO, came with Oñate in 1598. He had a good stature and a chestnut beard, and was a native of Jerez de los Caballeros.[1] He brought new troops to New Mexico in 1600, when his name was given as Xuares *de Figueroa,* but still his father's name was Pedro *Suares Montaño.* He was now an *Alférez* and was further described as having a swarthy complexion and a long face "recently bearded."[2] In 1603 he was with the wagon-train escort.[3] But it is not known if he stayed in New Mexico, or what connection he had with certain Montaño people in later times.

Vicente López Montaño came to New Mexico in 1628, but as owner of the wagon-train most likely returned with it to Mexico City.[4]

Lucas Montaño came in the escort of 1640.[5] But was he a native of New Mexico, or did he stay as a colonist?

Several Montaño individuals find more than passing mention in the middle of the century and after, all in the Salinas district.

Sebastiana López de Gracia had three daughters whose last name was Montaño: *Catalina, María,* and *Magdalena;* they were probably the children of a first husband of this name. These are in all likelihood the step-daughters of Diego de Apodaca, referred to in a case of incest.

Catalina, mother of Juana de Arzate (Maese or Apodaca), was the wife later on of Alonse Maese; *María* was a wife of Hernán Martín Serrano; and *Magdalena* was present at testimony given in 1668 regarding an itinerant German merchant, Bernardo Gruber. Also present was *Sebastián Montaño,* perhaps a brother of these women.[6]

Sebastián Montaño was reported very ill at Las Salinas in 1669; later a Captain, he had a house at La Cañada before the Rebellion of 1680.[7] He is most likely the same man just cited at Las Salinas in 1668. In 1680 he acted as interpreter for Governor Otermín;[8] and in the following year he was described as a native of New Mexico, married, a captain thirty-two years old, having a medium build, aquiline face, no beard, and long, black hair.[9]

Whatever Montaño people returned with Vargas in 1693, and were not children of Antonio Montaño de Sotomayor, belonged to this Salinas group.

1. Oñate, p. 200.
2. Ibid., p. 207.
3. AGI, Contad., leg. 704, **Data.**
4. Ibid., leg. 729, **Data.**
5. Ibid., leg. 735, **Data.**
6. AGN, Mex., Inq., t. 608, ff. 437-444; t. 666, f. 374.
7. Sp. Arch., I, No. 818; B-H, III, p. 273.
8. Revolt, I, p. 61.
9. Ibid., II, pp. 121-122.

MONTAÑO
(*Montaño de Sotomayor*)

(JUAN) ANTONIO DE SOTOMAYOR MONTAÑO, or names reversed, had come to New Mexico as a convict shortly before the Indian Rebellion, although he is not listed with the 1677 group under Lázaro de Mizquia. He married after his arrival. In 1680 he passed muster as a convict with a complete set of weapons, his wife, a female servant, but no children.[1] The next year he gave his age as thirty, when he was described as being of medium height, lisping in his speech, and with a fair and pimply skin.[2] He was a native of the City of Mexico.[3]

His wife was *Isabel Jorge de Vera*. Both returned to Santa Fe in 1693 with several children born at Guadalupe del Paso during the twelve-year exile. These were: *José, Lucas,* another *José, Polonia, Leonor, Magdalena,* and *Juana,* the last three becoming the wives of three sons of Don Fernando Durán y Chaves.

1. **Revolt,** I, p. 157.
2. **Ibid.,** II, pp. 77, 99.
3. **DM,** 1694, Nos. 19, 25, 29.

MONTOYA

BARTOLOMÉ de MONTOYA came with his entire family in 1600. He was a native of Cantillana (near Sevilla), the son of Francisco de Montoya, and was briefly described as being short of stature, blackbearded, and twenty-eight years old.[1] His wife was *María de Zamora,* born in Mexico City at San Sebastián, the daughter of Pedro de Zamora, who was a resident of that city and former *Alcalde Mayor* of Oaxaca. Her mother's name was Agustina Abarca.[2] María had married Montoya at Tezcoco,[3] and by the time they joined Oñate's colony they had three boys and two girls, who were all under sixteen in 1600: *Francisco, Diego, José, Lucía* and *Petronila.*[4] Bartolomé was an *Alférez* in 1609 when he escorted a band of friars from Zacatecas to Santa Fe.[5] This is the last we hear of him.

Of the girls, *Lucía* married Diego Robledo, and *Petronila* became the wife of Pedro Lucero de Godoy.

Francisco de Montoya appears to have been married to a daughter of Alonso Martín Barba, and is mentioned briefly in 1613.[6] Nothing more is known about him.

Diego de Montoya was an *Alférez* living in Santa Fe in 1628.[7] He married *Ana Martín,* daughter of Alonso Martín Barba, by whom he had a daughter, *Ynez de Zamora,* who married a certain Juan López.[8] There were at least two sons, *Pedro,* twenty-six in 1634, who was still living in 1663,[9] and *Bartolomé,* who inherited his father's *encomienda* of San Pedro Pueblo around the year 1660.[10]

After his first wife's death Diego, who was dead by 1661, had married *Doña María Ortiz de Vera,* or *Baca,*[11] daughter of Diego de Vera and María de Abendaño. She had three daughters prior to her marriage to Montoya. These were *Beatriz, Josefa,* and *Juana,* who sometimes were referred to as "Ortiz" and also as "Montoya." There was also a *Lucía de Montoya,* mentioned in 1663,[11a] perhaps a daughter by Diego, who became the wife of Francisco de Trujillo. Juana married Andrés Gómez Robledo.

José de Montoya is not mentioned again since his arrival in 1600 as a child.

* * * * * * * *

A **Pedro de Montoya** went on several journeys in the soldier-escort from New Spain in 1633, 1643, and 1646. In 1633 he is mentioned as one of twelve soldiers recruited at Zacatecas, along with Juan López and Nicolás Ortiz.[12] Hence he was a different man from Pedro de Montoya, son of Diego. In 1682, at the refugee settlement of San Pedro de Alcántara, a Rafael Telles Jirón married Mariana de Esparza, a native of New Mexico and daughter of *Pedro Montoya de Esparza* and Luisa Lucero de Godoy, both deceased.[13] This shows how the Zacatecas recruit was a different Montoya, the Pedro Montoya *"el Viejo"* mentioned in 1664 as being the son-in-law of Pedro Lucero and the nephew (by marriage) of an Antonia González.[14]

Another "Pedro de Montoya," whose real name was *Pedro de Moya,* was a Peruvian Indian in the entourage of Governor Peñalosa

[77]

who left New Mexico with his master.[15] He could easily be confused with the real Montoyas.

* * * * * * * *

There were several adult Montoyas who escaped the Indian massacre of 1680, but, because of insufficient data, they cannot be linked for certain with their respective parents of pre-Revolt times.

Bartolomé de Montoya passed muster in 1680, destitute, with a family of seven persons, including mother and brethren.[16] He is not heard of in 1681 or after. Most likely, he was the previously described son of Diego de Montoya; the mother with him could have been María Ortiz Baca.

Antonio de Montoya escaped in 1680 with his wife, three children, and two servants.[17] He was forty-one or forty-three years old, a native of New Mexico, married, having a good stature, a dark complexion, black eyes, a thick beard, and a somewhat bald head.[18] Like Diego, cited next, he was related by marriage to the wife (Isabel de Chaves) of Juan Domínguez de Mendoza.[19]

Antonio and his wife, *María Hurtado*, returned to New Mexico in 1693 with a family that had grown considerably by then.

Diego de Montoya passed muster in 1680 with his wife and two children. He was twenty-three in 1681, described as a New Mexican, married, of good stature, with broad shoulders, good features, a thick beard, and long straight hair.[20] Apparently he was a brother to Antonio, both being related by affinity to Juan Domínguez' wife.

Diego and his wife, *María Josefa de Hinojos*, returned to New Mexico with Vargas in 1693.

Felipe de Montoya declared in 1680 that he had four sons. He was twenty-nine in 1681 when he was described as a native of New Mexico, married, of a good slender stature, and having an aquiline face scarred by smallpox, and a thick beard.[21]

From later marriages of two children, *María* with Cristóbal Martín, and *Clemente* with Josefa Luján, we learn that his wife was *María de Paredes*, of the Domínguez de Mendoza clan; hence, Felipe was closely related to Antonio and Diego, perhaps a brother.

Francisco de Montoya (*de Esparza?*) passed muster with sixteen members of his family, which included his mother, brother, nephews and nieces, and servants. He was forty-eight years old and a widower in 1681, described as a native of New Mexico, of medium height, swarthy, with black hair and beard, and a wound-scar on the left temple.[22] He was among those who ran away from Guadalupe del Paso to New Spain.[23]

Juan de Montoya, perhaps the brother mentioned by Francisco, passed muster alone in 1680. He was single and eighteen or nineteen years old, described as slender and swarthy with curly hair and no beard.[24] He seems to be the Juan de Montoya ordered executed by Governor Posada for some crime in 1686.[25]

---

1. **Oñate**, pp. 203-204.
2. **AGN, Mex., Inq.**, t. 462, f. 351.
3. Ibid.
4. **Oñate**, p. 209. In 1607 Lucia mentioned a sister "Juana," who could not have been more than seven; or was this the Juana de Zamora named as one of the Baca girls?
5. **AGI, Contad.**, leg. 711, **Data.**
6. **AGN**, loc. cit. t. 316, f. 172.
7. Ibid., t. 363, ff. 4-11.
8. Ibid., t. 380, ff. 233-247.
9. Ibid., loc. cit.; t. 596, pt. 1, f. 75; B-H, III, p. 249.
10. Ibid., **Tierras**, t. 3268, pp. 194-195.
11. Cf. two preceding notes.
11a. **AGN, Mex., Inq.**, t. 507, f. 50.
12. **AGI**, loc. cit., legs. 738, 740, 845A, **Data.**
13. **DM**, 1682, No. 2.
14. **AGN**, loc. cit., t. 507, p. 133; t. 596, f. 157.
15. Ibid., t. 507, pp. 172, 228; **Troub. Times**, pp. 132-133.
16. **Revolt**, I, p. 149.
17. Ibid., pp. 35, 140.
18. Ibid., II, pp. 58, 115.
19. **Sp. Arch.**, II, No. 35.
20. **Revolt**, I, p. 145; II, pp. 60, 111.
21. Ibid., I, p. 140; II, pp. 59, 110-111, 200.
22. Ibid., I, p. 147; II, p. 116.
23. **BNM**, leg. 2, pt. 3, f. 302.
24. **Revolt**, II, pp. 66, 133.
25. **Sp. Arch.**, II, No. 39.

MONROY

(See *Sánchez de Monroy* and *Mondragón*)

MORAGA

DIEGO DE MORAGA lived in Santa Fe as early as 1632 with his wife, *Juana Bernal*, daughter of Juan Griego. He was forty-six in 1637, and a *Condestable de Artillería*.[1] Even after the Reconquest it was recalled that his house had stood near the spring of the Santa Fe swamp, or *cienega*, in the days of Governor de la Concha.[2] His children, to all appearances, were *Juan* and *Alonso*. A certain *Lázaro* de Moraga, mentioned in the soldier-escort of 1658, might have been another son.[3]

Alonso de Moraga passed muster in 1680-1681 as a captain in poor health. He had escaped the massacre with his wife and five small children, the eldest of whom was a boy of fourteen.[4] This boy was *Antonio* de Moraga, who passed muster in the fall of 1681 with his mother and brethren; hence, his sick father seems to have died. Antonio was described as being of medium height, with a beardless aquiline face and red hair.[5]

The house of Alonso de Moraga was still standing at La Cañada after the Reconquest.[6]

Juan de Moraga was mentioned in 1660 and 1661 as a blacksmith.[7] Nothing more is known about him so far.

Other Moragas mentioned in Revolt annals are as follows:

Juan de Moraga, twenty-one and single, passed muster in 1681. He was described as a native of New Mexico, of thick-set medium build, dark and beardless, and with thick black hair. With him was

Lazaro de Moraga, twenty-six or twenty-seven, married, and described as a native of New Mexico and looking exactly like Juan.[8] Presumably brothers, these two men were too old to be Alonso's sons, hence must have been the children of old Juan, or old Lázaro.

Antonia de Moraga, wife of Cristóbal Martín Serrano, was very likely a sister of these two. There also was an *Ana de Moraga*, wife of Captain Juan del Río, who perhaps was a daughter of old Diego de Moraga and Juana Bernal.

Some younger Moragas returned to New Mexico in 1693.

1. **AGN, Mex., Inq.**, t. 372, f. 10; t. 369, f. 6.
2. **Sp. Arch.**, I, No. 169; B-H, III, pp. 61, 142, 161.
3. **AGI, Contad.**, leg. 749, **Data.**
4. **Revolt**, I, pp. 119, 146; II, p. 46.
5. **Ibid.**, II, p. 120.
6. **Sp. Arch.**, I, No. 818.
7. **AGN, loc. cit.**, t. 587, pp. 154, 386-388.
8. **Revolt**, II, p. 121.

MORÁN

JUAN MORÁN, twenty-seven, the son of Juan Morán, and born in Mora del Toro, came with Oñate's troops of 1598. He was tall and thin, with a chestnut beard.[1] Nothing more is known about him.

Jerónimo Morán lived in Santa Fe in 1642, and had a grown son.[2]

Juan Morán was the jailer of Santa Fe in the middle of the century. His wife was *Cata-*

lina Durán. He and his son, *Juan Durán*, were mentioned together in 1663.³

Bernardina Morán, widow of Francisco Bernal, and in 1660 married to Pedro de la Cruz,⁴ was very likely Juan's sister.

Miguel Morán was the only adult male of this name among the refugees of 1680. He had a family of nine persons with him.⁵ He and his wife, *María Celestina de la Cruz*, returned with the Reconquest.

---

1. **Oñate**, p. 194.
2. **Ortiz Trial**, ff. 12, 18, 25-27.
3. **AGN, Mex., Inq.**, t. 608, f. 431; t. 566, pt. 2, f. 157.
4. **Ibid.**, t. 587, pp. 315, 316.
5. **Revolt**, I, p. 148.

NARANJO

ALONSO NARANJO, forty-two years of age, the son of Diego Carrasco and a native of Valladolid, was one of the Oñate soldiers in 1600. He had a good stature, a tawny beard, and a wound on the face.¹ What connection there is between him and later Naranjos cannot be ascertained.

Diego Martín Naranjo was killed by the Jémez Indians during the term of Governor Argüello.²

A man named Naranjo, apparently dead in 1680, was very likely the father of a two-year-old girl, *María Naranjo*, who was captured with her mother, Juana Hurtado, in 1680, and rescued in 1692 when she was fourteen.³

* * * * * * * *

Bartolomé Naranjo and the Naranjo boys, *Francisco Lorenzo* and *Juan Lorenzo*, part Indians, or else full-blooded Pueblo Indians who had adopted Spanish ways, lived with their mother at a ranch near San Felipe Pueblo. The eldest, Bartolomé, was killed by the Pueblo rebels of 1680 for refusing to side with them.⁴

* * * * * * * *

Pascual Naranjo, very poor, passed muster among the refugees of 1680 with his wife and six children. In 1681 he declared that he was married and thirty-eight years of age.⁵ This might be the man whom Pedro de Chaves II paid to go as his substitute in an Indian campaign.

Pascual's wife was *María Romero*, known as *"Cota, la Naranja,"* and residing in Guadalupe del Paso in 1706.⁶ For this family did not return with the Reconquest. Two known children were: *Juan*, who married Francisca Domínguez at Guadalupe del Paso in 1698; and *Antonia*, who married Asencio Pacheco Pérez in 1692.⁷

1. **Oñate**, p. 194.
2. **Revolt**, II, p. 266.
3. **First Expedition**, p. 237.
4. **Revolt**, II, p. 250.
5. **Ibid.**, I, p. 158; II, p. 64.
6. **AGN, Mex., Inq.**, t. 735, ff. 299-300.
7. **DM**, 1692, No. 1; 1698, No. 13.

NIETO

JOSÉ NIETO and his younger brother JUAN (also called *Juan de Leyva*) appear all of a sudden in the Salinas area after the middle of the century. In some way, they belonged to the Garcia Holgado clan. In 1662, José Nieto, Francisco Garcia, and Pedro de Leyva, were mentioned together as *"todos cuñados."*¹ In 1661 José was referred to as a forty-five-year old captain residing at the Salinas settlements, but a native of Santa Fe. His wife was *Lucía López de Gracia*.² They had a ten-year-old son in 1668, called *Fran-*

cisco *Garcia Nieto*. Fray Juan Bernal spoke highly of the character of José and his wife.³

In the Indian Rebellion of 1680, José Nieto, his wife, and two daughters were massacred. A Tano Indian of the same name, who had been reared in the Nieto home, later testified how the Galisteos, who killed the Padres of Galisteo, also slaughtered his master and his mistresses: *Lucía* (Nieto's wife), *María*, and *Juana* (their daughters).⁴

Francisco Garcia Nieto somehow escaped being killed with his parents and sisters at Galisteo. He reported that the enemy had killed his father, mother, two sisters, a sister-in-law, and four nephews and nieces.⁵ In this he was partly wrong, for the sister-in-law (Petrona Pacheco) and her children were taken captive instead, to be rescued in 1692. In 1681 Francisco passed muster, saying that he was twenty-six years old, single, and a native of New Mexico; he was described as robust, of medium height, beardless and pockmarked, and having black hair.⁶

Cristóbal Nieto, another son of José Nieto, also was away when the Indians fell on the colonists. In passing muster he declared himself to be a widower, twenty-nine years of age; and was described as being of medium height, slender, with an aquiline face, slight beard, and a scar on the right eyelid.⁷ Twelve years later, Roque de Madrid found Cristobal Nieto's wife, *Petrona* (*Pacheco*), with five daughters and a son, an increase of three since her captivity. Her husband was residing in Sonora at this time, 1692.⁸ Joined again with his family, he came back to Santa Fe with the Reconquest.

1. AGN, Mex., Inq., t. 512, f. 156.
2. Ibid., Tierras, t. 3268, p. 635.
3. Ibid., Mex., Inq., t. 666, ff. 374-380; t. 608, ff. 433-434.
4. Revolt, I, pp. 15, 24-25, 97.
5. Ibid., p. 146.
6. Ibid., II, pp. 65, 119.
7. Ibid., I, p. 147; II, p. 120.
8. First Expedition, pp. 143-144, 814; Doc. Hist. de Mex., p. 127.

NUÑEZ BELLIDO
(See *Rodríguez Bellido*)

OLGUÍN
(*López Holguín*)

JUAN LÓPEZ HOLGUÍN, *Alférez*, son of Juan López Villasana and a native of Fuente Ovejuna in Estremadura, came to New Mexico in 1600. He was of good stature, black-bearded, with a mark on the left eye, and forty years old.¹ His wife, who came with him, was *Catalina de Villanueva*. In 1626 he gave his age as sixty-four, saying that he was a "founder of the Kingdom."²

His children were: *Cristóbal*, who married Melchora de Carvajal; *Isabel*, wife of Juan de Vitoria Carvajal; and *Simón de Abendaño*, who married María Ortiz Baca.

Cristóbal Holguín was fifty years old in 1667, a native of Santa Fe residing in the Isleta jurisdiction. He was well spoken of by the Padres. His wife was *Melchora de Carvajal*, and they had a son, *Salvador*.³

Juan Holguín was referred to briefly with Cristóbal in 1668. Perhaps he was his brother, if not a son.⁴ This was very likely the Juan López Holguín who passed muster in 1680; he was married, and had one son and four servants.⁵ But he does not appear the next year or afterwards, hence might have died.

Juan López Holguín, "the Younger," age twenty-four and single in 1681,⁶ must have been the one son of the elder Juan. He later married *María Martín,* daughter of Captain Pedro Martín Serrano de Salazar; but he died prior to 1692, when his widow, twenty-five, married a Tomás de Bejarano at Socorro del Paso.⁷

Salvador Holguín, captain, the son of Cristóbal Holguín, escaped the Indian Revolt in 1680 with his wife, nine children, and ten servants.⁸ He was forty-four in 1681, when he was described as a native of New Mexico, married, very dark and pockmarked, with straight coarse hair. He took an active part in the Otermín campaign of that year.⁹

His wife was *Magdalena Fresqui.* They had a son, *Juan,* who ran away from the refugee colony in 1682;¹⁰ however, this Juan and his family appear in New Mexico after the Reconquest.

1. **Oñate,** p. 205.
2. **AGN, Mex., Inq.,** t. 356, f. 303v.
3. **Ibid.,** t. 608, ff. 437-444; t. 666, f. 374.
4. **Ibid.**
5. **Revolt,** I, p. 148.
6. **Ibid.,** II, p. 77.
7. **DM,** 1692, No. 4.
8. **Revolt,** I, p. 140.
9. **Ibid.,** II, pp. 99, 193, 319, 331-332, 391.
10. **BNM,** leg. 2, pt. 3, f. 284.

OLIVERA

JUAN DE OLIVERA, or *Olvera,* was a resident of Santa Fe who was allegedly hanged by order of Governor Eulate (1618-1625) for giving too much attention to church work.¹

Francisco de Olivera lived in Santa Fe in 1642 and was thirty-six years old at the time. He was sent to New Vizcaya to have the murderer of Governor Rosas intercepted by the Governor at Parral.² This is the first and last time he appears in any record, and the Olivera name as well. He could have been a son of Juan, or both could have been the natural children of Ysabel de Olvera, a free mulatto woman who came with Oñate's people of 1600.

1. **AGN, Mex., Inq.,** t. 356, f. 278v.
2. **Ortiz Trial,** f. 1.

ORTEGA

FRANCISCO DE ORTEGA, a native of Zacatecas, was a fifty-three-year-old captain residing in the Sandia district in 1667. His wife was *Isabel de Zamora.*¹ During the Otermín campaign of 1681 reference is made to his house near Sandia Pueblo. However, he must have died before the Indian Rebellion.²

Tiburcio de Ortega appears among the 1680 refugees more as a clerk than a military man. He was married, having his wife, son, and daughter with him, as well as his mother, some brothers and sisters, nephews and nieces, and servants.³ In 1681 he was described as a native of New Mexico, twenty-six or twenty-seven years of age, swarthy, with a good physique and curly hair.⁴ He was very like the eldest son of Francisco de Ortega.

Pablo de Ortega was a captain who passed muster in 1680 with his wife and six small children. The following year a "Pedro" de Ortega passed muster, which is very likely a mistake for "Pablo," or vice versa.⁵

Juan de Ortega was in the soldier-escort of 1658,⁶ and *Tomás de Ortega* was in New Mexico in 1639.⁷ They were most likely transients.

1. **AGN, Mex., Inq.,** t. 608, f. 390; t. 666, ff. 540-548; t. 507, pt. 6, f. 68.
2. **Revolt,** II, p. 341.
3. **Ibid.,** I, pp. 37 et seq., 147.
4. **Ibid.,** II, pp. 77, 97.
5. **Ibid.,** I, pp. 69, 141; II, p. 194.
6. **AGI, Contad.,** leg. 749, **Data.**
7. **B-H,** III, p. 52.

ORTIZ

Nicolás Ortiz, a native of Zacatecas, was a sixteen-year-old soldier who came to New Mexico around the year 1634.¹ He gave his age as twenty-four in 1642. He had married *María de Bustillo,* niece of Antonio Baca, whom he accused of infidelity with Governor Rosas while he was away with the Santa Fe-Mexico City wagon-train. Nicolás murdered the Governor on January 25, 1642. After being tried and acquitted in Santa Fe, he was sent to Mexico City for a final verdict; arrested on the way by the Governor of Nueva Vizcaya, he was re-tried and sentenced to hang. However, he escaped from prison and was not heard of again.² It seems as though he had no children by María de Bustillo, yet one single witness at his trial does refer once to their children.³

* * * * * * * *

Some women who bore the name "Ortiz" in this century belonged to the Baca family, thus carrying on the name of the first Baca's wife, Ana Ortiz. Still, one or more of these could have been María de Bustillo's children by her husband—or even by Governor Rosas, for she was visibly pregnant when Ortiz returned from Mexico City in 1642.

1. **AGN, Mex., Inq.,** t. 380, ff. 238-245.
2. **Cf. Ch. and State,** pp. 155-163; **Ortiz Trial,** ff. 1-81.
3. **Ortiz Trial,** f. 49v.

PACHECO

LUIS PACHECO was a soldier of Santa Fe in 1632, and forty years of age.¹ A Luis Pacheco and a *Vicente* Pacheco were in the soldier-escort of 1636.² On December 28, 1639, the soldiers Luis Pacheco and Juan de Estrada were killed with Fray Pedro Miranda by the Taos Indians.³ It seems to be the same Luis in every instance; Vicente is not heard of again.

GERONIMO PACHECO was a soldier reported in 1628 as having taken part in certain pagan games at San Juan Pueblo. He denied the charges.⁴ In 1631 he declared that he was twenty-five years old. His wife was *Francisca Cadimo,* twenty.⁵ He was the father of *Juan* Pacheco and *María* Pacheco, the latter the mother of Roque de Madrid's wife.⁶ Another daughter, apparently, was *Ana,* wife of Juan Garcia Holgado.⁷

Alonso Pacheco, captain, lived in New Mexico prior to 1668. His widow, *Lucía Montoya,* a native of Santa Fe, died at the age of thirty or so in February, 1669.⁸ An orphan daughter of theirs, *Juana,* escaped the 1680 massacre with relatives and married Juan Moro, an Isleta Tigua, at Guadalupe del Paso in 1683;⁹ widowed, she there married a Cristóbal Puga of Queretaro in 1702.¹⁰

Another daughter seems to have been an *Ana María* Pacheco, also known as Ana María Montoya, who married Nicolás Márquez, and later became the wife of Diego Arias de Quirós in 1694.¹¹

[83]

What relationship existed between Alonso and the foregoing Pachecos is hard to say.

Juan Pacheco was a son of Geronimo. He escaped in 1680 with his wife, three small children, and one servant.[12] In 1681 he passed muster as a native of New Mexico, married, and thirty-six years of age, and was described as tall and slim, dark, with an aquiline face, black hair and beard.[13]

His wife was *Antonia de Arratia*. Two of their children were *Silvestre* and *Josefa*, whose husband, José Baca, was killed by her brother Silvestre in 1687.[14] The entire family returned to Santa Fe in 1693.

Francisco Pacheco is the second male of this name in the Revolt lists. He declared in 1681, when he made his appearance at Guadalupe del Paso, that he had just arrived from San José del Parral, where he had been living for a long time. He was forty-six years old and married.[15] In 1682 he received permission to leave the refugee colony and return south.[16]

In 1692, an *Asencio Pacheco Pérez*, a native of San José del Parral, the son of *Francisco Pacheco* and *Catalina de la Concepción*, both dead, married Pascuala Naranjo at Guadalupe del Paso.[17]

1. **AGN, Mex., Inq.,** t. 304, f. 181.
2. **AGI, Contad.,** leg. 734, **Data.**
3. **Mission Monuments** p, 89.
4. **AGN,** loc. cit., f. 190.
5. **Ibid.,** t. 372, exp. 19, ff. 13-15.
6. **Sp. Arch.,** I, No. 486.
7. **AGN,** loc. cit., t. 608, f. 427.
8. **Ibid.,** t. 583, f. 316.
9. **DM,** 1683, No. 2.
10. **Ibid.,** 1702, No. 2.
11. **Ibid.,** 1694, No. 32.
12. **Revolt,** I, p. 147.
13. **Ibid.,** II, pp. 70, 116.
14. **Sp. Arch.,** II, No. 45.
15. **Revolt,** II, p. 70.
16. **BNM,** leg. 2, pt. 3, ff. 354-357.
17. **DM,** 1692, No. 1.

PADILLA

JOSÉ DE PADILLA had been living in "New Mexico" for more than twelve years when the Pueblos rebelled in 1680. He passed muster then as a captain, with his wife, five children, and six servants, and signed one declaration as "José de Padilla *Villaseñor*."[1] In 1681 he declared himself to be thirty-four years old, a native of Querétaro, and married in New Mexico. He was briefly described as having a robust medium stature.[2] Some years before, he had gone on a campaign as a substitute for Pedro de Chaves II; he said that he had twelve years' experience as *Alcalde Mayor* "on the frontier."[3] This means, very likely, that he had not always lived in New Mexico proper, but in the frontier district of Guadalupe del Paso.

In 1683 he left the exile colony with the *Sargento Mayor* Fernando de Chaves, without permission, to lay a petition of certain colonists before the Viceroy. His wife, *María López*, is mentioned in this connection.[4] Again, in 1689, he journeyed to Mexico City to escort some friars; he took this occasion to demand back-pay, declaring that he was a resident of Guadalupe del Paso, where his wife and children were, and that he had already served in New Mexico for twenty years.[5] Padilla's actual place of residence at this time was Senecú del Paso.[6]

Not having been a member of the northern New Mexico colony, he did not join the Vargas troops and colonists for the Reconquest, but remained in the Guadalupe del Paso area. However, some of his sons did come up to New Mexico shortly after, perhaps also taking part in the Reconquest.

1. **Revolt,** I, pp. 139, 177.
2. **Ibid.,** II, pp. 46, 132.
3. **Ibid.,** pp. 166, 327.
4. **BNM,** leg. 2, pt. 3, ff. 267, 291.
5. **AGN, Mex., Inq.,** t. 680, f. 104; **Ibid., Prov. Int.,** t. 35, pp. 163-166.
6. **DM,** 1699, No. 9.

PAREDES

ÁLVARO DE PAREDES was an *Alférez*, twenty-two years of age, residing in New Mexico in 1662. He was born in Mexico City. In New Mexico he had married *Damiana Domínguez de Mendoza*. Álvaro was killed by lightning in June or July, 1662. His brother was Fray José de Paredes, a Franciscan missionary in New Mexico at this time.[1]

This friar was the son of Don Esteban de Paredes and Doña Beatriz Cortés, the latter a native of the City of Mexico.[2] (A high-born lady according to her title, she was very likely descended from Hernán Cortés.)

Gonzalo de Paredes, captain, was with the Leyva escort party at Guadalupe del Paso when the Indians rebelled in 1680. He later passed muster with his wife and five small children. In the following year, claiming to be sick, he refused the salary of a soldier or settler.[3] If he did not die, he most likely went to New Spain with his relatives of the Domínguez clan.

A *Francisco de Paredes* deserted the refugee colony and left for New Spain.[4] Perhaps "Gonzalo" was meant, or else he was a brother.

María de Paredes, wife of Felipe de Montoya, both natives of New Mexico, was in all likelihood a daughter of Álvaro de Paredes and sister of Gonzalo.

1. AGN, Mex., Inq., t. 512, f. 176.
2. Bancroft, Mex. Mss., No. 218, f. 122v.
3. Revolt, I, pp. 36, 44, 139-140; II, p. 152.
4. BNM, leg. 2, pt. 3, ff. 267-268.

PARRA

Juan de la Parra lived in New Mexico prior to 1639. His widow, *María González*, a resident of the Rio Abajo, married a Juan Bautista Saragoza in 1654.[1]

Pascual Cobos de la Parra escaped in 1680 with a family of nine, wife, mother, brethren, nephews and nieces. The next year he passed muster as a native of New Mexico, married, and twenty-six years old; he was of medium height, swarthy, with curly hair, blue eyes, and a sparse beard.[2]

Gregorio Cobos de la Parra appeared at Guadalupe del Paso in 1681, having arrived from Parral where he had been living for many years. He was forty, a native of New Mexico but a citizen of Parral, where he had married. He was tall, slim and dark, with black eyes and partly gray hair. Sometime later he took part in the Otermín campaign, the only ex-New Mexican who volunteered.[3]

Manuel de la Parra and *María Brito*, both deceased by 1698, had a daughter, *Tomasa*, who returned with the Reconquest and became the wife of Marcos de Armijo.[4]

Antonio de la Parra was living at Casas Grandes in 1681.[5]

1. AGN, Mex., Inq., t. 571, exp. 8.
2. Revolt, I, p. 158; II, p. 133.
3. Ibid., II, pp. 73, 142, 156.
4. DM, 1698, No. 12; Sp. Arch., I, No. 731.
5. Revolt, II, p. 31.

PEDRAZA

JUAN DE PEDRAZA, thirty years old, the son of Alonso González and a native of Cartaya, came with the Oñate forces of 1598. He was dark and tall, with a black beard and a wound above the left eye.[1] It is not known who his wife was; two Pedraza women, *Beatriz* and *Isabel,* were in all likelihood his daughters.

Beatriz de Pedraza was twenty-six in 1631 and the wife of Captain Tomás de Albizu. *Isabel de Pedraza,* twenty-five, was married to Matías Romero. She was a cousin of María de Archuleta, widow of Captain Juan Márquez.[2] From this marriage came the "Romero de Pedraza" branch of the original Bartolomé de Romero family.

1. Oñate, p. 195.
2. AGN, Mex., Inq., t. 372, ff. 14, 18.

PERALTA

MANUEL DE PERALTA was in the soldier escort of 1641.[1] In 1643 he was condemned to death for sedition, but was not among the eight captains executed.[2] Evidently he fled from New Mexico and never returned.

Francisco de Peralta, nineteen years of age, appeared as a witness at Sandia in 1654.[3] He could have been a son of Manuel de Peralta.

Andrés de Peralta, an *Alférez* in 1661, was the son-in-law of Captain Diego de Santa Cruz, deceased, and Gregoria Archuleta. His wife's name was *Isabel de Santa Cruz*.[4] He was present at the dedication of the Guadalupe del Paso Mission in 1668.[5] He was presumably closely related to the foregoing Peraltas, but the exact link cannot be found.

And he was most likely the *Sargento Mayor* Andrés de Peralta killed by the Indians with the Padres and four soldiers at Santo Domingo in 1680.[6]

However, the slain officer's widow was a *María de la Escallada*.[7] If the same man, this was his second wife; or else she was married to a son of his having the same name.

Maria's sister, *Juana de la Escallada,* was the widow of *Manuel de Peralta*.[8] This man, a brother or son of Andrés, was very likely one of the four soldiers massacred with him at Santo Domingo. Or it could be that *Sargento Mayor* Andrés had two married sons, Andrés and Manuel, both soldiers, and all were killed together at Santo Domingo.

Regina Peralta was the wife of Cristóbal de Apodaca, and both were dead by 1707.[9]

1. AGI, Contad., leg. 735, Data.
2. Twit. Coll., No. 280; Ortiz Trial, f. 6v.
3. AGN, Mex., Inq., t. 571, exp. 8, ff. 227-229.
4. Ibid., Tierras, t. 3268, p. 298.
5. Ocaranza, p. 69.
6. Revolt, I, pp. 11, 66, 97.
7. DM, 1682, No. 4.
8. AGN, Mex., Inq., t. 1551, ff. 376-378.
9. DM, 1707, No. 2.

PEREA

JUAN DE PEREA, fifty years old and single (perhaps a widower), joined Otermín's troops as a soldier in 1681 at Guadalupe del Paso.[1] Presumably, he was a resident of that area, and not a colonist of New Mexico proper at the time the Indians rebelled.

Juan de Perea, eighteen and single, passed muster in 1681 with his mother and brethren.

He was slender and swarthy with thick straight hair.² Apparently these people were also residents of Guadalupe del Paso, not being listed among the refugees from the north in the preceding year. This appears to be the same Juan de Perea, married, who came to New Mexico with the Vargas colonists in 1693, being then twenty-four or twenty-five years of age.³

1. Revolt, II, p. 62.
2. Ibid., pp. 107-108.
3. DM, 1681, No. 1; 1690, No. 1; 1694, Nos. 22, 27.

Cristóbal de Perea, probably Juan's brother, offered himself as a recruit in 1681. He was twenty-six and single.⁴

Esteban de Perea was an interpreter referred to in 1689 as a *"feligrés natural"* of Corpus Christi de Ysleta.⁵ His wife was *Francisca Garcia,* and a son of theirs married in Santa Fe after the Reconquest.⁶

4. Revolt, II, p. 78.
5. AGN, Mex., Inq., t. 680, f. 105.
6. DM, 1711, No. 5.

PÉREZ

GASPAR PEREZ, armorer, arrived in Santa Fe on September 17, 1619.¹ By 1641 he was a captain when he declared that he was Flemish and a native of Brussels.² He made his last will in Santa Fe, April 26, 1646, leaving all his possessions to his only son and heir, *Diego Pérez Romero*. Gaspar died on May 21.³ His widow was *María Romero,* daughter of Bartolomé Romero and Luisa Robledo.

1. AGI, Contad., leg. 725, Data.
2. Ibid., leg. 926, Data.

Their son, *Diego Romero,* by which name he went afterwards, was deeply involved in matters of the Inquisition. Forbidden to return to New Mexico, he wrote his wife to join him in New Spain, and to marry off his *sister* to an Alonso Lucero.⁴ Diego's wife was *Catalina de Zamora,* daughter of Pedro Lucero de Godoy, who apparently did not heed her husband's wishes, as she appears among the refugees of 1680 with four grown nieces.⁵

3. Ibid., legs. 745, 755, Data.
4. AGN, Mex., Inq., t. 512, ff. 179-181.
5. Revolt, I, p. 151.

PÉREZ de BUSTILLO

JUAN PÉREZ DE BUSTILLO, forty years old, the son of Simón Pérez and a native of Mexico City, was an Oñate soldier of 1598. He was small of stature, gray-bearded, having a wart on the left side of the face.¹ With him came his wife, two sons, and seven daughters.² One son, *Simón,* was also listed as a soldier, as described later.

Juan's wife was *María de la Cruz,* and both were still living, it seems, in 1626.³ Their two sons were *Simón* and *Diego,* the latter having adopted the surname of "Santa Cruz." Four of the daughters accounted for were: *Ana,* fifty in 1631, the wife of Asencio de Arechuleta; *Yumar,* forty in 1631, married to Antonio Baca; *Beatriz,* thirty-eight in 1631, wife of Hernando de Hinojos; and *Catalina,* married to Alonso Varela.⁴

Simón Pérez de Bustillo (the plural, *Bustillos,* became common later in the century) was already a twenty-two-year-old soldier in 1598, when he was described as the son of Juan Pérez de Bustillo, a native of Mexico City, of medium height, dark and freckled, with a sparse beard.⁵ However, when declaring himself an "old colonist" in 1626, Simon said that he had been born in Zacatecas.⁶ In

1623 the Governor sent him, now a captain, to give an account of state affairs in New Mexico before the Viceroy.[7]

His wife, from a comparison of family charts, was *Juana de Zamora,* sister of Antonio Baca.[8] They had a son, *Nicolás,* evidently adopted. Three daughters were: *María,* wife of Nicolás Ortiz, who slew Governor Rosas because of her; *Juliana,* married to Blas de Miranda; and *Catalina,* wife of Pedro Márquez.

Diego Pérez de Bustillo is treated as Diego de Santa Cruz.

---

1. Oñate, pp. 188-189.
2. AGI, Patronato, leg. 22, pt. 5, f. 726.
3. AGN, Mex., Inq., t. 356, f. 268v.
4. Ibid., t. 356, ff. 266-269; t. 363, f. 13; t. 372, ff. 15-18; t. 380, ff. 253-254.
5. Oñate, loc. cit.

Nicolás Pérez de Bustillo, adopted son of Simón, played a brief and tragic political role. Involved in the murder of Governor Rosas, he was one of the men beheaded in 1643; among these were his double-uncle, Antonio Baca, and his close cousins, Juan de Archuleta, Diego Márquez, and Juan Ruiz de Hinojos.[9] Nicolás was a mestizo, a natural son of one of Simon's sisters or his own. In 1642 he declared that he was related to Nicolás Ortiz's wife "on her father's side."[10]

There were no people of this name left in New Mexico when the Pueblos rebelled in 1680.

---

6. AGN, loc. cit., t. 356, f. 268v; also, AGI, Mex., Aud., leg. 25, pt. 1.
7. AGI, Contad., leg. 725, Data.
8. BNM, leg. 1, pt. 1, pp. 470-504; see Baca and Montoya about his wife's identity.
9. Ch. and State, p. 175.
10. Ortiz Trial, ff. 4, 56.

PÉREZ GRANILLO

FRANCISCO PÉREZ GRANILLO appears as early as 1617 in the capacity of clerk of the colonial government.[1] In 1626 he was a captain; with another captain, Tomás de Albizu, he was reprehended by Governor Eulate for singing in the Santa Fe church choir.[2] His wife's name is not known, but a daughter of his had married Captain Bartolomé Romero II in the early part of the century. Two prominent Granillo men of the next generation, *Francisco* and *Alonso,* were in all likelihood his sons.

Francisco Pérez Granillo II and his brother Alonso were in charge of the wagon-train to and from Mexico City in 1661 and 1664.[3] Francisco and his wife, *Sebastiana Romero,* were dead by 1680, as attested by the marriage papers of their son, *Francisco Antonio.*[4] Other sons, most likely, were *Luis Pérez Granillo* and two younger brothers (besides Francisco Antonio) of military age whom Luis presented for muster in 1680.[5]

Alonso Pérez Granillo, Francisco's brother, had an *estancia* two leagues from Alamillo Pueblo.[6] By 1680 he was living in Nueva Vizcaya as *Alcalde Mayor* of the wagon-trains and of the jurisdiction of Janos. He was instructed by the Governor at Parral to prevent New Mexico refugees from passing on south into New Spain.[7]

Diego Pérez Granillo, who had married his cousin, *Juana Romero,* and had gone to Sonora before 1663, was Alonso's son if not a younger brother.[8]

Luis Pérez Granillo was a *Sargento Mayor* as well as *Alcalde Mayor* of the Jémez and Queres Pueblos, and Procurator General of the Kingdom, when the Indians rebelled in 1680. He escaped from Jémez with the friars, minus Fr. Juan de Jesús. His wife and nephews escaped from Santa Fe with its people under Governor Otermín.[9] In passing muster he declared that he was married and childless, but had three brothers of military age.[10] He gave his age as forty in 1681 and took an active part in the Otermín Campaign.[11] He was also very active as *Maese de Campo* and Lieutenant Governor in the Vargas Expedition of 1692,[12] and returned for the re-settlement of New Mexico in the following year. His childless wife was *Magdalena Varela de Losada*.[13] As Lieutenant Governor under Vargas, 1692-1695, he was also his *mayordomo* of the Conquistadora Confraternity.[14]

Francisco Antonio Granillo, a native of New Mexico, the son of Francisco Pérez Granillo and Sebastiana Romero, both deceased, married *María de Albizu* on October 6, 1681, at Guadalupe del Paso.[15] He was, to all appearances, one of the three brothers presented by Luis Granillo in 1680.

It seems as though the childless Luis Granillo was the only member of the family who returned to New Mexico. The name continued, however, at Guadalupe del Paso and Nueva Vizcaya. Some later marriages there were as follows: *María*, a native of New Mexico and widow of Juan Lucas, the daughter of Domingo Granillo and Catalina de la Cruz, married Nicolás de Ortega;[16] *Clara*, daughter of Ventura Granillo and María de la Concepción, married Pedro Fresqui at Socorro del Paso.[17]

* * * * * * * *

Tomás Perez Granillo, living in New Mexico after the middle of the century, was a freed slave, half Negro and half Indian. In 1660 he said that he was a native of Santa Fe (!) and a driver in the wagon-trains to Mexico City.[18] His wife took an illegitimate child of Governor Manso to Mexico City in 1656. By 1663 both Tomás and his wife were residing there, at Santa Catalina Martir, but he still journeyed to Santa Fe with the trains.[19]

1. **AGI, Contad.**, leg. 720, **Data.**
2. **AGN, Mex., Inq.**, t. 356, f. 285v.
3. **Ibid.**, t. 587, p. 17; t. 507, p. 265.
4. **DM,** 1681, No. 3.
5. **Revolt,** I, p. 137.
6. **AGN, loc. cit.**, t. 587, p. 17.
7. **Revolt,** I, p. 185.
8. **AGN, loc. cit.**
9. **Revolt,** I, pp. 56, 63, 66, 80.
10. **Ibid.**, p. 137.
11. **Ibid.**, II, pp. 34, 340.
12. **First Expedition,** p. 118.
13. **DM,** 1694, No. 1.
14. **OLC,** pp. 8, 63-64.
15. **DM,** 1681, No. 3.
16. **Ibid.**, 1716, No. 15.
17. **Ibid.**, 1719, No. 4.
18. **AGN, Mex., Inq.**, t. 583, f. 278.
19. **Ibid.**, t. 507, pp. 39-42; ibid., pt. 1, ff. 24-48.

PERRAMOS
(See *Ramos*)

QUINTANA

Luis de Quintana, a *Sargento Mayor* twenty-four or twenty-five years of age, passed muster in 1680 with his wife and infant daughter. He was a native of Valmaseda, a man of good stature, pockmarked, with a thick beard and very curly hair.[1] His residence was at La Cañada before the Indian Rebellion.[2] With Francisco Xavier and Diego Lopez he had become notorious among the Pueblos for his cruelty to the Indians, so that Vargas had to promise the Indians in 1692 that he would not allow these three men to return to New Mexico.[3]

The Quintanas of the next century were a different people.

1. **Revolt,** I, p. 139; II, pp. 35, 106.
2. **Sp. Arch.,** I, No. 818.
3. **First Expedition,** p. 83.

RAMÍREZ

FRANCISCO RAMÍREZ, twenty-four, was among the Oñate soldiers of 1598. He was a native of Cartaya, the son of Gómez de *Salazar,* described as small and red-bearded, and blind in the left eye.[1]

* * * * * * * *

ALONSO RAMÍREZ DE SALAZAR, forty-five, was a soldier living in New Mexico in 1631.[2] He had resided at Isleta with his wife up to the year 1626, if indeed he is the Captain Alonso Ramírez de Vargas who had arrived in New Mexico the previous year with his wife, *Juana Ordóñez.* She had died soon after their arrival.[3] Because of his age, and since he might be the Alonso Ramírez in the soldier escort of 1608,[4] he was not a son of the preceding man. He could be the Alonso Ramírez involved in the murder of Governor Rosas in 1642.[5]

* * * * * * * *

JUAN RAMIREZ DE SALAZAR, an *Alférez,* was a native of Mexico who arrived with the soldiers escorting the wagon-train of 1641.[6] He was active in the Rosas and subsequent political affairs between the years 1641 and 1643.[7] Any of these three pioneers might have been the progenitors of later Ramírez individuals.

* * * * * * * *

Francisco Ramírez (de Salazar), a captain thirty-five years of age, and born in New Mexico, was about to move down to Guadalupe del Paso in 1663. His wife was *María López de Gracia.*[8] Apparently this is the same man who was *Alcalde Mayor* of Casas Grandes in 1680, to whom Father Álvarez wrote concerning the Indian Rebellion in New Mexico.[9] A Francisco Ramírez who died there in 1682[10] was presumably a different man, for the captain was, to all appearances, the same Captain Francisco Ramírez de Salazar who was *Alcalde Mayor* of Casas Grandes in 1684 and as late as 1695.[11] (Or the latter might have been the son and successor as *Alcalde* of the former, who actually had died in 1682.)

* * * * * * * *

Andrés Ramírez del Prado, dead prior to 1680, had been the husband of *Petronila de Gamboa.* Their son, *Antonio Ramírez de Gamboa,* married a Luisa de Tapia at Ysleta del Paso in 1685.[12] This family appears to be totally distinct from the Salazar group.

Alonso Ramírez, captain, was with the Leyva escort party at Guadalupe del Paso when the Indians struck in 1680. He later passed muster with his wife and six children,[13] but he does not appear again.

Antonio Ramírez enlisted among the exiled soldiers at Guadalupe del Paso in 1681. He was thirty-six, and a native of Parral in Nueva Vizcaya. He was married, tall and corpulent, with a long beardless face, or at least having a scanty beard, and long straight hair.[14]

---

1. **Oñate**, p. 195.
2. **AGN, Mex., Inq.,** t. 364, f. 189.
3. **Ibid.,** t. 356, ff. 260, 271v.
4. **AGI, Contad.,** legs. 710, 850, **Data.**
5. **Ortiz Trial,** ff. 21v, 60v; **Twit. Coll.,** No. 280.
6. **Ibid.,** leg. 926, **Data.**
7. **Ch. and State,** pp. 140, 176, 185.
8. **AGN,** loc. cit., t. 587, pp. 361-362, 386, 454; t. 594, p. 340.
9. **Revolt,** I, p. 38; II, pp. 31, 154.
10. **BNM,** leg. 2, pt. 3, ff. 354-357.
11. **AGI, Guadalajara,** leg. 151, pt. 6, f. 1; **HSNM,** No. 2843.
12. **DM,** 1685, No. 1.
13. **Revolt,** I, pp. 35, 141.
14. **Ibid.,** II, pp. 135, 140.

RAMOS
(Perramos)

JUAN DE PERRAMOS was a soldier in New Mexico, 1626-1631, who was married to *Mariana Luján*. Their daughter, *María Ramos*, married her "uncle," Francisco Luján.[1] This is most likely the Juan Ramos mentioned in the escort of the 1616 wagon-train.[2]

The Ramos individuals reporting after the 1680 Indian Uprising were the following:

Juan Ramos, nineteen years old, married, was described as a native of New Mexico, of good build, with a scanty beard and long straight hair.[3]

Gabriel Ramos, not mentioned in 1680, passed muster in 1681 as a native of New Mexico, thirty years of age, and married; he was swarthy, with a curly beard and thick, black, curly hair.[4]

María Ramos, wife of Domingo de Herrera, was killed at Taos with her family in 1680.

* * * * * * * *

Marcos Ramos, soldier, was killed by the Indians at Santa Clara Pueblo on August 10, 1680.[5] However, he did not belong to the Ramos family of New Mexico, being one of the convicts brought to New Mexico three years before.[6]

1. **AGN, Mex., Inq.**, t. 587, pp. 305-311; t. 356, f. 311v.
2. **AGI, Contad.**, leg. 718, **Data.**
3. **Revolt**, I, p. 22; II, pp. 62, 125.
4. **Ibid.**, II, p. 141.
5. **Ibid.**, I, pp. 9, 10.
6. **B-H**, III, pp. 317-324.

RASCÓN

Don Francisco Rascón was in New Mexico for the Indian Revolt of 1680, when he declared that he was married, but without children. His name appears twice at San Lorenzo in 1681, when he said that he was thirty-five.[1] He did not return in 1693, but could have founded the prominent family of this name at Guadalupe del Paso.

1. **Revolt**, I, p. 142; II, pp. 57-58, 35, 197.

RIBERA

FRANCISCO DE RIBERA, an *Alférez* in Santa Fe in 1636, presumably born outside New Mexico, was the son of Juan de Ribera and María Pérez. Having lost his wife, *Melchora de Escarramán*, he asked to marry a widow by the name of *María de los Angeles*, twenty-seven, whose husband had been Gaspar de Arratia.[2] In 1636 Captain Pedro Lucero de Godoy testified that he had known Ribera for twenty years,[3] suggesting the possibility of their having come to New Mexico together.

No Ribera people appear in the lists of the 1680 Rebellion.

Juan de Ribera, thirty-three years old and married, was residing among the refugee colonists at Ysleta del Paso in 1685.[4] He came to New Mexico with them in 1693, and afterwards declared that he was a native New Mexican,[5] having been born, therefore, in the

Guadalupe del Paso district. He must have been living there when the Rebellion came. His wife was *Luisa de Ocanto,* and their son, *Francisco,* married a Juana Romero at Albuquerque in 1710.⁶

A Juan *Griego* Ribera is mentioned in 1682,⁷ and possibly is the same man. His middle name shows that he belonged in some way to the Griego and González Bernal people.

1. Oñate, p. 196.
2. AGN, Mex., Inq., t. 595, f. 407; t. 363, exp. 19, f. 10.
3. Ibid.
4. DM, 1685, No. 1.
5. Ibid., 1694, Nos. 15, 31.
6. Ibid., 1710, No. 10.
7. BNM, leg. 2, pt. 3, f. 388.

RÍO, del

ALONSO DEL RIO, twenty-eight years old, the son of Esteban Arias and a native of Puerto Real, came with the troops of 1598. He had a good stature and a bright reddish beard.¹ However, it is not known if he remained or what relationship he bore to succeeding generations of this name.

Diego del Rio de Losa was a twenty-four-year-old soldier in Santa Fe in 1632. He was secretary of the *Cabildo;* in 1624, when thirty-three, he witnessed the murder of Governor Rosas.² People of the next generation who added "de Losada" to their particular surname might have derived it from him, but there is no positive proof.

* * * * * * * *

Among the colonists who escaped the massacre of 1680 were the following individuals:

Alonso del Rio, Captain and Regent, was with the Leyva escort party at Guadalupe del Paso when the Pueblos fell on the colonists. He was married but had no children at this time.³ He signed up for the Otermín campaign in 1681, declaring that he was forty years old.⁴ His residence had been located at La Cañada,⁵ but he did not return to it at the time of the Reconquest. Still living at Guadalupe del Paso in 1709, he was considered an "elder and ancient" of that place.⁶ He had been the *mayordomo* of the Conquistadora Confraternity from 1685 to 1691, and continued remitting his dues to Santa Fe after the Reconquest.⁷

Juan del Rio was also a captain in 1680; he was married and had seven small children.⁸ In 1681 he gave his age as thirty-one or thirty-five, and was described as a native of New Mexico, of a slender and good build, with a large nose, wavy hair, and a black beard.⁹ He was also an officer of the Confraternity of La Conquistadora in 1693.¹⁰

His wife was *Ana de Moraga.* They had a son, *Diego,* who married Catalina Cisneros at Guadalupe del Paso in 1699. A daughter, *María,* became the wife of Felipe Durán in 1695; and another, *Juliana,* married Francisco Maese in 1701.¹¹ This, and their not appearing in New Mexico after the Reconquest, shows that this entire family remained at Guadalupe del Paso.

Francisco del Rio, eighteen, single, passed muster as a native of New Mexico in 1681. He was very tall, with a long beardless face and long straight hair.¹² Apparently, he was a younger brother of the two preceding men.

He married *Luisa Lucero*, daughter of Francisco Lucero de Godoy, and returned with her family to Santa Fe, where she sued him for maltreatment and non-support in 1695.¹³ Apparently, they had no children.

1. **Oñate**, p. 196.
2. **AGN, Mex. Inq.**, t. 304, f. 185; **B-H**, III, p. 57; **Ortiz Trial**, ff. 6v, 32-34.
3. **Revolt**, I, pp. 29, 40, 137.
4. **Ibid.**, II, pp. 48-49, 319.
5. **Sp. Arch.**, I, No. 818.
6. **DM**, 1705, No. 10; 1709, No. 2.

Domingo del Rio, dead before 1680, was married to *María Luján*. In 1695, their son, Diego, born in New Mexico but residing at San Lorenzo del Paso, married Isabel Romero of Senecú del Paso.¹⁴

7. **OLC**, pp. 5, 8, 55-59, 60, 67-68.
8. **Revolt**, I, pp. 119, 145.
9. **Ibid.**, II, pp. 46-47, 129.
10. **OLC**, p. 63.
11. **DM**, 1699, No. 6; 1695, No. 15; 1701, No. 2.
12. **Revolt**, II, p. 105.
13. **DM**, 1695, No. 5.
14. **Ibid.**, 1695, No. 17.

ROBLEDO

PEDRO ROBLEDO was a sixty-year-old *Alférez* when he accompanied Oñate's troops in 1598. He was a native of Maqueda (near Madrid and Toledo), the son of Alejo Robledo, of good stature and completely gray.¹ In the muster-roll of 1597 he stated that he had been born at the place of El Carmen or "El Carnero," and had lived in Toledo. With him were his wife and daughters, and five sons.² The four eldest sons were soldiers already, as described further on.

Old Pedro died shortly after the Oñate colony moved into what is now New Mexico, the first of the colonists to die here. He was buried on Corpus Christi Day, May 21, 1598,³ on the trail east of the Rio del Norte and a great bluff still called "Robledo." The varied birthplaces of his sons show how much this family had wandered all over New Spain before reaching New Mexico.

Pedro's family went on north with the colony to found San Gabriel. His widow was *Catalina López*, who had come to America with him from Toledo more than twenty years before.⁴ Their sons were *Diego, Alonso, Pedro*, and *Francisco*. Their two known daughters were *Luisa*, already married to Bartolomé Romero, and *Francisca*, who married Juan de Tapia.

Diego Robledo, twenty-seven in 1598, had been born at Maqueda, his father's place of origin. He was of good stature and red-bearded.⁵ With his brothers he distinguished himself as a soldier, and was still living at San Gabriel in 1607 with his wife, *Lucía de Zamora*, daughter of Bartolomé Montoya.⁶ Nothing more is known about him.

Alonso Robledo was twenty-one in 1598. He had been born at Cimapán in New Spain, and was described as having a good build and a scanty beard.⁷ By 1604 he was living at Cuencame in New Spain, at El Real de San Antonio de Padua. He was a miner there and had a wife and small son.⁸

Pedro Robledo II, twenty years old in 1598, had been born at Temazcaltepeque in New Spain, and was also described as having a good stature and a scanty beard.⁹ He was killed at Acoma in December, 1598. During a famous battle there, Pedro, with his brother Francisco and other soldiers, were forced to the edge of the Acoma cliff; all jumped down to the desert below, and all survived the fall except Pedro.¹⁰

Francisco Robledo, who survived the perilous drop at Acoma, was eighteen in 1598. He was born in Valladolid in New Spain.¹¹ Elsewhere, Zamora in New Spain was given as his birthplace.¹²

The fifth son is not mentioned anywhere; perhaps old Pedro had included his unmarried daughter, Francisca, among his five "*hijos.*" It seems as though all the Robledo men eventually left New Mexico, for they are not heard of again, nor is the name passed on through the male line. Their mother, Catalina López, might have left also, as there is evidence to show that this was her intention.[13] The two girls, however, remained with their husbands. The family name, assumed by Ana, daughter of Bartolomé Romero and Luisa Robledo, survived as Gómez Robledo when she married Francisco Gómez and bore him a large family.

Decades later, in 1663, Francisco Gómez Robledo, great-grandson of old Pedro Robledo and Catalina López, referred to them as his own maternal grandparents, and said that both of them had returned to Spain.[14]

1. Oñate, p. 196; AGI, Patronato, leg. 22, pt. 5, f. 747.
2. AGI, Mex., Aud., leg. 25, pt. 1.
3. Doc. Ined., p. 247.
4. AGN, Mex., Inq., t. 467, ff. 342-353.
5. Oñate, loc. cit.
6. AGI, Guadalajara, leg. 28, ff. 342-343.
7. Oñate, loc. cit.
8. AGI, loc. cit.
9. Oñate, loc. cit.
10. Ibid., p. 114.
11. Ibid., p. 196.
12. AGI, Mex., Aud., leg., 25, pt. 1.
13. AGN, Mex., Inq., t. 467, ff. 352-353.
14. Ibid., t. 583, ff. 341-346.

RODRÍGUEZ

ALONSO RODRÍGUEZ is mentioned in 1642 as Rodríguez *Cisneros*, twenty-three, the son-in-law of Francisco Anaya, and in 1663 as the brother-in-law of Cristóbal and Francisco de Anaya, together with his wife, *Ynez de Anaya,* and their daughter *Ana*.[1] An Alonso Rodríguez in the soldier escort of 1658 was very likely this same man.[2] The daughter, Ana, was the wife of Captain Ambrosio Sáez.[3]

* * * * * * * *

Only two Rodríguez men appear in the Revolt lists of 1681, none among the refugees of the previous year.

Alonso Rodríguez (Rodríguez *Varela* in one instance) was a native of New Mexico who had married down in Parral, but returned to Guadalupe del Paso in 1681 to enlist as a colonist. He was forty-two, with a good stature and a swarthy complexion, very thick black beard, a cleft upper lip, and a scar near the right eye.[4] He and his wife, *Juana de Valencia,* came with the Reconquest to Santa Fe, where he was known also as Alonso Rodríguez *Carcay.*

———

Nicolás Rodríguez Rey was a *Sargento Mayor* in the Otermín campaign of 1681.[5] He does not seem to belong to the New Mexico colonists, nor is he heard of again.

1. Ortiz Trial, ff. 21v, 48-50. AGN, Mex. Inq., t. 594, p. 378; t. 587, p. 119; t. 507, pt. 5, f. 601v.
2. AGI, Contad., leg. 749, Data.
3. AGN, loc. cit., t. 608, f. 391.
4. Revolt, II, pp. 132, 138.
5. Ibid., pp. 319, 321, 352-353.

RODRÍGUEZ BELLIDO

JUAN RODRÍGUEZ BELLIDO was the son of Francisco Núñez and a native of Xilbraleón in Castilla. He was forty in 1600, and was briefly described as well-bearded with a scar under the left eye.[1] He is perhaps the Juan Rodríguez in the soldier escorts of 1606 and 1609.[2]

His wife, it seems, was an *Isabel,* who was involved in some witchcraft dealings in 1607.[3] Later their son, *Diego,* was said to have died as a result of black magic.[4] In 1627 Juan was seventy years old and considered one of the "*antiguos pobladores.*"[5]

Besides Diego, whose name is found carved

on Inscription Rock, there were two daughters. *Lucía*, twenty in 1631, was married to Francisco Luján; *María* was the wife of Francisco Márquez.⁶

1. **Oñate**, p. 204.
2. **AGI, Contad.**, legs. 710, 726, **Data**.
3. **AGN, Mex., Inq.**, t. 467, f. 351.
4. **Ibid.**, t. 304, f. 188.
5. **Ibid.**, t. 356, f. 269.
6. **Ibid.**, t. 372, exp. 19, ff. 11-20.

RODRÍGUEZ de SALAZAR

SEBASTIÁN RODRÍGUEZ DE SALAZAR was a captain, forty-four years of age, living in Santa Fe with his wife in 1626. They had come up from New Spain seven years before. His wife's name was *Luisa Dias*.¹

1. **AGN, Mex., Inq.**, 1. 356, ff. 265-287; after Sebastián's death she must have married Agustín Romero (q.v.)

RODRÍGUEZ de ZEVALLOS

DON JUAN SEVERINO RODRÍGUEZ DE ZEBALLOS (*Zevalles, Zuballe*) was a young gentleman of twenty-two when he was sent to New Mexico with the convicts of 1677. He was sentenced to serve as a soldier without pay for an indefinite period. He had a good physique, a dark complexion, a large forehead, thick eyebrows, and a very large nose. He was born in Sevilla, the son of Captain Clemente Rodríguez.¹

By 1680 he was assistant *Alcalde* of the Sandia district.² From there he escaped the Indian massacre by fleeing south with the Rio Abajo people under the *Alcalde* and Lieutenant General, Alonso Garcia, who was his [grand] father-in-law.³ When passing muster the following year he declared that he was married and twenty-six years old. Later he was described as a native of Spain, of good stature, "fair" complexion, rather thick lips, and about thirty years of age.

His wife was *Ana María Varela*, granddaughter of Alonso Garcia. Their daughter, *María Leonor*, married Francisco de Valenzuela in 1694.⁵

1. **B-H**, III, pp. 317-324.
2. **DM**, 1680, No. 1.
3. **Revolt**, I, p. 30; **AGI, Guadalajara**, leg. 138, pt. 2.
4. **Revolt**, II, pp. 79, 96.
5. **DM**, 1694, No. 10.

ROMERO

BARTOLOMÉ ROMERO came as an *Alférez* in 1598. He was thirty-five then, the son of Bartolomé Romero and a native of Corral de Almaguer (east of Toledo), of good stature, dark, and black-bearded.¹ Already in 1597 he is mentioned as married to *Lucía López* (*Luisa López Robledo*), who came with him and her young family.² Bartolomé figured quite prominently in the Oñate annals; he was promoted to captain shortly after the colony arrived in New Mexico.³ His last recorded act was in 1632 when he reported strange rites performed by the Indians in the church of Alameda Pueblo.⁴

His children were: *Bartolomé* II, *Matías*, *Agustín*, *Ana*, wife of Francisco Gómez, and *María*, married to Gaspar Pérez.

Bartolomé Romero II, captain, was born at San Gabriel and later resided in Santa Fe,

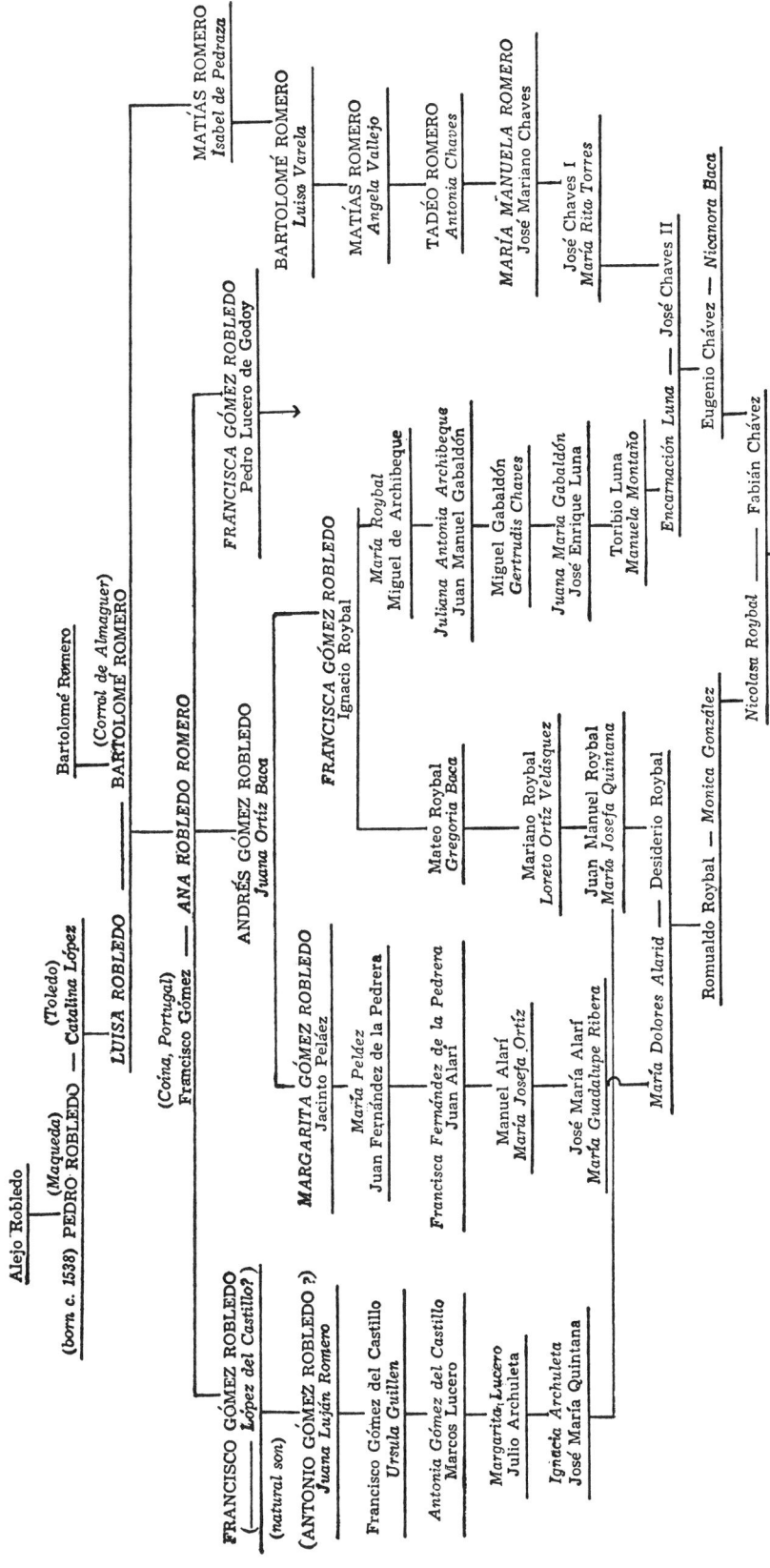

ROBLEDO-ROMERO CHART—Pedro Robledo is the oldest of the Oñate colonists who left any descendants, not by his several sons, but through a daughter. Moreover, he and his wife and his son-in-law, Bartolomé Romero, were *Manchegos* from the same spot in Central Spain around Toledo, the La Mancha country of Don Quixote. Note also "Apostle" given-names down Romero line, a distinctive feature of this family in the first century.

having been a Regent of New Mexico and *Alcalde* of Santa Fe. His wife was a daughter of Captain Francisco Pérez Granillo, by whom he had two sons and a daughter: *Bartolomé* III, living in Santa Fe in 1663; *Nicolás*, residing at the mines of Sonora; and *Juana*, wife of Diego Pérez Granillo, also at Sonora. Their father had died around the year 1643.[5]

In 1628, then twenty-six years old, Bartolomé had deposed before Father Benavides that his wife had failed to recover completely because of a spell cast on her by the wife of Juan Griego. Her name is not known, except that she was a Pérez Granillo; in 1632 she was at the Mission of Senecú taking treatments with her mother and grandmother.[6] The name "Bartolomé López Romero" on El Morro could very well belong to this man.

Matías Romero, second son of old Bartolomé, and most likely born before his parents reached New Mexico, was *Alférez Real* and also High Sheriff of Santa Fe in 1631, when he refused to testify against his brother-in-law, Gaspar Pérez.[7] His wife was *Isabel de Pedraza*, cousin of María de Archuleta, wife of Juan Márquez. In 1644, he and Juan Gómez de Luna were accused of trading illicitly with the Plains Indians and making captives for Governor Rosas.[8] Matías died in Santa Fe about the year 1648. The descendants of this couple can be identified later on by their use of "de Pedraza" with their Romero name.

Bartolomé and *Francisco* Romero de Pedraza of the next generation were in all probability their sons.

Agustín Romero, third son of old Bartolomé, was Secretary of War in 1642; he went to New Spain, later returned to Santa Fe, and was buried at the Pueblo of "Santiago." (The Inquisition scribe very likely meant to write "San Diego.") All this happened long before 1663.[9] His wife, in 1642, seems to have been a *Luisa Díaz*.[9]

* * * * * * * *

Bartolomé Romero III, son of Bartolomé II, was an *Alcalde* of Santa Fe in 1661. His wife was *Josefa de Archuleta*.[10] In 1669 he gave his age as forty-two and his military rank as *Sargento Mayor*. Father Bernal attested to his good character.[11]

Diego Romero, son of María Romero and Gaspar Pérez. (See *Perez*.)

Pedro Romero gets mention as the husband of *Petronila de Salas,* but there is no way of connecting him with the other Romeros of his day, except that he was named after one of the Twelve Apostles, as were most members of this family for several generations. In 1680 old Petronila was massacred at Pojoaque with all her children. (See *Salas*.)

Felipe Romero, captain, escaped in 1680 with his wife and six sons, one of military age and the rest small, as well as four grown daughters.[12] In 1681 he said that he was forty-two years old and married, and was pictured as slender, of good stature, with long straight hair. This time he presented his eldest son, *Sebastián*.[13]

In 1661 Felipe had been accused, along with Bartolomé Gómez Robledo, of killing some cattle that belonged to Alamillo Pueblo.[14] He and his wife, *Jacinta de Guadalajara y Quirós*, lived near this Pueblo at their hacienda of San Antonio de Sevilleta. She was twenty-seven in 1667.[15]

Their eldest son, *Sebastián*, passed muster in 1681 with his father. He was seventeen, tall and thin, with a long face and somewhat thick lips.[16] Two known daughters were *Juana*, who married Antonio Domínguez de Mendoza, and *Isabel*, wife of Diego del Rio.[17] The last marriage shows that the parents were already dead. The other five sons, small in 1680, and the other two grown daughters, cannot be traced so far. They could be any of the numerous Romeros who returned with the Reconquest, especially those with "apostolic" names who re-settled the Rio Abajo country.

* * * * * * * *

Bartolomé Romero de Pedraza was an Adjutant when he escaped from Santa Fe with

Governor Otermín and his people in 1680.[18] He was referred to in the following year as the Adjutant, not married at the time, a native of New Mexico, and forty years old. He was slender, of good stature, having a thick heavy beard and thick wavy hair.[19] A pre-Revolt house at La Cañada was mentioned in 1696 as that of Bartolomé Romero,[20] very possibly this man's, since Romero de Pedraza folk returned to this general area; or it could have belonged to any of the many Bartolomés of the century.

It appears, from post-Reconquest data, that his wife was *Luisa Varela,* and that they had a son, *Matías,* who married Angela Vallejo, and a daughter, *Juana,* who became the wife of Juan de Ribera.

Francisco Romero de Pedraza was mentioned (without "de Pedraza") as the assistant *Alcalde* of Santo Domingo in 1664; he was thirty-two years old and single.[21] He escaped in 1680 with his wife and four children, and was described the following year as forty-six or forty-seven years of age, married, a native of New Mexico, and ill at this time with the "*fríos.*" He was slender, with a turned-up nose, and somewhat deaf.[22]

His wife was *Francisca Ramírez de Salazar.* This family returned with the Reconquest.

* * * * * * * *

Two Romeros who reported at Guadalupe del Paso in 1681 evidently belonged to this large family of New Mexico, though they cannot be placed.

Salvador Romero, away at Casas Grandes in 1680, passed muster the next year as a native of New Mexico, twenty-one years old and single. He had a good slender build, a long beardless face, and long black hair.[23] Sometime later he married *María López de Ocanto,* and both returned with the Reconquest.

Juan Romero was also a native of New Mexico, twenty-six years old and married. He was of medium height, with red hair and beard, small eyes, and pockmarked.[24]

---

1. **Oñate**, p. 197.
2. **AGI, Patronato**, leg. 22, No. 3, pt. 5, f. 747.
3. Villagra, Canto XVIII.
4. **AGN, Mex. Inq.**, t. 304, ff. 187-196.
5. Ibid., t. 583, ff. 341-346.
6. Ibid., t. 304, f. 187.
7. Ibid., t. 372, f. 4.
8. Ibid., f. 18; **AGI, Patronato**, leg. 244, Ramo 7, doc. 22, p. 161.
9. **AGN**, loc. cit., t. 583, ff. 34-36; **Ortiz Trial**, ff. 11, 12, 20, 43v.
10. Ibid., **Tierras**, t. 3268, pp. 85-86.
11. Ibid., **Mex., Inq.**, t. 666, f. 532.
12. **Revolt**, I, p. 150.
13. Ibid., II, pp. 39, 140.
14. **AGN, Tierras**, loc. cit.
15. Ibid., **Mex., Inq.**, t. 608, ff. 417-427.
16. **Revolt**, II, pp. 64-65, 104, 198.
17. **DM**, 1681, No. 2; 1695, No. 17.
18. **Revolt**, I, pp. 16, 18, 119.
19. Ibid., II, p. 112.
20. **Sp. Arch.**, I, No. 818.
21. **AGN, Mex., Inq.**, t. 610, f. 99.
22. **Revolt**, I, pp. 69, 144; II, pp. 75-76, 98.
23. Ibid., II, p. 118.
24. Ibid., pp. 117, 195.

ROMERO
(Cadimo)

Alonso Romero, not a member of the preceding family, was a "*criado*" at the hacienda of Felipe Romero at Sevilleta. His real name was Alonso *Cadimo,* and he was nicknamed "*Jola.*" His wife was *María de Tapia.* All this information is from the year 1665.[1] Alonso himself does not appear in 1680 and 1681, having died before that time, evidently, but his family did return with the Reconquest as Romeros.

One son, *Diego,* married a María de San José, and a daughter, *María,* became the wife of Juan de Villalpando.

---

1. **AGN, Mex., Inq.**, t. 608, f. 427.

RUIZ

Pedro Ruiz, or *Ruiz de los Rios,* was in the soldier-escorts of 1608 and 1609.[1]

Juan Ruiz appears briefly in 1617 as a thirty-four-year-old soldier, single, who came with the wagon-train of that year.[2]

Cristóbal Ruiz, nineteen, was a Santa Fe soldier at Sandia in 1632. Ten years previously he had lived as a boy at some *estancias* in Nueva Vizcaya.[3]

* * * * * * * *

No Ruiz people are mentioned among the refugees from New Mexico in 1680 and 1681.

Cristóbal and *Nicolás Ruiz* find mention in Revolt records as residents of Casas Grandes.[4] In 1717, at Guadalupe del Paso, *Andrés Ruiz,* a soldier of Janos and Casas Grandes, and the son of Nicolás Ruiz and María Fontes, married Jacinta Valencia.[5]

---

1. **AGI, Contad.,** legs. 710, 711, **Data.**
2. **AGN, Mex., Inq.,** t. 304, f. 176.
3. **Ibid.,** f. 196.
4. **Revolt,** I, p. 186; II, p. 31.
5. **DM,** 1717, No. 4.

RUIZ CÁCERES

JUAN RUIZ CÁCERES, son of Pedro Ruiz and a native of the Isle of La Palma (Canaries), came to New Mexico in 1600. He was thirty years old, long-faced and well-bearded.[1] He was not only a countryman of Juan Luján, but evidently very closely related, so that later these two names became confused.

In 1631 Juan was a captain and also High Sheriff, and very active in political affairs.[2] It seems as though his wife was an *Isabel Baca,* who as a widow of fifty was cooking for the Padre at Tajique in 1662. Her son-in-law was Antonio de Avalos,[3] and Avalos' wife was a *Juana Ruiz Cáceres.* Moreover, Juan was closely allied with the Bacas in politics.[4] Decades later he was referred to also as the grandfather of Roque de Madrid, hence another daughter of his had married Francisco de Madrid, father of Roque.

A second *Juan Ruiz Cáceres,* most likely his son, is mentioned in the soldier escort of 1652.[5]

* * * * * * * *

Juan Ruiz de Cáceres, twenty-four and single, passed muster in 1681 as a native of New Mexico. He was described as tall, thin, and dark, with a black beard and wavy hair. Here he accompanied Domingo Luján in one instance, and Miguel Luján in another.[6] During the Otermín campaign of that year he acted as an interpreter for the Indians of Tesuque.[7] In 1692 Vargas made him a sergeant and sent him as a courier to Parral. Later he also continued as official interpreter for the Tanos and Tewas.[8] In both of the Vargas *entradas,* 1692 and 1693, he was associated with his brother, or brother-in-law, Miguel Luján.[9]

After the Reconquest he and Miguel Luján were appointed to inspect the homes at Santa Cruz,[10] and in 1698 he owned the property that had formerly belonged to Alonso del Rio.[11] But nothing is known about his immediate antecedents, or of his wife and children, if any.

A *Clara Ruiz Cáceres* was a poor widow living at San Lorenzo del Paso with other New Mexicans in 1682.[12]

---

1. **Oñate,** p. 202.
2. **AGN, Mex., Inq.,** t. 372, exp. 19, ff. 13-14.
3. **Ibid.,** t. 512, ff. 130, 156.
4. **Ch. and State,** pp. 32-33.
5. **AGI, Contad.,** leg. 747, **Data.**
6. **Revolt,** II, pp. 137, 195.
7. **Ibid.,** pp. 232-237, 383.
8. **First Expedition,** pp. 54, 80, 184.
9. **AGN, Hist.,** t. 37, f. 78; **Ritch Coll.,** Box 1, No. 25, ff. 107-108.
10. **Sp. Arch.,** I, No. 818.
11. **Ibid.,** No. 293.
12. **Ibid.,** No. 728.

RUIZ de HINOJOS
(See *Hinojos*)

SÁIZ

AMBROSIO SÁEZ, a captain residing in the Sandia area, was a native of El Valle de San Bartolomé in Nueva Vizcaya, and a former resident of San Felipe de Jesús (Chihuahua). His wife was *Ana Rodríguez de Anaya*. In 1665 he declared that he was twenty-five years old, and twenty-nine in 1667.[1] His home before the Rebellion was at La Cañada.[2]

He escaped the 1680 massacre with his wife, two sons, and eight smaller children.[3] A *Sargento Mayor* at this time, he stated that he was forty-two or forty-four years old, and a native of Nueva Vizcaya. He also presented a son nineteen years of age. He was pictured as having a good build, reddish hair and beard, watery eyes, and a long nose.[4] In 1682 he and a grown son, *Agustín*, ran away from the refugee colony at Guadalupe del Paso with their families.[5]

Agustín Sáez was described in 1681 as thirty-three years old, a native of New Mexico, married, with a good stature, curly hair, light blue eyes, and a fair and ruddy complexion.[6]

1. **AGN, Mex., Inq.,** t. 666, ff. 539, 553; t. 608, f. 391; t. 610, exp. 7, f. 66v.
2. **Sp. Arch.,** I, No. 818.
3. **Revolt,** I, p. 141.
4. **Ibid.,** II, pp. 42-43, 117.
5. **BNM,** leg. 2, pt. 3.
6. **Revolt,** II, pp. 142, 188.

SALAS

ANTONIO DE SALAS was a step-son of Pedro Lucero de Godoy.[1] Whether he was a child of Pedro's first wife in New Mexico, Petronila de Zamora (Montoya), or of a former wife in New Spain, cannot be ascertained. As late as 1663 Antonio was referred to as the brother of Catalina (de Zamora) and of Juan Lucero.[2] In 1639 he was a member of the *Cabildo* of Santa Fe.[3] He held the *encomienda* of Pojoaque Pueblo, where he lived with his wife, *María de Abendaño,* their son *Simón Salas,* and María's two daughters by her previous invalid marriage to Diego de Vera.[4] Antonio was accused in 1664 of having relations with one of these step-daughters, Petronila, and was said to be jealous of her husband, Pedro Romero.[5] Nothing more is known about the son, Simón de Salas. Antonio was a guard of Governor Rosas when the latter was murdered in 1642; he was twenty-five and single.[6]

The two step-daughters were *María Ortiz de Vera,* or *Baca,* and *Petronila,* who used the name of Salas. Women who used the Salas name later on, like the wife and some daughters of Andrés Hurtado, most probably owed it to the fact that a grandmother of theirs had been a step-child in the Salas family. María Ortiz de Vera had three daughters prior to her marriage with Diego de Montoya. Her sister Petronila was killed at Pojoaque in 1680 with all her children, eight or ten in number, which included three grown sons and some grown daughters, the rest of them young.[7]

Antonio de Salas himself was the only man of this name in the records of 1680, when as a *Sargento Mayor* he signed several *autos* and gave his opinions about the colony's returning to New Mexico.[8] He is not heard of again, having died by 1681 or gone to New Spain.

1. AGN, Tierras, t. 3268, p. 278.
2. Ibid., Mex., Inq., t. 596, pt. 2, f. 155.
3. B-H, III, p. 57.
4. AGN, Tierras, loc. cit.; Troubl. Times, pp. 42-43.
5. Ibid., Mex., Inq., t. 507, pp. 284-285.
6. Ortiz Trial, ff. 6v, 34-36.
7. Revolt, I, pp. 10, 96.
8. Ibid., I, pp. 68, 76.

SALAZAR

FRANCISCO DE SALAZAR first appears in the soldier-escorts of 1625, and then in 1643.[1] In 1634, if the same man, he was Procurator General of New Mexico.[2] Deeply involved in the Governor Rosas murder affair, he was beheaded with other officers in 1643. In the 1642 trial his full surname was given as Salazar *Hachero*.[3]

Bartolomé de Salazar had been *Alcalde Mayor* of the Zuñi and Moqui jurisdiction when he died prior to 1662. His widow was a certain *María*.[4] This woman seems to have belonged to the Martín Serrano and Martín Barba groups of Las Salinas, and so could be the *María Martín*, widow of Bartolomé de Ledesma, thus making Salazar and Ledesma the same man. But this is by no means a certainty.

A daughter, from descriptions given, was a *Juana de Salazar*, born at Zuñi, who was the wife of Diego Luján and mother of Sebastián Luján. A son, perhaps, was an *Agustín de Salazar*, who is met at the time of the Reconquest.

There were no Salazar individuals, that is, adult males, listed among the refugees of 1680 and 1681, or in the years immediately following. But minor children, not mentioned then, appear as adults in 1693 and after. It is impossible to say with any certainty whether or not they derived their name from these Salazar people, or from other individuals named "Ramírez de Salazar" and "Rodríguez de Salazar."

As explained in other sections, certain women of the period using this name were descendants of the step-daughters of Antonio de *Salas;* somehow, in many instances they stretched the name to Salazar.

1. AGI, Contad., legs., 729, 738, Data.
2. B-H, III, p. 47.
3. Ch. and State, p. 175; Ortiz Trial, ff. 8, 12 sqq.
4. AGN, Mex., Inq., t. 595, ff. 126-127.
5. DM, 1705, No. 6.

SÁNCHEZ

Juan Sánchez Cabello was a twenty-year-old convict, sentenced to six years' military service, who came to New Mexico in 1677. He was the son of Nicolás Sánchez, and was born in Mexico City at San Juan. He had a good physique, a long face, thick eyebrows, and a scar on the right side of the chin. His name here was given as Juan *Gómez* Cabello, but the son of Nicolás *Sánchez*.[1] In 1680 he passed muster with a family of six persons, and in the following year was described as a native of Mexico City, having a good stature, a long face and good features, thick eyebrows, and a scar on the right side of the chin.[2]

He did not return to New Mexico in 1693 but remained at Guadalupe del Paso, where his widow, *María López Cabello*, was living with her family in 1703. Prior to 1680 she had owned property in Santa Fe which Vargas gave to a José López, probably her brother.[3]

José Sánchez, twenty years old, also came with the convicts of 1677. He was the son of Nicolás de Olivares, and was born in Mexico City at the Arzobispal. He was of medium height, dark, flat-nosed, with a small forehead and black hair.[4] In 1680 he passed muster as a convict all alone, and was described again with the addition of scars on his face. He also added "Alejandro" to his last name.[5] He fled the colony at San Lorenzo del Paso in 1682.[6] Like the foregoing Sánchez, he did not establish a family in New Mexico.

JACINTO SÁNCHEZ (*de Iñigo*) gave his age as eighteen in 1681, but he was not described.[7] In 1685 he tried to run away from the refugee colony.[8] However, he and other relatives came to New Mexico with the Reconquest to found a large family of this name.

1. B-H, III, pp. 317-324.
2. **Revolt,** I, p. 159; II, pp. 81, 101.
3. Sp. Arch., I, No. 930.
4. B-H, loc. cit.
5. **Revolt,** I, pp. 150-151; II, pp. 136-137, 194.
6. BNM, leg. 2, pt. 3, ff. 354-357.
7. **Revolt,** II, p. 84.
8. Sp. Arch., II, No. 35.

SÁNCHEZ de MONROY

PEDRO SÁNCHEZ DE MONROY passed muster with Oñate's troops in 1597. With him were his wife and children. Again, in 1598, he passed muster as a native of Mexico City, fifty years old, the son of Hernán Martín de Monrroy, of good stature and gray-bearded.[1] Whether he stayed in New Mexico or not, it does seem as though a daughter, *Juana Sánchez,* remained with her husband, Juan de Mondragón.

The only man with this surname in 1680 was *Sebastián Sánchez de Monroy,* also known as Sebastián Sánchez de Mondragón. (See *Mondragón.*)

1. **AGI, Patronato,** leg. 22, pt. 5, ff. 729, 786; **Oñate,** p. 198.

SANDOVAL

Sebastián de Sandoval was an abusive individual who was murdered in Santa Fe in 1640, as a result of his open and continuous slanders against local citizens and their women. His talk about religious matters had earned him an excommunication, so that the question of his burial also created a public crisis.[1] He was not a native of New Mexico, and he died before establishing himself as a colonist, if he ever intended to do so. The Sandoval people of the next century come from a different source.

1. See **Ch. and State,** pp. 135-136.

SANTA CRUZ

DIEGO DE SANTA CRUZ, captain, was known as the son of Juan Pérez de Bustillo and María de la Cruz. He gave his age as twenty-six in 1617, and thirty-five in 1626, when he stated that he had been born in Zacatecas and reared in Santa Fe.[1] Diego was dead by 1661, when it was alleged that he had been allowed to marry his blood-niece,

Gregoria de Archuleta, daughter of his own sister.² What is more likely, he was not a real son of the Bustillo family, and the Padres, apprised of the secret fact, allowed him to wed a daughter of his adopted sister. Such accusations were often made against the friars, usually when the principals in the case were long dead and gone.

Diego had a daughter, *Isabel,* who married Andrés de Peralta in 1661.³ Perhaps a son of his was a *Pedro de la Cruz,* whose *encomienda* of "Cuquina" in Zuñi had been confiscated by Governor Mendizábal. Pedro boasted of being the son of a First Conquistador and of having served the King in New Mexico for forty-three years.

No one of this name appears at the time of the Rebellion in 1680, or after. Some "Cruz" people who appear later belong to other groups bearing this simple name, although it is possible that one or the other was descended from Diego de Santa Cruz.

1. **AGN, Mex., Inq.,** t. 316, f. 183; t. 356, f. 297.
2. **Ibid.,** t. 587, pp. 317-318.
3. **Ibid., Tierras,** t. 3268, p. 298.

SEDILLO
(Cedillo Rico de Rojas)

PEDRO DE CEDILLO was a native of Querétaro who arrived in New Mexico in the second half of the century. By 1680 he was a captain living in the Rio Abajo district. He escaped the Indian Rebellion with his family. He gave his age at "about seventy" in 1681, declaring that he had one grown son, twenty years old and ready to serve as a soldier, and eight other children.¹ His wife was *Isabel López de Gracia,* and the full family name was "Cedillo Rico de Rojas," as we learn from the marriages of their children after the Reconquest.

1. **Revolt,** I, pp. 78, 152; II, pp. 47, 124.

SERNA

DIEGO DE LA SERNA (or *Cierna*) came to Santa Fe before 1626 as an aide to Governor Sotelo.¹ He stayed in New Mexico, engaging several times in leading soldier-escorts to and from Mexico City.² As a captain he was involved in the intrigues of the times, and barely escaped execution for sedition under Governor Pacheco in 1643.³

Felipe de la Serna escaped the Indian massacre of 1680 with his wife and eight children. He was forty in 1681, described as a native of New Mexico, married, of medium height, pockmarked, and having straight hair.⁴ In all likelihood he was a son of Diego.

His wife was *Isabel Luján,* apparently the daughter of Juan Ramos and Mariana Luján. Some of their children were: *Cristóbal, Gregoria,* wife of Lazaro Duran, *Antonia,* wife of Matías Madrid, and perhaps a *María,* wife of Nicolás Garcia.

* * * * * * *

José de la Serna, not a member of the preceding family, had come with the convicts of 1677. He was thirty-one years old, the son of Esteban and a native of Puebla, a man of medium height, with a long dark face, and a large nose. He was sentenced to two years of military service.⁵ He was still in New Mexico when the Indians struck three years later,⁶ but was gone the following year, probably back home since his term was up.

1. **AGN, Mex., Inq.,** t. 356, f. 297.
2. **BNM,** leg. 1, pt. 1, ff. 470-504; **AGI, Contad.,** legs. 735, 845A, **Data.**
3. **Ch. and State,** pp. 125, 176; **Twit. Coll.,** No. 280.
4. **Revolt,** I, pp. 141-142, 176; II, pp. 82, 102.
5. **B-H,** III, pp. 317-324.
6. **Revolt,** I, pp. 142-143, 176.

SISNEROS
(Cisneros)

DIEGO DE CISNEROS, twenty-four years old, is mentioned in passing in the year 1632.[1]

Bartolomé de Cisneros and his brother *Vicente* were living in the Zuñi-Moqui jurisdiction in 1662.[2] They might or they might not have been the sons of Diego; anyway, their place of origin is not known. Vicente appears again in the Salinas area in 1668,[3] but is not heard of again.

Bartolomé was supposed to be in Hawikuh guarding the friars, but was absent when the Indians killed Fray Pedro de Avila y Ayala in 1670.[4] His wife was *Ana Gutiérrez*. A son of theirs, *Alonso*, married María Madrid at Guadalupe del Paso in 1690; a daughter, *Catalina*, married Diego del Rio at Socorro del Paso in 1699,[5] which indicates that this family did not return to New Mexico with the Reconquest.

Antonio de Cisneros is the only person of this name who appears with the refugees of 1680, or rather in 1681, when he passed muster as a twenty-one-year-old bachelor.[6] Since there were no Cisneros refugees in 1680, it seems as though they were all residing at Guadalupe del Paso by that time. Perhaps Antonio was another son of Bartolomé; or else he was the son of Vicente Cisneros of the Salinas country, for he later became *Alcalde Mayor* of Galisteo following the Reconquest.[7] (When the Salinas area was abandoned prior to the Rebellion, some of the Spanish folk moved to the Galisteo Basin.) Antonio's wife was *Josefa Luján*, and they had three children: *Hermenegildo*, *Felipe Neri*, and *Juana*, who married Juan de Santisteban.

1. AGN, Mex., Inq., t. 304, f. 197.
2. Ibid., t. 595, f. 125; see **Alonso Rodríguez Cisneros** as a possible ancestor.
3. Ibid., t. 608, ff. 437-444.
4. Vetancurt, Menologio, p. 109.
5. DM, 1690, No. 2; 1699, No. 6.
6. Revolt, II, pp. 61, 195.
7. DM, 1698, No. 14.

SOTO

Francisco de Soto was the real name of a soldier-of-fortune, fifty-eight years old when he came to New Mexico prior to 1626, under the alias of "Juan Donayre de las Misas." A religious scoffer, he claimed this to be his real name, saying that his father's name was Francisco Rodríguez *de las Misas* and his mother's, Catalina *Donayre*. His birthplace, he said, was Pedroche in the province of Cordoba. However, Fray Alonso Benavides, who had been a lay sheriff of the Inquisition in the Canary Islands before coming a Franciscan, recognized him as a Francisco de Soto who had received a sentence from the Holy Office many years previously. The Padre had a good talk with him, and he meekly changed his name to *Juan Pecador*.[1]

* * * * * * * *

Diego de Soto had lived and died in New Mexico, or perhaps in the Guadalupe del Paso district, prior to the Rebellion of 1680. A daughter, *Pascuala*, by his wife *Gregoria Trujillo*, married Diego Martín in Santa Fe after the Reconquest.[2] Pascuala later married an Antonio Valdés who, after her death, married a Manuela Sánchez.[3]

Pedro de Soto, son of *Gabriel de Soto* and Luisa de Albizu, married Francisca Lucero at Guadalupe del Paso in 1715.[4]

Antonio de Soto, twenty-five, born in Mexico City at El Reloj, and the son of Don Diego de Salazar, came with the convicts of 1677.[5] But he must have finished his term, or run away, before 1680, for he is not heard of again.

1. AGN, Mex., Inq., t. 356, ff. 293-294, 305.
2. DM, 1694, No. 9.
3. M-29, Sta. Cruz, Sept. 23, 1737.
4. DM, 1715, No. 5.
5. B-H, III, pp. 317-324.

SOSA

Miguel de Sosa was with the Leyva escort at Guadalupe del Paso when the Pueblos rebelled in 1680. In 1681 he passed muster with a family of seven persons, saying that he was twenty years old, married, and a native of New Mexico. He had a medium stature, a broad nose, large eyes, and black hair and beard.[1] Probably he was born in the Guadalupe del Paso area, which at the time considered itself a part of the "Kingdom of New Mexico," and now wished to join the northern colony. At any rate, the name vanishes as suddenly as it had appeared.

1. Revolt, I, pp. 37, 149; II, p. 114.

SUAZO

JUAN BAUTISTA SUAZO was an *Alférez* living in Santa Fe between the years 1646 and 1658.[1] Nothing more is known about him, or about any connection between him and later people of this name.

Juan de Suazo passed muster in 1681, saying he was twenty-five years of age and a native of New Mexico (perhaps of Guadalupe del Paso). He had a long face, a slender but good physique, no beard, and very thick black hair.[2] His name appears again in the Cruzate muster-roll of 1684.[3] Apparently, he is the same Juan de Suazo living at Senecú del Paso, after the Reconquest, who in 1699 said that he was fifty years old.[4] A daughter of his, *Beatriz*, by his wife *Ana María Bernal*, married Antonio González de Escalante at Guadalupe del Paso in 1718.[5] A Juan de Suazo testifying about a Santa Fe marriage in 1713 seems to be the same man.[6]

María de Suazo, wife of the *Sargento Mayor* Diego López of New Mexico, could well have been Juan's elder sister.

1. AGI, Contad., legs. 745, 755, Data.
2. Revolt, II, p. 141.
3. HSNM, No. 2845.
4. DM, 1699, No. 9.
5. DM, 1718, No. 3.
6. Sp. Arch., I, No. 2.

TAPIA

JUAN DE TAPIA finds first mention in 1607 as the husband of *Francisca Robledo*, daughter of Pedro Robledo and Catalina López.[1] Juan Fernández de Tapia was the name given once when acting as a church notary in 1617.[2] In 1625 he was an *Alférez*, and shortly after a captain and *encomendero*.[3]

A Juan de Tapia, condemned to death for treason in 1643 but not executed,[4] was more likely a son of his.

Cristóbal de Tapia owned lands two leagues below Isleta Pueblo prior to the Rebellion,[5] and he was described in 1681 as having a good thickset stature, an aquiline face, and black hair and beard.[6] He is the only Tapia among the male refugees. As a *Sargento Mayor* he was very active in the First Vargas Entry in 1692.[7] In that year he was the *Mayordomo* of the Conquistadora Confraternity.[8]

Francisco de Tapia had been living in New Mexico prior to 1680, but is not found among the refugee colonists. Mentioned as dead in 1685, when a daughter got married, he presumably had died before the Rebellion. His wife was *María de Chaves*, and their known children were: *Francisco*, *Luisa*, who married Antonio Ramírez de Gamboa in 1685,[9] and *María*, wife of Miguel Gutiérrez.[10]

1. AGN, Mex., Inq., t. 467, ff. 342-345.
2. Ibid., t. 316, f. 177.
3. Ibid., t. 356, f. 287; AGI, Contad., leg. 726, Data; Benavides, 1634, p. 110.
4. Twit. Coll., No. 280.
5. Revolt, I, pp. 79-80, 142.
6. Ibid., II, pp. 49, 127-128.
7. First Expedition, pp. 60, 73, 183, 254.
8. OLC, pp. 8, 63-69.
9. DM, 1685, No. 1.
10. AGN, loc. cit., t. 735, f. 299.

TELLES JIRÓN

JOSÉ TELLES JIRÓN had the *encomiendas* of San Felipe and Cochiti in 1661. He was married and had four children.[1] He was living at Senecú in 1667, when he declared that he was thirty-five or thirty-six years of age, and a native of Los Altos de San Jacinto in Cuyoacan. His wife was *Catalina Romero*.[2]

In 1680 he escaped with the refugees taking his wife, three sons, and four daughters. The next year he stated that he was forty-nine and married.[3] In 1684 his family was among those in dire need at Ysleta del Paso.[4] He and his wife were still living in that area in 1695,[5] hence they did not return with the Reconquest.

The three sons were adults in 1681 and so passed muster: *José*, *Juan*, and *Rafael*. Two known daughters were *María Zapata*, who later married Diego de Medina, and *Isabel*, who became the wife of Jacinto Sánchez de Iñigo.

José Telles Jirón II passed muster in 1681 as twenty-six years of age and married.[5]

Juan Telles Jirón reported in 1681, stating that he was married and with dependents, but ready to emulate his father and grandparents as a soldier; however, he was active with the Domínguez de Mendoza and Pedro de Chaves clans in the black market at Sonora.[6]

Rafael Telles Jirón appeared as a bachelor twenty-one years old in 1681. He was described as a native of New Mexico, of good stature, with a plump face, thick nose, large eyes and a budding mustache. He was appointed as an interpreter for the Piros.[7] In 1682 he married *Mariana Montoya de Esparza*.[8]

Made a captain by Vargas in 1692, he was placed in charge of troops and supplies at Halona during the Entry of that year.[9] In February, 1694, he and his sister, María Zapata, were marriage sponsors in Santa Fe, but the following June we find him back at Guadalupe del Paso acting in the same capacity with his wife.[10]

Although none of the sons returned to colonize New Mexico with the Reconquest of 1693, the name re-appeared generations later in the Rio Abajo area, and shortened to *"Telles."* The present *"Jirón"* surname derives from a different family, Jirón de Tejeda.

1. AGN, Tierras, t. 3268, pp. 234-250.
2. Ibid., Mex., Inq., t. 608, ff. 423-427.
3. Revolt, I, pp. 78, 144.
4. AGN, Prov. Int., t. 37, pp. 100-104.
5. Revolt, II, p. 35.
6. Ibid., pp. 152-165, 176.
7. Ibid., pp. 141, 188, 242.
8. DM, 1682, No. 2.
9. First Expedition, pp. 69, 207, 230.
10. DM, 1694, Nos. 11, 17.

TORRES

Juan de Torres, a native of Mexico City and the son of Baltasar de Torres, appears in the Oñate lists of 1597.¹ (See *Luna* for Melchor de Luna, son of Baltasar de Morales.)

In 1608, the *Alférez Juan de Torres* and a *Melchor de Torres* were in the same wagon-train escort.² A Melchor *Gómez* was in the escorts of 1652 and 1655.³ The Torres and Luna people (originally Gómez de Torres and Gómez de Luna) were mentioned as kinsfolk a generation later. Were Juan and Melchor brothers, or at least half-brothers, one the ancestor of the Torres folks, the other of the Lunas?

FRANCISCO GÓMEZ DE TORRES, a captain, led the wagon-train escorts in 1619 and 1621.⁴ He died suddenly in Santa Fe in 1636, when a large quantity of illegal quicksilver was found among his effects. He had a house in Santa Fe as well as an *estancia* at La Cañada.⁵

Among the Torres people living in New Mexico when the Indians rebelled in 1680, the following adult males are mentioned:

Cristóbal de Torres passed muster in 1681 as a native of New Mexico, married, and forty years of age. He was described as being thick-set, of medium height, rather fat, with a crooked nose, black hair, and an awkward gait.⁶

Francisco de Torres, not mentioned in the refugee rolls because he was a minor at the time, was nineteen years old in 1687, the son of Francisco de Torres and Gabriela Garcia. He married *Angela Trujillo* at Ysleta del Paso in that year. Both parties and their parents were all natives of New Mexico, and very poor at this time. The Torres were here mentioned as kinsfolk of Diego de Luna and his wife.⁷ This family did not return with the Reconquest, at least as a unit, for in 1699 both Angela and Francisco were living at Guadalupe del Paso.⁸ Eighty years old, and the widow of the soldier Francisco de Torres, Angela was still much alive there in 1745.⁹

Francisco de Torres and his wife, *Sebastiana de la Cruz,* were living at San Lorenzo del Paso in 1681 when a daughter, *Francisca,* married Pedro de Avalos. A *Lugarda Torres* married Salvador de Avalos at Guadalupe del Paso in 1718.¹⁰

* * * * * * * *

Sebastián de Torres, who was killed by the Indians at Nambé in August, 1680, together with his wife and child, did not belong to this New Mexico family. He was a brother of Fray Tomás de Torres, one of the twenty-one Franciscans martyred in 1680, who was a native of Mexico City, though given in the Revolt annals as a native of Teposotlán.¹¹

---

1. **AGN, Mex., Aud.,** leg. 25, pt. 1.
2. **AGI, Contad.,** leg. 710, **Data.**
3. Ibid., legs. 727, 748, **Data.**
4. Ibid., legs. 725, 738, **Data; AGN, Mex., Inq.,** t. 495, f. 103.
5. **BNM,** leg. 1, pt. 1, pp. 470-504.
6. **Revolt,** II, p. 132.
7. **DM,** 1687, No. 1.
8. Ibid., 1699, No. 6.
9. **AGN, Mex., Inq.,** t. 892, ff. 1-10.
10. **DM,** 1681, No. 1; 1718, No. 12.
11. **Revolt,** I, pp. 10, 96, 109; **AGN, Mex., Inq.,** t. 608, exp. 6, ff. 418-419; Rosa-Figueroa also makes this correction.

TRUJILLO

DIEGO DE TRUJILLO first appears in New Mexico as an *Alférez* and farmer, nineteen or twenty years old, in 1632.¹ He was in the soldier-escort of 1641.² In 1662 he was fifty, a *Sargento Mayor,* living in the jurisdiction of Sandia as Lieutenant General for the Rio Abajo area, as well as *Alcalde Mayor* of Zuñi. He then declared that he was born in Mexico City. His wife was *Catalina Vásquez.*³

In 1661 Governor Mendizábal confiscated his Zuñi *alcaldía*. There are reams telling of his troubles with this Governor. From them we learn that his home was four leagues from Sandia Pueblo, and that his two sons-in-law were Andrés Hurtado and Cristóbal Baca.[4] The name of his *estancia* was "Paraje de las Huertas." Diego gave his age as forty-eight in 1661.[5] By 1669 he was a *Maese de Campo* and also Syndic of the Franciscans at Sandia. His wife gave her age at this time as forty-eight, and said that she had been born in Santa Fe.[6] Diego also served a short term as second *Alcalde Mayor* of Guadalupe del Paso, succeeding the very first one, Andrés López de Gracia.[7]

In 1680 he gave his opinions about the causes and problems of the Indian Rebellion,[8] but is not mentioned in the following year. He died at Casas Grandes in 1682.[9] He had one son, *Francisco*, who was married to a daughter of María de Vera.[10]

Francisco de Trujillo was the only son of Diego de Trujillo and Catalina Vásquez.[11] It is not known which daughter of María de Vera, or Baca (step-daughter of Antonio de Salas) he married, but it could have been a *Doña Lucía de Montoya* mentioned in 1663.[12] (Her mother was the second wife of Diego de Montoya.) This Lucía seems to be the "Doña Luisa de Trujillo" whose hacienda, the present site of Albuquerque, is mentioned in later years.[13]

They had a daughter named *Bernardina de Salas y Trujillo*, wife of Andrés Hurtado, whose older daughters married several prominent and prolific colonists before and after the Reconquest. Several male Trujillos mentioned at the time of the Rebellion, and after, must have been his children or grandchildren, there being no other known Trujillo at this period.

Juan de Trujillo was thirty years old and married when he passed muster in 1681. He was tall, with a dark aquiline face and straight hair.[14] He and his wife, *Elvira Sánchez Jiménez*, returned to New Mexico in 1693.

Several other Trujillos also passed muster in 1680 and 1681, but how they were related to Francisco is impossible to say without further data. It seems as though one or two might have been natural sons of old Diego from certain indications.

Cristóbal Trujillo passed muster in 1680 with his wife and twelve other persons.[15] Among the families in distress at Ysleta del Paso in 1684 were those of Cristóbal Trujillo "*el Viejo*," Cristóbal Trujillo "*el Mozo*," Bartolomé Trujillo, and Juan Trujillo.[16]

Old Cristobal's wife was *María de Manzanares*, or *Sandoval*. Among their children were *José* and *Angela*, the latter the wife of Francisco de Torres; most likely, too, *Cristóbal "the Younger,"* and, perhaps, *Bartolomé, Mateo*, and *Juan*. A daughter might have been an *Antonia* who married Nicolás Durán.

Cristóbal Trujillo II, "*el Mozo*," passed muster in 1681 as a native of New Mexico, thirty years of age, tall, swarthy, and with several facial scars.[17] He and Bartolomé Trujillo were soldiers together at Guadalupe del Paso as late as 1694.[18]

His wife was *Micaela de Archuleta*. Their sons, *Cristóbal III* and *Diego*, married Rosa Varela and Maria de Herrera, respectively, at Guadalupe del Paso in 1709,[19] which indicates that this family did not return to New Mexico. Their father continued sending up his dues as a devotee of La Conquistadora as late as 1717.[20]

Bartolomé Trujillo reported in 1681 as a native of New Mexico, eighteen or twenty years old, and single. He was of medium height, with a round face scarred by smallpox.[21] In 1682 he married *María de Archuleta*, both parties declaring themselves children of "old Christians."[22] In 1693 Bartolomé married *Petrona Domínguez*.[23]

Mateo Trujillo passed muster in 1681 as a native of New Mexico, twenty-five or twenty-six years of age, and married. He was tall, slim, and dark, with long black hair. He enlisted with two other Trujillos, Juan and the younger Cristóbal.[24] His wife was *María de Tapia*, widow of Alonso Romero, who returned with him and their family to New Mexico in 1693.

1. AGN, Mex., Inq., t. 372, f. 7.
2. AGI, Contad., leg. 736, Data.
3. AGN, loc. cit., t. 595, ff. 121-127.
4. Ibid., t. 594, p. 358; ibid., Tierras, t. 3268.
5. Ibid., Mex., Inq., t. 596, pt. 1, f. 12.
6. Ibid., t. 666, ff. 552v, 565v.
7. Ibid., Prov. Int., pp. 352-357.
8. Revolt, I, pp. 116-118.
9. BNM, leg. 2, pt. 3, f. 354.
10. AGN, Mex., Inq., t. 596, pt. 2, f. 155v; t. 587, f. 51.
11. Ibid., ut supra; t. 594, p. 445.
12. Ibid., t. 507, f. 50.
13. Revolt, I, pp. 26-27; First Expedition, pp. 66-70; AGI, Guadalajara, title 265; Sp. Arch., I, No. 297.
14. Revolt, II, pp. 82, 102.
15. Ibid., I, p. 158.
16. AGN, Prov. Int., t. 37, pp. 100-104.
17. Revolt, II, p. 196.
18. DM, 1694, No. 11.
19. Ibid., 1709, Nos. 2, 14.
20. OLC, p. 73.
21. Revolt, II, pp. 105, 136.
22. DM, 1682, No. 7, incomplete.
23. Ibid., 1693, No. 6, incomplete.
24. Revolt, II, pp. 85, 103, 127, 196.

VALENCIA

BLAS DE VALENCIA was a soldier in Oñate's forces, twenty years old, with a round face and a light beard.[1] He appears later in Governor Zevallo's escort to Santa Fe in 1613.[2] He was most likely the father of Francisco de Valencia of the next generation.

Francisco de Valencia lived in the Isleta jurisdiction around the middle of the century. About the years 1661 to 1664 he declared himself to be from fifty to fifty-four years of age, and a native of Santa Fe. He was also Lieutenant General for the Rio Abajo area at this time, as also Syndic of the Franciscans at Isleta. His wife was *María Lopez Millán*, nicknamed "*la Maricota.*"[3] Francisco was dead by 1668, when his wife is referred to as a widow.[4] She was still living in 1684, as will be seen. Their estancia, referred to in 1680,[5] was on the site of the present town of Valencia.

Juan de Valencia, captain, is mentioned briefly in 1660.[6] He escaped the Pueblo massacre of 1680 with his six children, all grown, his widowed mother, as well as grandchildren and servants—a total of forty-six persons.[7] He is not mentioned in the lists of 1681, but in 1684 he was numbered with the refugee colony, specifically mentioned with his mother, the widow of the *Maese de Campo* Francisco de Valencia.[8] In 1692, as assistant *Alcalde* of Senecú, Ysleta, and Socorro del Paso, he received orders from Vargas to assemble troops for his first Entry into New Mexico.[9]

Juan's wife was *Juana Martín*. All their known children married at Guadalupe del Paso, even after the Reconquest, hence the conclusion that the family as a whole failed to return in 1693. These children were: *María*, who married José de Contreras in 1693; *Francisca*, married to Leonardo de Avalos in 1699; *Antonio*, who married Manuela Madrid in 1710; and *Jacinta*, who became the wife of Andrés Ruiz in 1717.[10] The last girl is mentioned as the daughter of Juana *Madrid*, either a mistake for "Martin" or a second wife of Juan de Valencia.

Manuel de Valencia passed muster in 1680, being ill at the time, with his wife and four small children. He was thirty in 1681 and still ailing with a throat ulcer.[11] His wife was *Angela de Tapia*. They had a daughter, *Josefa*, who married Francisco Luján in Santa Fe in 1694.[12]

1. AGI, Patronato, leg. 22, Ramo 4.
2. Ibid., Contaduria, leg. 718, Data.
3. AGN, Mex., Inq., t. 587, pp. 305-314, 321, 375-386; t. 507, pp. 722-723; t. 512, f. 102.
4. Ibid., t. 666, f. 406.
5. Revolt, I, p. 27; II, p. 175.
6. AGN, loc. cit., t. 587, p. 156.
7. Revolt, I, p. 152.
8. AGN, Prov. Int., t. 37.
9. First Expedition, p. 51.
10. DM, 1693, No. 7; 1699, No. 7; 1710, No. 13; 1717, No. 4.
11. Revolt, I, p. 142; II, p. 50.
12. DM, 1694, No. 31.

VARELA JARAMILLO

ALONSO VARELA and his brother *Pedro* came from Santiago de Compostela to the New World, and up to New Mexico in 1598 with Oñate's troops. The first man founded a family which came to be known as *Varela Jaramillo*, and the second founded the *Varela de Losada* family. The two men were specifically referred to as the Varela brothers in 1613.[1]

Alonso Varela was described in 1598 as a native of Santiago in Galicia, of good stature, with a chestnut beard, and thirty years old, the son of Pedro Varela.[2] In 1626 he referred to himself as an old settler sixty years of age, with a son, *Alonso*.[3] His estancia was at La Cienega in 1632, and his wife was *Catalina Pérez de Bustillo*, sister of Ana de Bustillo.[4]

There was a soldier, named *Francisco Varela*, in Santa Fe in 1631,[5] but it cannot be ascertained if he was the son of Alonso or of his brother Pedro.

Alonso Varela II is mentioned in 1626 as the adult son of the first Alonso Varela, and again in 1638 as the cousin of Pedro Varela (II). He was a public scribe in 1642.[6] Nothing more is known about him.

Pedro Varela Jaramillo, a captain sixty years of age, escaped the 1680 massacre with his wife and a twenty-year-old son.[7] He was the son of Alonso II, if not of the Francisco previously mentioned.

His wife was *Lucía Madrid*. He is mentioned as dead in 1692 when their son, *Juan Varela Jaramillo*, married Isabel de Cedillo.[8] Another son was *Cristóbal Varela Jaramillo*.[9] A *Luisa Varela*, wife of Bartolomé Romero, might have been a sister to these men.

Cristóbal Varela Jaramillo, son of Pedro, was described in 1681 as a native of New Mexico sixteen years old, with a family of mother and brethren; he was of medium build, with a ruddy, plump, and beardless face. Undoubtedly, he was the son, twenty, mentioned by his father as being of military age.[10]

He and his brother *Juan*, a minor in Rebellion times, returned to repopulate the Rio Abajo area after the Reconquest.

1. AGN, Mex., Inq., t. 316, f. 152.
2. Oñate, p. 199.
3. AGN, loc. cit., t. 356, ff. 296v, 303.
4. Ibid., t. 304, f. 187; t. 372, f. 6.
5. Ibid., t. 372, exp. 19, f. 15.
6. Ibid., t. 385, f. 9; Ortiz Trial, ff. 1-80.
7. Revolt, I, p. 79; II, p. 57.
8. DM, 1692, No. 5.
9. BNM, leg. 2, pt. 3, ff. 354-355.
10. Ibid.; Revolt, II, pp. 57, 115-116.

VARELA de LOSADA

PEDRO VARELA passed muster in 1598 with his brother Alonso. Pedro was six years younger, twenty-four years of age, and gave the same father and birthplace as Alonso. He had a good stature and a red beard.[1] Nothing more is known about him, save that his son, *Pedro Varela II*, active in a major campaign in 1638, was referred to as a cousin of Alonso Varela.[2]

Pedro Varela de Losada was an *Alférez*, thirty-six years old in 1644, and was referred to as a native of New Mexico in 1660.[3] His wife was *Ana Holguín*, and they lived in the Sandia district.[4] It was at his *estancia*, somewhere in the present site of Albuquerque, that a meeting was held in 1664 for founding an official settlement in the valley of Atrisco.[5] Captain Pedro was at death's door sometime prior to 1667, but it cannot be ascertained if he died then.[6] He and a Juan Varela had been condemned to death for treason in 1643, but escaped execution.[7] It is very likely that *Lucía* Varela de Losada, wife of Francisco Jurado de Gracia, was his daughter.

Juan Varela de Losada was forty years old in 1664 when residing in the Sandia area with his wife, *Francisca Madrid,* sister of Roque de Madrid.[8] He was referred to as a captain in 1661, thirty-five years of age.[9] He was also *Alcalde Mayor* of Cochiti, the only Spanish person there.[10] In 1695, a Juan Varela de Losada, resident of Casas Grandes, died there.[11] Perhaps he had fled there after altercations with different Governors, hence does not appear in the Revolt lists of 1680.

* * * * * * * *

Persons of this name appearing among the refugees of 1680 are the following:

Alonso Varela de Losada, an *Alférez,* passed muster in 1680 with his wife, five small children, and eight servants.[12] He is not mentioned in 1681.

Diego Varela de Losada, married, passed muster in 1680 with two children and five other people, including his mother and brethren.[13] In the following year he was pictured as an *Alférez* thirty years old, tall and fair, beardless, with chestnut hair.[14] In 1684 he went with the Domínguez Expedition into the Nueces country, when he was bitten by a rattlesnake but survived.[15] In 1692 he was the Adjutant General of troops under Vargas; he also conveyed the Governor's military reports to the Viceroy.[16]

His wife was *María Ana Fresqui*. The marriages of his sons, *Juan* with María Maese in 1709, and *José* with María Gallegos in 1710, show that the parents were living at Guadalupe del Paso, hence this particular family did not come back home with the Reconquest.

Francisco Varela passed muster with his mother and four brethren; the Indians had killed his wife.[17] In 1681 he passed muster as a native of New Mexico, twenty-six and a widower, having a tall and good build, good features, an aquiline face, thick mustache and chestnut hair, and large eyes.[18]

Eugenio Varela de Losada, twenty-eight and single, passed muster with his mother and a family of five persons.[19] These three men, Diego, Francisco, and Eugenio, seem to have been brothers who report the same mother and each other.

Pedro Varela de Losada passed muster in 1681 as a native of New Mexico, twenty-five and married, described as having a good stature with fair and good features, a thick chestnut mustache, and heavy eyebrows.[20] Residing at San Lorenzo del Paso in 1682, he was referred to as the son-in-law of Sebastián de Herrera and brother-in-law of Nicolás Lucero,[21] as also a cousin of José de Chaves.[22] His wife's name was *Juana de Herrera.*

José Lorenzano Varela de Losada presented himself in 1681 as a native of New Mexico, twenty years old and single. He had a good build, a plump beardless face, red hair, and a mole on the left side of the face.[23]

Cristóbal Varela de Losada, a native of New Mexico, nineteen years old and single, passed muster in 1681, described as having a good physique, a fair complexion, good features, no beard, and long chestnut hair.[24]

---

1. **Oñate**, p. 199.
2. **AGN, Mex., Inq.**, t. 385, f. 9.
3. **Ibid.**, t. 587, pp. 285-286; **AGI, Patronato**, leg. 244, Ramo 7, doc. 16, p. 108.
4. **AGN**, loc. cit., t. 583, f. 275.
5. Ibid., t. 507, p. 1322.
6. Ibid., t. 608, f. 388.
7. **Twit. Coll.**, No. 280.
8. **AGN**, loc. cit., t. 507, pp. 222-226.
9. Ibid., t. 587, pp. 362, 375, 386.
10. Ibid., t. 507, p. 145.
11. **AGI, Guadalajara**, leg. 151, pt. 6, f. 1.
12. **Revolt**, I, p. 144.
13. Ibid.
14. Ibid., II, pp. 85, 103.
15. **AGN, Prov. Int.**, t. 37.
16. **First Expedition**, pp. 121, 166.
17. **Revolt**, I, pp. 40, 140.
18. Ibid., II, pp. 41, 108.
19. Ibid., I, p. 153; II, p. 38.
20. Ibid., II, pp. 41, 111, 184.
21. **Sp. Arch.**, I, No. 728.
22. **AGN, Mex., Inq.**, t. 1551, ff. 383-384.
23. **Revolt**, II, pp. 37, 136.
24. Ibid., pp. 138-139.

VÁSQUEZ

FRANCISCO VÁSQUEZ came in 1598. He was a native of Cartaya, twenty-eight years of age, the son of Alonso Alfrán. He had a good stature and a red beard.[1] He next appears in the soldier escort of 1608,[2] but there is no further information on him. However, the following women could well have been his daughter and grand-daughter:

Bernardina Vásquez, widow of Diego Márquez, living at the *estancia* of Los Cerrillos with her daughter Margarita in 1660, played a role in major happenings of her day. (See *Gerónimo de Carvajal.*)

Catalina Vásquez was the wife of Diego de Trujillo, and most likely a daughter of Bernardina, from whom her grand-daughter, Bernardina de Salas y Trujillo, got her name.

No Vásquez males appear during the rest of this century; a Vicente Vásquez acting as a witness in 1642 is not heard of again.[3]

1. **Oñate,** p. 129.
2. **AGI, Contad.,** leg. 710, **Data.**
3. Ortiz Trial, f. 25v.

VERA

DIEGO DE VERA came to Santa Fe sometime before 1622, and on January 16 of that year he married *Maria de Abendaño,* daughter of Simón de Abendaño and María Ortiz (Baca), both deceased. The witnesses were Don Pedro Durán y Chaves and his wife, Isabel de Bohórquez (Baca), aunt of the bride. Three years later, Fray Alonso Benavides came to Santa Fe as head of the Church in New Mexico, but also representing the Inquisition; as a layman he had been its sheriff in the Canary Islands. Now, Diego de Vera had a wife in Tenerife in the Canaries. The presence of Father Benavides finally compelled him to go to the Padre and disclose his bigamous status. When he left New Mexico in 1626, Father Benavides took him along to Mexico City, and there Diego was tried by the Holy Office. But because Benavides pleaded that he had confessed the crime voluntarily, and had been a good *encomendero* in New Mexico, personally teaching the catechism to the Indians under him, Diego got off with an easy sentence from the Holy Office. He was to return to his wife in the Canaries and never come back to New Mexico. He sailed for Europe in the company of good Fr. Benavides.

Diego was thirty-three in 1626 when he revealed his bigamy. His Santa Fe wife was mentioned as a grand-daughter of Captain Juan López Holguín. They had two little children, both girls.[1] These were *Maria,* who became the wife of Manuel Jorge,[2] and then of Diego de Montoya; and *Petronila,* who married Pedro Romero. After the annulment, their mother married Antonio de Salas.

Since Diego de Vera, through his two daughters, became the ancestor of leading New Mexicans in later generations, it is well to give his own genealogy, which came out during his trial. His parents were Pedro de Vera Perdomo and María de Betancur, residents of the City of La Laguna on Tenerife. His paternal grandparents were Hernán Martín Baena, a native of Jerez de los Caballeros in Estremadura, and Catalina Garcia, native of La Laguna on Tenerife. His maternal grandparents were Antonio Pérez, born on the Canary Island of La Graciosa, and Catalina Aponte, native of Garachico on Tenerife.[3]

1. **AGN, Mex., Inq.,** t. 495, ff. 89-103; t. 356, ff. 267v, 270v, 303v, 306.
2. This is only a supposition, from charts of related families.
3. See Note 1.

XAVIER

FRANCISCO XAVIER first appears in the wagon-train escort that brought Governor Mendizábal to Santa Fe in 1658.[1] In 1661 he said that he was thirty-three years old.[2] His wife, mentioned in 1663, was *Graciana Griego*, daughter of Juan Griego.[3] In 1680 Francisco was Secretary of Government and War and *Alcalde Ordinario*, holding the rank of *Maese de Campo*. He escaped the Indian massacre with four daughters and two sons, declaring he had lost two mulatto slaves at Picuris.[4] The following year he passed muster as a widower, fifty-one or fifty-two years of age, with two sons and three daughters. (One of the girls had married in the meantime.) He was a native of Sevilla in Spain, and was described as having a good build, very gray hair, and the scar of a wound on the left side of the forehead.[5]

In 1682 Francisco Xavier left Guadalupe del Paso for New Spain, with permission, being then in very poor health.[6] Permission to leave had been readily granted, for Otermín had promised the Indians the year before that he would never allow Xavier and two other men to return because of their extreme cruelty to the Pueblo Indians.[7] The Indians made this same request to Vargas in 1692, but by this time the Xaviers were gone.

José Xavier was with the Leyva escort party at Guadalupe del Paso in August, 1680, when the Indians struck. He was referred to as a married man with a small child and two servants.[8] He does not appear again.

Francisco Xavier II signed *autos* with the elder Francisco in 1680. He was a widower with a child of three or four years, and was described as a captain born in New Mexico, twenty-five years of age, having a good physique, front teeth missing, very little hair, and a toe missing from the left foot.[9] In departing for New Spain, he left his child with relatives who later brought her back to New Mexico with the Reconquest. She was *Josefa Xavier*, "orphan and poor," who married Luis Garcia at Bernalillo in August, 1704. Her mother was *Juana Francisca Baca;* her father at this date was stationed at the Presidio del Gallo in Nueva Vizcaya.[10]

---

1. **AGI, Contad.,** leg. 749, **Data.**
2. **AGN, Mex., Inq.,** t. 587, pp. 361, 375, 386.
3. **Ibid.,** t. 596, pt. 2, f. 212v.
4. **Revolt,** I, pp. 98, 137.
5. **Ibid.,** II, pp. 34, 94.
6. **BNM,** leg. 2, pt. 3, f. 357.
7. **Revolt,** II, pp. 239, 386.
8. **Ibid.,** I, pp. 38, 152.
9. **Ibid.,** I, pp. 8, 16, 18, 119, 152; II, pp. 62, 136.
10. **DM,** 1704, No. 5.

XIMENEZ
(See *Jiménez*)

ZAMORA

Diego de Zamora appears in the soldier escort of 1608; again, or another man of the same name, in that of 1655.[1]

Nicolás de Zamora, a native of Mexico City, came with Governor Pacheco in 1641.[2]

José de Zamora was in the escort of 1661.[3]

This family name, like the Ortiz surname, is used during this century by females of the Baca and Montoya families, perpetuating the name of some pioneer grandparent in the New World—in New Mexico, that of pioneer grandmothers. However, there is no connection found with any male of this name in New Mexico. The individuals given above were most likely transients, travelling with the wagon-trains to and from Mexico City.

Juan de Zamora is the only adult male of this name in 1681, none passing muster with the refugees of the previous year. He claimed to be a native of New Mexico, married, with a good stature, a long pockmarked face, blond hair and beard.[4] Most likely he was born at Guadalupe del Paso, which at that time was considered part of the Kingdom of New Mexico, and in 1681 had decided to cast his lot with the exiles from the north. He is, to all appearances, the man of this name who came with the Reconquest and settled in Santa Cruz.

1. AGI, Contad., legs. 850, 748, Data.
2. Ibid., leg. 926, Data.
3. Ibid., legs. 754, 755, Data.
4. Revolt, II, p. 128.

ZAMORANO

Salvador Zamorano was in the convict list of 1677, the son of Lucas and born in Mexico City at El Carmen. He was twenty-four years old, with a good build, a broad face, small forehead, and thick eyebrows.[1] He is without doubt the man of this name who passed muster in 1680, alone and poor. He said he was a bachelor, thirty years old, and ready to serve as a soldier.[2] But he is not heard of again.

1. B-H, III, pp. 317-324.
2. Revolt, I, p. 149; II, pp. 41-42.

PART TWO
THE EIGHTEENTH CENTURY

. . . en manos tuyas, Conquistadora,
abrirme han puertas de fino amor.

ABEYTA

DIEGO DE VECTIA was living in Santa Fe in 1701.[1] When his daughter, *Manuela Rosalía*, married Juan Antonio Luján in 1727, the *Alférez Diego de Abeytia* was already dead. His widow's name was *Catalina Leal*.[2] He and his wife came, most probably, with the colonists from Zacatecas in 1695. Catalina Leal, fifty years old and widow of Diego de *Beitia,* died in Santa Fe, July 8, 1727.[3] Besides Rosalia, they had a son *Antonio* and, very probably, *Baltasar* and *Paulín*.

Antonio de Beytia, or *aBeytia*, son of Diego, was an *Alférez* of the militia at Santa Cruz in 1735, and was mentioned also as the son-in-law of José Luján.[4] In 1731 he gave his age as thirty-two and claimed the Río Arriba area as his residence.[5] He made his will in 1765, then holding the rank of captain, at his place in "San Antonio del Bequiú del Guyqui," jurisdiction of Santa Cruz. After giving his parents' names, Antonio named his wife, *Rosalía Luján*. He had only one son, *Miguel,* but had adopted several boys and girls, not named. Some of these heirs were the children of Juan Antonio Luján (who had married *Rosalía Abeyta*). He also mentioned "my son, *Nicolás*," chosen executor, and a *Juan de Jesús Beytia* was a witness to the will.[6]

Baltasar de Beytia lived in the Río Arriba area in 1728 when a son, *Juan Manuel,* was born to his wife, *Rosalía Martín*.[7] They had been married there on February 9, 1728, with Antonio de Beytia and wife as sponsors.[8] Baltasar was twenty-five in 1732.[9] In 1741 he was a widower and serving as a soldier at the Albuquerque garrison when he married Antonia Durán y Chaves, on March 20.[10] After his death Antonia married a Miguel Lucero around the year 1756.[11]

They had two sons: *José,* born January 16, 1745, and *Diego Antonio,* March 6, 1746.[12]

Paulín de Abeytia married Angela Martín on July 6, 1737, with Juan Antonio Luján and Rosalía de Abeytia as sponsors.[13] He was very likely a brother of Antonio, Baltasar, and Rosalía.

A daughter, *Juana,* was the wife of a José Baca.[14]

María Rosa ———, wife of *Juan de Beitia,* died in Santa Fe on June 15, 1726.[15] He was perhaps another brother, the Juan de Jesús mentioned in Antonio's will.

Miguel Manuel de Beitia married *María Francisca Chaves* in Santa Fe, September 12, 1744, with Juan Luján and Rosalía Abeytia as witnesses.[16] He appears to be the only son of Antonio, mentioned in his father's will.

In time the family name took the form *Abeyta*. The settlement of Los Abeytas in the Río Abajo was composed of descendants of Baltasar.

---

1. Sp. Arch., I, No. 77.
2. DM, 1727, No. 15.
3. Bur-48, Santa Fe.
4. Sp. Arch., I, Nos. 20, 743; II, No. 382.
5. Bancroft, NMO, 1731; Crespo, pars. 116, 119.
6. Sp. Arch., I, No. 110.
7. B-27, S. Juan.
8. M-27, S. Juan.
9. Bancroft, NMO, 1732.
10. M-3, Albuq.
11. Sp. Arch., I, No. 454.
12. B-3, Albuq.
13. M-29, Sta. Cruz.
14. Sp. Arch., I, No. 117.
15. Bur-48, Sta. Fe.
16. M-50, Sta. Fe.

ABREGO

JUAN DE ABREGO was a *primer sargento*, forty-nine years old, of the Santa Fe garrison in 1790. He was a native of Mexico City. His wife was *Juana Fernández*, twenty-eight; they had two boys, six and seven years old, and two girls, four and two.[1] One child, *José Guadalupe*, was born on June 4, 1800.[2] The mother died on October 3, 1818, and was buried from the military chapel in Santa Fe.[3]

José de Abrego and his wife, *María Soledad Roybal*, had a child baptized on January 3, 1818.[4] The father enlisted as a soldier in 1805, when twenty years old.[5]

1. **Twit. Coll.,** No. 179.
2. **B-Sta. Fe.**
3. **Bur-51, Castrense.**
4. **B-Sta. Fe.**
5. **HSNM,** Mil. Papers.

ABREU

SANTIAGO ABREU was the first person in New Mexico of this name, unless the preceding *Abrego* name suffered change; then he would be another son of Juan de Abrego.

Santiago was living in Santa Fe in 1805 when a daughter, *María Jacoba Marcelina*, was born to his wife, *María Soledad de la O*.[1] A son of theirs, *Ramón*, married María Pelegrina Domínguez in the military chapel, May 23, 1827.[2] Another son, *Marcelino*, had married Brigida Olona of Tomé, where their child, *Justa*, was born on May 15, 1832.[3] Santiago died in 1814.[4]

Santiago Abreu II was married to *Josefa Baca*. On August 15, 1818, they had a son, *José María Asención Agapito;* a girl, *María Soledad,* was born in 1821, and another son, *José de Jesús,* in 1823.[5]

In 1837 Don Santiago Abreu, a former *Jefe Político,* was captured near Los Cerrillos by the Chimayó insurgents and cruelly put to death at Santo Domingo Pueblo. The rebels had already killed Ramón and Mariano Abreu,[6] presumably his brothers.

1. **B-Sta. Fe,** Jan. 18.
2. **M-51, Castrense.**
3. **B-72, Tomé.**
4. **Sp. Arch.,** II, No. 2537.
5. **B-Sta. Fe.**
6. **Leading Facts,** Vol. II, p. 62; **Ritch Coll.,** Box 4, No. 164.

AGÜERO

PEDRO NOLASCO AGÜERO was a native of Zacatecas, of unknown parentage, who married *María Domínguez,* of like estate, in Santa Fe in 1708.[1] He might be the "Juan Nolasco Armijo," widower of María Acosta, who married María de Silva, widow of José Gallegos, July 27, 1732.[2] Anyway, the name did not survive beyond the following individual who might have been his son:

Miguel Agüero married Antonia Martín January 12, 1726.[3]

1. **DM,** 1708, No. 2.
2. **M-3, Albuq.**
3. **M-29, Sta. Cruz.**

AGUILAR

Alonso Rael de Aguilar (see *Rael*).

* * * * * * * *

Nicolás de Aguilar, villainous character of the preceding century, did not return to New Mexico. If his children remained until the 1680 Indian Rebellion, they went under their mother's name of Márquez. Of the four children, only one was a boy, Nicolás.

* * * * * * * *

Francisco de Aguilar was the only Aguilar among the refugees of 1680, a *Sargento,* married, but with no children.[1] He had come to New Mexico three years before, with the convicts of 1677, when he was described as being thirty-eight years old and a native of Puebla, sentenced to two years without pay.[2] Since his term was up he must have returned home, for he does not appear in 1681 or after.

* * * * * * * *

Miguel Gerónimo del Aguila and his family appear in the Velasco list of colonists in 1693. He was thirty, the son of Nicolás del Aguila and a native of Baeza, with large eyes, a sharp nose, and a scar next to his right eye. His wife was *Gerónima Días Flores,* daughter of Ignacio and born in Mexico City, having large eyes and two moles on the face.

They had a ten-year-old daughter, *Josefa Antonia,* born in Mexico City at La Merced; she was pockmarked and had big eyes.[3] It is not known if this family had any male descendants; the name does not appear again as such.

* * * * * * * *

Pedro de Aguilera and his family were also among the Velasco colonists. He was twenty-seven, the son of Rodrigo and a native of Mexico City, with a fair complexion, a large nose, and small eyes. His wife was *Juana de Torres,* twenty-eight, the daughter of Francisco and also born in Mexico City; she had a round face, a high forehead, and a small nose.

They had a son, *Rodrigo,* six years old, born in Mexico City, having a broad face, large and rather deep-set eyes, and a flat nose. There were two daughters, both born in Mexico City: *María Casimira,* eleven, of medium height, with an aquiline face, gray eyes, and a small nose; and *Mariana,* five, who was fair, with a round face, high forehead, and small eyes. An infant of a year and a half, also born in Mexico City, was *José* (or *Josefa*) *María,* with a high forehead, large eyes, and small nose.[4]

As with the preceding family, it is not known if they arrived in New Mexico, or stayed permanently. At any rate, the name is not found in succeeding years.

* * * * * * * *

Antonio de Aguilera Yssasi, or *Yssasi Aguilera,* often appears as an official in civil documents following the Reconquest. He came in 1693, the son of Matías and a native of Mexico City, thirty-eight years of age, of medium height, with large eyes and a wound on the nose. His wife was *Gertrudis Hernández,* twenty-eight, the daughter of Mateo and also born in Mexico City; she was of medium height, with a round, dark face.

They brought along an adopted child, *José Benito,* three years old, with a round face, small eyes, and a rather flat nose.[5]

But after the first years of the Reconquest, Antonio and his name disappear.

* * * * * * * *

Manuel de Aguilar, origin unknown, lived in Santa Fe in the last quarter of the century with his wife, *Rosa Beltrán.* He died on February 1, 1789.[6]

* * * * * * * *

CRISTÓBAL AGUILAR, son of Vicente Aguilar and Nicolasa *Rinan* (?), was a native of Zacatecas, twenty-seven years old when he enlisted as a soldier of the Santa Fe Presidio in 1837. He was a shoemaker by trade.⁷ Though he came after 1820, during the Mexican period, he is included here because he is evidently the ancestor of the Aguilar family in New Mexico.

1. Revolt, I, pp. 143, 176.
2. B-H, III, pp. 317-324.
3. Sp. Arch., II, No. 54c.
4. Ibid.
5. Ibid.
6. Bur-49, Sta. Fe.
7. HSNM, Mil. Papers.

AGUIRRE

JOSÉ CALIXTO MARIANO DE AGUIRRE, origin not known, married *María Magdalena Durán y Chaves* on February 27, 1752, with Bernardo de Chaves and María Quintana as witnesses.¹ The marriage is also entered in the register of Isleta, where the name is spelled *Aguerri*.²

1. M-4, Albuq.
2. M-11, Isleta.

ALARID

JUAN BAUTISTA ALARÍ was a Frenchman who married *María Francisca Fernández de la Pedrera,* childless widow of Captain Juan Rodríguez, on March 24, 1741.¹ Bancroft wrote that about the year 1740 a party of nine Frenchmen came to Taos, and two of them remained in Santa Fe. One of these, "Jean d'Alay," became a good Spanish citizen practising his trade of barber (medic), and married a local woman.² Bancroft's information was from a letter of Governor Codallos, who wrote the name, "Juan de Alarí." "Jean d'Alay" looks like Bancroft's guess, repeated by Read.³ Others say that he belonged to a party of thirty-three Frenchmen who visited New Mexico in those times.⁴ Was Juan de Alarí, then, the "Petit Jean" or "Jean David" among the eight members of the Mallet Expedition that reached New Mexico in 1739? He was the only European Frenchman among these Creoles of Canada and Louisiana. His alleged companion, Louis Moreau, or Morín, is also among these men.⁵

The year prior to their marriage, his wife had bought the house and lot in Santa Fe where La Fonda now stands.⁶ Their known children were *Juan Antonio, José Ignacio, María Francisca,* who married Francisco Xavier Fragoso, *Manuel Isidoro,* and *María Josefa de Loreto,* born March 29, 1754.⁷ Their mother died on November 22, 1757, at the age of forty.⁸

Juan de Alarí, now referred to as a soldier, married *Ana María Tenorio* on June 13, 1758,⁹ by whom he had another son, *José Antonio,* April 22, 1763.¹⁰ Old Juan died on October 5, 1772.¹¹

In their efforts to spell the name phonetically, the Spanish Padres and others wrote it variously as *Alarij, Alaríe, Alejaríe,* and *Alarí,* the last soon becoming the accepted form. The correct French spelling would be *Alaríe*. It was not until the Nineteenth Century that *Alarid* came into being, an effort to hispanicize the name, like "Madrid."

Juan Antonio Alarí, son of the above, was a *Sargento* in 1764 when he married *Dominga Roybal.*¹² She was a daughter of Mateo Roybal and Gregoria Baca who had been reared by a childless aunt, the wife of Juan José Moreno.¹³ He re-enlisted as a soldier in 1777, when thirty-four.¹³ᵃ

Two known children were *José Francisco,*

born October 4, 1771, and *María Estéfana*, October 26, 1773.¹⁴ Their mother died on November 23, 1798, and was buried from the military chapel.¹⁵

José Ignacio Alarí enlisted as a soldier when thirty-three, in 1779.¹⁵ᵃ

Manuel Isidoro Alarí was born on April 6, 1751, the son of "Don Juan de Alaríe" and Doña María Francisca Fernández de la Pedrera.¹⁶ He first married a *María (Josefa) de Armenta*,¹⁷ by whom he had a son, *José de Jesús*, November 23, 1773, who later married Antonia Romo;¹⁸ and a daughter *María Rita de Jesús*, May 29, 1776.¹⁹ Their mother died on March 9, 1781.

Manuel Alarí then married *Josefa Ortiz Bustamante* in the military chapel of Our Lady of Light on December 21, 1781.²¹ Both were active members of the Confraternity of La Conquistadora.²² He was twenty-eight in 1779, when he enlisted as a soldier.²²ᵃ In the Santa Fe Presidio census of 1790 he was listed as "Manuel Alarye, forty, and a native of New Mexico." His wife, Josefa Ortiz, was twenty-five. Their four sons were sixteen, eight, three, and one; their one daughter was six.²³

These children were as follows: *Joaquín*, who married María Luz Chávez of Tomé;²⁴ *José María*, who married María Guadalupe Ribera (see below); *José Manuel*, born in 1804, who married Isabel Urioste;²⁵ *Mariano José*, born in 1801, who married María Luz Martínez;²⁶ and the girl, *Ana María*, who became the wife of Vicente Villanueva. Old Manuel died on April 14, 1804, and was buried from the military chapel.²⁷

José de Jesús Alarí, son of old Juan Alarí by his second wife, Ana Tenorio, was a thirty-one-year-old soldier of Santa Fe in 1790. His wife was *Polonia Rael*.²⁸

* * * * * * * *

José María Alarí, son of Manuel Alarí and Josefa Ortiz Bustamante, married *María Guadalupe Ribera*, daughter of Manuel Ribera and Josefa Labadía, on April 20, 1814.²⁹ Their children were:³⁰ *María de Jesús*, born 1816, who married José Pino; *María Manuela*, born 1820; *María Dolores*, born February 5, 1824, wife of Desiderio Roybal;³¹ *José María Apolinario*, 1818; *María Nicolasa Severa*, 1821; and *María Josefa Juliana*, 1829. Their Ribera mother died on June 21, 1829.³²

José María was transferred from Santa Fe to the new military outpost of San Miguel del Vado where he married *Antonia Ruiz Esparza* on August 17, 1830.³³

---

1. M-50, Sta. Fe.
2. Hist. Ariz. and N. M., p. 243, ftn.
3. Ill. Hist. of N. M., p. 329.
4. Cf. Colorado Magazine, Vol. XVI, No. 5, p. 169; Twitchell in Sp. Arch., I, pp. 148-151.
5. Cf. Folmer in **NMHR**, Vol. XVI, No. 3, p. 262; **Colorado Magazine**, Vol. XVI, pp. 167-171; see Mora, Luis María.
6. Sp. Arch., I, No. 272.
7. B-62, Sta. Fe.
8. M-50, Sta. Fe.
9. Ibid.
10. B-62, Sta. Fe. He enlisted as a soldier in 1781 (HSNM, Mil. Papers).
11. Bur-48, Sta. Fe.
12. M-50, Sta. Fe, Feb. 15.
13. Sp. Arch., I, No. 552.
13a. HSNM, Mil. Papers.
14. B-Sta. Fe.
15. Bur-51, Castrense.
15a. HSNM, loc. cit.
16. B-62, Sta. Fe.
17. M-50, Sta. Fe, Feb. 20, 1772.
18. B-Sta. Fe; B-66, Castrense, f. 66v.
19. B-Sta. Fe.
20. Bur-51, Castrense.
21. M-51, Castrense.
22. AASF, Bk. LXX; El Palacio, Vol. 57, No. 10, p. 306.
22a. HSNM, loc. cit.
23. Twit. Coll. No. 179.
24. Grandparents given, bapt. of child, Dec. 8, 1829, **B-72**, Tomé.
25. B and M-51, Castrense.
26. B-Castrense; B-23, Nambé-Pojoaque, M. Sec.
27. Bur-51, Castrense.
28. Twit. Coll., loc. cit.
29. M-52, Sta. Fe.
30. All bapt. dates in B-66, Castrense.
31. GENEALOGY: María Dolores Alarí, Romualdo Roybal, María Nicolasa Roybal, Fr. A. Chávez.
32. Bur-51, Castrense.
33. M-San Miguel, 1829-1848; M-51, Castrense. At eighteen he had enlisted as drummer of the Santa Fe Presidio in 1807 (**HSNM**, loc. cit.).

ALDERETE

JUAN DE ALDERETE, a native of the Mines of Talpujagua in Michoacán, left home on November 20, 1690, to join Vargas' forces at Guadalupe del Paso. His parents were Juan de Alderete and María Galindo. He was seventeen years old in 1691, when he married *María Lucero de Godoy* at the Real de San Lorenzo on August 26. She was fourteen, a native of Santa Fe, the daughter of Francisco Lucero de Godoy and Josefa Sambrano de Grijalva.[1] In 1697 he and his wife's family sold some property in Santa Fe.[2]

1. **DM**, 1691, No. 4.
2. **Sp. Arch.**, II, No. 3.

ALIRE

MIGUEL DE ALIRE (*Aliri*) was a native of Mexico City who came to Santa Fe early in the century. In the census of 1790 he is listed as a widower eighty-four years old, living with an unmarried daughter, forty-six.[1]

Miguel married *Isabel de la Vega y Coca* in Santa Fe, on May 18, 1728.[2] In 1732 he gave his age as twenty-five.[3] He was an uncle of a José Baca, husband of Juana de Beytia.[4] In 1758 he and Toribio Ortiz were after land in La Ciénega that had belonged to his father-in-law, Miguel de la Vega y Coca. He was a charter member of Our Lady of Light.[5] Miguel de Alire, widower of Isabel Coca, died in Santa Fe on May 15, 1798.[6] Direct connections with any sons have not been found, except with *Tomás*, who enlisted as a soldier in 1757 when he was twenty-one.[6a]

José, or *José Antonio*, Alire was living in Santa Fe in the middle of the century with his wife, *Margarita Lobato*. They had the following children:

José Miguel, born February 20, 1755; *Tomás Antonio*, January 25, 1760; *Bartolomé*, December 9, 1761; *Manuela Candelaria*, February 6, 1764; *Martín*, February 1, 1776; and *María Josefa*, April 19, 1773.[7]

Tomás Alire, son of Miguel de Alire and Isabel de la Vega, also resided in Santa Fe with his wife, *Luz* (or *Nicolasa*) *Tafoya*. Their children were:

Diego Antonio, born March 10, 1767; *Francisco Esteban*, August 16, 1768; *María Valvanera*, February 28, 1770; *María Gertrudis*, June 19, 1774; and *Tomás Faustín*, December 15, 1775.[8]

Benito Alire and his wife, *María Luz Tenorio*, had one son, *Manuel de Jesús*, December 28, 1765.[9]

1. **Sp. Arch.**, II, No. 1096a.
2. **M-50, Sta. Fe.**
3. **Bancroft, NMO,** 1732.
4. **Sp. Arch.**, I, No. 117.
5. **Ibid.**, No. 652; **NMHR**, Vol. X, No. 3, p. 188.
6. **Bur-49, Sta. Fe.**
6a. **HSNM,** Mil. Papers.
7. All in **B-Sta. Fe.**
8. **Ibid.**
9. **Ibid.**

ANAYA
(Anaya Almazán)

FRANCISCO DE ANAYA ALMAZÁN was the only male survivor of the large Anaya Almazán family which was wiped out by the Rebellion of 1680, including his second wife and his children by his first two wives. In 1682 he had married *Felipa Cedillo Rico de Rojas*. Both returned with the Reconquest, being mentioned as marriage sponsors before the turn of the century.[1] He left his name on El Morro in 1692.[1a]

Old Francisco was dead by 1716, when his son by his third wife, *Joaquín*, married *Margarita de Ortega*.[2] There was another son, *Salvador*; and a daughter, *Juana*, who was married consecutively to three men, Lucas Montaño, Juan Lorenzo de Medina, and Lucas Miguel Moya. Their Cedillo mother was married a second time, to Francisco González.[3]

Joaquín de Anaya, who married *Margarita de Ortega* in 1716, was still living in 1733,[4] but nothing is known about his children, if any.

Salvador de Anaya, brother of Joaquín, had married *Magdalena de Espínola*, by whom he had a daughter, *María Antonia*, born on August 20, 1703.[4] Salvador was dead by 1733, his wife having died several years before, since his widow was *María Francisca Esquibel*, who now referred to María Antonia as her "daughter."[5] This girl married Salvador Días Blea in 1724.[6] What sons there were is not known.

* * * * * * * *

Diego de Anaya Almazán married *Juana de Sena*, adopted child of Bernardino de Sena and Manuela Roybal, who acted as wedding sponsors, January 25, 1728.[7] But Diego died at the age of twenty-four on November 19 of the same year.[8] His widow, referred to merely as "Juana María ——," widow of Diego de Anaya, married an Andrés Trujillo in 1730.[9] It is not known if Diego was an Anaya brother, or only a servant, or if a child was born of his brief marriage.

---

1. **DM**, 1695, No. 6; 1696, No. 10.
1a. **Mesa, Canyon, etc.**, p. 473.
2. **DM**, 1716, No. 8.
3. **Sp. Arch.**, II, No. 386.
4. **B-13, Bernalillo.**
5. **Sp. Arch.**, loc. cit.
6. **DM**, 1724, No. 1.
7. **M-50, Sta. Fe.**
8. **Bur-48, Sta. Fe.**
9. **M-50, Sta. Fe.**

ANCIZO

Among the colonists from Zacatecas were a *Juana de Ancizo de la Cruz*, who married Francisco Pérez de la Rosa in 1698;[1] *Josefa de la Encarnación*, wife of Ignacio Losano; and *María de Ancizo*, wife of Agustín de la Cruz. They were the daughters of Miguel de la Cruz de Lara and *Juana de Ancizo*.[2] The latter, or else the younger Juana, is referred to as the mother (mother-in-law?) of Cristóbal Crespín,[3] and was very likely the Juana de la Cruz, called *"La Mozonga,"* who died in Santa Fe, May 9, 1727.[4]

---

1. **DM**, 1698, No. 7.
2. **AGN, Mex., Inq.**, t. 735, ff. 273, 299.
3. **Sp. Arch.**, I, No. 167.
4. **OLC**, p. 70.

ANGEL

Miguel Angel was among the Mexico City colonists who settled in Santa Cruz in 1696, being single at the time.[1] The name appears afterwards, but not enough to be traced effectively.

1. Sp. Arch., I, No. 817.

ANSURES

GABRIEL DE ANSURES, son of the same, was a native of Puebla, and thirty-eight years old when he came in 1693. He had an aquiline face and large deep-set eyes. His wife was *Felipa de Villavicencio Pérez Lechuga*, twenty-one, the daughter of Domingo, and born in Mexico City; she had a round face, large eyes and forehead, and a small nose.

Their children were: *José*, nineteen, the son of Gabriel by a previous marriage, born at Oaxaca, tall and dark, with a round face, joined eyebrows, and a low forehead; and *María*, child by the second wife, nine years old, fair and freckled, with large eyes and forehead.[1] *María* became the wife of José de Atienza. *Juana*, perhaps a sister born in New Mexico, married a Diego Martín.

* * * * * * * *

Bartolomé de Ansures, sixty-two years old in 1695, was a native of Puebla,[2] probably an uncle of Gabriel. His marriage to *Ynez Martín* was under question in that year.[3]

1. Sp. Arch., II, No. 54c.
2. DM, 1695, No. 13.
3. Ibid., No. 7.

APODACA
(*González de Apodaca*)

JOSÉ GONZÁLEZ DE APODACA returned to New Mexico in 1693 with his wife, *Isabel Gutiérrez*, and their known children, *Juan Esteban* and *Juan Antonio*. His daughter *María*, by his first wife, was married to Carlos López. Old José was still living in Chama in 1729, when he gave his age as seventy-four.[1]

Juan Esteban de Apodaca married *Francisca Moya* in Santa Fe in 1709.[2] In 1716 he rebought ancestral lands in Santa Fe.[3] According to testimony given in 1728, he had been reared by his aunt, María Gutiérrez, wife of Juan (Cedillo) Rico de Rojas.[4] Juan Esteban died on February 12, 1727, and was survived by his widow.[5] It is not known who his children were, if any.

Juan Antonio de Apodaca of Santa Cruz, brother of Juan Esteban, was bereft of his first wife, *María Durán*, before he was twenty-six, when he married *Francisca Lucero de Godoy* at Albuquerque, on November 8, 1716.[6] He was still residing at Santa Cruz in 1727, but is mentioned as a soldier of Santa Fe the following year.[7] He is very likely the Juan de Apodaca mentioned with his daughter *María* as being related to Ana Bernal of Santa Cruz.[8]

A known son of his was *Felipe de Apodaca*.[9]

* * * * * * * *

FRANCISCO DE APODACA was a brother of José González de Apodaca, and uncle of the two preceding men.[10] He had died, and was buried in Santa Fe, before 1695, when his widow, *Juana Martín de Salazar*, married

Juan Olguín.[11] She was still living at Río Arriba in 1734.[12]

A daughter, *Josefa,* married Juan Márquez at Santa Cruz in 1709.[13] A grown son, not named, was reported killed by the Jémez Indians with his step-father, Captain Juan Olguín, in the uprising of 1696, but an Indian witness declared that the youth had been taken captive instead.[14]

Cristóbal de Apodaca, who had a wife and two children in 1680, returned to Santa Fe in 1693.[15] Both he and his wife, *Regina Peralta,* were dead by 1707, when their son, *Juan Andrés,* married Margarita Martín;[16] this Margarita Martín died in Santa Fe on August 25. 1727.[17]

Cristóbal might have been a brother of José and Francisco.

* * * * * * * *

Other Apodacas who returned with the Reconquest were the sons of any of the above-cited men, or else, like Ventura below, were of unknown parentage, yet all members of the same family group.

Ventura de Apodaca, a soldier of Santa Fe, and born before the 1680 Rebellion in the Salinas country, was twenty-one to twenty-five years old in 1695, when he married *Angela Varela.*[18] He did not know who his parents were.

José de Apodaca and his wife, *Josefa Martín,* were living in Santa Cruz in 1713, when a son, *Diego,* was born to them.[19]

Sebastián de Apodaca, twenty-six years of age and married, was living in Santa Fe in 1716.[20] He is also mentioned as a civil witness in 1744 and 1749.[21] In 1732 he was referred to as a resident of Santa Fe and forty-nine years old.[22]

José Manuel de Apodaca married *Josefa del Castillo* at Jacona, June 21, 1733.[23] She died in Santa Fe, December 21, 1737.[24]

Antonio de Apodaca, husband of *María Antonia Fernández,* died in Santa Fe, March 22, 1727.[25]

Marcos de Apodaca married *Mónica Valverde* on August 19, 1733; he died at the age of forty-four on January 10, 1766.[26]

---

1. **DM**, 1729, No. 1.
2. Ibid., 1709, No. 5.
3. **Sp. Arch.**, I, No. 11.
4. Ibid., No. 747.
5. **Bur-48, Sta. Fe; Sp. Arch.,** I, No. 514.
6. **DM**, 1716, No. 4.
7. Ibid., 1727, No. 1; 1728, No. 5.
8. **AASF**, No. 15.
9. **Twit. Coll.**, fragment.
10. **DM**, 1691, No. 1; **Maese-Montaño** charts.
11. Ibid., 1695, No. 8.
12. **Sp. Arch.,** I, No. 19.
13. **DM**, 1709, Nos. 6, 12.
14. **Crusaders**, p. 251; **Old Santa Fe**, III, pp. 332-373.
15. **DM**, 1696, No. 1.
16. Ibid., 1707, No. 2.
17. **Bur-48, Sta. Fe.**
18. **DM**, 1694, No. 17; 1695, No. 10.
19. **M-33, Sta. Cruz.**
20. **DM**, 1716, No. 9.
21. **Sp. Arch.,** I, Nos. 334, 648.
22. **Bancroft, NMO,** 1732.
23. **Bur-16, Nambé, M-Sec.**
24. **Bur-48, Sta. Fe.**
25. Ibid.
26. **M-50 and Bur-48, Sta. Fe.**

ARAGÓN

IGNACIO DE ARAGÓN, thirty-two, the son of Juan and a native of Mexico City, came with his family in 1693. He was of medium height, with an aquiline face, high forehead, and small, deep-set eyes. His wife was *Sebastiana Ortiz,* twenty-seven, also born in Mexico City, the daughter of Nicolás (Ortiz). She had an aquiline face, large eyes and forehead, and a small, sharp nose.

They had two girls at this time: *María,* eight years old and born in Mexico City, having an aquiline face, a high forehead, black eyes, and a small nose; and *Antonia,* three years old, born in Mexico City, and of exactly the same description as her sister.[1]

Another list has Aragón with his wife and three children.[2] Perhaps one child died on the way, or else an elder boy had joined the Vargas troops. The wife was in all probability a sister of Nicolás Ortiz, another settler who brought his family in the same group, for both are natives of Mexico City and children of Nicolas Ortiz.

Ignacio still resided in Santa Fe in 1705, but by 1710 had settled in Bernalillo, when he gave his age as fifty.[3] His wife had died prior to 1708, when he married *Luisa Baca* on April 25.[4] She was, apparently, a daughter of Cristóbal Baca of Bernalillo, and the reason for his moving there after his marriage.

There a son, *Salvador Manuel,* was born on April 21, 1710.[5] A *Nicolás de Aragón* of Bernalillo, thirty years old in 1731,[6] was in all likelihood a son by his first (Ortiz) wife. *Maria,* the eight-year-old child of 1693, became the wife of Antonio Baca, June 12, 1706.[7]

The numerous Aragón clan of the Río Abajo area stems from this family of Ignacio de Aragón.

* * * * * * * *

Felix de Aragón was a different individual who enlisted at Guadalupe del Paso and then deserted with two others in 1693, being apprehended soon after.[8] In 1694 he married *Juana de Torres* in Santa Fe, when he stated that he was twenty-one, a soldier of the garrison, and born in Guadiana (now Durango), the son of Diego de Aragón and Josefa Martínez, both still living in Durango. The bride was the orphan daughter of Blas Navarro and Matiana Gómez of La Villa de León in New Spain.[9] It is not known if he had any descendants. Perhaps the Rio Arriba Aragons are descended from him.

1. **Sp. Arch.,** II, No. 54a.
2. **BNM,** leg. 4, Pt. 1, pp. 830-834.
3. **DM,** 1705, No. 12; 1710, No. 9.
4. **B-13, Bern.,** M. sec.
5. **Ibid.**
6. **DM,** 1731, unnumbered.
7. **B-13, Bern.** GENEALOGY: **María de Aragón,** Gregoria Baca, Mariano Roybal, Juan Manuel Roybal, Desiderio Roybal, Romualdo Roybal, Nicolasa Roybal, Fr. A. Chávez.
8. **Crusaders,** p. 148.
9. **DM,** 1694, No. 22.

ARCE

ANTONIO DE ARCE was an *Alférez,* stationed at the Presidio of San Buenaventura, Chihuahua, in 1792.[1] By 1797 he had been transferred to Santa Fe.[2] He married *Soledad Holguín,* by whom he had at least two children: *María Luisa Veronica,* May 29, 1800; and *Jesús María Hermenegildo,* August 25, 1804.[3] Apparently he had been married before, and brought two young sons, *Juan* and *José María.*

Martina de Arce was married to Francisco de Paula Ortiz, son of Antonio Ortiz and Teresa Miera. According to the baptism of their child, Martina was the daughter of a Francisco Quirós and *Soledad Holguín.*[4] Hence, she was a step-daughter of Antonio de Arce.

Juan de Arce, a native of Chihuahua, was twenty-six when he enlisted as a soldier in 1831. He was the son of José Antonio de Arce and María de Hinojos.[5]

José María de Arce, a second lieutenant of the Santa Fe garrison, is mentioned in dispatches in the beginning of the Nineteenth Century.[6] He was very likely a son of Antonio by his first wife in Chihuahua, and a brother of Juan. At any rate, he does not appear in any marriage or baptismal register; hence he can be presumed to have left no descendants. An adopted son of his, *José María,* enlisted as a soldier in 1831 when fourteen years old.[7]

1. **Sp. Arch.,** II, No. 1201.
2. **Ibid.,** Nos. 1409, 1470, 1638.
3. **B-Castrense.**
4. **B-65, Sta. Fe,** Dec. 4, 1810.
5. **HSNM,** Mil. Papers.
6. **Sp. Arch.,** II; **NMHR,** Vol. IV, pp. 146-164.
7. **HSNM,** loc. cit.

ARCHIBEQUE

JEAN L'ARCHEVEQUE was born in Bayonne, France, in 1671, the son of Claude L'Archeveque and Marie d'Armagnac. In 1684, at the age of thirteen, he joined the La Salle Expedition in search of the Mississippi Delta. The ships landed by mistake on the Texas coast, and there, in 1687, some of the men plotted to assassinate their leader. On March 18, they got young l'Archeveque to lead La Salle into an ambush where he was shot. Soon after the youth went to live with the Indians with a certain Grolet and others.[1]

Two years later, in 1689, he and Grolet learned of Spanish troops near their Texas Indian camp, and contacted the commander by means of a message on a curiously decorated parchment, surrendering themselves sometime after. Both men were naked, save for an antelope skin, with faces, chests, and arms painted Indian style. They were taken to Coahuila, and thence to Mexico City. In the same year they were sent to Spain.[2] A Spanish source says that they were first taken to San Luis Potosí, then to Mexico City, and condemned to work in the mines.[3]

By 1693 the two Frenchmen were back in New Spain, being numbered with a third Frenchman, "Pedro Munier," among the settlers recruited by Velasco at Zacatecas. They were described as "streaked on the face,"[4] which shows that their Indian markings were more than mere paint.

In 1697, l'Archeveque married *Antonia Gutiérrez,* presumably at Santa Clara, where Bandelier found the matrimonial papers. Antonia had joined the colonists with her husband, Tomás de Hita (Itta), when she was described as a native of Mexico City, sixteen years old, and the daughter of Mateo, tall, broad-faced, with brown hair and eyes.[5] Her husband, however, was murdered at Zacatecas before the colony started north.[6] She had two children by l'Archeveque, *Miguel* and *María,* and died prior to 1719. This daughter became the wife of Francisco José de Casados.

In this year Jean married *Manuela Roybal* at San Ildefonso on June 23.[7] They had no children. Both were sponsors for a Mestas child on April 1, 1720,[8] and shortly after he left on the Villasur Expedition to the eastern plains where he was killed by Frenchmen and, ironically, by a loyal survivor of the La Salle Expedition thirty-three years before.[9] The estate of *Juan de Archibeque,* this was the Spanish form his name had taken, was probated in 1721, and from it we have a clear picture of his family, including two other sons, not legitimate, *Agustín* and *Juan.*[10]

———

Miguel de Archibeque, legitimate son of Captain Juan de Archibeque and Antonia Gutiérrez, married *María Roybal,* daughter of Captain Ignacio Roybal and Francisca Gómez, at San Ildefonso, November 2, 1716. Both parties gave their age as twenty.[11] Three years later his widowed father married María's elder sister. Miguel was absent from Santa Fe, trading in Sonora for his merchant father, when the latter was killed.[12]

Miguel made his own last will in 1727, dying on August 15 of that year.[13] In it he declared that he had been married to María Roybal for eleven years, and that they had only two children: a boy, *Lorenzo Claudio,* who died in infancy, and a girl, *Juliana.*[14]

Juliana married Juan Gabaldón on July 26, 1735, with her aunt María de Archibeque and husband Francisco Casados as witnesses.[15]

* * * * * * * *

Agustín de Archibeque is referred to in Juan de Archibeque's estate as a "bastard by an unwed woman" during his father's first marriage.[16] He married a *Manuela Trujillo.* Their son, *Antonio Domingo,* married Casilda Gonzalez on April 6, 1750,[17] by whom he had two sons: Juan Domingo, January 5, 1751, and Agustín Antonio, June 20, 1753.[18]

Sample page of *Diligencia Matrimonial*, 1716, No. 17, dated October 24. Formal Application of Miguel de Archibeque to marry María de Roybal.

Juan de Archibeque is referred to in his father's estate as a "natural son" by a young servant girl while his father was a widower. Both Agustín and Juan were reared in the Archibeque home. The servant-girl remembered in the estate was a *María de Mascareñas,* an orphan reared in the family.[19] She was undoubtedly Juan's mother, for after his father's death he went under the name of Mascareñas.

The name "Archibeque" was passed down through Agustín, since Miguel, the only legitimate son, had only one male child that died in infancy, while Juan chose his mother's family name.

---

1. **Gilded Man,** pp. 289-302. Bandelier took the data from a **DM** he found in the Mission of Santa Clara in 1888, but which is not in the Archives of the Archdiocese. It related to the Frenchman's first marriage, in 1697, to Antonia Gutiérrez. Cf. Twitchell in **Sp. Arch.,** I, p. 14.
2. **B-H,** II, Appendix, pp. 470-4; message reproduced facing p. 257.
3. **AGN,** Hist., 43, pt. 23, f. 4.
4. **BNM,** leg. 4, pt. 1, pp. 830-4.
5. Ibid., pp. 790-5; **Sp. Arch.,** II, No. 54c.
6. **Sp. Arch.,** I, p. 14.
7. **DM,** 1719, No. 9, incomplete.
8. **M-24, S. Ild.**
9. Cf. **El Palacio,** Vol. 54, No. 8, pp. 179-82; in this my maiden research opus, I futilely try to exonerate him of La Salle's murder.
10. **Sp. Arch.,** I, No. 13.
11. **DM,** 1716, No. 17; **M-24, S. Ild.**
12. **Sp. Arch.,** loc. cit.
13. **Bur-48, Sta. Fe.**
14. **Sp. Arch.,** I, No. 17.
15. **M-50, Sta. Fe.** GENEALOGY: **Juliana Archibeque,** Miguel Gabaldón, Juana María Gabaldón, Toribio Luna, María Encarnación Luna, Eugenio Chávez, Fabián Chávez, Fr. A. Chávez.
16. **Sp. Arch.,** I, No. 13.
17. **M-50, Sta. Fe.**
18. **B, Sta. Fe.**
19. **Sp. Arch.,** loc. cit.

ARCHULETA

There were only two male adults of this name among the refugees of 1680, and both were called **Juan de Archuleta**. One was married, twenty to twenty-six years of age, and without children as yet; the other, nineteen or twenty, was single and accompanied by his mother and many relatives.[1] Their descriptions are alike, hence they were most likely first cousins, one the son of Juan de Archuleta II and the other of Melchor de Archuleta. But which son belonged to which father is impossible to say.

One *Juan de Archuleta* apparently remained at Guadalupe del Paso, for a person of this name was living there after the Reconquest.[2] But he could belong to the family of Francisco de Archuleta and Bernardina Baca, the first Spanish couple married in the new Mission of Guadalupe del Paso in 1678. (See *Archuleta,* preceding century.)

A Juan de Archuleta, with his wife and children, was killed by Indians at the Janos Misssion of Santa Gertrudis del Ojito in 1682.[3] Was he a New Mexico refugee of 1680, or a member of the Guadalupe del Paso family? Anyway, only one of these is mentioned among the Archuletas in New Mexico at the time of the Reconquest and the years immediately following.

* * * * * * * *

JUAN DE ARCHULETA, the one who came back to New Mexico in 1693, was very likely the son of Juan de Archuleta II and María Luján, since generally the natives who returned were the eldest sons of eldest sons, to reclaim their patrimony. His wife was *Isabel González*. In 1690, while still at Guadalupe del Paso, both were witnesses for a marriage.[4] Juan had a sister, Antonia de Archuleta, who married Miguel de Herrera.[5]

In the Indian uprising of June 4, 1696, happening to be at Santa Cruz, Juan went to rescue Fray Blas Navarro at San Juan Pueblo, and brought him to Santa Cruz; then he went on the same mission to San Ildefonso, but found the Padres already murdered and the church sacked.[6] He also carried out orders for Vargas regarding the protection of the people at Bernalillo and the loyal Indians of Zia Pueblo.[7] In 1698 and 1699 he received grants of land in Santa Fe and another at San Juan from Governor Cubero, and in 1697 and 1698 he purchased lands at Santa Cruz. He was dead by 1703, when his widow acquired more Santa Cruz property. In 1713 she bought more land at San Juan next to the grant made to her husband, and again in 1715 she acquired a ranch in Santa Cruz; she also transferred title to some of her own land in Taos.[8] On her Santa Cruz property were the ruins, visible in 1712, of the old church and government houses.[9] Isabel González died at the age of seventy on October 16, 1729.[10] The Padre wrote her late husband's name as "Luis," probably a slip of the pen, as there was no one of that name old enough to be her husband. A *Luis de Archuleta,* who married María Martín in Santa Cruz on November 14, 1718,[11] was very likely one of her sons.

Known children were: *Diego, Andrés,* and *María,* wife of Miguel Martín Serrano.

Diego de Archuleta, young son of Isabel González and her late husband, was accused in 1719 of beating somebody's wife.[12] He died at the age of forty on January 20, 1731, when he is mentioned as married,[13] but the names of his wife, or of any children they had, are not known.

Andrés de Archuleta, son of Juan de Archuleta and Isabel González, was an *Alférez* already in 1715.[14] He was a member of the Conquistadora Confraternity.[15] He and his wife, *Josefa Martín,* were sponsors for a child in 1713.[16] In 1711 he was thirty-one years of age, and therefore an older brother of Diego.[17]

His known children were *Juan, Hilario,* and *Asencio,* the latter's name harking back to the first Archuleta of 1598. Evidently, there was also a natural son, *Juan Antonio.*

* * * * * * * *

Salvador de Archuleta, who did not know who his parents were, married a *Juana García,* of similar status in 1698 in Santa Fe.[18] He was thirty in 1701.[19] Between 1710 and 1715 he hauled vigas and other freight for the building of the parish church in Santa Fe and the restoration of San Miguel Chapel.[20]

A daughter of his, *Josefa,* married Tomás Segura in 1730.[21]

Other Archuletas of the early part of the century were:

Agustín de Archuleta, married to *María de la Cruz,* whose daughter *Ana María* married Diego Velásquez in 1705.[22]

Bernardo Pascual de Archuleta and *Antonia Martín* were married on January 3, 1733.[23]

Nicolás de Archuleta, twenty-five, husband of *Antonia de Herrera,* died on July 25, 1749.[24] Perhaps he was a son of Asencio Archuleta and Lugarda Quintana.

* * * * * * * *

Juan de Archuleta, son of Andrés de Archuleta and Josefa Martín, both deceased, and widower of *María Valerio,* married *María Candelaria Córdoba* in 1766.[25] His children are not known.

Hilario de Archuleta, son of Andrés de Archuleta and Josefa Martín according to his last will, left a numerous progeny in Cuyamungué. His first wife was *Bernarda Trujillo,* by whom he had five children, *Antonio Diciano, Andrés Santiago* (died in infancy), *Bernardo Antonio* (died in infancy), *Julio Antonio* (died in manhood), and *Felix Victor,* living and married.[26] Hilario and Bernarda were married on May 3, 1734.[27] *Julio Antonio,* born on April 22, 1741, married Margarita Lucero on November 1, 1766.[28] *Felix Victor* married Barbara Gómez del Castillo on May 13, 1774, and died on December 3, 1789.[29]

Hilario's second wife was *Antonia de Ontiveros,* who bore him five more children: *María Isabel, Juliana de la Encarnación, Bernardo Antonio, Juan* and *Bernardo Crisóstomo.* Part of his estate also went to the children of his deceased son, Julio.[30] A son by this wife, *Cristóbal Marcelino,* not mentioned in the will, was born on June 6, 1755, and inherited land next to that of his sister Juliana.[31]

María Antonia de Ontiveros had a first husband, Juan Andrés González, by whom she had children. She died in 1806.[32]

Asencio de Archuleta is mentioned in Hilario's will as his brother. He married *Lugarda Quintana,* by whom he had three children, *Cristóbal, Juana Josefa,* and *Nicolás Marcos,* according to a will she made in 1749 when Asencio was absent from New Mexico.[33] Lugarda died on June 10, 1749, at the age of 50.[34]

* * * * * * * *

Juan Antonio Archuleta claimed Juan Andrés de Archuleta as his father by his mother who was known as *"La Mala Hora."* He had been known as *"Juan Antonio de los Rios"* until her death, when he changed his name.[35] In 1742 he was asking for land in Santa Fe.[36] He died on June 17, 1755, at the age of seventy; his late wife had been a *María Carvajal*.[37]

1. **Revolt**, I, pp. 157, 149; II, pp. 71, 116, 61, 106-7, 129.
2. **DM**, 1699, No. 6; 1714, No. 9.
3. **AGN, Prov. Int.**, t. 35, p. 53.
4. **DM**, 1690, No. 1.
5. **Sp. Arch.**, II, No. 298.
6. **Old Santa Fe**, Vol. III, pp. 332-73.
7. **Ibid.**
8. **Sp. Arch.**, I, Nos. 293, 311, 1136.
9. **Doc. Hist. de Mex.**, p. 193.
10. **Bur-33, Sta. Cruz.**
11. **DM**, 1718, No. 8, incomplete.
12. **Sp. Arch.**, II, No. 298.
13. **Bur-32, Sta. Cruz.**
14. **Sp. Arch.**, I, No. 311.
15. **OLC**, p. 72.
16. **B-33, Sta. Cruz**, April 20.
17. **DM**, 1711, No. 2.
18. **Ibid.**, 1698, No. 9.
19. **Ibid.**, 1701, No. 1.
20. **OLC**, pp. 39, 72-3; Kubler, p. 19.
21. **DM**, 1730, unnumbered.
22. **Ibid.**, 1705, No. 11.
23. **M-50, Sta. Fe.**
24. **Bur-32, Sta. Cruz.**
25. **DM**, 1766, unnumbered.
26. **Twit. Coll.** No. 180.
27. **Bur-16, Nambé**, M. Sec.
28. **Ibid.; M-25, S. Ild.** GENEALOGY: Julio Archuleta, María Ignacia Archuleta, María Josefa Quintana, Desiderio Roybal, Romualdo Roybal, Nicolasa Roybal, Fr. A. Chávez.
29. **M-25, S. Ild.; B-33, Sta. Cruz,** Bur. Sec.
30. **Twit. Coll., loc. cit.**
31. **Bur-16, Nambé, B. Sec., Twit. Coll.**, Nos. 29, 40.
32. **Twit. Coll.**, No. 40.
33. **Sp. Arch.**, I, No. 968.
34. **Bur-32, Sta. Cruz.**
35. **Sp. Arch.**, II, No. 354. See family of Diego Velásquez and Juana del Rio.
36. **Ibid.**, I, No. 24.
37. **Bur-22, Pojoaque.**

ARELLANO

CRISTÓBAL DE ARELLANO deposed that he was born in La Villa de Aguas Calientes in New Spain, and was twenty-one years of age in 1695.[1] In 1698, then twenty-four and stationed as a soldier in Santa Fe, he married *Graciana Romero*, eighteen, the daughter of Captain Francisco Romero and Francisca Ramírez de Salazar. His own parents were Nicolás de Arellano and Leonor Ruiz de Esparza, both deceased.[2] In 1702, Cristóbal was stationed out in the Acoma-Zuñi country,[3] and two years later he was a Captain and Alcalde Mayor of Santa Cruz.[4] He was Alcalde Mayor of the Pueblos of Santa Ana, Zia, and Jemez, in 1716.[5]

1. **DM**, 1695, No. 13.
2. **Ibid.**, 1698, No. 2.
3. **Bancroft, NMO.**, 1702.
4. **Sp. Arch.**, I, No. 1339.
5. **NMHR**, Vol. VI, No. 2, pp. 160-66.

ARGÜELLO

JUAN DE ARGÜELLO, a soldier of Santa Fe in 1716, was a native of Zacatecas and twenty-five years of age.[1] He was the son of Joaquin de Argüello and Juana Gutiérrez. In 1715 he married *Juana Gregoria Brito*.[2] He might have come with the colonists of 1695 with his parents, or at least his mother; a sister of his seems to be a Juana de Dios Gutiérrez, natural daughter of Juana Gutiérrez of Zacatecas, who married a Cristóbal Montoya in 1716.[3]

A daughter, *Juana Gertrudis*, married Luis Francisco Leyva, on July 23, 1731.[4] His son, in all likelihood, was *Juan José*, whose family with that of old Juan was among the first settlers of Trampas in 1751.[5] Juan himself, "more than eighty years old," was still living at Trampas in 1776, the person chiefly instrumental in gathering contributions for the church there.⁶

Juan José de Argüello was a pioneer resident of San José de Gracia (Trampas), Picuris jurisdiction, living there in 1753 with his wife, *Joaquina Rodríguez,* daughter of Melchor Rodríguez and Clara de Villaroel.⁷ He and Joaquina were married on October 13, 1746.⁸

Their son, *Juan Salvador,* was born on February 20, 1749.⁹

Esteban Rodríguez Argüello, living in Isleta in 1757 with his wife, *Juana de Mata Espinosa,* had a daughter, *Teresa,* who married a Juan Luis Romero of Santa Cruz.¹⁰ He was, to all appearances, a younger brother or a son of Melchor Rodríguez who had been reared by Joaquina and her Argüello husband.

---

1. DM, 1716, No. 2.
2. Ibid., 1715, No. 9.
3. Ibid., 1716, No. 16.
4. M-50, Sta. Fe.
5. Sp. Arch., I, No. 975.
6. BNM, Leg. 10, No. 43, **Picuris.**
7. Sp. Arch., I, No. 1049.
8. M-50, Sta. Fe.
9. B, Sta. Fe.
10. M-11, Isleta, July 17.

ARIAS de QUIROS

DIEGO ARIAS DE QUIRÓS, a native of Asiera in Asturias, was one of the soldiers recruited in Spain by Vargas. His parents were Juan de Quirós Prieto and Ynez de Arias. He was the *Real Alférez* in Santa Fe when he married *María (Ana) Montoya,* widow of Nicolás Márquez, on July 20, 1694.¹ He was active in the campaigns of his day and received important grants from the Governor.² In 1695 a process regarding bigamy was instituted against him, but the charge seems to have been proven false.³

Ana Maria Montoya died in 1712, and Diego then married *María Gómez Robledo* at San Ildefonso on July 28, 1714.⁴ It is not known if he had any children by either wife; he is referred to indirectly regarding descendants of his first wife and her own first husband.⁵ In 1746 his widow sold his Santa Fe estate, the block east of the Governors' Palace, to Bernardino de Sena.⁶ It was recalled in 1776 that Diego had founded the Confraternity of the Poor Souls in Santa Fe, leaving the interest of the proceeds of his house to its suffrages.⁷ He had also been a member of the Confraternities of La Conquistadora and San Miguel.⁸

A *Francisco Arias Quirós* was living at Santa Cruz in 1735,⁹ but nothing more is known about him.

* * * * * * * *

The earliest *Arias* people (without *Quirós*), appearing in Santa Fe in the middle of the century, were as follows:¹⁰

Toribio Arias and *Beatriz* ———— had a child, *María Luisa,* August 31, 1749.

José Miguel Arias and *Ana María Luz Sáenz* had four sons: *Manuel de la Merced,* September 30, 1749; *Francisco de la Concepción,* November 28, 1762; *Bernardo de la Concepción,* December 9, 1765; and *Diego de la Encarnación,* April 4, 1767.

---

1. DM, 1695, No. 32.
2. Sp. Arch., I, Nos. 294, etc.
3. AGN, Mex., Inq., t. 595, f. 293v.
4. DM, 1714, No. 7.
5. See Nicolás Márquez.
6. Sp. Arch., I, No. 846.
7. BNM, leg. 10, No. 43, **Miscellaneous.**
8. OLC, p. 69; Kubler, p. 19.
9. Sp. Arch., I, No. 20.
10. All in B, Sta. Fe. Perhaps their ancestor was **Nicolás Arias** of Zacatecas. See wife of **Vásquez de la Cruz, Juan Antonio.**

ARMENDARIS

PEDRO DE ARMENDARIS, a Lieutenant of the Company of Janos, was stationed at the Santa Fe garrison when he married *Josefa Ortiz* in 1809.[1] His transfer orders had been issued at Chihuahua, August 3, 1807, and he reached Santa Fe in May, 1808.[2] Josefa had two children while in Santa Fe: *José Manuel*, December 19, 1819, and *Enrique Francisco de Paula*, July 15, 1822.[3] In this year their father was an Alcalde of Santa Fe.[4]

In 1820 Armendaris had been given a grant of land at Valverde, south of Socorro, which he was forced to abandon because of Indian depredations. He then left New Mexico for Chihuahua.[5]

1. **DM**, 1809, unnumbered.
2. **Sp. Arch.**, II, Nos. 2069, 2103.
3. **B., Sta. Fe.**
4. **Sp. Arch.**, I, No. 58.
5. Twitchell commentary in **Sp. Arch.**, I, p. 335.

ARMENTA

ANTONIO DE ARMENTA was a thirty-six-year-old resident of Santa Fe in 1732.[1] His wife was *Juana Beitia*, sister of *Manuela Beitia*. Their daughter, *Manuela*, married a José Antonio Naranjo on September 4, 1749.[2] They also had a son, *Antonio*. The father was one of the survivors of the ill-fated Villasur Expedition.[3] He died at the age of eighty-five on December 10, 1779.[4]

Luis de Armenta died in Santa Fe on January 3, 1756, at the age of sixty.[5] Being a contemporary of Antonio, he was very likely his brother, but their origin is not known. Luis had owned a tract of Santa Fe land on the road to Pecos since 1732; it was claimed by his son, *Nicolás*, in 1759, who was married and had children at the time.[6]

Nicolás de Armenta and his wife, *Eulalia Sánchez*, had a child, *Ana Teresa*, born January 30, 1750.[7]

Cristóbal de Armenta, also a contemporary of the preceding men, might have been a third brother. He married *Francisca Tenorio* on April 13, 1735.[8] They had a daughter, *Gertrudis Ynez*, January 30, 1750.[9]

Antonio de Armenta II was a Santa Fe soldier in 1765.[10] The son of Antonio de Armenta and Juana Beitia, he enlisted when he was twenty-five, in 1756.[11] He acquired a grant in the Jémez country in 1789,[12] and by 1805 was *Alcalde* of the Jémez area.[13]

1. Bancroft, NMO, 1732.
2. **Sp. Arch.**, II, No. 437; **M-50, Sta. Fe.**
3. **DM**, 1720, No. 4.
4. **Bur-48, Sta. Fe.**
5. **Ibid.**
6. **Sp. Arch.**, I, No. 357.
7. **B, Sta. Fe.**
8. **M-50, Sta. Fe.**
9. **B, Sta. Fe.**
10. **Sp. Arch.**, II, No. 579.
11. **HSNM, Mil. Papers.**
12. **Sp. Arch.**, I, No. 52.
13. **Ibid.**, II, Nos. 1914, 2503.

ARMIJO
(Durán de Armijo)

JOSÉ DE ARMIJO and his wife, *Catalina Durán,* were natives of Zacatecas who arrived with the Zacatecas colonists in May, 1695, with their four sons: *Antonio, Marcos, José,* and *Vicente,* all of whom used the double surname of "Durán de Armijo."

José was dead by 1706, when Catalina Durán was referred to as his widow and fifty years old.[1]

Antonio Durán de Armijo, eighteen, born in Zacatecas, the son of José de Armijo and Catalina Durán, was residing in Santa Fe when he married *María Quirós* on October 17, 1695. She was also eighteen, the daughter of José de Quirós and María de la Cruz, natives of Sombrerete.[2] A literate man and versed in medicine, Antonio appears in many documents either as a notary or a physician, being known as *"el Maestro Barbero."* In this capacity he is met either in Santa Fe or in Santa Cruz. As early as 1695 he gave his office as that of a "barber."[3] By 1731 he was a sergeant of the militia, then fifty-eight years old.[4] He belonged to the Conquistadora Confraternity.[5] His burial entry refers to him as the "Master Barber" when he died on June 22, 1753, more than eighty years old.[6]

His known children were *Antonio II* and *Juan,* and a girl *Ynez,* who is mentioned in a document of 1724.[6a]

Marcos Durán de Armijo, twenty years of age, a native of Zacatecas and the son of José de Armijo and Catalina Durán, married *Tomasa de la Parra,* also twenty, on February 3, 1698.[7] Both are mentioned together in 1716 and in 1731 when acting as sponsors.[8]

There are several early marriages and baptisms of Armijos in Santa Fe, not identifiable, who could have belonged to this particular family.

José Durán de Armijo, brother of the above men, married *María Manuela Velásquez* in 1710.[9] He gave his age as thirty in 1718, and Santa Fe as his place of residence.[10] In 1710 he worked on the restoration of San Miguel Chapel in Santa Fe.[11]

He had a son, *Antonio,*[12] and a daughter, *Rosa.* It seems as though the mother died young, for José had given the girl to the childless wife of Antonio de Ulibarrí. José was still living in 1732 when Rosa was suing Ulibarrí for her adopted mother's inheritance.[13]

Vicente Durán de Armijo, the fourth son of José de Armijo, deceased, and Catalina Durán, was already married to *María de Apodaca* in 1706 and living in Santa Fe. At this time he gave his age as twenty-two, saying that his family was from Zacatecas.[14] His wife was the daughter of Juana de Apodaca, who had been captured as a girl by the Indians and used by them during her twelve years' captivity; her little girl María was baptized with Governor Vargas as her godfather when they were liberated in 1692.

Vicente's house was outside Santa Fe by the "Alto del Río" in 1718.[15] He worked on the restoration of San Miguel Chapel in 1710.[16] In 1739 he was given royal possession of land near Nambé which he later sold to the Ortiz family.[17] But he died as a resident of Santa Fe in 1743, when he made his last will. In it he mentions his wife, to whom he had been married for forty years, and their three sons, all named alike: *Manuel el Primero, Manuel el Segundo,* and *Salvador Manuel el Tercero.* The "second" Manuel and his mother were named as executors.[17]

* * * * * * * *

Antonio Durán de Armijo II, son of the first Antonio and María Quirós, was living at Taos when he was killed by wild Indians in 1748.[18] In 1742 he had married *Barbara Montoya* of Chimayó, the widow of Diego Romero of Taos. They were married only three years when Barbara felt that she must make her last will. Their only living child, *Barbara Gertrudis*, was born shortly before her mother's death. She was three years old when Antonio was killed in 1748. She became the wife of Manuel Vigil, pioneer resident of Ranchos de Taos.[19]

Juan Durán de Armijo, also a son of the first Antonio, was taken to Chihuahua as a boy by his grandfather, José Quirós. He must have been brought back after his mother applied for his return in 1715.[20]

Juan's young son, *José Antonio*, served as a blacksmith's apprentice to his uncle Antonio of Taos, for whose forge he was petitioning in 1748.[21] The names of Juan's wife and his other children, if any, are not known.

* * * * * * * *

José Antonio de Armijo, who married *María Antonia Fernández* on April 6, 1729,[22] was most probably the son of José D. de Armijo and a brother of Rosa, or Rosalía, who was a witness of his marriage. This Rosalía married a Juan de Leyba in January of the following year.[23]

* * * * * * * *

Salvador Manuel de Armijo, apparently the "First," son of Vicente D. de Armijo, caused a great commotion in Santa Fe and Albuquerque when he wooed and married *Francisca Baca* against the will of her father, Antonio Baca, and the sentiment of higher "society" in the Kingdom. They were married at Albuquerque on August 10, 1733.[24] A more solemn ceremony took place in 1735, and the fact was officially noted in Santa Fe.[25]

Alfonso, a boy who died on September 22, 1737, the son of a Manuel Armijo, might have been their child.[26] By 1748 they were living in Nambé, where *Lucía Antonia* was born on July 9. They were still there in 1754 when they acted as sponsors for a child on January 28.[27] What other children they had is not known.

Salvador Manuel de Armijo, "the Second," son of Vicente D. de Armijo, and who had been executor for his father's will in 1743, drew up his own will in 1764, in which he refers to himself as the "second" son of that name. From it we have a comprehensive picture of his entire family.[28] He had married *Francisca Alfonsa Lucero de Godoy* in Santa Fe on October 19, 1734.[29] According to the will, he had been a poor soldier who by hard work had acquired plenty of worldly goods in Albuquerque, where his military duties had taken him. There he reared twelve children, whom he named, in part: *Vicente, Ana (Antonia), Manuela, María de la Luz, Santiago, Pablo, José, Isabel,* and "four other little ones, all legitimate," which he left in the care of his brother, Manuel de Armijo.[30] His wife, Francisca Alfonsa, and their eldest son, Vicente, were named executors of the estate when he died on December 4, 1764.[31]

Data on the above-named children are as follows, showing how a great part of the family intermarried with that of Diego Antonio Durán y Chávez. *Vicente* married Bárbara D. y Chávez in September, 1769;[32] *Antonia* married Antonio D. y Chávez, November 24, 1774;[33] *Manuela* married Pablo D. y Chávez, January 12, 1776;[34] *María de la Luz* became the wife of Francisco Antonio Candelaria, August 28, 1767;[35] *Pablo* married Josefa D. y Chávez in 1775, this girl a daughter of Ignacio D. y Chávez;[36] *José* married María Guadalupe D. y Chávez on June 16, 1774;[37] *Isabel* married Bernardino D. y Chávez, April 20, 1769;[38] *Santiago* might be the one who married a Rosalía Chávez on February 2, 1782.[39] Nothing is known for certain of the four minor children placed in their uncle's care.

Salvador Manuel de Armijo ["the Third," by elimination], when ten years old, in 1720, was placed by his father Vicente as an apprentice under a José García of Guadalupe del Paso, to learn the tailor's trade; after four years he would get a master's certificate.[40] Did he remain there and marry, thus being the "Manuel Durán de Armijo," husband of Ignacia Molinar, who died there on May 21, 1747?[41] Or did he return to Santa Fe, and is he the following person?

[137]

Salvador Manuel de la Cruz Armijo married *Rosalía Romero* on October 29, 1735.[42] Some of their children were born in Santa Fe: *Salvador Manuel*, April 7, 1749; *María Gerónima*, May 21, 1754; *María Valvanera*, January 14, 1756; and *María Josefa*, April 6, 1752.[43] *María Antonia* was baptized at Nambé on April 17, 1758.[44]

Their father died in Santa Fe in November, 1761, at the age of forty-five.[45] If this age is correct, he could not have been the boy sent to Guadalupe del Paso. Their mother, mentioned in connection with her brother, Joaquín Romero, in 1762, died on August 6, 1789, when it was remarked that they had been from Sandía.[46] The question remains: was this Salvador Manuel one of the three sons of Vicente, or a first cousin of theirs?

A serious problem with the Armijo family, both in the north and in the Río Abajo, in this century as well as the following, is that scores of contemporary individuals were named "Manuel" or "Salvador," or both names combined and interchangeable.

1. AGN, Mex., Inq., t. 735, f. 297.
2. DM, 1695, No. 12.
3. Ibid., No. 22.
4. Bancroft, NMO, 1731.
5. OLC, pp. 70-72.
6. Bur-48, Sta. Fe.
6a. Sp. Arch., II, No. 334.
7. DM, 1698, No. 12.
8. Sp. Arch., I, No. 731; B-2, Albuq., Mar. 27.
9. DM, 1710, No. 14.
10. Ibid., 1718, No. 1.
11. Kubler, pp. 17, 20.
12. Sp. Arch., I, No. 979.
13. Ibid., No. 236.
14. AGN, loc. cit.
15. Sp. Arch., II, No. 291.
16. Kubler, p. 20.
17. Sp. Arch., II, No. 26.
18. Ibid., I, No. 240.
19. Ibid., II, Nos. 48, 240; BNM, leg. 10, No. 43, Taos.
20. Ibid., II, No. 239d.
21. Ibid., I, No. 240.
22. M-50, Sta. Fe.
23. Ibid.
24. Crespo, pp. 302-343; entire story related by me in New Mexico Quarterly, Vol. XX, No. 4, pp. 471-480.
25. M-50, Sta. Fe.
26. Bur-48, Sta. Fe.
27. Bur-16, Nambé, B. Sec.
28. Sp. Arch., I, No. 246.
29. M-50, Sta. Fe.
30. Sp. Arch., loc. cit.
31. Bur-2, Albuq.
32. DM, 1769, in Albuq., no number.
33. M-3, Albuq.
34. Ibid.; also DM, 1776, in Albuq., no number.
35. M-3, Albuq.
36. DM, 1775, in Albuq., no number.
37. Ibid., 1774, in Albuq., no number; M-3, Albuq. GENEALOGY: José Durán de Armijo, María Isabel Armijo, María Rita Torres, José Chávez, Eugenio Chávez, Fabián Chávez, Fr. A. Chávez.
38. M-3, Albuq.
39. M-4, Albuq.
40. Sp. Arch., II, No. 312.
41. Bur., Guad. del Paso.
42. M-29, Sta. Cruz.
43. B-62, Sta. Fe.
44. B-16, Nambé.
45. Bur-48, Sta. Fe.
46. Sp. Arch., II, No. 552; Bur-49, Sta. Fe.

ARTEAGA

MANUEL DE ARTEAGA, a native of Mexico City, married *Isabel López* of Santa Cruz on March 29, 1761. His parents were Luis de Arteaga and María Manuela Pérez, both deceased.[1] He was *Mayordomo* of the Conquistadora Confraternity in 1774.[2] In the census of 1790 he stated that he was fifty-three years old, a native of Mexico City, and a resident of Isleta, and had a son twenty-three years old.[3] This son, *Gregorio*, enlisted as a soldier in 1792.[4]

On October 5, 1797, as a resident of Belén and native of Mexico City, and widower of Isabel "Gabaldón," he married Ursula Durán y Chávez of Los Padillas.[5] He was *Alcalde Mayor* of the district when he and Ursula acted as sponsors in 1802,[6] having held such posts in the Río Abajo since 1785.[7]

1. M-29, Sta. Cruz.
2. OLC, p. 15.
3. Sp. Arch., II, No. 1092b.
4. HSNM, Mil. Papers.
5. M-49, Isleta; DM, 1797, no number.
6. B-54, Tomé, Feb. 7.
7. Sp. Arch., 1, Nos. 122, 204, 371, 462; II, Nos. 1815, 1829.

ARRATIA

Felipe de Arratia is the only male of this name mentioned after the Reconquest. He was living in Santa Fe in 1703, but owned property between Santa Cruz and Chimayó.[1] His wife was *Juana Martín*.[2] He was living at Santa Cruz in 1712,[3] but seems to have left no descendants.

1. **Sp. Arch.**, II, No. 89.
2. Ibid., I, No. 270; II, No. 137b.
3. Ibid., I, No. 161.

ATENCIO

JOSÉ DE ATIENZA DE ALCALÁ Y ESCOBAR was a native of Villa Berguera in the Archbishopric of Toledo, and boasted at a son's wedding that he was a member of the Third Order of Saint Dominic.[1] He and his wife, *Gertrudis Sevillano de Mancilla* came with the Velasco colonists of 1693, with two adult sons, *Juan* and *José*, and two minor ones, *Manuel*, fifteen, and *Joaquín*, thirteen.[2] In 1698, old José signed his full name again during another marriage deposition, again mentioned his Dominican affiliation, and gave his age as forty-nine.[3] He gave his age as sixty-four in 1713.[4] In 1716 he was granted permission to return to New Spain,[5] and it seems as though the family did leave, except José II and his family, and Joaquín, who seems to have died before that time.

Juan de Atienza Sevillano, son of old José and Gertrudis Mancilla Sevillano, was born in Puebla. He was thirty years old and a weaver by trade when he proposed to María Luisa Godines in 1696; the young lady, however, changed her mind after the wedding depositions were made. Juan had been married to *Juana de Carranza*, who died on the trip to New Mexico at the Real de Sacualpa on June 20, 1693.[6]

Juan is listed with his parents and brothers in the Velasco roll as a widower with two sons: *Cayetano*, five, and *Ignacio*, one year old.[7] In 1710 he stated that he was forty years old and had lost his wife at Sacualpa.[8] He was official "Protector of the Indians" in 1715, asking for justice for the Pueblos as land grants were being made to the colonists.[9]

José de Atienza Sevillano II, brother of Juan, was described in 1693 as a native of Mexico City at the Arch of San Agustín, seventeen years old, of medium height, fair, with an aquiline face and a mole on the left cheek. His wife was *Estefánia Trujillo*, also seventeen, the daughter of Nicolás [Moreno Trujillo]; she was born in Mexico City at the Calle Real, and had a round face, large eyes, and a small nose. They had no children, as yet, but brought along two of her small brothers, José Damián and José Joaquín Trujillo, whose parents came in the same colony.[10]

José, called "El Mozo," and known also by his father's long name, was thirty-three in 1713; his wife gave her age as thirty-six.[11] In 1724 he sued a Santa Cruz man for wounding him and his young son, *Gregorio*.[12] Other sons were *Lázaro*, *José*, *Cayetano*,[13] and most likely *Antonio*, who married a María Romero of Taos in 1737.[14]

Lázaro de Atienza married *Gertrudis Martín*, widow of Bernardo Madrid, on January 20, 1727,[15] and both were living at Ojo Caliente of Río Arriba in 1735.[16] He made his will in 1767 as Lázaro Atencio, leaving his wife but no children.[17]

José de Atienza III married a María Manuela Chávez at Santa Cruz on October 17, 1734. He died in 1752, when his brothers and widow are mentioned, but no children.[18]

Nothing more is heard of the third of the four original brothers, **Manuel de Atienza**.

Joaquín de Atienza, fourth and youngest son of old José de Atienza, gave his age as twenty-five in 1710, stating that he was born in Mexico City.[19] He married a *María Ansures*, who was dead by 1737, when their daughter, *Gabriela*, married Marcial Martín.[20]

1. DM, 1696, No. 14.
2. BNM, leg. 4, Pt. 1, pp. 790-795.
3. DM, 1698, No. 11.
4. Sp. Arch., II, No. 196.
5. Ibid., Nos. 262, 263.
6. DM, 1696, No. 14.
7. BNM, loc. cit.
8. DM, 1710, No. 4.
9. Sp. Arch., I, No. 7.
10. BNM, loc. cit.; Sp. Arch., II, No. 54c.
11. Sp. Arch., II, No. 196.
12. Ibid., No. 330.
13. Ibid., No. 522.
14. M-27, S. Juan; Sp. Arch. I, No. 760.
15. M-29, Sta. Cruz.
16. Sp. Arch., I, No. 20.
17. Ibid., No. 49.
18. M-29, Sta. Cruz; Sp. Arch., II, No. 522.
19. DM, 1710, No. 12.
20. M-27, S. Juan, August 28.

ÁVILA

Pedro de Ávila, known as "El Piojo," lived in Santa Cruz with his wife in 1708, having resided in Santa Fe in 1703.[1] It could be that he was the Pedro de Aguilera described among the colonists of 1693; anyway, neither name appears in the next generation.

1. Sp. Arch., II, Nos. 137b, 930.

AVILES

Ignacio de Aviles, a thirty-year-old widower, native of the Villa de Sinaloa and son of Andrés de Aviles and María de Vergara, asked to marry *María Varela* of Santa Fe, fifteen-year-old daughter of Francisco Varela and Antonia de Carvajal.[1] It is not known if the wedding took place, nor is the name seen afterwards.

1. DM, 1698, No. 4, incomplete.

AYALA

Miguel de Ayala, single, was one of the original settlers of Santa Cruz in 1696.[1] He was perhaps closely related to, if not the son of, *Angela González*, widow of *Francisco de Ayala*, a colonist who did not reach New Mexico, having been shot at the Villa of Jerez in New Spain. Angela then married Melchor de Herrera in 1696.[2] Miguel might have changed his name to Herrera.

1. Sp. Arch., I, No. 817.
2. DM, 1696, No. 11.

BACA

IGNACIO BACA (see preceding century) died some years prior to the Reconquest. His widow, *Juana de Anaya Almazán,* returned to New Mexico with her family, to be massacred in the Indian uprising of 1696, as also two sons, *Alonso* and *Andrés,* and two daughters, *Leonor,* wife of Pedro Sánchez, and *Rosa,* not yet married. Of three surviving girls, *María* was the wife of Tomás Gutiérrez Carrera, *Gerónima* later married Francisco Rodríguez Calero, and *Margarita* became the wife of Diego Lucero de Godoy.[1]

* * * * * * * *

Juana Baca, niece of Ignacio Baca and orphan daughter of JOSÉ BACA, murdered at Guadalupe del Paso, returned in 1693 with her mother, *Josefa Pacheco,* and later married Nicolás Ortiz II.[2]

* * * * * * * *

MANUEL BACA, surviving brother of Ignacio and José, returned to Santa Fe in 1693 with his wife, *María de Salazar,* and a growing family. Soon after, he established himself at Bernalillo on lands that had belonged to his father, Cristóbal aca.[3] There in 1699 he gave his age as forty,[4] and there also a post-Reconquest daughter was born in 1702.[5] In 1716 he gathered forty Queres Indians for the Moqui Campaign and also led the Albuquerque contingent.[6] The Indians of the three Queres Pueblos of Cochití, Santo Domingo, and San Felipe complained more than once of mistreatment by him and his sons; for this cause he was deprived of the *Alcaldía* of Cochití in 1718 and sentenced to go on the next two forays against infidel Indians.[7] Both he and his wife were dead by 1727.[8]

His sons were: *Antonio, Juan Antonio, Diego Manuel,* and *Cristóbal.*

His daughters were: *María Magdalena,* who married José Vásquez de Lara in 1694; *Juana* and *Josefa,* who, though unmarried, have prominent descendants; and a second *María Magdalena,* born on June 5, 1702,[9] who married Diego Antonio Montoya, and then a Juan Márquez in 1735, by whom she was murdered in 1740.[10]

———

Antonio Baca married *María de Aragón* at Bernalillo on June 12, 1706,[11] but later moved up to Santa Fe. Not only was Antonio accused of mistreating the Indians with his father, but his wife also.[12] She died on September 1, 1751, and he followed ten years later, on December 4, 1761, being then "more than eighty years old."[13] Antonio had made his will in 1755, in which he gave the names of his parents and his wife, and those of his son and seven daughters with their respective husbands:[14]

Ana (*Antonia*) *María,* deceased, wife of Antonio Montoya; *María Francisca,* wife of Manuel de Armijo;[15] *Juana,* married to Francisco Montoya; *Gregoria,* wife of Mateo Roybal;[16] *Ynez,* wife of another Antonio Montoya; *Rosa,* married to Antonio Ortega; and *María,* deceased. The only son, *Pablo,* was married to Lorenza Juana de Ribera.[17]

Three of the girls had been born in Bernalillo before the parents moved to Santa Fe: *María,* July 19, 1707, *María Antonia,* December 2, 1710; and *María Francisca,* August 17, 1712.[18] Their brother, *Pablo* (*Antonio*), married Lorenza, daughter of Felipe de Ribera and María Estela Palomino, on May 27, 1743.[19]

———

Juan Antonio Baca, the second son, married *María Gallegos* at Bernalillo on August 2, 1716,[20] by whom he had one daughter, *Teodora.*[21] He next married *Petronila García Jurado,* by whom he had two children: *Juan Francisco* and *Rafaela.*[22] This Rafaela became the wife of Diego de Torres,[23] and then of Baltasar Baca.

———

Diego Manuel Baca, the third son, lived with his wife, *María de la Vega y Coca,* at La Cañada de Guicú (La Ciénega). He made his will in 1727 in which he named his deceased parents, his wife, and his three children:

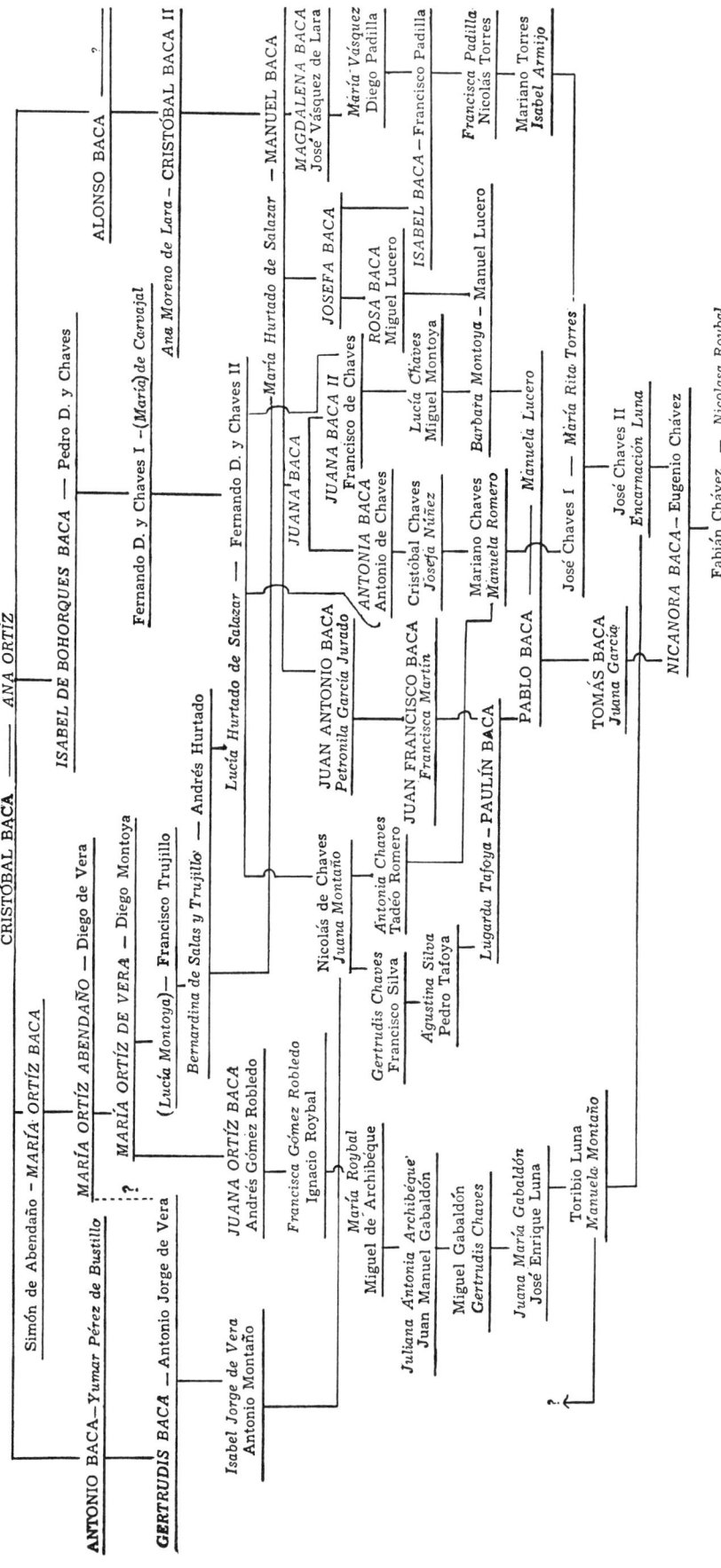

BACA CHART ONE—This diagram, and the one following, present a visual picture of how one single family like the Bacas descended and transcended in the production of a Chávez-Roybal combination, so much so that two separate charts had to be made. Note how the preponderance of Rio Abajo people pushes the names to the right side of the page, while the Santa Fe-Rio Arriba ancestors in the chart following pull the names in the opposite direction.

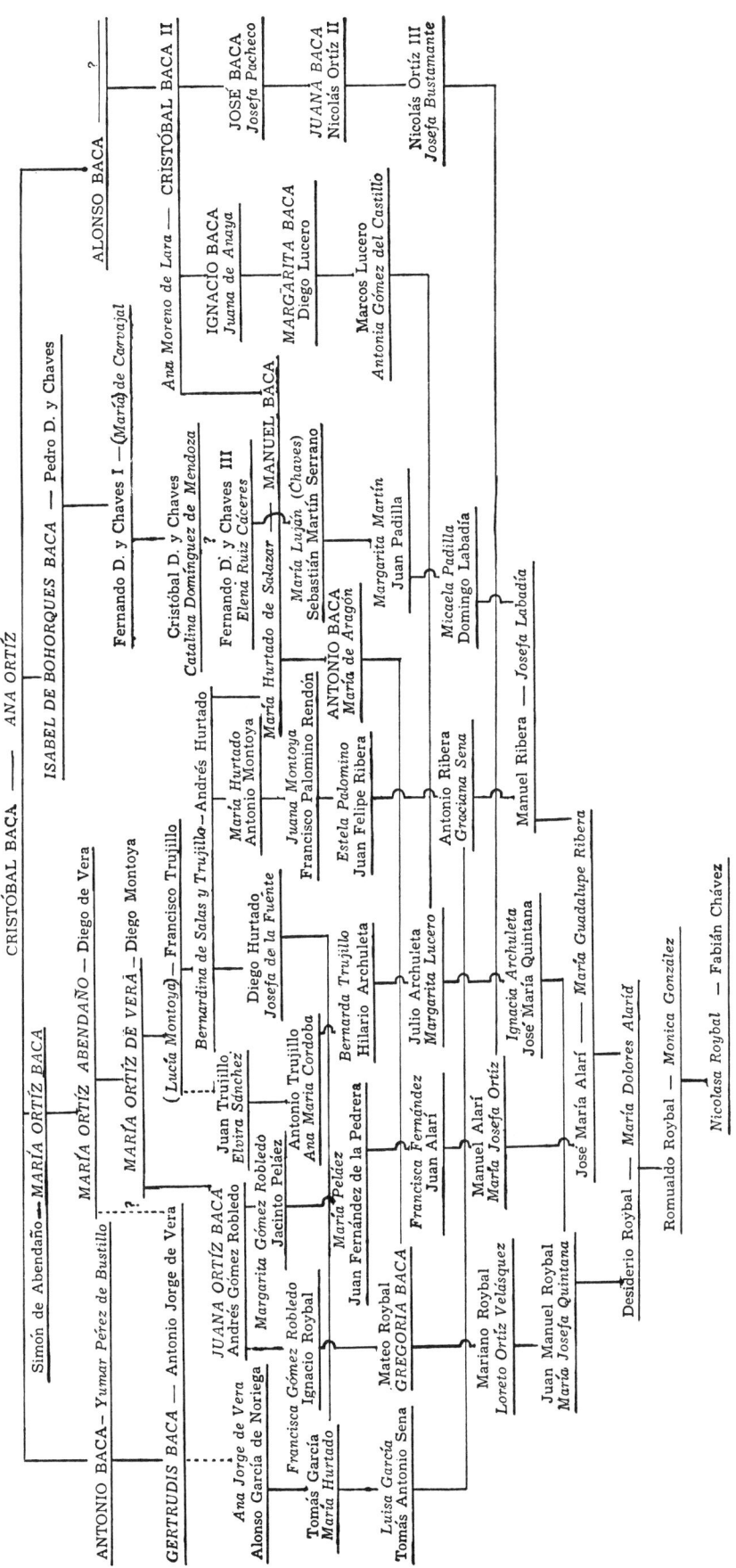

BACA CHART TWO—The first generations are the same in both diagrams. Then different children start divergent lines; but in some cases the same line contributes to both parents of this Chávez-Roybal combination. This saturation by the Bacas is a phenomenon that applies to practically every old New Mexico family. Certain ones tended to form separate groups or clans, due to social and regional influences, but the Baca influence cemented them all.

Manuel, Nicolás, and *Juan Esteban.*²⁴ He died on March 29, 1727.²⁵

Manuel married Leonarda Fernández, then Margarita Tafoya in 1750, and finally Juana Silva in 1768.²⁶ *Nicolás* married Teodora Fernández de la Pedrera in 1747.²⁷ *Juan Esteban* married Teodora Terrus.²⁸

Cristóbal Baca, the fourth son, had been married to *Apolonia de la Vega y Coca,* who died at the age of thirty-three on March 7, 1734.²⁹ He then married *Manuela Márquez* at San Juan on November 9 of the same year.³⁰

In his last will, drawn up before he died in 1739,³¹ after declaring his parents and two successive wives, Cristóbal outlined his fourteen children. By Apolonia Coca: *Juana* (dead), *Juana María, Antonio* (dead), *Marina de Jesús, Rosa, Nicolasa, Diego* (dead), *José Francisco, Cristóbal Silvestre, Juan Antonio,* and *Antonia Rosaura* (dead). By Manuela Márquez: *Juan Tomás* (dead), *Agustina,* and *María Francisca.*³²

Juana Baca, daughter of Manuel Baca and María de Salazar, and sister of the preceding four men, had two daughters, *Juana, "la Moza,"* who married Francisco Durán y Chávez,³³ and *Antonia,* who became the second wife of his brother, Antonio Durán y Chávez.³⁴ Relationships of mother and daughters are deduced from Chávez family charts.³⁵

Josefa Baca, sister of the above Juana, made her last will in 1746, leaving her Pajarito property to her six natural children, all Bacas: *Antonio, José, Domingo, Manuel, Rosa,* and *Isabel.*³⁶

The marriages and families of her four sons are treated below. As for the girls, *Rosa* married Miguel Lucero,³⁷ and *Isabel* married Francisco Padilla.³⁸

* * * * * * * *

Antonio Baca, eldest son of Josefa Baca, married *Mónica de Chávez* in Albuquerque, June 16, 1726.³⁹ They had the following children. First of all, *Juan Antonio* and *Bárbara Antonia,* who together establish the relationship; then *Pedro Antonio,* born September 25, 1733; *Josefa Apolonia,* March 29, 1736; *Diego Antonio,* June 3, 1738; *Juan Domingo,* November 3, 1741; *José Antonio,* February 23, 1744; and *María Ignacia,* April 23, 1746.⁴⁰

The daughters married as follows: *Bárbara Antonia* married José Pablo Rael of Santa Fe, and then Juan Bautista Durán.⁴¹ *Josefa Apolonia* became the wife of Clemente Gutiérrez, and *María Ignacia* married Francisco Trebol Navarro.

Of the sons, *Juan Antonio,* brother of Bárbara Antonia and uncle of her son Nicolás Rael de Aguilar,⁴² married María Romero. *Diego Antonio* married Juana Sáenz Garvisu, October 17, 1759,⁴³ by whom he had at least eight children up to 1786; he was a *Mayordomo* of La Conquistadora with Francisco Trebol Navarro in 1773.⁴⁴ *Juan Domingo* married Loreta Garvisu in 1765, and then Gertrudis Ortiz in 1782,⁴⁵ having five children by the first wife and eleven by the second.

José Baca, second son of Josefa Baca, and his wife Josefa Gallegos had one son and four daughters when he made his will in 1766: *José Antonio, Bárbara Antonia, Ana María,* wife of Juan José Chávez, *María Isidora,* and *María Rosa.* One of the other three girls [Isidora?] was married to a Vicente Armijo.⁴⁶

Diego Domingo Baca, who married *Juana Chávez* in 1736,⁴⁷ was most likely the third son of Josefa Baca; however, no definite connection can be made. They had twelve children. Of these, *Juana María* married José Chávez in 1758, *María Febronia* married José Manuel Silva in 1757,⁴⁸ and *José Antonio* married Victoria Ana Chávez in 1784.⁴⁹ In this same year their father took a second wife, *Antonia Montoya.*⁵⁰

Manuel Baca, who married Feliciana Chávez, daughter of Antonio D. y Chávez and Antonia Baca, February 22, 1746,⁵¹ seems to be the fourth son of Josefa Baca. He lived for several years at Laguna Pueblo as *Alcalde Mayor.* His children were: *Antonio Vicente,* born March 28, 1748, who married María Gertrudis Sánchez on May 31, 1775;⁵² *Narcisa,* born November 29, 1750, and *José Antonio,* April 18, 1753;⁵³ *María de la Luz,* who married Pedro Sánchez, October 25, 1761;⁵⁴ *María Josefa,* married to José Silva, October, 1787;⁵⁵ and *Antonia,* who became the wife of Antonio Sedillo, July 1, 1770.⁵⁶

* * * * * * * *

Ignacio Baca, whose parents cannot be ascertained, married *Margarita Romero* on October 29, 1737, with Diego Domingo Baca and Juana Chávez as witnesses.⁵⁷ They had at least four children, of whom *Diego Antonio* married María Antonia Sánchez in 1776, and *María Catalina* married Pedro Antonio Durán y Chávez in 1772.⁵⁸ He might have been a son of Juana Baca "La Vieja," daughter of Manuel Baca and Maria de Salazar.

* * * * * * * *

Bernabé Baca is often mentioned after the Reconquest, but it is not known who his parents were. He is possibly the Bernabé *Jorge,* not heard of again as such, to whom Vargas granted the Pueblo Viejo at La Ciénega in 1701.⁵⁹ On May 28, 1718, he married *Margarita Baca (Mata).*⁶⁰ He was *Alcalde Mayor* of Ácoma and Laguna in the third decade of the century, and very unpopular with the Indians and missionaries.⁶¹

His son, *Baltasar Baca,* was as unpopular as his father when *Alcalde Mayor* of the Lagunas.⁶² Baltasar married *Manuela Rael de Aguilar,* July 17, 1738.⁶³ In her will, drawn up at Isleta in 1758, she named their six children: *José Francisco, Laureano, Miguel Hermenegildo, María Isabel, Juana Leocadia,* and *Juana Vita.*⁶⁴ After her death, Baltasar married his second cousin, *Rafaela Baca,* the widow of Diego de Torres,⁶⁵ by whom he had a daughter, *Micaela,* who married Antonio José Ortiz II.⁶⁶

The Baca family is by far the most widespread in New Mexico. While other old names, even the more common ones, are restricted to certain family or regional groupings, the Bacas permeate all of New Mexico's people and history.

---

1. GENEALOGY: **Margarita Baca,** Marcos Lucero, Margarita Lucero, María Ignacia Archuleta, María Josefa Quintana, Desiderio Roybal, Romualdo Roybal, Nicolasa Roybal, Fr. A. Chávez.
2. GENEALOGY: **Juana Baca,** Nicolás Ortiz III, Josefa Ortiz Bustamante, José María Alarí, María Dolores Alaríd, Romualdo Roybal, Nicolasa Roybal, Fr. A. Chávez.
3. Sp. Arch., I, No. 1136.
4. DM, 1699, No. 2.
5. B-13, Bern., June 5.
6. Sp. Arch., II, No. 250.
7. Ibid., No. 287.
8. Ibid., No. 83.
9. B-13, Bern.
10. M-50, Sta. Fe; Sp. Arch., II, No. 437.
11. B-13, Bern., M. Sec.
12. Sp. Arch., II, Nos. 287, 431.
13. Bur-48, Sta. Fe.
14. Sp. Arch., I, No. 101.
15. Their love story, New Mexico Quarterly, Vol. XX, No. 4, pp. 471-480.
16. GENEALOGY: **Gregoria Baca,** Mariano Roybal, Juan Manuel Roybal, Desiderio Roybal, Romualdo Roybal, Nicolasa Roybal, Fr. A. Chávez.
17. Sp. Arch., loc. cit.
18. B-13, Bern.; the first Bapt. Book of Santa Fe, where the other children appeared, has long been lost.
19. M-50, Sta. Fe.
20. DM, 1716, No. 10.
21. Sp. Arch., I, No. 236b.
22. Ibid., II, Nos. 344, 592a. GENEALOGY: **Juan Francisco Baca,** Paulín Baca, Pablo Baca, Tomás Baca, Nicanora Baca, Fabián Chávez, Fr. A. Chávez.
23. Ibid., No. 592a. GENEALOGY: **Rafaela Baca** (stepmother of Nicolás Torres), Mariano Torres, María Rita Torres, José Chávez, Eugenio Chávez, Fabián Chávez, Fr. A. Chávez.
24. Sp. Arch., I, No. 83; also, Nos. 109, 539.
25. Bur-48, Sta. Fe.
26. M-50, Sta. Fe; DM, 1768, in Albuq., no number.
27. M-50, Sta. Fe; Sp. Arch., I, Nos. 109, 991.
28. Bapt. of children from 1759 to 1777, B, Sta. Fe.
29. Bur-48, Sta. Fe.
30. M-27, S. Juan.
31. Bur-48, Sta. Fe, May 4.
32. Sp. Arch., I, No. 88. This **María Francisca** seems to be the one who married her cousin Juan Francisco Baca (Note 22), but this is by no means certain.
33. GENEALOGY: **Juana Baca** II, Lucía Durán y Chávez, Bárbara Montoya, Manuela Lucero, Tomás Baca, Nicanora Baca, Fabián Chávez, Fr. A. Chávez.
34. GENEALOGY: **Antonia Baca,** Cristóbal D. y Chávez, Mariano Chávez, José Chávez II, Eugenio Chávez, Fabián Chávez, Fr. A. Chávez.
35. Also, Sp. Arch., II, No. 437; DM, 1766, in Albuq., **José Baca-Juana Chávez;** ibid., 1735, **Juan Antonio Baca-Bárbara Montoya.**
36. Sp. Arch., I, No. 94; relationship deduced from ibid., Nos. 177, 1231; Crespo, **Armijo-Baca** case; Chávez and Baca charts.
37. GENEALOGY: **Rosa Baca,** Manuel Lucero, María Manuela Lucero, Tomás Baca, Nicanora Baca, Fabián Chávez, Fr. A. Chávez.
38. GENEALOGY: **Isabel Baca,** Francisca Padilla, Mariano Torres, María Rita Torres, José Chávez, Eugenio Chávez, Fabián Chávez, Fr. A. Chávez.
39. M-3, Albuq.
40. These six in B-57, Isleta.
41. Sp. Arch., I, No. 1231; AGN, Tierras, No. 426, ff. 7-11.
42. Bancroft, NMO, 1764; cf. Cabeza de Baca Family.
43. M-50, Sta. Fe.
44. OLC, p. 11.
45. M-50, Sta. Fe.
46. Sp. Arch., I, No. 1231.
47. M-4, Albuq., April 22; M-11, Isleta, May 5.
48. M-11, Isleta.
49. DM, 1764, in Albuq., no number.
50. M-3, Albuq.
51. Ibid.
52. B-57, Isleta; M-3, Albuq.
53. B-57, Isleta.
54. DM, 1761, in Albuq., no number; M-11, Laguna.
55. DM, 1787, in Albuq., no number.
56. M-12, Laguna.
57. M-3, Albuq.
58. DM, 1776, 1772, in Albuq., no number. These were the grandparents of Col. Manuel A. Chaves.
59. Sp. Arch., I, No. 732.
60. DM, 1718, No. 9.
61. Sp. Arch., II, No. 394; Bancroft, NMO, 1732.
62. BNM, leg. 10, No. 12; Bur-13, Laguna, Jan. to Mar. 1772; Sp. Arch., I, No. 523.
63. M-50, Sta. Fe.
64. Sp. Arch., I, No. 774.
65. DM, 1762, in Albuq., no number; M-11, Isleta.
66. Sp. Arch., II, No. 592a; Twit. Coll., No. 27 and another not numbered.

BACHICHA
(See *Durán*)

BARRERAS

Domingo de la Barrera, thirty years old in 1694, appears twice as a witness in that year. He was a native of Zamora, Spain.[1] But in several civil documents, 1694-1703, acting as an official, his name is spelled "*Barreda.*" It is not known if he married and remained in New Mexico.

* * * * * * * *

Ignacio Barrera and *Micaela López* had two children, *Salvador Vicente*, January 20, 1727, and *Antonio*, November 15, 1733.[2]

Manuel Barreda and *María García* had a son, *Juan Miguel*, October 5, 1749; its sponsors were Marcial Barreda and Rosa Trujillo.[3]

Marcial Barreda, or *Barrera*, married Rosa Trujillo on November 14, 1743.[4] They had a son, *Antonio Albino*, April 8, 1752.[5]

Manuel Barrera and *María Torres* had two children: *Juan Miguel*, May 18, 1748, and *Bernardino*, June 1, 1752.[6]

The origin of these people is not known, nor their relationship with each other.

1. DM, 1694, Nos. 1, 23.
2. B-2, Albuq.
3. B-57, Isleta.
4. M-11, Isleta.
5. B-57, Isleta.
6. Ibid.

BARRIOS

Juan Antonio Barrios was one of Vargas' soldiers in 1696.[1] He and his wife, *María González*, were living in Santa Fe in 1705. They had a step-daughter, Antonia Rodríguez.[2]

1. Old Santa Fe, Vol. III, pp. 332-373.
2. DM, 1705, No. 11; AGN, Mex., Inq., t. 735, f. 277.

BAZÁN

IGNACIO RICARDO BAZÁN (or *Basán*), a widower, and his brother, *Juan Bazán*, single, made a contract with the government in Mexico City, September 3, 1805, to come to New Mexico to teach the craft of weaving. They had to live in Santa Fe and remain six years. With Ignacio Ricardo came his two sons, *Francisco Xavier*, fourteen, and *José Manuel*, ten.[1] Nothing more is heard of Juan, the brother, or of the two sons.

In February, 1807, Ignacio Ricardo Bazán asked to marry *Juana Apolonia Gutiérrez* of Pajarito, stating that he was born in Puebla, the son of José Bazán y Lobato and Josefa Álvarez y Trujillo, both deceased. His first wife was Ignacia Ledesma of Mexico City.[2] He made a claim for some pay as "Master Weaver" in 1809.[3]

He and his Gutiérrez wife had a son, *Joaquín Alejandro*, and a daughter, *Ignacia Juana Paula*, born June 27, 1809,[4] who married a Manuel Baca.[5]

Joaquín Alejandro Bazán married *María Luz*

Ortiz, daughter of Antonio Ortiz and Juana Gertrudis Baca.[6] He died at the age of sixty-four in Los Pueblitos, on August 28, 1871, some time after his wife's death.[7]

1. Sp. Arch., II, No. 1885.
2. DM, 1807, no number.
3. Sp. Arch., II, No. 2198.
4. B, Sta. Fe.
5. B-72, Tomé; bapt. of their child, Juan Francisco, Jan. 1, 1833.
6. B-12, Belén; bapt. of their child, Higinia, Jan. 12, 1844.
7. Bur-7, Belén.

BEJARANO

Tomás de Bejarano (*Vejarano*) gave his age as thirty-five in 1693.[1] He was fifty-six when he married a *Teresa Madrid*, or *Perea*, native of New Mexico of unknown parentage, in 1714. His parents were Nicolás de Bejarano and Josefa Ruiz de Ontiveros.[2] Tomás died at the age of seventy on May 15, 1731.[3]

1. DM, 1693, No. 7.
2. Ibid., 1714, No. 1.
3. Bur-48, Sta. Fe.

BENAVIDES

JUAN ESTEBAN DE BENAVIDES, origin unknown, seems to have been a soldier, or colonist, of 1695 who came with his wife, *María de Diezma*. Or, as it happened in other instances, he died on the way from Zacatecas, and his wife reached New Mexico with her children. In 1695 she and Cristóbal de Arellano were sponsors for a wedding in Santa Fe.[1]

Nicolás de Benavides, son of Juan Esteban de Benavides and María de Diezma, both deceased, married *Juana de Ojeda* on March 4, 1702. He was a soldier stationed in Santa Fe.[2] He was dead by 1739, but his widow was still living in 1762.[3]

Their children were: *Juan, Domingo,* and *Tomasa*, wife of Francisco Valdés; also, perhaps, a contemporary, *José Antonio Benavides*.

* * * * * * * *

Francisco Xavier Benavides, apparently a brother of Nicolás, had a son, *Juan Antonio*, by his wife, *Jacinta Romero*.[4] A soldier in Santa Fe of the same name declared in 1711 that his wife had been *Josefa de Tamaris*, deceased, and that they had one son, also dead.[5] If the same man, the Tamaris woman might have been the first wife.

* * * * * * * *

Juan de Benavides, son of Nicolás, is mentioned in connection with his sister Tomasa and brother Domingo in 1739, 1762, and 1770. He was a soldier.[6] But nothing is known about his family.

Domingo de Benavides, son of Nicolás, made his last will in Santa Fe in 1770. His wife was *Francisca Luján*, to whom he was married for twenty-seven years. They had ten children, eight of whom are named: *Juan Domingo, María de Loreto, José Manuel Victorino, Juan Antonio, Luisa, Rosalía, José Manuel "el Vitorino,"* and *Bartolo*. It seems as though Bartolo was the only one living at this time.[7]

José Antonio de Benavides was very likely a brother of Juan, Domingo, and Tomasa. He was dead by 1766 when his widow, *Josefa Montoya*, made her last will. They had six children: *Manuela*, wife of Antonio Lucero, *Xaviera*, wife of Nicolás García, *Gertrudis, Ignacia, Antonio Gervasio,* and *Juan Domin-*

go. Ignacia had been adopted by Manuela Urioste,⁸ who was the wife of Alejandro Valdés and daughter-in-law of Tomasa de Benavides.

1. DM, 1695, No. 2.
2. Ibid., 1702, No. 1.
3. Sp. Arch., I, Nos. 90, 104.
4. B-2, Albuq., Dec. 8, 1710.
5. Sp. Arch., I, No. 300.
6. Ibid., Nos. 90, 104, 115.
7. Ibid., No. 115.
8. Ibid., No. 569.

BERNAL

FRANCISCO BERNAL, sixty years old and a soldier at Guadalupe del Paso in 1691,¹ very likely returned to New Mexico with the Reconquest two years later, as well as the children and grandchildren of Catalina Bernal who escaped the massacre with her in 1680. But no definite connections can be made.

Antonio Bernal was living in Santa Cruz in 1729 when he sold some property in Santa Fe.² He and a Maria Rosa (Romero) de Pedraza had acted as sponsors for a Taos Indian child in 1706.³

* * * * * * * *

José Ramón Bernal, son of Buenaventura Bernal and Feliciana Montoya, was a native of Guadalupe del Paso who enlisted as a soldier in Santa Fe, in 1806. He was twenty-eight years old.⁴ From the names of both parents, it can be seen that he was a New Mexican returning home a century after the Reconquest.

1. DM, 1691, No. 2.
2. Sp. Arch., I, No. 683.
3. B-54, Taos, June 12.
4. HSNM, Mil. Papers.

BETANZOS

ANDRÉS DE BETANZOS (*Bettancos*) was a forty-year-old widower, the son of Don Geronimo and born in Mexico City, who joined the 1693 colonists with two grown sons. He was of medium height, bald, with a round face, large eyes, and a Greek nose. His sons were *Francisco* and *Diego*.¹

In 1694 Andrés deposed that he was forty years old and a native of Mexico City.² He was still living in Santa Fe in 1701. A fragmentary book of Santa Cruz has a "Memoria" by Andrés de Betanzos, Master Carpenter, and his sons Diego, nineteen, and Francisco, sixteen, for some work done.³

Francisco de Betanzos, born in Mexico City at San Francisco, was twenty years old in 1693. He had an aquiline face, a broad forehead, and a thick nose.⁴ In all probability, he is a *"Francisco Afán de Ribera"* who appears later on. (See *Ribera.*)

Diego de Betanzos, also born in Mexico City, was nineteen in 1693, having chestnut hair, a small nose, and a mole on the cheek.⁵ A chanter for the Padres, he was killed with them at San Cristóbal near Santa Cruz in the Indian uprising of 1696.⁶

1. Sp. Arch., II, No. 54c.
2. DM, 1694, No. 6.
3. Sp. Arch., II, Nos. 80, 82; Bur-33, Sta. Cruz, flyleaf.
4. Ibid., No. 54c.
5. Ibid.
6. Old Santa Fe, Vol. III, pp. 332-73

BLEA

CARLOS DÍAS BLEA was twenty-two in 1694, a native of Puebla, and married.[1] His wife was *Pascuala de Herrera,* daughter of a María Rodríguez.[2] They had two children, *Francisco* and *Salvador.*

Francisco Días Blea, son of Carlos Días Blea and Pascuala de Herrera, was twenty-eight years old and living in Santa Fe when he married a widow, *María Gertrudis Muñiz,* in 1722.[3]

Salvador Días Blea, son of Carlos Días Blea and Pascuala de Herrera, the latter deceased, married a widow, *Antonia Anaya Almazán,* in Santa Fe in 1724.[4]

1. DM, 1694, Nos. 23, 24.
2. AASF, No. 16.
3. DM, 1722, No. 1.
4. Ibid., 1724, No. 1.

BORREGO

DIEGO VÁSQUEZ BORREGO was in New Mexico as early as 1733.[1] The following year he bought some land south of Isleta Pueblo.[2] He had a wife in New Spain, and also a son, *Manuel Borrego;* this son married in Mexico City, where he had six children, and later moved up to Chihuahua.[3]

During his first New Mexico sojourn, around 1733 and some years following, old Diego first sired two natural sons, *Francisco* and *Diego,* both of whom lived in Bernalillo and herded their father's flocks from the year 1745 (when he came to New Mexico "a second time") until his death in 1753.[4]

Also during his first stay in New Mexico, Diego had married a New Mexican woman, *Rosa de Tafoya Altamirano,* who bore him two boys, one of whom died. The sole surviving legitimate son was *Juan Diego Borrego.*[5] Old Diego, "married outside the country" (a third time?), died in Santa Fe on May 10, 1753.[6]

Francisco Borrego, natural son, married *Victoria Mora;* they had a daughter, *Ana María,* August 8, 1786.[7]

Diego Borrego, natural son, married *Francisca Gurulé,* by whom he had a son, *Juan Domingo,* July 4, 1763.[8]

(Juan) Diego Borrego, probably reared by his mother's family, the Tafoyas of the Rio Arriba country, married *Vibiana Sandoval,* by whom he had a child, *María de la Luz,* November 7, 1787.[9]

1. B-2, Albuq., Dec. 27.
2. Sp. Arch., I, No. 178.
3. Ibid., No. 103.
4. Ibid.
5. Ibid.
6. Bur-48, Sta. Fe.
7. B-4, Albuq.
8. B-3, Albuq.
9. B-23, Pojoaque.

BRITO

JUAN DE LEÓN BRITO, son of Juan Brito and Antonia Ursula Durán, had married *Sebastiana Madrid* at Guadalupe del Paso in 1692.[1] At Santa Fe, on January 10, 1694, Brito, now a widower, married a *María Granillo,* of unknown parentage.[2] He was a member of the Conquistadora Confraternity; he and a Diego Brito made adobes for the reconstruction of San Miguel Chapel in Santa Fe in 1710.³

Brito and his Granillo wife had at least two children: *María Magdalena,* who married Antonio Olguín in Santa Fe in 1710;⁴ and *Juana Gregoria,* who married Juan de Argüello in 1715.⁵ He was dead by 1732 when his widow, eighty years old, died on July 21 of that year.⁶ Brito's ancestral property was in the Analco section of Santa Fe.⁷

Pedro Brito, a native of New Mexico and the son of Antonio Brito and Magdalena de Dios, was married in Santa Fe to *María Apodaca de la Rosa,* of unknown parentage, in 1706.⁸

José Brito, evidently a member of the family, was still living at San Lorenzo del Paso in 1697.⁹

1. **DM,** 1692, No. 3.
2. **Ibid.,** 1694, No. 12.
3. **OLC,** p. 70; **Kubler,** p. 20.
4. **DM,** 1710, No. 11.
5. **Ibid.,** 1715, No. 9.
6. **Bur-48, Sta. Fe.**
7. **Sp. Arch.,** I, No. 85.
8. **DM,** 1706, No. 2.
9. **Ibid.,** 1697, No. 5.

BUSTAMANTE

DON JUAN DOMINGO DE BUSTAMANTE was Governor of New Mexico for two terms, 1722-1731. He had been Lieutenant General for the Guadalupe del Paso area before being promoted to Santa Fe.¹ He was a nephew as well as son-in-law of another Governor, Don Antonio de Valverde y Cosío.²

Relatives of his, of the same name, followed him to Santa Fe, but their exact relationship is hard to ascertain, except for that of a brother, *Francisco Antonio de Bustamante*³ who, however, is not heard of again.

Don Bernardo de Bustamante y Tagle was Lieutenant Governor under Don Domingo.⁴ He was a native of Spain, and thirty-seven years of age in 1745, when he was still residing in Santa Fe.⁵ He was either a younger brother or a nephew of the Governor, if not a son. His wife was *Doña Feliciana de la Vega y Coca,* who on the occasion of a daughter's wedding gave her full name as *de la Vega Lazo Vique y Coca.*

They had two daughters who married in Santa Fe, *Josefa* and *Rosa.* Josefa became the second wife of Nicolás Ortiz III in 1751,⁶ when she was specifically referred to as an "adopted daughter." Rosa married a son of this Nicolás Ortiz by his first wife, Antonio José Ortiz, in 1754. It is very likely that both girls were daughters of either parent by a former marriage. Bernardo was transferred to the Presidio of Goajoquilla in New Spain, where he and his wife were residing in 1776.⁷

José de Bustamante y Tagle was a resident of Santa Fe as late as 1757. He was a native of Aranda de Duero in Spain, the son of Juan Antonio de Bustamante y Tagle (Advocate in the Royal Councils) and Maria Antonia Bracho Bustamante. He had a brother, Pedro Isidro, residing in Mexico City.⁸ He seems to be the same José Bustamante who married a *María de Chávez,* or *Montoya,* on October 7, 1728,⁹ and then married again. He died on June 17, 1759.¹⁰

In 1762 his widow, *Bartola Hurtado,* made her last will. She declared that they had been married for twenty years, and that she was the natural daughter of Maria Hurtado. Her brothers were Santiago and José Hurtado.¹¹

José and Bartola had five children: *Bernardo, José, María Antonia, Isidro,* and *Juan Antonio,* the last one deceased. The chief executor of the will was Don Bernardo de Bustamente y Tagle.¹² Other records of their children are as follows: *Antonio,* their infant son, died on June 17, 1750,¹³ apparently the *"Antonio Norberto"* born eleven days before, on June 6; *María Antonia Bernarda* was born on August 23, 1752; and *Pedro Isidro* on April 30, 1756.¹⁴ Bernardo, José, and María Antonia appear in a land transfer of 1767.¹⁵

Don José de Bustamante was a secular priest who represented the Bishop of Durango as his Vicar in Santa Fe from 1733 to 1736. With Don Santiago Roybal, he was one of the two New Mexicans ordained by Bishop Crespo at that early period.¹⁶ He was a son, nephew, or brother of Governor Bustamante, and is not heard of again after 1736, probably having rejoined the Governor's family at Guadalupe del Paso or elsewhere in New Spain.

* * * * * * * *

Bernardo Bustamante and *María Lobato* had a child, *María Josefa Rita*, February 22, 1767. Perhaps he is the same man, married a second time, who had three children by *Anastasia Griego*: *María Martina*, February 21, 1799; *Policarpio*, January 29, 1802; and *José María*, December 20, 1803.¹⁷

Pedro Antonio Bustamante and *Ana Antonia de Armijo* had a girl, *Dominga*, August 10, 1763—two years later, a "Pedro Bustamante" (same man?) and Antonia Arias (same woman?) had a son, *Andrés Antonio*, October 23, 1765.¹⁸

José de Bustamante, known also as "Mirabal," lived in the valley of Taos in 1770. He had married *Monica Tomasa Martín*, widow of Francisco Romero. They had no children. He is also very likely the "José Hurtado" mentioned there in 1776.¹⁹

1. **Bancroft, NMO,** 1731; **Sp. Arch.,** I, No. 13.
2. **Sp. Arch.,** I, No. 1031; II, No. 319.
3. **Bancroft, loc. cit.**
4. **Ibid.; Sp. Arch.,** II, Nos. 437, 486.
5. **Bancroft, NMO,** 1745.
6. GENEALOGY: **Josefa Bustamante,** Josefa Ortiz Bustamante, José María Alari, María Dolores Alarid, Romualdo Roybal, Nicolasa Roybal, Fr. A. Chavez.
7. **BNM,** leg. 10, No. 43, **Santa Fe.**
8. **AGN, Mex., Inq.,** t. 932, ff. 1-2.
9. **M-50, Sta. Fe.; Ibid.,** Alire-Coca wedding, May 18.
10. **Bur-48, Sta. Fe.**
11. **Sp. Arch.,** I, No. 409.
12. **Ibid.;** perhaps José and Bernardo were brothers, or at least first cousins.
13. **Bur-48, Sta. Fe.**
14. All three in **B, Sta. Fe.**
15. **Sp. Arch.,** I, No. 364.
16. Crespo, par. 304; **DM,** 1736, No. 1; ministry: **B-24, S. Ild.,** April 21, 1732; **Bur-16,** Nambé, B. Sec., Sept. 6, 1734; **M-50, Sta. Fe,** Oct. 5, 1734. Cf. **El Palacio,** Vol. 55, No. 8, pp. 239-40, 246; **NMHR,** Vol. XXV, No. 4, p. 265.
17. All in **B, Sta. Fe.**
18. **Ibid.**
19. **Sp. Arch.,** I, No. 590; **BNM, loc. cit.,** Taos.

BUSTILLOS

JUAN DE PAZ BUSTILLOS was among the Velasco colonists of 1693. He was twenty-nine, the son of Francisco, and born in Mexico City at the Calle de Vergara; he was of medium height with a high forehead, deep-set eyes, and a sharp nose. His wife was *Manuela Antonia de Alanis,* twenty-eight, the daughter of José and a native of Istlehuaca. She was of medium height and had an aquiline face.¹

They brought two children: *Josefa Antonia,* nine, who was their own daughter, born in Mexico City at the Calle del Parque; she had a round face and flat nose. The other was a nephew, *Antonio,* seven years old, the son of Antonio Xavier and born in Mexico City at the Calle del Reloz. He had a round face, large eyes, and a thick nose.²

Juan gave his age as forty-five and fifty some fifteen years later, when he stated that he was a native of Mexico City, married, and residing in Santa Fe.³

* * * * * * * *

Andrés de la Paz (without Bustillos), thirty years of age, appeared as a witness in 1693.⁴ In 1719, as a resident of Santa Fe, he sold some land in Santa Cruz. His wife was *Fran-*

*cisca Antonia de Guijosa.*⁵ It is not known if he was related to the preceding man. His wife was the widow of Antonio de Moya.

This Bustillos family was entirely different from the important *Pérez de Bustillo* family of the preceding century which was not carried over to the eighteenth. But is the following *Bustos* family one and the same?

1. **Sp. Arch.,** II, No. 54c.
2. **Ibid.**
3. **DM,** 1707, No. 1; 1709, No. 5.
4. **Ibid.,** 1693, No. 4.
5. **Sp. Arch.,** I, No. 742.

BUSTOS

JUAN DE BUSTOS and his wife, not named, were among the 1693 colonists.¹ He owned land in Santa Cruz in 1699.² In 1719, three Bustos individuals, all natives of Mexico City, *Juan, Francisco,* and *Josefa,* acted as sponsors for Taos Indian children.³

1. **BNM,** leg. 4, pt. 1, pp. 830-4.
2. **Sp. Arch.,** I, No. 819.
3. **B-45, Taos,** May 9 and July 30.

CABEZA de BACA

LUIS MARÍA CABEZA DE BACA was born in Santa Fe, the eldest son of **Juan Antonio Baca** and María Romero. According to Twitchell, he and his father had come to New Mexico in the early part of the century, being descendants of Alvar Núñez Cabeza de Vaca.¹ However, his parents belonged to the one and only Baca family descended from Cristóbal Baca of Oñate's colony.

Juan Antonio Baca was the son of Antonio Baca and Monica de Chávez (*q.v.*). He married María Romero on September 17, 1753.² She was a daughter of Antonio Romero and Nicolasa del Castillo, both natives of New Mexico.³ Both were still alive in 1790 with two sons and two daughters still living with them; he gave his age as sixty-eight, and she as sixty-two.⁴ Their known children were as follows, all plain Bacas:

LUIS MARÍA, born October 26, 1754; *Bernardo Antonio,* October 22, 1757; *José María,* April 26, 1761; *José Miguel,* June 16, 1765; *José Manuel,* January 10, 1767; *Juan Esteban,* December 31, 1768; and *Manuel José María,* April 8, 1776.⁵ Three known daughters were: *Antonia de la Trinidad,* who married Juan Bautista González in 1777;⁶ *María Magdalena,* who sued a Gallegos youth, but married Cristóbal Pantaleón Romero the following year;⁷ and *María Josefa,* who in this same year married Manuel Antonio Sánchez.⁸

Of Luis María's brothers, *Bernardo Antonio* married María Josefa Quintana in 1781; *José (María)* married her sister Ignacia Quintana in 1785;¹⁰ *José Miguel* was married to Juana María Baca;¹¹ and *José Manuel* married María Guadalupe Sánchez on the same day his sister María Josefa married his bride's brother.¹² Now to Luis María's change of name and his family.

"Luis María Cabeza de Baca" thus signed his name in 1803, while his brother signed "José Miguel Baca," during an investigation regarding the death at La Cienega of a Salvador Armijo, allegedly killed by Apaches. Armijo was the guardian of their late brother Bernardo's children and property.¹³ Like his ancestors before him, he was accused of mistreating the Indians of Galisteo and Santo Domingo.¹⁴

Luis María was married three times, and Twitchell published a list of the wives and children as relayed to him by the family;¹⁵

documentary information, rather different, is the following:

"**Luis Baca**," soldier of the Santa Fe garrison, married *María Josefa López* on November 24, 1777.[16] Children born to them in Santa Fe were: *María Margarita*, February 22, 1782; *Juan Antonio*, December 1, 1783; *María de la Luz*, October 19, 1785; *Antonio José*, February 18, 1789; *Guadalupe*, February 12, 1791; and *José Ramón*, April 2, 1797.[17] There was an older *Guadalupe*, daughter of Luis María Cabeza de Baca and Josefa López, deceased, who married Santiago Mariano Trujillo, September 20, 1785.[18] Another son, *Miguel*, married Maria Dolores Sánchez in 1820.[19] These two had been born ahead of those listed in Santa Fe. A son, *José*, married Maria Dolores González of Jémez in 1811. Their mother, María Josefa ———, wife of Luis Baca, died on April 2, 1797.[20]

On April 11, 1798, "**Luis María Baca**," widower of Josefa López, married *Ana María Sánchez*, "familiar" of the house of the Corporal, Román Sánchez.[21] A son, *José Mateo Mauricio*, was born on September 25, 1803.[22] Another son was *Luis María* II, who married Maria Isabel López, April 14, 1829;[23] a daughter, *Josefa*, married Juan Luis Montoya of Santa Fe on August 2, 1827.[24]

In 1810, "**Luis María Cabeza de Baca**," widower of Ana María Sánchez, of the Ranchos called "de la Peña Blanca," married *María Encarnacion Lucero*, daughter of Gaspar Antonio Lucero and María Francisca Salas, of Jémez.[25] A son of theirs, *Manuel*, married María Antonia Chavez in 1849.[26]

* * * * * * * *

The marriages and other data about various sons of Luis María Cabeza de Baca are as follows:

Juan Antonio Cabeza de Baca, son of Luis María Cabeza de Baca, was "*Teniente Politico*" of Cochiti and Santo Domingo when the Padre and Indians of these Pueblos made complaints against him and his father in 1808. The family was living at the Rancho de Peña Blanca. His father signed as "Luis María Cabeza de Baca," fifty-three years old and a widower, while he signed simply as "Juan Antonio Vaca," twenty-seven years old and married.[27] He was killed during a Navajo campaign in February, 1835, leaving a widow, *Josefa Gallegos y Chávez*, with thirteen children, eight of them small.[28]

A grown son of Juan Antonio at this time was *Francisco Tomás Baca*.[29] As Francisco Tomás Cabeza de Baca, and the widower of Isabel Ortiz, he married *Manuela Ortiz*, daughter of Juan Rafael Ortiz and María Gertrudis Pino, on June 10, 1844.[30]

———

(Antonio) José Baca, son of Luis María Baca and María Josefa López, deceased, of La Peña Blanca, married *María Dolores González*, daughter of Miguel González and Apolonia Chávez, of Jémez, in 1811.[31]

———

Miguel Cabeza de Baca, son of Luis María Cabeza de Baca and Josefa López, deceased, of La Peña Blanca, married *María Dolores Sánchez*, widow of Antonio Mares, of San Miguel de la Bajada, April 10, 1820.[32]

———

(José) Mateo (Mauricio) Baca, son of Luis Baca and Ana María Sánchez, married *Margarita Sánchez* at the "Plaser de Dolores," in 1845.[33]

———

Luis María Cabeza de Baca, son of Luis María Cabeza de Baca and Ana María Sánchez, married *María Isabel López*, daughter of Jesús López and Manuela Martínez, on April 14, 1829, in the military chapel at Santa Fe.³⁴

Manuel Baca, son of Luis Baca and Encarnacion Lucero, of La Peña Blanca, married *María Antonia Chávez*, daughter of Antonio Chávez and Ynez Apodaca, of Jémez, in 1849.³⁵

1. Biography in **Sp. Arch.**, I, p. 376.
2. **M-50, Sta. Fe.**
3. **Sp. Arch.**, I, No. 776.
4. Ibid., II, No. 1096a.
5. All in **B, Sta. Fe.**
6. **M-50, Sta. Fe**, May 4.
7. **Sp. Arch.**, II, No. 1382; **M-50, Sta. Fe**, July 25, 1798.
8. **M-52, Sta. Fe**, April 11, 1798.
9. **DM**, 1781, in Sta. Cruz, no number.
10. **M-31, Sta. Cruz**, Oct. 24.
11. **Sp. Arch.**, I, No. 465; **M-50, Sta. Fe**, April 6, 1790, wedding of son, Miguel.
12. **M-52, Sta. Fe**, April 11, 1798.
13. **Sp. Arch.**, I, No. 54.
14. Ibid., II, No. 1188.
15. See **Sp. Arch.**, I, p. 47.
16. **M-50, Sta. Fe.**
17. All in **B, Sta. Fe.**
18. **M-35, Sto. Domingo.**
19. Ibid., April 10.
20. **Bur-49, Sta. Fe.**
21. **M-51, Castrense.**
22. **B, Sta. Fe.**
23. **M-51, Castrense.**
24. **M-35, Sto. Domingo.**
25. **DM**, 1810, no number.
26. Ibid., 1849, no number.
27. **Sp. Arch.**, II, No. 2154.
28. **Twit. Coll.**, Nos. 142, 146, 163, 164; facsimile of will, NMHR, Vol. VIII, No. 4, facing p. 241.
29. **Twit. Coll.**, No. 145.
30. **M-54, Sta. Fe.**
31. **DM**, 1811, no number.
32. Ibid., 1820, no number.
33. Ibid., 1845, no number.
34. **M-51, Castrense.**
35. **DM**, 1849, no number.

CABRERA

Josefa de Cabrera, a widow thirty years old and a native of Mexico City, came in 1693 with her son-in-law, Miguel de la Vega y Coca, who was married to her young daughter, Manuela de Medina. Another daughter, María, was the wife of José Luis Valdés. Josefa's late husband was *Alonso de Medina*.¹

Gabriel de Cabrera is mentioned as a wedding witness on August 21, 1714.² He is also mentioned in 1715.³ He eventually went to Guadalupe del Paso, where he was living in 1745 with his wife, *Micaela de Contreras*. They had a daughter, *Francisca*.⁴

Juan Antonio Cabrera, parents unknown, married *Teodora Pacheco* in Santa Fe, October 6, 1728.⁵

Ana Bernal *de Cabrera* was the wife of Luis López of Pojoaque in 1703, but no connection between her and the Cabreras can be found.⁶

1. **Sp. Arch.**, II, No. 54c.
2. **M-24, S. Ild.**
3. **Sp. Arch.**, I, No. 434.
4. **AGN, Mex., Inq.**, t. 892, f. 1 et seq.
5. **M-50, Sta. Fe.**
6. **AASF**, No. 15.

CADENA
(Cruz)

Francisco de la Cadena, fifty years old, a native of New Mexico, the son of Francisco de la Cruz and Antonia de Hinojos, had been married to Ana de la Cruz, a Tesuque Indian. In 1716 he married Leonor Montaño, widow of Luis de Chávez.¹ Francisco died at the age of ninety on July 14, 1757, and Leonor died at the age of seventy on November 17, 1762.²

In 1710 he had worked in the reconstruction of San Miguel chapel.³

José Antonio de la Cadena was married to a *Gertrudis Rodriguez*, who died on September 4, 1727.⁴

Francisca Cadena was the wife, in 1753, of

the soldier Francisco González of Santa Fe.⁵ *María Luisa Cadena*, wife of Juan Lorenzo Carvajal, sold some land inherited from her parents.⁶

1. **DM**, 1716, No. 1.
2. **Bur-48, Sta. Fe.**
3. Kubler, p. 19.
4. **Bur-48, Sta. Fe.**
5. **Sp. Arch.**, I, No. 9..
6. **Ibid.**, No. 978.

CALVES

JOSÉ CALVES (or *Galves*?) was living in Santa Fe as early as 1773, when his wife, *María Miera*, bore him a daughter, *María Rita del Rosario*, November 5. They had two other girls, which explains why this family name died out: *María Ygnacia*, January 12, 1776, and *María Manuela Rafaela*, December 14, 1781.¹ Their father was a mayordomo of the restored Confraternity of La Conquistadora in 1775.²

1. All in **B, Sta. Fe.**

2. **OLC**, p. 11.

CAMPOS

JOSÉ CAMPOS REDONDO was a soldier of the Santa Fe garrison in 1790 who had enlisted in 1777. He was thirty-seven at this latter date, and had been born in Mexico City, the son of Alejandro Campos Redondo and Joaquina de Arteaga. His wife was *Feliciana Ortiz*, twenty-five. They had three boys, thirteen, eight, and two years old, and two girls, fifteen and seven.¹

Their known children were: *José María Francisco de Paula*, born January 20, 1785; *José Francisco de Jesús*, March 12, 1787;² *Juan Pedro*, who married at Pojoaque;³ and *Domingo*, married to María Guadalupe Baca.⁴ One of the sons named "*José*" married María Concepción Valencia on May 22, 1827.⁵

Feliciana Paula Ortiz Bustamante, widow of José Campos Redondo, made her last will in Santa Fe in 1815. She stated that she had borne thirteen children, most of whom died in infancy, and two premature ones that had been baptized.⁶ She was a daughter of Nicolás Ortiz III, and he most likely a brother or nephew of Fray Francisco Campos Redondo.

1. **Twit. Coll.**, No. 179; **HSNM**, Mil. Papers.
2. Both in **B-23, Nambé, Poj., S. Ild.**
3. **M-22, Pojoaque**; other data misplaced.
4. **B-65, Sta. Fe**, bapt. of child, Mar. 13, 1811. He enlisted as a soldier in 1798, when twenty years old. (**HSNM**, Mil. Papers.)
5. **M-4, Albuq.**
6. **Sp. Arch.**, I, No. 666.

CANDELARIA

BLAS DE LA CANDELARIA had died before 1680, when his widow *Ana de Sandoval y Manzanares* escaped the Indian massacre with her family. These returned to New Mexico with the Reconquest.

Felix de la Candelaria, son of Blas de la Candelaria and Ana de Sandoval y Manzanares, lived in the Rio Abajo district with his mother and the rest of the family. In 1716 Ana was claiming the Rancho de San Clemente as having formerly belonged to her own father.¹ In that year Felix was forty-eight years old, married, and living in Albuquerque.² He took part in the Moqui campaign of that same year.³

"*Feliciano*" de la Candelaria seems to be the same man as "Felix." He and Francisco de la Candelaria took their families from Bernalillo to be among the founding settlers of Albuquerque in 1706.⁴

Feliciano and his wife, *Petrona Varela,* had at least four children: *José,* April 25, 1700; *María,* February 8, 1702; a second *María,* February 4, 1704;⁵ and *Catalina,* March 8, 1708.⁶

Francisco de la Candelaria was most likely another son of Blas. In 1694 he declared that he was born in the Rio Abajo and was twenty-six years old.⁷ In 1699 he was a witness again at Bernalillo.⁸ His family, with that of Feliciano, was believed to be among the "twelve" founding families of Albuquerque. He acted as a civil witness in Albuquerque in 1709.⁹

His wife was *Francisca Montoya,* by whom he had a daughter, *Isabel,* July 17, 1703.¹⁰

---

1. Document quoted by Twitchell in **Sp. Arch.,** I, p. 141.
2. **DM,** 1716, No. 14.
3. **NMHR,** Vol. VI, No. 2, p. 184.
4. **Ibid.,** Vol. IV, No. 3, p. 274.
5. The three in **B-13, Bern.**
6. **B-2, Albuq.**
7. **DM.,** 1694, No. 9.
8. **Ibid.,** 1699, No. 8.

Ventura de la Candelaria had a first wife by the name of *Francisca Torres;* their son, *Salvador,* married a María Durán in Albuquerque in 1725.¹¹

On January 16, 1727, a son, *Manuel,* was born to him and *Efigenia* ———;¹² the mother must have died in childbirth or soon after, for on July 20 of the same year he married Ynez Gutiérrez.¹³ Ventura was very probably a brother of Felix and Francisco.

Juan de la Candelaria was twenty-six years old in 1720, when he appeared as a marriage witness.¹⁴ On May 30, 1728, he married *Manuela Varela.*¹⁵

He seems to be the aged man who penned or dictated a brief history of New Mexico, faulty but interesting, in 1776. He claimed to have been born in 1692, relying on the old belief that Vargas re-colonized New Mexico in 1692. He was the son of Francisco or Feliciano, both of whom he named among the first founding families of Albuquerque.¹⁶

---

9. **Sp. Arch.,** I, No. 716.
10. **B-13, Bern.**
11. **DM,** 1725, No. 4.
12. **B-2, Albuq.**
13. **B-3, Albuq.**
14. **DM,** 1720, No. 7.
15. **M-3, Albuq.**
16. "Noticias of Juan Candelaria," **NMHR,** loc. cit., pp. 274-97.

CANSECO

(See *Sebastian de Salas*)

CÁRDENAS

ANDRÉS DE CÁRDENAS, a native of Puebla, came in 1693. He was forty-six, swarthy, with a high forehead and small eyes. His wife, *Juana de Ávalos,* was thirty, a native of Mexico City, the daughter of Nicolás. She, too, was dark, with a blind right eye.

They had two girls, *Petrona María,* eleven, born in Mexico City, swarthy, with a mole on the left cheek; and *María Teresa,* two, with an aquiline face and a high forehead.¹ Both parents were still living in Santa Cruz in 1716.² Apparently they had no sons to pass on the name. *Petrona,* wife of Roque Jaramillo, made her last will at Santa Cruz in 1767.³

---

1. **Sp. Arch.,** II, No. 54c.
2. **DM,** 1716, No. 3.
3. **Sp. Arch.,** I, No. 126.

CARRILLO

MIGUEL CARRILLO appears for the first time in 1694, when he declared that he was thirty-five years old and knew a certain man from Jerez since he was sixteen.[1] He and his wife, *María de Mondragon*, died in the same year 1727.[2]

In this same year, their son, *Manuel*, got married in Albuquerque. In 1714, August 21, a *Juana Carrillo*, very likely their daughter, had married Bartolomé Lobato.[3]

Manuel Carrillo, son of Miguel Carrillo and María de Mondragon, both deceased, married *María Varela*, daughter of Juan Varela and Isabel Sedillo, November 30, 1727.[4]

Their four known children were: *Juan María*, born September 6, 1728; *Anastasia de la Cruz*, May 6, 1730; and *Mateo Antonio*, September 24, 1735.[5] In 1745, November 4, *María de la Luz* was baptized. Here the mother's name is given as *Juana Varela*.[6]

1. DM, 1694, No. 2.
2. Bur-48, Sta. Fe, Feb. 7 and May 7.
3. M-24, S. Ild.
4. M-3, Albuq.
5. These three in B-2, Albuq.
6. B-57, Isleta.

CARVAJAL

Juan Antonio de Carvajal, son of Alonso de Carvajal and Ana Varela, both natives of New Mexico and deceased, married *Josefa Martín*, daughter of Luis Martín and María de la Vega, on June 8, 1701.[1]

Lorenzo de Carvajal, born in the Rio Abajo, was twenty years old in 1692.[2] By 1699 he was residing in Bernalillo, when he gave his age as twenty-six.[3] In 1706 he received a grant of land in Albuquerque.[4] Perhaps he was a brother of Juan Antonio, both obscure remnants of a once great family.

1. DM, 1701, No. 1.
2. Ibid., 1692, No. 3.
3. Ibid., 1699, No. 8.
4. Sp. Arch., II, No. 156.

CASADOS

FRANCISCO LORENZO DE CASADOS, a widower already in 1704, was a native of Cádiz in Spain, where he had known Juan Páez Hurtado.[1] By 1716 he was a Captain, when he stated that he was forty-six years old and married.[2] But it is not known who his first and second wives were. He was a member of the Confraternity of St. Michael which restored the ancient chapel of San Miguel in 1710.[3]

He had a son, *Francisco José*, by his first wife.

Francisco (José) de Casados, son of Francisco (Lorenzo) de Casados, was married to *María de Archibeque*, daughter of Juan de Archibeque.[4] He was thirty-two years old in 1731 and living in Santa Fe.[5]

This couple had a son, *Miguel*, who married María Diega Domínguez on June 26, 1750.[6]

1. DM, 1704, No. 6.
2. Ibid., 1716, No. 17.
3. Kubler, p. 19.
4. Sp. Arch., I, Nos. 13, 748; II, No. 239d.
5. Bancroft, NMO, 1731.
6. M-50, Sta. Fe.

CASTELÁ

JOSÉ ANTONIO CASTELÁ and *María Montaño* had a child, *Juana Gertrudis*, born September 8, 1755.[1]

A José Casteló and a *María Lerchunda* had a son, *Salvador José*, at the same place, on April 24, 1759.[2] Apparently they were the same couple.

The daughter, Juana Gertrudis *Casteló*, then living in the jurisdiction of Santo Domingo, married Juan Cristóbal Baca of Santa Fe, on October 30, 1782.[3] In 1794 she is mentioned as the wife of Cristóbal Baca and mother-in-law of Miguel Baca, son of Juan Antonio Baca.[4]

A *Mariano Castelá* sold some land in Santa Fe in 1812.[5]

1. B-3, Albuq.
2. Ibid.
3. M-35, Sto. Domingo.
4. Sp. Arch., I, No. 465.
5. Ibid., No. 888.

CASILLAS

BERNARDO CASILLAS and *María Vigil* were sponsors, November 29, 1703.[1] She was his wife, mentioned as such when she died on May 19, 1741.[2] In 1716 Casillas sold some land in Santa Fe.[3] As an *Alférez* he took part in a campaign against the Utes and Comanches in 1719.[4] Nothing more is known about this couple, their origin, and their descendants.

Manuel Casillas, very likely a son of the above, married *Elena Montoya* on September 12, 1729.[5] As a soldier of the Santa Fe garrison he sold some property in 1731; his wife was a daughter of Antonio Montoya and Catalina de Ribera.[6] They lost their infant twin girls, February 5, 1736.[7]

1. M-24, S. Ild.
2. Bur-48, Sta. Fe.
3. Sp. Arch., II, No. 11.
4. Bancroft, NMO, 1719.
5. M-50, Sta. Fe.
6. Sp. Arch., I, No. 749.
7. Bur-48, Sta. Fe.

CASTILLO
(*Álvarez del Castillo*)

JUAN MIGUEL ÁLVAREZ DEL CASTILLO was married in the early part of the century to *Barbara Baca*, sister of Captain Baltasar Baca. They had several children, four of whom were living when his estate was probated in 1765. His second wife was *Gertrudis Montoya*, sister of Miguel Montoya; she bore him a boy and a girl. His third wife was *Rosalia García*, who had no children. Juan Miguel died suddenly at Guadalupe del Paso.[1]

The children by Barbara Baca were: *Ana María Olaya*, born on February 24, 1740,[2] who married Diego Antonio Sánchez, April 6, 1756;[3] *María Manuela*, born on June 1, 1741, who was dead by 1765;[4] *María Gertrudis*, born on February 12, 1743, who married Francisco Chávez;[5] *José Antonio Nicolás*, born December 15, 1744;[6] and *Joaquín Jacinto*, born September 17, 1747,[7] who married Ana María Andrea Vallejos.

Gertrudis Montoya, the second wife, was the daughter of Lucia de Chávez and sister of Miguel Montoya of Atrisco, who was the guardian of her two minor children after her death.⁸ She had died at the age of twenty-five in February, 1761.⁹

Miguel married his third wife, the widow Rosalía García de Noriega, at Guadalupe del Paso, on December 28, 1761.¹⁰ She had taken the girl by the second wife whom her uncle, Miguel Montoya, was trying to get back in 1768.¹¹

Joaquín del Castillo, son of Miguel by his first wife, married *Ana María Andrea Vallejo*, by whom he had at least two children,

María and *Antonio José*. María became the wife of Francisco Xavier Chávez in 1799;¹² and Antonio José married María Guadalupe Pino on June 22, 1810.¹³

Joaquín must have married again, for when he died, May 18, 1821, at the age of seventy-eight, his widow was a *Juana Sánchez*.¹⁴

The Castillos of the Rio Abajo belong to this Álvarez del Castillo family. For other Castillos see *López del Castillo, Gómez del Castillo,* and *Francisco Afán de Ribera*.

1. Sp. Arch., II, No. 586.
2. B-57, Isleta.
3. M-11, Isleta.
4. B-57, Isleta; Sp. Arch., loc. cit.
5. B-57 and M-11, Isleta; Sp. Arch., loc. cit.
6. Ibid.
7. Ibid.

8. Sp. Arch., II, Nos. 586, 642.
9. Bur-2, Albuq.
10. M, Guad. del Paso (Juárez).
11. Sp. Arch., I, No. 642.
12. DM, 1799, in Belén, no number.
13. B-54, Tomé, M-Sec.
14. Ibid., Bur. Sec.

CERDA

JUAN JOSÉ DE LA CERDA, a native of Valladolid in Michoacan, thirty-six years old and the son of Juan de la Cerda and María de Chavarría, was living in Santa Cruz when he married *Antonia Sánchez*, daughter of Pedro Sánchez and María Luján, in 1721.¹

They had a son, *Juan*, born on September 7, 1723.² Another son could be the *Francisco de la Cerda* who married Antonia Olaya Jirón on March 4, 1743.³

1. DM, 1721, No. 2.
2. M-24, S. Ild.
3. M-29, Sta. Cruz.

CERVANTES

MANUEL DE CERVANTES, eighteen years old and the son of Manuel de Cervantes, was a native of Mexico City who came with the 1693 colonists. He was described as able-bodied, with a round face and a scar on the right side of the chin. His wife was *Francisca Rodríguez*, daughter of Juan, and also born in Mexico City; she was of medium height, with an aquiline face and a mole on the right temple.¹

In 1696, Manuel said that he was twenty, a native of Mexico City, and residing in Santa Cruz. The occasion was the wedding investigation of Juan Manuel Chirinos, son of Juan Martínez *de Cervantes* and Antonia Chirinos.² It can be seen that he and the Martínez Chirinos family were related. Since the Cervantes name did not continue, it is possible that any descendants would be "Martínez" instead.

* * * * * * * *

Toribio Aniceto Cervantes, a native of San Juan del Rio, married *Juana Pacheco* in Santa Fe, August 17, 1801.³

1. Sp. Arch., II, No. 54c.
2. DM, 1696, No. 8.
3. M-52, Sta. Fe.

CHACÓN

The first members of the *Chacón* family of New Mexico appear as adults living in the Rio Arriba area near San Juan Pueblo shortly before the middle of the century. Their parents and their place of origin are so far unknown. They most likely came to this area with the Velarde family from El Paso.

Cristóbal Chacón married *Rosa Madrid* on July 23, 1741.[1] But three years later a *Cristóbal Chacón* had a legitimate daughter, *María*, by a *Rita Luján*, February 3, 1744. Francisco Xavier Chacón and Lugarda Martin were the godparents.[2] Apparently it was the same man, who had married a second time.

Francisco Xavier Chacón married *Josefa Velásquez*, December 29, 1748.[3] They had a son, *Antonio José*, on April 18, 1755.[4]

A *Francisca Chacón* married José Pacheco, April 24, 1732.[5]

Cayetano Chacón married *Rosa Chávez* at La Soledad, May 7, 1755.[6] Two known sons of theirs were: *José Antonio*, born February 2, 1756, who married Guadalupe Archuleta, January 27, 1782;[7] and *Juan Pedro*, born June 29, 1759.[8]

José Chacón and *Clara Trujillo* had three children who married as follows: *María Luz* with José Antonio Romero, January 8, 1791; *Juan Antonio* with Andrea Quiteria Martín, February 4, 1792; and *Francisco Antonio* with Encarnación Atencio, October 11, 1810.[9]

Pedro Ignacio Chacón married *María de Jesús Martín*, February 12, 1787, and then *María Pascuala Martín*, August 17, 1801.[10] *José María*, a son by the second wife, married Serafina López in 1833; both parties lived at El Rito Colorado.[11]

Felipe Chacón and *Guadalupe Villalpando* had a son, *Baltasar*, January 7, 1787.[12]

José Albino Chacón, son of Felipe Chacon and Nicolasa Trujillo, married *Refugio López*, daughter of Francisco López and María Fernández, in the military chapel at Santa Fe, January 23, 1830.[13] But by 1854, the family was living in the Peñasco country where a son, *José Pablo*, was born, January 27, 1854.[14]

---

1. M-27, S. Juan.
2. B-27, S. Juan.
3. M-27, S. Juan.
4. B-27, S. Juan.
5. M-27, S. Juan.
6. Ibid.
7. B-42, S. Juan; M-1, Abiquiú.
8. B-42, S. Juan.
9. All three in M-1, Abiquiú.
10. Ibid.
11. DM, 1833, no number.
12. B-42, S. Juan.
13. M-51, Castrense.
14. B, Picurís; both parents and grandparents given.

CHÁVEZ
(*Durán y Chaves*)

DON FERNANDO DURÁN Y CHAVES, who escaped in 1680 from the Sandia district with his wife, *Lucía Hurtado*, and four small children, was the only member of the large Durán y Chaves clan to return with his family at the time of the Reconquest.[1] During the 1680-93 exile at Guadalupe del Paso he took part in the futile Otermín Expedition, and was one of the *Regidores* of the colony,[2] and with the arrival of Governor Vargas he became one of his councillors.[3] In the grand *Entrada* into Santa Fe, December 16, 1693, Don Fernando led with the Royal Standard as *Real Alférez*,[4] but soon after moved to the ancestral lands at Bernalillo; here and at San Felipe Pueblo he maneuvered the colonists and Indians so as to forestall disaster during the uprising of 1696, though he had to disagree with Vargas as to tactics; subsequently he vanquished the Jémez Indians at San Diego Canyon, when they fled into the Navajo country.[5] Governor Vargas, taken ill during an Apache campaign in the Sandias in 1704, was carried to Bernalillo where he made his will and died, presumably in the Chaves house, for Don Fernando and his eldest son, Bernardo, signed as official witnesses of the last will and testament.[6]

By 1707 he and the family had moved to Atrisco, while Bernardo and his young family remained at Bernalillo. At Atrisco Don Fernando made his last will on February 11, 1707, but he was still living as late as 1712.[7] By 1716 he was referred to as dead.[8]

His widow, Lucía Hurtado de Salas, lived with some of her sons until her death on February 3, 1729.[9] Their ten children are named in their father's will in this order: *Bernardo, Pedro, Antonio, Isabel, Francisco, Luis, Nicolás, María, Catalina,* and *Pedro Gómez Durán.*[10] The four eldest had been born before 1680 in the Sandia-Bernalillo area; the rest at Guadalupe del Paso.

Before his marriage Don Fernando had a natural daughter, *Clara de Chaves,* mother not known, who became the wife of Juan de la Mora Pineda.[11]

Of his three daughters, *Isabel* married Jacinto Peláez, and then Baltasar de Mata; *María,* wife of Antonio de Ulibarrí, died without issue; and *Catalina* became the wife of Matías de Miranda.

Bernardo D. y Chaves, who signed the will of Vargas with his father in 1704, remained with his wife and children at Bernalillo. He gave his age as twenty in 1695.[12] In 1705, when playing an Indian-scare prank, he was accidentally shot and mortally wounded by a Gallegos cousin, leaving his young wife and three small children. He was buried on November 19, 1705.[13]

Bernardo had married *Francisca de Mizquia,* at Santa Fe in 1699.[14] They had two boys and a girl: *José,* April 24, 1700; *María Manuela,* June 15, 1703; and *Juan,* February 26, 1705.[15] In their mother's last will in 1714, the girl is mentioned as *Lucia* Manuela; their mother was married to Juan de Ulibarrí at this time.[16] One son, *José,* was married and living at Guadalupe del Paso in 1769, while his brother Juan resided in Santa Fe; *Luisa* (or *Lucia*) was already dead.[17]

Pedro D. y Chaves married *Juana Montoya* on January 27, 1703.[18] His was one of the supposed "twelve" founding families of Albuquerque in 1706.[19] In 1713 he was a squadron leader of the militia and conducted ex-Governor Felix Martínez back to Mexico City; but he resigned in 1716 because of illness; yet he is numbered among those who took part in the Moqui campaign of this year.[20]

In March, 1735, his estate was probated due to the fact that he was dying, having been out of his senses for some time. But he rallied enough to draw up his will, and died on December 7, 1735. After Bernardo's death he had come into possession of his father's will, but due to his illness it had passed into the hands of the next brother, Antonio, who was absent from "the Kingdom" at this time.[21]

Pedro had ten children by Juana Montoya, named in the will as follows: *Manuela,* wife of Sebastian Marcelino; *Monica,* wife of Antonio Baca; *Josefa,* married to Francisco Sánchez; *Efigenia,* wife of Jacinto Sánchez; *Francisco Xavier; Quiteria; Juana;* and three minors who had been placed with their uncle, Francisco D. y Chaves, when Pedro married a second time. These minors were: *Diego Antonio,* twelve; *María Luisa,* ten, and *Eusebio,* eight.[22]

Pedro's second wife was *Gertrudis Sánchez,* by whom he had five children, one of them dead, but none are mentioned by name in the will. This marriage took place on January 12, 1728.[23] The four living children are found elsewhere as follows: *Salvador Manuel,* born on June 9, 1731; *José,* born on June

1, 1733,[24] who married twice, lived in Bernalillo, had many children,[25] and was the "José Chaves of New Mexico" killed by Apaches near el Paso, December 9, 1772;[26] a daughter, not named, who was married to Antonio Gutiérrez;[27] and a *Pedro II*, referred to years later as a son of old Pedro,[27a] who was therefore the fourth living child of this marriage.

Of the unmarried daughters by the first wife mentioned in Pedro's will, *Quiteria* finally married a Bernardo Padilla after some trouble;[28] *María Luisa* (Lucia) reared by her uncle Francisco, could very well be the woman who married Miguel Montoya as Francisco's daughter; *Juana* seems to be the one who married Domingo Baca.

Of the sons by the first wife, *Francisco Xavier*, the eldest son among many girls, was considered a wastrel by his sisters;[29] he was the man of this name who married *Manuela Padilla* on September 29, 1735.[30] *Diego Antonio*, the next son but very much younger, among the minors of his father's will, married his third cousin, *Juana Silva*, December 14, 1740.[31] If his elder brother was the wastrel that his sisters accused him of being, it explains how Diego Antonio could have inherited the original Chaves document and signet-ring later inherited by Colonel Manuel Antonio Chaves of Civil War fame.[32] *Eusebio*, the youngest son, married *Vibiana Martín Serrano* on August 19, 1752;[33] he vainly tried to get grants and honors on the merits of his ancestors for himself and his sons, Blas and Juan Miguel, in 1774, and is said to have voyaged to Spain for the purpose.[34]

Antonio D. y Chaves was ailing in 1705 when his father, Don Fernando, asked for his position as commander of the soldiers at Atrisco,[35] but in 1712 he was perfectly healthy when engaged in fights with his father and brother Francisco against a certain individual.[36] He was first married to *Magdalena Montaño*, by whom he had at least two children: *María*, born in 1707, and *Fernando*, in 1708.[37]

On March 23, 1718, after complicated dispensations were granted, Antonio, widowed of his first wife, married a cousin, *Antonia Baca*.[38] As previously stated, Antonio was in possession of his famous father's last will, which in the nineteenth century was in the family of General José María Chávez.[39] Antonio died on May 12, 1738; his widow died many years after at the age of seventy-five, on February 15, 1770.[40]

No wills by Antonio or his wife Antonia Baca are extant. Some of their sons, gathered from different sources, are as follows: *Cristóbal, Miguel, José, Juan Antonio, Tomás, Francisco,* and *Santiago*. Three known girls were: *Feliciana*, who married Manuel Baca; *Lucia Ana*, wife of Felipe Romero;[41] and *María*, who drowned in the Rio del Norte at the age of eleven in 1742.[42]

Of the sons, *Cristóbal*, on a trip to Mexico City brought a bride, *María Josefa Núñez*, and they had their *velación* at Laguna, where his sister Feliciana's husband was Alcalde Mayor, on June 30, 1756.[43] *Miguel*, mentioned as brother of Cristóbal, perhaps his twin, and a sponsor with his mother,[44] married *Gertrudis Santisteban* of Santa Fe, October 10, 1754.[45] *José* married *Juana Baca* on October 15, 1758.[46] *Juan Antonio*, who appeared as a sponsor with his mother,[47] married a first cousin, *Barbara Montoya*.[48] *Tomás*, who also appeared as a sponsor with his mother and with his sister Feliciana, married *Tomasa Padilla*, December 3, 1742.[49] *Francisco* appeared once as a sponsor with his mother.[50] *Santiago*, born in 1733, married *María Luisa Páez*, daughter of Ramon Páez and Manuela Velarde, at Guadalupe del Paso in 1761, and brought her back home; his mother and brother Juan Antonio were sponsors for a child of theirs in 1768.[51]

Francisco D. y Chaves married *Juana Baca*, "the younger," daughter of Juana Baca, "the Elder."[52] In his brother Pedro's will he is mentioned as having adopted Pedro's three minor children by his first wife.

He and Juana Baca had at least eight children: *Miguel Antonio*, born November 26, 1735, who married Francisca Baca, August

29, 1781;⁵³ *José Vicente*, born February 14, 1730;⁵⁴ *Agustín*, who died young on January 7, 1741;⁵⁵ *Ignacio*, who married Gregoria Maese, and then Ursula Sánchez in 1770;⁵⁶ *Margarita*, born January 3, 1734, who married Salvador Garcia in 1761;⁵⁷ *Juana*, born January 10, 1744; *Maria*, who died young, May 9, 1744;⁵⁸ and *Lucia*, very likely the child of his brother Pedro, who became the wife of Miguel Montoya.⁵⁹

Luis D. y Chaves married *Leonor Montaño*, by whom he had a daughter, *Antonia*. He died relatively young prior to 1716, when his widow remarried in Santa Fe.⁶⁰ His brother Antonio bought his Atrisco inheritance from his widow.⁶¹

Nicolás D. y Chaves was twenty-four and a resident of Atrisco when he had at least one natural child, already four years old in 1714, when he decided to marry its mother, *Juana Montaño*, of Santa Fe. The wedding took place on July 20.⁶² She was the sister of two other Montaño girls, Magdalena and Leonor, who had married his brothers Antonio and Luis. The men were second cousins of the women.⁶³ Nicolás acquired much property south of Isleta, and appears in several land litigations.⁶⁴

He made his last will on May 19, 1768, in which he gave the names of his parents and of his wife, followed by his eight sons and five daughters: *José, Gertrudis, Bernardo, Luis, Fernando, Isabel, Antonio, María Francisca, María Antonia, Juan, Vicente, María,* and *Francisco*.⁶⁵ Of the girls, *Gertrudis* married Francisco Silva,⁶⁶ and *María Antonia* married Tadeo Romero,⁶⁷ and later a Domingo Baca.

The sons are as follows: *José* married Luisa de Aragón, February 3, 1732;⁶⁸ *Bernardo* married an Apacha, María Benavides, and then his first cousin's widow, María Josefa Núñez;⁶⁹ *Luis* married Eduarda Yturrieta, April 20, 1747;⁷⁰ *Fernando* married Antonia Sánchez;⁷¹ and *Francisco* married María Gertrudis Álvarez del Castillo, April 6, 1756.⁷²

Pedro Gómez Durán y Chaves was born when aging Don Fernando must have been pre-occupied with the past. For, although he had an elder brother named "Pedro," this last child received the full name of Don Fernando's grandfather, *"Pedro Gómez Durán,"* as his baptismal name. Later he was referred to also as *"Pedro de Chaves el Menor,"* or by the nickname of *"Perico"* (little Pedro), when living with the family at Atrisco.⁷³ He was still there in 1732 when he sold the lands of his inheritance to Bernabé Baca and to the widow of his brother Antonio.⁷⁴ But three years later he was living in the Rio Arriba country.⁷⁵

On July 6, 1737, Pedro Gómez de Chaves married *Petrona Martín*.⁷⁶ They were still living in Ojo Caliente of Rio Arriba in 1742.⁷⁷ He is the only son of Don Fernando who settled in the country north of Santa Fe, but so far it is not known who his children were.

---

1. For more detailed treatment see **El Palacio**, Vol. 55, No. 4, pp. 103-21. Some emendations in this present work are the result of more data found.
2. **Revolt**, II, pp. 25-6, 96, 336-7, 391; **Sp. Arch.**, II, No. 38a.
3. **AGN, Hist.**, t. 37, pt. 3, ff. 322-3; **AASF**, No. 5.
4. **Ibid.**, t. 38, pt. 2, f. 61; **Sp. Arch.**, II, No. 54c, ff. 4-16.
5. **Sp. Arch.**, I, No. 423; **B-H**, III, p. 351; **Old Santa Fe**, Vol. III, pp. 332-373.
6. **Sp. Arch.**, I, Nos. 99, 1027.
7. **Ibid.**, II, No. 170.
8. **Ibid.**, No. 269.
9. **Ibid., Bur-2, Albuq.**
10. **Twit. Coll.**, No. 261, copy, extract of original in possession of descendants of Gen. José María Chávez, USA.
11. **DM**, 1708, No. 3.
12. **Ibid.**, 1695, No. 19.
13. **Sp. Arch.**, II, No. 120, **B-13, Bern.**, Bur. Sec.
14. **DM**, 1699, No. 4.
15. All in **B-13, Bern.**
16. **Sp. Arch.**, I, No. 495; **DM**, 1711, No. 7.
17. **AGN, Tierras**, 426, III, f. 11; **Sp. Arch.**, I, No. 875.
18. **B-13, Bern.**
19. **NMHR**, Vol. IV, No. 3, p. 274.
20. **Sp. Arch.**, I, No. 1117; II, Nos. 198, 250, 297; **Bancroft, NMO**, 1716.
21. **Sp. Arch.**, I, No. 177.
22. **Ibid.**
23. **M-3, Albuq.**
24. Both in **B-2, Albuq.**
25. **Sp. Arch.**, I, No. 250.
26. **Bur., Guad. del Paso** (Juárez).
27. **Sp. Arch.**, loc. cit.
27a. **DM**, 1766, in Albuq., no number; evidently the man who became PEDRO OTERO.
28. **Sp. Arch.**, I, No. 196.
29. **Ibid.**, No. 177.
30. **M-11, Isleta.** GENEALOGY: **Francisco Xavier Chávez**, Tomás Chávez, Governor Francisco Xavier Chávez.
31. **M-3, Albuq.**, also Jan. 16, 1741; **Sp. Arch.**, II, No. 513.
32. GENEALOGIES: (1) **Diego Antonio Chávez**, Pedro Antonio Chávez, Julián Chávez, Col. Manuel A. Chávez, USA.
   (2) **Diego Antonio Chávez**, María Guadalupe Chávez, María Isabel Armijo, María Rita Torres, José Chávez, Eugenio Chávez, Fabián Chávez, Fr. A. Chávez.
33. **M-3, Albuq.**
34. **Sp. Arch.**, II, Nos. 675, 686; Twitchell's note, **Ibid.**, pp. 254-5.—For more details on this family, see **El Palacio**, Vol. 60, No. 4, pp. 154-160.
35. **Ibid.**, No. 106.
36. **Ibid.**, No. 170.
37. Both in **B-2, Albuq.**, pp. 3, 6.
38. **DM**, 1718, No. 11.

The marvelous growth of this family from a single source is due to the fact that each generation had more sons than daughters. As with the Bacas and Armijos of the Rio Abajo, the repetition of identical names among contemporaries makes it impossible to distinguish them one from another, except when a will, or some other document, provides some relationships. But there are not enough of these.

---

39. See note 49 below.
40. Both in **Bur-2, Albuq.**
41. **AGN, Tierras,** 426, III, ff. 7-11.
42. **Bur-2, Albuq.,** f. 28v.
43. **M-12, Laguna;** cf. **El Palacio,** Vol. 54, No. 11, p. 255n; **DM,** 1773, No. 4, marriage of son Mariano. GENEALOGY: **Cristóbal D. y Chávez,** José Mariano Chávez, José Chávez, José Chávez II, Eugenio Chávez, Fabián Chávez, Fr. A. Chávez.
44. **DM,** loc. cit; **M-3, Albuq.,** f. 16.
45. **M-3, Albuq.**
46. **M-11, Isleta.**
47. **Ibid.,** f. 29; **M-12, Laguna,** f. 21, wedding of sister Feliciana's daughter.
48. **DM,** 1770, in Albuq., no number.
49. **M-3, Albuq.,** ff. 13, 16v; **M-11, Isleta,** f. 16; **B-3, Albuq.,** pp. 36, 67, 115. GENEALOGY: **Tomás Baca (Chávez),** Francisco Antonio Chávez, Gen. José María Chávez, USA. (**TWit. Coll.,** No. 204, if family's information was correct.)
50. **M-3, Albuq.,** f. 13.
51. **B-2, Albuq.; M, Guad. del Paso; B-3, Albuq.,** p. 262.
52. **DM,** 1766, in Albuq., **Marcos Baca; Ibid.,** 1770, **Baca-Montoya.**
53. **B-2, Albuq.; M-49, Isleta.**
54. **B-2, Albuq.**
55. **Bur-2, Albuq.**
56. **DM,** 1770, in Albuq., no number.
57. **B-2, Albuq.; DM,** 1761, in Albuq., no number.
58. **B-3,** and **Bur-2, Albuq.**
59. GENEALOGY: **Lucía D. y Chávez,** Barbara Montoya, Manuela Lucero, Tomás Baca, Nicanora Baca, Fabián Chávez, Fr. A. Chávez.
60. **DM,** 1716, No. 1.
61. **Sp. Arch.,** I, No. 175.
62. **Ibid.,** II, No. 208.
63. **Ibid.;** also, No. 213.
64. **Ibid.,** I, Nos. 92, 178, 841; II, Nos. 299, 465, 516.
65. **Ibid.,** I, No. 201.
66. GENEALOGY: **Gertrudis D. y Chávez,** Agustina Silva, María Lugarda Tafoya, Pablo Baca, Tomás Baca, Nicanora Baca, Fabián Chávez, Fr. A. Chávez.
67. GENEALOGY: **María Antonia D. y Chávez,** María Manuela Romero, José Chávez, José Chávez II, Eugenio Chávez, Fabián Chávez, Fr. A. Chávez.
68. **M-3, Albuq.**
69. **M-11, Isleta,** f. 52; **DM,** 1762, no number.
70. **M-4, Albuq.; Sp. Arch.,** II, No. 516.
71. **Sp. Arch.,** II, No. 465.
72. **M-4, Albuq.; M-11, Isleta.**
73. **Sp. Arch.,** II, Nos. 208, 213.
74. **Ibid.,** I, No. 86; **AGN, Tierras,** 426, III, ff. 20-2.
75. **Ibid.,** I, No. 20.
76. **M-29, Sta. Cruz** and **Sta. Clara.**
77. **B-31, Sta. Clara,** Feb. 2.

CHÁVEZ

(Others)

Juan de Chaves Medina, natural son of Juana de Medina, and a native of Zacatecas, was a new colonist of forty-two who married *Petronila de la Cueva*, widow of Juan de Gongora, in 1694.[1] He is heard of again in 1714 in connection with his wife, accused of malicious gossip.[2] It is not known if he had any children.

Juan de Aparicio Chaves, a nineteen-year-old soldier of unknown parentage, married a girl of like estate, *María Rosa Velásquez*, in 1723.[3] She died on April 3, 1737.[4]

Their son, *Diego*, got married at Guadalupe del Paso, October 29, 1753.[5] Nothing more is known about these people.

Miguel de Figueroa Núñez de Chaves, a native of Puebla, is listed with his family among the Velasco colonists of 1693. He was the son of Diego, thirty-six years old, of medium height, with a broad face, large eyes and forehead, a thick nose, and a mole on the left cheek. His wife, *María de Mirabal*, daughter of Juan, and born in Mexico City, was fifteen, having an aquiline face, white and fair, large eyes, and a sharp nose. With them came her widowed mother and her ten-year-old brother.[6]

Miguel is not heard of again under any of his surnames.

---

1. **DM,** 1694, No. 4.
2. **AGN, Mex., Inq.,** t. 758, ff. 468 et seq.
3. **DM,** 1723, No. 4.
4. **Bur-48, Sta. Fe.**
5. **M, Guad. del Paso (Juárez).**
6. **Sp. Arch.** II, No. 54c; see **Mirabal.**

CHIRINOS
(See *Martinez*)

COCA
(See *Vega y Coca*)

CONTRERAS

JOSÉ DE CONTRERAS was at Guadalupe del Paso as early as 1687,[1] where he married a *Magdalena de Carvajal*, or *Garcia*, and after her death married a *María de Valencia* in 1693. He was a Sergeant in command of a hundred soldiers from New Mexico, the son of Andrés de Contreras and María de Salinas y Valdés, both deceased, natives of San Luis Potosí.[2] Around this period he gave his age as forty or forty-one,[3] and was still stationed at Guadalupe del Paso. In 1705 he was in Santa Fe, but as a member of the Conquistadora Confraternity sent up his dues from Guadalupe del Paso.[4]

Two daughters by his first wife were married down there: *María* to José de la Cruz, and *Josefa* to José Madrid, both in 1709.[5] *Antonia*, a daughter by his second wife, married a widower, Juan de Gamboa, also at Guadalupe del Paso, in 1710.[6]

A Casilda Contreras was the wife of Francisco Martín, both living at Santa Cruz in 1709, and at Embudo in 1736.[7]

Simón de Contreras, twenty-one years of age and a native of Zacatecas, was living at Santa Cruz in 1696 with his wife, *Manuela Negrete*.[8]

1. **DM**, 1687, No. 1.
2. **Ibid.**, 1693, No. 7.
3. **Ibid.**, 1695, No. 3; 1696, No. 2.
4. **Sp. Arch.**, I, No. 479; **OLC**, p. 65.

5. **DM**, 1709, Nos. 1, 13.
6. **Ibid.**, 1710, No. 21.
7. **Sp. Arch.**, II, No. 137b; I, No. 753.
8. **Ibid.**, I, No. 817; **DM**, 1696, No. 11.

CORDOBA

ANTONIO DE CÓRDOBA was a native of the City of Mexico who had married *Eugenia de Herrera*, born in New Mexico, at Guadalupe del Paso. He was still acting as notary there in 1695, two years after the Reconquest.[1] But his wife, or widow, came to Santa Cruz with her children, for Antonio was referred to as deceased when their son, *Lazaro Antonio*, married Ana Valdés at Santa Cruz in 1710.[2] A daughter, *Ana María*, married Antonio Trujillo there in 1711.[3]

Lazaro de Córdoba and others of the same name appear in land documents from 1712 to 1762, always in the Santa Cruz or Rio Arriba area.[3] Although his wife was *Ana Valdés* as late as 1712, some children by a second wife appear several years later, if the father is the same Lazaro. These were: *Francisco Xavier*, born on February 2, 1727, child of Lazaro de Córdoba and *Petronila de Ávila;* and *Germán*, June 13, 1731, child of Lazaro de Córdoba and *Petrona Martín*.[4]

* * * * * * * *

Simón de Córdoba, of a different origin from the preceding family, was in New Mexico in 1714 with his wife, *María de Guada-*

lupe. He was twenty-five at this time.⁵ He was very likely a brother of *María de Córdoba* of Santa Cruz, married to a Bernardo Romero, and a daughter of Simón de Córdoba I, and Juana de la Encarnación, both natives of Zacatecas.⁶

---

1. **DM,** 1695, No. 15.
2. **Ibid.,** 1711, No. 2, GENEALOGY: **Ana María de Córdoba,** Bernarda Trujillo, Julio Archuleta, María Ignacia Archuleta, María Josefa Quintana, Desiderio Roybal, Romualdo Roybal, Nicolasa Roybal, Fr. A. Chávez.
3. **Sp. Arch.,** I, Nos. 161, 187, 188, 189, 933; II, No. 560.
4. Both in **B-52, S. Juan.**
5. **DM,** 1714, No. 4.
6. **Ibid.,** 1727, No. 7.

CORTÉS

JUAN CORTÉS, son of Don Fernando, thirty-six years old and born in Mexico City, brought his family with the colonists of 1693. He was of medium height, dark, with a sharp nose and somewhat deep-set eyes. His wife, *María de Ribera,* was thirty, the daughter of Juan and a native of Los Angeles (Puebla). She was small, freckled, with a small nose and large eyes.

They had four children, all born in Mexico City: *Andrea,* no age given, having a rather broad nose; *Diego,* twelve, fair with chestnut hair and large eyes; *Juana,* eleven, broad-faced with a flat nose, and pockmarked; and *Joaquín,* three, with a fair and ruddy complexion and large eyes.¹

Juan Cortés was at Nambé in June, 1696, when the Indians rebelled, killing him with a daughter, not named, and her husband, José Sánchez.²

A *Juana* Cortés, mentioned in 1705 as the sister-in-law of Juana Rodríguez, daughter of Alonso Rodríguez and Juana Valencia, seems to be the second daughter described in 1693.

* * * * * * * *

JOSÉ CORTÉS DEL CASTILLO and *María de Carvajal,* residents of Mexico City, were married in the church of Santiago, Querétaro, prior to starting out for New Mexico. They had a daughter, *Andrea,* before their marriage, and two other children after, *Rafaela* and *Dionisio.*³ In the Velasco list of colonists the family is given as follows:

José Cortés, son of Pedro, born in Puebla, forty years old, of medium height, with an aquiline face, large eyes and forehead, and a scar under the nose. His wife, *María de Carvajal,* was twenty-one, the daughter of Ignacio and a native of Querétaro; she was fair with a broad face and large eyes.⁴

Only two children are listed with them: *Rafaela,* five years old, born at San Miguel el Grande, having a round face and forehead, and large eyes; and *Leonisio Daniel,* born in Mexico City, having large eyes and a large forehead.⁵ The other Velasco list gave three children: *Andrea,* nine, *Rafaela,* six, and *Dionisio,* six months old.⁶ The oldest girl, Andrea, absent in this list, is therefore the girl accompanying the other Cortés, Juan, and his family. Hence it can be presumed that these two families were closely related. The other girl, Rafaela, became the wife of Mateo de Mestas in 1720 at Santa Cruz.⁷

As a marriage witness in 1694, the father gave his age as forty and forty-two, his birthplace as Puebla, and his full name as José Cortés del Castillo.⁸

---

1. **Sp. Arch.,** II, No. 54c.
2. **Old Santa Fe,** Vol. III, pp. 332-73.
3. **DM,** 1693, No. 10, copy of marriage certificate.
4. **Sp. Arch.,** loc. cit.
5. **Ibid.**
6. **BNM,** leg. 4, pt. 1, pp. 790-5.
7. **DM,** 1720, No. 1.
8. **Ibid.,** 1694, Nos. 21, 24.

CRESPÍN

CRISTÓBAL CRESPÍN was living in Santa Cruz in 1714, a member of the families recruited in Zacatecas. His mother (mother-in-law?) was Juana de Ancizo. He and others were granted some land at Chama in that year.[1]

Gregorio Crespín was living in Santa Fe in the middle of the century.[2]

At Pojoaque, on June 5, 1740, *Ricardo Crespín* and *Rosa de Ortega* had a child, María.[3] Presumably, Gregorio and Ricardo were sons of Cristóbal Crespín.

1. Sp. Arch., I, Nos. 167, 437.
2. Ibid., Nos. 180, 194, 775.
3. B-16, Nambe.

CRUZ

Francisco de la Cruz, fifty years old in 1698, declared that he was a native of New Mexico,[1] hence one of the adult refugees of the 1680 Indian Rebellion.

He was very likely the father of *Francisco de la Cadena* (q.v.), son of Francisco de la Cruz and Antonia de Hinojos;[2] perhaps also of *Domingo Matías de la Cruz*, son of Francisco de la Cruz and María de la Cruz, who married Margarita Domínguez, of unknown parentage, at Santa Cruz in 1727.[3]

A Francisco de la Cruz was tried for the murder of Juan Chaves in 1735.[4] Both were Indian servants of Rio Abajo families.

These individuals, and other unidentifiable men and women of the same name, if natives of New Mexico at the start of the century, were in all probability the descendants of Juan (Catalán) de la Cruz and Pedro de la Cruz of pre-Revolt times. The Reconquest brought others of this name who were low-caste people, servants or slaves of officials.

* * * * * * * *

Agustín de la Cruz was living in Santa Fe in 1706, the husband of María de Ancizo of Zacatecas. In the same connection there is mention of a *Diego Felipe de la Cruz*, deceased, whose widow was Josefa de Ortega.[5] Agustin furnished adobes for the reconstruction of old San Miguel Chapel in 1710.[6]

Marcos Montoya, parentage not known, married *María Antonia de la Cruz*, daughter of Agustín de la Cruz and Ana María de Almazán, in Santa Fe, in 1718.[7]

Hernando de la Cruz, twenty, a native of Oaxaca, was living in Santa Fe in 1698;[8] also, a *Miguel de la Cruz*, twenty-two, who furnished adobes for San Miguel in 1710.[9]

Juan Antonio Vásquez de la Cruz, native of Tepozotlán, married *Josefa de la Rosa*, daughter of Nicolas Arias and Lorenza de la Cruz, all natives of Zacatecas, at Santa Fe, in 1697.[10]

Bernardo de la Cruz Samorano, servant of Governor Valverde, married *Josefa Xaviera de los Angeles*, former slave of Governor Vargas, and widow of Ignacio de Zepeda, who had died in Santa Fe.[11]

1. DM, 1698, No. 15.
2. Ibid., 1716, No. 1.
3. Ibid., 1727, No. 3.
4. Sp. Arch., II, No. 405.
5. AGN, Mex., Inq., t. 735, ff. 273-6.
6. Kubler, pp. 18, 20.
7. DM, 1718, No. 4.
8. Ibid., 1698, No. 4.
9. Ibid., 1694, No. 12; Kubler, p. 20.
10. Ibid., 1697, No. 8.
11. Ibid., 1705, No. 13.

CUÉLLAR

CRISTÓBAL DE CUÉLLAR, born in Granada (Spain or New Spain?), was thirty-six years old when he married *Juana Hurtado* in Santa Fe, on February 21, 1694. His parents were Tomás de Cuéllar and Gabriela Domínguez, both living in Granada.[1] He was residing in Bernalillo in 1696, when he testified that he was thirty-nine and forty-four years old and a native of Granada.[2] He died on November 8, 1700,[3] and his widow later married Tomás Garcia.

He and Juana had a daughter, *María de Cuéllar*, who became the wife of José Montaño.[4]

1. DM, 1694, Nos. 3, 30.
2. Ibid., 1696, Nos. 2, 12.
3. B-13, Bern., Bur. Sec.
4. Sp. Arch., II, No. 215.

DIEZMOS

José Diezmos, or *Dias Morales*, was the name of a man whose widow lived in Santa Fe in 1706; she was a *María Rodríguez*, native of San Luis Potosí.[1] A *María de Diezmo*, or *Diezma*, also appears in 1695,[2] but nothing else is known about her.

1. AGN, Mex. Inq., t. 735, f. 287.
2. DM, 1695, No. 2.

DIMAS

Antonio Dimas and *Lucia Ortega* had a son, *Geronimo*, September 5, 1748.[1] The name could be a derivation of "Diezma," or it could be a different family of unknown origin.

1. B. Sta. Fe.

DELGADO

MANUEL DELGADO was a native of Pachuca. The 1790 census of the Santa Fe Presidio shows him as holding second place in command, a *Primer Teniente*, fifty-one years old. His wife at this time was *Josefa Garcia de Noriega*, twenty-three. They had two sons, five and one, and a girl, eleven years old.[1] The disparity in ages of husband and wife points to the probability of his having been married before. In 1775, Manuel had been stationed as an *Alférez* at the Presidio of Carrizal, thirty leagues from Guadalupe del Paso.[2] Later transferred to the latter post, he there perhaps married Josefa Garcia.[3]

While living in the Nambé-Pojoaque area, Manuel and Josefa had twins, *Manuel* and *Manuela*, baptized on June 28, 1792.[4] These, and the two boys and one girl recorded in 1790, brought the number up to five, three boys and two girls: *Manuel, Marcos, Fernando, Josefa,* and *Manuela*, (given in this order by Francisco Delgado).[5] An *Estéfana Delgado*, daughter of Manuel Delgado and Josefa Garcia, was married to Juan Rafael Ortiz.[6]

Josefa Garcia died on May 9, 1811,[7] and

Manuel then married *Ana María Baca* on November 30, 1814.[8] He died suddenly on August 13, 1815.[9] When his estate was probated in that year, Ana María was named as his widow; those of his children named were *Fernando, Marcos, Manuel Salustiano,* and *Manuela,* wife of Jose Francisco Baca. Also mentioned, but not named individually, were his grandchildren, the children of Juan Rafael Ortiz.[10]

Fernando Delgado, married *Ana María Ortiz,* daughter of Antonio Ortiz and Teresa Miera. He was a merchant of Santa Fe in 1814.[11] A daughter, *María Josefa de Jesús del Pilar,* was born on January 25, 1814.[12] As an *Alférez,* he was killed during an Indian campaign, and his bones and those of two soldiers were buried in the military chapel of Our Lady of Light on June 16, 1821.[13]

His widow then married José Antonio Vizcarra, at the time assistant colonel in charge of ordnance in New Mexico. The wedding took place in the same military chapel on April 14, 1824.[14]

Marcos Delgado. Further data on him and his brothers, and sisters Josefa and Manuela, are outlined by Twitchell as relayed to him,[15] but it is not known if the material is documentary.

Manuel Delgado II married *María de la Luz Baca,* daughter of Juan Domingo Baca and Gertrudis Ortiz, on April 20, 1814, a few months before his widowed father married Ana María Baca.[16]

Five children of theirs were born as follows: *José de la Encarnación,* March 25, 1815; *María Josefa Gregoria,* November 19, 1816; *José Manuel de Jesús Tranquilino,* July 11, 1819; *José Vicente,* April 7, 1821; and *José Pablo,* March 24, 1822.[17]

* * * * * * * *

Tomás Delgado and *José Antonio Delgado* were contemporaries of the first Manuel Delgado, too old to be the sons of Josefa Garcia. Perhaps they were brothers of his, if not sons by a first wife in Nueva Vizcaya; or maybe they were not related at all, to him or to each other. Tomás Delgado and his wife, *Ana María Rodríguez,* had a child, *María Rita,* born May 27, 1805.[18]

José Antonio Delgado and his wife, *Gertrudis Atencio,* or *González,* had two children: *María Dominga,* March 3, 1811, and *Juan Nepomuceno* (Juana Nepomucena?), July 15, 1808.[19]

1. **Twit. Coll.,** No. 297.
2. **BNM,** leg. 10, No. 22.
3. **Twit. Coll.,** No. 279. Twitchell published some information in **Sp. Arch.,** II, pp. 315-18, furnished by Francisco Delgado, who said that old Manuel was born at Pachuca on December 30, 1738, and had married Josefa Garcia at El Paso.
4. **B, Nambé, Poj., S. Ild.**
5. See Note 3.
6. **B-65, Sta. Fe.,** Jan. 20, 1812, bapt. of their child.
7. **Bur-51, Castrense.**
8. **M-52, Sta. Fe.**
9. **Bur-51, Castrense.**
10. **Sp. Arch.,** I, No. 252.
11. **HSNM,** Estate of Rosa Bustamante.
12. **B, Sta. Fe.**
13. **Bur-51, Castrense.**
14. **M-51, Castrense.** See **NMHR,** Vol. XXV, pp. 267-70 and footnotes.
15. Ut supra, Note. 3.
16. **M-52, Sta. Fe.**
17. All in **B, Sta. Fe.**
18. **B, Castrense.**
19. **B, Sta. Fe.**

DOMÍNGUEZ

The large and influential *Domínguez de Mendoza* family of the preceding century did not return home with the Reconquest, except for some women married to individuals who did return, and one lesser male member of the family.

José Domínguez de Mendoza, natural son of one of the old Dominguez brothers, Tome II or Antonio, by Ana Velásquez, had married *Juana López* at Guadalupe del Paso in 1682.[1] By 1692 he was an *Alférez,* twenty-six years of age, and a widower.[2] In this year he rescued his sister, Juana Domínguez, with her four daughters and one son, from Indian captivity.[3]

In 1705, Capt. José Dominguez and his wife, *Geronima Varela*, were sponsors for a wedding; also in 1714, when he gave his age as fifty and his residence as Santa Cruz.[4] Geronima was a widow in 1727 when she died, on April 11.[5]

Two known children of theirs were: *María*, wife of Dimas Jirón;[6] and *Manuel*, who was fourteen years old in 1719.[7]

* * * * * * * *

Benito Domínguez, a resident of Santa Fe in 1715, had come to New Mexico in 1693 with his mother, Agueda Morán,[8] most likely from Zacatecas.

Juan Antonio Domínguez, deceased, had a daughter, *Simona Antonia*, living in 1728, who was the step-daughter of Francisco Rendón.[9] According to this, his wife was *Catalina Maese*. A Domínguez man of this name had gotten into trouble with the authorities prior to 1716, and had offered, if pardoned, to go on the Moqui campaign of that year.[10]

Antonio Domínguez was living in Santa Fe between 1739 and 1750, during which time he made some land transfers.[11]

* * * * * * * *

José Vicente Domínguez, a native of Chihuahua, and two years a resident of Albuquerque, married *María Candelaria Garcia*, on November 1, 1774. He was the son of Tomás Domínguez and Isabel Durán y Chávez of Chihuahua.[12] Here it can be readily seen that the pre-Revolt families of Domínguez de Mendoza and Durán y Chaves, which had left for New Spain instead of returning to New Mexico, were still inter-marrying down there; and here a descendant had returned to the land of his forefathers.

1. DM, 1682, No. 5.
2. Ibid., 1692, No. 1.
3. First Expedition, p. 184.
4. M-24, S. Ild., Sept. 5; DM, 1714, No. 4.
5. Bur-48, Sta. Fe.
6. Sp. Arch., I, Nos. 233, 1223.
7. Ibid., II, No. 296.
8. Ibid., I, No. 232.
9. Ibid., No. 839.
10. Ibid., II, No. 272.
11. Ibid., I, Nos. 239, 345, 959.
12. M-3, Albuq.

DURÁN

Many members, both men and women, of the Durán family of the preceding century returned with the Reconquest, but they are hard to identify and keep apart.

SALVADOR DURÁN of pre-Revolt times and his wife, *Ana Márquez*, both deceased, had several children, some of whom came back in 1693. These were *Miguel, Diego, Lazaro*, and *Juana*. The latter became the wife of Tomás Núñez. A *Josefa Durán*, widow of Agustín Griego, and mentioned in conjunction with Juana, might have been her sister.[1]

Miguel Durán remained at Guadalupe del Paso as a soldier, where he asked to marry a *María Gamboa* in 1705. He had been born in his father's prolonged absence and given to Apaches to rear. To impede the marriage, someone deposed that both parties were bastards of Francisco de Madrid.[2] It is not known if the charge was proved untrue, or if a marriage took place.

Diego Durán came to Santa Fe and there, at the age of twenty-five, married *Pascuala Montaño*, or *Martín*, in 1694.[3] He appeared as a witness a number of times.[4]

Lazaro Durán, the third brother, married *Gregoria de la Serna* at Santa Cruz in 1698. He was twenty at the time.[5]

Luis Durán asked for a grant of land in 1713, originally made to his mother, Ana de Archuleta.[6] He was twenty years of age in 1698.[7] He is in all likelihood the Luis Durán, husband of María Romero, both natives of New Mexico, whose daughter, *María*, married Salvador Candelaria in 1725.[8]

Lazaro Durán, the second man of this name, was the son of Nicolás Durán and Juana Martín, both deceased, who married *María de Cárdenas* at Santa Cruz in 1716. His first wife had been a *Juana Lobón*.[9] He might be the same man, thirty years old in 1694, who is mentioned as having lived with the Lucero family at San Lorenzo del Paso before the Reconquest.[10]

Juan Durán married *Gertrudis Trujillo*, November 11, 1731.

Xavier Durán married *María Luján*, May 27, 1736.

Miguel Durán married *Josefa Luján* at Pojoaque, November 24, 1738, with Xavier Durán and wife as witnesses.[11] Miguel died at Pojoaque, July 25, 1753.[12]

All three men seem to be brothers, the latter two marrying two sisters, but their parents cannot be ascertained.

Nicolas Durán married *Francisca López*, January 20, 1726.[13]

* * * * * * * *

Estéban Durán from El Valle de San Buenaventura in Nueva Vizcaya, widowed of *Margarita Carvajal*, married *Margarita de Luna* at Bernalillo in 1727.[14]

1. Sp. Arch., II, No. 187.
2. DM, 1705, No. 10.
3. Ibid., 1694, No. 29.
4. Ibid., 1692, No. 1; 1694, No. 3; 1696, No. 4; 1698, No. 8.
5. Ibid., 1698, No. 10.
6. Sp. Arch., I, No. 2.
7. DM, 1698, No. 8.
8. Ibid., 1725, No. 4.
9. Ibid., 1716, No. 2.
10. Ibid., 1694, No. 34.
11. All in B-16, Nambé, M. Sec.
12. Ibid., Bur. Sec.
13. M-29, Sta. Cruz.
14. DM, 1727, No. 6.

DURÁN
(Bachicha)

JUAN BAUTISTA DURÁN was a "European,"[1] and, therefore, a Durán from Spain if not a Durand from France. He was also referred to, in one instance, as *"alias, Bachicha."*[2] Sometime around the year 1740 he had married *Antonia Mestas*, daughter of Ventura Mestas and Catalina Jurado,[3] by whom he had two daughters, *Tomasa*, born January 31, 1741; and *María Guadalupe*, February 6, 1744.[4]

After his Mestas wife's death he married *Barbara Antonia Baca*, on July 6, 1747.[5] Barbara was a daughter of Antonio Baca, sister of Diego Antonio Baca and Juan Antonio Baca, and grand-daughter of old Josefa Baca of Pajarito.[6] Durán's trade was that of a merchant. During the last years of his life until his death in 1782, he was without the use of his mental faculties.[7] The children by his second wife are as follows:

María Ursula, born July 2, 1749; *José Nicolás*, December 9, 1750; *María Gertrudis*, February 19, 1753; *Ana María*, June 1, 1757 (father's name here given as "Don Juan Bachicha"); *María Soledad*, February 19, 1761; *Ana María Antonia*, March 9, 1766; and *Juan Manuel Antonio*, October 15, 1772.[8]

Of the girls, Ursula married Manuel Bernardo Sáenz de Garvizu, Gertrudis married Francisco Suárez Catalán, and Ana María Antonia was the wife of a certain Mestas.

1. DM, 1771, no number, marriage of d. Gertrudis.
2. Sp. Arch., II, No. 841.
3. Ibid., No. 845.
4. B-27, S. Juan and B-31, Sta. Clara.
5. M-4, Albuq., and M-11, Isleta.
6. Sp. Arch., I, No. 1231; Bancroft, NMO, 1756, 1764.
7. Ibid., No. 845.
8. All in B-57, Isleta.

ENCINAS

Francisco Xavier Carlos de Encina, single, married *María Antonia de Anaya*, single, on September 23, 1757.[1] This is the first appearance of the name; the man's origin is not known.

1. **M-50, Sta. Fe.**

ESPÍNOLA

DON FRANCISCO DE ESPÍNOLA was a smelter of precious metals who joined the colonists in 1693 with his wife, *Doña María de las Heras*, and three daughters: *Catalina*, thirteen, *María Magdalena*, nine, and *Juana Antonia*, seven years of age.[1] He was forty-seven years old, the son of Don Antonio, and born in Genova (in the Valley of Mexico); he was tall, red-faced, with a low forehead and a mole on the left side of the throat. His wife was thirty-five, the daughter of Don Andrés and a native of Tenango in the Valley (of Mexico); she had an aquiline face, a broad forehead, and a small nose.

Doña Catalina, the oldest girl, born in Mexico City, was white and fair with large eyes; *Doña María Magdalena*, also born in Mexico City, had a round face, a rather broad and flat nose, and large eyes and forehead; *Doña Juana Antonia*, born in Zacatecas, was white and fair, with an aquiline face, large eyes and forehead.[2]

But Don Francisco and his wife did not reach New Mexico. They probably died at Guadalupe del Paso, if not on the journey from Zacatecas, for their three daughters continued the trek alone with the colonists up to Santa Fe. In late December, 1694, Antonio Jorge married *Catalina*, daughter of Francisco de Espínola and Doña María de las Heras, both dead.[3] Catalina's husband died within a year, and she married a widower, Francisco Lucero de Godoy, in 1695.[4]

María Magdalena became the wife of Salvador Anaya Almazán. (q.v.).

Juana Antonia married Ramón García Jurado in 1697.[5]

1. **BNM**, leg. 1, pt. 1, pp. 814-16.
2. **Sp. Arch.**, II, No. 54c.
3. **DM**, 1694, No. 28.
4. **Ibid.**, 1695, No. 6.

5. **Ibid.**, 1697, No. 3. GENEALOGY: **Juana Antonia de Espínola**, Petronila García Jurado, Juan Francisco Baca, Paulín Baca, Pablo Baca, Tomás Baca, Nicanora Baca, Fabián Chávez, Fr. A. Chávez.

ESPINOSA

NICOLÁS DE ESPINOSA was an original settler of Santa Cruz.[1] His parents were José Gómez and María de Espinosa, both natives of Villa de los Lagos and deceased in 1697, when Nicolás asked to marry *Josefa de la Cruz*, twenty-four years old, a native of San Luis Potosí and of unknown parentage. She was the widow of a Laureano Gómez, killed at Cochiti pueblo and buried in its church the previous year.[2]

* * * * * * * *

PEDRO DE ESPINOSA was living in Santa Fe after the Reconquest. He was a native of Guanajuato, and thirty years old before the turn of the century.[3] He and his wife, *Micaela Hernández*, had a child, *María*, born August 19, 1703, in Bernalillo.[4]

DON MIGUEL RAMÍREZ DE ESPINOSA was in the Velasco list of colonists from Mexico City, with his wife, *Josefa Sedano,* their two boys, *Diego,* thirteen, and *José,* nine years old; also a nephew, *Miguel de Correa,* three years of age.⁵ However, it is not known if this family actually reached New Mexico.

* * * * * * * *

Among the heads of families who asked to settle at Nuestra Señora del Rosario, Rio de Truchas, in 1754, were four Espinosas, apparently brothers, or at least members of one and the same family: *Salvador, Ventura, Miguel,* and *Tadeo.*⁶ Salvador had bought land in Chimayó as early as 1736.⁷ These men were descended from any one of the three different colonists previously treated.

1. **Sp. Arch.,** I, No. 817.
2. **DM,** 1697.
3. **Ibid.,** 1697, No. 6; 1698, No. 6; **Sp. Arch.,** II, No. 111.
4. **B-13, Bern.**
5. **BNM,** leg. 4, pt. 1, pp. 790-5.
6. **Twit. Coll.,** No. 4; **Sp. Arch.,** I, No. 771.
7. **Sp. Arch.,** I, No. 260.

ESQUIVEL

JUAN ANTONIO DE ESQUIVEL, his wife and their two children, not named, were mentioned among the colonists of 1693.¹ However, only one daughter appears in the Viceroy's list. Juan Antonio was the son of Francisco, a native of Mexico City, and thirty years of age, with a broad swarthy face and a scar between the eyebrows. His wife, *María de San Nicolás,* also born in Mexico City, was twenty-one, the daughter of Francisco Rangel; she was dark, with large eyes and forehead, and a sharp nose. They had a daughter, *Magdalena,* twelve, born in the City of Mexico; she had a round face, dark and pockmarked.²

María Rangel, eighty years old, and widow of José (*sic*) Esquivel, died on June 18, 1737.³

Buenaventura (Ventura) de Esquivel seems to have been the other child of Juan Antonio; having joined the military section of the colony, most likely, he was excluded from the family group in the civilian section, as often happened. He was thirty-one years old in 1716, when he stated that he was born in Mexico City and was now residing in Santa Fe.⁴ His wife was *Rosa Lucero de Godoy.*⁵

A daughter of theirs, *María Francisca,* became the wife of Salvador Anaya Almazán, and was a widow by 1733.⁶ Another, *Gertrudis,* married Diego Antonio Márquez at Santa Cruz in 1730.⁷

———

José de Esquivel was a resident of Santa Cruz in the middle of the century, and Alcalde of the town in 1764.⁸

Francisco Esquivel and *María Clara Gonzales* had a twenty-one-year-old son, *Ventura,* who enlisted as a soldier in 1769.⁹

1. **BNM,** leg. 4, pt. 1, pp. 830-34.
2. **Sp. Arch.,** II, No. 54c.
3. **Bur-48, Sta. Fe.**
4. **DM,** 1716, No. 10.
5. **Sp. Arch.,** I, No. 432.
6. **Ibid.,** II, No. 386.
7. **DM,** 1730, no number.
8. **Sp. Arch.,** I, Nos. 261, 262, 361.
9. **HSNM,** Mil. Papers.

ESTRADA

JUAN DE ESTRADA, mentioned in 1693, was married to *Micaela de la Rosa* in 1694. He was a soldier of Santa Fe, twenty years old, the son of Geronimo de Estrada and Teresa Rodríguez.¹ A Rosa Rodríguez, wife of Juan de Estrada, died on June 13, 1726.²

Don Luis de Estrada y Nora (Nova?) married Rosa Barbara López at Santa Cruz, May 8, 1745.³

1. **DM,** 1693, No. 8; 1694, No. 14.
2. **Bur-48, Sta. Fe.**
3. **M-29, Sta. Cruz.**

FAJARDO

Miguel Fajardo is mentioned among Vargas' soldiers in 1695.[1]

Antonio Fajardo of Santa Fe married *Rita Márquez* at Santa Cruz, September 16, 1738.[2] In 1742, November 5, he married *María Gómez,* or *Chávez.*[3]

Two children by this second marriage are known: *Francisco,* born May 22, 1748;[4] and *Antonio,* who died in infancy, May 2, 1755.[5]

1. Crusaders, p. 226.
2. M-29, Sta. Cruz.
3. Ibid.
4. B, Sta. Fe.
5. B-16, Nambé.

FEBRO

Louis Febre was one of three Frenchmen found at Taos in 1749 and brought to Santa Fe for questioning. He was a native of New Orleans, twenty-nine years old, and a tailor and barber by trade.[1] The following year, as *Luis Febro,* a Frenchman of "la Villa de la Cañada," he married *María Antonia (Tafoya) Altamirano,* June 12, 1750.[2] They had a daughter, *María Francisca,* born on December 12, 1753.[3]

On April 7, 1754, he married *Tomasa Romero.*[4] A girl, *María Geronima,* was born on October 6, 1755.[5] Here the name ended, apparently; it must not be confused with the "La Febre" name which came a hundred years later.

1. Bolton, Pacific Ocean, pp. 389-407.
2. M-50, Sta. Fe.
3. B, Sta. Fe.
4. M-50, Sta. Fe.
5. B, Sta. Fe.

FERNÁNDEZ

JUAN FERNÁNDEZ DE LA PEDRERA was a native of Mondoñedo in Galicia. His parents, Santiago Fernández de la Pedrera and Francisca Lopez de Rios, were living in Madrid when he came to the New World. On April 24, 1695, Juan married *María Jurado de Gracia,* a native of Bosque (present Albuquerque), jurisdiction of Sandia.[1] He gave his age as twenty-five the previous year.[2]

After his wife's death, Captain Juan was living with the Ignacio de Roybal family near San Ildefonso, and there in 1710 he married *María Peláez,* reared in that family.[3] By 1719 he was residing in Albuquerque, his wife's section of the country, when he gave his age as fifty-one.[4] He died there at the age of eighty on July 28, 1745.[5]

Two women known for certain as theirs were: *María,* born in 1712, who died as a young maiden on March 12, 1729;[6] and *Francisca,* who first married Captain Juan Rodríguez, by whom she had no children, and then Juan Bautista Alarí.[7]

The following men and women, from their name and connections, were in all likelihood his children also.

Juan Fernández de la Pedrera II (by the first wife) married *María Hurtado,* who bore him two children: *Margarita,* who died on May 9, 1741,[8] and *Bartolomé.*[9] This Bartolomé married Luisa Tenorio de Alba, May 8, 1740; the pair had at least seven children between 1750 and 1763.[10] Bartolomé was a charter member of the Confraternity of Our Lady of Light, as well as *Alcalde Mayor* of Jémez at this latter date.[10]

Teresa Fernández de la Pedrera married Felipe de Sandoval Martínez in 1743, with Juan Bautista Alarí and wife Francisca Fernández de la Pedrera as witnesses. She next married Felipe Tafoya in 1750.[11]

Teodora Fernández de la Pedrera married Miguel Tenorio de Alba in 1758. Presumably the same woman, she had first married a Nicolás Baca in 1747.[12]

Leonarda Fernández de la Pedrera had married a Manuel Baca, who later married Margarita Tafoya, June 12, 1750.[13]

Santiago Fernández de la Pedrera, soldier, married María de los Dolores Gallegos, March 20, 1741.[14]

Antonio Fernández de la Pedrera, who died October 17, 1760, at the age of twenty-seven, was most likely a son of Juan Fernandez II and María Hurtado.[15]

* * * * * * * *

MANUEL and SEBASTIAN FERNÁNDEZ DE VARGAS were brothers, natives of Guadalajara in New Spain, the sons of Gabriel and Ana (or Juana), their last names being confused in the matrimonial data. See *Vargas*.

* * * * * * * *

JUAN FERNÁNDEZ DE ATIENZA LADRON DE GUEVARA, son of the same, twenty-five years old and a native of Puebla, joined the 1693 colonists with his wife, child, and mother-in-law. He had an aquiline face, large eyes and forehead. *Teresa Fernández*, his wife, also born in Puebla, was twenty-two, the daughter of Martín; she had a round face, large eyes and forehead, and a thick nose.

Their son, four, was *Diego Manuel*, born in Mexico City; he also had an aquiline face, large eyes and a broad nose. Teresa's mother was María de Ribera, forty years old and a widow.[18]

In another list, Juan was set down simply as "Juan Fernández," worker in filigree, with his wife Teresa Fernández and a child, Diego Manuel Fernández de la Santísima Trinidad.[19]

* * * * * * * *

BERNARDINO FERNÁNDEZ appears as early as 1705, as sponsor with María González at the wedding of Bernardino de Sena y Valle and Tomasa Martín González.[20] He disappeared in New Spain while conducting a prisoner who also escaped,[21] but was back two years later. In 1715 he was a soldier at Santa Fe, forty to forty-three years of age. His birthplace was Sombrerete.[22] In 1718 he was referred to as "Martín Fernández," but signed "Bernardo." He was then living in Chimayó.[23]

His first wife was apparently a *Valerio*, who could have been the mother of two individuals who married in Santa Cruz: *Antonio Marcelino Valerio Fernández* with Luisa Martín, June 24, 1742; and *Lorenza Fernández Valerio* with Manuel Gregorio Montes Vigil, April 8, 1742.[24]

His wife, the second if the first supposition is correct, was *Antonia Martín*, by whom he had at least four children: *Isabel*, born November 8, 1726; *Antonio*, December 26, 1728; and *María*, February 5, 1731.[25] An older daughter, *Ana María*, married Cristóbal Garcia on October 6, 1740.[26]

Bernardino died a widower at the age of eighty-seven, May 13, 1752.[27]

Alonso Fernández, twenty-four years old in 1695, and also a native of the Mines of Sombrerete, the son of Juan Fernández and Melchora de los Reyes, asked to marry *Catalina Martín de Salazar*.[28] He could have been a close relative, perhaps even a brother, of Bernardino.

* * * * * * * *

CARLOS FERNÁNDEZ XIRALDO was born in Villacampo, Zamora, Spain, the son of Alonso Fernández Xiraldo and María de Ribera. He was seventy-two when he enlisted in 1772 at the Presidio of Santa Fe; he was still there in 1790. His wife was *Juana Padilla*.²⁹ They had been married as early as 1744 when they resided at Taos, she being the daughter of Juan Padilla and Margarita Martín.³⁰ From his wife's ancestral lands in Taos Valley he had moved down to Santa Cruz, where he was Alcalde in 1762-3.³¹ In 1757 he had asked for the post of *Teniente* at the Santa Fe garrison, but it was not until 1763 that he finally got the commission. Some years later he bought property in Santa Fe.³² He was the first *Mayordomo* of the Conquistadora Confraternity when it was revived in 1771, and was also a charter officer of Our Lady of Light.³³ By 1795 Don Carlos, a retired *Teniente*, was mentioned as dead; he died in 1793.³⁴

1. **DM**, 1695, No. 1.
2. Ibid., 1694, No. 1.
3. Ibid., 1710, No. 15.
4. Ibid., 1719, No. 3.
5. **Bur-2, Albuq.**
6. **M-24, S. Ild., B. Sec.; Bur-2, Albuq.**
7. GENEALOGY: **Francisca Fernández de la Pedrera,** Manuel Alarí, José María Alarí, María Dolores Alarid, Romualdo Roybal, Nicolasa Roybal, Fr. A. Chávez.
8. **Bur-2, Albuq.**
9. **Sp. Arch.**, II, No. 392.
10. **M-50 and B, Sta. Fe; NMHR,** Vol. 10, No. 3, p. 188; **BNM,** leg. 10, No. 12.
11. Both in **M-50, Sta. Fe.**
12. **Ibid.**
13. **Ibid.**
14. **M-3, Albuq.**
15. **Bur-2, Albuq.**
16. **DM,** 1694, No. 18.
17. **Ibid.,** 1695, No. 10.
18. **Sp. Arch.,** II, No. 54c.
19. **BNM,** leg. 4, pt. 1, pp. 790-5.
20. **DM,** 1705, No. 12.
21. **Sp. Arch.,** II, No. 187.
22. **DM,** 1715, No. 3; 1716, No. 10.
23. **Sp. Arch.,** II, No. 293; he might have signed for **Martín Valerio,** q.v.
24. **M-29, Sta. Cruz.**
25. All in **B-27, S. Juan.**
26. **M-27, S. Juan.**
27. **Bur-2, Albuq.**
28. **DM,** 1695, No. 19.
29. **Twit. Coll.,** No. 179; **HSNM,** Mil. Papers.
30. **Sp. Arch.,** I, Nos. 530, 698.
31. **Ibid.,** Nos. 359, 369; II, No. 556.
32. **Ibid.,** II, No. 537; I, Nos. 276, 278.
33. **OLC,** p. 11; **NMHR,** Vol. X, No. 3, p. 188.
34. **Sp. Arch.,** II, No. 1324; **HSNM,** Mil. Papers.

FLORES

LUCAS FLORES was a native of Parras, and twenty-five years old in 1694.¹ His wife was *María Ramos*. Lucas worked as a laborer during the restoration of old San Miguel Chapel in Santa Fe in 1710.²

———

Manuel Flores of Santa Fe, son of Lucas Flores and María Ramos, married *Ana María de Vega,* a widow of unknown parentage, in 1710; witnesses were Blas Lobato and *Juana Flores*.³ Manuel's wife died on December 24, 1726.⁴

* * * * * * * *

Don Agustín Flores Vergara was an aide and member of the household of the Governor, the Marqués de la Peñuela, and also Standard-Bearer, when he supervised the restoration of old San Miguel in Santa Fe in 1710; this reconstruction was carried out by the Confraternity of St. Michael, of which Don Agustín was *Mayordomo* at the time.⁵ No doubt, he returned with his master to New Spain when his term was up as Governor.

1. **DM,** 1694, No. 7.
2. **Kubler,** p. 20.
3. **DM,** 1710, No. 10.
4. **Bur-48, Sta. Fe.**
5. **Kubler,** pp. 5 **et seq.** Historians in the past credited the Marquis with the deed, while Kubler thinks it was Flores Vergara.

FRAGOSO

FRANCISCO XAVIER FRAGOSO, fifty-six years of age and a native of Guadalajara in New Spain, was stationed in the Santa Fe garrison in 1790. His wife was *Francisca Alarí,* forty-three.¹ He had made his last will as early as 1766, declaring that his parents were Domingo Fragoso and Beatriz de Hijar. He and María Francisca Alarí had been married ten years and had three children: *José Manuel, María Josefa de la Luz,* and *María Antonia Dolores.*² His wife had been reared from childhood by Tomasa Benavides, wife of Francisco Valdés.³

The only son, *José Manuel,* born on January 22, 1758, died at the age of nineteen, March 19, 1778, of smallpox.⁴ Thus the name died, too.

1. Sp. Arch., II, No. 1096a.
2. Ibid., I, No. 275.
3. Ibid., No. 104.
4. B, Sta. Fe; HSNM, Mil. Papers.

FRÉSQUEZ

AMBROSIO FRESQUI was an *Alférez* of the militia at Santa Cruz in 1703.¹ He was very ill in 1709 when another man was appointed to replace him.² He and a *Francisco Fresqui* were members of the Conquistadora Confraternity.³ Ambrosio had a nephew by the name of Sebastian de Apodaca.⁴

José Fresqui, son of Ambrosio Fresqui, was married to *María de Herrera* and lived at Santa Cruz.⁵ He was dead by 1720, when his wife was mentioned as a widow.⁶

They had a daughter, *Gertrudis,* who married an Antonio Martín in Santa Cruz, August 25, 1725,⁷ and a son, *Adaucto Isidro,* mentioned as José's son in 1754.⁸

Pedro Fresqui, a soldier of Guadalupe del Paso in 1719, was the son of Francisco Fresqui, deceased, and María Ortiz, both natives of New Mexico. Widowed of Micaela de Archuleta, Pedro married Clara Granillo.⁹

The name in New Mexico finally evolved into "Frésquez," to go with "Márquez" and other such names.

1. Sp. Arch., II, No. 89.
2. Ritch Coll., Box 2, No. 46.
3. OLC, p. 69.
4. Sp. Arch., II, No. 355.
5. Ibid., I, No. 641.
6. Ibid., II, No. 310.
7. DM, 1725, No. 7.
8. Sp. Arch., I, No. 1002.
9. DM, 1719, No. 4.

GABALDON

JUAN MANUEL GABALDÓN was in New Mexico as early as 1731.¹ In 1737 he acted as attorney in Santa Fe for Catalina Varela de Losada, widow of Tomé Domínguez de Mendoza, residing in Chihuahua.² He married *Antonia Juliana Archibeque* on July 26, 1735.³ In 1744 he probated the estate of his mother-in-law, María de Roybal, widow of José Reaño.⁴ Her first husband was Miguel de Archibeque.

He drew up his own will on July 14, 1745, when he stated that he was born in the City of Los Angeles (Puebla), the son of Antonio Gabaldón and Micaela de Córdoba y Rendón. He had been married to Antonia Juliana Archibeque for eleven years, by whom he had six children: *Antonio* (died in infancy), *Antonio Manuel, Juan, María Ignacia, Esteban* (died in infancy), and *Micaela.* One of the executors named was Fray Antonio Gabaldón, by permission of his superior.⁵ This Franciscan was then stationed at Santa Cruz, and seems to have been Juan's elder brother, or an uncle.

Juan did not die after making his will. He and Juliana had five more children: *Miguel Baltasar,* baptized on January 8, 1749, by his uncle, the Vicario Roybal; *Juan Antonio,*

March 3, 1753; *Manuela Rafaela,* March 28, 1755; *José Joaquín,* October 21, 1758; and *José Miguel,* October 1, 1759.⁶

Miguel Baltasar Gabaldón married *María Gertrudis Chávez,* on February 12, 1775, at Los Chávez.⁷ In 1790 he was the *Comisionado* of the first Plaza of Los Chávez and forty-one years old. His wife was twenty-six, and they had five sons ranging from fourteen years of age to three months, and a daughter who was ten. With him lived two of his brothers, not named, twenty-one and thirteen years of age.⁸ Miguel died on November 11, 1807, and his widow on February 2, 1829.⁹

Their sons were: *José Miguel, Manuel,*¹⁰ who married María Josefa Pino in 1814;¹¹ *Pedro José Mariano,* born on June 21, 1795; and *José Pablo,* January 28, 1808.¹²

Of their daughters, *Juana María* married José Enrique Luna in 1796;¹³ *María Antonia* was born on January 26, 1778, at Tomé;¹⁴ *María Juliana Encarnación,* born on March 31, 1794, married José Bruno Luna in 1809, and then José Antonio Otero in 1827;¹⁵ and *María Antonia Nestoriana* was born on February 26, 1797.¹⁶

* * * * * * * *

Juan Ignacio Gabaldón was a native of Chihuahua, the son of Juan Gabaldón, deceased, and Francisca Gradillas, both of Chihuahua. He was thirty years old when he married *Micaela Sánchez,* January 30, 1797.¹⁷ Perhaps he was related to the Gabaldón family already established in New Mexico for two generations.

---

1. B-16, Nambé, sponsor, Dec. 3.
2. Sp. Arch., II, No. 422; here the name is once spelled, "Bagaldón."
3. M-50, Sta. Fe.
4. Sp. Arch., II, No. 458.
5. Ibid., I, No. 339.
6. All in B, Sta. Fe.
7. M-11, Isleta; her family cannot be ascertained without further data.
8. Sp. Arch., II, No. 1092b.
9. B-54, Tomé, Bur. Sec.
10. AASF, No. 30.
11. DM, 1814, in Belén, no number.
12. Both in B-54, Tomé.
13. B-54, Tomé, M. Sec. GENEALOGY: **Juana María Gabaldon,** Toribio Luna, María Encarnación Luna, Eugenio Chávez, Fabián Chávez, Fr. A. Chávez.
14. B-54, Tomé.
15. Ibid., B. and M. Sec.; DM, 1827, in Belén, no number.
16. B-54, Tomé.
17. Ibid., M. Sec.

GAITÁN

José Gaitán, twenty-two years old and a native of San Luis Potosí, the son of Andrés Gaitán and María de la Concepción, married *Cecilia de la Cruz* in Santa Fe in 1694.¹ The girl came as a servant of the Martínez de Cervantes family in 1693.² After her death José married an Indian woman by the name of Geronima.³

---

1. DM, 1694, No. 21.
2. Sp. Arch., II, No. 54c.
3. DM, 1697, No. 6.

GALINDO

Antonio José Galindo, son of José María *Galindo* and Teodora Rita Santillanes, married *María Dolores Barreras,* on December 29, 1793, at Tomé.¹ His father's place of origin is not known.

---

1. B-54, Tomé, M. Sec.

GALLEGOS

The brothers JOSÉ and ANTONIO GALLEGOS were treated in the preceding century. The following are their descendants who returned to New Mexico with the Reconquest:

Diego Gallegos, sixteen years old and born in Bernalillo, the son of José Gallegos, deceased, and Catalina Hurtado, married *Josefa Gutiérrez*, on November 25, 1709.[1] He acquired a land grant in 1730 on the north side of the old Pueblo of Cochiti in the mountains. His widow and children, the latter not named, were interested in the grant in 1748.[2]

Nicolás and **Juan Gallegos**, brothers, were first cousins of Nicolás D. y Chávez. Juan killed his cousin, Bernardo D. y Chávez, by accident.[3] Therefore, they were the sons of José Gallegos and Catalina Hurtado, sister of Lucia Hurtado who was the mother of these Chávez men. A sister of theirs, *María*, married José Varela at Guadalupe del Paso in 1710.[4]

Nicolás Gallegos married *Paula Molina*, August 8, 1707, and they had a son, *Juan*, April 1, 1709.[5]

* * * * * * * *

Antonio Gallegos, II, husband of *Rosa Montoya*, was the son of the first Antonio and Catalina Baca.[6] He was twenty-two in 1699 and living in Bernalillo.[7] His sister *Elena* married Santiago Grolé (Gurulé) in 1699.[8]

Antonio died as a *Sargento* at Bernalillo in 1715, leaving his widow, *Rosa Montoya*, and eight children: *María, José, Juan Antonio, Margarita, Juana, Gertrudis, Josefa*, and one "*en el vientre.*"[9] Most of them were born in Bernalillo: *María*, February 27, 1701; *José*, October 14, 1702; *Juan Antonio*, July 7, 1704; *Margarita*, February 10, 1706; *María (Josefa?)*, May 11, 1710.[10]

The elder María married Juan Antonio Baca in 1716.[11] Juan Antonio married Juana Varela in 1722.[12] A José Gallégos who married María Silva prior to 1730, and died before 1732, seems to have been one of these children.[13]

Felipe Gallegos was also a son of the first Antonio Gallegos and Catalina Baca.[14] He married *Antonia Aragón*, September 2, 1708.[15] Two known children of theirs were: *Juana*, born October 12, 1710, and *Paula*, June 28, 1730.[16]

Cristóbal Gallegos married *Juana (Romero)*, widow of Juan de Ribera, August 16, 1728.

Nicolás Gallegos married *Isabel Jaramillo*, March 9, 1734.[17] These two men belonged to any one of the preceding families.

---

1. **B-13, Bern.**, M. Sec.; **DM**, 1709, No. 7.
2. Sp. Arch., I, No. 1346.
3. Ibid., II, Nos. 208, 120.
4. DM, 1710, No. 8.
5. **B-13, Bern**, M. Sec.; **B-2**, Albuq.
6. Relationships deduced, DM, 1716, No. 10.
7. DM, 1699, No. 8.
8. Ibid., No. 5.
9. Sp. Arch., I, No. 310.
10. **B-13, Bern.**
11. DM, 1716, No. 10; Sp. Arch., II, No. 334.
12. Ibid., 1722, No. 2.
13. M-3, Albuq., Armijo-Silva, July 27, 1732.
14. Sp. Arch., II, No. 379, uncle of Ant. Gurulé.
15. **B-13, Bern..**, M. Sec.
16. **B-2**, Albuq. Section between these dates is missing.
17. Both in M-3, Albuq.

GALVÁN

Juan Galván was living at Zia Pueblo in 1727, a man of low estate and unknown origin.[1] His sister, or sister-in-law, was a Lucia Hurtado, who named him guardian of her two children, Matías and María, ten and two years of age. The names of their respective consorts are not given.² Galván was assistant Alcalde of Zia by 1744.³

A *Juana Galván, mestiza* of Zia, died and left some property there in 1753.⁴ Known as "La Galvana," she had been captured by the Navajos as a child, and was rescued sixteen years later.⁵

1. **Sp. Arch.,** II, No. 345.
2. **Ibid.,** No. 406.
3. **Ibid.,** No. 459.
4. **Ibid.,** I, No. 193.
5. **B-H,** III, pp. 404-405.

GAMBOA

Cristóbal de Gamboa, son of Lucas de Gamboa and Isabel de Archuleta, both natives of New Mexico and deceased, married an *Antonia López, "La Manca,"* at Guadalupe del Paso in 1695, two years after the Reconquest. She was a Tigua of the pre-Rebellion Pueblo of Sandia, and both were related in the second degree of affinity.¹

Juan de Gamboa, widowed of Gertrudis Jorge, married *Antonia de Contreras* in 1710, also at Guadalupe del Paso.²

None of the seventeenth-century Gamboas, it seems, came back to New Mexico in 1693.

* * * * * * * *

Juan de Gamboa, a native of Puebla, came with the colonists of 1693 recruited in Mexico City. He was then thirty-four years old, the son of Santiago, having small eyes, a sharp nose, and was pockmarked. His wife was *María de Zépeda,* thirty, a native of Mexico City of unknown parentage; she had an aquiline face, a high forehead, and small deep-set eyes.

Their children, all born in Mexico City, were: *Juan,* eleven, swarthy, with a high forehead and a small nose; *Juana,* eight, with a dark aquiline face and three moles on it; and *Catalina,* one year old, dark, with large eyes and a small nose.³

Diego de Gamboa and *Ynez de Herrera,* both of unknown parentage, were married at Santa Cruz in 1704.⁴

1. **DM,** 1695, Nos. 4, 9.
2. **Ibid.,** 1710, No. 20.
3. **Sp. Arch.,** II, No. 54c.
4. **DM,** 1704, No. 2.

GÁONA

JOSÉ DE GÁONA and his wife, *Manuela Rodríguez,* were living in the "Rancho de José Miguel de la Peña" in 1777.¹ The earliest mention of this couple is in 1751, when she had twins in Santa Fe: *Juan Vicente Nepomuceno* and *Vicente de San Juan Nepomuceno,* October 30, 1751.² One of them died on January 31, 1752.³ A daughter, *María Josefa,* was born on April 21, 1760.⁴

Vicente Gáona, son of José Gáona and Manuela Rodríguez, of the Rancho de Nuestra Señora de Guadalupe, jurisdiction of Santo Domingo, married Manuela Armijo of Vallecito, daughter of José Antonio Armijo and Rosa Aragón, in 1775.⁵

They had two children, *Antonio,* April 12, 1778, and *Juana,* May 21, 1780.⁶

Juan Antonio "Gabona," natural son of Juana "Gabona," was born on June 14, 1767. The godmother was Doña Barbara de la Peña.⁷

1. **M-35, Sto. Domingo.**
2. **B, Sta. Fe.**
3. **Bur-48, Sta. Fe.**
4. **B, Sta. Fe.**
5. **DM,** 1775, no number.
6. **M-35, Sto. Domingo, B. Sec.**
7. **B-14, Cochiti.**

GARCÍA HOLGADO

Of this 17th century family of New Mexico, some members returned with the Reconquest, but they cannot be connected with their ancestors. Others stayed at Guadalupe del Paso.

Cristóbal García married *Isabel Romero* (or *López, Salazar*) in 1702.[1] They had a son, *Cristóbal,* November 29, 1703,[2] and another child on January 20, 1708, whose name the Padre forgot to enter,[3] probably a miscarriage that did not survive. In 1710, January 14, they had another boy, *Nicolás*.[4] *María Petrona Candelaria* was born on February 4, 1727, and *Alonso* in 1730.[5]

Cristóbal García II, widowed of *Gertrudis López,* married *Ana María Fernández,* October 6, 1740.[6]

1. DM, No. 4, incomplete.
2. M-24, S. Ild., B. Sec.
3. B-2, Albuq.
4. Ibid., section missing for next several years.
5. Ibid.
6. M-27, S. Juan.

GARCÍA de NORIEGA

Of the descendants of **Alonso García de Noriega I**, some remained at Guadalupe del Paso, to prosper and, generations later, to intermarry with New Mexico families. But the majority returned with Vargas in 1693. One daughter, *Juana,* was the wife of Antonio Domínguez de Mendoza; another, *Josefa,* came to Santa Fe with her husband, Alonso Rael de Aguilar.

JUAN GARCÍA DE NORIEGA remained at Guadalupe del Paso with his second wife, *Francisca Sánchez de Yñigo,* and their children. A daughter, *María Ana,* by his first wife, had married Miguel de Herrera three years before the Vargas Reconquest.[1]

Of the known children by the second wife, *Francisco* married María Jirón de Tejeda at Guadalupe del Paso in 1710,[2] and *María* became the wife of Juan Martín Navarro de Quesada, also at Guadalupe del Paso, in 1704.[3]

ALONSO GARCÍA DE NORIEGA II took part in the Reconquest as a Captain.[4] His first wife, *Ana Jorge de Vera,* had died at Guadalupe del Paso, and in 1694 Alonso married *María Luisa Godines* in Santa Fe.[5] He gave his age as fifty-five in 1695.[6] In 1696 he was wounded by an Apache arrow at the Paraje del Agua Escondida, while on his way to Santa Fe, and he died some time after at Sevilleta.[7]

Alonso's children by his first wife were: *Luis, Alonso III, Tomás,* and *Vicente*.

Luis García de Noriega married *Josefa Xavier y Baca,* reared in the Valverde family, on August 27, 1703.[8] With his brothers Alonso and Vicente he was a grantee of San Antonio in the Rio Abajo.[9] His wife died on January 20, 1735.[10]

His will in 1747 gave Josefa *"Valverde"* as his first wife, whose only child, *Rosalía,* was married to a Salvador Martínez. His second wife was *Barbara García Jurado,* by whom he had four children: *Luis, Ana María, María Rosa,* and *Lazaro Antonio*.[11] The last child was baptized on February 21, 1745, with Tomás de Sena and Luisa Garcia as sponsors.[12] One girl, María Rosa, became the wife of Ventura Romero.[13]

Tomás García de Noriega married *Juana Hurtado*, widow of Cristóbal de Cuéllar, on January 7, 1705.[14] While soldiering in Santa Fe in 1725, but claiming Albuquerque as his residence, he stated that he was forty years old.[15]

His known children were: *Francisca*, born on June 21, 1706, who married José González in 1719;[16] *María Luisa*, born August 12, 1708, who married Tomás Antonio de Sena in 1723;[17] and *Salvador Matías*, born March 8, 1711, who first married Catalina Sánchez, and then Margarita D. y Chávez in 1761.[18]

Vicente García de Noriega married *Catalina González* of Bernalillo on February 7, 1710.[19] He gave his age as thirty-five in 1727.[20] By 1733 he was living in Alameda when his family was believed to have been hexed by some Isleta Indians.[21] A daughter, *Juana Antonia*, was born on June 20, 1731.[22] Vicente died on January 11, 1740.[23]

* * * * * * * *

Juan García de Noriega, nicknamed *"El Cojo,"* lived in Santa Fe in the decades following the Reconquest. In 1736 he made his will, in which he stated that he and his first wife, *María Vega*, had been married for thirty-five years. They had five children: *María Francisca*, now married to José Baca; *Lazaro*, married to María Antonia Nieto; *Antonia Camila*; *Santiago*; and *Francisco*.

His second wife was *Barbara Baca*, whom he had married the previous year and who had one child, *Feliciana*.[24]

María de la Vega, wife of "El Cojo," died on July 5, 1735. Juan then married *Barbara Baca* on August 29, 1735. After his death, September 5, 1736, she married a Francisco Velásquez, August 11, 1737.[25] His relationship with the preceding Garcias cannot be ascertained.

Francisco García de Noriega, widowed of *María de Ribera*, married *Juana Sedillo*, widow of Carlos López, on March 17, 1732.[26] The first wife had died on January 28, 1732.[27]

Children by this first wife were: *Lazaro*, who married Nicolasa López, and then Francisca Varela;[28] *María Francisca*, born December 14, 1705;[29] and *Antonia*, February 20, 1711.[30]

* * * * * * * *

Juan Esteban García de Noriega was a prominent individual of the Rio Arriba district. On June 23, 1721, he married *Luisa Gómez Luján*, or *Gómez del Castillo*, with ex-Governor Valverde as sponsor.[31] He was thirty-five years old in 1731 and residing in Santa Cruz.[32] This connection with Valverde points to his being a close relative of Luis García and Josefa Xavier.

Their known children were: *José Anselmo*, born April 25, 1722; *Juan Tomás*, December 26, 1723;[33] *José Joaquín*, who married María Concepción Garcia de la Mora, October 13, 1761;[34] *José*, born January 20, 1730; and *Antonio*, February 20, 1742.[35]

---

1. DM, 1690, No. 1.
2. Ibid., 1710, No. 3.
3. Ibid., 1704, No. 3.
4. First Expedition, pp. 68, 45.
5. DM, 1694, No. 20.
6. Ibid., 1695, No. 15.
7. Ibid., 1696, No. 23.
8. Ibid., 1703, No. 5; B-13, Bern.
9. Sp. Arch., I, No. 340.
10. Bur-2, Albuq.
11. Sp. Arch., I, Nos. 340, 341, 343; II, No. 1221.
12. B-2, Albuq.
13. Sp. Arch., II, No. 620.
14. B-13, Bern., M. Sec.
15. DM, 1725, No. 1.
16. B-2, Albuq.; DM, 1719, No. 6.
17. B-2, Albuq.; DM, 1723, No. 2. GENEALOGY: María Luisa García de Noriega, Graciana Prudencia Sena, Manuel Ribera, María Guadalupe Ribera, María Dolores Alarid, Romualdo Roybal, Nicolasa Roybal, Fr. A. Chávez.
18. B-2, Albuq.; DM, 1761, in Albuq., no number.
19. B-13, Bern., M. Sec.; DM, 1710, Nos. 18, 22.
20. DM, 1727, No. 4.
21. Sp. Arch., II, No. 381.
22. B-2, Albuq.
23. Bur-2, Albuq.
24. Sp. Arch., I, No. 1225.
25. Bur-48 and M-50, Sta. Fe.
26. M-3, Albuq.
27. Bur-2, Albuq.
28. M-3, Albuq., Sept. 22, 1728.
29. M-24, S. Ild., B. Sec.
30. B-2, Albuq.
31. M-24, S. Ild.
32. Bancroft, NMO, 1731; Crespo, pars. 120-24.
33. Both in M-24, S. Ild., B. Sec.
34. M-29, Sta. Cruz; Sp. Arch., II, No. 556.
35. Both in B-31, Sta. Clara.

GARCÍA de la RIVA

MIGUEL GARCÍA DE LA RIVA, or *Riba* (also often written *"de la Rivas"*), was a native of Mexico City and a weaver by trade, who joined the colonists of 1693 with his wife, *Micaela Velasco,* and their five children: *Miguel,* fourteen, *María,* twenty, *Antonia,* fifteen, *María Francisca,* ten, and *Teodora,* seven.[1] His wife became a member of the Confraternity of La Conquistadora on arrival.[2] Miguel received a grant in the Pajarito area sometime after the Reconquest.[3]

Of the children, *Juan,* an older son who must have enlisted as a soldier and was not listed with the family, married Feliciana Rael de Aguilar.[4] He was an Alcalde of Santa Fe in 1716, when he gave his age as thirty-four, and his birthplace, Mexico City; in that year he declared his intention to return there.[5] *Teodora* married Juan Paez Hurtado in 1705, and *Manuela (María)* became the wife of Salvador Montoya.[6]

By 1716, old Miguel had died, either in New Mexico, or, more likely, in Mexico City, where the rest of the family had returned.[7] In that year the mother came back to visit her two married daughters, and to see about the patrimony due a natural child of another daughter by ex-Governor Cuervo y Valdés.[8] Teodora and Manuela died on the same day and were buried together in the Conquistadora Chapel, November 17, 1736.[9]

1. **BNM**, leg. 1, pt. 1, p. 790.
2. **OLC**, p. 67.
3. **Sp. Arch.**, I, No. 517.
4. **Ibid.**, II, No. 294.
5. **DM**, 1716, No. 17; **AGN, Mex., Inq.**, t. 533, exp. 32, f. 180.
6. GENEALOGY: **Manuela García de la Riva,** Miguel Montoya, Barbara Montoya, María Manuela Lucero, Tomás Baca, Nicanora Baca, Fabián Chávez, Fr. A. Chávez.
7. **Sp. Arch.**, I, No. 512.
8. **Ibid.**, II, No. 265.
9. **Bur-48, Sta. Fe.**

GARCÍA JURADO

JOSÉ GARCIA JURADO was a native of Mexico City, the son of Fernando, and forty years old, when he joined the 1693 colonists with his family. He was tall, with a broad forehead and nose, and small deep-set eyes. His wife, *Josefa de Herrera,* was thirty, the daughter of Agustín Mazín, and born in Oricana. Of medium height, she had big eyes, a low forehead, and heavy eyebrows.

They had two sons, both born in Puebla: *Antonio,* seventeen, with a high forehead, small eyes, and a scar beneath the chin; and *Ramón,* thirteen, with a broad face, large eyes, small nose, and a scar on the left cheek.[1] The older boy ran away before the journey started north from Zacatecas.[2]

Old José was much mistreated by Governor Valverde; by 1702 he was in Mexico City, representing the Council of Santa Fe against Valverde's confirmation as Governor.[3]

Ramón García Jurado carried on his father's feud, for as late as 1723 he also was at the Viceregal Court presenting grievances against the Bustamante-Valverde clique.[4] He had married *Antonia de Espínola* in Santa Fe, May 4, 1697, when he was eighteen. Here he gave José García Jurado as his father, but *María Rodríguez de Alava* as his mother;[5] hence, Josefa de Herrera in the Velasco list must have been his step-mother; and it explains his elder brother's running away from the colony.

Ramón and Antonia had one daughter, *Petronila,* who became the wife of Pedro Asencio López, and later of Juan Antonio Baca.[6]

After his first wife's death, Ramón married *Bernardina Hurtado* at Albuquerque in 1710.[7] He was *Alférez Real* in the Moqui campaign of 1716.[8] As Alcalde of Bernalillo and nearby Pueblos in 1732, he was accused by the Padres and others of mistreating the Indians.[9] On August 5, 1709, he had carved his name on Inscription Rock, while on the way to Zuñi.[10] He died on April 6, 1760, at the age of eighty.[11]

The known children by his second wife were: *Pedro Alcántara,* born February 2, 1711, who married Manuela Quintana, February 25, 1732;[12] *Ramón II,* who married Andrea Gallegos, and then Rosalia Baca, but had no surviving children when he died in 1768;[13] *Toribio,* who married Brigida Vallejo in 1766;[14] and *Teresa,* born on January 1, 1727.[15]

1. **Sp. Arch.,** II, No. 54c.
2. **BNM,** leg. 4, pt. 1, pp. 790-5.
3. **Crusaders,** pp. 315, 336, 339.
4. **Sp. Arch.,** II, No. 319.
5. **DM,** 1697, No. 3.
6. GENEALOGY: **Petronila García Jurado,** Juan Francisco Baca, Paulín Baca, Pablo Baca, Tomás Baca, Nicanora Baca, Fabián Chávez, Fr. A. Chávez.
7. **DM,** 1710, No. 20.
8. **Sp. Arch.,** II, Nos. 239j, 250.
9. **Ibid.,** No. 367.
10. **Art and Arch.,** Vol. 34, p. 147; **Mesa, Canyon, and Pueblo,** p. 472; Lummis misread it as "Paez Hurtado."
11. **Bur-2,** Albuq.
12. **B-2** and **M-3,** Albuq.
13. **Sp. Arch.,** I, No. 366.
14. **DM,** 1766, in Albuq., no number.
15. **B-2,** Albuq.

GARCÍA de la MORA

JUAN GARCÍA DE LA MORA was born in La Villa de Pozuelo de Almagro, in the Archbishopric of Toledo, the son of Juan García de la Mora and Manuela González. On January 10, 1725, he married María de Hornero at Pozuelo de Calatrava. A few months later, suspecting his wife of infidelity, he murdered her, fled to Sevilla, and from there shipped to the Indies. From Habana he found his way to New Mexico, where he married *Josefa Martín* on August 3, 1735. Her parents were Marcial Martin and Leogarda de Medina of La Soledad, near San Juan Pueblo.[1] A previous wedding ceremony had taken place on November 11, 1733.[2]

His New Mexican family was as follows: *Antonio,* born October 16, 1734; *Josefa,* February 9, 1736; *Juan,* June 13, 1737; *Antonia Manuela,* March 14, 1740; *María Concepción,* December 16, 1742; *Manuel Manchego,* January 1, 1745; *José,* March 21, 1747; and *Juan Simón,* February 23, 1749.[3]

María Concepción married Joaquín García de Noriega in 1761. A *María del Rosario* García de la Mora married Santiago Ortiz, April 23, 1759.[4] A *Manuel* Garcia de la Mora was Alcalde of Abiquiu in 1809.[5]

All, no doubt, were children of old Juan. An *Antonio* García de la Mora and Josefa Griego had an eighteen-year-old son, Francisco, who enlisted as a soldier in 1790.[6]

1. **AGN,** Mex., Inq., t. 849, ff. 55-68.
2. **M-27,** S. Juan.
3. All in **B-27,** S. Juan.
4. **M-27,** S. Juan.
5. **Sp. Arch.,** I, No. 606.
6. **HSNM,** Mil. Papers.

GARCÍA
(*Others*)

Manuel García PAREJAS, native of Tembleque near Toledo, married a widow, *Rosalía Abeytia,* on November 4, 1755. He had a first wife, *Isabel Vicenta Lozano,* presumably in Spain, by whom he had a son who was also dead. Manuel had no children by his second wife, with whom he had resided at La Soledad in Rio Arriba.[1]

Florencio García de LIRA, twenty, a native of San Juan del Rio, the son of Salvador de Lara (*sic*) and Magdalena García, servants of General Antonio Valverde, married *Juana Padilla* of Santa Fe, January 7, 1717.[2]

Martín García, thirty-eight, from Sombrerete, was in Santa Fe in 1693. Also, a *Miguel García*, forty, a native of Mexico City, in 1694.[3] It is not known if they were transients, oxen-train drivers, or actual residents.

José García, a native of San Juan del Rio in New Spain, the son of Manuel García and María de Estrella, made his last will in 1754. He had been married for twenty years to his first wife, *María de Guadalupe y Mendoza*, who had no children.

His second wife was *Tomasa Romero*, sister of Salvador and Felipe Romero of Santa Cruz. They had seven children: *María* (dead), *Juan Antonio* (dead), *Isabel* (dead), *Nicolás Antonio, María Josefa,* and *Antonio José*.[4] The seventh is not named.

José Manuel García SANDARTE, or *LECHUGA*, a native of San Miguel de Horcasitas in Sonora, settled in the Rio Abajo in the middle of the century. His parents were Juan María García Sandarte and María del Rosario Lechuga. José married *María Barbara Baca* of Belen, daughter of Ventura Jojola and Jacinta Baca, on February 12, 1769.[5] In 1790 he was the head of the community of Los Jarales, with his wife, three sons, and four daughters.[6] He died, a widower, on April 16, 1793, leaving one son and five daughters.[7]

Juan García y MORENO married *María Antonia Montaño* in March or April, 1783, "*con dispensa de Ultramarino.*"[8] In other words, he came from overseas (Spain).

Other Garcías are mentioned in early records of this century who cannot be identified without further data. If not members of the *Holgado* group, they were either *García de Noriega* or *García Jurado*, if not members of the odd families just treated. By the end of the century, practically all of the Garcías had dropped the second surname. By this token the Garcías ought to be the most numerous in New Mexico, though stemming from widely different sources.

---

1. **M-27, S. Juan; Sp. Arch., I, No. 359.**
2. **DM, 1717, No. 2.**
3. **Ibid., 1693, No. 10; 1694, No. 19.**
4. **Sp. Arch., I, No. 359.**
5. **DM, 1769, in Albuq., no number; M-11, Isleta.**
6. **Sp. Arch., II, No. 1092b.**
7. **B-54, Tomé, Bur. Sec.**
8. **M-4, Albuq.**

GARDUÑO

BARTOLOMÉ GARDUÑO and his wife, *Catalina Durán*, lived in Santa Fe in the years following the Reconquest. When he married her in 1695, he gave his name as Bartolomé *Sánchez*, a native of Queretaro, the son of Juan Sánchez and Ana González, and twenty-one years old at the time.[1] In 1713 he was assigned to carry some official papers to the Viceroy.[2] His widow died sometime before 1752; a grandson, *José Miguel*, was a soldier in Santa Fe at this time.[3]

Bartolomé had a son, *Gregorio*, who married Juana Sedillo in 1720.[4] The two men following, Francisco and Felipe, were very likely his sons also.

Francisco Garduño acted as a godfather in 1714; he was twenty-nine in 1727 and living in Santa Fe.[5]

Felipe Garduño of Santa Fe married *Leonarda Córdoba*, on September 29, 1733.[6]

José Garduño had a sister *María Diega*

Garduño, who died prior to 1752, and had been the wife of a certain "Vitón." Gabriel, her son, was a cousin to *José Miguel Garduño*, grandson of old Bartolomé.⁷

1. **DM**, 1695, No. 13.
2. **Sp. Arch.**, II, No. 198.
3. **Ibid.**, I, No. 243.
4. **DM**, 1720, Nos. 3, 5.
5. **M-24, S. Ild.**, Nov. 25; **DM**, 1727, No. 5.
6. **M-27, S. Juan.**
7. **Sp. Arch.**, I, No. 351.

GILTOMÉY

José Manuel Giltoméy most likely came as a soldier of the Reconquest. His name appears in Santa Fe land deeds from 1696 on.¹ In that year he also acted as a church notary.² He died on April 21, 1727, the husband of *Isabel de Olivas*.³

A daughter, *Mariana*, married Ignacio Martín, January 17, 1730;⁴ another, *Rosalia*, was the wife of Juan Manuel Varela.⁵

1. **Sp. Arch.**, I, Nos. 2, 293, 298, 639; II, No. 94.
2. **DM**, 1696, No. 8.
3. **Bur-48, Sta. Fe.**
4. **M-27, S. Juan.**
5. **Sp. Arch.**, I, Nos. 37, 862.

GINZO

Vicente Ginzo Rón y Tobar was the Teniente of the Santa Fe Presidio under Governor Marín del Valle.¹ He had married *Prudencia González Bas*, widow of Antonio Tafoya, in 1743.²

They had at least two sons: *Juan Antonio*, born December 23, 1748,³ and *Diego Antonio*, who married María Gertrudis Domínguez, daughter of Vicente Domínguez and María Garcia de Noriega, in 1802.⁴

1. **Bancroft, NMO**, 1756.
2. **Sp. Arch.**, I, No. 25; **M, Sta. Clara.**
3. **B-27, S. Juan.**
4. **DM**, 1802, in Albuq., no number.

GODINES

ANTONIO GODINES, a widower, joined the 1693 colonists with his daughter, *María Luisa*, who was twenty years old.¹ He was described in the other Velasco list as a native of Mexico City, thirty-three, the son of Don Francisco, of medium height, with a narrow forehead, joined eyebrows, and large eyes. His daughter, fourteen (a more likely age), was also born in Mexico City; she had a round face, a large forehead, and big eyes.² He was named one of the first Alcaldes of Santa Fe after the Reconquest.³

In 1694 Antonio married *María Domínguez de Mendoza*, when he gave his parents as Don Francisco de Godines and Josefa de Estrada, both natives of Mexico City.⁴ His house, up until 1714, was on the Calle Real of Santa Fe between the Plaza and the Church then being built.⁵ He worked on the restoration of San Miguel Chapel.⁶ In 1714 he made his last will, declaring the names of his parents and of his first wife, *Mariana de Villavicencio*, by whom he had three children: *Manuel* and *Antonia*, both living in the City of Mexico, and *María Luisa*, who had accompanied him and resided in Santa Fe with her husband, Antonio Tafoya. He had no children by his second wife. Nephews of his were Captain Juan Garcia de la Riva and Captain Miguel de Sandoval Martínez.⁷

María Luisa was first married to Alonso Garcia de Noriega II, who was killed by Apaches in 1696; then she was spoken for by Juan de Atienza, but she changed her mind, and finally married Antonio Tafoya.⁸

1. **BNM**, leg. 4, pt. 1, pp. 790-5.
2. **Sp. Arch.**, II, No. 54c.
3. **DM**, 1694, No. 28.
4. **Ibid.**, 1694, No. 27.
5. **Sp. Arch.**, I, No. 498.
6. Kubler, p. 19.
7. **Sp. Arch.**, I, No. 305.
8. **DM**, 1694, No. 20; 1696, No. 23; **Sp. Arch.**, I, No. 995; see Genealogy, **Tafoya**, note 17.

GÓMEZ
(*Gómez del Castillo*)

It looks as though no male descendants of the seventeenth century Gómez families returned with the Reconquest. Some women of the Parra and Barragán group appear in early records. Other early Gómez people had long adopted the second part of the name, like the Torres and Luna families. Of the once prominent Gómez Robledo family, only the daughters of Andrés Gómez Robledo, killed during the siege of Santa Fe in 1680, returned in 1693.

But early in the century there appears the mysterious family of GÓMEZ DEL CASTILLO: *Francisco, Juan,* and *Luisa,* all children of *Juana Luján,* daughter of Matías Luján and Francisca Romero, who had a prosperous homestead near San Ildefonso, including Apache and other Indian servants. These three children were already adults in 1732, sometimes called "Luján," but mostly "Gómez del Castillo," a name which became permanent. In her last will in 1762,¹ their mother mentioned her marriage to Francisco Martín, by whom there was no issue, then declared the three Gómez del Castillo as her carnal children and heirs.

The mystery arises, not from the mere fact of illegitimacy, but because there was no "Gómez del Castillo" family in New Mexico before or during this time. What seems very likely is that Juana Luján had her three children at Guadalupe del Paso by Antonio or Bartolomé Gómez Robledo,² sons respectively of Francisco and Bartolomé Gómez Robledo by some López del Castillo woman; for Juana Luján and her children were very close to the family of Ignacio Roybal, whose wife was a Gómez Robledo.

Francisco Gómez del Castillo was twenty-two in 1732,³ and was already married to *Ursula Guillén,* as attested by the baptisms of their children. Once he is referred to as "Gómez del Castillo, alias Luján."⁴ He was dead by 1762 when his mother made her last will and included his orphans among her heirs. His widow was still living at their ranch in 1766, when she declared that two of her boys had been killed by raiding Utes that May.⁵

These were their children: *Lugarda,* born July 6, 1728; *Juana María,* January 6, 1730; *Francisco Simón,* October 31, 1733; *Prudencia,* April 10, 1737; *Barbara,* 1739;⁶ *María Josefa,* March 29, 1741; *Tomás,* March 11, 1743; *Antonio,* April 15, 1745; *Sebastián,* February 3, 1747;⁷ and *María Antonia,* who married Marcos Lucero de Godoy.⁸ Barbara married Cayetano de Atienza in 1757, and Josefa became the wife of a Pedro Trujillo in 1757.⁹

Juan Gómez del Castillo married *Antonia Quintana,* by whom he had several children. *Juliana* was born on March 2, 1732.¹⁰ The mother was abducted for some days by a negro in August, 1734, an event which created quite a stir.¹¹ Other children were born as follows: *Nicolás,* December 11, 1736; *María Manuela,* January 17, 1739; *Juan Domingo,* February 12, 1742; *Antonia Apolonia,* February 10, 1745; and then twins on September 10, 1747, *Eugenio* and *Rosalia.*¹²

Luisa Gómez del Castillo, sister of Francisco and Juan, married Juan Esteban Garcia de Noriega.

* * * * * * * *

Laureano Gómez, thirty, a native of Guanajuato, or Sombrerete, appeared twice as a witness in 1696.¹³ He was killed at Cochiti shortly after, and his widow, *Josefa de la Cruz,* married Nicolás de Espinosa.

1. Sp. Arch., II, No. 556.
2. See **Gómez Robledo,** preceding century.
3. Bancroft, NMO, 1732.
4. Sp. Arch., II, No. 422.
5. Ibid., I, No. 1351; II, No. 556.
6. All in B-24, S.Ild.
7. All in M-31, Sta. Clara, B. Sec.
8. Sp. Arch., I, No. 1351. GENEALOGY: **María Antonia Gómez del Castillo,** Margarita Lucero, María Ignacia Archuleta, María Josefa Quintana, Desiderio Roybal, Romualdo Roybal, Nicolasa Roybal, Fr. A. Chávez.
9. M-31, Sta. Clara.
10. B-24, S. Ild.
11. Sp. Arch., II, No. 400.
12. All in B-24, S. Ild.
13. DM, 1696, Nos. 12, 13.

GONGORA

JUAN DE GONGORA, a wax-worker of Mexico City, joined the colonists of 1693 with his wife, *Petronila de la Cueva,* and their five children: *Cristóbal,* twenty, *María Gertrudis,* nine, *Francisca,* six, *Gregorio,* five, and *Juan José,* seven months old.¹ Juan died in Mexico City before starting out,² but his widow undertook the journey to New Mexico with her family.

Petronila de la Cueva was born in the City of Mexico, the daughter of Lorenzo, and was thirty-three years old in 1693. All the children were also born in Mexico City. *Cristóbal* was fair-skinned, pockmarked about the eyes, and had three moles on the left cheek. *Gertrudis* had a broad face, and large eyes and forehead. *Francisca* had an aquiline face with big eyes and a thick nose. *Gregoria* was white and ruddy with large black eyes, and *Juan* (*José*), the same, but with large gray eyes.³

The widow married Juan de Chaves Medina in Santa Fe in 1694 where she later acquired notoriety as a local gossip.⁴ *Josefa,* who had first married Felipe Jiménez, became the wife of Antonio Molinar in 1696. *Gregoria* and her husband, Antonio Gutiérrez, were living at Isleta in 1719.⁵ *María,* twenty-two and single, was living with her mother in Santa Fe in 1714.⁶

Cristóbal de Gongora lived in Santa Fe with his wife, *Ynez de Aspeitia,* known as "La Memela." He left her on grounds of adultery and witchcraft.⁷ He was a soldier of the Presidio and also sang in the church choir.⁸ A Gongora who collected alms for the restoration of San Miguel chapel in 1710 was in all likelihood this same man.⁹

1. BNM, leg. 4, pt. 1, pp. 790-5.
2. DM, 1694, No. 4.
3. Sp. Arch., II, No. 54c.
4. DM, loc. cit.; AGN, Mex., Inq., t. 758, ff. 468 et seq.
5. DM, 1719, No. 2.
6. AGN, loc. cit.
7. DM, 1696, No. 15; 1703, No. 2; 1705, No. 4.
8. AGN, loc. cit., t. 735, f. 277
9. Kubler, p. 19.

GONZÁLEZ
(*Bernal* and *Bas*)

JUAN GONZÁLEZ BERNAL died before the Reconquest, but some of his children returned to Santa Fe. Two daughters of his were *Antonia Bas González* and her sister *Melchora*. Antonia lived with her daughter and two grandchildren in Santa Fe, while Melchora had moved to Santa Cruz. In 1704, they deposed that land in the center of Santa Fe, unfairly granted to Diego Arias de Quirós, had belonged to Isabel Bernal before 1680.[1]

Melchora had a niece, Ana Bernal, the wife of Luis López. She lived with *Diego González*, and a *Juan González* was also Ana Bernal's uncle.[2] Juan testified in 1691 as "Juan González Bernal" that he was a native of New Mexico and twenty-three years old.[3] In short, both Diego and Juan seem to be brothers of Antonia and Melchora.

SEBASTIÁN GONZÁLEZ BAS, who returned with the Reconquest, is in all likelihood the one described in 1680-81; he must not be confused with the Adjutant of the same name who stayed at Guadalupe del Paso.[4]

Sebastián died in Santa Fe on June 11, 1726, and his widow, *Lucia Ortiz*, passed away on March 3, 1738.[5] He was an uncle of Juan González Bas of the Rio Abajo,[6] and therefore a brother, or half-brother, of Juan González Bernal. He was a member and officer in 1693 of the Conquistadora Confraternity.[7]

Apparently, he had no children of his own. His heirs, *Sebastiana González*, wife of Geronimo de Ortega, and *Salvador González* of Santa Fe, were orphans (very likely close relatives) reared by him.[8]

Salvador Gonzalez married Leonicia de la Vega, April 13, 1730.[9]

JUAN GONZÁLEZ BAS, late in 1731 when he was Alcalde Mayor of Albuquerque, boasted that he had returned at the time of the Reconquest with his family, to re-occupy the house where he had been born. He gave his parents' names as Juan González Bas and Nicolasa Zaldívar Jorge. His two brothers were already dead; Captain Sebastián González Bas, also deceased, was his uncle.[10] By 1710 he was already a Captain and residing in Bernalillo, when he gave his age as forty.[11] In 1712 he was appointed Alcalde Mayor of Albuquerque, which so angered old Don Fernando Durán y Chaves that the latter assaulted Juan, calling him a "*perro yndio Griego*," an epithet he had used on Juan's father without being contradicted. Whatever Don Fernando's right in acting so rudely, the incident shows that González belonged to the old "Bernal-Griego" clan.[12] Juan prospered, nevertheless, both as an official and landholder in the Rio Abajo,[13] until his death at Alameda on November 14, 1743; his widow, *María López del Castillo*, survived him.[14] He had been a member of the Confraternity of La Conquistadora, whose flocks of sheep were in his care in 1700.[15] His name is on El Morro with those of two contemporaries, Salvador Holguín and José Naranjo.[15a]

He had many daughters: *Catalina*, who married Vicente Garcia in 1710 at Bernalillo;[16] *Antonia*, who married Juan de Tafoya in 1716;[17] *Juana*, born July 30, 1701, who married Pedro Varela in 1716;[18] *Prudencia*, born May 8, 1704, who married Antonio de Tafoya, and then Vicente Ginzo;[19] *Ynez*, born January 30, 1703; *Valentina*, November 4, 1706; and *María Quiteria*, May 28, 1708.[20]

His known sons were *José* and *Juan II*.

José González Bas married *Francisca Garcia de Noriega* at Albuquerque in 1719.[21] Two children born to them were *María Casilda*, April 15, 1731, and *Lorenza*, August 18, 1734.[22] Presumably, there were several others born before them. Both her parents were dead when Casilda married Antonio Domingo Archibeque in Santa Fe on April 6, 1750.[23]

Juan González Bas II was born on January 10, 1710.[24] He built a church in Alameda, *Nuestra Señora de la Concepción,* at the time Bishop Crespo visited New Mexico, and its license was re-approved by Bishop Tamarón in his visitation of 1759, when it was in charge of his son, *Alejandro González Bas.* The latter left it to his son, *Gaspar González.*[25] Another son was *Antonio González,* mentioned as Alejandro's brother, who was married to Josefa Varela.[26] Alejandro's wife was *Teresa Fernández de la Pedrera.*[27]

The wife of Juan II was *Manuela Baca*, if, indeed, he is the man of this name whose wife had a child, *Andrés Facundo*, November 30, 1734.[28]

* * * * * * * *

Diego González, of the Bernal group, resident of Santa Fe and then of Santa Cruz in the same year, 1698, was twenty-four or twenty-five years old, and a native of New Mexico.[29] He is, to all appearances, the Diego in whose house Melchora González was living in 1704.[30] In 1702 he bought land in the vicinity of Chimayó, and in the following year he was an *Alférez* of the militia.[31]

His wife was *María de Benavides.*[32] Her husband was dead by 1736 when some of their children are mentioned. These were *Juan Angel,* married to Antonia D. y Chaves, *Diego II* (their mother had married Tomás de Vargas), *Leonardo,* and *Teodora,* wife of Antonio Garcia.[34]

Juan Angel González, a soldier of Santa Fe, died on April 6, 1741.[35] His widow, *Antonia de Chaves*, was still living in 1767 with three children of her late daughter, *Nicolasa González.*[36]

Diego González II, husband of *Elena Vigil,* and who died in Santa Cruz at the age of forty, December 1, 1745,[37] was most likely the brother of Juan Angel.

* * * * * * * *

The following González people were most likely members of the González Bernal family, or the González Bas sub-group.

Antonio González, husband of María Sánchez, died on April 28, 1727.

Juan Andrés Gonzalez, husband of Antonia Ontiveros, was killed by a bull on June 14, 1745.[38]

Juan González married Francisca Rael de Aguilar on January 20, 1747.[39]

Francisco González married Josefa Gutiérrez on August 6, 1730.[40]

Juan Antonio González, eighteen, was living in Bernalillo in 1726.[41]

Francisco Antonio González acted as church notary in Albuquerque in 1727.[42]

---

1. **Sp. Arch.**, I, Nos. 295, 929.
2. **AASF**, No. 15.
3. **DM**, 1691, No. 1; 1694, No. 12.
4. See preceding century.
5. **Bur-48, Sta. Fe.**
6. **Sp. Arch.**, I, No. 316.
7. **OLC**, pp. 64-6, 74-5.
8. **Sp. Arch.**, I, Nos. 316, 336, 948.
9. **M-50, Sta. Fe.**
10. **Sp. Arch.**, I, No. 316.
11. **DM**, 1710, No. 9.
12. **Sp. Arch.**, II, No. 170.
13. **Ibid.**, I, Nos. 25, 29, 605; Crespo, par. 105; **Bancroft, NMO,** 1732.
14. **Bur-2, Albuq.; Sp. Arch.,** I, No. 426.
15. **OLC**, pp. 70-3, 77.
15a. **Mesa, Canyon, etc.,** p. 474.
16. **DM**, 1710, No. 18.
17. **Ibid.,** 1716, No. 19; here she is called both "**Bas**" and "**Bernal.**"
18. **B-13, Bern.; DM,** 1716, No. 14.
19. **B-13, Bern.; DM,** 1722, No. 3; **M, Sta. Clara,** July 29, 1743.
20. The three in **B-13, Bern.**
21. **DM**, 1719, No. 6.
22. **B-2, Albuq.**
23. **M-50, Sta. Fe.**
24. **B-13, Bern.**
25. **BNM**, leg. 10, No. 43, **Albuq.**
26. **Sp. Arch.**, I, No. 990.
27. **DM**, 1766, in Albuq., no number, M. of daughter Antonia to Manuel Sánchez.
28. **B-2, Albuq.**
29. **DM**, 1698, Nos. 8, 11.
30. See first Note.
31. **Sp. Arch.,** I, No. 292; II, No. 89.
32. **Ibid.,** II, No. 197.
33. **Ibid.,** I, No. 324.
34. **Ibid.,** No. 325.
35. **Bur-48, Sta. Fe.**
36. **Sp. Arch.,** I, Nos. 365, 856.
37. **Bur-32, Sta. Cruz.**
38. Both in **Bur-50, Sta. Fe.**
39. **M-50, Sta. Fe.**
40. **M-3, Albuq.**
41. **DM**, 1726, No. 3.
42. **Ibid.,** 1727, No. 4.

GONZÁLEZ
(Others)

ANDRÉS GONZÁLEZ, a native of Zacatecas, came to New Mexico in 1693. He is very likely the soldier from Parral who joined Vargas' forces in 1692.[1] He was living in Santa Fe up until the year 1710, when he gave his age as sixty. He wrote very legibly.[2] He directed the restoration of San Miguel Chapel in that year.[3] In 1715 and 1716 he lived in Santa Cruz,[4] but was back in Santa Fe in this year to direct the repairing of the Palace of the Governors.[5]

He and his wife, *Francisca de Gambo* (*Gamboa* or *Ogamo*?), a native of New Mexico, had a son, *Diego*, who married Olaya Sánchez at Santa Cruz in 1720.[6]

FRANCISCO (GONZÁLEZ) DE LA ROSA was a native of Guejocingo in the diocese of Puebla. He gave his age as thirty-eight or forty in 1695.[7] He did not use the "González" surname when he signed up with the Velasco colonists of 1693. He said then that he was thirty-six years old, the son of Don Antonio, and was described as swarthy, with a large forehead and large eyes, and a somewhat thick nose. His wife, *Antonia de la Cerda*, twenty-four, was born in Mexico City; she was able-bodied and had large eyes. Francisco was a tailor by trade.[8]

Manuel de la Rosa was living in the Rio Arriba country in 1751; and an *Antonio González de la Rosa* lived at Santa Rosalía del Vallecito in 1763.[9]

González Vallejo. See *Vallejo.*

Antonio Sayago, twenty-five years old and born in Mexico City, came with the Velasco colonists with his wife, *María de Mora*, thirty, also born in Mexico City. They brought along a four-year-old nephew, *Juan de Sayago*, born in Tezcoco, and María's nine-year-old son, *Diego de Arroyo*, by her first husband.[10]

Since they are listed after Francisco de la Rosa, there is a possibility that this family also survived as "González." For example, *Diego Sayago GONZÁLEZ*, a witness in 1719 who was twenty-nine years old and a native of Mexico City,[11] is none other than Diego de Arroyo. Another example: *Margarita Sayago* married Felipe Tafoya on April 2, 1728; she was also called Margarita *Gallego* when acting as a sponsor with her husband in 1741;[12] but in his last will, her husband referred to her as Margarita González de la Rosa.[13] Likewise, Felipe's sister, Lugarda Tafoya, had been married to a man whose name is written down as "Juan *Gallego*," though her children adopted their mother's name.[14] This man was very likely the *Juan de Sayago* who came as a child in 1693.

A possible solution is that Juan Sayago and his cousin, Margarita Sayago, the latter born in New Mexico, married a brother and sister of the Tafoya family; but through some connection with the González de la Rosa family, even if by adoption, were known also by this name. The use of "Gallego" in two rare instances, where there were no Gallegos people involved, merely shows that the scribe was not used to the Sayago name.

---

1. **Ritch Coll.**, Box 1, No. 25; **AGN, Hist.**, 37, pt. 3, ff. 887-400.
2. **DM**, 1694, No. 17; 1709, No. 6; 1710, No. 16.
3. **Kubler**, pp. 11, 16.
4. **DM**, 1715, No. 6; 1716, No. 5.
5. **Kubler, loc. cit.**
6. **DM**, 1720, No. 2.
7. **Ibid.**, 1695, Nos. 6, 18.
8. **Sp. Arch.**, II, No. 54c; **BNM**, leg. 4, pt. 1, pp. 790-5.
9. **Sp. Arch.**, I, Nos. 538, 1068.
10. See Note 8.
11. **DM**, 1716, No. 10.
12. **M-50, Sta. Fe.**
13. **Sp. Arch.**, I, No. 995.
14. **AGN, Mex., Inq.**, t. 862, ff. 186-95.

GRIEGO

AGUSTÍN GRIEGO, still alive in 1690,[1] was most probably dead by 1693, but his widow, *Josefa Luján,* did return at the time of the Reconquest with her children. One of them was *Miguel Angel Griego.*[2]

In the meantime she had married Antonio Cisneros. In 1712, *Nicolás Griego,* in his name and of his brother *Pedro* and his sisters *Josefa* and *María,* all Griegos, brought suit against Josefa Luján, widow of Antonio Cisneros, regarding some Griego land and property. Apparently, her own children by her first husband were bringing suit.[3] Yet these same four brethren appear as *"Cisneros"* some time afterwards. (See *Sisneros, Antonio.*)

* * * * * * * *

JUAN GRIEGO was living in Albuquerque in 1718, when he sold some land in Santa Fe. His wife was *Juliana Sáiz,* sister of Francisco Sáiz.[4] Without doubt, he was one of the two young "Juan Griego" men who passed muster in 1680.

Two known children were: *Joaquín,* who married Francisca de la Luz Candelaria in 1768,[5] and *Tomasa,* born on January 6, 1736.[6]

Lorenzo Griego of Albuquerque sold some land to his father-in-law, Geronimo Jaramillo in 1733. His wife was *Casilda Jaramillo.*[7] She was the widow of Antonio Vallejo, and had married Griego in 1728.[8] A daughter, *Rosalia,* was born on July 22, 1730.[9]

Pedro Griego and his wife, *Juana Mestas,* were living at Santa Cruz, or visiting, in 1726.[10]

José Griego married *Ana María Baca (Ortiz),* natural daughter of Juana Baca; the latter afterward married Nicolas Ortiz II. This Ana María also had a child before her marriage to Griego; he was known as "José Antonio de la Fuente." A legitimate daughter by Griego was *Petrona Griego.*[11] After a year and a half of married life, Ana María died at the age of twenty-six on June 27, 1729.[12]

---

1. DM, 1690, No. 1.
2. Sp. Arch., I, No. 187.
3. Ibid., No. 301.
4. Ibid., No. 717.
5. DM, 1768, in Albuq., no number.
6. B-2, Albuq.
7. Sp. Arch., I, No. 18.
8. M-3, Albuq.
9. B-2, Albuq.
10. M-29, Sta. Cruz, sponsors, Nov. 12.
11. Sp. Arch., I, No. 964(2).
12. Bur-48, Sta. Fe.

GUERRERO

JOSÉ MIGUEL GUERRERO, a native of San Juan del Rio, and resident of Pajarito, married *María Antonia Rafaela Suárez,* in 1798. His parents were Santiago Guerrero and Juana Rosa Fierro.[1] They had a son, *Pablo de Jesús,* born in Santa Fe, January 25, 1813.[2]

* * * * * * * *

FRANCISCO GUERRERO was an *Alférez* of Santa Fe in 1752, when his son *Antonio,* twenty-one, joined the militia. His wife was *María Páez.*[3] He was also a charter officer of the Confraternity of Our Lady of Light.[4]

Antonio Guerrero, sixty years old, was First *Alférez* of the Santa Fe Presidio in 1790, and noted down as a native of New Mexico. His wife was *Polonia Casados,* fifty; they had one widowed daughter.[5] Antonio was the son of *Alférez* Francisco Guerrero and María Páez.

He was twenty-one when he enlisted in 1752.⁶

* * * * * * * *

Antonio Guerrero, Indian, married *Agustina* Archibeque, *coyota,* January 27, 1732. His widow died May 6, 1752.⁵

Francisco *Guerrero* de la Mora. (See *Mora*)

1. DM, 1798, no number.
2. B-65, Sta. Fe.
3. HSNM, Mil. Papers.
4. NMHR, Vol. X, No. 3, p. 188.
5. Twit. Coll., No. 179.
6. M-50 and Bur-48, Sta. Fe.

GUILLÉN

Pedro Guillén, a native of New Mexico, was a soldier of Santa Fe, thirty-five years old, in 1716.¹ His wife, *María Ramos,* died on February 28, 1730, at the age of forty-three.² He was still serving at the Santa Fe Presidio in 1732.³

1. DM, 1716, No. 12.
2. Buf-48, Sta. Fe.
3. Sp. Arch., II, No. 375.

GURULÉ

SANTIAGO GROLÉ was the *Jacques Grolé* (or *Grolet*), member of the ill-fated de la Salle Expedition, who deserted the stranded colony in Texas and later was picked up by Spanish troops with Jean l'Archeveque. (See *Archibeque.*) He was born in La Rochelle, France, the son of Yvon Grolé and Marie Odom, and baptized in the church of St. Jean. Leaving France with M. de la Salle, he was "lost" for five years among savage Indians, then sent to Spain by order of the Viceroy, the Conde de Galve. After returning to New Spain, he came up to New Mexico. This is the gist of his testimony in 1699 when he asked to marry *Elena Gallegos* in Bernalillo. Also testifying for him were Pedro Meusnier, twenty-seven, a native of Paris, and Juan "Archibec," twenty-seven, native of Bayonne.¹

Santiago and Elena had a son, *Antonio,* born April 2, 1703.²

Antonio Grolé and his wife, *"Teresa" Gallegos,* had a son, *Antonio,* born on July 9, 1730.³

Antonio Grolé or **Gurulé**, a farmer in the Sandia Jurisdiction, was married to *Antonia Quintana,* in the first half of the century. (Was he first married to a Teresa Gallegos? Or is the preceding Antonio his father, married to "Elena" Gallegos?)

Antonia Quintana bore Antonio the following children: *Luisa,* born June 27, 1731; *Juan Antonio,* June 3, 1733; *Fabiana,* January 22, 1736; and *Francisca,* January 22, 1743.⁴ Another daughter, *Elena,* was the widow of Jose D. y Chávez of Alameda in 1783, while a sister of hers, not named, was married to a Nicolás Montoya.⁵

The one son mentioned above, *Juan Antonio,* appears to be the man of this name who was involved in land disputes around Cieneguilla and Los Cerrillos in 1775. His wife was *María Montoya.*⁶

The French name, Grolé or Grolet, soon evolved into Gurulé, and this was further hispanicized by nineteenth-century Padres into Guruléd, as happened with Alarí into Alaríd. But the spelling went back midway to the present *Gurulé.*

1. DM, 1699, No. 5.
2. B-13, Bern.
3. B-57, Isleta.
4. B-2 and B-3, Albuq.
5. Sp. Arch., I, No. 250.
6. Ibid., No. 798.

GUTIÉRREZ

ROQUE GUTIÉRREZ and *María de Tapia* had children who returned with the Reconquest; he had died prior to 1686, according to a daughter's marriage testimony. These children were: *Alejo* and his sisters *María* and *Lucía*, all living in 1749;[1] another sister, *Isabel*, who had married José González de Apodaca in 1686; and perhaps a *Juan Roque*, a contemporary whose name links him to the family, though there is no other definite proof.

María became the wife of Juan Sedillo in 1698, and *Lucía* married Baltasar Francisco de la Peña in 1694.

Alejo Gutiérrez, a soldier in Bernalillo, married *María Naranjo*, or *Hurtado*, in 1699; six years previously she had been rescued from Indian captivity, a witness testififed.[2] She was, therefore, the fourteen-year-old girl rescued with her mother, Juana Hurtado, by her uncle Martín Hurtado.[3]

A known daughter of theirs was *Ynez*, who married Ventura Candelaria, July 20, 1727.[4] Her parents were still living in that year.[5]

Juan Roque Gutiérrez was a native of New Mexico, and a soldier twenty years of age, in 1692.[6] In 1707 he was a captain in charge of the garrison at Halona.[7] He and his wife, *Antonia Martín*, were dead in 1709 when their daughter, *Josefa*, married Diego González at Bernalillo.[8]

* * * * * * * *

Felipe Gutiérrez was more likely a younger brother of the pre-Rebellion Roque Gutiérrez, and was described in the muster-rolls of 1681. In 1693 he returned to New Mexico with his wife, *Isabel de Salazar*. He was thirty-eight, and a soldier of Santa Fe, in 1698, but the following year he was in Bernalillo, when he gave his age as forty.[9] He died at the age of eighty, the widower of Isabel de Salazar, on August 9, 1737.[10]

They had a daughter, *Francisca Antonia*, born on February 28, 1705,[11] and a much older son, *Francisco*, who married Manuela Lucero, or Montoya, at Bernalillo, October 29, 1709.[12] These latter had a son, Juan Francisco, born on October 12, 1710.[13]

* * * * * * * *

Other Gutiérrez people of this period, without doubt members of this New Mexico family, were:

Francisco Gutiérrez, tried at Guadalupe del Paso in 1683 for the needless killing of a Janos Indian during an expedition under Captain Ramírez of Casas Grandes;[14]

Catalina Gutiérrez, first wife of Diego de Padilla, *Francisca Gutiérrez*, wife of Marcos de Herrera, and *Ana Gutiérrez*, married to Bartolomé Cisneros;

Antonio Gutiérrez, who in 1716 asked for lands below Isleta Pueblo that had belonged to Cristóbal de Tapia before 1680.[15] He was thirty-eight in 1710 and a resident of Albuquerque.[16] Antonio and his wife, *Gregoria Góngora*, were living in the Isleta jurisdiction in 1719.[17]

* * * * * * * *

TOMÁS GUTIÉRREZ CARRERA was a native of Sianca Parbayón, Valley of Piélagos, in the Mountains of Burgos, the son of Juan Gutiérrez Carrera and Catalina del Cotero. He was twenty-seven in 1692 when he married *María Baca*, fifteen, a native of New Mexico.[18] After coming to the New World he had been at Zacatecas until 1689, when he came to Guadalupe del Paso as an aide to Governor Reneros de Posada. He returned with this governor at the end of his term, but was back at Guadalupe del Paso for Vargas' first Expedition in 1692.[19] In 1695 he and María Baca were still at Guadalupe del Paso, he being the *Sargento* of the Presidio there.[20]

* * * * * * * *

ANTONIO GUTIÉRREZ DE FIGUEROA, a native of Zacatecas newly arrived at Guadalupe del Paso in 1681, was described in the muster-rolls of that year.[21] From 1694 to 1698 he was still soldiering in Santa Fe. Twice in separate years he acted as sponsor with the same woman, *Jacinta Telles Jirón*, and so one can presume that she was his wife.[22]

* * * * * * * *

CLEMENTE GUTIÉRREZ, a native of Spain, and the son of Pedro Gutiérrez and María García, married *Apolonia Baca* on October 13, 1755.[23] In 1768 he bought the Rancho de los Padillas.[24] He made his last will in 1789 at San Isidro de Pajarito, declaring that he was from Aragón. Besides his Baca widow, the following children were named the heirs of his wealthy estate:

Lorenzo, Lorenza, wife of Francisco Antonio García, *María Manuela de la Soledad*, married to Mariano de la Peña, and two minors: *María Luisa* and *Juana*.[25] Another son, who must have died in infancy, was *Manuel*, born on March 31, 1768.[26]

Lorenzo Gutiérrez was living at Pajarito in 1802 with his mother, Apolonia Baca, his wife, *Candelaria García*, and his children: *José Matías, Juan José*, and *Juana Apolonia*. With them lived two nieces: Dolores García and Francisca de la Peña.[27]

* * * * * * * *

MIGUEL GUTIÉRREZ, a native of San Luis Potosí, was living in New Mexico in 1706. His wife was *María de Tapia*, a native of New Mexico, daughter of Francisco de Tapia and María de Chaves.[28]

Juana Gutiérrez, a native of Zacatecas, was the mother of a *Juana de Dios Gutiérrez* who married Cristóbal Montoya.[29] These women were possibly related to *Isabel Gutiérrez*, wife of Felipe de Tamaris.

1. **Twit. Coll.**, two fragments.
2. **DM**, 1699, No. 2.
3. **First Expedition**, p. 237.
4. **M-3, Albuq.**
5. **B-2, Albuq.**, Feb. 4.
6. **DM**, 1692, No. 1; 1695, No. 9.
7. **Ritch Coll.**, Box 2, No. 44.
8. **DM**, 1709, No. 7.
9. **Ibid.**, 1694, No. 19; 1693, No. 3; 1699, No. 8; 1716, No. 11.
10. **Bur-48, Sta. Fe.**
11. **B-13, Bern.**
12. **DM**, 1709, No. 8; **B-13, Bern.**, M. Sec.
13. **B-13, Bern.**
14. **Sp. Arch.**, II, No. 16.
15. **Ibid.**, I, No. 315; therefore, perhaps a son of old Roque and María de Tapia.
16. **DM**, 1710, No. 20.
17. **Ibid.**, 1719, No. 2.
18. **Ibid.**, 1692, No. 2.
19. **AGN, Prov. Int.**, t. 35, pp. 19, 79; **First Expedition**, p. 50.
20. **DM**, 1695, Nos. 3, 15.
21. **Revolt**, II, pp. 63-64, 140.
22. **DM**, 1694, No. 19; 1696, Nos. 1, 2; 1697, No. 7; 1698, No. 6.
23. **M-11, Isleta; M-4, Albuq.**
24. **Sp. Arch.**, I, No. 695.
25. **Ibid.**, No. 371.
26. **B-57, Isleta.**
27. **AASF**, No. 30.
28. **AGN, Mex., Inq.**, t. 735, ff. 299-300.
29. **DM**, 1716, No. 16.

HERNÁNDEZ

Nicolás Hernández, of Mexico City, twenty-one-year-old son of Domingo Hernández, deceased, and Francisca de la Cruz, married *Petrona Gómez* in Santa Fe, July 8, 1696.[1]

Francisco Hernández, husband of *Juana García*, the latter a native of Zacatecas, was killed in Santa Fe prior to 1696.[2]

Ana Magdalena Hernández, whose late husband was a Miguel de Zárate, by whom she had one daughter, was living in Santa Fe in 1712. She and her husband had been recruited by Juan Páez Hurtado in Zacatecas.[3]

1. **DM**, 1696, No. 1.
2. **Ibid.**, No. 13.
3. **Sp. Arch.**, I, No. 402.

HERRERA

JUAN DE HERRERA and *Ana López del Castillo* had several sons and daughters prior to 1680: *Antonio; Juan; Miguel; Isabel,* wife of Cristóbal Tafoya; *Eugenia,* who married Antonio de Córdoba;[1] *Ana María;* and also, perhaps, *Josefa,* wife of Domingo Martín Serrano.

The two eldest sons are treated in the section on the Seventeenth Century. Their sister, Ana María, had at least two natural sons, Francisco and Juan Manuel de Herrera,[2] and a natural daughter, Antonia López, wife of José Trujillo.[3]

Miguel de Herrera, apparently younger than his sisters, came to Santa Fe after the Reconquest, very likely in 1705 when the family, excluding Juan and Antonio, came up from Guadalupe del Paso.[4] His first wife at Guadalupe del Paso was *Mariana García;* their daughter *María* married Diego Trujillo at Santa Cruz in 1709.[5] Miguel and his sister Eugenia owned land jointly in Santa Cruz.[6]

His second wife was *Antonia de Archuleta,* by whom he had at least three children: *Miguel, Casilda,* and *Juan Antonio.* Their father was murdered by Diego Velasco in 1712 or 1713. His sisters, Ana María, Isabel, and Eugenia, are mentioned during the trial.[7] Another youth, *José,* soldiering in Santa Fe in 1728, is mentioned as the son of Antonia de Archuleta;[8] perhaps he was a baby, or not yet born, when his father was killed. Many years later, in a property dispute in 1784, descendants of his referred to Miguel as the son of old Juan de Herrera, and that he had nine children altogether by both wives.[9]

* * * * * * *

TOMÁS DE HERRERA SANDOVAL came from Mexico City among the colonists of 1693 with his wife, *Pascuala de la Concepción,* and two children: *Antonio* and *Teresa,* the latter eight years old.[10]

With them came **Manuel de Herrera** and his wife, *Francisca Rodríguez.*[11] He must have been a son, brother, or nephew, of Tomás.

Tomás and his family were living in Santa Cruz in 1698, when he gave his age as seventy-four and Valladolid (in New Spain) as his birthplace.[12] However, he was referred to as a native of Mexico City when he asked for Chimayó land in 1700.[13]

Besides *Antonio* and *Teresa,* he had two other daughters, *Gertrudis* and *Ana María,* and perhaps a fourth, *Pascuala,* wife of Carlos Días Blea.

Teresa married Diego Martín;[14] *Ana María* seems to be the woman of this name who married Antonio Martín;[15] *Gertrudis* was the wife first of José Núñez, and then of Juan de Dios Sandoval Martínez. Teresa and Ana María, involved in a suit in 1697, could easily be confused with namesakes of the preceding Herrera family.[16]

Antonio de Herrera Sandoval, born in Salvatierra and reared in the City of Mexico, was living in Santa Cruz with his family when he married *María Rodríguez,* a native of Zacatecas, in 1703. He was eighteen years old, and both his parents were still living.[17]

* * * * * * *

MELCHOR JAIMES DE HERRERA was born in Guanajuato, the son of Nicolás Jaimes de Herrera and Juana Barón. At the age of thirty he married *Angela González,* widow of Francisco de Ayala, in Santa Fe, March 15, 1696.[18] They had a daughter, *Juana,* who married Francisco Sáiz in 1718.[19]

A Melchor de Herrera, husband in 1714 of *Catalina Griego,* widow of Diego Trujillo,[20] might be the same man. He could even be the "Manuel de Herrera" who came in 1693 with Tomás de Herrera Sandoval.

These people soon dropped the second half of their name and became plain "Herrera."

The Sandoval families derive from the "Sandoval Martínez" colonists.

1. GENEALOGY: **Eugenia de Herrera**, Ana María de Córdoba, Bernarda Trujillo, Julio Archuleta, María Ignacia Archuleta, María Josefa Quintana, Desiderio Roybal, Romualdo Roybal, Nicolasa Roybal, Fr. A. Chávez.
2. **Bancroft, SWO,** 1784.
3. **DM,** 1710, No. 12.
4. **Sp. Arch.,** II, No. 108.
5. **DM,** 1709, No. 4.
6. **Sp. Arch.,** I, No. 828.
7. **Ibid.,** II, No. 172.
8. **Ibid.,** I, No. 327.
9. **Bancroft, loc. cit.**
10. **BNM,** leg. 4, Pt. 1, pp. 790-795.
11. **Ibid.**
12. **DM,** 1698, No. 11; 1712, No. 4.
13. **Sp. Arch.,** I, No. 400.
14. **Ibid.,** No. 401; **DM,** 1720, No. 1.
15. **Ibid.,** No. 33; ibid., 1719, No. 9.
16. **Sp. Arch.,** II, No. 68.
17. **DM,** 1703, No. 2.
18. **Ibid.,** 1696, No. 11.
19. **Ibid.,** 1718, No. 5.
20. **Sp. Arch.,** I, No. 926.

HINOJOS

Aparicio Alonso de Hinojos was a resident of Zacatecas before he came to New Mexico in a military capacity. In 1731 he was appointed as assistant to José Romo de Vera in drawing up the *residencia* of Governor Bustamante.[1] He is very likely the ancestor of any old New Mexicans of this name that are left, unless a female of the Hinojos family of the preceding century passed on the name.[2]

1. **Bancroft, NMO,** 1731.
2. See **El Palacio,** Vol. 56, No. 4, pp. 99-101.

HURTADO

MARTÍN HURTADO appears to be the only son of Andrés Hurtado and Bernardina de Salas[1] to have returned with the Reconquest. His several married sisters also came back with their husbands and families. In 1694 he gave his age as thirty-five,[2] and by 1709 he was a captain.[3] In 1714 he was *Alcalde Mayor* of Albuquerque, and in 1731 he stated that he was fifty-nine.[4] He died on October 17, 1734, aged "more than fifty," leaving his widow, *Catalina Varela.*[5] Several civil documents mention him, one of 1723 in particular, when he was involved in a political feud between his son-in-law, Ramón García Jurado, and Governor Bustamante.[6]

Martín and his wife, Catalina *Varela Jaramillo,* find mention as sponsors in several baptismal and marriage entries of his day. She had a sister, Luisa Varela.[7] While they might have had one or more sons, only two daughters are known for certain: *María,* wife of Juan Fernández de la Pedrera, and *Bernardina,* second wife of Ramón García Jurado.

* * * * * * * *

JOSÉ HURTADO DE MENDOZA came to New Mexico in the second half of the century. He was a native of Jerez de la Frontera in Spain, the son of Juan Hurtado de Mendoza and Josefa Fernández Ponce de León. He was first married to *María Teresa de la Fuente,* who died at Xalpa in New Spain in 1660. From there he came up to Albuquerque and in March, 1766, asked to marry *Feliciana Sánchez,* daughter of Jacinto Sánchez and Efigenia Chaves.[8] He was severely criticized by ecclesiastical authorities of Chihuahua for overstepping certain bounds in examining a rape case in 1767-1768.[9]

A known son of his was *Antonio José,* born on July 18, 1767.[10]

The family of Colonel Manuel A. Chávez confused the surname of this late-comer, applying it to the wife of Don Fernando Durán y Chaves, Lucía *Hurtado*, who belonged, however, to the seventeenth-century family of this name.[11]

1. **DM**, 1766, in Albuq., no number, **García Jurado-Vallejo**.
2. **Ibid.**, 1694, No. 10.
3. **Ibid.**, 1709, No. 7.
4. **Bancroft, NMO,** 1731.
5. **Bur-2, Albuq.**

6. **Sp. Arch.,** II, No. 319.
7. **Ibid.,** No. 79.
8. **DM,** 1766, in Albuq., no number.
9. **Sp. Arch.,** II, No. 611.
10. **B-3, Albuq.**
11. See C. F. Lummis, **A New Mexico David,** pp. 190-217.

JÁQUEZ

Although perhaps of French origin far back in history, this surname is very old in Spain. In New Spain, a certain Gil *Jáquez* had an hacienda at Zacatecas as early as 1620.[1] The name first appears in New Mexico in 1704, borne by Catalina *Xáquez* de Salazar, of Sombrerete, the mother of Beatriz Sedillo who married Pedro Montes de Oca in 1694.[2]

Juan José Jáquez was living in Río Arriba in 1754.[3]

1. **AGI, Guadalajara,** leg. 33, No. 8642.
2. **DM,** 1694, No. 13; **AASF,** No. 16.
3. **Sp. Arch.,** II, No. 529.

Julián Jáquez and his wife *Paula Martín* had a child, *María Gertrudis,* January 25, 1787.[4] His previous wife, *Jacinta Torres,* was killed by Cumanches prior to 1763.[5] A nephew of Julián Jáquez and Paula Martín was *Juan Manuel Jáquez,* an eighteen-year-old soldier of Río Arriba in 1808.[6]

All these were, to all appearances, descendants of Juan José Jáquez of 1754, who, in turn, came from a prominent family at Guadalupe del Paso, as did the Velardes of Río Arriba.

4. **B-42, S. Juan.**
5. **Sp. Arch.,** I, No. 987.
6. **HSNM,** Mil. Papers.

JARAMILLO

PEDRO VARELA JARAMILLO died at Guadalupe del Paso, but his sons, *Cristóbal* and *Juan,* came back to New Mexico in 1693 to re-settle their ancestral lands in the Río Abajo.

Cristóbal Varela Jaramillo, the sixteen-year-old described in the 1680-1681 lists, married *Casilda Cedillo Rico de Rojas* some years later. They had at least three children: *Gerónimo,*[1] *Salvador,* born September 18, 1701;[2] and a girl, *Francisca,* who married Antonio Lucero de Godoy in 1712.[3] He and his brother Juan were living in Bernalillo, possibly near the present site of Algodones.[4] He is listed as a member of the Confraternity of La Conquistadora.[5]

Cristóbal married again, between the years 1701 and 1704. His second wife, *Leonor Luján Domínguez,* bore him at least five children: *Juana,* born January 11, 1705; *Francisco,* October 12, 1706; *María,* February 13, 1707; *Luis,* in 1710,[6] who married María Antonia Lucero de Godoy on November 3, 1729;[7] and *Gregorio,* who married Francisca Hurtado, July 21, 1727.[8]

The *Alférez* Cristóbal Jaramillo was dead by 1736 when Leonor Domínguez was mentioned as his widow.[9]

Juan Varela Jaramillo, son of Captain Pedro Varela Jaramillo, deceased, and Lucía de Madrid, said that he was born in New Mexico, and was twenty-one years of age when he married *Isabel de Cedillo* at the Real de San Lorenzo, February 11, 1692.[10] In 1719, at Albuquerque, he gave his age as fifty.[11] Right after the Reconquest he settled in Bernalillo with his brother Cristóbal, but both later moved to Albuquerque, as may be seen in the baptisms of some of their children.

His known children were: *Josefa,* born on February 21, 1701; *Juana,* October 30, 1704;[12] *María,* October 20, 1706; *Teresa,* October 21, 1708; and *Francisca Antonia,* June 24, 1710.[13] Their son, *Pedro,* who married Juana González Bas in 1716,[14] must have been older than these girls. Of the latter, *Juana* married Juan Antonio Gallegos, *María* married Manuel Carrillo, *Teresa* married Isidro Sánchez Bañales, and *Francisca Antonia* became the wife of Lázaro García.

Gerónimo Jaramillo, son of Cristóbal Jaramillo and Casilda Cedillo, was thirty or thirty-five in 1716, and a resident of Albuquerque.[15] His wife was *Gertrudis Silva,* by whom he had a son, *José,* born on January 23, 1710,[16] and a girl, *Casilda,* who became the wife of Antonio Vallejo, and later of Lorenzo Griego.[17]

The son, *José,* married a Francisca *Vallejo* or *Hurtado,* of unknown parentage, by whom he had at least two children: María Rosa, January 23, 1728, and José Timoteo, January 20, 1731.[18]

Gregorio Jaramillo, son of Cristóbal and his second wife, married *Francisca Salas y Hurtado,* July 21, 1727.[19] Of their known children, *Josefa Antonia* was born on July 21, 1731;[20] *Antonio Xavier,* November 1, 1742; *Ana María,* January 2, 1745;[21] and *José Casimiro* married a Manuela Montoya, or Baca, of unknown parentage, in 1766.[22]

As may be seen, some of the Varela Jaramillos became simply "Jaramillo," while others of the same family branch might have kept the "Varela" name instead.

* * * * * * * *

JOSÉ JARAMILLO NEGRETE, a native of Mexico City, thirty-eight years old, the son of Nicolás, brought his family in the colony of 1693. He had an aquiline face, a broad forehead, and a mole on the left side. His wife, *María de Sotomayor,* thirty, was also born in Mexico City, the daughter of Mateo; she had large eyes and a mole on the left eyebrow.

Their children were: *Pedro José,* six, fair, with dark hair, a small nose, large eyes and forehead; *María Antonia,* three, having an aquiline face, large eyes, and a small nose,[23] and *Roque,* eleven, who was included in the other Velasco list, when his father gave his trade as that of a mason.[24] This boy must have joined up as a soldier, to be excluded from the later list of colonists.

Roque Jaramillo was married and living at Santa Cruz by 1711, when he stated that he was twenty-six years old and a native of Mexico City.[25] In 1723, at Santa Cruz, he gave his age as thirty-eight.[26]

His wife was *Petrona de Cárdenas,* also of the 1693 colonists, who made her last will at Santa Cruz in 1767. In it she declared that she was the daughter of Andrés de Cárdenas and Juana de Ávalos, and the wife of Roque Jaramillo, by whom she had fourteen children: *Lorenzo, Miguel* (both dead), *Juan, Juana, Sebastián* (dead), *Manuel, Gertrudis, Francisco, José, Antonio, María, Francisca Xaviera,* and two *Marías* (the last three dead). Two of these daughters were married, one to Domingo de Herrera, and the other to José Medina.[27]

Except for later migrations, the Jaramillos

of the Río Arriba area north of Santa Fe descend from this Jaramillo Negrete family, while those of the Río Abajo come from the Varela Jaramillo group.

1. **Sp. Arch.,** I, No. 751.
2. **Ibid.,** No. 418; **B-13, Bern.**
3. **DM,** 1712, No. 1.
4. **Sp. Arch.,** I, No. 78.
5. **OLC,** p. 63.
6. All four in **B-2, Albuq.**
7. **M-50, Sta. Fe; Sp. Arch.,** I, No. 418.
8. **M-3, Albuq.**
9. **Sp. Arch.,** I, No. 238.
10. **DM,** 1692, No. 5.
11. **Ibid.,** 1719, No. 6.
12. Both in **B-13, Bern.**
13. The three in **B-2, Albuq.**; Cristóbal Jaramillo and Juan "Barela" are included among the people from Bernalillo who were the "twelve" founding families of Albuquerque in 1706. (**NMHR,** Vol. 4, No. 3, p. 274.)
14. **DM,** 1716, No. 14.
15. **Ibid.,** Nos. 3, 19.
16. **B-2, Albuq.**
17. **Sp. Arch.,** I, No. 18.
18. Both in **B-2, Albuq.**
19. **M-3, Albuq.**
20. **B-2, Albuq.**
21. Both in **B-57, Isleta.**
22. **DM,** 1766, in Albuq., no number.
23. **Sp. Arch.,** II, No. 54c.
24. **BNM,** leg. 4, Pt. 1, p. 790.
25. **DM,** 1711, No. 2.
26. **Ibid.,** 1723, No. 5.
27. **Sp. Arch.,** I, No. 198.

JIMÉNEZ

Felipe Jiménez, a native of San Luis Potosí, the son of José Jiménez and Josefa de Ulloa, both deceased, married *Josefa de Góngora* in 1694.¹ He died sometime later on the road to the Salinas area and was buried in Santa Fe. His widow married Antonio Molinar in 1696.²

1. **DM,** 1694, No. 24.
2. **Ibid.,** 1696, No. 5.

JIRÓN
(Jirón de Tejeda)

DIEGO JIRÓN DE TEJEDA and *María Zúñiga y Cervantes* lived in Mexico City prior to the Reconquest, but they most likely did not accompany their sons, *Diego* and *Tomás,* who came to New Mexico with the colonists of 1693.

Diego Jirón de Tejeda II brought his young family among the Velasco colonists. He was twenty-six, the son of Diego, and born in Mexico City; he was dark, with a large forehead and eyes, and somewhat pug-nosed. His wife was *María de Mendoza,* twenty-two, the daughter of Gabriel, and also a native of Mexico City; she had a broad face, large eyes and forehead.

The two children with them, also born in Mexico City, were: *José,* two years old, white and ruddy with large, gray eyes; and *Gertrudis,* four, with a broad face, big black eyes, and a small nose.¹ Another daughter, *Josefa,* five, was mentioned in the earlier list, when her father's trade was given as that of a weaver,² but she either died, remained behind with relatives, or came with some other family. Another son, *Vicente,* most likely born in New Mexico, gave his mother's name as María de *Leyva* when he married Lugarda Salazar at Santa Cruz in 1723.³

Tomás Jirón de Tejeda and his family are in the earlier Velasco list. Apparently he joined up as a soldier, and so is not included among the colonists of the subsequent list. He was a painter *(pintor)* by trade. His wife was *Josefa González de Aragón,* and they had two small children: *Dimas,* six, and *María,* five.⁴ An older married son, *Nicolás,* came with his wife.⁵

The girl, María, became the wife of Francisco García de Noriega in 1710.

Their mother died in Santa Fe shortly after their arrival, and on October 25, 1694, Tomás married *Antonia Domínguez de Mendoza*, widow of Andrés Hurtado.[6] In 1710 he worked on the reconstruction project of San Miguel Chapel.[7] He died on May 12, 1736, at the age of seventy; his second wife died on August 23, 1748.[8]

———

Nicolás Jirón de Tejeda, fifteen years old and son of Tomás, born in Mexico City at the Calle de los Cordobanes, had a round, fair face with some moles on it. His wife, *Josefa Sedano*, was only thirteen, the daughter of Pedro, and a native of Querétaro. She was of medium build, with an aquiline face, white and fair, and large eyes. Nicolás was a painter like his father.[9]

Josefa Sedano gave her age as twenty-three in 1706, and declared that her parents were Pedro Sedano and María Coronel, both of Querétaro. Her husband was still living in 1713, but it is not known if they had any children.[10] He was dead by 1722. A sister of his wife was married to Juan Lorenzo Medina.[11]

———

Dimas Jirón de Tejeda married *María Domínguez,* a native of New Mexico, whose father had owned land in the Taos Valley.[12] In 1736 Dimas made his last will in which he named his parents as Tomás Jirón de Tejeda and Josefa *Muñoz de Castro* (Josefa González de Aragón, or else a first wife of his father), both natives of Mexico City. Dimas stated that he and his wife had been married for thirty-one years, and that they had two children, *Juan Antonio* and *Antonio*.[13] He died on November 20, 1736.[14]

———

Dropping the second part of the name, this family came to be known as "Jirón." The altogether distinct family of *Telles Jirón* also dropped the second part and became "Telles."

---

1. **Sp. Arch.,** II, No. 54c.
2. **BNM,** leg. 4, Pt. 1, pp. 790-795.
3. **DM,** 1723, No. 1.
4. **BNM, loc. cit.**
5. **Ibid.**
6. **DM,** 1694, No. 25
7. Kubler, p. 19.
8. **Bur-48, Sta. Fe.**
9. **BNM, loc. cit.; Sp. Arch., loc. cit.**
10. **AGN, Mex., Inq.,** t. 758, ff. 468 sqq.
11. **Sp. Arch.,** I, No. 508.
12. **Ibid.,** No. 510.
13. **Ibid.,** No. 1223.
14. **Bur-48, Sta. Fe.**

JOJOLA
(See *Lente*)

JOLLANCO

Bonifacio Jollanga, or *Joyanga,* was living in the Río Abajo country in 1748.[1]

Juan Isidro Jollanco and *María García* of Tomá had a son, *Andrés*, who married María Ana Antonia Montoya in 1823, daughter of José Antonio Montoya and María Trinidad Flores.[2]

---

1. **Sp. Arch.,** II, No. 462.
2. **DM.,** 1823, in Albuq., no number.

LABADÍE

DOMINGO LABADÍA, a "native of France," married *Micaela Padilla* in Santa Fe on November 2, 1766, with Tomás and Juana Padilla as witnesses.[1] But when or how he came to Santa Fe is not known. The earliest civil document that mentions him is of the same year.[2] In 1777 he witnessed the contract for the erection of a new church in Sandía Pueblo.[3] He lived for some time in the Río Arriba country, his wife's home, and also in Santa Fe, as may be seen from the birthplaces of their children. In 1790 the census of San Juan described the family as follows:

Don Domingo Labadía, European, age fifty-two, married to María Micaela Padilla, forty-two. They had three sons, aged twenty-one, nine, and five; and four daughters, eighteen, twelve, six, and three.[4] According to what descendants told Twitchell, his wife was a daughter of Juan de Padilla and Margarita Martín, the latter a daughter of Sebastián Martín.[5] The many Labadía children appear as follows in baptismal registers:

Ana María Ignacia, August 14, 1767; *Pedro Antonio*, February 6, 1769; *María de la Cruz*, May 4, 1772; *María Trinidad*, May 29, 1774; *José Miguel*, October 8, 1775; *María Rita Encarnación*, March 25, 1777; *Francisco Xavier*, December 3, 1779;[6] *Margarita*, February 23, 1783; *Juan Pablo*, May 24, 1784; *José Miguel*, in 1788; *María Andrea*, in 1789; and another *Margarita* in 1792.[7]

Two other daughters, very likely born in between the preceding children, were *Bárbara*, wife of Andrés Pacheco,[8] and *Josefa*, mentioned as their daughter when she married Manuel José Ribera in 1783.[9]

Pablo Labadía married *María Rosa de los Reyes Sisneros*, by whom he had at least three children: *José Lorenzo*, August 15, 1825;[10] *María Manuela*, April 12, 1827; and *María Vicenta*, October 29, 1829.[11]

The original French name (*Labadie* or *L'Abadie*?) was hispanicized by the Padres from the start, but it reverted to a Gallic semblance in the Nineteenth Century.

---

1. **M-50, Sta. Fe.**
2. **Bancroft, NMO,** 1766.
3. **BNM,** leg. 10, No. 45.
4. **Sp. Arch.,** II, No. 1110c.
5. Commentary in **Sp. Arch.,** II, p. 198.
6. All in **B-62,** and **63, Sta. Fe.**
7. All in **B-42, S. Juan.**
8. **B-29, S. Juan,** bapt. of their children in 1827.
9. **M-51, Castrense;** both were active members of La Conquistadora Confraternity. (**El Palacio,** Vol. 57, No. 10, p. 305.) GENEALOGY: **Josefa Labadía,** María Guadalupe Ribera, María Dolores Alarid, Romualdo Roybal, Nicolasa Roybal, Fr. A. Chávez.
10. **B-71,** Tomé.
11. **B-72,** Tomé; Vicenta married Col. Manuel A. Chávez.

LADRÓN de GUEVARA

Pedro Ladrón de Guevara was a soldier of the Presidio of Guadalupe del Paso who married *María Gómez Lozada* on July 16, 1684.[1] In the same year he was Secretary to Governor Petriz de Cruzate.[2] He was still there in 1692 acting as a notary for the friars.[3] He never settled in New Mexico proper; Twitchell interpolated "Ortiz Niño" in his name to link him with the Nicolás Ortiz family of Santa Fe, but there was no connection.[4]

Cristóbal Marzelino, eighteen years old, and the son of Bartolomé de *Guerra* [sic, perhaps the scribe's error], was a native of Osuna in Spain. He joined the colonists of 1693, and was described as round-faced with a large nose and forehead.

His wife was *Juana de Góngora*, fourteen, the daughter of Juan and a native of Mexico City; she was of medium height, with an aquiline face and large eyes.[5]

Sebastián Marzelino Niño Ladrón de Guevara and his wife, *Manuela de Chaves,* had a son, *Lugardo,* born on February 20, 1730.⁶ He was referred to simply as "Sebastián Marcelino" when named administrator of the estate of his father-in-law, Pedro D. y Chaves, in 1735.⁷ Evidently, he is the same man of this full name who moved down to Guadalupe del Paso, and there married an *Ana Lucero,* June 7, 1740.⁸

From his name, and the time in which he lived, he seems to be a son of Cristóbal Marzelino and Juana de Góngora.

* * * * * * * *

Miguel Ladrón de Guevara was a native of Puebla, twenty-six years old in 1694.⁹ He had joined the colonists from Mexico City the previous year with his wife, *Felipa Guerrero,* and a child, *Juana,* two years old. In 1696 he was *Sargento* of the militia at Santa Cruz, as also *Alcalde.*¹⁰ By 1700 he was living in Santa Fe.

———

The name of *Ladrón de Guevara* disappeared from New Mexico in the early part of the century, except when appended to the Ortiz surname occasionally by Nicolás Ortiz II and Nicolás Ortiz III. But there was a prominent Ladrón de Guevara family in Guadalupe del Paso which stemmed from any, or all, of the three distinct sources just treated.

---

1. First M-Book of **Guadalupe del Paso,** Bandelier Notes.
2. **Bancroft, SWO,** 1684; **Sp. Arch.,** II, No. 31f.
3. **DM,** 1691, No. 3; 1692, No. 3.
4. **Sp. Arch.,** I, p. 2; **NMHR,** Vol. XXV, No. 4, p. 267.
5. **Sp. Arch.,** II, No. 54c.
6. **B-2, Albuq.**
7. **Sp. Arch.,** I, No. 177.
8. **M-Book, Guad. del Paso** (Juárez).
9. **DM,** 1694, No. 21.
10. **Ibid.,** 1696, No. 14; **Sp. Arch.,** I, No. 293.

LAIN

JOAQUÍN LAIN HERREROS married *Josefa Tafoya* on September 25, 1768.¹ Three children of theirs were: *María Antonia,* born on January 6, 1774; *José Agatón,* January 12, 1776; and *Ana María Luciana,* January 12, 1780; *José Nicolás,* December 9, 1798.²

In 1787, widowed of Josefa Tafoya, he married *María Micaela Sánchez,* daughter of Diego Antonio Sánchez and Ana María Álvarez del Castillo. On this occasion he gave Spain as his country of birth, and the Padre wrote his "Herrero" surname to make it seem as though his trade was that of a blacksmith.³ A civil source describes him as Joaquín Lain *de Herreros,* European.⁴ Likewise, the 1790 census gave this correct name, with the added information that he was born at Santa Cruz, near Coca, in Castilla la Vieja, and that he was forty-eight years old. His wife, Micaela Sánchez, was twenty-five; and they had three girls, aged thirteen, eleven, and five.⁵ Joaquín died in 1799.⁶

———

Nicolás Lain, husband of María Isabel Tafoya, died on September 9, 1843.⁷

---

1. **M-50, Sta. Fe.**
2. All in **B, Sta. Fe.**
3. **DM,** 1787, no number; **M-49, Isleta.**
4. **Sp. Arch.,** II, No. 640.
5. **Twit. Coll.,** No. 179.
6. **Sp. Arch.,** II, No. 1473a.
7. **Bur-7, Belén.**

LARA

Miguel de Lara was very active as a soldier during the Indian uprising of 1696.[1] He and a *María Rodarte* were marriage witnesses together in 1695,[2] but it is not known if she was his wife.

Or he might have been the Miguel de la Cruz de Lara whose wife was *Juana de Ancizo*, and their daughter, *Josefa de la Encarnación*, was married to Ignacio Losano.[3]

1. **Old Santa Fe**, Vol. III, pp. 332-373.
2. **DM**, 1695, No. 14.
3. **AGN, Mex., Inq.**, t. 735, f. 2⁰⁹.

LARRAÑAGA

CRISTÓBAL DE LARRAÑAGA married *María Gertrudis Mestas* on June 14, 1775.[1] He had come to New Mexico as a military surgeon, his name being found in several extant orders, including the practice of vaccination.[2]

He had two sons: *José Mariano*, born on March 22, 1780, at La Cañada;[3] and *José Antonio*. A son, referred to simply as *José*, twenty-one years old, enlisted as a soldier in 1804.[3a]

José Mariano Larrañaga, twenty-eight, the son of Cristóbal Larrañaga and María Gertrudis Mesa [sic], married María de Jesús Ortiz, daughter of Matías Ortiz and Francisca Baca, June 3, 1813.[4]

José Antonio Larrañaga, son of Cristóbal Larrañaga and (he did not know his mother's name), married *María Loreta Luna*, daughter of Isidro Luna and María Luz Valdés, April 5, 1815.[5]

José Ramón Larrañaga was probably a third son. He married *Bárbara Baca*, widow of Manuel Pino, on February 23, 1817.[6] She made her will twenty-two years later in which reference is made to both husbands.[7]

1. **M-11, Isleta**.
2. **Sp. Arch., II**, at least ten documents; last date of service is 1809.
3. **B-24, S. Ild**.
3a. **HSNM, Mil. Papers**.
4. **DM**, 1813, no number.
5. **M-1, Abiquiú**.
6. **DM**, 1817, no number.
7. **Twit. Coll.**, No. 141.

LEDESMA

Juan de Ledesma was a soldier who escaped the massacre of the Villasur Expedition.[1] His wife was *Juana de la Cruz*, known also as "*La Mozonga*," who died on May 9, 1727. She was a member of the Conquistadora Confraternity.[2]

1. **DM**, 1720, No. 4.
2. **Bur-48, Sta. Fe; OLC**, p. 70.

LENTE

"Matías el Ente" was an Indian or *genízaro* living at or near Isleta Pueblo in 1736.¹ As Matías Ente, he and his wife, *Juana* ———, are entered as the parents of a child, *Nicolás Andrés*, born on September 11, 1730.² He is also written down as "Clente" at the marriage of another son, *Juan Blas*, with a María Lucero in 1771.³

Juan Felipe Lente, son of Andrés Lente and Antonia Montoya, married María Lucero in 1771. They were all designated as Indians.⁴ *Juan Rey Lente*, son of Andrés Lente and Antonia Lente, enlisted as a soldier in 1808, when twenty-six years old.⁵

* * * * * * * *

Another name similar in origin seems to be that of "Jojola," which begins to appear around the same period and same Isleta area.

Angelina Jojola, widow of Juan Vallejo, died at Fuenclara, January 19, 1762. She was also called "Jaramillo" and "Vallejo."⁶

Bárbara Jojola, or Baca, daughter of *Ventura Jojola* and Jacinta Baca, married José García Lechuga, or Sandarte, in 1769. She was called a *mestiza* and a *coyota*.⁷

---

1. B-57, Isleta.
2. Ibid.
3. M-11, Isleta.
4. DM, 1771, no number.
5. HSNM, Mil. Papers.
6. Bur-2, Albuq.; DM, 1716, No. 1; Bur-2, Albuq., June 4, 1718, death of her husband.
7. M-11, Isleta; DM, 1769, in Albuq., no number; Sp. Arch., II, No. 1092b.

LEYVA

PEDRO DE LEYVA II returned to New Mexico with the Reconquest,¹ but was dead three years later when his daughter *Angela* married Sebastián Fernández de Vargas.² He had been a member of the Confraternity of La Conquistadora.³ Whatever Leyvas existed in following generations were descendants of his and his wife, *María de Nava;* for his only surviving brother, *José de Leyva*, seems to have stayed permanently at the Presidio of Janos in Nueva Vizcaya.

Some Leyva women mentioned in the early years of the Reconquest were members of this New Mexico family. However, the name was also used by the wives of some of the new colonists from Mexico City and Zacatecas.

José de Leyva of Santa Fe, who received a grant in 1728 from Governor Bustamante, at or near the site of the old Pueblo of La Ciénega,⁴ was most likely a son of the above Pedro; at any rate, he belonged to the same family.

The name came to be spelled "Leyba" more commonly than the original "Leiva" or "Leyva."

---

1. DM, 1694, No. 6.
2. Ibid., 1696, No. 10.
3. OLC, p. 69.
4. Sp. Arch., I, No. 441.

LOBATO

BARTOLOMÉ LOBATO was a native of Sombrerete, Zacatecas, thirty or thirty-three years old in 1696.[1] A captain by 1712, he then declared that he was one of the (Páez Hurtado) colonists who arrived in 1695. While residing in Santa Cruz, he asked for lands at Yunque and Chama in 1714.[2] He acted as a sponsor in 1704 with his wife, Lucía Ana,[3] who was *Lucía Ana Negrete,* a native of Zacatecas like himself; he also declared that he was a Franciscan Tertiary *"de Avito descubierto."*[4]

Two known sons were *Juan Cayetano* and *Agustín,* and also, perhaps, a young *Bartolomé.* Another contemporary Lobato, *Matías,* could have been the older Bartolomé's brother, as he was too old to be his son.

Juan Cayetano Lobato, eighteen years old and a soldier of Santa Fe, married *Lucía Chirinos,* fifteen, in Santa Fe, February 25, 1716.[5] In 1724, Cayetano and his brother Agustín were mentioned as sons of Bartolomé Lobato.[6]

He had a son, *Bartolomé,* who enlisted as a soldier in 1745, when twenty-five years old.[6a] This Bartolomé married *María Encarnación de Sena,* October 21, 1749.[7] He and his Sena wife had the following children: *María Josefa,* June 2, 1750; *José Baltasar,* January 9, 1752; *Juana de la Luz,* June 3, 1753; *María Juliana,* February 25, 1757; *María Xaviera,* April 5, 1759; *Manuela Josefa,* March 26, 1761; *José Mariano,* February 7, 1763; *Margarita,* April 14, 1765; *Bernardo José de Jesús,* January 18, 1767.[8]

Agustín Lobato, brother of Cayetano, had a contemporary of the same name in Santa Fe, very likely a first cousin, the son of Matías Lobato. Both lost their wives the same year, and it is impossible to say which is which without further data.

1. *Agustín Lobato* was married to *Bárbara Márquez,* who had a child, *Juana Teresa,* November 2, 1747. Then she died on April 10, 1748.[9]

2. *Agustín Lobato* was married to *Juana Tafoya,* who died on July 20, 1748.[10]

Bartolomé Lobato II married *Juana Carrillo* in 1714.[11] Very likely, he was a brother to Cayetano and Agustín. Years later he moved to the Río Abajo, possibly a military transfer, where two children are recorded: a boy (name not given) born on August 30, 1733, and *Rita,* November 3, 1734.[12] He died at "the age of seventy" and was buried in the military chapel in Santa Fe, September 30, 1779.[13]

* * * * * * * *

Matías Lobato was a soldier already in 1696, when he was rescued from a massacre at San Juan Pueblo with Fr. Blas Navarro.[14] His age and "Apostle's" name would make him a brother of old Bartolomé. The names of his wife and children are not known; he died as a soldier of Santa Fe in 1715, having belonged to a soldiers' insurance pool that was to provide for his heirs.[15]

* * * * * * * *

Other early Lobatos, children of Bartolomé or Matías, were the following:

Blas Lobato and his wife were witnesses in 1723, in Santa Fe, of the wedding of Antonio Tafoya and Prudencia González Bas.[16] He died on March 5, 1727.[17] His daughter, *Francisca Xaviera,* married Cayetano Segura.

Juan (José) Lobato married *Elena Martín* at San Juan, November 27, 1733.[18] Their son, *Juan Agustín,* was born at Ojo Caliente, September 5, 1746.[19]

---

1. **DM,** 1696, Nos. 9, 11.
2. **Sp. Arch.,** I, No. 433; II, No. 178.
3. **M-24, S. Ild.,** Feb. 9.
4. **DM,** 1716, No. 10.
5. **Ibid.**
6. **Sp. Arch.,** I, No. 1035.
6a. **HSNM,** Mil. Papers.
7. **M-50, Sta. Fe.**
8. All in **B, Sta. Fe.**
9. **B.** and **Bur-48, Sta. Fe.**
10. **Ibid.**
11. **M-24, S. Ild.**
12. **B-2, Albuq.**
13. **Bur-51, Castrense.**
14. **Old Santa Fe,** Vol. III, pp. 332-373.
15. **Sp. Arch.,** II, No. 239a.
16. **DM,** 1723, No. 10.
17. **Bur-48, Sta. Fe.**
18. **M-27, S. Juan.**
19. **B-31, Sta. Clara.**

LOBERA

Francisco Lobera is mentioned once at Santa Fe, in 1767.¹ He also served as *Alcalde Mayor* at Acoma prior to 1792.²

The names "Lobera" and "Luera" occur, but rarely, in the Río Abajo area from this period on.

1. Sp. Arch., I, No. 654.

2. Ibid., II, No. 1193.

LÓPEZ

PEDRO LÓPEZ DEL CASTILLO returned at the time of the Reconquest with his wife, *María de Ortega*. In 1699 he was in Bernalillo.¹ His family and that of *Juana López del Castillo* (most probably his sister) were supposed to be among the original founding families of Albuquerque in 1706.²

His known children were: *José*³ *Pedro Asencio*, and *María*, who was the wife of *Juan González Bas*.

Pedro Asencio López was involved in a fracas with Nicolás D. y Chaves in 1719, from which some of his family relationships are known.⁴ In this same year he married *Petronila García Jurado*,⁵ who later married Juan Antonio Baca.

* * * * * * * *

Of the other López families of the preceding century, those called simply *López*, as well as the *de Gracia*, *Mederos*, *de Ocanto*, and *Sambrano* clans, no males seem to have returned in 1693, or else no connection can be made with López individuals who appear with the Reconquest and immediately after.

NICOLÁS LÓPEZ, killed at Santo Domingo Pueblo in 1680, might have belonged to the López de Gracia group. His widow, *Ana Luján*, returned in 1693 with three sons, *Carlos*, *Luis*, and *Juan*.

Carlos López was transferred back to the Presidio of Guadalupe del Paso, where he married *María González de Apodaca*, resident of Ysleta del Paso, on December 13, 1698.⁶ Both came back eventually to Santa Fe, where she died in 1712; Carlos then married *Juana de Cedillo*, on January 12, 1716. He was thirty-five at the time.⁷ Carlos and his brother Juan were claiming certain lands at Pojoaque in this same year.⁸ While living in the country north of Santa Fe with his first wife, they had at least three girls after the turn of the century: *Nicolasa*, August 10, 1704; *Gregoria Paula*, January 20, 1707;⁹ and *Lorenza Gertrudis*, August 17, 1709.¹⁰

Carlos was dead by 1736 when his widow, Juana Cedillo, was mentioned as the wife of Captain Francisco García.¹¹

Luis López was married to *Ana María Bernal* as early as 1704.¹² She was at least a half-sister to Tomasa Martín González, wife of Bernardino de Sena, since López considered himself an uncle of Sena's son, Tomás.¹³ In 1728, Luis made his last will in Santa Cruz, giving his parents as Nicolás López and Ana Luján, both natives of New Mexico and deceased. His wife was (*Ana*) *María de la Concepción*, to whom he had been married for thirty years. They had one daughter, *Micaela Antonia*.¹⁴ His age was given as fifty-one and fifty-seven in 1731.¹⁵

Ana María died on March 3, 1762, being more than eighty years old; and Luis followed, June 4, 1772, aged more than ninety-seven years.¹⁶

Of the colonists who came with the Reconquest, or shortly afterwards, the following López people appear in early documents.

Juan López, "*alias el Grande*," was a native of Guadalajara.[17]

José López, forty-one, who had a wife in Mexico City, joined the New Mexico exiles at Guadalupe del Paso in 1681. He had a good build, a thick beard, an aquiline nose, and a red moustache.[18]

José López, forty-eight or fifty, a native of Villa de los Lagos, was living in Santa Fe in 1695.[19]

José López, the son of José López and María de Espinosa, natives of New Spain, married *Sebastiana Rodríguez* in Santa Fe in 1696.[20] He could be the son of either of the two preceding men.

Pedro López Gallardo, a master-builder, worked on the restoration of San Miguel Chapel in 1710. A small daughter of his was buried in this same year.[21]

Other López individuals, who could have belonged to any one of all the preceding groups, are the following:

Andrés López was married to *Ana Varela*. Two sons born to them were *Gregorio Ignacio*, February 5, 1729, and *Nicolás Antonio*, April 3, 1730.[22]

Pedro Marcial López married *Isabel Cedillo* at Alameda, October 8, 1730; they had a child, *María Apolonia*, July 4, 1731.[23] This man most likely was a López *del Castillo*. Likewise,

Miguel López, whose wife, *Juana García*, bore him a son, *Pedro Asencio*, July 10, 1744.[24]

Nicolás López of Chimayó was dead prior to 1736; his widow was *María Rosa Martín*, daughter of Captain Luis Martín.[25]

Manuel López married a *María de Herrera*, November 12, 1736.[26]

Gerónimo López married *Gertrudis Montaño*, August 25, 1737.[27]

---

1. DM, 1699, No. 5.
2. NMHR, Vol. IV, No. 3, p. 274.
3. Sp. Arch., I, No. 426.
4. Ibid., II, No. 299.
5. DM, 1719, No. 3.
6. Ibid., 1698, No. 15.
7. Ibid., 1716, No. 3.
8. Sp. Arch., I, No. 234.
9. Both in M-24, S. Ild., B. Sec.
10. B-18a, Nambé.
11. Sp. Arch., I, No. 178.
12. Ibid., II, No. 137b; AASF, No. 16.
13. Twit. Coll., No. 287.
14. Sp. Arch., I, No. 442.
15. Bancroft, NMO, 1731.
16. Bur-48, Sta. Fe.
17. DM, 1705, No. 9.
18. Revolt, II, pp. 74, 134-135.
19. DM, 1695, Nos. 2, 12.
20. Ibid., 1696, No. 9.
21. Kubler, pp. 16, 19-20.
22. B-2, Albuq.
23. M-3 and B-2, Albuq.
24. Ibid.
25. Sp. Arch., I, No. 260.
26. M-29, Sta. Cruz.
27. M-50, Sta. Fe.

LOSANO

Ignacio Losano and his wife, not named, were sponsors in 1694.[1] He died on February 23, 1728; his widow, Josefa ———, died on September 11, 1729.[2] This woman was *Josefa de la Encarnación*, daughter of Miguel de la Cruz de Lara and Juana de Ancizo. She was also called "La Losana" and "La Lara." Both she and Ignacio were from Sombrerete.[3]

---

1. DM, 1694, No. 26.
2. Bur-48, Sta. Fe.
3. AGN, Mex., Inq., t. 735, ff. 288, 291-299.

LUCERO
(Lucero de Godoy)

JUAN LUCERO DE GODOY, so very active before the Rebellion, returned to New Mexico in 1693 with his third wife, *Isabel (Hurtado) de Salazar,* and her mother, Doña Bernardina de Salas y Trujillo. They were living on his old property in Santa Fe right after the Reconquest, the "Pueblo Quemado." He gave his age as sixty-nine in 1693.[1] The following two years he signed two statements in which his age was given as seventy and seventy-one.[2]

Of his four sons by either, or both, of his first two wives, three are known to have returned in 1693, *Juan, Antonio,* and *Nicolás.* These had their own families.

Juan de Dios Lucero de Godoy II, brother of the *Alférez* Antonio Lucero,[3] seems to be the Juan Lucero who was killed by Indians with two other Spanish soldiers on March 4, 1703. As he was a member of the Conquistadora Confraternity, it had Masses said for the repose of his soul.[3a]

Antonio Lucero de Godoy, *Alférez,* the son of Juan and his second wife, Juana de Carvajal, came to New Mexico with his second wife, *Antonia Varela de Perea,* or *de Losada.* (The two children by his first wife could be any of the unidentified Luceros appearing in various documents.) Early in the century he was asking for Santa Fe lands that had belonged to his father, Juan.[4] In 1695 and 1696, he gave his age as forty-five, in 1699 as forty-eight, and in 1705 as fifty.[5] He belonged to the Conquistadora Confraternity,[6] and was dead by 1712, when his widow made her last will.

Antonia Varela named their children as follows: *Rosa,* wife of Ventura de Esquivel, *Antonio, Juan,* and *Diego.*[7]

Antonio Lucero married *Francisca Jaramillo* at Albuquerque, on September 27, 1712.[8]

Juan Lucero lived in Santa Fe near the site of the old post-Reconquest Church of Saint Francis by the ancient north wall of the city.[9] His wife was *Isabel Luján.* He died in 1741 and was buried in the Conquistadora Chapel on November 23; she died on August 9, 1771.[10] When Isabel made her will in 1771 she listed their five children: *María Antonia, Francisca Alfonsa,*[11] *Pedro,* married to Margarita Lobato; *María Ignacia,* and *Juan* (dead).[12]

Diego Lucero married *Margarita Baca,* July 5, 1716, at San Ildefonso, with his brother Juan and wife Isabel Luján as witnesses.[13] Three known sons of theirs were: *Miguel,* who married Nicolasa González;[14] *Diego,* husband of Ana María Martín; and *Marcos,* who married María Antonia Gómez del Castillo.[15]

The name of Diego Lucero de Godoy is found on El Morro with those of three contemporaries.

Nicolás Lucero de Godoy, who married *María Montoya,* seems to be a son of old Juan and a brother of Antonio, there being no conclusive proof. He settled in the Río Abajo, giving his age as fifty in 1696.[16] In 1710 he was living in Albuquerque, and by 1716 he gave his age as seventy.[17] His family, and that of Bernardina de Salas y Trujillo [his father's third mother-in-law] were considered among the original founders of Albuquerque in 1706.[18] Nicolás died on April 27, 1727, and María Montoya on January 12, 1740.[19]

Their known children were: *Pedro;*[20] *Francisca,* who married Juan Antonio Apodaca in 1716; and *Manuela,* who married Francisco Gutiérrez in 1709.[21] A *Luis Lucero,* who married María Romero at Isleta in 1719 might also have been his son,[22] and also *Miguel Lucero,* husband of Angela Vallejo, treated further on.

* * * * * * * *

FRANCISCO LUCERO DE GODOY, Armorer and Captain of Artillery, took part in

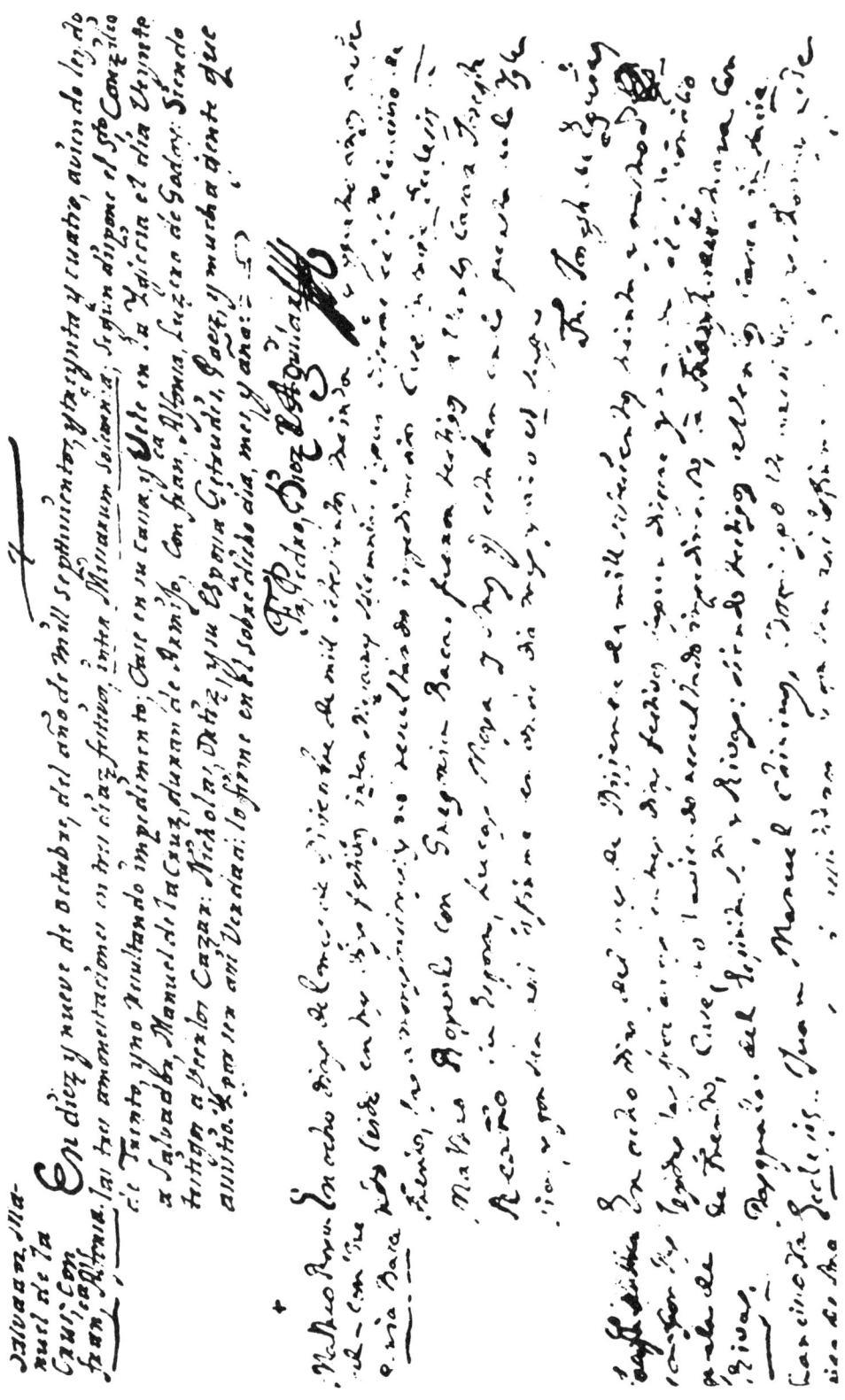

Sample page of *Marriage Book 50* of Santa Fe, showing marriage entries of Manuel de la Cruz Durán de Armijo and Francisca Alfonsa Lucero de Godoy, October 19, 1734; and of Mateo de Roybal and Gregoria Baca, December 8, 1734.

the Vargas Expedition of 1692, when he rescued a nephew, the son of Cristóbal de Anaya.²³ He was stationed in Santa Fe after the Reconquest with his wife, *Josefa Sambrano de Grijalva;* he gave his age as fifty-three in 1698.²⁴

Their known children were *Francisco Mateo, Beatriz, María Josefa,* and *Lucía,* the last-named married to Francisco del Río of Guadalupe del Paso.²⁵ Beatriz and Josefa were asking for ancestral lands in Santa Fe in 1704.²⁶ In 1691 Beatriz had been asked for by Gabriel Tapia, but it looks as though the wedding request was rejected because of impediments.²⁷ In that same year, María married Juan de Alderete.

Francisco Mateo sometimes called himself "*López de Godoy,*" combining his mother's family name (López Sambrano) with his father's.²⁸ His wife's name is not known, but he had three daughters: *Ana María, María Magdalena,* and *Francisca.*²⁹ A Francisca Lucero who married Andrés Montoya could be one of these girls, if not a daughter of the elder Francisco.

* * * * * * * *

Miguel Lucero, living in the Río Abajo, was already married to Angela Vallejo at the start of the century. Their children were *Manuel,*³⁰ *María,* born December 1, 1708, and *Miguel* II, born on January 6, 1710, after the untimely death of his father,³¹ who was wounded at El Morro and died shortly after at Zuñi, June 15, 1709, when he was buried in the Mission's sanctuary, on the Epistle side.³² On December 8, 1710, his widow acted as sponsor with a Pedro Lucero,³³ who could well be her brother-in-law, and one of the sons of old Nicolás Lucero de Godoy.

———

Miguel Lucero II made his last will at his home in Fuenclara, on January 20, 1766, being then *Alcalde Mayor* of Albuquerque. After naming his parents, Miguel Lucero and Angela Vallejo, he stated that he had been married to *Rosa Baca* for twenty-six years, and then to *Antonia Chaves,* widow of Baltasar de Beytia.³⁴ Rosa Baca had died on June 29, 1755, at Tomé.³⁵ Miguel had been *Alcalde Mayor* of Albuquerque already in 1763.³⁶

The children named in the will are as follows: By Rosa Baca: *Josefita, Miguel, Manuel, Loreta* (these four already married), *Lugarda, Graciana, Mariano,* and *Ana.* By Antonia Chaves: *María de la Luz, María Bárbara, José, Antonio José, María Antonia, Tomás,* and *María Gertrudis.* Miguel also mentioned his brother, Manuel Lucero.³⁷ He died on January 25, 1766.³⁸

Of the above-named children, *Manuel,* born June 18, 1740,³⁹ married Teresa Chaves of Los Padillas, and then a second cousin, Bárbara Montoya, of Atrisco.⁴⁰ *Lugarda* married Francisco Silva, and then Pedro Bautista Pino in 1781, *María Bárbara* married Julián Rael in 1776, *María de la Luz* became the wife of Manuel Pacheco in 1771, *Ana* married Juan José Silva in 1769, and *Mariano* married Anamaría Silva in 1776.⁴¹

1. **Sp. Arch.,** I, No. 422.
2. **DM,** 1694, No. 8; 1695, No. 10.
3. **BNM,** leg. 2, Pt. 3, f. 338.
3a. **Doc. Hist. de Mex.,** p. 183; **OLC,** p. 70.
4. **Sp. Arch.,** I, Nos. 422, 423.
5. **DM,** 1695, No. 10; 1696, No. 15; 1699, No. 1; 1705, No. 6.
6. **OLC,** pp. 64, 69.
7. **Sp. Arch,** I, No. 432.
8. **DM,** 1712, No. 1.
9. **Sp. Arch,** I, No. 758.
10. **Bur-48, Sta. Fe.**
11. GENEALOGY: **Francisca Alfonsa Lucero de Godoy,** José D. de Armijo, María Isabel Armijo, María Rita Torres, José Chávez, Eugenio Chávez, Fabián Chávez, Fr. A. Chávez.
12. **Sp. Arch.,** I, No. 458.
13. **DM,** 1716, No. 5; **M-24, S. Ild.; Sp. Arch.,** I, No. 953.
14. **DM,** 1766, in Albuq., no number.
15. GENEALOGY: **Marcos Lucero de Godoy,** Margarita Lucero, María Ignacia Archuleta, María Josefa Quintana, Desiderio Roybal, Romualdo Roybal, Nicolasa Roybal, Fr. A. Chávez.
16. **DM,** 1696, No. 10.
17. **Ibid.,** 1710, No. 7; 1716, No. 1; 1718, No. 9.
18. **NMHR,** Vol. IV, No. 3, p. 274.
19. **Bur-2, Albuq.**
20. **Sp. Arch.,** I, No. 238; perhaps the youth, **Pedro,** of 1691 (**Revolt,** II, pp. 113, 141-142).
21. **DM,** 1716, No. 14; 1709, No. 4.
22. **Ibid,** 1719, No. 2.
23. **First Expedition,** p. 134.
24. **DM,** 1694, No. 34; 1695, No. 5; 1698, No. 1; **AGN, Mex., Inq.,** t. 701, f. 322; **Twit. Coll.,** Nos. 111, 2836.
25. **DM,** 1694, No. 34.
26. **Twit. Coll.,** loc. cit.
27. **DM,** 1691, No. 1.
28. **Revolt,** I, p. 119; **AASF,** No. 1, Inventory, f. 3.
29. **Sp. Arch.,** I, No. 3.
30. **Ibid.,** No. 454.
31. **B-2, Albuq.**
32. **Bur-45, Zuñi.**
33. **B-2, Albuq.**
34. **Sp. Arch.,** I, No. 454.
35. **Bur-2, Albuq.**
36. **Bancroft, NMO,** 1763.
37. **Sp. Arch.,** loc. cit.
38. **Bur-2, Albuq.**
39. **B-57, Isleta.**
40. **DM,** 1781, in Albuq., no number; **M-4, Albuq.** April 27, 1781. GENEALOGY: **Manuel Lucero,** María Manuela Lucero, Tomás Baca, Nicanora Baca, Fabián Chávez, Fr. A. Chávez.
41. **DM,** in Albuq., no number; **M-3, Albuq.**

LUERA

Felipe Santiago de Luera, a native of Rancho de las Cuevas, Valle de San Bartolomé, came as a soldier to New Mexico at the age of 25. His parents were Bartolomé Luera and Ursula Villanueva.[1] By 1805 he was a sergeant, when reference was made to his twenty-five years of military service. In 1808 he asked to be transferred back to New Spain.[2]

On January 7, 1814, a *Felipe Luera*, husband of *Francisca Mañas* [?], died at the age of "sixty or seventy."[3]

1. **HSNM**, Militia Papers.
2. Sp. Arch., II, Nos. 1881, 1892, 2012, 2013, 2019, 2176.
3. **B-54**, Tomé.

LUJÁN

DOMINGO LUJÁN, apparently the man of this name killed in an accident in 1693,[1] had come to re-settle New Mexico. His widow, *Juana Domínguez*, who afterwards married Lorenzo de Madrid, made her last will in 1717, in which she named a son, *Juan*, and three daughters, *Antonia, Josefa,* and a third [Leonor?] whose name is obliterated.[2] She left land in Analco to two sons-in-law, José de Quintana and Cristóbal Jaramillo, to her daughter Josefa, and to a María Luján[3] [Martín], who was the wife of her son Juan.

Her children by Domingo Luján had the following consorts: *Juan* married María Martín in 1698;[4] *Antonia* became the wife of José de Quintana in 1696;[5] *Josefa* married Matías Martín after refusing his cousin, Antonio Martín;[6] and *Leonor* was the wife of Cristóbal Jaramillo.

Juan Luján and María Martín were married for forty years when he died as a corporal. She made her last will in 1769, mentioning her parents and nine children, but naming only eight of them: *Antonio* (dead), *José, Cristóbal* (dead), *Juan* (dead), *Santiago* (dead), *Domingo, María,* and *Francisco*.[7]

* * * * * * * *

SEBASTIÁN LUJÁN was the son of Diego Luján and Juana de Salazar, both of whom had fled from the exile colony at Guadalupe del Paso to reside in the Parral country of Nueva Vizcaya. Sebastián, born there or in the El Paso area after 1680, came to Santa Fe; he was twenty-four in 1705 when he married *Juana Teresa Moreno Trujillo* on February 24.[8] His wife's family was not of the New Mexico Trujillos, having come up with the 1693 colonists from Mexico City, and at their own expense; for this reason they were allowed to return home in 1705.[9] Sebastián also applied to leave, but was refused permission as being technically a New Mexican.[10] The following year he and his wife, referred to as *"La Trujilleta,"* were still in Santa Fe.[11] Her sister, married to Miguel de Quintana of Santa Cruz, also stayed in New Mexico.

* * * * * * * *

PEDRO LUJÁN was the son of Juan *Luis* Luján [Ruiz Cáceres branch].[12] He was but a minor in 1680-1681, and hence not included in the Revolt lists; but he returned with the Reconquest, accompanied by his wife, *Francisca Martín de Salazar*. He was twenty-seven in 1693.[13] As a company captain he took part in an Apache campaign in 1713, and was on the Governor's staff during the Moqui campaign of 1716.[14]

One known child was a daughter, *Isabel*, who became the wife of Juan Lucero de Godoy.[15]

MATÍAS LUJÁN, described in 1680-1681, came back to his pre-Revolt lands at Santa Cruz.[16] He had been born and reared at the place called "San Cristóbal" after the Reconquest.[17] In 1693-1695 he gave his age as fifty.[18] His wife was *Francisca Romero*.

His known children were: *Miguel, María, Antonia,* and *Juana*. María was married to Pedro Sánchez, Antonia to José Trujillo, and Juana was the author of a unique family.[19]

Miguel Luján was married to Catalina Valdés, nicknamed "La Prieta," whom he murdered in 1713.[20]

A bastard daughter of a "Matías Luján," by some Indian servant, became the wife of José López Naranjo; but since there was another Matías Luján, husband of Catalina Varela, who lived in the same northern district,[21] it is not known which of the two was her father.

Perhaps children also of Matías Luján and Francisca Romero, if not their nephews, were two brothers living in the same neighborhood, *Juan* and *Felix*.

Juan Luján (Romero) married *María Trujillo* on January 13, 1717, with Baltasar Trujillo and Juana Luján as witnesses.[22] They had the following children: *Matías Jorge,* April 28, 1718; *Josefa,* March 28, 1720; *José,* March 18, 1725; and *Antonio,* September 24, 1723,[23] who married Micaela Griego on August 5, 1748.[24]

Felix Luján, brother of Juan Luján, was married to *Francisca Gómez de Torres*. A daughter, *María,* was born on December 14, 1705.[25]

* * * * * * * *

MIGUEL LUJÁN, brother or brother-in-law of the *Sargento* Juan Ruiz Cáceres, was a soldier of the Reconquest. On reaching Santa Fe, Vargas assigned him and his family to the Palace of the Governors, where he was to guard the old chapel which the Indians had converted into an *estufa*. On December 28, 1693, the family escaped from it when the occupying Tanos decided to fight for the town.[26] This seems to be the same man who had joined as a recruit in 1681,[27] and who was killed on April 19, 1694, during a campaign at Cochití.[28]

He had a young son, referred to as *Agustín* and as *Cristóbal* in the 1693 incident.[29]

Antonio Luján, described in 1680-1681, had died in 1682; but his widow, *María Martín,* who had married Domingo de Herrera in 1683,[30] returned to Santa Fe.

Her daughter, *Antonia,* by her first husband, married Mateo de Ortega in 1797.[31]

Agustín Luján, of unknown parentage, was a Santa Fe soldier who married *María (Luisa) Perea,* widow of Miguel Maese, in 1701.[32] She is mentioned in a hexing incident, and as the sister of Catalina Varela, wife of Martín Hurtado.[33]

They had a daughter, *María de la Candelaria,* born on February 4, 1725.[34]

* * * * * * * *

JUAN LUJÁN (really Juan *Barba*) came to New Mexico as a colonist from Parral, where he had fled in 1682. (See preceding century.) He was now described, in 1693, as thirty-four years old, the son of Esteban Barba and a native of New Mexico, swarthy, with rather deep-set eyes and a scar beneath the left eye. His wife, *Petrona Ramírez,* thirty, a native of Parral and daughter of Isidro, had a reddish skin, a round face, and large eyes.

They had a four-year-old child, *Juan,* born in Parral, having a reddish skin and a round face.[35] Juan was in Mexico City when he joined up, saying that he had to pick up his wife and child at Cuencame.[36]

Juan Luján and *Teresa de Herrera* had two known children, born at Taos: *María,* February 7, 1715, and *Juana,* October 5, 1718, perhaps the first Spanish baptisms at that Mission after the Reconquest.[37]

With so many mix-ups after the Reconquest, besides those before the Rebellion, it is most difficult to identify the people who went by the name of Luján: the *Luján* family proper, the *Martín Barba group,* and the *Luis* and *Ruiz Cáceres* clans.

1. **AGI, Guadalajara,** leg. 140, f. 68.
2. **Sp. Arch.,** I, No. 235.
3. **Ibid.,** No. 508.
4. **DM,** 1698, No. 16.
5. **Ibid.,** 1696, No. 15.
6. **Ibid.,** No. 16; **Sp. Arch.,** I, No. 231.
7. **Sp. Arch.,** I, No. 587.
8. **DM,** 1705, No. 6.
9. **Sp. Arch.,** II, No. 108.
10. **Ibid.,** No. 109.
11. **AGN, Mex., Inq.,** t. 735, ff. 289-298.
12. **Sp. Arch.,** I, No. 758; see **Luis** family.
13. **DM,** 1693, No. 7; 1694, No. 31; **Sp. Arch.,** I, No. 490.
14. **Sp. Arch.,** II, No. 198; I, No. 250.
15. **Ibid.,** I, Nos. 458, 867. GENEALOGY: **Isabel Luján,** Francisca Alfonsa Lucero de Godoy, José D. de Armijo, María Isabel Armijo, María Rita Torres, José Chávez, Eugenio Chávez, Fabián Chávez, Fr. A. Chávez.
16. **Sp. Arch.,** I, No. 818; II, No. 250.
17. **Ibid.,** II, No. 89.
18. **DM,** 1693, No. 5; 1695, No. 8.
19. See **Gómez del Castillo.** GENEALOGY: **Juana Luján,** Francisco Gómez del Castillo, María Antonia Gómez del Castillo, Margarita Lucero, María Ignacia Archuleta, María Josefa Quintana, Desiderio Roybal, Romualdo Roybal, Nicolasa Roybal, Fr. A. Chávez.
20. **Sp. Arch.,** II, No. 187.
21. **AGN, Tierras,** t. 426; **ibid., Mex., Inq.,** t. 735, f. 306.
22. **M-24, S. Ild.**
23. **All ibid., B. Sec.**
24. **B-16, Nambé,** M. Sec.
25. **Sp. Arch.,** II, No. 196; **M-24, S. Ild., B. Sec.**
26. **Ritch Coll.,** Box 1, No. 25.
27. **Revolt,** II, p. 195.
28. **Crusaders,** pp. 70, 144-147, 180.
29. **Ritch Coll., loc. cit.**
30. **DM,** 1683, No. 1.
31. **Ibid.,** 1697, No. 2.
32. **Ibid.,** 1701, No. 4.
33. **AASF,** No. 16; **Sp. Arch.,** II, No. 79.
34. **M-24, S. Ild.**
35. **Sp. Arch.,** II, No. 54c.
36. **BNM,** leg. 1, Pt. 1, pp. 814-816.
37. **B-45, Taos.**

LUNA

DIEGO DE LUNA was still living shortly before the Reconquest, being mentioned as a member of the Conquistadora Confraternity in 1689.[1] An old man by this time, he must have died soon after, for he is not heard of again. But members of his large family settled in the Río Abajo district. All the following Lunas apparently belong to this one family.

* * * * * * * *

ANTONIO DE LUNA is the oldest man of this name appearing after the Reconquest, and only as an obituary. He was married to *Jacinta Peláez* when he died on August 9, 1729.[2] His widow then married Captain Antonio Montoya in 1737; surviving her second husband, she herself died at Tomé, January 27, 1766.[3]

The next generation contains several men, any or all of whom could have been Antonio's sons. These were: *Domingo, Joaquín, Felipe, Antonio, Bernardo, Salvador,* and *José.*

Of early Luna women, *María Rosa,* wife of Juan Chaves, died October 6, 1738; on October 12, her baby of the same name also died.[4] *Gregoria* became the wife of Pedro Romero, August 26, 1728.[5]

Domingo de Luna married *Josefa Lucero,* December 21, 1745, with Antonio Baca and daughter Josefa Baca as witnesses.[6] In 1758, they were sponsors together for Paulín, son of Juan and Francisca Baca.[7]

Their known children were: *José Manuel,* born March 5, 1747; *Vicente,* September 21, 1750; *María Manuela,* June 13, 1757;[8] and *Antonio,* who married Catalina Pino. Vicente married Victoria Chaves in 1774, when both his parents are mentioned as dead.[9]

Domingo had been married a second time, to *María Baca,* daughter of Nicolás Baca and Teodora Fernández. She bore him a son, *Rafael Antonio,* March 25, 1773,[10] who married Ana María Tafoya, November 11, 1793.[11] Domingo and his second wife were living at San Clemente in 1766, while he was suing for her inheritance at La Ciénega.[12]

Joaquín de Luna married *María Torres,* July 17, 1743, with Antonio Baca and wife Mónica de Chaves as witnesses.[13] But she must have died soon after, for within the next two years he began to have children by a new wife, *Juana Ángela de Salazar.*

These children were: *Miguel de San Juan,* September 10, 1745; *Bernardo Paulo,* July 9, 1747; *Antonio Xavier,* May 11, 1751;[14] and

Tomás, who married Margarita Antonia Sena at Bernalillo in 1773.¹⁵ The eldest son, Miguel, widowed of Juana Rael de Aguilar, married María Catalina Valdés of Jémez jurisdiction.¹⁶ Bernardo married Catalina García and resided at Alameda.¹⁷

Felipe de Luna married *Bárbara Yturrieta* on September 8, 1753, with José de Luna and Rosalía Vallejo as sponsors; Juan Antonio de Chaves and his mother Antonia Baca were *padrinos* for the *velación* on September 20.¹⁸ This pair had quite a large family.

The boys were: *Francisco,* July 6, 1755; *Tomás Antonio,* December 28, 1765;¹⁹ *José,* who married María Paula D. y Chaves, September 14, 1799;²⁰ *Juan Dionisio,* who married Bárbara Antonia Romero, March 23, 1793;²¹ *Juan,* who married María Guadalupe García Jurado, June 15, 1782; *Pedro Secundino,* who married Joaquina Aguirre, May 23, 1802; *Manuel,* who married Luisa García, May 21, 1791; and *Mariano,* who married Bárbara Aragón, February 15, 1789.

Two daughters were: *Manuela,* who married José Torres in Belén, October 16, 1781;²² and *Guadalupe,* born September 19, 1773.²³

In 1790, their widowed mother, Bárbara Yturrieta, fifty-six years old, was living in the second Plaza of Belén with five sons, ranging from thirty-one down to thirteen years.²⁴

Antonio de Luna married a María Magdalena ———, December 22, 1735.²⁵

Bernardo de Luna married Antonia Quintana in 1743. That same year they had a daughter, *María Francisca,* June 16, 1743.²⁶ This girl, or another named simply María, married Ignacio Vallejo in 1756.²⁷

Salvador de Luna died on November 6, 1743, while in Guadalupe del Paso. It was not known if he was married or single, wrote the Padre, "for he was an outsider."²⁸

José de Luna married Rosalia Vallejo, April 29, 1743,²⁹ while a Bernardo Vallejo married a *Juana de Luna,* June 21, 1759.³⁰

IN THE EIGHTEENTH CENTURY

ANTONIO DE LUNA, son of Domingo de Luna and Josefa Lucero, was killed by Apaches prior to 1782. His wife was *María Catalina Pino,* sister of José Francisco Pino. He left four children: *José Enrique, María Josefa, Antonio Encarnación,* and *José Bruno.* His brother Vicente is mentioned in the probation of the estate.³¹

The daughter, *María Josefa,* born April 24, 1774, became the wife of Ventura Chaves.³² Her widowed mother married Anacleto Miera y Pacheco. The three sons married as follows:

José Enrique Luna, born on July 18, 1771, married *Juana María Gabaldón* in 1795.³³ Their known children were:

José Tomás Mariano, born December 23, 1796; *José Toribio,* April 18, 1799; *José Valentín Mariano,* February 20, 1803; *María Soledad Emiliana,* baptized January 8, 1805, with Paulín Baca and Lugarda Tafoya as sponsors; *Juan Antonio,* December 27, 1808;³⁴ *Jesús María,* and *José Antonio.*

José Tomás married María Manuela Pino.³⁵ *José Toribio* married Manuela Montaño.³⁶ *José (Valentín?)* married Lugarda Baca in 1828, and *Jesús María* applied to marry Preciliana Salazar in 1848.³⁷ *José (Antonio)* married Isabel Baca, daughter of Juan Cruz Baca and María Luisa Castillo.³⁷ᵃ

Antonio Encarnación Luna married *Antonia Marcelina Chávez,* May 11, 1798.³⁸ A son, *Ramón,* married Guadalupe Sarracino, November 30, 1832, and a daughter, *Juana María,* married Salvador Apodaca, July 17, 1821.³⁹

José Bruno Luna married *María Juliana Gabaldón.* After his death she married José Antonio Otero, widower of Bárbara Sedillo, in 1827.⁴⁰

* * * * * * * *

Bartolomé de Luna [Oliva?] Bautista, eighteen years old, and born in San Juan Teoteguacán, was among the Mexico City colonists of 1693. The son of Tomás Bautista, he was a nephew of Gertrudis Bautista, wife of Tomás Palomino, with whom he was listed.⁴¹

It is not known if he arrived in New Mexico, or if he had descendants by any other name.

1. OLC, p. 70.
2. Bur-2, Albuq.
3. Ibid.
4. Ibid.
5. M-11, Isleta.
6. M-3, Albuq.
7. B-57, Isleta, June 28.
8. Ibid.
9. DM, 1774, no number.
10. B-57, Isleta.
11. M-52, Sta. Fe.
12. Sp. Arch., I, No. 991.
13. M-11, Isleta.
14. All in B-57, Isleta.
15. M-23, San Felipe (Pueblo).
16. DM, 1772, in Albuq., no number.
17. B-3 and B-4, Albuq., bapts. of children.
18. M-11, Isleta.
19. Both in B-57, Isleta.
20. B-54, Tomé, M. Sec.
21. Ibid.
22. All in M-49, Isleta.
23. B-57, Isleta.
24. Sp. Arch., II, No. 1092b.
25. M-11, Isleta.
26. M-29, Sta. Cruz; B-31, Sta. Clara.
27. M-11, Isleta.
28. Bur., Guadalupe del Paso (Juárez).
29. M-3, Albuq.
30. M-11, Isleta.
31. Sp. Arch., I, No. 462.
32. B-57, Isleta; Sp. Arch., I, No. 212.
33. B-57, Isleta; B-54, Tomé, M. Sec.
34. All in B-54, Tomé.
35. B, Belén, bapt. of child., Aug. 10, 1852.
36. DM, 1845, in Belén, no number; M, Belén, Oct. 3, 1845, daughter's marriage. GENEALOGY: Toribio Luna, María Encarnación Luna, Eugenio Chávez, Fabián Chávez, Fr. A. Chávez.
37. DM, 1828 and 1848, in Albuq., no number.
37a. B-73, Tomé, bapt. of son, Jesús María y José, July 9, 1837; the family that became prominent in this century. Cf. Twitchell, Old Santa Fe, p. 465, and Leading Facts, Vol. II, pp. 493, 551.
38. Both in M-49, Isleta.
39. Ibid.
40. DM, 1827, in Belén, no number.
41. Sp. Arch., II, No. 54c.

MADRID

LORENZO DE MADRID, *Sargento Mayor*, returned to New Mexico in 1693 with his second wife, *Ana de Almazán*. Just before the Reconquest he declared that he was an *encomendero* with forty-one years in royal military service. He and Ana had no children, but had reared six adopted ones: *Luisa*, thirty years of age, *Paula*, nine, *Eusebia*, eight, *Juan Francisco*, eight, *Cristóbal*, fourteen, and *Pedro*, still in the nursing stage.¹

In 1697 Lorenzo got into trouble with civil and church authorities for supposedly living in concubinage with a widow, Juana Domínguez; both parties denied the charges, especially Lorenzo, who boasted of his years and honors as oldest living Conquistador of the Kingdom.² But when he made his last will in 1715, this same *Juana Domínguez* was his third wife, old Ana having died in the meantime.³

ROQUE DE MADRID became *Sargento Mayor* of all troops by 1688, when he gave his age as forty-four.⁴ He took a leading part in the Vargas Expeditions of 1692 and 1693, and also in the serious Pueblo uprising of 1696.⁵

His wife, *Juana López (Pacheco, de Ar-*

vid), returned with him and their family, settling at Santa Cruz. They had a grown son, *José*, in 1702,⁶ and a daughter *Josefa*, who married Cristóbal de la Serna in 1694.⁷ Two other young Madrids of the same generation, also living at Santa Cruz, and married into the same Serna family, were in all likelihood the sons of Roque. They were *Pedro* and *Matías*.

Roque must have married again, for in 1723, *Julián Madrid*, born in New Mexico, the son of *Maestre de Campo* Roque Madrid, deceased, and of *Josefa Durán*, married Estefanía Martín in Santa Cruz.⁸ Roque had belonged to the Conquistadora Confraternity.⁹

José Madrid, son of old Roque, was mentioned as a soldier of Santa Fe, twenty years of age in 1698, together with Pedro and Matías Madrid.¹⁰ It is not known who his wife and family were, if any.

Pedro Madrid, soldier of Santa Cruz and twenty-five years old in 1698,¹¹ and his wife, *Isabel de la Serna*, had a son, *Bernardo*, who married Gertrudis Martín, July 7, 1714.¹² Another son, *Nicolás*, married Antonia Luján, August 29, 1735. Both Pedro and Isabel were already dead.¹³

Matías Madrid, resident of Santa Cruz, and twenty-three years old in 1698, was a wedding sponsor with his wife *Antonia de la Serna* for Lázaro Durán and Gregoria de la Serna.¹⁴ They had two daughters: *Isabel*, who married Agustín Sáiz in 1709,¹⁵ and *María*, who became the wife of Juan Trujillo of Santa Cruz in 1715.¹⁶ By this time he was a captain. He died on February 18, 1727.¹⁷

1. AGI, Guadalajara, leg. 139.
2. AASF, No. 17.
3. Sp. Arch., I, No. 502.
4. DM, 1688, No. 1.
5. First Expedition, pp. 184, sqq.; Old Santa Fe, Vol. III, pp. 332-373; Bancroft, Hist. of N. M., p. 207.
6. Bancroft, NMO, 1702.
7. DM, 1694, No. 11.
8. Ibid., 1723, No. 3.
9. OLC, p. 58.
10. DM, 1698, No. 11.
11. Ibid..
12. M-24, S. Ild.
13. M-27, S. Juan.
14. DM, loc. cit.
15. Ibid., 1709, No. 9.
16. Ibid., 1715, No. 6.
17. Bur-48, Sta. Fe.

MAÉS

LUIS MAESE and his wife, *Josefa de Archuleta*, might have returned to Santa Fe in 1693, but it is certain that two daughters of theirs, *Antonia* and *Francisca*, were living there in 1727, when they sold some paternal lands. Both parents were referred to as dead.¹

Antonia had married Mateo Martín, and was a widow in 1767 with two twin sons, both named Joaquín Martín, and known as "los Joaquines."²

Francisca had married Simón Nieto, a Santa Fe soldier, and was dead by 1728.³

Miguel Maese had returned to New Mexico with his wife *María Perea*. But, sometime before 1701, on a trip back to Santa Fe from Guadalupe del Paso, he was killed by Apaches. His widow then married Agustín Luján.⁴ In her last will, made in 1715, María Perea mentioned her only child by Miguel, *Catalina Maese*, who was married at that time to Juan Antonio Domínguez.⁵

In this will she also mentioned a boy, *Miguel Maese*, fifteen, whom she had reared from birth.⁶

Other early Maese people, who cannot be classified for lack of data, were the following:

Cristóbal Maese and his wife, *Gertrudis Sánchez*, were living in Santa Fe in 1705.⁷

Alonso Maese married *Catalina Hurtado* at Bernalillo, November 13, 1701.⁸

Juan Maese was living in Santa Fe in 1708 with his wife, *Rufina Severiana*.⁹

Marcial Maese, also called *Marcial Sangil*, was married to Rosalia Abeytia. They had at least two sons: *Antonio*, born April 5, 1734, and *Bartolomé*, December 17, 1735.¹⁰

The Maese families which remained at Guadalupe del Paso (Socorro, San Elzeario, Ysleta, and Senecú) kept the old spelling of the name even to this day. During the past century, the descendants of those who returned to New Mexico dropped the final vowel, and pronounced it as one syllable, "Més."

1. Sp. Arch., I, No. 16.
2. Ibid., No. 40.
3. Ibid., No. 642.
4. DM, 1701, No. 5.
5. Sp. Arch., I, No. 680.
6. Ibid.
7. Ibid., II, No. 105; DM, 1705, No. 6.
8. B-13, Bern., M. Sec.
9. Sp. Arch., II, No. 150.
10. B-2, Albuq.

MAESTAS

JUAN DE MESTAS PERALTA returned to Santa Fe in 1693 with his wife, *Casilda López de Osura*, who died soon after and was buried in Santa Fe. When Juan applied to marry *María Trujillo* in November, 1695, he stated that he had been born in Santa Fe, but did not know who his parents were.[1] By 1710 he had established himself at Pojoaque, giving his age as fifty-eight in 1714.[2] In 1715, he and a son, Mateo, received permission to visit New Vizcaya, very likely to see relatives who had remained at Guadalupe del Paso.[3]

The only son by the first wife was this *Mateo*, who married *Rafaela Cortés* in 1720.[4]

María Trujillo bore Juan the following large family: *María*, born February 7, 1707,[5] who married Lorenzo Inocencio Velásquez; *Casilda*, who married Nicolás Sisneros in 1714; *Juana*, who became the wife of Pedro Sisneros in the same year;[6] *Antonio*, who married María Luisa Montoya in 1728;[7] *Joaquín*, born March 25, 1713, who married Teresa Tafoya; *José*, born March 25, 1715; *Manuela*, born April 1, 1720;[8] *Juan Manuel*, born June 17, 1709, who married Francisca Martín; *Francisco Xavier*, born April 14, 1711; *Josefa Micaela*, born May 18, 1717;[9] and *Ventura*, who married Catalina Jurado.

Joaquín Mestas married *Teresa Tafoya*, by whom he had a son, *Manuel*, born in 1742.[10]

After her death he married *Victoria Sánchez*, May 16, 1756,[11] by whom he had the following children:

Juan Ignacio, born April 20, 1763; *José Joaquín*, February 14, 1760;[12] *Josefa*, April 18, 1771;[13] and *Gertrudis*, wife of Cristóbal Larrañaga.[14]

Ventura Mestas married *Catalina Jurado*, daughter of Juan Jurado and Rosa de Misquia (most likely of Guadalupe del Paso), who left him two children in 1767, *Antonia* and *Juan Ignacio*.[15]

Antonia, the first wife of Juan Bautista Durán, was dead by 1767.[16]

Ventura was married a second time, to *María Juana Vigil*.[17]

Antonio Mestas married *María Luisa Montoya* at Santa Cruz in 1728.[18] They had these children: *María Juliana*, June 5, 1729; *Antonio*, June 9, 1731; *Pedro Joaquín*, March 30, 1735.[19]

During the Nineteenth Century the name came to be spelled "Maestas," probably influenced by the family name of *Maes*, which was pronounced "Més." But in spite of its corrupted spelling, "Maestas" is still pronounced "Mestas."

---

1. DM, 1695, No. 14.
2. Ibid., 1710, No. 15; 1714, No. 7.
3. Sp. Arch., II, No. 183a.
4. DM, 1720, No. 1.
5. B-18a, Nambé.
6. Both in M-24, S. Ild.
7. DM, 1728, No. 1.
8. These three in M-24, S. Ild., M. Sec.
9. These three in B-18a, Nambé.
10. B-31, Sta. Clara.
11. M-29, Sta. Cruz.
12. Both in B-27, S. Juan.
13. B-14, Cochití.
14. B-24, S. Ild., bapt. of child, Mar. 22, 1780.
15. Sp. Arch., II, No. 419.
16. Ibid., II, No. 845.
17. Ibid., No. 667.
18. DM, 1728, no number.
19. All in B-16, Nambé.

MALDONADO

SEBASTIÁN ANTONIO MALDONADO was a witness, forty-two years of age, at the marriage of Antonio Durán y Chaves at Bernalillo in 1718.[1] In 1714 an order had been issued in Mexico City for the arrest of the soldier Sebastián Maldonado, for murdering a governor down in New Spain; it was proclaimed in New Mexico in April, 1715.² If this was the same man, he had not been arrested three years later. However, nothing more is known about him.

José Maldonado, a soldier of Santa Fe, married *María Luisa Tenorio*, March 19, 1754.³ When he made his last will in 1789, he was Second *Teniente* of the garrison. After naming his wife, he gave these seven children as their progeny: *José Miguel, Gaspar, Teodora, Francisca, José Miguel, Baltasar,* and *Antonio*.⁴ Gaspar and the younger José Miguel enlisted as soldiers in 1779 and 1783.⁵

He died on June 14, 1789, and was buried in the military chapel.⁶

A ———— *Baldonado* (Christian name omitted) and his wife, *Catalina Vallejo*, had a son *Fabián*, born February 2, 1744.⁷

1. DM, 1718, No. 10.
2. Sp. Arch., II, No. 211.
3. M-50, Sta. Fe.
4. Sp. Arch., I, No. 598.
5. HSNM, Mil. Papers.
6. Bur-51, Castrense.
7. B-57, Isleta.

MANZANARES

Ana (Antonia) de Sandoval y Manzanares had come up to New Mexico before the 1680 Pueblo Rebellion. She was a daughter of Mateo de Sandoval y Manzanares and wife of *Blas de la Candelaria*. She returned to the Río Abajo area after the Reconquest with her Candelaria children.¹

A child, Andrés, was baptized in Albuquerque, December 16, 1709, the son of Feliciano *Manzanares* and Petronila *de Ávila*;² however, this couple seems to be none other than Feliciano *Candelaria* and Petrona *Varela*.

María de Manzanares was the wife of Cristóbal Trujillo.³

Tomasa de Manzanares, a nineteen-year-old girl, lived in the Santa Cruz country in 1713; and as late as 1748, a woman of the same name was practicing the art of herb-healing, "for lack of surgeons in the Kingdom."⁴

Juan Manzanares and his wife, *María Madrid*, had a child, *Bárbara*, born on May 28, 1737.⁵ He acquired land in Chama in 1751.⁶

Andrés and *Manuel Manzanares*, probably his sons, were living in Pojoaque in 1769.⁷

1. See Candelaria.
2. B-2, Albuq.
3. DM, 1694, No. 17.
4. Sp. Arch., II, Nos. 187, 498.
5. M-31, Sta. Clara.
6. Sp. Arch., I, No. 1045.
7. Ibid., Nos. 588, 589.

MANCHEGO

Manuel Manchego, a weaver, sixty-nine years old, lived in Belén in 1790 with his wife, *Rosa Miranda*. They had three sons, twenty, thirteen, and eleven years of age, and four daughters, sixteen, six, four, and two.¹ He died on December 22, 1802, leaving his wife with two sons and two daughters.²

A son, *Juan Francisco*, married María Gertrudis Silva in Belén, May 2, 1793.³

1. Sp. Arch., II, No. 1092b.
2. B-54, Tomé, Bur.. Sec.
3. Ibid., M. Sec.

MARES

JOSÉ MARES, who did not know who his parents were, married *Ana Rodríguez*, fifteen-year-old daughter of Lorenzo Rodríguez and Teresa López Olguín, in 1716.[1] They had at least two sons, *Nicolás* and *José*, who was evidently the "José Julian," twenty-five years old, who enlisted as a soldier in 1746.[2]

Simón de Ortega and a *María Mares* were marriage witnesses in 1694.[3]

Nicolás Mares, a soldier of Santa Fe, made his last will in 1766. His parents were José Antonio Mares and Ana Antonia Rodríguez, both deceased. His wife was *Josefa de los Reyes de Vargas,* to whom he had been married for thirty-two years. He also mentioned a brother, José.

Their ten children were: *Lorenzo, Manuel, Luis, Cristóbal, José, María de la Luz, Francisco Esteban, José Manuel, Juan Domingo,* and *Nicolás.*

A **Manuel Mares** made his last will in Santa Fe in 1804.[5]

1. DM, 1716, No. 9.
2. HSNM, Mil. Papers.
3. DM, 1694, No. 6.
4. Sp. Arch., I, No. 567.
5. Ibid., No. 604.

MARIÑO

LUIS MARIÑO married *Isabel de Aguirre* on May 21, 1778.[2] He was a native of San Miguel el Grande, and thirty-three years old in 1790, residing at Los Padillas with his wife, thirty-one years of age. They had three boys, seven, six, and four years old, and two girls, nine and seven.[3]

One known son, *Rafael*, married Bernarda Luna, July 23, 1810.[4] A son, *José Dolores,* was born on September 18, 1825.[5]

Luis was most likely a brother of Fray José Mariño, also a native of San Miguel el Grande, who was the thirty-six-year-old Padre at Acoma in 1776.[5]

1. M-49, Isleta.
2. Sp. Arch., II, No. 1092b.
3. B-54, Tomé, M. Sec.
4. Ibid., B. Sec.
5. BNM, leg. 10, No. 43, Acoma.

MÁRQUEZ

Few members of the prominent and numerous Márquez family of the preceding century returned with the Reconquest; the few who did are hard to place.

FRANCISCO MÁRQUEZ and his wife, *Estela Luján,* were living in Santa Cruz in 1709, when their son *Juan* married Josefa Apodaca on August 18.[1] In all probability, a *Diego Márquez* who married Juana Martín Serrano was another son.

Juan Márquez and *Josefa Apodaca* had the following children: *Manuela,* who became the second wife of Cristóbal Baca in 1734; *María,* wife of Andrés Sandoval; *Domingo,* born on August 11, 1726; *Antonia Simona,* June 4, 1728; and *Alejandro,* in 1731.²

Their mother died in Santa Fe, March 2, 1758.³

Diego Márquez made his last will at Santa Cruz in 1729, in which he named his wife, *Juana Martín Serrano,* and their three children: *María Estela,* wife of Domingo Montes Vigil; *Diego,* eighteen and single; and *Francisca,* wife of Pablo Trujillo.⁴

Their son, *Diego* II, married Gertrudis Esquivel in Santa Fe, August 25, 1730.⁵

* * * * * * * *

Juan Márquez, a different man from the preceding namesake, married a widow, *Magdalena Baca,* January 16, 1735.⁶ The following year he was prosecuted for adultery with another woman,⁷ and on February 23, 1741, Magdalena was found dead in bed,⁸ murdered by her husband. They had no children; her heirs were two boys by her first husband: *Nereo* and *Cristóbal Manuel Montoya.*⁹

Nicolás Márquez had been the husband of *Ana María Montoya,* who married Diego Arias de Quirós in 1694.¹⁰ She had two Márquez children: *Antonia* and *Mateo.* *Antonia,* wife of Agustín Sáez, had died before 1709. *Mateo* married *Agustina Romero* in Santa Fe in 1702;¹¹ they had a daughter, *Ana María,* who married Domingo Valdés.

This Nicolás Márquez might well have been the son of Catalina Márquez by her infamous husband, Nicolás de Aguilar, of the preceding century.

* * * * * * * *

DIEGO MÁRQUEZ DE AYALA was a native of Zelaya in New Spain who joined the colonists of 1693. He was the son of Don Juan, nineteen years old, with an aquiline face, large eyes, the left one darker than the other. His wife was *María de Palacios Bolívar,* fifteen, daughter of Antonio and born in Vera Cruz; she was fair with a round face and big eyes.¹²

Diego was a coppersmith by trade.¹³ But by 1716 he held the rank of captain in the militia.¹⁴ Either he or his contemporary of the same name (without *Ayala*) was a member of the Confraternity of La Conquistadora.¹⁵

A known child of his, *María,* became the wife of Lázaro Trujillo.¹⁶ Another was, in all probability, a *Juana* Márquez *de Ayala* who was the wife of José Antonio Naranjo.

---

1. **DM**, 1709, Nos. 6, 12.
2. These three in **B-27, S. Juan.**
3. Bur-48, Sta. Fe.
4. Sp. Arch., I, No. 513; two girls evidently named for Márquez grandparents.
5. **DM**, 1730, no number.
6. **M-50,** Sta. Fe.
7. Sp. Arch., II, No. 437.
8. Bur-48, Sta. Fe.
9. Sp. Arch., loc. cit.
10. **DM,** 1694, No. 32.
11. Ibid., 1702, No. 3.
12. Sp. Arch., II, No. 54a; I, No. 404; **BNM,** leg. 4, Pt. 1, pp. 790-795.
13. **DM,** 1705, No. 12.
14. Sp. Arch., I, No. 404.
15. **OLC,** p. 70.
16. **B-17, Nambé,** 1797, second M. of son Mariano.

MARTÍN BARBA

Some members of this pre-Rebellion family very likely came back to New Mexico in 1693 as plain *"Martín."* Hence they would be hard to separate from any Martín Serrano people who also dropped the second part of the name.

We do know that one Martín Barba came back as *Juan Luján.*

MARTÍN SERRANO

I: LUIS MARTÍN SERRANO of the preceding century, and his wife *Catalina de Salazar*, had many descendants to resettle New Mexico in 1693 through at least two sons, **Luis II** and **Pedro**. (The progeny of his brother HERNÁN are treated further on.)

1. LUIS MARTÍN SERRANO II and his wife, *Antonia de Miranda*, had these children, as well as they can be distinguished and sorted out: *Luis* III (not heard of again after the Reconquest), *Domingo* (?), *Antonio, Francisco, María*, wife of Antonio Luján, and *María Rosa*, married to Nicolás López.

Domingo Martín Serrano (was he a son of Luis II or Hernán II?) was married to Josefa de Herrera. A witness in 1694, he declared that he was born in Santa Fe, giving his age as forty-seven in that year, and as eighty in 1726.[1] He died at the age of ninety on February 27, 1735.[2] His children were:

Diego, who married Pascuala de Soto at Santa Cruz in 1694;[3] *María*, wife of Juan Luján; *Blas*, who married Rosa de Vargas Machuca in 1705;[4] and *Matías*, husband of Josefa Luján Domínguez.[5]

Antonio Martín Serrano, son of Captain Luis Martín, was twenty-six in 1681 and thirty-three in 1690.[6] He was married to *Ynez de Ledesma* before 1680, then by 1703 to *María de Carvajal*, a native of Querétaro and widow of José Cortés, when Antonio is referred to as "El Tecolote." He was married a third time, to *Gertrudis Fresqui*, August 25, 1725, at Santa Cruz. He was living in Chimayó when he died at the age of eighty.[7]

In 1696, after his first wife's death, he had asked to marry Josefa Luján, daughter of Domingo Luján, but she changed her mind.[8]

He then married María de Carvajal in 1698, when he gave both his parents' names and said that he was a charter settler of the new town of Santa Cruz.[9] It is not known who his children were, if any.

Francisco Martín Serrano, son of Luis Martín, still living in 1694, and of Antonia Miranda, had lost his wife, *Juana Laurera*, when he married *Juana García* in Santa Fe, October 26, 1694.[10] This second wife, Juana García de los Ríos,[10a] made her last will in 1752, where she named their twelve children:

Juan Martín, Nicolás, Lorenzo, María, Francisco Xavier, Marcial, Ana, Petrona, Josefa, Ángela, Manuel, and *Blas* (the last two dead).[11] Of these, *Francisco (Xavier)* married Felipa Ribera at Albuquerque in 1721;[12] *Marcial* was sued for heart-balm by Ynez Griego in 1736,[13] but married Gabriela de Atienza on August 28, 1737.[14]

Margarita, a daughter by the first wife, married Juan Andrés Apodaca in 1707.[15]

2. PEDRO MARTÍN SERRANO DE SALAZAR and his wife, *Juana de Argüello*, also returned in 1693 to re-settle the ancestral La Cañada country.[16] He was dead by 1700, when a son got married. But Juana, seventy years old in 1718, was still living with her daughter *Josefa*, widow of Andrés Archuleta, in Santa Fe.[17]

The known sons were: *Miguel*, husband of Leonor Domínguez de Mendoza; *Antonio*, who married Ana María Gómez, and then Magdalena Sedillo; *Francisco*, "El Ciego," married to Casilda Contreras; and *Sebastián*, husband of María Luján.

Three known daughters were: *María*, widow of Juan Olguín, who married Tomás de

---

1. DM, 1694, No. 26; 1726, No. 2.
2. BuF-32, Sta. Cruz.
3. DM, 1694, No. 9.
4. Ibid., 1705, No. 1.
5. Sp. Arch., I, No. 231.
6. Revolt, II, pp. 167, 197; DM, 1690, No. 1.
7. DM, 1725, No. 7; AGN, Mex., Inq., t. 735, ff. 304 sqq.
8. DM, 1696, No. 16.
9. Ibid., 1698, No. 11.
10. Ibid., 1694, No. 8.
10a Perhaps of family of Diego Velásquez and **Juana del Río** (q.v.).
11. Sp. Arch., I, No. 353.
12. DM, 1721, No. 1.
13. Ibid., 1736, no number.
14. M-27, S. Juan.
15. DM, 1707, No. 2.
16. Sp. Arch., I, No. 818; II, Nos. 67, 68.
17. Ibid., I, No. 505.

Bejarano; *Juana,* widow of Francisco de Apodaca, who then married a different Juan Olguín in 1695, and then Felipe de Arratia; and *Josefa,* wife of Andrés de Archuleta.[18]

Miguel Martín Serrano married *Leonor Domínguez de Mendoza* in 1707.[19] Both are mentioned in a hexing case in 1708. His wife's aunt, Petrona Domínguez, was married to a Simón Martín.[20]

Antonio Martín Serrano was twenty-seven when he married *Ana María Gómez* of Guadalupe del Paso, at Santa Fe in 1700. His father Pedro was here mentioned as deceased.[21] He next married *Felipa de Villavicencio,*[22] widow of Gabriel de Ansures, and then *Magdalena Sedillo,* widow of Juan de Dios Martínez, in 1734.[23]

One known daughter of his, by his first wife, was *Ynez Martín,* who married Juan José Pacheco in 1732.[24] This pair was living at La Soledad in 1758, when her father was mentioned as dead.[25]

Francisco Martín Serrano, called *"El Ciego,"* must have been blind, or very much nearsighted, to deserve the nickname. His wife was *Casilda Contreras.*[26] He was living at El Embudo with his wife in 1764 when he made his last will.[27]

Of their children, *Salvador Manuel* married Feliciana Rael de Aguilar, April 25, 1743;[28] *Juan Francisco* married Paula Villalpando; *María Luisa* was born on May 20, 1729;[29] and *Josefa* married Luis Suazo of Guadalupe del Paso, October 2, 1734.[30]

One son, *Juan Francisco,* made his last will at El Embudo in 1767, naming *Paula Villalpando* as his wife, and their eleven children: *Rosalia* (dead), *Valentín, Tomás* (dead), *Tomás* II (dead), *Juan Gabriel, Margarita, Miguel, Rosalia, Juan Bautista, José,* and *Ana María.*[31]

Another son of old Francisco might have been an *Antonio,* married to *Catalina de Villalpando,* who made his will at Embudo in 1763. Their children were: *María,* second wife of Marcial Torres, and *Pascuala,* wife of Joaquín Torres, son of Marcial by a first wife.[32]

Sebastian Martín Serrano is the most famous of the whole clan. He and his wife, *María Luján,* were still in Santa Fe in 1698, when he gave his age as twenty-seven.[33] But within a few years he had moved north to the ancestral Río Arriba country.[34] In 1714 he was *Alcalde* of Santa Cruz.[35] He built up his large grant at La Soledad, north of San Juan Pueblo, and there reared a large family; he himself became a legendary figure as an Indian campaigner.[36] The chapel that he built at La Soledad was mentioned by Father Domínguez in his report of 1777.[37] In 1730 he was made to vacate grant lands in Taos Valley that were too close to the Pueblo, and he brought suit against Governor Bustamante for the loss of crops and stock. His complaints, proven false, brought him a fine for perjury and misrepresentation.[38]

His wife, *María Luján,* made her last will in 1765, when she declared that she was the legitimate daughter of Don Fernando Durán y Chaves and Elena *Ruiz Cáceres* (another example of interchanging this name with *Luján*). Her father was, then, not the progenitor of the post-Reconquest family of the Río Abajo, but the *Sargento Mayor* whose family was massacred in Taos in 1680. María might have been made captive as a baby,[38a] or she was with relatives away from Taos at the time; anyway, some of her husband's

---

18. GENEALOGY: **Josefa Martín Serrano,** Hilario Archuleta, Julio Archuleta, María Ignacia Archuleta, María Josefa Quintana, Desiderio Roybal, Romualdo Roybal, Nicolasa Roybal, Fr. A. Chávez.
19. DM, 1707, No. 1.
20. Sp. Arch., II, No. 137b.
21. DM, 1700, No. 1.
22. Sp. Arch., I, No. 686.
23. B-16, Nambé; M-27, S. Juan.
24. M-27, S. Juan.
25. Sp. Arch., I, No. 687.
26. Ibid., II, No. 137b.
27. Ibid., I, No. 565.
28. M-50, Sta. Fe.
29. B-27, S. Juan.
30. M-27, S Juan.
31. Sp. Arch., I, No. 600.
32. Ibid., No. 987.
33. DM, 1694, No. 8; 1695, No. 10; 1698, No. 1.
34. Sp. Arch., I, No. 484; II, Nos. 154, 137b.
35. Bancroft, NMO, 1714.
36. An interesting account by Twitchell in Sp. Arch., I, p. 431; the story rings true, but dates and persons are jumbled.
37. BNM, leg. 10, No. 43, S. Juan.
38. Bancroft, NMO, 1731.
38a. See First Expedition, p. 156.

lands in Taos Valley were those she had inherited from Don Fernando. (q.v.).

María mentioned her husband as already dead, and named their children as follows: *Marcial, Margarita* (dead), *Rosa, Manuel, Ángela, José Antonio, Josefa, Juan,* and *Francisco* (the last three dead). The estate of Captain Sebastián Martín was probated again in 1772, with the last wills of both parents in evidence. Lands in question included those in Taos Valley, Truchas, and Chamisal; surviving children and grandchildren also found mention.[39]

Their eldest son, *Marcial,* the executor of his father's will, married *Lugarda Medina,* who bore him a son, *Salvador,* April 6, 1726.[40]

Juan Manuel Martín, who married *Elena Roybal,* with Bernardo Roybal and Margarita Martín as sponsors, September 27, 1731,[41] was, to all appearances, Margarita's brother, the "Juan" mentioned in the will.

Of the daughters, *Margarita* had married Juan de Padilla early in the century,[42] and later became the wife of Bernardo Roybal in 1731; on the same day, September 26, her younger sister, *Ángela,* married Bernardo's younger brother, Ignacio.[43] Here are three Martíns, two sisters and one brother, married to three Roybals, two brothers and one sister.

* * * * * * * *

II. HERNÁN MARTÍN SERRANO, who survived his brother LUIS I, and was so healthy and active when "more than eighty" during and after the Pueblo Rebellion of 1680, appears to have had three wives, at the least: *María Montaño, Catalina Griego,* and *Josefa de la Asención González.* Having been born at San Gabriel del Yunque around the year 1606, he actually was about seventy-four in 1680; and if he did come back to New Mexico in 1693, he was then about eighty-seven years old.

His children by the first wife appear to have been: *Juan,* husband of Ana López de Gracia; *José; María,* wife of Bartolomé de Ledesma (all dead before 1680); *Cristóbal,* certainly known to be María Montaño's son, who married Antonia Moraga;[44] and *Pascuala,* daughter of Hernando Martín and María Montaño, who married Diego Durán in Santa Fe in 1694.

Cristóbal Martín II, twenty, son of Hernando Martín and Catalina Griego, married a *Juana de la Cruz* at Guadalupe del Paso in 1697. Evidently he had remained there with some of his mother's people, Juan Griego being a witness.[45]

Children by Josefa de la Asención González were: *Mateo,* who married Antonia Maese; *Andrés,* husband of Lucía de Torres; *Tomasa,* first wife of Bernardino de Sena;[46] and *María,* married to Bernardo (or Bernardino) Fernández. Their mother, Josefa de la Asención, survived her aged husband for many years, ending her days in the house of the Vicar, Don Santiago Roybal.[47] The Vicar's sister, Manuela Roybal, had married Bernardino de Sena after Tomasa Martín's death.

———

Cristóbal Martín Serrano returned in 1693 with his wife, *Antonia Moraga,* and their known children: *Cristóbal,* who married María Montoya at Bernalillo in 1698, after being rejected by Gerónima Baca that same year;[48] *Diego,* who married Manuela de Vargas in 1714 at Santa Fe;[49] *María,* wife of Manuel Antonio Domínguez;[50] and *Josefa,* mentioned with her mother and brethren in 1713.[51]

Cristóbal and his wife were arguing for lands in Chimayo in 1714.[52] In 1715, Antonia de Moraga and two sons, Diego and younger Cristóbal, got leave to visit relatives in Sonora.[53] Her husband died at Santa Cruz at the age of seventy, November 28, 1736.[54]

---

39. **Sp. Arch.**, I, Nos. 195, 698.
40. **B-27, S. Juan.**
41. **Bur-16, Nambé,** M. Sec.
42. GENEALOGY: **Margarita Martín,** Micaela Padilla, Josefa Labadía, María Guadalupe Ribera, María Dolores Alarid, Romualdo Roybal, Nicolasa Roybal, Fr. A. Chávez.
43. **M-27, S. Juan.**
44. **Sp. Arch.**, I, No. 491.
45. **DM,** 1697, No. 5.
46. GENEALOGY: **Tomasa Martín González,** Tomás Antonio de Sena, Graciana Prudencia Sena, Manuel Ribera, María Guadalupe Ribera, María Dolores Alarid, Romualdo Roybal, Nicolasa Roybal, Fr. A. Chávez.
47. **Sp. Arch.**, I, No. 40.
48. **DM,** 1698, Nos. 3, 11, 18.
49. **Ibid.,** 1714, No. 6.
50. **Ibid.,** 1723, No. 5.
51. **Sp. Arch.**, II, No. 197.
52. **Ibid.,** No. 496.
53. **Ibid.,** No. 183a.
54. **Bur-32, Sta. Cruz.**

Mateo Martín and *Antonia Maese* had twin sons, both named Joaquín, and called *"los Joaquines,"* born in Santa Fe in 1730, five years before their mother married Mateo. Their grandmother was Josefa de la Asención, widow of Hernando Martín.[55]

They also had a daughter, *Ynez Griego* [adopted?], who sued Marcial Martín, son of Francisco Martín, for breach of promise in 1736.[56]

Andrés Martín, brother of Mateo and son of Josefa de la Asención, inherited his mother's lands in Chimayó.[57] On March 3, 1723, he married *Lucía de Torres*, a widow.[58]

This seems to be the same Andrés Martín who moved from the Santa Cruz country down to Alameda, where he married *Quiteria García de Noriega*, August 16, 1734.[59] They had a son, *Juan Pablo Toribio*, born April 23, 1745,[60] and a daughter, *María Vibiana*, who became the wife of Eusebio Durán y Chaves.[61]

Andrés next married *María Dolores Gallegos*, July 15, 1747; this young wife brought suit against Eusebio de Chaves in 1765 for beating up her fifty-seven-year-old husband, and his own father-in-law. Andrés was still living in 1812, being then eighty years old.[62]

* * * * * * * *

Other Martín Serrano people of the Reconquest period, surely the sons and daughters of any of the foregoing heads of families, cannot be placed in their proper categories without additional data.

Miguel Martín Serrano, residing at Santa Cruz in 1713, was married to *María Archuleta*, daughter of Juan de Archuleta and Isabel González. In his last will, drawn up in 1753, he listed their children: *Agustín, Juan, Pablo, Isidro, Juan Pablo, Manuela,* and *José*.[63] One son, Juan Pablo, was the principal witness in a celebrated case in 1728 involving one Francisco Xavier Romero.[64] An Isidro Martín, soldier of Santa Fe in 1757, married to the widow of Francisco Trujillo, and step-father to Antonio Trujillo, seems to be another of his sons.[65]

Miguel died in 1754; one of his daughters (Manuela) was mentioned as the wife of Francisco Quintana.[66]

Alejo Martín was living in Santa Fe in 1701 with his wife, *María de la Roche*, or *Rocha*.[67] Shortly after, he moved to the Río Arriba area. He and Captain Sebastián Martín witnessed a wedding officially at La Soledad, December 25, 1729.[68] In all likelihood, he was Sebastián's brother, as some of his children used the "Martín Serrano *de Salazar*" name.[69]

A son, *Nicolás Jacinto*, married María de la Serna at Santa Cruz in 1712, and these had a child, Juan Ricardo, April 8, 1731.[70]

A daughter, *María*, was the wife of Diego de Torres.[71]

An Alejo Martín who married Catalina de Ribera on February 20, 1730,[72] might be the old man himself, or else a son of the same name.

Diego Martín was already married to *Teresa de Herrera* in 1706. Both were sponsors at the marriage of Diego Lucero and Ana María Martín, February 3, 1726.[74] Diego Martín died on October 1, 1743.[75]

Antonio Martín, husband of *María de Herrera*, died on March 17, 1749.[76]

This looks like another case of two brothers marrying two sisters.

Diego Martín, a younger man, and *Rosa de Atienza*, had the following children: *María Antonia*, February 9, 1726; *Juan Ignacio*, March 18, 1729; and *Diego*, May 22, 1731.[77]

---

55. **Sp. Arch.,** I, No. 40.
56. **DM,** 1736, no number..
57. **Sp. Arch.,** loc. cit.
58. **M-16, Nambé.**
59. **M-3, Albuq.**
60. **B-3, Albuq.**
61. **Sp. Arch.,** I, Nos. 605, 609.
62. **M-3, Albuq.; Sp. Arch.,** II, Nos. 590, 605.
63. **Sp. Arch.,** I, Nos. 509, 546.
64. **Ibid.,** II, No. 353.
65. **Ibid.,** I, No. 980.
66. **Ibid.,** II, No. 529.
67. **Ibid.,** I, No. 480. She was a native of the Province of Sonora. (Marriage of daughter María.)
68. **M-27, S. Juan.**
69. **Sp. Arch.,** I, No. 752.
70. **DM,** 1712, No. 4; **B-27, S. Juan.**
71. **Sp. Arch.,** I, No. 752. GENEALOGY: María Martín, Nicolás Torres, Mariano Torres, María Rita Torres, José Chávez, Eugenio Chávez, Fabián Chávez, Fr. A. Chávez.
72. **M-50, Sta. Fe.**
73. **Sp. Arch.,** I, No. 401.
74. **M-27, S. Juan.**
75. **Bur-32, Sta. Cruz.**
76. **Sp. Arch.,** I, No. 33; **Bur-32, Sta. Cruz.**
77. All in **B-27, S. Juan.**

In 1740, Diego Martín and a different woman, *Juana de Ansures,* had a legitimate son, *Baltasar.*[78]

Ignacio Martín married *Mariana Giltoméy,* January 17, 1730. They had a son, *Simón,* October 28, 1730.[79]

It can be seen how large this Martín Serrano family was from the start, since practically all of its members returned with the Reconquest. During the Nineteenth Century they gradually came to be known as *"los Martines,"* and the later addition of a final *z* turned this plural form into the patronymic *"Martínez."* But this was the name of different families treated next.

---

78. Ibid.

79. M-27 and B-27, S. Juan.

MARTÍNEZ
(*Various*)

Don Felix Martínez was one of the "hundred" soldiers recruited by Vargas in Spain. He was a native of Galicia. After signing up at Zacatecas in April, 1693, he came up to Guadalupe del Paso to play an active role in the Reconquest. He was Vargas' Adjutant in 1694, Commander of the Guadalupe del Paso Presidio in 1695, and of Cavalry in 1705.[1] He is mentioned as having been escorted back to Mexico City by Pedro Durán y Chaves just prior to 1713,[2] but is listed as acting or interim Governor of New Mexico in 1715-1717, after which he left New Mexico.[3] There is no evidence of his having had a family in New Mexico.

* * * * * * * *

Manuel Martínez de Gamboa was in the Velasco list of 1693. He was eighteen years old, the son of Nicolás and a native of Mexico City; he had a round face and a large scar down the entire left side of his face and forehead. His wife was *Ysabel Cano Montezuma,* sixteen, the daughter of Don Manuel de Proenza, and also born in Mexico City; she had big eyes and a pointed nose.[4]

The other Velasco list had a *Doña Juana Cano Montezuma,* a widow, with her mother, *Doña Polonia García,* and four children: *Isabel María,* seventeen; *Manuel,* fourteen; *Josefa,* ten; and *Alonso Francisco,* six.[5] This appears to have been a superior sort of family which, unfortunately, backed out, leaving only the girl, *Ysabel,* who meanwhile had married young Manuel Martínez de Gamboa. But there is no evidence to show that even this young pair ever reached New Mexico.

* * * * * * * *

JUAN MANUEL MARTÍNEZ DE CERVANTES, son of the same, twenty-seven years old and a native of Mexico City, came with the colonists of 1693. He had a dark, round face, large eyes, and a broad nose. His wife was *Catalina de los Ángeles,* twenty-four, the daughter of Francisco Collacos, and also a native of Mexico City; she had a dark, aquiline face, large eyes and forehead.

With them came a thirty-six-year-old servant, Cecilia de la Cruz.[6]

The wife died on the journey during childbirth, at the post of Ojo Caliente, Hacienda of Tabalopa and Paso del Norte, in April, 1694. Her husband reached Santa Fe with the colonists, and he settled in Santa Cruz, where he married another native of Mexico City, *María de Guadalupe Navarro,* sixteen, daughter of Antonio Navarro and Antonia González de Vargas, both deceased. He gave his own parents as Juan *Martínez* de Cervantes and María Antonia *Chirinos.* Here he also gave his own last name as "Chirinos."[7]

This is the name he went under when working in the reconstruction of San Miguel Chapel in 1710,[8] and also when he married again in this same year; his third wife was *Juana Montoya,* widow of Francisco Palomino Rendón.[9]

He had two daughters by his second wife: *Lucía,* who married Juan Cayetano Lobato of Santa Fe; and *María de Guadalupe,* who married José Trujillo of Santa Cruz. Both marriages took place in 1716, and both girls were using the "Chirinos" name.[10] This surname did not survive; if Juan Manuel had any male children, they might have reverted to "Martínez."

Juan de Dios Martínez, sixty years old and a native of Mexico City, and **Pedro Martínez,** thirty and a native of Puebla, and also married, appeared together as testimonial witnesses for the marriage of María de Guadalupe Chirinos. Hence, they may have been closely related.

Juan de Dios was married to *Magdalena Cedillo,* who, after his death, married a widower, Antonio Martín, in 1734.[11]

Pedro had appeared as a witness before, in 1708, when he said that he was born in Puebla, was married, and resided in Santa Fe.

He signed his name "Pedro Martínez."[12] It is not known who his wife was, or his children, if any.

* * * * * * * *

SALVADOR MARTÍNEZ CLEMENTE, place of origin not known, married *Rosalia García de Noriega* early in the century. They appeared together as sponsors, October 8, 1728.[13] Known children of theirs were:

Antonio Facundo, born December 6, 1731; *Luis,* March 7, 1734; *Vicente,* October 28, 1745; *Coleta Bárbara,* in 1750;[14] and *Joaquín,* who married Teresa Tenorio de Alba, October 20, 1749.[15]

Salvador was accused of trying to kill his father-in-law, Luis García, by running him down with his horse.[16]

The Martínez people were few when compared with the old Martín Serrano group. But when the latter became "Martínez" also, this name became, perhaps, the most numerous in New Mexico, especially in the north.

1. **AGI, Mex., Aud.,** leg. 377.
2. **Sp. Arch.,** II, No. 198.
3. **NMHR,** Vol. VI, No. 2, p. 158.
4. **Sp. Arch.,** II, No. 54c.
5. **BNM,** leg. 4, Pt. 1, pp. 790-795.
6. **Sp. Arch.,** loc. cit.
7. **DM,** 1696, No. 1.
8. **Kubler,** pp. 11, 17, 20.
9. **DM,** 1710, No. 16.
10. **Ibid.,** 1716, Nos. 10, 13.
11. **B-16, Nambé.**
12. **DM,** 1708, No. 1.
13. **B-2, Albuq.**
14. **B-2 and B-3, Albuq.**
15. **M-50, Sta. Fe.**
16. **Sp. Arch.,** I, No. 1221.

MARZELINO
(See *Ladrón de Guevara*)

MASCAREÑAS

JOSÉ MASCAREÑAS, twenty-six years old, the son of Felipe, and born in Mexico City, brought his family with the colonists of 1693. He had a medium build, large eyes, and scars on the eyebrow and chin. His wife, *María de Acosta,* eighteen, the daughter of Nicolás, was also born in Mexico City; she was of medium height, dark, with large eyes and a small nose.

They had an eight-year-old daughter, *Josefa Melchora,* born in Mexico City, who had a broad face, large eyes, and a thick nose.[1]

Jose was a *calderero* by trade.[2] He gave his age as twenty-seven in 1695, and twenty-eight in 1697, giving Mexico City as his birthplace. First he lived in Santa Cruz, and then was in Santa Fe, when he signed his name as "José Bernardo Mascareñas."[3] In 1701 he and his wife were living in Bernalillo, where a boy, *Francisco*, was born on February 27.⁴ Another child, *María*, is treated further on in connection with the Archibeque family.

Their father must have died in the early part of the century, as their mother had married a Juan Nolasco Armijo or Agüero, and died prior to 1732.⁵ The children were known in Santa Fe as "the orphans of José Mascareñas" in 1736.⁶

One girl, *María*, was reared in the household of Juan de Archibeque, who had a natural son by her. This boy, *Juan*, was reared in his father's house and bore his name. But after Archibeque's death he took his mother's name instead.⁷

Francisco Mascareñas is heard of in connection with his nephew, the son of Archibeque and his sister María,⁸ and finds mention in other documents, but nothing is known of his wife and family.

1. Sp. Arch., II, No. 54c.
2. BNM, leg. 4, Pt. 1, pp. 790, 795.
3. DM, 1695, No. 1; 1697, No. 3.
4. B-13, Bern.
5. M-3, Albuq.
6. Sp. Arch., I, No. 754.
7. Ibid., I, Nos. 13, 339; II, No. 373.
8. Ibid.

MATA

José de Mata, forty-six, was with the exiled colonists at Guadalupe del Paso in 1681.¹

Baltasar de Mata married *Isabel de Chaves*, widow of Jacinto Peláez, in 1705.² They had two children: *Pedro*, born August 12, 1708,³ and *Margarita*, October 30, 1705,⁴ who became the wife of Bernabé Baca.

1. DM, 1681, No. 3.
2. B-13, Bern., M. Sec
3. B-2, Albuq.
4. B-13, Bern.

MEDINA

JUAN LORENZO DE MEDINA and his wife *Antonia Sedano* were among the colonists of 1693.¹ He was twenty years old, the son of José, and born in Mexico City, of medium height, with joined eyebrows, large eyes and nose. She was fourteen, the daughter of Pedro and a native of Querétaro, fair and pockmarked, with a scar on the left eyebrow.² Her sister, *Josefa*, was the wife of Nicolás Jirón.³

It is not known if Juan Lorenzo and Antonia had any children. He was married a second time, to *Juana Anaya Almazan*, by whom he had during five years of married life up until his death: *Juan Francisco, María Antonia,* and *Margarita Antonia*.⁴ He died on July 4, 1731.⁵

DIEGO DE MEDINA, who did not know who his parents were, was born in the City of Durango. He was a soldier in Santa Fe in 1694 when he married *María Zapata Telles Jirón*.⁶ Two known children of theirs were *Ramón* and *Josefa*. The girl married Diego Romero of Santa Cruz in 1714.⁷

Ramón de Medina, soldier of Santa Fe, the son of Captain Diego de Medina, deceased, and María Telles Jirón, had been married to a *Juana Rodríguez*. After her death he married *Valentina Montes de Oca*.⁸

* * * * * * * *

JUAN DE MEDINA, twenty, the son of Melchor, and born in Mexico City, was described as tall, long-faced, with large eyes, a thick nose, and a scar on the left cheek. His wife was *Juana Márquez,* twenty-six, of medium height, with a dark aquiline face and big eyes.⁹

Either this Juan, or the one first treated, was the carpenter who made the altar for the Conquistadora Chapel in 1714.¹⁰

* * * * * * * *

Other Medinas of the Reconquest period were several women, the wives or mothers of new colonists. For example, two daughters of *Alonso de Medina,* who died before the colony set out for New Mexico, were *Manuela* and *María,* wives of Miguel de la Vega y Coca and of José Luis Valdés, respectively. Then, *Andrea de Medina* was the wife of Nicolás Rodríguez, and *Micaela de Medina* of Simón de Molina.

―――

Juan Antonio de Medina married *Francisca Fernández,* April 19, 1739.¹¹

Salvador de Medina and his wife *Manuela Martín* were witnesses for the marriage of *Juan Tiburcio de Medina* and Manuela Márquez, February 6, 1759.¹²

These people were descended from any of the above-mentioned distinct families, but more data is necessary to link them definitely.

1. **BNM,** leg. 4, pt. 1, pp. 790-5.
2. **Sp. Arch.,** II, No. 54c.
3. **Ibid., I,** No. 508.
4. **Ibid.,** I, No. 1226.
5. **Bur-48,** Sta. Fe.
6. **DM,** 1694, No. 23.
7. **Ibid.,** 1714, No. 3.
8. **Ibid.,** 1718, No. 1.
9. **Sp. Arch.,** II, No. 54c.
10. **OLC,** pp. 39, 76.
11. **M-27,** S. Juan.
12. **B-16,** Nambé, M. Sec.

MEUSNIER

Pedro Meusnier did not settle in New Mexico proper, but the facts incidental to his coming and his marriage affect two other Frenchmen who did stay; moreover, his name is encountered in histories of the period covering Nueva Vizcaya and what is now Texas.

Meusnier married *Lucía Madrid,* a native of Guadalupe del Paso, the daughter of Pedro Madrid and Yumar Varela, both pre-Revolt New Mexicans. He was a native of Paris, the son of Luis Meusnier and Ysabel German. "Juan de Archibec" and "Santiago Grolé," soldiers of Santa Fe, stated that they had known Meusnier for fifteen years, having left France together in 1684 with the "General, Monsiur de La Sala," who considered Pedro as though he were his own son; for old Meusnier, treasurer of the French King, had entrusted the boy to the General's personal care.

The marriage took place at Guadalupe del Paso, on December 28, 1699.¹ Earlier in the same year, Pedro had given testimony for Grolé's marriage. At that time he gave Paris as his birthplace, and his age as twenty-six.²

1. **DM,** 1699, No. 9.
2. **Ibid.,** No. 5.

MIERA
(*Miera y Pacheco*)

BERNARDO MIERA Y PACHECO, a Captain of the Cavalry of Cantabria, was a native of Valle de Carriedo of the Mountains of Burgos in Spain. His father was a Don Luis de Miera who served under the Conde de Aguilar in the Army of Philip V. His grandfather, Don Antonio Pacheco, Governor of Navarra and Colonel of the "Terzio" of Lombardy, died in the battle of Mantua. His mother's name was Isabel Ana Pacheco.[1]

Bernardo arrived in Santa Fe as early as 1756, when he was *Alcalde Mayor* of Galisteo and Pecos.[2] In a Memorial which he wrote to the Spanish King, he said that he had arrived at El Paso del Norte in 1743, where he first resided and participated in five campaigns. From there he moved to Santa Fe with his family at the beginning of Governor del Valle's term, when he was made *Alcalde* and War Captain of Pecos and Galisteo.[3] Outlining his ancestry, as previously given, he asked for military titles for himself and for his son, Anacleto.[4]

Bernardo was an accomplished jack-of-all-trades. He tried, though he failed, to recast old ordnance pieces in Santa Fe.[5] He carved the wooden statue of St. Philip the Apostle still to be seen on the high altar at San Felipe Pueblo.[6] And he accompanied Fathers Domínguez and Veléz Escalante as guard commander and explorer on their famous tour of exploration, from which noteworthy maps from his hand came into being, including a detailed map of New Mexico in 1779. He was also a charter officer and first secretary of the Confraternity of Our Lady of Light.[7]

The wife who came with him was *Estefánia Domínguez de Mendoza*, evidently a member of the old New Mexico family which settled in the Chihuahua country instead of returning north with the Reconquest. She died in Santa Fe on December 13, 1783; her husband followed her on April 11, 1785.[8]

They had two sons: *Anacleto* and *Manuel*.

Anacleto (also **Cleto**) **Miera y Pacheco** was born in Chihuahua around the year 1742. As a member of the Santa Fe garrison in 1790 he gave his age as forty-eight. His wife, *Catalina Pino*, was thirty-seven, and they had five sons, eighteen, twelve, ten, three, and one, and three girls, fifteen, nine, and six.[9]

He had first married *Maria Felipa Tafoya*, May 29, 1768,[10] by whom he had some of the children just enumerated. These were: *María Josefa*, born September 12, 1769; *Francisco Xavier*, February 19, 1772; *Teresa Rosalía*, November 8, 1773; and *María de las Nieves*, August 6, 1776.[11] Of these girls, María Josefa married José Francisco Ortiz, and Teresa became the wife of Antonio Ortiz, both of Santa Fe. María de las Nieves was involved in an affair in the Rio Abajo country in 1805.[12] Their Tafoya mother had died on April 9, 1782.[13]

Anacleto then married *Catalina Pino*, widow of Antonio de Luna, November 20, 1782.[14] In 1786, while residing in Santa Fe, as a Sergeant of the Presidio, he was suing Miguel Lucero for property at Tomé that belonged to his wife's Luna children.[15] In 1805 he was *Alcalde Mayor* of Alameda, but by 1815 Catalina Pino was a widow once more.[16] Of their children, two sons are known: *Manuel* and *Ignacio*, who married two sisters on the same day, May 16, 1820. Manuel married María Vibiana Rael, and Ignacio married María Quiteria Rael, daughters of Eusebio Rael and María Tomasa Montoya.[17]

Manuel Miera y Pacheco, "soldado distinguido" of Santa Fe, widower of Barbara Torres, and son of Don Bernardo Miera y Pacheco and Doña María Estefania Domínguez de Mendoza, married *María Josefa Quintana*, daughter of Juan Quintana and Paula Sánchez, at Santa Cruz, May 24, 1781.[18] He had been born at Guadalupe del Paso, and gave his age as thirty-six when he enlisted in 1779.[18a]

Manuel and his first wife had been wedding sponsors at Laguna in 1774.[19]

Two children by his second wife were: *Joaquin* and *Ignacia*. The boy married Cayetana Montoya in 1824, and the girl married Ramón Trujillo in 1818.[20]

* * * * * * * *

Don José de Mier was an *Alférez* at Guadalupe del Paso in 1694.[21] He had taken part as an officer in Vargas' staff during the Reconquest of 1693. But he did not establish himself in New Mexico. Records at Juárez point to the probability of his having founded the prominent family of this name there, which must not be confused with the Miera y Pacheco surname and family.

1. **BNM,** t. 10, pt. 2, ff. 4080-81; **HSNM,** Mil. Papers.
2. **Bancroft,** NMO, 1756.
3. **Ayer Coll., Sp. Amer.,** No. 1134.
4. **Ibid.**
5. **Bancroft,** loc. cit.
6. **BNM,** leg. 10, No. 43, S. Felipe.
7. **NMHR,** Vol. III, No. 12, pp. 41-72; ibid., Vol. X, No. 3, p. 188.
8. **Bur., Castrense.**
9. **Twit. Coll.,** No. 297; **HSNM,** loc. cit.
10. **M-50, Sta. Fe.**
11. All in **B, Sta. Fe.**
12. **Sp. Arch.,** II, No. 1829.
13. **Bur-49, Sta. Fe.**
14. **DM,** 1782, no number.
15. **Sp. Arch.,** I, No. 597.
16. **Ibid.,** I, No. 381; II, No. 1869.
17. **M-50, Albuq.; DM,** 1820, in Albuq., no number.
18. **M-31, Sta. Cruz; DM,** 1781, in Sta. Cruz, no number.
18a. **HSNM,** loc. cit.
19. **M-12, Laguna,** May 25.
20. **DM,** 1818 and 1824, in Sta. Cruz, no number.
21. **Ibid.,** 1694, No. 2.

MIÑON

Juan Miñon (Jean Mignon) was a Frenchman who landed in Santa Fe in the middle of the century. At the time of his marriage, July 23, 1752, he is referred to as a Frenchman, and his bride, *Regina Roybal*, as an Indian, the widow of Francisco.¹ She was one of the many non-Pueblo Indian captives reared in the household of Ignacio Roybal at Jacona;² Ignacio donated land in Santa Fe to Miñon in 1775.³ He died on December 20, 1762.⁴

His known children were: *Santiago,* November 12, 1752; *Micaela Bautista,* May 2, 1754; *María Josefa,* November 2, 1755; *Ynez Sebastiana,* January 22, 1758; and *Juan Antonio,* February 27, 1762.⁵

Juan Antonio Miñon of San Isidro Labrador, Rio de Tesuque, son of Juan Miñon and "*La Gavacha,*" both deceased, married María de la Luz Quintana, daughter of Juan Quintana and Juana Montoya at Santa Cruz, September 23, 1785.⁶

1. **M-50, Sta. Fe.**
2. **B-24, S. Ild.,** April 28, 1748.
3. **Sp. Arch.,** I, No. 551.
4. **Bur-48, Sta. Fe.**
5. All in **B, Sta. Fe.**
6. **M-31, Sta. Cruz; DM,** 1785, in Sta. Cruz, no number.

MIRABAL

JOSÉ DE MIRABAL, child of Juan López de Mirabal, native of Mexico City and deceased, came in 1693 with his widowed mother, *Antonia de Tordezillas,* in the family of Miguel de Figueroa Núñez de Chávez, who was married to José's sister, *María de Mirabal.* José, born in Mexico City, was then ten years old; he had a white and ruddy complexion, an aquiline face, large eyes and forehead.¹

It is not known if this family actually reached New Mexico.

* * * * * * * *

CARLOS JOSÉ PÉREZ MIRABAL and his wife *Beatriz de Tafoya Altamirano* were wedding sponsors in 1734, February 13, and again on September 14, 1738.² In most cases he dropped the "Pérez" part of the name. He lived in the Santa Clara area during the first half of the century,³ but seems to have moved to Santa Fe by 1758, then to the Rio Abajo, to judge from his connections with the González Bas family.⁴ Two known sons were: *Juan Paulino,* born July 3, 1741,⁵ and *Miguel,* who lived at San José de las Huertas in 1808.⁶ Don Carlos was still alive in 1784.⁷

His place of origin is not known. From his age, full name, and his place of marriage and early residence, he seems to have been a brother of Fray José Pérez Mirabal, missionary of the Rio Arriba Pueblos from 1722 to 1763.

1. Sp. Arch., II, No. 54c.
2. M-29, Sta. Cruz.
3. Sp. Arch., II, No. 401; M-31, Sta. Clara, July 29, 1743.
4. Sp. Arch., I, Nos. 178, 651.
5. M-31, Sta. Clara, B. Sec.
6. Sp. Arch., I, No. 605.
7. Bancroft, SWO, 1784.

MIRANDA

MATÍAS DE MIRANDA was a native of the Mines of Sombrerete, the son of Benito de Miranda and María de Aguilar. His first wife was *Ynez Núñez de Ybarra y Bracamontes*. After coming to New Mexico he married *Catalina Durán y Chaves* in 1711.[1] The ceremony was performed by Fray Antonio de Miranda, stationed at Albuquerque; hence it seems as though Matías was his brother. Several cases are known of some missionary's brother coming to New Mexico and settling there; it happened in every century, including our own times.

Francisco Xavier de Miranda, who sold some land in Atrisco in 1735,[2] might have been a son of Matías; also a descendant, perhaps, was a *Jacinto Miranda* living in the Rio Abajo in 1771.

1. DM, 1711, No. 1.
2. Sp. Arch., I, Nos. 321, 601.

MOLINA

SIMÓN DE MOLINA first came to New Mexico as a convict in 1677, when he was described as the son of Don Tomás, born in Mexico City at San Juan, of medium height, with a broad face and large eyes and nose. He was sentenced to six years of military service without pay.[1] In 1680 he escaped the Indian massacre with the New Mexican people; from Guadalupe del Paso he went to Mexico City to see his family, returning in 1681 to enlist as a soldier. He was then thirty-three years old, and was described as having a fair complexion and ruddy face, with a scant beard and straight hair.[2]

Simón went back home to Mexico City prior to 1693, and there he joined the colonists under Velasco. He was described again as the son of Tomás, born in Mexico City at San Juan, forty years old, pockmarked, with large eyes and a rather thick nose. His wife was *Micaela de Medina*, daughter of Cristóbal, and born in the same place as her husband; she was thirty, with an aquiline face and large eyes.

They brought three children, all born in Mexico City: *María Teresa*, four, with a dark face, big eyes and a thick nose; *Paula Antonia*, three, who looked like her sister; and *Nicolás Francisco*, one year old, fair with large eyes.[3] Their father's civilian trade was that of a carpenter.[4]

While building the new Mission at Nambé in 1696, Simón was killed by the rebel Indians at San Cristóbal with Fathers Arbizu and Carbonel.[5] Poor Simón, twice attracted to New Mexico after his first involuntary trip, and having escaped one Indian massacre in 1680, he was destroyed by another one sixteen years later.

1. B-H, III, pp. 317-24.
2. Revolt, I, pp. 148-9; II, pp. 71, 134.
3. Sp. Arch., II, No. 54c.
4. BNM, leg. 4, pt. 1, pp. 790-5.
5. Old Santa Fe, Vol. III, pp. 332-73.

MOLINAR

Antonio Molinar, a native of Sombrerete, thirty-three years old, was a soldier of Santa Fe in 1694.[1] He was the son of Domingo de Molinar, deceased, and Isabel de Montemayor, both natives of Sombrerete. On April 6, 1696, he married *Josefa de Gongora* in Santa Fe.[2]

1. **DM**, 1694, Nos. 4, 15.
2. **Ibid.**, 1696, No. 5.

MONDRAGÓN

SEBASTIÁN SÁNCHEZ DE MONDRAGÓN, or, DE MONROY, returned with the Vargas Reconquest. A widower in 1693, he got married on December 27; the wedding feast was going on just as the Tanos Indians within the walls of Santa Fe were about to rebel and start Vargas' famous battle for Santa Fe.[1] The bride's name was a *María*, called "María de Mondragón," widow of Sebastián "Monrroy," when she died in 1727.[2]

Juan Alonso Mondragón and his wife, *Sebastiana Trujillo*, or *Martín*, were living in the Pojoaque area in 1715. He was twenty-eight years old.[3] In 1719 he said that he was forty-four, a native of New Mexico, and a resident of Santa Cruz.[4]

Known children of theirs were: *Juana*, born February 30 (sic), 1711;[5] *Catalina* (perhaps) mentioned with Juan Alonso in 1719;[6] *Francisco Xavier*, born September 20, 1721;[7] and *Salvador*, mentioned with his mother, February 2, 1742.[8] Very likely another daughter was a *María de Mondragon*, wife of Miguel Carrillo.

———

A relic of the preceding century was old *Sebastiana de Mondragón*, who returned with the Reconquest to claim property in Santa Fe owned by her father, Juan de Mondragón, prior to the "uprising of the Indians." Her (grand) daughter was *Tomasa Martín Serrano*, wife of Bernardino de Sena, whom she called her son-in-law.[9] Hence, her daughter, the mother of Tomasa, was Josefa de la Asención González.[10]

Old Sebastiana died on November 25, 1728, a widow eighty-eight years old.[11]

1. **Ritch Coll.**, Box 1, No. 25, ff. 109-10.
2. **Bur-48, Sta. Fe.**
3. **Sp. Arch.**, I, No. 740; II, No. 239c.
4. **DM**, 1719, No. 1.
5. **B-33, Sta. Cruz.**
6. **DM, loc. cit.**
7. **B-33, Sta. Cruz.**
8. **B-24, S. Ild.**
9. **Sp. Arch.**, I, Nos. 289, 826.
10. GENEALOGY: **Sebastiana de Mondragón**, Josefa de la Asención González, Tomasa Martín González (or Serrano), Tomás Antonio de Sena, Graciana Prudencia Sena, Manuel Ribera, María Guadalupe Ribera, María Dolores Alarid, Romualdo Roybal, Nicolasa Roybal, Fr. A. Chávez.
11. **Bur-48, Sta. Fe.**

MONTAÑO

Alonso Montaño and *María de la Cruz* had a daughter, *María de las Nieves*, who married a Sebastián Luis, native of San Miguel el Grande, at Santa Fe in 1699.[1]

Alonso is the only male member of the old New Mexico Montaño family, if indeed he belonged to it, to return with the Reconquest. It is not known if he had any male descendants to pass on the name.

* * * * * * * *

JUAN ANTONIO MONTAÑO DE SOTO-

MAYOR and his wife, *Isabel Jorge de Vera,* returned with Vargas in 1693 and settled in Santa Fe; after her husband's death, Isabel moved to the Rio Abajo.

His antecedents are told in the preceding century. Twice referred to as a native of Mexico City, he appeared as a witness in three nuptial investigations of 1694.[2] But he was dead by 1696 when reference was made to his widow, Isabel Jorge de Vera, as a grand-daughter of Captain Antonio Baca of pre-Revolt times.[3] She died on November 25, 1736.[4]

Three known sons were *José, Juan,* and *Lucas.* Three of their daughters, *Leonor, Magdalena,* and *Juana,* married three Durán y Chaves brothers, Luis, Antonio, and Nicolás,[5] respectively. A fourth, *Polonia,* became the wife of Salvador de Santisteban.

José Montaño, living in Santa Fe, was twenty years old in 1695.[6] He married *María de Cuéllar* and went to live in the Rio Abajo, where in 1715 he wounded a man, because of jealousy, at the home of his mother-in-law, then married to Tomás Garcia.[7] He was still living in 1734 when he and María were sponsors for a child of his sister Juana and Nicolás de Chaves.[8] In 1750 he trespassed on Alameda Pueblo lands and got a fine imposed by Governor Gachupín.[9] He is in all probability the José Montaño who died a *"muerte violenta"* at Tomé, June 29, 1756.[10]

His widow was still much alive in 1772 as one of the first settlers of the Rio Puerco country with three of her sons.[11]

Their children were: *Pedro,* who married Paula Gallegos in 1748;[12] *Joaquín,* who died at the age of eleven, April 28, 1742;[13] *Juan Bautista,* husband of Rosalia Jaramillo; and *Bernabé Manuel,* who married Eduarda Yturrieta, or Varela. The latter two were among the first Rio Puerco settlers with their mother.

Juan Montaño, known as *"el Cuate,"* was very likely José's twin.[14] He married *Juana Gallegos,* sister to a Joaquín Gallegos,[15] by whom he had two children: *Quiteria,* born January 23, 1729,[16] and *Nicolás.*[17] When their mother died on March 6, 1729,[18] two months after the girl's birth, the children must have been reared by the Tomás Garcia family, since both bore this name up to the time of their marriage, but reverted to Montaño after that time. Both were married on the same day, August 16, 1734: *Nicolás* to a Quiteria Romero, and his sister *Quiteria* to Andrés Martín Serrano.[19]

It seems as though their father married again. Two sons of Juan Montaño and Ignacia Lucero appear in the records, *Luis,* who married Luisa Jaramillo, January 26, 1745, and *José,* who married María Benavides, October 20, 1770.[20]

Lucas Montaño, unlike his brothers, stayed in Santa Fe, where he had married *Juana de Anaya Almazán* prior to 1710.[21] He died after eleven years of marriage, and his widow married twice after that. In her last will, in 1736, she named her five children by Lucas Montaño: *María Gerónima, María Josefa,* wife of Manuel Martin, *Antonio Urbano, María Gertrudis,* and *Lucas Tadéo.*[22]

Of the girls, María Geronima had married José Rodríguez in 1729,[23] and María Josefa de la Candelaria had married Manuel Martín of Santa Cruz in 1730.[24]

One son, Antonio Urbano, married Juana María Ortega, November 31, 1740.[25]

---

1. **DM,** 1699, No. 3, incomplete.
2. **Ibid.,** 1694, Nos. 19, 25, 29.
3. **Sp. Arch.,** I, No. 411.
4. **Bur-2, Albuq.**
5. GENEALOGY: **Juana Montaño: a)** María Antonia D. y Chávez, María Manuela Romero, José Chávez I, José Chávez II, Eugenio Chávez, Fabián Chávez, Fr. A. Chávez.
   b) Gertrudis D. y Chávez, Agustina Silva, Lugarda Tafoya, Pablo Baca, Tomás Baca, Nicanora Baca, Fabián Chávez, Fr. A. Chávez.
6. **DM,** 1695, No. 17.
7. **Sp. Arch.,** II, No. 215.
8. **B-2, Albuq.,** Feb. 3.
9. **Sp. Arch.,** I, No. 29.
10. **Bur-2, Albuq.**
11. **Sp. Arch.,** I, No. 277.
12. **M-3, Albuq.**
13. **Bur-2, Albuq.**
14. **Sp. Arch.,** II, No. 299.
15. **Ibid.,** No. 416a.
16. **B-2, Albuq.**
17. **DM,** 1767, in Albuq., no number.
18. **Bur-2, Albuq.**
19. **M-3, Albuq.**
20. **Ibid.**
21. **DM,** 1710, No. 2.
22. **Sp. Arch.,** I, No. 1226.
23. **DM,** 1729, No. 1.
24. **Ibid.,** 1730, No. 3.
25. **M-50, Sta. Fe;** See **Urban.**

MONTES
(*Montes de Oca*)

PEDRO MONTES DE OCA was a native of Zacatecas, twenty-one or twenty-two in 1694.[1] He was a soldier at Santa Fe in this same year when, widowed of his first wife, *Micaela Garcia*, he married *Beatriz Sedillo de Salazar*, herself a new colonist from Sombrerete. Pedro gave his parents as Domingo Montes de Oca and María de la Concepción, residing in the Pueblo de Escapusalco.[2] Beatriz was dead by 1718 when their daughter, *Valentina*, married Ramón de Medina.[3] Pedro belonged to the Conquistadora Confraternity.[4]

* * * * * * * *

Nicolás de Montes and his wife, *Nicolasa de Herrera*, were in the earlier Velasco list of 1693,[5] but it is not known if they actually reached New Mexico.

1. **DM**, 1694, Nos. 4, 10, 15.
2. **Ibid.**, No. 13.
3. **Ibid.**, 1718, No. 1.
4. **OLC**, p. 72.
5. **BNM**, leg. 4, pt. 1, pp. 790-5.

MONTES VIGIL
(See *Vigil*)

MONTIEL

José de Montiél, thirty-eight, was at Guadalupe del Paso in 1705.[1] He was a native of Talpujagua and related to Juan de Alderete.[2]

1. **DM**, 1705, No. 8; 1710, No. 8.
2. **Ibid.**, 1691, No. 4; 1693, No. 1.

MONTOYA

ANTONIO MONTOYA and his wife, *María Hurtado*, were witnesses for the wedding of Andrés Hurtado (her brother) and Antonia Domínguez at Guadalupe del Paso in 1689.[1] They returned home with Vargas four years later with a large increase over the three children of 1680. In 1707, by then a Captain, Antonio gave his age as sixty, and sixty-six in 1715.[2] In 1716 he took part in the Moqui campaign with the Santa Fe Militia.[3] A 1704 suit shows that his father had owned land in Santa Fe before the Rebellion.[4] Antonio died before 1725, the year his widow made her last will. He had been *mayordomo*, in Vargas' name, of the Confraternity of La Conquistadora in 1696.[5]

In her last testament, María Hurtado declared that she and Antonio had been married for forty-six years, and then named their children: *Juan Antonio, Andrés, Angela, Juana, Antonia, Nicolasa, Antonio, Manuela, Tomasa,* and *María*. She also mentioned a grandson, Miguel Ortiz.[6] She died on March 22, 1726, and was buried in the Conquistadora Chapel of Santa Fe.[7]

Of these children, *Andrés* married Antonia Lucero, and then María Sisneros; *Antonio* is very likely the man of this name whose young wife, Catalina de Ribera, died early in June, 1727.[8] Of the girls, *Juana* married Francisco Palomino Rendón in 1693,[9] and then Juan Manuel Chirinos in 1710; and *María* became the wife of Miguel de la Vega y Coca in 1699.[10]

Andrés Montoya, son of Antonio and María Hurtado, lived in Santa Fe until his death, where he acquired considerable property.[11] He also was *Alcalde Mayor* of the three north Queres Pueblos in 1731-32.[12] He appears to be the man who furnished the *vigas* and other lumber for the Santa Fe parish church in 1714 and the chapel of San Miguel in 1710.[13]

Andrés made his last will in 1740. After giving the names of his parents, he declared that he had ten children by his first wife, *Antonia Lucero de Godoy*, and none by the second, *María Sisneros*.

These children were: *Josefa*, wife of José Santisteban; *Manuela*, late wife of Joaquín Sánchez; *Andrés*, married to Ana Baca; *Isidro*, husband of Manuela Silva; *José*, married to Juana Quintana; *Francisco*, husband of Juana Baca; *Antonio*, husband of *Ynez Baca*; *Cristobal* (dead); *Nicolás* and *Diego*, both single.[14] Of the children just mentioned, Josefa had first married Manuel Silva in 1717, and then Santisteban in 1720; Francisco married Juana Baca, on June 14, 1733.[15]

Captain Andrés Montoya died on August 31, 1740; his first wife had died on December 6, 1736.[16]

DIEGO MONTOYA went to live in the Indian-occupied city of Santa Fe as soon as the colonists arrived there in 1693. But, warned beforehand of the impending rebellion, December 27, he left to join the others in the camp outside the walls.[17] Two or three years later he moved down to Bernalillo with other old settlers who preferred the Rio Abajo.

Diego and his wife, *Josefa de Hinojos*, had at least five children: *Salvador*, who married Manuela Garcia de la Riva;[18] *Juana*, first wife of Pedro Durán y Chaves;[19] *Antonio*, who married Bernarda Baca; *Isabel*, wife of Miguel de San Juan; and another girl, name not known, who was the second wife of Baltasar Romero.

Salvador Montoya married *Manuela Garcia de la Riva* in Bernalillo on April 25, 1700,[20] where he had gone to live with his parents after the Reconquest, and in 1715 he was a Regent of the "Kingdom."[21] He was a member of the Confraternity of La Conquistadora.[22]

He made his last will in 1727, while residing in Santa Fe as *"Regidor."* After naming his parents and his wife, he declared the following three sons and two daughters as his children: *José Francisco, Miguel, José Manuel, Francisca,* and *Josefa*.[23]

Of the sons, *José (Francisco)* was born on July 30, 1701, and was living in Valle de San Buenaventura in Nueva Vizcaya as late as 1733.[24] *Miguel* married Rosa Baca in 1729, and then Lucía de Chávez in 1734.[25] One of the girls, *Josefa*, became the wife of José Antonio Benavides.[26]

Antonio Montoya, brother of Salvador, married *Bernarda Baca*, May 20, 1707.[27] In 1731 he was the Captain in charge of the distribution of alms from church titles, and of the sheep of the church used for relief of the needy.[28] The following year he was *Alcalde* of Santa Fe, on January 22, 1736, at the age of forty.[30] Antonio also belonged to the Conquistadora Confraternity.[31]

The known children by Bernarda Baca were: *María Francisca*, born September 15, 1708; *Juan Manuel*, May 11, 1710; *Miguel*, October 8, 1711;[32] and *Bernardo Baltasar*, mentioned with his two brothers as grantees of the Old Pueblo of Abiquiú in 1741.[33]

Antonio married again, this time a widow, *Jacinta Peláez*, in 1736.[34] He then bought property in Santa Fe,[35] but by 1745 he was living at Santa Rosa de Lima, Abiquiú, as a stockman and farmer, being then fifty-five years of age.[36] There he died on August 8, 1745.[37]

Sample page of *Spanish Archives of New Mexico*, Vol. II, No. 179, dated September 16, 1712. Signatures of Lt. Gov. Juan Páez Hurtado, inaugurating the Santa Fe Fiesta, with Council Members: Alfonso Rael de Aguilar, Don Felix Martínez, Salvador Montoya, Miguel de Dios Sandoval Martínez, Lorenzo Madrid, Antonio Montoya, Juan García de la Riva, and Francisco Lorenzo de Casados.

FELIPE MONTOYA and his wife *María de Paredes* also came to Bernalillo after the Reconquest battles were over. There two known children of theirs were married: *María* became the wife of Cristóbal Martín of Santa Cruz in 1699, and *Clemente* married Josefa de Herrera (Luján) at Santa Cruz, September 19, 1701.[38] Their parents were dead in this latter year.[39]

Clemente Montoya made his last will in 1753, in which he lists his seventeen children by two wives.[40]

---

1. **DM**, 1689, No. 2.
2. **Ibid.**, 1707, No. 2; 1715, No. 6.
3. **Sp. Arch.**, II, No. 250.
4. **Ibid.**, I, No. 481.
5. **OLC**, pp. 8, 64-5, 74-5.
6. **Sp. Arch.**, I, No. 405.
7. **Bur-48, Sta. Fe**.
8. **Ibid**.
9. GENEALOGY: **Juana Montoya**, María Estela Palomino Rendón, Antonio Ribera, Manuel Ribera, María Guadalupe Ribera, María Dolores Alarid, Romualdo Roybal, Nicolasa Roybal, Fr. A. Chávez.
10. GENEALOGY: **María Montoya**, Feliciana de la Vega y Coca, Josefa Bustamante, Josefa Ortiz Bustamante, José María Alarí, María Dolores Alarid, Romualdo Roybal, Nicolasa Roybal, Fr. A. Chávez.
11. **Sp. Arch.**, I, Nos. 511, 526, 836, 837, 840.
12. **Bancroft, NMO**, 1732; Crespo, par. 255.
13. **OLC**, pp. 39, 72, 74-5; Kubler, p. 19.
14. **Sp. Arch.**, I, No. 526.
15. **M-50, Sta. Fe**.
16. **Bur-48, Sta. Fe**.
17. **Ritch Coll.**, Box 1, No. 25, ff. 108-10.
18. GENEALOGY: **Salvador Montoya**, Miguel Montoya, Barbara Montoya, María Manuela Lucero, Tomás Baca, Nicanora Baca, Fabián Chávez, Fr. A. Chávez.
19. GENEALOGY: **Juana Montoya**, Diego Antonio Chávez, María Guadalupe Chávez, María Isabel Armijo, María Rita Torres, José Chávez, Eugenio Chávez, Fabián Chávez, Fr. A. Chávez.
20. **B-13, Bern.**
21. **DM**, 170, No. 6; 1707, No. 7; 1715, No. 8.
22. **OLC**, p. 70.
23. **Sp. Arch.**, I, No. 512.
24. **B-13, Bern.; Sp. Arch.**, I, No. 517.
25. **M-3, Albuq.**
26. **Sp. Arch.**, I, No. 569.
27. **B-13, Bern.**
28. Crespo, pars. 277-7.
29. **Bancroft, NMO**, 1732.
30. **Bur-48, Sta. Fe**.
31. **OLC**, p. 70.
32. All in **B-13, Bern.**
33. **Sp. Arch.**, I, No. 571.
34. **M-3, Albuq.**
35. **Sp. Arch.**, I, No. 272.
36. **Bancroft, NMO**, 1745.
37. **Bur-33, Sta. Cruz.**
38. **DM**, 1701, No. 3.
39. This is the only known link with the Paredes family of the seventeenth century; anyone connecting with **María** or **Clemente** would have good reason for claiming possible descent from Hernán Cortés, Conqueror of Mexico.
40. **Sp. Arch.**, I, No. 494.

MORA

This name is hard to pin down, due to the fact that it is combined with several double surnames, and also for lack of early documentary evidence. A family of this name would have to be traced back, step by step, to arrive at any of the following sources.

Juan de la Mora was a native of Guadalajara serving as a soldier in Santa Fe in 1697, when he married *María de la Encarnación*, a native of Santa Fe of unknown parentage. He was twenty-seven years old, and she was thirty.[1]

Antonio de Mora and his wife, not named, were in the early Velasco list of new colonists in 1693.[2] But it is not known if they actually came to New Mexico.

* * * * * * * *

Francisco de la Mora was one of the three deserters from the new colony on the way to Santa Fe.[3] He was a native of La Villa de Zamora, and twenty-nine years old in 1694.[4] In 1696, and even in 1708, he declared his age as "forty," and said that he was a settler of Santa Fe.[5] He also appeared as a civil witness in 1696, and sold some lands at Santa Cruz in 1702.[6]

He might have been the Francisco Guerrero de la Mora, married to *María Luisa de Solorga (Senorga?)*, whose daughter Francisca married Joaquín Sánchez at Albuquerque in 1725.[7] The wife seems to be the Luisa de Senorga who came in 1693 as the wife of Diego de Salas,[8] a man who was later tried for bigamy.

Alejandro Mora was godfather for a child on September 21, 1728.[9] He could have been a son of the preceding couple. In 1751 he was tried for beating his wife.[10]

Juan de la Mora Pineda (See *Pineda*) could have contributed to this family name through some of his descendants, for the Pineda name did not last: likewise,

Juan García de la Mora (q.v.). In 1753, a Captain at Santa Cruz del Ojo Caliente, in Rio Arriba, was referred to as "Manuel Dias del Castillo, *alias Mora*."[11]

Among the Frenchmen who came to New Mexico in 1739, there was a *Louis Morin*, or *Moreau*.[12] This man stayed in Santa Fe where, on October 12, 1740, as **Luis María Mora**, Frenchman, he married *Juana Muñiz*.[13] It is not known if they had children to perpetuate his name in the hispanicized form the Padre used in recording the marriage.

1. **DM**, 1697, No. 4.
2. **BNM**, leg. 4, pt. 1, pp. 830-4.
3. **Crusaders**, p. 148.
4. **DM**, 1694, No. 21.
5. **Ibid.**, 1696, No. 6; 1708, No. 2.
6. **Sp. Arch.**, I, Nos. 2, 292.
7. **DM**, 1725, No. 5.
8. **Sp. Arch.**, II, No. 54c.
9. **B-2, Albuq.**
10. **Sp. Arch.**, II, No. 515.
11. **Ibid.**, I, No. 544.
12. **NMHR**, Vol. XVI, No. 3, p. 262; **Colorado Magazine**, Vol. XVI, No. 5, pp. 167-8.
13. **M-50, Sta. Fe.**

MORAGA

Felipe Moraga, brother of Antonia Moraga, the wife of Cristobal Martín, was the only male member of this family to return in 1693. He was involved in a hexing affair with San Juan Indians in 1703. By 1711 he had "left the kingdom."[1]

1. **AGN, Mex., Inq.**, t. 735, ff. 306-8; **Sp. Arch.**, I, No. 490.

MORAN

Miguel Morán returned to his native Santa Fe in 1693 with his wife, *Celestina de la Cruz*. He gave his age as thirty in 1692 and 1694.[1] He was dead by 1728 when his son, *Antonio*, married Juana Dorotea de Sila, of unknown parentage.[2] Another son, *Nicolás*, widowed of Micaela Gerónima de la Cruz, married Bernarda Varela, May 6, 1743.[3] Another son could have been a *Juan Morán*, whose wife, Micaela Cadena, died on May 2, 1735.[4]

Their mother, Celestina, died in June or July 1737.[5]

1. **DM**, 1692, No. 4; 1694, No. 29.
2. **Ibid.**, 1728, No. 5.
3. **M-50, Sta. Fe.**
4. **Bur-48, Sta. Fe.**
5. **Ibid.**

MORENO

Juan José Moreno was a native of Spain, and forty-two years old in 1745; he had been living in Santa Fe as early as 1732.[1] In 1756 he made his last will, in which he named his childless wife, *Juana Roybal*, and an adopted daughter, *Antonia Dominga*.[2] He was a charter officer of the Confraternity of Our Lady of Light.[3]

The girl belonged to the numerous family of Juana Roybal's brother, Mateo, and later became the wife of Juan Antonio Alarí.

1. **Bancroft, NMO**, 1732 and 1745.
2. **Sp. Arch.**, I, No. 552.
3. **NMHR**, Vol. X, No. 3, p. 187.

MORQUECHO

Vicente Morquecho was a native of Guichapa, Valley of Mexico, and forty-seven years old in 1790, then living in Santa Fe with his (second) wife, *Rosalia Torres*, thirty-one years of age. They had two daughters, nineteen and seven years old.[1] He was thirty-one when he enlisted in 1776, and gave his parents as Cristóbal Morquecho and Ana María Gutiérrez.[2]

His first wife had been *Agustina Rodríguez*. A daughter, *María*, was born to them at Chama on April 23, 1770,[3] and was very likely the nineteen-year-old girl mentioned before.

1. Sp. Arch., II, No. 1096a.
2. HSNM, Mil. Papers.
3. B-31, Sta. Clara.

MOYA

ANTONIO DE MOYA was a mason by trade who joined the colonists of 1693 with his wife, *Francisca Antonia Morales*, or *de Guijosa*. He was a native of Mexico City, born at Santa Teresa, the son of Juan, and twenty-one years old. He had a broad face, large eyes and forehead, and a rather wide nose. His wife, seventeen, the daughter of Juan, and born in Mexico City at Las Escalerillas, had a round face and big eyes.[1]

By 1715 Antonio was dead and his widow was married to Andrés de la Paz.[2] Francisca herself passed away on April 20, 1752, "more than eighty years old."[3]

Their children were: *Pedro Antonio, Lucas Miguel,* and *María Francisca*, the eldest. For she had been born on the way from Mexico City at the Presidio del Gallo; in 1709 she married Juan Esteban de Apodaca in Santa Fe.[4]

Pedro Antonio Moya and his sister Francisca were sponsors for Indians at Taos in July, 1715. There he died, leaving a widow, *Ana María Domínguez*, December 8, 1716.[6]

Lucas Miguel Moya became the third husband of *Juana Anaya Almazán*, and in five years of married life had two children by her: *Lucas de Jesús* and *Pedro Antonio*.[7] She died on November 17, 1736.[8] Lucas was a charter officer of Our Lady of Light.[9]

1. BNM, leg. 4, pt. 1, pp. 790-5; Sp. Arch., II, No. 54c.
2. Ritch Coll., Box 2, No. 54; Sp. Arch., I, Nos. 9, 309.
3. Bur-48, Sta. Fe.
4. Sp. Arch., I, No. 514; DM, 1709, No. 5.
5. B-45, Taos.
6. Ibid., Bur. Sec.
7. Sp. Arch., I, No. 1226.
8. Bur-48, Sta. Fe.
9. NMHR, Vol. X, No. 3, p. 188.

MUÑIZ

ANTONIO MUÑIZ was a native of Zelaya in New Spain. As a twenty-seven-year-old soldier of Santa Cruz, he married *Angela de Olivas*, twenty, a native of Sombrerete. His parents were Lorenzo Muñiz and Ana María de la Cruz, both deceased.[1] He appeared as a witness on two occasions.[2]

A daughter, *Gertrudis*, married Antonio

Vásquez in 1714, when both her parents were mentioned as dead,³ and after his death she married Francisco Dias Blea in 1722.⁴

1. **DM**, 1695, No. 2.
2. Ibid., 1694, No. 3; 1698, No. 7.
3. Ibid., 1714, No. 11.

José Muñiz and his wife, not named, are entered in the other Velasco list,⁵ but it is not known if they arrived in New Mexico.

4. Ibid., 1722, No. 1.
5. **BNM**, leg. 4, pt. 1, pp. 830-4.

NARANJO

DOMINGO NARANJO was an Indian of New Spain who cast his lot with the Taos Indians when the Pueblos rebelled against the Spanish colony in 1680. He seems to have died by the time Vargas' Expedition came to Taos in 1696. But a son of his, *José López Naranjo,* "lobo de Yndio mulato," had joined the Spaniards.¹

José López Naranjo, it appears, had joined the forces of Vargas before 1696, possibly when the First Expedition visited the Pueblos in 1692. For he appeared as a marriage witness for some Tiguas at Guadalupe del Paso in that year, when he gave his age as twenty-two.² During the Indian uprising of 1696, he was referred to as a Spaniard by Roque de Madrid, when Naranjo was rendering valuable services to Vargas through his Indian contacts.³ In 1702 he was *Alcalde Mayor* of Zuñi, and very hopeful about pacifying the Moqui Pueblos.⁴ He was Captain of thirty Indian scouts in the Sandia Apache campaign, when Vargas died, in 1704.⁵ In 1715 he commanded the Pueblo Indian forces in the Navajo campaign of that year.⁶ He left his name on Inscription Rock during one of his Zuñi and Moqui excursions.⁶ᵃ

José married a bastard daughter of a Matías Lujan of Santa Cruz.⁷ He acquired lands across the Rio del Norte from Santa Cruz, south of those owned by an Antonio Salazar.⁸ One known son of his was *José Antonio*.

José Antonio Naranjo married *Juana Márquez de Ayala*. They had a son, *José Antonio*, who married Manuela Armenta, and a daughter, *Catalina*, who was the wife of Salvador de Torres.⁹ Most likely another son was *Geronimo* Naranjo, who married María Trujillo, February 2, 1743, with Salvador de Torres and Catalina Naranjo as sponsors.¹⁰ And possibly another son was *Matías Naranjo,* living in the same district with his wife María Varela, who bore him two children: José Joaquín, March 28, 1741, and Gabriela, March 25, 1743.¹¹

In 1731, Naranjo killed a man and "fled the Kingdom."¹¹ᵃ

José Antonio Naranjo II, son of José Antonio Naranjo and Juana Márquez de Ayala, married *Manuela Armenta*, daughter of Antonio Armenta and Juana Abeytia, on September 4, 1749.¹² His military career had taken him to the Capital; two years previously he had asked for the title of *"Capitán de Gente de Guerra"* in Santa Fe, which was granted.¹³ He made the most of it, and this did not settle well among the officials and people. In 1759 they charged that Naranjo's title was as a Captain for Indian troops only, and that he had acquired it by representing himself to the Viceroy as a descendant of Spanish Conquistadores, whereas his great-grandfather was none other than the Indian Domingo Naranjo who had apostatized in 1680; his grandfather, José López Naranjo, had been of great help to the Spaniards as a Captain, but a Captain of Indians only. Some citizens, who took Naranjo's part in this controversy, were from the Chimayó district.⁴

In 1766 Governor Gachupín reviewed Naranjo's rustling activities in Guadalupe del

Paso as well as New Mexico proper, and called him to Santa Fe from Taos.¹⁵ As a result, the Viceroy ordered Naranjo's title revoked in 1767, as well as his arrest for sedition two years later, at which time the Viceroy also discussed the matter of founding settlements for the restless *genízaros*.¹⁶ Here, no doubt, were the first stirrings of the Santa Cruz-Chimayó insurrections of the following century.

Other recorded activities of Naranjo are a real estate deal with Diego de Torres in 1752, a trial in 1756 for mistreating his Armenta wife, and still other charges for assault in 1758.¹⁷

———

A **Diego Naranjo**, thirty years old, was in Santa Fe in 1698.¹⁸ He was, perhaps, a brother of José López Naranjo.

1. AGN, Tierras: Civil, t. 426, ff. 72-84.
2. DM, 1692, No. 3.
3. Old Santa Fe, Vol. III, pp. 332-73.
4. Bancroft, NMO, 1701; Crusaders, p. 348.
5. Sp. Arch., II, No. 99.
6. Bancroft, NMO, 1715.
6a. Mesa, Canyon, etc., p. 474.
7. AGN, loc. cit.
8. Ritch Coll., Box 2, No. 52.
9. Sp. Arch., I, No. 643.
10. M-31, Sta. Clara.
11. Ibid., B. Sec.
11a. Sp. Arch., II, No. 363.
12. M-50, Sta. Fe.
13. Sp. Arch., II, No. 478.
14. AGN, loc. cit.
15. Ibid., ff. 85-8, 94.
16. Sp. Arch., II, Nos. 613, 651, 2580.
17. Ibid., I, No. 643; II, Nos. 535, 923.
18. DM, 1698, No. 16.

NAVARRO

Antonio Navarro and his wife, *Antonia González de Vargas*, were both dead in 1696, when their sixteen-year-old daughter, *María de Guadalupe*, married Juan Manuel Chirinos. She had been born in Mexico City.¹

* * * * * * * *

Blas Navarro and his wife, *Matiana Gómez*, had a daughter, *Juana de Torres*, twenty-one, born in Leon, who married Felix de Aragón in Santa Fe, in 1694.²

A *Luisa Navarro* received mention in passing, in 1704, in Santa Fe.³

Juan Martín Navarro was the son of Jacinto de Quesada and Micaela de Quintanilla, all native of San Felipe de Jesus on the Rio de Conchos. He married *María Garcia de Noriega* at Ysleta del Paso in 1704.⁴

———

José Navarro and *Antonia Archuleta* had a daughter, *Rosa*, who married Cristóbal Durán at Socorro del Paso in 1719.⁵

1. DM, 1696, No. 8.
2. Ibid., 1694, No. 22.
3. AASF, No. 15.
4. DM, 1704, No. 3.
5. Ibid., 1719, No. 5.

NIETO

CRISTÓBAL NIETO returned to Santa Fe with the Reconquest with his wife, *Petrona Pacheco*, and their family. He received a grant of land on August 5, 1697.¹ Petrona, widow of Cristóbal Nieto, died on May 18, 1750.²

Of their known children, *María Magdalena* married Francisco de Tapia, and *Lucía* became the wife of Salvador Olguín. Nothing is known so far of the other two legitimate children, and the three others which Petrona had during her twelve-year captivity among the Indians.

———

Simón Nieto, perhaps a son of Cristóbal,

was a soldier of Santa Fe in 1700.³ Still soldiering in 1728, he had lost his wife, *Francisca Maese*, daughter of Luis Maese. Simón sold some land in Santa Fe in that year.⁴

1. Sp. Arch., I, No. 638.
2. Bur-48, Sta. Fe.
3. Sp. Arch., I, No. 639.
4. Ibid., No. 642.

NOÁNEZ

Juan Antonio de Unanue was in Santa Fe as early as 1731, apparently as a government clerk.¹ He and his wife, *María Francisca Garcia* had a son, *Juan Cayetano*.

Felipe de Unanue appears as an official witness in 1746.² In 1747 he and Polonia Baca were sponsors for the marriage of Juan Bautista Durán and Barbara Baca.³ Polonia married Clemente Gutiérrez in 1755, but she might have been married previously to Unanue.

Were these two men brothers, or father and son?

Juan Cayetano Unanue, son of Juan Antonio Unanue and María Francisca Garcia, was twenty-three when he enlisted in 1757.³ᵃ He and his wife, *Ana María Garduño*, were living in Santa Fe where these three sons were born: *José Miguel*, June 5, 1760; *Juan Antonio*, March 6, 1762; and *Francisco Gerónimo*, September 17, 1770.⁴ Juan Cayetano bought a house in Santa Fe in 1766.⁵

The family still resided in Santa Fe in 1790. Juan Cayetano was fifty-eight years old, and a farmer. Ana María was fifty-one. With them lived a son, twenty (Francisco Gerónimo).⁶

José Miguel Unanue, the eldest son, and thirty-one in 1790, was married to Andrea Candelaria, twenty-eight. They had two sons, five and three years of age, and a girl, seven.⁷

Francisco Gerónimo, the youngest, married *Barbara Maese*. In 1821, their son, *José Guadalupe NUANES* went to Albuquerque and married Antonia Garcia, daughter of Juan Garcia and Isabel Romero.⁸

A **Felipe Noanes** married *Manuela Montaño* in Albuquerque, April 5, 1832.⁹

Here, and throughout the following century, may be seen the evolution of *"Unanue"* to the present *"Noánez"* and *"Nuánez."*

1. Bancroft, NMO, 1731; Sp. Arch., I, Nos. 236, 316, 515, 517, 357.
2. Sp. Arch., I, Nos. 213, 340.
3. M-11, Isleta, July 6.
3a. HSNM, Mil. Papers.
4. All in B, Sta. Fe.
5. Sp. Arch., I, No. 1023.
6. Ibid., II, No. 1096a.
7. Ibid.
8. DM, 1821, in Albuq., no number.
9. M-5, Albuq.

NÚÑEZ

TOMAS NÚÑEZ DE HARO was living at Ysleta del Paso in 1684 with some of the New Mexico exiles. His wife was *Juana Durán*, daughter of Nicolás Durán.¹ His own parents were Alonso Núñez and Francisca Garcia, and he had been born in Zacatecas. He next married a *Gerónima López* and with her came up to New Mexico at the time of the Reconquest; she died in Santa Fe, and fourteen months later, at Santa Cruz, he married another (and younger) *Juana Durán*, April 6, 1697. She was twenty, the daughter of Salvador Durán and Ana Márquez.²

Tomás was "sixty" in 1729 and 1731, and still residing in Santa Cruz.³ He also belonged to the Conquistadora Confraternity.⁴

* * * * * * * *

JOSÉ NÚÑEZ came with the new colonists of 1693. He was twenty-two, the son of Nicolás, and born in Mexico City. He had a round face and a mole on the chin. With him came his twelve-year-old wife, *Gertrudis de la Candelaria Herrera*, the daughter of Tomás, and a native of Zelaya; she was dark and pockmarked, with large eyes. José was a tailor by trade.⁵

José was killed on the way from Zacatecas to New Mexico, when a wagon fell on him at a place called "Las Cruces." Gertrudis then married Juan de Dios Sandoval Martínez.⁶

1. **AGN, Prov. Int.**, t. 37, pp. 100-4.
2. **DM**, 1697, No. 1.
3. **Ibid.**, 1729, No. 2; 1731, no number; Crespo, par. 229.
4. **OLC**, pp. 72-3, 75.
5. **Sp. Arch.**, II, No. 54c. **BNM**, leg. 4, pt. 1, pp. 790-5.
6. **DM**, 1695, No. 1.

O, de la

JOSÉ DE LA O was the armorer of the Presidio in Santa Fe who succeeded Martín Yrigoyen at the start of the nineteenth century. Yrigoyen's wife was Gertrudis de la O,¹ very likely an elder sister of José. His full name was José Santiago, the son of Tiburcio de la O and María Josefa Herrera. He was born at the Presidio of Guajoquilla in New Vizcaya, and was twenty-four when he signed up as armorer in 1805.²

José's wife was *Ana María Sena*, by whom he had the following children: *José Toribio*, September 11, 1803; *José Santiago Mariano*, July 26, 1805;³ *María Guadalupe*, August 22, 1807; *José Luis*, August 27, 1809; and a second *María de Guadalupe*, May 2, 1812.⁴ The second son, Santiago, was twenty-five years old and married when he enlisted in 1832.⁵

1. **B-66, Castrense**, Aug. 8, 1805, Aug. 22, 1807.
2. **HSNM**, Militia Papers.
3. These two in **B, Sta. Fe**.
4. These three in **B-66, Castrense**.
5. **HSNM**, loc. cit.

OJEDA

Bartolomé de Ojeda was a literate Indian leader of Zia who was very active on the side of the Spaniards and especially the missionaries during the Indian uprising of 1696.¹

Antonio de Ojeda, origin unknown, was the husband of *Bernardina Bernal*, of New Mexico, whose daughter, *Juana de Ojeda* married Nicolás Benavides in 1702.²

1. **Old Santa Fe**, III, pp. 332-73.
2. **DM**, 1702, No. 1.

OLGUÍN

JUAN OLGUÍN (*Holguín*), Captain, was the sole survivor of the once prominent López Holguín family to return to New Mexico with his family; other Olguíns remained at Guadalupe del Paso. The son of Salvador Olguín and Magdalena Fresqui, both deceased, he had lost his first wife, *María Luján*, at Guadalupe del Paso in 1693. In 1695 he married *Juana Martín de Salazar*, widow of Francisco de Apodaca, in Santa Fe.[1] He belonged to the Confraternity of La Conquistadora.[2]

Juan had taken part in Vargas' Expedition of 1692; when he rescued two captive nieces, the daughters of José (de Leyva) Nevares.[3] While *Alcalde Mayor* of San Juan de Jémez, he was killed during the uprising of 1696, as also a son of his, name not given, at San Diego de Jémez. Two Spanish women and another youth also perished; but, according to the testimony of a captured Indian, the two women and two youths were made captives instead.

Two of Juan's sons by his first wife were *Salvador* and *Antonio*.

Salvador Olguín, the son of Captain Juan Olguín and María Luján, both deceased, married *Lucía Nieto* in 1705. He was twenty-four at the time.[5] His name is carved on El Morro with those of three other contemporaries.[5a]

Antonio Olguín, son of the same parents as Salvador, married *María Magdalena Brito de Leon* in 1710.[6]

Tomás Olguín, probably another son, was an officer in the Moqui campaign of 1716.[7]

Bartolomé Olguín and *María Romero* had a son, *Bartolomé*, born July 19, 1730, at Chama.[8] In 1751 he asked for Picurís lands, but these were not granted.[9] Either the father or the son tried in vain to obtain a grant in 1763.[10]

1. DM, 1695, No. 8.
2. OLC, p. 69.
3. First Expedition, p. 184.
4. Crusaders, p. 251; Old Santa Fe, Vol. III, pp. 332-73.
5. DM, 1705, No. 14.

5a. Mesa, Canyon, etc., p. 474.
6. Ibid., 1710, No. 11.
7. NMHR, Vol. IV, No. 2, pp. 158-226.
8. B-27, S. Juan.
9. Sp. Arch., I, No. 649.
10. Ibid.., II, No. 576.

OLIVAS

JUAN BAUTISTA DE OLIVAS (*Olivos*) was a native of Zacatecas, and forty-eight years old in 1695.[1] His wife was *Magdalena Juárez*, also a native of Sombrerete. Their daughter, *Angela*, twenty, married Antonio Muñiz in 1695 at Santa Fe.[2] *Juana Bautista de Olivas*, wife of Santiago Romero of Santa Cruz in 1719,[3] was most likely another daughter.

José Bautista, also testifying at a nuptial investigation in 1695, was twenty-six years old, and a native of Sombrerete.[4] In all likelihood he was a son of Juan.

This family was very likely related closely to that of Gertrudis *Bautista*, a native of Mexico City and daughter of Martín *Bautista*. With her and her husband, Manuel Palomino, came her nephew, *Bartolomé de Luna Bautista*.[5] (Perhaps the scribe intended to write "*de Oliva Bautista*.")

1. DM, 1695, No. 12.
2. Ibid., No. 2.
3. Sp. Arch., I, No. 742.

4. DM, 1695, No. 20.
5. Sp. Arch., II, No. 54c.

[245]

OLONA

MIGUEL DE OLONA was a Spaniard from Aragón who was registered in 1790 with his New Mexico family: his wife, *María Luz Ortiz*, thirty-four, with a twelve-year-old daughter, and a son who was six.[1]

His wife was an illegitimate daughter of Rosa Bustamante, by a certain José Baca, who had been born on February 16, 1755, less than two months after her mother's marriage to José Antonio Ortiz; the latter knew all about it and generously gave her his name. She married Miguel de Olona, on April 21, 1773, and her origin was forgotten until 1814, when Pedro Bautista Pino used the hidden fact to break the Bustamante will.[2]

The Olona children were: *Miguel* II, twenty-eight years old in 1814 and residing in Tomé; *José de los Reyes*, also at Tomé; and *María Rosa*, wife of Manuel Tafoya of Santa Fe.[3]

The elder Miguel had troubles in 1777 with the Padre of Santa Fe regarding the enslavement of an Indian woman.[4]

1. Sp. Arch., II, No. 1096a.
2. HSNM, Estate of Rosa Bustamante.
3. Ibid.
4. Bur-48, Sta. Fe: note, Dec. 15.

ORTEGA

TIBURCIO DE ORTEGA was secretary of the 1692 Santa Fe Council at Guadalupe del Paso.[1] As late as 1695, two years after the Reconquest, he was still at Guadalupe del Paso acting as notary for the friars.[2] But in 1715 he was back in New Mexico as *Alcalde Mayor* of Jémez, Zia, and Santa Ana.[3] From Vargas' arrival until 1712 he held the office of "Protector of the Indians" for the Crown; Lieutenant Governor Valverde threw him into prison because of his opposition to Indian slave-labor.[4]

Gerónimo de Ortega married *Sebastiana de Jesús*, July 9, 1715.[5] She was an adopted daughter of Sebastián González Bas. Their eleven children are mentioned in the probation of her estate in 1744; *Antonio, Juana María*, wife of Antonio Urban Montaño, *Gertrudis*, and *Lucía;* and seven minors: *Francisco, Tomás, Juan Francisco, Antonio José, Felipa, Sebastiana,* and *Victoria.*[6]

Gerónimo was married a second time, to *Rosa de Archibeque*, when he died in 1750. Three children by her were: *Gerónima, María Antonia,* and *María Guadalupe.*[7]

Mateo de Ortega, twenty, a native of Guadalupe del Paso, of unknown parentage, married *Antonia Luján*, eighteen, in Santa Fe, June 14, 1697.[8] She once accused a San Juan Indian woman of making her worse through her healing art.[9] They had a daughter, *Margarita*, who married Joaquín de Anaya in 1716.

A Mateo Ortega, his son if not himself, was the husband of *María Rosa Mestas*, living in the north country, who had the following children: *Juan Manuel*, born December 28, 1731; *José Alejandro*, March 21, 1734; and *Juan*, February 11, 1739.[10]

Antonio de Ortega, most likely the eldest son of Gerónimo de Ortega, first married *Rosa Baca*, daughter of Antonio Baca.[11] They had four children during twenty-nine years of married life, mentioned in his last will in 1785: *Domingo, Alejandro, Petrona,* and *Catalina*. Alejandro was the only one living.[12]

Antonio next married *María Antonia Romero*. During seventeen years of marriage they had two boys and a girl: *José, María,* and *Francisco.*[13]

The wills of later Ortegas may be found in *Sp. Arch.*, I, Nos. 654, 659, and 660. The Ortega wives of Pedro López del Castillo and Cristóbal Varela, both of Albuquerque, undoubtedly belonged to this old Ortega family, and were possibly daughters of Tiburcio de Ortega.

1. Cf. **Sp. Arch.**, II, p. 81; **First Expedition**, p. 119.
2. **DM**, 1695, No. 4.
3. **Bancroft, NMO**, 1715.
4. **BNM**, leg. 6, No. 11.
5. **M-24, S. Ild.**
6. **Sp. Arch.**, I, No. 336.
7. **Ibid.**

Nicolás de Ortega was a native of Villa de San Felipe, in Nueva Vizcaya, the son of Lorenzo Gómez and María Marmolejo. He was twenty-seven in 1696, when he came to Santa Fe and married *Juana Garcia*, widow of Francisco Hernández.[14]

8. **DM**, 1697, No. 2.
9. **Sp. Arch.**, II, No. 225.
10. All in **B-16, Nambe**.
11. **Sp. Arch.**, I, No. 101; II, No. 403.
12. **Ibid.**, I, No. 661.
13. **Ibid.**
14. **DM**, 1696, No. 13.

ORTIZ

NICOLÁS ORTIZ and his wife, *Doña Mariana Coronado*, joined the new colonists with their family of six in 1693.[1] At Zacatecas, on November 30, he was referred to as a *Sargento* with a family of seven,[2] but the other Velasco list shows him as a civilian colonist, not as a soldier, and with only six children.[3] A girl by the name of *Ana*, six years old, must have died before the caravan started north from Zacatecas.

This was the description of the family: *Nicolás Ortiz*, forty, son of the same and born in Mexico City, of medium height, with a sharp nose, large eyes, and bald head. His wife was the daughter of Francisco Hernández, and born at Jimiquilpa; she was twenty-eight, with a broad face and a mole on the cheek.

Their six children were: *Josefa*, fourteen, born in Pachuca, having a dark aquiline face, a high forehead, and a sharp nose; *Manuela*, three, born in Mexico City, with a ruddy aquiline face, black eyes, and small nose; *Nicolas* II, ten years old, born in Mexico City, having a freckled aquiline face, a high forehead, and a broad nose; *Antonio*, eight, also born in Mexico City, reddish, with a rather thick nose and large eyes; *Luis*, six years of age, born in Mexico City, also reddish, with big eyes and a small flat nose; and *Francisco*, one year old, a native of Mexico City, white and ruddy, with an aquiline face and large eyes.[4]

Sebastiana Ortiz, twenty-seven, wife of Ignacio de Aragón, was also a daughter of Nilás and a native of Mexico City;[5] hence, in all likelihood, a sister of Nicolás Ortiz, head of the family just described.

Nothing more is known about the parents, or about the girls, and very little about the boys, except the junior Nicolás.

Antonio Ortiz deeded his Santa Fe house to (brother) Nicolás Ortiz in 1714.[6]

Luis Ortiz, with Bernardino Fernández, was sent to Mexico City in 1714, to take a convicted murderer for final disposition. The prisoner escaped them on the way, and Ortiz returned with the news and was jailed.[7] He and a Nicolás Ortiz went together as soldiers in the Moqui campaign of 1716.[8]

Francisco (Nicolás) Ortiz was banished with his family to the post of Bernalillo by Governor Cuervo in 1705.[9]

Nicolás Ortiz II, "Niño Ladrón de Guevara," used this lengthy name in 1720, when he appeared as a nuptial witness, being then thirty-seven years of age.[10] He used it again in his last will, applying it also to his departed father; here he gave his mother's name as María Ana de Vargas Barba Coronado.[11] In 1702 he married *Juana Baca* at Bernalillo on November 12.[12] They were sponsors at Ber-

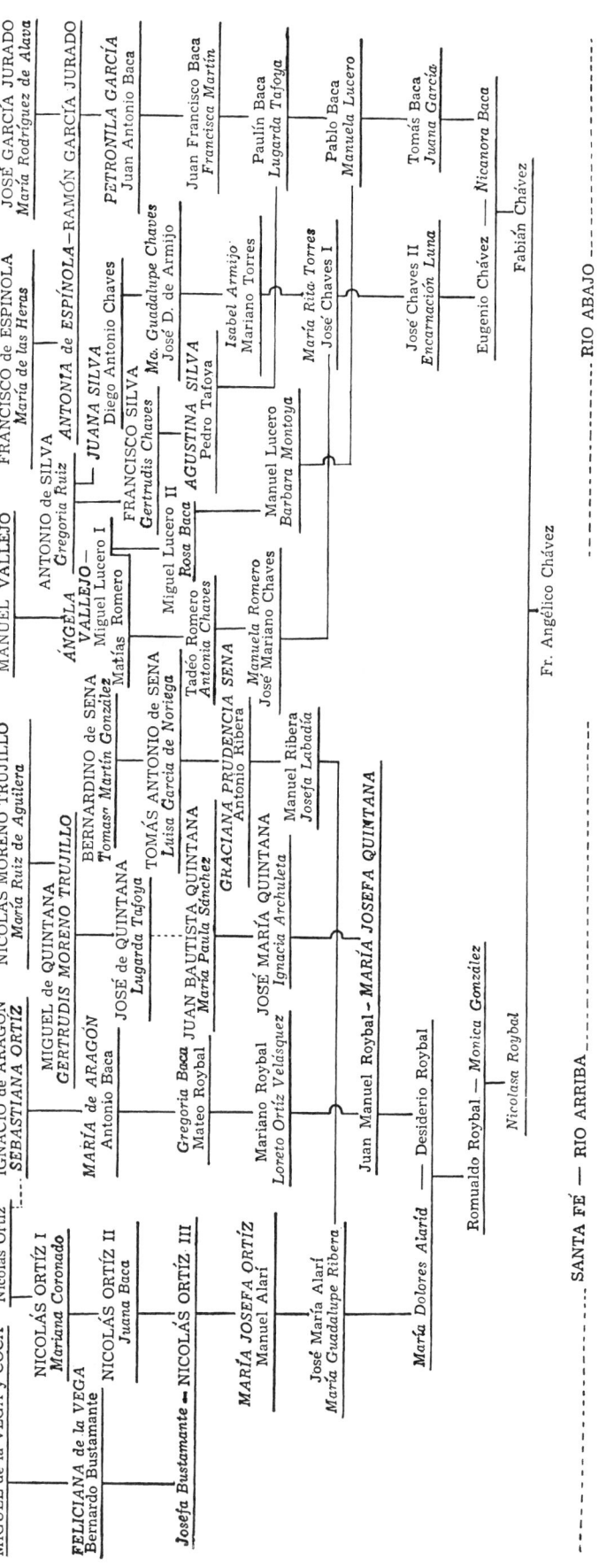

ESPAÑOLES-MEXICANOS CHART.—The term "Español" was first applied to Spanish people born in the New World; Spaniards born in Spain were designated according to their Province, such as "Castellanos, Gallegos, Andaluces, Estremeños," etc. Likewise, the only "Mexicanos" in colonial times were the Nahua (Aztec) Indians native to the Valley of Mexico. Spanish people born or residing in the City or Valley of Mexico were called "Españoles-Mexicanos." Those families sent to Vargas in 1693 were handpicked by the Viceroy himself. This diagram shows how six of them (*left*) contributed to a Santa Fe-Rio Arriba Roybal family, and four (*right*) to a Rio Abajo Chávez family. Though two distinct groups, they were integrated in the over-all New Mexico Family through other strains, especially the Bacas. (See BACA Chart.)

nalillo for some Apache captives in 1705.¹³ In 1713 he was a Captain of the Santa Fe militia,¹⁴ but in the 1716 Moqui Campaign he is designated as an ordinary soldier¹⁵ (but this Nicolás might have been a younger Nicolás, perhaps the son of Luis Ortiz, with whom he was listed). In this year Nicolás had received permission to go on a trip outside New Mexico.¹⁶

Nicolás had received a citation for military valor in 1697 from Governor Vargas himself; it stated that he had come from Mexico City to "this Kingdom" as a colonist in 1693, when twelve years old; that in 1696 he had distinguished himself at the battles of the Black Mesa, of the Mountains of Taos and Picurís, during the Ute attack at the San Diego de Jémez Mesa, and also at Chimayó and the Cañada of Santa Clara.¹⁷

Well established in Santa Fe, Nicolás acquired many pieces of property, among them a house directly in front of the Church of St. Francis; he was also involved in some property suits.¹⁸ His widow and sons sold their more important site to Governor Codallos in 1746, to clear the space in front of the parish church.¹⁹ Nicolás made his last will in 1742, naming his parents, his only wife, and their three sons: *Francisco, Nicolas* III, *and Toribio.*²⁰

Before her marriage to Ortiz, Juana Baca had an illegitimate daughter, *Ana María*, who married a José Griego;²¹ he must have died young, for his widow was only twenty-six when she died on June 27, 1729.²²

* * * * * * * *

The families of the three sons of Nicolás Ortiz II and Juana Baca are as follows, according to documentary evidence.

Francisco Ortiz married *Francisca Montoya* around the year 1730. He was *Alcalde* of Santa Fe in 1744; in the same year he registered a mine in the Picurís country.²³ He died on March 11, 1749, and his widow followed on April 8, 1750.²⁴

He had made his last will shortly before, in which he stated that he and Francisca had been married for nineteen years. The ten children named in the will were:

José (died in infancy), *Ana María, Nicolás* (died when four), *Luis Fernando* (died when two), *Santiago, Juana Manuela, José Miguel, Nicolás Francisco, Antonia Teresa,* and *María de Loreto.*²⁵

Nicolás Ortiz III married *Gertrudis Páez Hurtado,* daughter of the Lieutenant General, Juan Páez Hurtado, on May 28, 1730.²⁶ She died after twenty years of married life on April 12, 1750, when Nicolás was the *Teniente* of the Santa Fe Presidio.²⁷ They had five children,²⁸ whose marriages were as follows:

Antonio José, born September 6, 1734, who married Rosa Bustamante, December 31, 1754;²⁹ *Juan Antonio,* who married María Loreto Ribera;³⁰ and *Teodora,* wife of Nicolás Rael de Aguilar.³¹ The two others were *Gaspar,* who married Josefa Martín, October 23, 1765, and then Dolores Alarid, November 27, 1810;³² and *Tomás,* who married María Rosa de los Reyes Martin at the same ceremony in Santa Clara in 1765 (two brothers marrying two sisters). The last two are mentioned as their sons when they enlisted as soldiers in 1771 and 1779.³²ᵃ

Nicolás III married a second time, ten months after Gertrudis died. He gave the full "Ortiz Niño Ladrón de Guevara" name, February 6, 1751, when he married Doña Josefa Bustamante, adopted daughter of Don Bernardo Antonio de Bustamante y Tagle.³³ Josefa and Rosa Bustamante (the latter married Nicolás' eldest son) were otherwise considered full sisters and actual daughters of Don Bernardo.³⁴ In 1769, Captain Nicolás was killed by savage Indians during a campaign, and was buried in Santa Fe on September 4, 1769.³⁵ In memory of his death, and to obtain divine aid during the Cumanche menace of the times, his widow, Doña Josefa, was instrumental in re-establishing the fiesta and Confraternity of La Conquistadora.³⁶

Josefa also donated vestments to the military chapel of Our Lady of Light, as well as paintings and other gifts to the church at

Pojoaque.[37] She sold her Santa Fe property to Antonio José Ortiz, her brother-in-law and step-son, in 1789,[38] and eventually lost her Pojoaque estate to him for not being able to meet a loan,[39] so that by 1790 she was depending on a small insurance from the *"Monte Pio"* of the Presidio.[40]

The known children of Nicolás Ortiz III and Josefa Bustamante were: *Ana María Feliciana,* born August 18, 1761,[41] who married José Campos Redondo; *María Josefa de Jesús,* December 18, 1762,[42] who married Manuel Alarí; *Feliciana María Joaquina,* August 1, 1765; and *José Vicente,* April 5, 1767.[43] This boy enlisted as a soldier in the Santa Fe Presidio in 1779.[43a]

Toribio Ortiz married *Leonarda de la Vega y Coca* on June 14, 1735.[44] In 1758 he was after part of the Cienega grant which had belonged to his late father-in-law, Miguel de la Vega y Coca.[45]

His known children were: *María Isidora,* born April 6, 1750; *María Barbara,* December 8, 1751; *María Josefa,* April 5, 1753; *María Gertrudis,* December 16, 1754; *María Guadalupe,* October 27, 1757; *José Antonio,* March 12, 1759;[46] and *Antonio Matías,* who ran away and perished with the demented José Reaño, husband of his first cousin, Ana María Ortiz.[47]

Toribio was *mayordomo* of the Conquistadora Confraternity in 1774, and was also a charter officer of the Confraternity of Our Lady of Light.[48]

Manuel Ortiz was a contemporary of the three sons of Nicolás Ortiz II, and therefore, most likely, his nephew, the son of Antonio, Luis, or Francisco, about whose lives so little is known. Manuel married *Marcelina de la Vega y Coca,* on November 6, 1735.[49] Their known children were as follows:

Mateo Mauricio, born September 6, 1750;[50] *Manuel José,* May 11, 1748; *Manuel Antonio,* December 28, 1749; *Ana María Monica,* May 13, 1752; and *Salvador Manuel,* April 14, 1754.[51]

After his wife's death Manuel married *Tomasa Romero,* a widow, on May 3, 1757.[52] They had at least four children before she died, September 5, 1779.[53] These were: *Ventura José,* July 20, 1758; *Manuel Antonio,* February 2, 1760; *José Antonio,* July 14, 1762; *José Alejandro,* in 1764.[54]

* * * * * * * *

PEDRO ORTIZ DE ESCUDERO was a totally different Ortiz, yet perhaps related to his contemporary, the original Nicolás Ortiz. Pedro was a silversmith born in Oaxaca, the son of Pedro Ortiz Escudero and Lucía de Quiñones. He was twenty when he married *Ana Páez Hurtado,* daughter of Juan Páez Hurtado by his first wife. The wedding took place in Santa Fe, January 6, 1715.[55] In 1713 Pedro was listed with the soldiers of the Presidio,[56] and in March 1716, he asked for permission to leave New Mexico and return to New Spain.[57] Whether or not this permis-

---

1. **BNM**, leg. 4, pt. 1, pp. 814-16.
2. Ibid., pp. 830-4.
3. **Sp. Arch.**, II, No. 54c.
4. Ibid.
5. Ibid.
6. Ibid., I, Nos. 1072, 1073.
7. Ibid., II, No. 187.
8. **NMHR.**, Vol. VI, No. 2, p. 181.
9. **Sp. Arch.**, II, No. 119.
10. **DM**, 1720, Nos. 3, 5.
11. **Sp. Arch.**, I, No. 647.
12. **B-13, Bern.**, M. Sec.
13. Ibid.
14. **HSNM**, No. 2102.
15. **NMHR**, loc. cit.
16. **Sp. Arch.**, II, No. 183a.
17. **BNM**, leg. 4, No. 1a; Fr. Morfi copied this item in 1781 from "originals" in possession of Don Antonio José Ortiz.
18. **Sp. Arch.**, I, Nos. 498, 1072, 1073, 1074, 1078; II, Nos. 145b, 150, 317a.
19. Ibid., II, No. 181.
20. Ibid., I, No. 647.
21. Ibid., No. 964.
22. **Bur-48, Sta. Fe**.
23. **Sp Arch.**, I, Nos. 27, 763.
24. **Bur-48, Sta. Fe**.
25. **Sp. Arch.**, I, No. 648.
26. **M-50, Sta. Fe**.
27. **Bur-48, Sta. Fe**.
28. **Sp. Arch.**, II, No. 841.
29. **Bur-16, Nambé**, B. Sec.; **M-50, Sta. Fe**.
30. **Santa Fe County**, Vol. R, pp. 212-14, in Santa Fe Court House.
31. **Sp. Arch.**, II, No. 841; **M-50, Sta. Fe.**, Dec. 31, 1754.
32. **M, Sta. Clara**; **M-51, Castrense**.
32a. **HSNM**, Militia Papers.
33. **M-50, Sta. Fe**.
34. **Sp. Arch.**, I, Nos. 652, 662.
35. **Bur-48, Sta. Fe**.
36. **BNM**, leg. 10, No. 43, **Miscellaneous**; **El Palacio**, Vol. 54, No. 10, pp. 304-5.
37. Ibid.
38. **Sp. Arch.**, I, No. 662.
39. Ibid., I, No. 120; II, No. 980.
40. **Twit. Coll.**, No. 179.
41. **Bur-16, Nambé**, B. Sec.
42. **B-62, Sta. Fe**. GENEALOGY: María Josefa Ortiz Bustamante, José María Alarí, María Dolores Alarid, Romualdo Roybal, Nicolasa Roybal, Fr. A. Chávez.
43. Ibid.
43a. **HSNM**, Mil. papers.
44. **M-50, Sta. Fe**.
45. **Sp. Arch.**, I, No. 652.

sion was granted is not known. If he stayed, the preceding Manuel Ortiz could well have been his son.

46. All in **B**, Sta. Fe.
47. Bancroft, NMO, 1763.
48. OLC, p. 11; **NMHR**, Vol. X, No. 3, p. 188.
49. **M-50**, Sta. Fe.
50. **B-16**, Nambé.
51. All in **B.**, Sta. Fe.

An *Antonio Escudero* married *Gertrudis Madrid* on January 19, 1753.[58] Nothing more is known about him.

52. **M-50**, Sta. Fe.
53. **Bur-48**, Sta. Fe.
54. All in **B**, Sta. Fe.
55. **DM**, 1715, No. 8.
56. **HSNM**, No. 2102.
57. **Sp. Arch.**, II, No. 297a.
58. **M-50**, Sta. Fe.

OTERO

PEDRO OTERO married *María Juliana Alarí* as "**Pedro Durán y Chaves**" on September 2, 1759.[1]

Some of their children were: *José Lorenzo*, born July 8, 1773, the son of Pedro *Chaves* and Juliana Alarí;[2] *Antonio Rafael*, December 3, 1775, the son of Pedro *Otero* and Juliana Alarí;[3] *Vicente Antonio*, December 25, 1781, the son of Pedro *Chaves* and Juliana Alarí,[4] and *José Estanislao*, son of Pedro *Otero* and Juliana Alarí, and husband of Margarita Garcia.[5]

Pedro *Otero* was mentioned as an eye-witness in 1769 in a case involving Efigenia Chaves, wife of Jacinto Sánchez.[6] Now, Efigenia was a daughter of Pedro Durán y Chaves and his first wife, Juana Montoya. Old Pedro had a minor son by the name of "Pedro"[7] who is not mentioned by name in his father's will; therefore, he was one of the four minor children, none mentioned by name, of his second wife, Gertrudis Sánchez. Since there had been no Otero family in all of New Mexico, it seems as though Pedro Otero is this young Pedro Durán y Chaves. But where did he get his name? As the youngest orphan by a second wife of so a vast a family, broken up by litigations besides, he might have been reared in the household of the pastor of Albuquerque in those times, Fray Cayetano Otero, the only Otero individual in New Mexico up to that time.

José Lorenzo Otero and his wife *María Sedillo* lived in Valencia. Their existence is known from the marriage of a son, *Antonio*, to Feliciana Sanchez.[8] They are also mentioned as grandparents in the baptisms of some children of Antonio and Feliciana.[9]

Another son was *José Antonio*, married to Petra Sedillo; the grandparents are given in the baptism of a son, Manuel de Jesús, April 4, 1836.[10]

A third son was *José de Jesus*, married to María Aguirre; grandparents given in baptism of child, Juan Pablo, June 8, 1836.[11]

Antonio Otero, son of Pedro Otero and Juliana Alarí, was thirty-one when he enlisted as a soldier in 1813.[11] He is most likely Antonio Rafael, born in 1775, since there are no other Oteros in New Mexico. He and his wife *Lugarda Garcia* are also known from the baptisms of their grandchildren.

One son, *Francisco Antonio*, who married Elena Aragón on May 6, 1823,[12] had several children at whose baptisms Antonio Otero and Lugarda Garcia are given as paternal grandparents: Juana María, June 24, 1825;[13] Manuel de la Trinidad, February 28, 1829; Manuel Antonio, October 17, 1840;[14] and four others in between.

Another son was *Miguel*, married to Josefa Chaves. Miguel's parents are known in the same way, two of whose children were: José Gregorio, May 19, 1833, and José Andrés, December 9, 1835.[15]

A third son, *Juan*, was married to Josefa Sánchez; Juan's wife and parents likewise known through the baptism of a son, José Margarito, February 22, 1841.[16]

Old Antonio, his wife Lugardia Garcia still living, died on March 30, 1845.[17]

Vicente Otero was reported by his family to local historians as the son of Pedro Otero, who came to Santa Fe from Spain and married a "Miss Alarid" of Santa Fe.[18] He would be the *Vicente Antonio* born in 1781. Vicente was married to *Gertrudis Chaves*, by whom he had several children, the following appearing in the records:

Miguel Luis Senón, born June 23, 1829;[19] *María Candelaria,* February 6, 1827;[20] *Antonio José,* married to Francisca Chávez;[21] *Pedro,* who married Serafina Otero at San Miguel, June 14, 1840;[22] *Juana,* wife of Mariano Yrisarri;[23] *Juliana,* married to Pablo Salazar;[24] *Juan,* who married Mercedes Chaves, May 27, 1837; *Manuel Antonio* who married María Victoriana Chaves y Perea, March 19, 1844;[25] and *María de Jesús,* wife of Vicente Armijo.[26]

Estanislao Otero, son of Pedro Otero and Juliana Alarí, both deceased, married *Barbara Garcia* on August 2, 1813.[27] Their known younger children were: *María Agapita,* January 18, 1829; *José Ponciano,* November 27, 1831;[28] *Petra,* wife of José Antonio Otero (q.v.); and *Antonio José,* married to María Gertrudis Herrera.[29]

---

1. M-50, Sta. Fe.
2. B-3, Albuq.
3. B, Sta. Fe.
4. B-4, Albuq.
5. B-71, Tomé; bapt. of son, Juan Rafael, Mar. 1, 1824.
6. AGN, Tierras, leg. 426, III, ff. 7-11.
7. DM, 1766, in Albuq., Vallejo-Hurtado.
8. Ibid., 1824, no number.
9. B-73, Tomé. Antonio José, April 28, 1834; Francisco Antonio, Feb. 5, 1839; María Carlota, Feb. 21, 1846.
10. Ibid.
11. Ibid.
12. M-56, Tomé.
13. B-71, Tomé.
14. B-72, Tomé.
15. Ibid.
16. Ibid.
17. Bur-54, Tomé.
18. Anon., Hist. of N. M. (N.Y., 1907), pp. 536-7; Twitchell, Leading Facts, Vol. II, pp. 273-4n.
19. B-72, Tomé.
20. B-71, Tomé.
21. B-73, Tomé; bapt. of four children, 1838-46.
22. M, San Miguel del Vado.
23. M-11, Tomé; March 26, 1836; DM, 1836, in Albuquerque, no number.
24. B-72, Tomé; bapt. of son, Jan. 18, 1828.
25. Both in M-49, Isleta.
26. B-73, Tomé; bapt. of son, Feb. 26, 1835.
27. M-56, Tomé.
28. Both in B-72, Tomé.
29. B-73, Tomé; bapt. of son, Oct. 17, 1845, at Manzano.

PACHECO

JUAN PACHECO returned to New Mexico at the time of the Reconquest, perhaps with his wife *Antonia de Arratia,* if she was still living. His family went to live inside the Indian-occupied city of Santa Fe upon arrival, but had to vacate it and join the other colonists outside when the Tanos decided to resist Vargas.[1] Juan gave his age as fifty-two in 1694.[2] He was an officer of the Conquistadora Confraternity in 1693.[3]

His children were: *Silvestre; Josefa,*[4] widow of José Baca, who was murdered by her brother Silvestre; *Maria,* mother-in-law of Roque de Madrid, who had died before 1693; and, very likely, *Petrona,* wife of Cristóbal Nieto who was captured in 1680 and rescued in 1692.

Silvestre Pacheco killed José Baca, husband of his sister Josefa, during an altercation at Guadalupe del Paso in 1687.[5] In 1708 he is mentioned in Santa Fe with his father, sister Josefa, and other relatives.[6] It is not known who his wife was, or if he had any children. He sold his lands in Santa Fe at this time to Antonio Montoya and Nicolás Ortiz, as he was leaving "the Kingdom" with his family.[7]

Matías Pacheco and *Felipe Pacheco,* perhaps brothers, were relatives of Josefa Pacheco, very likely her nephews, who were living with her and her second husband, Juan de Tafoya, in 1706-7. Matías was twenty years old at this time, when he deposed that he did not know who his parents were.[8]

He later married *María Cisneros,* and was dead by 1728 when their daughter, *Teodora,* married Juan Antonio Cabrera.[9] Another daughter, *Valentina,* was the wife of José González and a niece of María Griego.[10]

Felipe Pacheco, mentioned with *Matías*, was a *Sargento* by 1731 and living at or near San Juan Pueblo.[11] His wife was *Rosa Martín*. Some of their children were: *Juan José*, who married Ynez Martín, May 9, 1732;[12] *Isabel*, married to Francisco Xavier Sánchez, August 20, 1743;[13] *José Antonio*, born February 2, 1727; *Salvador Vicente*, April 19, 1729; *Diego Antonio*, November 19, 1730; and *Cayetano*, February 18, 1732.[14]

1. **Ritch Coll.**, Box 1, No. 25, f. 108.
2. **DM**, 1694, No. 1.
3. **OLC**, p. 63.
4. GENEALOGY: **Josefa Pacheco**, Juana Baca, Nicolás Ortiz III, Josefa Ortiz Bustamante, José María Alarí, María Dolores Alarid, Romualdo Roybal, Nicolasa Roybal, Fr. A. Chávez.
5. **Sp. Arch.**, II, No. 45.
6. **Ibid.**, I, Nos. 485, 486, 487, 488.
7. **Ibid.**, Nos. 486, 487, 679.
8. **AGN, Mex., Inq.**, t. 735, f. 304; **Sp. Arch.**, II, No. 134b.
9. **DM**, 1728, No. 2.
10. **Sp. Arch.**, I, No. 337.
11. Crespo, pars. 227-9.
12. **M-27, S. Juan**; **Sp. Arch.**, I, Nos 686-7.
13. **Ibid.**
14. These four, **Ibid.**, B. Sec

PADILLA

JOSÉ DE PADILLA and his wife, *María López*, not being refugees from the Kingdom of New Mexico, remained at Guadalupe del Paso instead of coming up with the Vargas Reconquest. He was still living there, at Senecu, in 1699.[1] From the marriages of their children we learn that his wife was dead by 1711, while José himself died less than two years later.[2] His known sons were: *José*, *Diego*, and, most likely, *Juan Antonio*.

José de Padilla II, born in Guadalupe del Paso, there married *Antonia de Herrera* in 1711.[3] His wife died on November 30, 1729.[4] He appears to be the same man, if not a son of the same name, who married *María Rosa Ladrón de Guevara,* May 7, 1732.[5]

Diego de Padilla came to New Mexico proper and married *Catalina (Gutiérrez) de Salazar*, November 3, 1706.[6] She died and Diego then married *María Vásquez Baca*, also of Bernalillo, in 1713.[7] They were wedding sponsors together as late as 1730.[8]

He made his last will in 1736 at El Puerto de San Andres, Isleta jurisdiction, where he had lived and acquired property, known as *"lo de Padilla."* He named one son by his first wife, *Pedro Nolasco*, and also an older natural son, born prior to his first marriage but reared by him, who went under the name of *Luis Suazo*.

His second wife bore him eight children: *Francisco*, twenty-four and executor of the will; *Manuela*, wife of Francisco Chavez; *Diego*, seventeen; *Nicolás*, fourteen; *Bernardo*, twelve; *Tomasa*, eight; *Pedro*, six, and *María Barbara*, three.[9]

Other facts about some of these children are as follows: *Francisco* married Isabel Baca on March 13, 1732;[10] *Manuela* married Francisco Xavier Chávez on September 29, 1735;[11] *Diego* married María Luisa Chávez; she died on December 23, 1741;[12] *Bernardo* married Quiteria Chávez after she had illegitimate children;[13] *Tomasa* became the wife of Tomás Chávez, December 3, 1742;[14] *Pedro*, born May 26, 1731, married Victoria Chávez, January 28, 1755;[15] *María*, born August 29, 1733,[16] must have died young; *María Barbara*, born February 27, 1735, married Antonio Chávez, April 13, 1750.[17] Pedro, referred to as the "seventh child," sold his father's estate to Clemente Gutiérrez in 1768.[18]

Juan Antonio Padilla came up from Guadalupe del Paso to the Santa Cruz-Rio Arriba area in the beginning of the century. He signed his name, "Juan de Padilla," in 1720.[19] Since his arrival he had been married to *Margarita Martín*, daughter of Captain Sebastián Martín of La Soledad,[20] but had died by the year 1731, when his widow married Bernardo Roybal.[21]

Their daughter *Juana* was the wife of Carlos Fernández of Taos, who was after his wife's inheritance in 1744. Her younger sister, *Barbara*, was living with her, while

Julián and *Tomás,* minor children, went from the care of Bernardo Roybal (their stepfather) to that of one of their Martín uncles. They had two half-sisters and one half-brother, "all Roybals," who stayed with their widowed father.[22] Julian was born on April 12, 1726.[23] He and his sister Juana were witnesses at the marriage of another sister, *Micaela,* when she married Domingo Labadía in 1766.[24] Tomás was thirty-one when he enlisted as a soldier of the Santa Fe Presidio in 1766.[24a]

Felipe de Padilla, a native of the Rio Abajo was twenty years old in 1694.[25] He married *Juana María de Ogama* in 1698,[26] the daughter of Magdalena de Ogama. In 1703 he was still living in Santa Fe.[27] A daughter, *Juana,* married Florencio Garcia de Lira in Santa Fe in 1717.[28]

Antonio Padilla married *Francisca Xaviera Vásquez,* November 7, 1728.[29] They had a son, *Andrés,* born May 4, 1730.[30]

There is no way of classifying these two men.

1. **DM**, 1699, No. 9.
2. **Ibid.**, 1711, No. 4; 1713, No. 1.
3. **Ibid., loc. cit.**
4. **Bur, Guad. del Paso (Juárez).**
5. **M, Guad. del Paso (Juárez).**
6. **B-13, Bern., M. Sec.**
7. **DM**, 1713, No. 1.
8. **M-11, Isleta,** April 30.
9. **Sp. Arch., I,** No. 685.
10. GENEALOGY: **Francisco Padilla,** Francisca Padilla, Mariano Torres, María Rita Torres, José Chávez, Eugenio Chávez, Fabián Chávez, Fr. A. Chávez.
11. **M-11, Isleta.**
12. **Sp. Arch., II,** No. 460; **Bur-2, Albuq.**
13. **Sp. Arch., I,** No. 196.
14. **M-11, Isleta.**
15. **B-57** and **M-11, Isleta.**
16. **Ibid.**
17. **Ibid.**
18. **Sp. Arch., I,** No. 695.
19. **Ibid., II,** No. 310.
20. **Ibid., I,** No. 530.
21. **M-27, S. Juan,** Sept. 26; **Bancroft, NMO,** 1731.
22. **Sp. Arch., loc. cit.**
23. **B-27, S. Juan.**
24. **M-50, Sta. Fe.** GENEALOGY: **Micaela Padilla,** Josefa Labadía, María Guadalupe Ribera, María Dolores Alarid, Romualdo Roybal, Nicolasa Roybal, Fr. A. Chávez.
24a. **HSNM, Mil. Papers.**
25. **DM**, 1694, No. 26.
26. **Ibid.,** 1698, No. 1, incomplete.
27. **Sp. Arch., I,** No. 1071.
28. **DM**, 1717, No. 2.
29. **M-11, Isleta.**
30. **B-57, Isleta.**

PÁEZ HURTADO

JUAN PÁEZ HURTADO was born in Villafranca de los Palacios, near Las Cabezas in Andalucía, the son of Domingo Hurtado and Ana Rubio y Vásquez, both deceased.[1] Vargas got him for the Reconquest of New Mexico and appointed him as the leader of other recruits, both military and civilian colonists.[2] He was Lieutenant Governor and General under Vargas during both his terms, and his actual commander of many of his expeditions. He was also the executor of Vargas' last will in 1704, interim Governor, and a very active *mayordomo* of the Conquistadora Confraternity, as well as a member of that of San Miguel.[3]

His first wife was *Pascuala López Vera,* who died in 1693, shortly before the Reconquest Army and colony set out for New Mexico.[4] He brought along his little girl, *Ana,* who later married Pedro Ortiz Escudero in Santa Fe.[5]

Juan himself married *Teodora Garcia de la Riva,* on June 20, 1704.[6] Three known children of theirs were: *Antonia,* who became the wife of José Terrus;[7] *Gertrudis,* first wife of Nicolás Ortiz III; and *Juan Domingo.* Juan died in 1742 and was buried under the main altar of La Conquistadora on May 5; his second wife was buried in the same chapel, November 17, 1736.[8] His name is carved on El Morro, with the date "July, 1736."[8a]

It seems as though his son, *Juan Domingo,* mentioned only once in the will of his Terrus brother-in-law,[9] went to live at Guadalupe del Paso, being very likely the founder of a prominent family there later known as "Páez." His father was referred to simply as "Don Juan Páez" in at least one official document.[10]

The name "Páez," later "Páiz," begins to appear in Santa Fe registers from 1771 on, and is most difficult to trace, for lack of wills and other civil documents. These people were very likely some descendants who moved back north from Guadalupe del Paso.

1. **DM,** 1704, No. 6.
2. **First Expedition,** pp. 55, 116; **Sp. Arch.,** I, No. 402; **Bancroft, NMO,** 1694; **NMHR,** Vol. 25, No. 3, p. 248.
3. **Sp. Arch.,** I, Nos. 99, 1027; **OLC,** pp. 66-7; **Kubler,** p. 19.
4. **DM, loc. cit.**
5. **Ibid.,** 1715, No. 8.
6. **Ibid.,** 1704, No. 6.
7. **Sp. Arch.,** I, No. 966.
8. **OLC,** pp. 41, 66-7.
8a. **Mesa, Canyon,** etc., p. 475; Lummis also read his name in an inscription dated 1709, but actually it is "Ramon Garcia Jurado" (p. 472).
9. **Sp. Arch., loc. cit.**
10. **Bancroft, NMO,** 1731.

PALOMINO RENDÓN

FRANCISCO PALOMINO RENDÓN was a native of Puerto de Santa María in Spain, the son of Juan Gallegos and Catalina Palomino Rendón. After four years in southern New Spain, and one at Guadalupe del Paso, he reached Santa Fe with the Reconquest colony in 1693, to marry *Juana Montoya* on December 17, a few days before the battle of Santa Fe. The final nuptial papers had been drawn up at Santo Domingo Pueblo on the way up to Santa Fe.¹ Francisco died before 1710, when his widow married Juan Manuel Chirinos.²

They had one daughter, *María Estela*, who married Juan Felipe de Ribera.³

This surname represents a family distinct from the "Rendón" family, and it ended witth María Estela.

1. **DM,** 1693, No. 8.
2. **Ibid.,** 1710, No. 16.
3. GENEALOGY: **María Estela Palomino Rendón,** Antonio de Ribera, Manuel Ribera, María Guadalupe Ribera, María Dolores Alarid, Romualdo Roybal, Nicolasa Roybal, Fr. A. Chávez.

PALOMINO

TOMÁS PALOMINO, his wife, and a "youth" joined the 1693 colonists at Zacatecas.¹ He was the son of Fernando, twenty-six years old, and was a native of Puerto de Santa María in Spain. He was of medium height, fair and pockmarked. His wife was *Gertrudis Bautista Ulibarri (Olivares?)*, twenty, a native of Mexico City at the Calle del Reloz, the daughter of Martín Bautista; she had an aquiline face, a high forehead, and small nose. They had a son, *Manuel Palomino*, fourteen years old, born in Mexico City; he was fair-complexioned, with large eyes and a rather broad nose.

With them also came a young nephew of his wife, Bartolomé de Luna Bautista.²

Tomás was perhaps related to Francisco Palomino Rendón, since both were from the same Spanish city. He settled in Santa Cruz in 1696, and sold his land grant in 1699 to Antonio de Silva.³ On March 4, 1703, he was killed by Indians inside the mission church of Zuñi with two other soldiers.⁴ His son is not heard of again, nor did the family name survive.

1. **BNM,** leg. 4, pt. 1, pp. 830-4.
2. **Sp. Arch.,** II, No. 54c.
3. **DM,** 1694, No. 26; 1697, No. 1, **Sp. Arch.,** II, No. 820.
4. **Doc., Hist. de Mex.,** p. 183.

PELÁEZ

JACINTO PELÁEZ, a native of Villanueva in Asturias, was the son of Gonzalo Peláez and Elvira Méndez. He was twenty-one when he married *Margarita Gómez Robledo* at Guadalupe del Paso in 1691.[1] Another Spanish soldier, Alonso Romero, had married Margarita's sister, María. Peláez denounced Romero as a bigamist and the charge was proven true.[2] The grant made to him by Vargas was at Jacona near San Ildefonso.[3]

Margarita bore him two daughters: *María*, who married Juan Fernández de la Pedrera,[4] and *Jacinta*, first married to Antonio de Luna and then to Antonio Montoya.

After Margarita's early death Jacinto married *Isabel de Chaves* in 1700;[5] but he died shortly after, for in 1705 his widow married Baltasar de Mata.

1. **DM**, 1691, No. 2.
2. **AGN**, Mex., Inq., t. 507, f. 343.
3. **Sp. Arch.**, I, No. 1261.
4. GENEALOGY: **María Peláez**, María Francisca Fernández de la Pedrera, Manuel Alarí, José María Alarí, María Dolores Alarid, Romualdo Roybal, Nicolasa Roybal, Fr. A. Chávez.
5. **B-13, Bern.**, M. Sec.

PEÑA

BALTASAR FRANCISCO DE LA PEÑA was a native of Zacatecas, and a soldier of Santa Fe in 1694, when he married *Lucía Gutiérrez*. His parents were Francisco Gabriel de la Peña and Manuela Gómez de Medina, deceased.[1] He gave his age as twenty-three a couple of years after.[2]

Nothing more is known about him except that he later brought some boys, apparently nephews, from Mexico City to New Mexico, as shown further on.

José Miguel de la Peña seems to have been a son of Baltasar Francisco and Lucía Gutierrez. He married *María Francisca Rael de Aguilar* on April 23, 1737; she was a sister of Nicolás Rael.[3] Sometime in the third quarter of the century he was *Alcalde* at Jémez,[4] and was living in Santa Fe in 1790, when he gave his age as seventy, and that of his Rael wife as sixty-five.[5]

They had a son, *Juan de Dios*, born March 18, 1748,[6] who married Loreta Ortiz, by whom he had a son, Mariano. The father followed a military career.[7]

Another son, to all appearances, was *José Miguel* II, chanter in the church at Santa Fe, who received a grant near Santo Domingo Pueblo.[8] This homestead of his was known as "*El Rancho de José Miguel de la Peña*" from 1777 to 1780; by 1791 it was shortened to "*Rancho de Peña*," and from 1792 on it was "*Rancho de la Peña Blanca*." His wife was *Dolores Martín*.[10]

* * * * * * * *

José Mariano de la Peña was born in Mexico City, the son of Juan Antonio de la Peña and María Antonia Álvarez. On March 10, 1783, he married *María Soledad Gutiérrez*.[11] In 1785 he declared that he had been brought to New Mexico, when eight years old, by a Don Baltasar (*illegible*).[12] In 1789 he was executor of the will of Clemente Gutiérrez, his father-in-law.[13] He was living at Pajarito in 1790, when he was described as a native of Mexico City, thirty-one years old, and a merchant by profession. His Gutiérrez wife was twenty-six. With them was a *brother*, twenty-one, also born in Mexico City.[14]

A census in 1802-3 named him, his wife, and four children: *Mariana, Lorenzo, Rafael,* and *Bartolomé*.[15]

José de la Peña, a native of Mexico City,

who married *Francisca Silva*, widow of Manuel Salazar, December 2, 1802,¹⁶ was, no doubt, the younger brother of José Mariano just mentioned living with him at Pajarito in 1690. Besides, Juan Antonio de la Peña and María Antonia Álvarez are given as grandparents at the baptism of his daughter, María Francisca, August 1, 1810.¹⁷

1. DM, 1694, No. 15.
2. Ibid., 1696, No. 5; 1697, No. 4.
3. M-50, Sta. Fe; Sp. Arch., II, No. 841.
4. BNM, leg. 10, No. 12.
5. Sp. Arch., II, No. 1096a.
6. B, Sta. Fe.
7. B-65, Sta. Fe, bapt. of grandson, Fernando, April 18, 1812; HSNM, Estate of Rosa Bustamante; Sp. Arch., II, No. 1874.
8. Sp. Arch., I, Nos. 699, 904; II, No. 1188.
9. M-35, Sto. Domingo.
10. Ibid., M. of son, Juan de Jesús, Sept 1. 1825
11. M-49, Isleta.
12. AGN, Tierras, t. 1257, ff. 1-2.
13. Sp. Arch., I, No. 371.
14. Ibid., II, No. 1092b.
15. AASF, No. 30.
16. DM, 1802, no number.
17. B-65, Sta. Fe.

PERALTA

Pedro de Peralta, fifty-five years old and a widower, was living in Santa Fe in 1710. He was a native of Valladolid.¹ His name appears in 1703 and 1705, but with no hints regarding his wife or family.²

Of the seventeenth-century Peraltas, only Juan de Mestas Peralta returned in 1693, and he used this name only once, at his wedding. But there could have been others at the time, minors perhaps, or descendants of those who remained at Guadalupe del Paso might have come up later on.

1. DM, 1710, No. 12.
2. Sp. Arch., II, Nos. 94, 116

PEREA

JUAN DE PEREA came up to New Mexico from Guadalupe del Paso with the Reconquest colonists. He and his wife were nuptial witnesses at Santa Fe in 1694.¹ He was a soldier, a "native of New Mexico," and thirty years old in 1697.² His wife, *Aldonsa Varela*, and he were both dead by 1701, when their daughter, *María* (*Luisa*), widow of Miguel Maese, married Agustin Luján.³

Other known daughters were *Catalina*, the wife of Martín Hurtado, and another girl, apparently, the wife of Antonio Lucero de Godoy.

Francisco de Perea and *María Varela* had a son, *Francisco*, born January 22, 1709.⁴

He might be the same man, or his son of the same name, who married *Rosa de Torres*, who bore him two children: *Lucas Francisco*, October 23, 1731, and *Isabel*, April 29, 1733.⁵

* * * * * * * *

Esteban de Perea and his wife might or might not have come to New Mexico with the Reconquest. Both were dead by 1711, when their son, *Jacinto*, also a "native of New Mexico," married *Josefa Pacheco*, born in Santa Fe of unknown parentage.⁶ Jacinto was one of the few survivors of the Villasur Expedition.⁷ He bought and sold land in Santa Fe in 1761 and 1765.⁸

1. DM, 1694, No. 22.
2. Ibid., 1697, No. 2.
3. Ibid., 1701, No. 4.
4. B-2, Albuq.
5. Ibid.
6. DM, 1711, No. 5.
7. Ibid., 1720, No. 4.
8. Sp. Arch., I, Nos. 644, 985.

PÉREZ

Jesús María Pérez Serrano, married to *María Candelaria Baca,* was living in Belén at the start of the nineteenth century. They had a daughter, *María Guadalupe,* born May 6, 1813, and a son, *José Miguel Antonio,* April 24, 1818.[1] He was, to all appearances, the son of Francisco Pérez Serrano, *Alcalde* of Albuquerque in 1782, and brother-in-law of Governor de Anza.[2]

* * * * * * * *

Francisco Perez de la Rosa. (See *Rosa*).

José Miguel Pérez registered a mine at Abiquiú in 1818.[3]

1. B-8, Belén.
2. AASF, No. 19.
3. Sp. Arch., I, No. 706.

PINEDA

JOSÉ DE LA MORA PINEDA was a military man who came from Mexico City, perhaps at the time of the Reconquest.[1] He seems to be the Juan de Pineda y Guzmán, twenty-three years old and a native of Sombrerete, who was in Santa Fe in 1695.[2] In 1708 he was mentioned as the husband of *Clara de Chaves.*[3] Between the years 1715 and 1720 he was *Alcalde Mayor* of Taos.[4] He died on January 17, 1727.[5]

Jacinto Pineda, widower of *Simona Domínguez,* married *Juana de Castro Rodarte,* widow of Lazaro Saenz, May 16, 1751.[6] His first wife had died on November 26, 1736.[7]

1. Ocaranza, pp. 133-6.
2. DM, 1695, No. 19.
3. Ibid., 1708, No. 3.
4. B-45, Taos; Ritch Coll., Box 2, No. 54; Sp. Arch., I, No. 240.
5. Bur-48, Sta. Fe.
6. M-50, Sta. Fe.
7. Bur-48, Sta. Fe.

PINO

JUAN BAUTISTA PINO was a traveling merchant from Mexico City who resided in the vicinity of Isleta Pueblo and Rancho de San Clemente as early as 1747.[1] It is not known if his wife, *Petra Teresa Dávila y Calle,* came with him and his two adult sons, likewise merchants and traders, who make mention of their parents later on. These sons were *Joaquín José* and *Mateo José.*

Joaquín José Pino, born in Mexico City and residing in Tomé, the son of Juan Bautista Pino and Petra Dávila y Calle, both deceased, married *Barbara Sánchez,* August 28, 1764.[2] New Mexico products, intended for trade in Mexico City, were stolen from him at Santa Cruz in 1763.[3] He died in 1768 at the age of fifty-nine at the Rancho de San Clemente.[4]

In this same year he had made his will, in which he again gave his parents and birthplace, declaring that he and Barbara had been married four years and three months. They had had three children: *Joaquín Mariano, Ana María (Catalina),* and *Joaquín Mariano.* Only the girl was living.[5] The second boy had been born on January 6 of this same year.[6]

Joaquin José named his brother Mateo José as executor, and also mentioned his brothers-in-law, Juan Cristóbal Sánchez and Diego Antonio Sánchez, the latter married to Ana María del Castillo. Also mentioned were two step-children, *Cristóbal* and *Bartolo*. Among his many effects, he left fifteen published tomes by various authors, and six closely written sheets of persons who owed him money.[7]

Besides Cristóbal and Bartolo, his wife had another illegitimate son prior to her marriage with Pino, *José Francisco Pino*, who married Barbara Chávez in 1775,[8] and then Juana María Baca in 1780.[9] *Bartolo* (or *Bartolomé*) *Pino* married Manuela Chávez, and then Antonio Josefa Torres in 1790.[10]

The only surviving child of the marriage, *Ana María*, was *María Catalina Pino* (unless she, too, was illegitimate), sister of Bartolo,[11] who married Antonio de Luna,[12] and then Anacleto Miera y Pacheco, November 20, 1782, when Joaquín Pino and Barbara Sánchez were given as her deceased parents.

Mateo José Pino, executor of his brother Joaquín's will, turned down the assignment after his brother died, and sued the Sánchez in-laws, complaining about the poverty of his own large family.[13] In 1752, referred to as a native of Mexico City, he had been suggested as a candidate for High Sheriff of the Holy Office in New Mexico.[14]

His wife was *Teresa Sánchez*, presumably a sister of Joaquín's wife, Barbara. They had several children: *Pedro José, Pedro Bautista, Joaquín Mariano, Mariano Antonio*, born February 6, 1752; *Juan Francisco*, March 19, 1753;[15] *Alejandro Ricardo*, April 7, 1756, and *Carlos Casimiro*, baptized on December 15, 1761.[16]

Their mother, Teresa Sánchez, died on November 28, 1761,[17] in childbirth evidently, and their father then married *María Concepción Roybal*, who bore him two children: *Francisco Mariano*, February 6, 1769, and *María Josefa Andrea*, December 8, 1763.[18]

Some of the children of Mateo José Pino married as follows:

Pedro José Pino apparently had brought his wife from Mexico City, or from Chihuahua, where the Pinos also traded.[19] For her name was *María Josefa Caballero,* a name unknown in New Mexico. He was twenty-eight years old in 1767,[20] and was mentioned as already forty years dead in 1822 by his brothers.[21] As *Alcalde Mayor* of Laguna he caused the friars much trouble and even held some of them in debt.[22]

His known children were: *José Mateo*, born October 2, 1768; *Justa Gertrudis María*, July 19, 1772; *María Guadalupe Susana*, August 14, 1774;[23] and *José Manuel Francisco*, January 7, 1780.[24]

Pedro Bautista Pino did not always use the "Bautista" part of his name early in his career, hence it is sometimes difficult to distinguish him from his brother, Pedro *José*, also referred to simply as "Pedro," until the latter's death about the year 1781.[25] Pedro Bautista resided at the Rancho de San Clemente near Isleta when he married *Manuela Gabaldón* in Santa Fe, December 24, 1772.[26] He was assistant *Alcalde* of Laguna in 1780 when he acted as godfather for a child of his brother Pedro José.[27] His first wife died within a decade after bearing the following daughters: *María Vicenta*, November 1, 1773;[28] *María Gertrudis*, July 9, 1775;[29] and the twins, *María Barbara* and *María de la Luz*, at Tomé, September 3, 1778.[30] María Barbara married Isidro Antonio Baca of Belen at Santa Fe in 1793.[31] Another daughter, *María Rita,* married Juan Dionisio Baca, October 11, 1785.[31a]

On September 30, 1781, Pedro Pino, widowed of Manuela Gabaldón, son of the deceased Don Mateo Pino and Tomasa (Teresa) Sánchez, married *Lugarda Lucero*, widow of Francisco Silva. The marriage took place in Santa Fe, though both parties gave Tomé as their residence. They were third cousins.[32] They were still living at Tomé in 1790, when he gave his age as thirty-eight and Lugarda's as thirty-seven. They had five sons, twenty-two, eighteen, sixteen, nine, and seven, respectively; and four girls, thirteen, ten, eight, and three.³³ But in 1786 they were living in Santa Fe, when they went to Tomé to act as sponsors for a grandchild.³⁴ At this period he held offices in Santa Fe or acted as an attorney.³⁵ Lugarda Lucero, "married first to Francisco Silva, and then to Don Pedro Bautista Pino," died on March 8, 1813, leaving eight children.³⁶ Some children by her were: *Juan Esteban*, December 29, 1782, who married Nicolasa Troncoso;³⁷ *María Gertrudis*, July 5, 1786, who as the widow of Mariano Durán became the third wife of Juan Rafael Ortiz in 1816;³⁸ and *Juan Francisco*, August 22, 1788.³⁹

Pedro Bautista Pino then married *María Baca*, with a dispensation, on March 24, 1816.⁴⁰ Known children of this marriage were: *María Guadalupe de la Trinidad*, May 16, 1818; *Nicolás de Jesús*, December 4, 1819,⁴¹ who married Juana Rascón in 1842;⁴² *Miguel Estanislao*, May 6, 1821, who married *María de la Luz Ortiz*, December 31, 1842;⁴³ and *José Facundo*, November 27, 1823.⁴⁴

Pedro Bautista is best known for his being the first and only Deputy from New Mexico to the Spanish Cortes in 1810, when he composed an "Exposition" concerning New Mexico for the Court of Madrid.⁴⁵ His brother Joaquín, during a land dispute at Pajarito in 1821, still boasted of his brother Pedro Bautista who had been the "*Sr. Diputado en Cortes*."⁴⁶

Juan Francisco Pino, mentioned with his brother Pedro José in 1767,⁴⁸ married *María Victoria Chávez*, November 9, 1782,⁴⁹ by whom he had at least six children at Los Chaves. Of these, *Francisco* married Soledad Rael,⁵⁰ and *Mateo* married María Manuela Baca.⁵¹

Joaquín (Mariano) Pino, mentioned with his brothers in civil documents already cited, married *Josefa de la Luz Chávez*, widow of Felipe Varela, November 17, 1783.⁵² They had at least seven children.

1. Sp. Arch., II, No. 480.
2. M-3, Albuq.; DM, 1763, in Albuq., no number.
3. Sp. Arch., II, No. 562.
4. Bur-2, Albuq.
5. Twit. Coll., No. 2813.
6. B-3, Albuq.
7. Twit. Coll., loc. cit.
8. M-11, Isleta, May 3.
9. DM, 1780, no number; M-49, Isleta, Sept. 18; B-3, Albuq., sponsor with his mother, Dec. 11, 1774.
10. M-49, Isleta, Oct. 3.
11. Ibid., sponsors together, May 2, 1782.
12. GENEALOGY: **María Catalina Pino**, José Enrique Luna, Toribio Luna, María Encarnación Luna, Eugenio Chávez, Fabián Chavez, Fr. A. Chávez.
13. Twit. Coll., loc. cit.
14. AGN, Mex., Inq., t. 592, ff. 1-34.
15. These two in B-57, Isleta.
16. These two in B-3, Albuq.
17. Bur-2, Albuq.
18. Both in B-3, Albuq.
19. Sp. Arch., II, No. 623.
20. Ibid.
21. Ibid., No. 212.
22. BNM, leg. 10, Nos. 12, 42.
23. These three in B-57, Isleta.
24. B, Laguna (in Gallup); his godfather was Don Pedro Bautista Pino, **Teniente** of Acoma.
25. Sp. Arch., I, No. 212.
26. M-50, Sta. Fe.
27. B, Laguna, loc. cit.
28. B-57, Isleta, at San Clemente.
29. B-3, Albuq.
30. B-4, Albuq.
31. M-50, Sta. Fe.
31a. M, Laguna, in Gallup.
32. Ibid.
33. Sp. Arch., II, No. 1096a.
34. B-54, Tomé, July 10.
35. Sp. Arch., I, Nos. 54, 126; II, No. 2620; HSNM, Estate of Rosa Bustamante.
36. Bur-50, Sta. Fe.
37. B, Sta. Fe; Ibid., bapts. of these children, 1809, 1812, 1813.
38. Ibid.; M-52, Sta. Fe. Feb. 14.
39. Ibid.
40. M-52, Sta. Fe.
41. Both in B, Sta. Fe.
42. M-54, Sta. Fe, Feb. 16.
44. B, Sta. Fe.
45. Cf. Three New Mexico Chronicles; Note faulty genealogy in Introduction.
46. Sp. Arch., I, Nos. 216, 217.
47. Bur-52, Sta. Fe.
48. Sp. Arch., I, No. 623.
49. DM, 1782, no number; M-49, Isleta.
50. B-54, Tomé, bapt. of son, May 23, 1825.
51. M-49, Isleta, Oct. 24, 1813.

PORRAS

Francisco de Porras, forty, the son of Juan, and born in Madrid, was listed among the colonists of 1693. He had a broad forehead and was blind in one eye. His wife, *Damiana González*, was thirty years of age, a native of Mexico City, and daughter of Santiago; she had an aquiline face, a high forehead, and a broad nose.

They had one daughter, *María,* thirteen years old and born in Mexico City, who had a broad face.¹

Francisco was a Captain at Santa Cruz in 1696; his wife was a sister of Guadalupe Navarro, who married Juan Manuel Chirinos in 1696.²

1. **Sp. Arch.,** II, No. 54c.
2. **DM,** 1696, No. 8.

PRADA

José Prada, a native of Chihuahua, was twenty-seven years of age in 1790 when listed among the soldiers of the Santa Fe garrison. He had come as a widower prior to 1787, when he enlisted at the age of twenty-four. His parents were José Manuel Prada and María de la Rosa. His Santa Fe wife was *Loreta Sandoval,* twenty-two in 1790; they had one son and three daughters.¹ Two known children were *José Manuel,* born January 1, 1798, and *María Antonia Josefa,* May 23, 1810.²

1. **Twit. Coll.,** No. 179; **HSNM,** Mil. Papers.
2. **B, Castrense.**

PRADO

Juan del Prado was a Spaniard from Galicia, married in New Mexico. He and fifteen other New Mexico soldiers fled to Mexico City from Abiquiú and Ojo Caliente in 1763. Among them was his brother-in-law, a son of Inocencio Velásquez.¹ But two years later he was back in Chama.²

While he was gone his wife, *María Antonia Velasco,* had a natural son, *Juan Julián,* January 28, 1764.³ In 1774, July 2, they had twin-boys, *Manuel* and *Juan Pedro.*⁴

1. **Bancroft, NMO,** 1763.
2. **Ibid.,** 1765.
3. **B-31, Sta. Clara.**
4. **Ibid.**

QUINTANA

MIGUEL DE QUINTANA came with the colonists of 1693. He was born in Mexico City, the son of José, and was twenty-two years old; he had a round face, small forehead, large eyes, and a hole (dimple) in the chin. His wife was *Gertrudis (Moreno) Trujillo,* fifteen, the daughter of Nicolás, and also a native of Mexico City; she had an aquiline face, large eyes, and a small nose.¹

A brother of his, José de Quintana, came as a soldier, and from his marriage, given further on, we learn that their parents in Mexico City were José de Quintana and Nicolasa Valdés de Cervantes.

Miguel lived in Santa Cruz all his life.² He died there on April 9, 1748, at the age of seventy.³ He had gained local fame as a poet and composer of *coloquios,* which got him into no small trouble with some injudicious friars at a time when he was mentally perturbed. Here he stated that he had a large family.⁴

His known children were: *Nicolás,* born September 2, 1712;⁵ *Micaela,* wife of Pedro Sánchez;⁶ and some other Quintanas of the same place and ages appearing together, who in all probability were his children: *Lugarda,* wife of Asencio Archuleta;⁷ *Juan, Francisco,*

José, and *Antonia,* who married Juan Gómez del Castillo.

Nicolás Quintana and (mother) Gertrudis Moreno Trujillo were sponsors for a child of Juan Gómez del Castillo and (sister) Antonia Quintana in 1736.[8] His wife was *María Antonia de Herrera;* they had a son, *Hilario,* born January 10, 1743.[9]

Juan Quintana married *Francisca Xaviera Sánchez,* September 6, 1734, with Pedro Sánchez and wife Micaela Quintana as witnesses,[10] apparently Quintana brother and sister marrying Sanchez sister and brother. Juan was killed by Cumanches in 1773, leaving a son, *José Julian,* and other children with his widow.[11]

Francisco Quintana married *Juana Martín,* September 12, 1737, a daughter of Miguel Martín.[12] A child of theirs, *Manuela Antonia,* was born at Abiquiú, August 12, 1741.[13]

If he is the same man later married to a *Rosa Trujillo,* he had two sons by her at Chama: *Juan Francisco,* February 3, 1764, and *Tomás,* January 1, 1766.[14]

José Quintana was older than the preceding sons. He was fifty years old when killed by savage Indians in August, 1748. His widow was *Lugarda Tafoya.* Nothing else is known about him.

* * * * * * * *

Juan Bautista Quintana, a little too young to be a son of Miguel de Quintana, was the son of any of the preceding brothers. He married *María Paula Sánchez* on April 17, 1746.[15] They were still living at Santa Cruz in 1790, when he gave his age as sixty-two, and María Paula's as fifty-eight. They lived alone with two mestizo servants,[16] as all their children were married. María Paula died a widow on May 23, 1815.[17]

Their known children were: *José Julian,* born January 31, 1749, who married María de Jesus Lucero, June 27, 1772;[18] *José María,* born November 12, 1757,[19] who married María Ignacia Archuleta;[20] *José Mariano,* born October 20, 1760;[21] *María Josefa de Jesús,* who married Bernardo Antonio Baca of La Cieneguilla in 1781; *María Josefa,* second wife of Manuel Miera y Pacheco; and *María Ignacia,* who married José María Baca of La Cieneguilla in 1785.

* * * * * * * *

JOSÉ DE QUINTANA, seventeen, and born in Mexico City, the son of José de Quintana and Nicolasa de Valdés y Cervantes, married *Antonia (Luján) Domínguez* in Santa Fe, May 31, 1696.[22] He was still in Santa Fe in 1697,[23] but from 1709 on he was living in Bernalillo.[24] By 1722 he had the title of Captain, and was still a resident of Bernalillo when he sold Santa Fe lands that had belonged to his mother-in-law.[25]

His known children were: *Juan Manuel,* born December 31, 1709, most likely the man who married Rosalia Garcia Hurtado at Albuquerque in 1731;[26] *Manuela,* born June 17, 1707; *Juana,* May 6, 1711;[27] and *Josefa,* mentioned in a land document.[28]

---

1. Sp. Arch., II, No. 54c; BNM, leg. 4, pt. 1, pp. 830-4.
2. Sp. Arch., II, Nos. 178, 330.
3. Bur-32, Sta. Cruz.
4. Cf. "The Mad Poet of Santa Cruz," **New Mexico Folklore Record,** Vol. III, 1948-49, pp. 10-17.
5. B-33, Sta. Cruz.
6. Sp. Arch., II, No. 330.
7. Ibid., I, No. 968; his **compadre** Pedro Sánchez was executor of his will.
8. B-24, S. Ild., Dec. 11.
9. B-31, Sta. Clara.
10. M-29, Sta. Cruz.
11. Sp. Arch., I, Nos. 723, 728.
12. M-29, Sta. Cruz; Sp. Arch., II, No. 529.
13. B-31, Sta. Clara.
14. Ibid.
15. M-27, Sta. Cruz.
16. Sp. Arch., II, No. 1110b.
17. Bur-34, Sta. Cruz.
18. M-25, S. Ild.; DM, 1772, in Albuq., no number.
19. B-34, Sta. Cruz.
20. GENEALOGY: **José María Quintana,** María Josefa Quintana, Desiderio Roybal, Romualdo Roybal, Nicolasa Roybal, Fr. A. Chávez.
21. M-29, Sta. Cruz, B. Sec.
22. DM, 1696, No. 15.
23. Ibid., 1697, No. 3.
24. Ibid., 1708, No. 3; 1710, No. 9.
25. Sp. Arch., I, Nos. 235, 508.
26. B-13, Bern.; DM, 1731, no number.
27. Both in B-13, Bern.
28. Sp. Arch., I, No. 235.

QUIRÓS

JOSÉ DE QUIRÓS, a native of Sombrerete, came to New Mexico shortly after the Reconquest with his wife, *María de la Cruz*.¹ In 1696 he was listed as a widower of Santa Cruz with a son eighteen years of age.² He was living there with Antonio de Armijo in 1715,³ who had married his daughter *María* in 1695.⁴ In that same year of 1715 he ran away to the mines of Chihuahua, taking a young grandson, Juan de Armijo; the youth's mother was trying to get the boy back.⁵ It may be that the son mentioned in 1696 was actually his son-in-law, Antonio de Armijo, for the Quirós name is not met afterwards.

1. DM, 1695, No. 12.
2. Sp. Arch., I, No. 817.
3. Ibid., No. 7.
4. DM, loc. cit.
5. Sp. Arch., II, No. 239d.

RAEL
(*Rael de Aguilar*)

ALONSO RAEL DE AGUILAR was at Guadalupe del Paso as early as 1683, when he married *Josefa* (*Ana*) *García de Noriega* on October 24.¹ He was a native of the City of Lorca in Múrcia.² He took part in both Reconquest *Entradas* of 1692 and 1693, his name appearing in so many documents as Secretary of Government and War, Lieutenant General, *Alcalde* of Santa Fe, and Protector of the Indians, as to defy quoting countless sources.³ In 1697 he had been a *mayordomo* of La Conquistadora for Vargas.⁴ He died on April 10, 1735, and was buried in the Conquistadora chapel; his wife followed him on August 12 of the same year.⁵

Their known children were: *Alonso II, Eusebio, Juan, Antonia, Francisca*, who married Felix Sánchez, and *Feliciana*, wife of Juan García de la Riva.

One son, **Eusebio**, seems to have remained a bachelor all his life, although he could have had a wife and family about whom nothing is known.⁶ He served as an *Alférez* with his father in the Moqui campaign of 1716. In 1720 he was stationed with the guard at Laguna Pueblo.⁷ A servant of his died at Albuquerque in January, 1729.⁸ In 1733 he is mentioned with his brothers and sisters.⁹

Another son, **Juan**, twenty-four in 1723 and twenty-seven in 1727, is then mentioned as a resident of Santa Fe,¹⁰ but is not heard of again.

Alonso Rael de Aguilar II, often referred to as "*El Mozo*," followed in his father's steps as a military figure. In 1715 he was involved in a serious case when he stabbed a soldier fatally and then sought sanctuary in various mission churches.¹¹ In 1745 he made his last will, in which he stated that he was a native of New Mexico who had lived in Santa Fe for forty-eight years.

His first wife was *Tomasa Montoya*, married eighteen years when she died, by whom he had the following six children: *Alonso III, Josefa, Francisca, Manuela, Margarita* (died when five), and *Julián Lorenzo*.

He had been married a second time, for eighteen years also, to *Melchora de Sandoval Martínez*, by whom he had two children, *Tomasa* and *José*.¹²

Tomasa Montoya had died on May 20, 1727, and was buried near the altar of La Conquistadora.¹³ Alonso then married Melchora at her home (because she was ill) on February 9, 1729.¹⁴ He died on May 15, 1745; Melchora lived on until October 21, 1783.¹⁵ Both Alonso and his father left behind a reputation of heavy gamblers.¹⁶

Of his children, *Alonso* III went to study

in New Spain in 1750,[17] and is not heard of again; *Josefa* married Juan Manuel Sandoval in 1733;[18] *Francisca* became the wife of Juan González in 1747;[19] *Manuela* married Baltasar Baca (q.v.); *Julián Lorenzo* married Teresa González, and died on January 24, 1799, at the age of seventy-two,[20] and *Feliciana*, not mentioned in her father's will, had married Salvador Martín in 1743.[21]

Of the two children by the second wife, *Tomasa* married Salvador de Ribera in 1747,[22] while *José* (*Pablo*) married María Bárbara Baca; he enlisted as a soldier in 1759 when twenty-five years of age.[23]

---

1. 1st M-Book, **Guadalupe del Paso,** Bandelier Notes.
2. **AGN, Mex., Inq.,** t. 735, f. 280.
3. E. g.: **Sp. Arch.,** I, Nos. 31, 769; II, Nos. 250, 297a, 382; Crespo, par. 253; **DM,** 1691, No. 4; B-H, III, p. 336; **Vargas Journals,** etc.
4. **OLC,** pp. 19, 25.
5. **Bur-48, Sta. Fe.**
6. More than a generation later, when all the principals were long dead, Eusebio was accused of fathering Cristóbal and Miguel de Chaves by Antonia Baca, wife of Antonio D. y Chaves (**HSNM,** no number).
7. **Sp. Arch.,** II, No. 311; **NMHR,** Vol. VI, No. 2, p. 212.
8. **Bur-2, Albuq.**
9. **Sp. Arch.,** II, Nos. 239j, 382.
10. **DM,** 1723, No. 5; 1727, No. 5.
11. **Sp. Arch.,** II, No. 239j.
12. **Ibid.,** I, No. 765.
13. **Bur-48, Sta. Fe.**
14. **M-50, Sta. Fe; DM,** 1728, No. 3.
15. **Bur-48 and 49, Sta. Fe.**
16. **Sp. Arch.,** I, No. 31.
17. **Ibid.**
18. **M-50, Sta. Fe,** May 10.
19. **Ibid.,** Jan. 20.
20. **Bur-2, Albuq.**
21. **M-50, Sta. Fe,** April 25.
22. **Ibid.,** July 17.
23. **Sp. Arch.,** I, No. 1207; II, Nos. 841, 855; **HSNM,** Mil. Papers.

RAMÍREZ

Gregorio Ramírez, twenty, a native of Zacatecas and soldier of Guadalupe del Paso, married *María Fresqui* in Santa Fe in 1696.[1] He died in 1715.[2]

Nicolás Ramírez, twenty-five, also a native of Zacatecas, the son of José Ramírez, deceased, and María Pineda, married *Isabel de la Rea Gaitán* in 1696.[3] He was living at Santa Cruz in this same year.[4] He worked as a laborer in 1610 during the reconstruction of San Miguel Chapel in Santa Fe.[5]

Felipa Ramírez, sister of *Nicolás* and *Lorenzo* Ramírez, was the wife of an Antonio Pacheco of Santa Fe.[6]

---

1. **DM,** 1696, No. 2.
2. **Sp. Arch.,** II, No. 239a.
3. **DM,** 1696, No. 7.
4. **Sp. Arch.,** I, No. 817.
5. Kubler, p. 18.
6. **Sp. Arch.,** I, No. 1222.

RAMOS

Juan Antonio Ramos, eighteen or twenty and a native of Salvatierra, appeared as a witness in 1694.[1] He had known Diego Velasco of Guadiana for eleven years.[2] He gave his parents as Juan Ramos and Sebastiana de San Antonio when he married *Catalina Jirón* in Santa Fe in 1694.[3]

He died in 1715, his widow at this time being a *María Canseco*.[4]

Nicolás Ramos, a resident of Santa Cruz, was dead by 1706 when his widow, *Ana Rodríguez*, or *Reinoso*, was mentioned as being forty-four years old. She was also known as "*La Rana,*" and they had a daughter, *Antonia*.[5] Ana de Reinoso, a widow eighty years old, died on May 24, 1727.[6]

---

1. **DM,** 1694, Nos. 5, 14.
2. **Ibid.**
3. **Ibid.,** No. 26.
4. **Sp. Arch.,** II, Nos. 239a, 239e.
5. **AGN, Mex., Inq.,** t. 735, f. 285.
6. **Bur-48, Sta. Fe.**

REAÑO
(Riaño)

JOSÉ DE REAÑO was in New Mexico as early as 1732, married to *María Roybal*, widow of Miguel de Archibeque.[1] He made his last will in Santa Fe, April 15, 1743, in which he said that he was born in the Villa de Santillana in the Mountains of Santander, the son of Jacinto de Reaño and Teresa de Tagle Bustamante. (Hence, it appears that he was closely related to Governor Bustamante and came to Santa Fe in his household.) He had been married to María Roybal for fifteen years, by whom he had one son, *José*. His brother-in-law, the Vicar Roybal, was named an executor with Reaño's *concuño*, Juan José Moreno.[2]

His widow married Felipe Rojas y Sandoval on July 13, 1755.[3]

José Reaño II married *Ana María Ortiz* on June 14, 1747,[4] by whom he had three children: *Antonio José Joaquín*, July 4, 1756; *María Manuela*, March 22, 1758; and *Ana María Josefa*, December 26, 1759.[5]

Around the year 1759, José was thrown off his horse, and later lost his mind as a result. While held in custody inside the Santa Fe Presidio because of his dementia early in 1763, he escaped after midnight of February 20, taking along a youth, Antonio Matías Ortiz, who was his wife's cousin, four *genízaros*, and some army horses. The following July a Nataje chieftain reported to the *Alcalde* of Galisteo that he had found the human remains of two *españoles* and three *genízaros* out on the bison plains. Arrowheads were found among the remains.[6]

Riaño is the correct spelling, but the name is spelled with an *e* in eighteenth-century documents. The name survives only among San Felipe and Santo Domingo Indians who adopted it, and they now pronounce it "*Reyno*."

1. Sp. Arch., II, No. 373.
2. Ibid., I, No. 963.
3. M-50, Sta. Fe.
4. Ibid.
5. All in B, Sta. Fe.
6. Sp. Arch., II, No. 557; Bancroft, NMO, 1763.

RENDÓN

FRANCISCO RENDÓN was thirty-two years old in 1711 and living in Santa Fe.[1] He twice bought and sold land there between 1721 and 1739.[2] He participated as a soldier in the Moqui campaign of 1719 when he proved himself most useful as an interpreter of Indian languages,[3] a proficiency also noted years later, in 1732 and 1737.[4]

His wife was *Catalina Maese*, who died on May 20, 1751.[5] A step-daughter was a Simona Antonia Domínguez.[6] Francisco himself died on March 18, 1757.[7]

1. DM, 1711, No. 5.
2. Sp. Arch., I, Nos. 743, 748, 839, 957.
3. NMHR, Vol. VI, No. 2, pp. 190, 218.
4. AGI, Escribanía, leg. 239, No. 6755; Bancroft, NMO, 1737.
5. Bur-48, Sta. Fe.
6. Sp. Arch., I, Nos. 839, 680.
7. Bur-48, Sta. Fe.

RESENES

Isidro Resenes, of San Luis Potosí, married *María Antonia Benavides*, December 2, 1761.[1]

1. M-50, Sta. Fe.

RIBA

Manuel George de la Riba Solar was a native of El Real de Santa Eulalia who came to the Río Abajo district and there married a *María Josefa Escobedo,* daughter of José Escobedo, deceased, and Teresa García, in 1763.[1]

José María de la Riba was second in command at San Elzeario del Paso in 1799-1800, and came up to Sabinal with troops at this time.[2]

1. **DM**, 1763, in Albuq., no number.
2. **Sp. Arch.**, II, Nos. 1491, 1506.

RIBERA

JUAN DE RIBERA, son of Juan de Ribera and Luisa de Ocanto, came to New Mexico with the Reconquest, or shortly after, residing in Albuquerque in 1710, when he married *Juana Romero*.[1] He died prior to 1721, and his widow then married Cristóbal Gallegos in 1728.[2]

His known children by Juana Romero were: *Francisco Antonio,* July 6, 1710;[3] *Felipa,* who married Francisco Martín of Chimayó in 1721;[4] and *María Antonia,* wife of Salvador Varela.

* * * * * * * *

FRANCISCO AFÁN DE RIBERA BETANZOS was living in Santa Cruz in 1718.[5] He appears to be the Francisco de Ribera who was *Alcalde* of Santa Cruz in 1705,[6] and is in all likelihood the Francisco de Betanzos who came with his widower father and younger brother in 1693. (See *Betanzos*.) A merchant by profession, he figured in a trial for assault and battery in 1724 when his stores of goods were embargoed; here it was mentioned that he was an original settler of Santa Cruz, and, though not married, had a large family to support.[7]

For some reason he left New Mexico and died in Nueva Vizcaya sometime before 1728, perhaps on a trading trip. He left an estate at Santa Cruz which was to be divided among the following "heirs": *Nicolasa del Castillo,* wife of Antonio Romero; *Francisco del Castillo,* not heard from in twelve years; *Josefa del Castillo,* twenty years old; and *María del Castillo,* wife of Felipe Nereo Cisneros. The last two girls had been living with the Ignacio Roybal family for the past three years.[8] Josefa married José Manuel Apodaca at Jacona on June 21, 1733, and died four years later in Santa Fe.[9]

When Ribera's estate was probated, a *María de Leyba,* or *María de Piña Días de Brito* (if the same person) was mentioned as the mother of these Castillo people.[10] Moreover, "María de Leyba y Mendoza" had appeared in a land-suit with Francisco de Ribera in 1706.[11] And again, in 1737, "María de Piña" was mentioned as the mother of Francisco Xavier del Castillo.[12] But at no time is Francisco de Ribera referred to as husband or father.

It seems as though this "María" of the many surnames was the "María de Carvajal" who came with her husband, José Cortés *del Castillo* in 1693. After having these children, and after her husband's death, she could have married Francisco Afán de Ribera Betanzos. Or she could be the grandmother of the Castillos, Ribera having married her eldest daughter, *Andrea,* for example. Whatever the solution, these three girls, from whom later prominent families descended, belonged to the ill-fated Cortés families that settled in the Santa Cruz country.

SALVADOR MATÍAS DE RIBERA was born in Puerto de Santa María in Spain, and was twenty years old in 1695.[13] Recruited at Zacatecas by Juan Páez Hurtado, he had arrived in Santa Fe in 1695 with his wife and family. Her name was *Juana de Sosa Canela.*[14] In 1704 he lost his Vargas grant in the center of Santa Fe through a law-suit, and by 1713, his widow and son were after other grants in the Torreón de la Ciénega section of Santa Fe.[15]

Their only known child was *Juan Felipe.*

Juan Felipe de Ribera was twenty-two years old and married in 1716, when he stated that he had been born in Zacatecas,[16] so that he was about four years old when his parents came to Santa Fe. He was a soldier all his life, and a charter officer of Our Lady of Light.[17] He died on October 1, 1767,[18] leaving his widow, *María Estela Palomino Rendón,* and several sons and daughters. By 1770, when their mother was seventy years old, there were seven children living, out of fifteen. Ten children, as found in records, are as follows:

Vicente, fourteen years old when killed by Apaches *"en el monte,"* May, 1743;[19] *Francisca,* who died while a girl, December 22, 1737, and was buried in the Conquistadora chapel;[20] *Lorenza,* who married Pablo Antonio Baca on May 24, 1743;[21] *María de Loreto,* wife of Juan Antonio Ortiz;[22] *Juliana,* married to José Rodriguez;[23] *Juan Miguel, Salvador, Antonio, Luis,* and *José.*[24] Luis (Felipe) enlisted as a soldier in 1757.[24a] Of these sons, three married as follows:

Juan Miguel de Ribera was dead by 1770.[25] His widow, *Manuela Olguín,* married José Miguel Tafoya.[26] He had made his will in 1769, stating that in four years of marriage he and Manuela had two children, *Juana Antonia* and *Miguel de Jesús.*[27]

Salvador de Ribera married *Tomasa Rael de Aguilar* on June 17, 1747.[28] He gave his age as seventy in 1790, being then married to *Juana Abeyta.*[29]

Antonio de Ribera married *Graciana (Prudencia) Sena* on December 24, 1745.[30] He bought land in Santa Fe in 1762, and both he and Graciana were very active members of the Conquistadora Confraternity.[31] He was nineteen when he enlisted as a soldier of Santa Fe; still listed at the Presidio in 1790, he gave his age as sixty-eight, and that of his wife as forty. A son, twenty-six and single, was living with them.[32] Antonio died February 27, 1794,[33] and his wife followed, June 22, 1810, leaving four surviving children.[34]

Their known children were: *Matías,* born March 7, 1750, who married Juliana de la Peña;[35] *María Josefa,* born March 6, 1752; *Viterbo,* March 11, 1754; *Manuel Antonio,* June 29, 1756,[36] who married Josefa Labadía, April 28, 1783;[37] *Antonio José,* born January 8, 1759, and who died November 30, 1765;[38] *Santiago Francisco,* November 30, 1760; *Nicolasa María,* September 12, 1748; *María Rosalia,* November 5, 1762; and *Julián Rafael,* April 13, 1765.[39] José and Matías enlisted as soldiers in 1779.[39a]

---

1. **DM,** 1710, No. 10.
2. **Ibid.,** 1721, Nos. 1, 4; **M-3, Albuq.,** Aug. 16.
3. **B-2, Albuq.**
4. **DM, loc. cit.**
5. **Sp. Arch., II,** No. 298.
6. **Ibid., I,** No. 401.
7. **Ibid., II,** No. 330.
8. **Ibid.,** No. 335.
9. **B-16, Nambé,** M. Sec.; **Bur-48, Sta. Fe,** Dec. 13.
10. **Sp. Arch., loc. cit.**
11. **Ibid., I,** No. 401.
12. **AGI, Escribanía,** leg. 239, No. 6769.
13. **DM,** 1695, No. 13.
14. **Sp. Arch., I,** No. 491; **DM,** 1696, No. 9.
15. **Ibid., I,** Nos. 181, 481, 162, 491.
16. **DM,** 1716, No. 2.
17. **Ibid.; Sp. Arch., II,** No. 162; **Bancroft, NMO,** 1732; **NMHR,** Vol. X, No. 3, p. 188.
18. **Bur-48, Sta. Fe.**
19. **Ibid.**
20. **Ibid.**
21. **M-50, Sta. Fe.**
22. **Sp. Arch., I,** No. 793.
23. **Ibid.**
24. **Ibid.**
24a. **HSNM, Mil. Papers.**
25. **Sp. Arch., loc. cit.**
26. **Ibid.,** No. 793.
27. **Ibid.,** No. 788.
28. **M-50, Sta. Fe.**
29. **Twit. Coll.,** No. 179.
30. **M-50, Sta. Fe;** velados, April 18, 1746.
31. **Sp. Arch., I,** No. 775; **AASF,** Bk. XXIV.
32. **Twit. Coll., loc. cit.; HSNM, Mil. Papers.**
33. **Bur-51, Castrense.**
34. **Bur-50, Sta. Fe.**
35. **B-62, Sta. Fe; M-51, Castrense,** Jan. 6, 1786, her re-marriage to Pedro Ortiz.
36. The three in **B-62, Sta. Fe.**
37. **M-51, Castrense. GENEALOGY: Manuel Antonio Ribera,** María Guadalupe Ribera, María Dolores Alarid, Romualdo Roybal, Nicolasa Roybal, Fr. A. Chávez.
38. **B-62** and **Bur-48, Sta. Fe.**
39. All in **B-62, Sta. Fe.**
39a. **HSNM, loc. cit.**

Juan de Ribera, living in Pojoaque, and a member of the Conquistadora Confraternity in 1715,[40] cannot be placed in the preceding categories for lack of data. He was already married to *María García de Noriega* in 1702 (too old to be the son of Salvador Matías de Ribera), and was also mentioned as an uncle of *María (Griego) Bernal*.[41] Hence he belonged in some way to the Ribera family of the preceding century.

40. **OLC**, p. 72.
41. **AASF**, No. 15; **Sp. Arch.**, I, Nos. 518, 291.

RINCÓN

Antonio Rincón de Guemes, the son of Don Andrés, thirty-six, and born in Mexico City, was tall and swarthy, with an aquiline face and large eyes. He signed up for the 1693 colony, with his wife, *Antonia de Valenzuela*. She was twenty-eight, the daughter of Juan, and also born in Mexico City, having an aquiline face and a sharp nose.

Their three children, all born in Mexico City, were: *José*, eight, having a round, reddish face, large eyes, and a broad nose; *María*, five, with a round face, big eyes and forehead; and *Manuel*, one year old, dark, with large eyes and forehead, and a small nose.[1] A certificate made out at the Cathedral of Mexico, April 15, 1693, testified to the fact of their previous marriage.[2]

A José Rincón sold some land in Santa Fe in 1755.[3]

1. **Sp. Arch.**, II, No. 54c.
2. **DM**, 1693, No. 3; 1694, No. 4.
3. **Sp. Arch.**, I, No. 550.

RODARTE

Cristóbal (or **Xavier**?) **de Rodarte** was among the new settlers of Santa Cruz in 1696.[1] Perhaps he is the man of the same name in the Valverde campaign against the Utes and Comanches in 1719.[2]

Baltasar Rodarte, thirty-six, was living at Santa Cruz in 1713.[3] In 1703 he and his wife, *Francisca García*, were mentioned as residents of that place.[4] A suit was filed against him in Santa Fe in 1702.[5]

1. **Sp. Arch.**, I, No. 817.
2. **Bancroft, NMO**, 1719.
3. **Sp. Arch.**, II, No. 187.
4. **AASF**, No. 15.
5. **Sp. Arch.**, II, Nos. 87, 88.

RODRÍGUEZ

ALONSO RODRÍGUEZ VARELA (or *Carcay*) returned to Santa Fe with his wife, *Juana de Valencia*, in Reconquest times. In 1703 she was accused of sorcery.[1]

Their known children were: *Micaela de la Rosa*, who married Juan de Estrada;[2] *Juana*, who married Antonio Velásquez;[3] *Rosa*, and *Antonio*.[4] A son, not named, was the husband of a Juana Cortés.[5]

* * * * * * *

JOSÉ RODRÍGUEZ was born in Santa María la Real de Nieva, bishopric of Segovia, and was living at Santa Cruz in 1696, when he gave his age as forty-six.[6] He had signed up with the colonists of 1693 as the son of Juan, forty years old, and a native of Santa María Real de Nieva; and was described as of medium height, with a round face, a broad nose, and a large number of moles on the face. His wife was *María de Samano,* twenty-eight, the daughter of Juan and a native of Mexico City. She was dark, with big eyes and a small, sharp nose.

They brought along three children, all born in the City of Mexico: *Gertrudis,* six, with large eyes and forehead, a small nose, and chestnut hair; *Juan Antonio,* four, with a round, ruddy face, large eyes, and a small nose; and *Juana,* two, same description as her brother.[7]

José Rodríguez married again. He and his second wife, *María López Conejo,* sold some Santa Fe property in 1718. They had a son, *José Antonio,* mentioned as a brother to Gertrudis and Juan Antonio.[8]

Juan Antonio Rodríguez, Captain, had been married to *Francisca Fernández de la Pedrera* for four years,[9] when he made his last will in 1738. They had no children, but he mentioned two natural sons of his, *Francisco Xavier* and *Marcos.* Executors of the will were his Fernández father-in-law, his wife, and his brother José Antonio; he also mentioned his sister Gertrudis.[10] He was buried in the Conquistadora chapel on January 2, 1738.[11]

José Antonio Rodríguez, the son by María López Conejo, was married to *Juana Gertrudis de Tapia,* who died on May 24, 1727; their baby, *Juana Gertrudis,* seventeen days old, died on June 9.[12] He then married *Gerónima Montaño,* August 4, 1730.[13] She died on December 11, 1760.[14]

* * * * * * * *

FRANCISCO RODRÍGUEZ CALERO, a soldier and armorer in Santa Fe, married *Gerónima Baca* in 1698. He had left Mexico City on June 1 of that year with Governor Cubero, who testified to his freedom to marry.[15] In 1704 he killed a certain Luisa Gómez de Arellano,[16] and was most likely exiled for it, for in 1715 he was residing at Guadalupe del Paso, when he said that he was born in Mexico City.[17]

* * * * * * * *

Lorenzo Rodríguez, a soldier of Guadalupe del Paso and native of Zacatecas, was twenty years old in 1697.[18] He married *Teresa García (López Olguín),* born in the Río Abajo of unknown parentage. His own parents were Nicolás Rodríguez and Ángela Ortega, both deceased.[19] In 1712 he purchased land in Santa Fe.[20]

Their daughter *Ana* married José Mares in Santa Fe in 1716.[21]

Nicolás Rodríguez was among the 1696 settlers of Santa Cruz with *Agustín Rodríguez,* the latter's wife, Nicolasa Ortiz, and their daughter.[22]

His wife was *María (López) de Tapia.* Apparently they moved down to Socorro del Paso, where two of their children were married: *Tomasa* to Juan Olguín in 1715,[23] and *Marcial* (*vaquero* for the Governor) to Juana Ignacia Méndez, whose parents were farming for the Governor at El Paso del Norte.[24]

Agustín Rodríguez, just mentioned with his Ortiz wife and daughter at Santa Cruz, was born in Zacatecas and reared there with a Cristóbal Rodríguez, who married Teresa de la Cruz.[25]

Cristóbal Rodríguez was born in Zacatecas, the son of Juan Rodríguez and Isabel de la Cruz, both deceased. His first wife had died there in 1694; now at Santa Fe, in 1695, he married *Teresa de la Cruz,* native of San Luis Potosí, and widow of Nicolás Rodríguez.[26]

Nicolás Rodríguez and the above *Teresa de la Cruz* had a daughter, *María de la Rosa,* who married Antonio de Herrera y Sandoval in 1703. At this time her mother (re-married in 1695) was also dead.[27]

The five families in this section, as can be

discerned, were people of low quality, recruited in a hurry at Zacatecas, or brought up by officials as family servants.

* * * * * * * *

MANUEL RODRÍGUEZ, twenty-seven, the son of Juan, was born in Mexico City at the Calle del Reloz, and joined the 1693 colonists with his wife, *María de la Encarnación*. He was tall, with a round face, large eyes, and a sharp nose. She was the daughter of Antonio de Palacios, and born in Mexico City at the Alameda; her complexion was dark, her face pock-marked, and she had circles under the eyes. Manuel was a tailor.[28]

* * * * * * * *

SEBASTIÁN RODRÍGUEZ was Vargas' drummer and town crier, or herald.[29] He said he was fifty in 1692 (and forty in 1694), a native of Río Llanero, San Pablo de Loanda, in Guinea (Africa), the son of Manuel Rodríguez and María Fernández, both jungle Negroes of Loanda. On one occasion Sebastián was referred to as *"de nación moreno,"* evidently a euphemism for "colored" in those days.[30]

He had arrived at Guadalupe del Paso prior to 1689 with Governor Reneros de Posada, under whom he served for three years.[31] In 1692 he asked to marry Antonia Naranjo, but she refused because of a rumor that he was already married. Here Sebastián was referred to as *"de nación Angola."*[32] However, he did succeed in marrying a widow, *Isabel Olguín*, who was dead by 1697, when he married *Juana de la Cruz*, or *Apodaca*, in Santa Fe on May 12.[33] This Juana and her family were involved in sorcery trials in Santa Fe in 1706.[34] She was a member of the Conquistadora Confraternity.[35] Sebastián had property in Santa Fe, both by grant and by purchase, and he continued as official drummer even as late as 1704 when Vargas died.[36]

Known children of his were *Melchor* and *Esteban*.

Melchor Rodríguez married a woman by the name of *Clara de Villareal* (or *Almazán*, or *de los Reyes*).[37] He bought land in Santa Fe in 1738, and was co-owner with his brother Esteban of other properties. As a child he was also connected with the hex practices just mentioned. His was one of the first twelve families that settled the village of Trampas.[38] Both he and his wife were sponsors in 1736.[39] She died in April, 1752, and her estate was probated the following year, when Melchor was mentioned as already re-married.[40]

Their known children were: *Bernardina*, who died single on June 2, 1734;[41] *Pedro Felipe*, mentioned in his mother's estate; and *Joaquina*, wife of Juan José de Argüello.[42]

Esteban Rodríguez succeeded his father as military drummer, and as such took part in the Moqui campaign of 1716.[43] He was also mentioned as official *pregonero* in 1732.[44] As late as 1757, the entire Spanish garrison of Santa Fe petitioned the Governor to recall Esteban to active service, in order to teach a successor the art of drumming.[45] In 1734 he had kidnapped a housewife of Santa Cruz, but the woman, Antonia Quintana, soon was returned to her husband.[46]

---

1. **AGN, Mex., Inq.**, t. 735, f. 306.
2. **DM**, 1694, No. 14.
3. **Ibid.**, 1705, Nos. 2, 5, 6.
4. **Ibid.**, No. 6.
5. **Ibid.**, No. 1.
6. **Ibid.**, 1695, No. 1; 1696, No. 8.
7. **Sp. Arch.**, II, No. 54c; **BNM**, leg. 4, Pt. 1, pp. 790-795.
8. **Sp. Arch.**, II, Nos. 939, 756.
9. Married, Sept. 1, 1733 (**M-3, Albuq.**).
10. **Sp. Arch.**, I, No. 756.
11. **Bur-48, Sta. Fe**.
12. **Ibid.**
13. **M-50, Sta. Fe**.
14. **Bur-48, Sta. Fe**.
15. **DM**, 1698, No. 5.
16. **Sp. Arch.**, I, No. 953.
17. **DM**, 1715, No. 7.
18. **Ibid.**, 1697, No. 4.
19. **Ibid.**, 1696, No. 6.
20. **Sp. Arch.**, I, No. 738.
21. **DM**, 1716, No. 9.
22. **Sp. Arch.**, I, No. 817.
23. **DM**, 1715, No. 2.
24. **Ibid.**, 1717, No. 1.
25. **Ibid.**, 1695, No. 20.
26. **Ibid.**
27. **Ibid.**, 1703, No. 2.
28. **Sp. Arch.**, II, No. 54c; **BNM**, leg. 4, Pt. 1, pp. 790-795.
29. **El Palacio**, Vol. 56, No. 5, pp. 131-138.
30. **DM**, 1692, No. 1; 1694, No. 32; 1697, No. 7; 1698, No. 6.
31. **Ibid.**, 1689, No. 2.
32. **Ibid.**
33. **Ibid.**, 1697, No. 7.
34. **AGN**, loc. cit., t. 735, ff. 277-278, 292-295; **AASF**, No. 15.
35. **OLC**, p. 67; for her fateful life, see Apodaca, Maese, Montaño.
36. **Sp. Arch.**, I, Nos. 102, 730; II, Nos. 94a, 1028.
37. **Ibid.**, I, Nos. 757, 960.
38. **Ibid.**, No. 975.
39. **B-24, S. Ild.**, May 10.
40. **Sp. Arch.**, I, No. 1049.
41. **Bur-48, Sta. Fe**.
42. **Sp. Arch.**, loc. cit.
43. **Ibid.**, II, No. 250.
44. **Bancroft, NMO**, 1732.
45. **Sp. Arch.**, II, No. 538.
46. **Ibid.**, No. 400.

ROMERO
(*Seventeenth-Century New Mexico Family*)

FRANCISCO ROMERO DE PEDRAZA gave his age as forty-eight at Guadalupe del Paso in 1683, and as fifty-nine in Santa Fe at the time of the Reconquest.[1] He was *Alcalde* of Santa Fe the following year when he said that he was sixty; in 1699 his age was given as sixty-five.[2] He belonged to the Confraternity of La Conquistadora.[3]

In 1698, *Graciana,* an eighteen-year-old daughter of his, and of his wife *Francisca Ramírez de Salazar,* married Cristóbal de Arellano.[4]

Diego Romero de Pedraza remained at Guadalupe del Paso with his wife, *Isabel de Gracia.* He was dead by 1715, when their daughter *Gerónima,* fourteen years old, married her first cousin, Dionisio (González) de Escalante, soldier of Guadalupe del Paso.[5]

Matías Romero, son of Bartolomé Romero and Luisa Varela,[6] returned in 1693 with at least his mother and a sister, *Juana;* this girl married Juan de Ribera at Albuquerque in 1710, when their father Bartolomé was mentioned as dead.[7] Matías was, therefore, a nephew of the foregoing Francisco Romero de Pedraza. His name appears in civil documents in conjunction with that of a son, *Tadeo.*[8]

His wife was *Ángela Vallejo,* widow of Miguel Lucero, by whom he had these children: *Rosalia,* who married Lugardo Vallejo in 1730;[9] *Quiteria,* wife of Nicolás Montaño; *Pascual,* killed as a youth "by an arrow," November 20, 1744;[10] and *Tadeo,* who married Antonia Durán y Chaves, March 20, 1751.[11]

Antonio Romero de Pedraza married *Nicolasa del Castillo* on April 30, 1726.[12] He was, perhaps, a son of Francisco Romero de Pedraza. His residence and property were at La Cieneguilla, south of Santa Fe, in which general area his immediate descendants lived. Antonio died on November 19, 1736,[13] and his widow, who had married Miguel Ortiz, died a widow on January 8, 1783.[14]

Their children were: *Juana,* wife of Nicolás Chaves, and then of Cristóbal Montoya;[15] *María,* who married Juan Antonio Baca;[16] *Miguel,* husband of Rosa Montoya;[17] and *Domingo.*[18]

Baltasar Romero was twenty-six years old in 1699, when he stated that he was a native of New Mexico and a resident of Bernalillo.[19] He married *Francisca Góngora* on January 22, 1703.[20] In 1732 he bought some land in Taos in favor of his brothers and sisters, Juan José, Ana María, Antonia, and Domingo Mariano, signing the deed with his sons, *Felipe* and *Pedro.*[21]

His known children were: *Gregorio,* born May 7, 1704;[22] *María Gregoria,* January 19, 1707; *Felipe de Santiago,* May 7, 1709;[23] *José;*[24] and *Pedro,* mentioned above with his brother Felipe.

A *Baltasar* Romero and wife Josefa de Herrera had a son, *Pedro,* born at Guadalupe

---

1. DM, 1683, No. 2; 1693, No. 8.
2. Ibid., 1694, Nos. 23, 27; 1699, No. 1.
3. OLC, p. 69.
4. DM, 1698, No. 2.
5. Ibid., 1715, No. 4.
6. Relationship in DM, 1771, in Albuq., no number.
7. Ibid., 1710, No. 10.
8. Sp. Arch., I, No. 751; II, No. 746.
9. M-3, Albuq., May 10.
10. Bur-2, Albuq.
11. M-11, Isleta. GENEALOGY: Tadeo Romero, María Manuela Romero, José Chávez I, José Chávez II, Eugenio Chávez. Fabián Chávez, Fr. A. Chávez.
12. M-29, Sta. Cruz; DM, 1726, No. 2, incomplete; Sp. Arch., II, No. 235.
13. Bur-48, Sta. Fe.
14. Bur-49, Sta. Fe.
15. Sp. Arch., I, No. 776.
16. See Cabeza de Baca.
17. Sp. Arch., I, No. 779.
18. Ibid., Nos. 776, 1003.
19. DM, 1699, No. 2.
20. B-13, Bern., M. Sec.
21. Ritch Coll., Box 2, No. 54.
22. B-13, Bern.
23. Both in B-2, Albuq.
24. Sp. Arch., I, No. 765.

del Paso in 1699,²⁵ but this was most likely a different man—unless it was an Andrés Romero later living at Taos with a wife of the same name.

Andrés Romero and *Josefa de Herrera* were living in Taos, where a son, *Miguel,* was born on September 19, 1717, and a girl, *Clara Rosa,* in 1722.²⁶

Salvador Romero, a native of New Mexico, returned in 1693 with his wife, *María López de Ocanto.* A daughter, *Pascuala,* was born in Bernalillo on April 7, and baptised *in extremis* on April 11, 1702.²⁷ A grown daughter, *Agustina,* married Mateo Márquez in this same year;²⁸ and in 1714, a son *Diego,* married Josefa de Medina of Santa Cruz.²⁹

Several other Romeros, men and women, who appear in civil and church documents in the first quarter of this century, cannot be identified or classified for lack of more explicit data.

25. B, Guad. del Paso (Juárez).
26. B-45, Taos.
27. B-13, Bern.
28. DM, 1702, No. 3; Sp. Arch., II, No. 91c.
29. DM, 1714, No. 3.

ROMERO
(Others)

José Antonio Romero was a native of Carmona, and twenty years of age in 1696, when a soldier in Santa Fe.¹ Nothing more is known about him.

Alonso Romero, a native of Sevilla, married *María Gómez Robledo* at Guadalupe del Paso, September 2, 1693, but he was found to be a bigamist and the marriage was annulled.² He had two still-born children by her, and did not return to New Mexico after his trial in Mexico City.³

Juan Romero, *Alférez* and miller, joined the 1693 colonists at Zacatecas with his wife, *María de Ávila.* He ran away from the colony, and very likely did not reach New Mexico.⁴

Juan Luis Rionuevo, origin unknown, married *María Romero,* widow of Juan Antonio López, in 1736.⁵ Because of family connections, he is otherwise referred to as "Romero." His second marriage was with *Teresa Rodríguez Argüello,* July 17, 1757.⁶

DIEGO ROMERO, not a true Romero, but the son of Alonso *Cadimo,* who had lived in the Felipe de Romero *estancia* before the 1680 Rebellion,⁷ returned to New Mexico with his wife, *María de San José.* He established himself at Taos where he acquired considerable land and the title of *teniente.* He had three children by his first wife: *Francisco Xavier, Juan,* and *Ana María.*⁸

In 1735, June 14, he married Bárbara Montoya,⁹ but died soon after.¹⁰ Of his three children, *Francisco* married Mónica Martín on September 9, 1737, and had three children, Juan and Juan Andrés, dead by 1770, and María Antonia, wife of Julián Luján.¹¹ *Ana María* married Antonio de Atienza, July 1, 1737.¹²

* * * * * * * *

FRANCISCO XAVIER ROMERO was a native of Mexico City, the son of Matías Romero and Andrea de la Cruz, still living at the Barrio del Carmen in Mexico City, when their son came up to Santa Fe in 1693 and married *María de la Cruz,* widow of Cristóbal Domínguez.¹³ He moved to Santa Cruz

(Chimayó), where he was a shoemaker and also practiced medicine.¹⁴ In 1715 he was tried for killing someone's ox;¹⁵ for this reason, and very likely for others far more serious, he was exiled to Albuquerque. But in the following year the people of Santa Cruz petitioned the Governor for his return, because they needed a doctor. In 1728 he was convicted of soliciting a young male patient, a crime evidently committed more than once previously, according to testimonies given.¹⁶

In his 1728 defense, Francisco mentioned six legitimate children by his wife, María *de Ynojos*, as well as two natural ones by someone else. His known children were: *Micaela*, married to Ambrosio de Balbeinci in 1719;¹⁷ *Juana María*, widow of Juan Antonio López, who married Juan Luis Romero (Rionuevo) in 1736;¹⁸ *Santiago*, husband of Juana Bautista de Oliden [Olivas?]; *Bernardo; Juan de Dios*, married to Efigenia Núñez;¹⁹ and *Nicolás*.²⁰

These Romero sons and their brother-in-law, Juan Luis Romero, were among the first settlers of Truchas.²¹

---

1. **DM**, 1696, Nos. 9, 11.
2. Ibid., 1693, No. 1; 1714, No. 7.
3. **AGN, Mex., Inq.**, t. 701, ff. 319-388.
4. **BNM**, leg. 4, Pt. 1, pp. 790-795, 830-834.
5. **M-29, Sta. Cruz.**
6. **M-11, Isleta.**
7. **Sp. Arch.**, I, No. 1002.
8. Ibid., Nos. 755, 759; **Bancroft, NMO**, 1731.
9. **M-29, Sta. Cruz.**
10. **Sp. Arch.**, loc. cit., and No. 240.
11. Ibid., No. 590; **M-27, S. Juan.**

---

12. **M-27, S. Juan.**
13. **DM**, 1693, No. 10; 1714, No. 1.
14. **Sp. Arch.**, II, No. 330.
15. Ibid., No. 239c.
16. Ibid., No. 353, incomplete; the missing section in **Bancroft, NMO**, 1728.
17. **DM**, 1719, No. 1.
18. See Note 5.
19. **DM**, 1717, No. 6.
20. **Sp. Arch.**, I, No. 742; II, Nos. 310, 239c.
21. **Twit. Coll.**, No. 4.

ROMO

JOSÉ ROMO DE VERA came from the City of Mexico prior to 1731 and settled in Santa Fe.¹ When he made his last will in 1754, he declared as his parents Don Francisco Pérez Romo and Doña Petronila de Vera, both deceased. His first wife had been *María Maldonado y Solís*, by whom he had nineteen children (in Mexico City), all now dead.

His second wife was *Ángela Valdés*, daughter of Domingo Valdés and Ana Márquez. Of their three children, only one was living, *José Manuel*.² Ángela had died on April 13, 1749, and José followed on March 12, 1754.³

José Manuel Romo de Vera married *María Marta Martín* on April 21, 1774.⁴ Three known children of theirs were: *Juan José*, born February 13, 1775; *Juan Nepomuceno*, August 2, 1778; and *María Antonia*, June 29, 1782.⁵ José Manuel had enlisted as a soldier, thirty-seven years of age, in 1783.⁶

---

1. **Bancroft, NMO**, 1731.
2. **Sp. Arch.**, I, No. 1052.
3. **Bur-48, Sta. Fe.**

4. **M-50, Sta. Fe.**
5. All in **B, Sta. Fe.**
6. **HSNM, Mil. Papers.**

ROYBAL

IGNACIO DE ROYBAL Y TORRADO, twenty-one years old, the son of Pedro de Roybal y Torrado and Elena de la Cruz, was a native of Caldas de Reyes, a few miles south of Compostela, in Galicia, who came as a soldier of the Reconquest in 1693. On February 8, 1694, he married *Francisca Gómez Robledo*.¹

Perhaps a brother of his was a *(Santiago) Domingo Roybal*, treated at the end of this

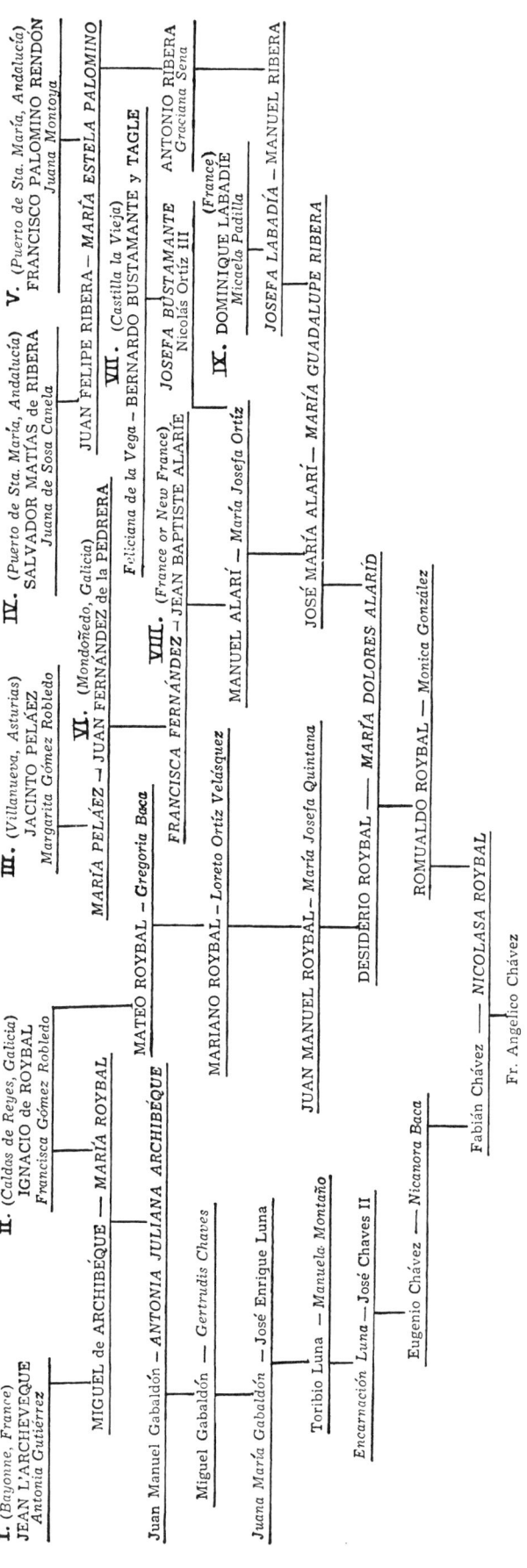

A FRENCH, NORTH SPANISH, AND ANDALUCIAN COMBINATION.—The statement that the old Spanish life-pattern and bloodstream in New Mexico are Extremeño-Manchego is questioned by some New Mexicans who happen to have a French or North Spanish name or ancestor. Here are three Frenchmen, three northern Spaniards, one North Castilian, and two deep-south Spaniards, all pouring their blood and characteristics down into one family. However potent their contribution, it is absorbed by an immense century-old background, and a vast contemporary millieu, of Extremeño-south Castilian factors, whether these latter folk came directly from Extremadura and Castilla la Nueva, or indirectly through the Canary Islands and the Valley of Mexico.

section. Other brothers and sisters were: *Martina*, born November 14, 1655; *María*, February 20, 1659; *Antonio*, May, 1662; and *Marcos*, January 29, 1665.[2]

Ignacio received land grants in Santa Fe and the San Ildefonso (Jacona) district,[3] and was active in Vargas' campaigns in Reconquest years.[4] He also served most of his life as High Sheriff of the Inquisition.[5] He died in Santa Fe at the age of "eighty and more years" on July 14, 1756; his widow followed him on March 2, 1763, "more than a hundred years old."[6] Ignacio had belonged to the Confraternity of La Conquistadora.[7]

Their children were the following: *María Manuela*, who married Juan de Archibeque in 1719, and then Bernardino de Sena, but had no children by either husband; *María*, wife of Miguel de Archibeque,[8] then of José Reaño, and later of Felipe de Rojas Sandoval; *Juana*, wife of Juan José Moreno; *Elena*, who married Juan Manuel Martín in 1731; and the sons: *Santiago, Bernardo, Mateo, Ignacio*, and *Pedro*.

Santiago de Roybal was sent to Mexico City for his education and chose an ecclesiastical career. Ordained by Bishop Crespo of Durango, he was sent to Santa Fe, where soon after he began serving as his Vicar and Ecclesiastical Judge, in 1730, until the end of his days. For one short period, 1733-1736, he served in the same capacity at Guadalupe del Paso. He died in Santa Fe, just having celebrated Mass, on February 4, 1774. He was the first native priest of New Mexico as well as the first native secular priest and prelate of what is now the United States.[9]

Bernardo de Roybal was born in 1709.[10] He married *Margarita Martín*, widow of Juan de Padilla, on September 20, 1731.[11] Their children were: *María Margarita*, October 19, 1733, who married José Antonio López, June 27, 1758;[12] *Rosa María*, May 22, 1739, who married Miguel Sánchez, May 23, 1757;[13] *Juan Inocencio*, January 6, 1738;[14] and *Tomás*.[15]

Bernardo was married a second time to *Bárbara Pacheco*, September 14, 1744,[16] by whom he had: *José Ignacio*, who married Manuela Lucero;[17] *José Antonio*, March 20, 1750; and *María Josefa*, February 3, 1756.[18]

Mateo de Roybal was born on September 23, 1710.[19] On December 8, 1734, he married *Gregoria Baca*,[20] who once was reported by the Padre for cruelty to her Indian servants.[21] Mateo succeeded to his father's lands at Jacona, as well as the portion belonging to his younger brother Pedro.[22] Both he and his wife were active members of the Conquistadora Confraternity.[23] They had the following children:

Eugenio, born November 19, 1739;[24] *Teodora*, November 14, 1741; *Matías*, March 3, 1743; *Santiago José*, February 3, 1745,[25] who married Gertrudis Ortega, and then Candelaria Benavides in 1781;[26] *Antonia Dominga*, May 18, 1746, adopted by her childless aunt, wife of José Moreno,[27] and later married to Juan Antonio Alarí; *Pedro*, March 3, 1748;[28] *Juana*, April 5, 1750; *Antonio José*, March 18, 1751;[29] *Cornelio*, who married María Ignacia Pacheco in 1775;[30] *Ambrosio Mariano*, December 12, 1756, who married María Loreto (Ortiz) Velásquez, June 27, 1781;[31] *Felix*, December 2, 1758, who married María Josefa

---

1. **DM**, 1694, No. 1; 1695, No. 3.
2. I found these entries in extant baptismal books of the parish of Santo Tomás, Caldas de Reyes, in June, 1952.
3. **Sp. Arch.**, I, Nos. 1136, 1261, etc.; **DM**, 1704, No. 7.
4. **B-H**, III, p. 132; **Old Santa Fe**, Vol. III, pp. 332-373.
5. **AGN, Mex., Inq.**, t. 952, ff. 1-34; t. 553, exp. 32, f. 180.
6. **Bur-48, Sta. Fe**.
7. **OLC**, p. 70; **El Palacio**, Vol. 54, No. 10, p. 302.
8. GENEALOGY: **María de Roybal**, Juliana Archibeque, Miguel Gabaldón, Juana María Gabaldón, Toribio Luna, María Encarnación Luna, Eugenio Chávez, Fabián Chávez, Fr. A. Chávez.
9. Detailed account of his life and ancestry, **El Palacio**, Vol. 55, No. 8, pp. 231-252.
10. **M-24, S. Ild.**, f. 12.
11. **M-27, S. Juan**.
12. **B-27, S. Juan; M-25, S. Ild.**
13. **Ibid.**
14. **Ibid.**
15. Mentioned with sisters María and Rosa as minors in mother's estate. (**Sp. Arch.**, I, No. 530.)
16. **M-27, S. Juan.**
17. **B-24, S. Ild.**, bapt. of child, Mar. 27, 1780.
18. Both in **B-24, S. Ild.**
19. **M-27, S. Ild., B. Sec.**
20. **M-50, Sta. Fe; Sp. Arch.**, I, No. 101.
21. **Sp. Arch.**, II, No. 596.
22. **Ibid.**, I, No. 1261.
23. **AASF**, Books LXXIX, LXXX.
24. **Bur-16, Nambé, B. Sec.**
25. These three in **B-24, S. Ild.**
26. **DM**, 1781, no number.
27. **B-24, S. Ild.; Sp. Arch.**, I, No. 552.
28. **B-34, Sta. Cruz.**
29. Both in **B-24, S. Ild.**
30. **DM**, 1775, no number.
31. **B-24, S. Ild.; M-33, Sta. Clara.** GENEALOGY: **Ambrosio Mariano Roybal**, Juan Manuel Roybal, Desiderio Roybal, Romualdo Roybal, Nicolasa Roybal, Fr. A. Chávez.

Miera y Pacheco in 1784;[32] and *María Marta,* February 20, 1763, who became the wife of Bartolomé García in 1783.[33]

Ignacio de Roybal married *Ángela Martín* in the same ceremony that united his elder brother Bernardo with her elder sister Margarita. Their known children were: *Margarita,* June 14, 1732; *Manuela,* January 1, 1734; *Antonio,* December 7, 1735; *María,* May 14, 1738;[34] and *Juan,* living with his widowed mother at La Canoa in 1766.[35]

Pedro de Roybal had donated his inheritance to his brother Mateo[36] around the time he moved to Guadalupe del Paso. He probably went there with his eldest brother, the Vicar, when the latter was stationed there in 1733-1736. And there he remained and perhaps married a local girl, whose name is not known. All that we know is that he died there on March 1, 1777.[37]

* * * * * * * *

Domingo de Roybal married *Juana Gómez* on May 3, 1713.[38] He died on January 28, 1729, at the age of fifty.[39] Since he was only five or six years younger than Ignacio de Roybal y Torrado, he could not have been his son. The fact that he married a Gómez Robledo, as did Ignacio, points to the probability of his being a younger brother. Nothing more is known about him.

Their only recorded child was *Basilio,* son of *Santiago (Domingo) Roybal* and *Juana Gómez,* born at Jacona, July 16, 1713.[40] Basilio is not heard of again either.

---

32. **B-24, S. Ild.**; **M-22, Pojoaque**; he enlisted as a soldier of the Santa Fe Presidio in 1789. (HSNM, Mil. Papers.)
33. **B-24, S. Ild.**
34. All in **B-27, S. Juan.**
35. **Bancroft, NMO, 1766.**
36. **Sp. Arch., I, No. 1261.**
37. **Bur., Guad. del Paso (Juárez).**
38. **M-24, S. Ild.**
39. **Bur-48, Sta. Fe.**
40. **M-24, S. Ild.**

RUBÍ

MANUEL RUBÍ, son of Don Antonio Rubín de Celis and Doña Mariana Maldonado, married *Juana Gutiérrez* on April 8, 1798.[1] They both were living at the Hacienda del Pajarito in 1803.[2]

This family was perhaps descended from Alonso Victores Rubín de Celis, who was *Alcalde* of Guadalupe del Paso and Commander of its Presidio in 1736-1747.[3]

The priest who performed the wedding ceremony of Manuel Rubí and Juana Gutiérrez was Fray José Pedro Rubí de Celis, who came to Santa Fe for it and received permission from the secular pastor; hence, he might have been the groom's uncle or brother.

---

1. **M-52, Sta. Fe.**
2. **AASF, No. 30.**
3. **Ocaranza, p. 168; Sp. Arch., I, No. 27, II, Nos. 411, 479, 483.**

RUELAS

Juan José Ruelas was an ox-team driver, born in Mexico City, and forty-five years old in 1790, when residing in Santa Fe with his wife, *Josefa García,* who was thirty-five. He had three step-sons and four step-daughters.[1] In 1792 he underwent trial for wounding a Juan García in Santa Fe.[2]

---

1. **Sp. Arch., II, No. 1096a.**
2. **Ibid., I, No. 1209.**

RUIZ

Juan Ruiz Cáceres. (See preceding century.) What sons of his, if any, returned with the Reconquest is not known. It is possible that any descendants of his continued as "*Luján.*"

* * * * * * * *

JUAN RUIZ CORDERO, a native of Medina Sidonia and son of Gerónimo, was twenty-two in 1693 when he joined the colony for New Mexico. He was dark and had a scar on the left side of the face. His wife was *María Nicolasa Carillo,* twenty, the daughter of Nicolás and born in Mexico City. She was of middle height, dark, with large eyes and mouth, and a rather flat nose.[1] He again gave his birthplace, and his age as thirty-eight, in 1710.[2] In 1722, a retired adjutant, he sold some Santa Fe land.[3] He was dying early in 1724, on February 17, when he brought serious charges of malfeasance against certain persons.[4]

Shortly before, he had made his last will, in which he stated that he and María Carrillo *Terrazas* had been married for thirty-one years. Their five children were: *Juana Serena, María Antonia, Manuela de Gracia, María Daria,* and *Francisco Xavier.* All were given the surname "Cordero" without the "Ruiz."[5]

* * * * * * * *

ANTONIO RUIZ VILLEGAS was a native of Puebla, the son of Juan de Villegas Ruiz and Ana María Castellanos. He came to New Mexico as an orphan and was reared by Fray José Mariano Rosete, priest of Acoma.[6] In 1790 he was living at the Plaza de San Antonio, in Albuquerque, with his wife, *Isabel Armijo.* He was thirty-five, and she was twenty.[7] They had been married on April 6, 1785.[8]

---
1. Sp. Arch., II, No. 54c.
2. DM, 1710, No. 7.
3. Sp. Arch., I, No. 1032.
4. Ocaranza, pp. 136-139.
5. Sp. Arch., I, No. 1206.
6. DM, 1785, no number.
7. Sp. Arch., II, No. 1092b.
8. M-4, Albuq.

SÁENZ

MANUEL SÁENZ DE GARVISU married *María Ignacia Lucero de Godoy* on February 25, 1743.[1] He was a native of Spain, and *Teniente* of the Santa Fe garrison in 1745, when he gave his age as thirty-eight.[2] At that time he purchased property in Santa Fe.[3] He was a *mayordomo* of the Conquistadora Confraternity with Toribio Ortiz in 1774.[4]

His known children are the following: *Manuel Bernardo,* who married Ursula Durán in 1766, and made his home in the Rio Abajo;[5] *María de Loreto,* wife of Juan Domingo Baca;[6] *Juana de la Cruz,* born December 1, 1744;[7] *Antonio José,* October 22, 1749; *Juan Manuel,* March 8, 1755; and *María Andrea,* February 7, 1752.[8] Juan Manuel enlisted as a soldier in 1776.[9]

---
1. M-50, Sta. Fe.
2. Bancroft, NMO, 1745.
3. Sp. Arch., I, No. 846.
4. OLC, p. 11.
5. DM, 1766, in Albuq., no number; M-11, Isleta; AGN, Tierras, leg. 426, III, ff. 7-10.
6. M-11, Isleta.
7. Bur-48, Sta. Fe.
8. All in B, Sta. Fe.
9. HSNM, Mil. Papers.

SÁIZ

AGUSTÍN SÁEZ, son of Captain Ambrosio Sáez and Ana Rodríguez,[1] enlisted at Parral for the Reconquest of 1693. His was one of the families that had to vacate Santa Fe on December 27, 1693, when the Tanos decided to fight for the town instead of departing peacefully; he was warned beforehand by an Indian who had served his father before the Rebellion of 1680.[2]

His first wife, *Leonor de Herrera,* seems to have died at Guadalupe del Paso before 1692. The wife who came up to Santa Fe with him was *Antonia Márquez,* who was dead by 1709, when he applied to marry Isabel Madrid, a marriage that did not take place.[3] In 1701, Agustín was banished from Santa Fe for adulterous relations while his Márquez wife was still living.[4] He died intestate prior to 1725, when his long-dead second wife was referred to as "Pascuala Vásquez," daughter of the first wife of Captain Diego Arias de Quirós;[5] but the woman's name was actually Antonia Márquez, daughter of Nicolás Márquez and Ana María Montoya.[6]

His known children by Antonia Márquez were *Francisco* and *Juliana.*[7] Francisco married Juana de Herrera in 1718, when his mother is mentioned as deceased,[8] and Juliana became the wife of Juan Griego of Albuquerque.[9]

1. DM, 1709, No. 9.
2. Ritch Coll., Box 1, No. 25.
3. DM, loc. cit.
4. Sp. Arch., II, No. 79.
5. Ibid., I, Nos. 838, 717.
6. Ibid.
7. Ibid.
8. DM, 1718, No. 5.
9. Sp. Arch., loc. cit.

SALAÍCES

JOSÉ QUIRINO SALAÍCES, a native of Chihuahua, was a twenty-three-year-old soldier of Santa Fe in 1790. His wife was *Rita Ortiz.* He was the son of Xavier Salaíces and Rosalia Gabaldón; he was twenty-one when he enlisted in 1789.[1]

1. Twit. Coll., No. 179; HSNM, Mil. Papers.

SALAS

SEBASTIÁN DE SALAS, son of Bernardo de Salas and a native of Sevilla, was twenty-five years old in 1693 when he joined the colonists for New Mexico. He was of medium height, with large eyes, and a scar on the forehead. His wife was *María García,* twenty-three, a native of Puebla and daughter of Nicolás; she was fair, with a small nose and somewhat deep-set eyes.[1] He again gave his age as twenty-five and his birthplace the City of Sevilla in 1694.[2]

In 1701 he sold some land in Pojoaque, and again some more at Santa Cruz in 1703.[3] He seems to be the Sebastián *Canseco* who sold Pojoaque lands in 1702, and had been tried for robbery in 1697.[4]

A son, *Sebastián Higinio,* was born to Sebastián de Salas and María García, January 18, 1717.[5]

* * * * * * * *

DIEGO DE SALAS, the son of Antonio and born in Mexico City at San Fernando, joined the 1693 colonists when nineteen years of age; he was dark, with a round face and a mole on the right cheek. His wife was *María Luisa de Senorga,* fifteen, the daughter of Diego and also born in Mexico City at Santa Catalina Martir; she was of medium height, with large eyes and forehead, and a sharp nose.

They brought along a brother of María Luisa, *Diego de Senorga,* seventeen, and also a native of Mexico City. He was of medium height, with a high forehead and small eyes.[6]

In 1720 a "Diego de Salas, alias Herrera, Treviño," was investigated on a charge of bigamy.[7] This could have been the younger Diego de Senorga.

* * * * * * * *

José de Salas remarried *Bernardina Hurtado* in Albuquerque, February 27, after some question about the validity of their previous marriage.[8] He might be the "Diego" with several aliases just mentioned.

José gave his age as forty-six in 1747. A daughter of his, *Francisca,* was the wife of Gregorio Jaramillo.[9] José de Salas could have been the son of either of the two Salas colonists just treated.

---

1. **Sp. Arch.,** II, No. 54c; **BNM,** leg. 4, Pt. 1, pp. 790-795.
2. **DM,** 1694, Nos. 4, 27.
3. **Sp. Arch.,** I, Nos. 927, 678.
4. **Ibid.,** No. 928; II, No. 64.
5. **B-2, Albuq.**

6. **Sp. Arch.,** II, No. 54c.
7. **AGN, Mex., Inq.,** t. 595, ff. 293-301.
8. **DM,** 1718, No. 11, fragment.
9. **Sp. Arch.,** II, Nos. 453, 476.

SALAZAR

AGUSTÍN DE SALAZAR was a blind interpreter, "proficient in his mother's tongue," who reported the impending Indian resistance late in December, 1693, while Vargas was waiting for the Tanos to vacate Santa Fe. He was helped to safety by Miguel Luján.[1] In 1698 he gave his age as thirty-three.[2] His father, perhaps, was Bartolomé de Salazar, pre-Rebellion *Alcalde* of Zuñi and Moqui.

Agustín and his wife *Felipa de Gamboa* had the following children: *Lugarda,* who married Vicente Jirón in 1723, when her parents were living in Santa Cruz;[3] *Josefa,* who married Juan Lorenzo de Valdés;[4] and *Antonio.*

Antonio de Salazar, son of Agustín de Salazar and Felipa de Gamboa, married *María de Torres* in Santa Fe, November 27, 1708.[5] In 1714 he asked for Santa Cruz lands west of the Rio del Norte that had belonged to his grandfather, Captain Alonso Martín Barba, and the Governor ordered the grant made.[6]

---

1. **Ritch Coll.,** Box 1, No. 25; **Doc. Hist. de Mex.,** p. 145.
2. **DM,** 1698, No. 11.
3. **Ibid.,** 1723, No. 1.
4. **Ibid.,** 1729, No. 2.

5. **Ibid.,** 1708, No. 1.
6. **Ritch Coll.,** Box 2, No. 52. Martín Barba was more likely his great-grandfather, whose daughter married Bartolomé de Salazar.

SÁNCHEZ
(*Sánchez de Iñigo*)

Pedro and **Jacinto Sánchez de Iñigo** were two natives of New Mexico, evidently brothers, who escaped the 1680 Indian massacre as minors, and returned to re-settle New Mexico in 1693. Or else they were born at Guadalupe del Paso, considered then a part of New Mexico.

PEDRO SÁNCHEZ DE IÑIGO was born "in New Mexico," the natural son of Ana (Juana) López. On January 7, 1692, he married *Leonor Baca* at El Real de San Lorenzo.[1] A Francisca Sánchez de Iñigo, the wife of Captain Juan García de Noriega, was most likely his sister. And he could well be a "Pedro López de Yñíguez" who was soldiering at Guadalupe del Paso prior to the Reconquest.[2] Pedro first settled in the Rio Arriba area, and in 1696 his wife was killed by the Indians of San Ildefonso with her mother, a brother, and her two children.[3]

By the turn of the century Pedro had married a *María Luján* at Bernalillo, moving shortly afterwards back to the Rio Arriba country.[4] At Santa Cruz, in 1710, he gave his age as thirty-six, stating that he was a resident there, and married.[5] In 1713 he was mentioned as a brother-in-law of Diego Martín, son of Domingo Martín.[6] He was dead by 1720 when a daughter got married.

He had a son, *Pedro II*, who gave his age as twenty-seven in 1727,[7] being therefore a son by the second wife. Other children were: *Manuela*, born January 13, 1701;[7a] *Olaya*, who married Diego Gonzalez of Santa Cruz in 1720;[8] *Francisca Xaviera*, December 13, 1715, who became the wife of Juan Quintana;[9] and *Antonia*, wife of Juan José de la Cerda.[10]

Pedro Sánchez II, grandson of Juana (Ana) Lopez, the old lady still much alive in 1724, was the son-in-law of Miguel de Quintana of Santa Cruz.[11] The name of his wife was *Micaela Quintana*.[12]

Two known children of theirs were *Bernardo Antonio*, born on April 9, 1733,[13] and *Francisco Xavier*, who married Isabel Pacheco, August 20, 1743.[14]

JACINTO SÁNCHEZ DE IÑIGO was also a "native of New Mexico," who was twenty-two years old in 1685, when he tried to run away from the exile colony with Juan Domínguez de Mendoza.[15] He was first married to *Isabel Telles Jirón*. After her death in Santa Fe, he married *María Rodarte de Castro Xabalera* in 1696. Here his parents were given as unknown. The bride was a native of Sombrerete, the daughter of Miguel de Castro Xabalera and Juana Guerrero, or de Herrera.[16] He gave his age as thirty-five in 1697, saying that he was a native of New Mexico.[17] In 1703 he received a grant of land on the Rio del Norte, on the east side opposite Cochiti Pueblo.[18] In 1713 he was *Alcalde Mayor* of Santa Cruz, but not considered too competent by the Governor; here he was mentioned together with Pedro Sánchez.[19] In 1715 he asked for a permit to visit outside New Mexico with his son, Francisco.[20] On his return he settled down in the Rio Abajo district.

In 1728 Jacinto led an unauthorized small expedition into the Moqui country,[21] but by 1734 both he and his wife were dead; she was sixty at the time of her death on May 13, and he was "more than fifty" when he died on December 14 of the same year, 1734.[22]

Known children by Isabel Telles Jirón were: *José*, who married Teresa Jaramillo; *Joaquín*, who married Manuela Montoya and then Francisca Guerrero de la Mora; and (*Ana*) *Juana* (*Isabel*), who married Manuel Montoya in January, 1705.[23] These three are recalled together in 1763.[24]

Children by his second wife were: *Francisco*, who married Josefa Chaves, *Gertrudis*, and *Miguel*.[25] Three of the above sons married as follows:

---

1. DM, 1691, No. 3.
2. Ibid., 1694, No. 3.
3. **Old Santa Fe**, Vol. III, pp. 332-373.
4. Sp. Arch., II, Nos. 187, 828.
5. DM, 1710, No. 3.
6. Sp. Arch., I, No. 430. María Luján could very well be a daughter of Juan Luján and Juana Domínguez.
7. DM, 1727, No. 1.
7a. B-13, Bern.
8. DM, 1720, No. 2.
9. M-24, S. Ild.; Sp. Arch., I, No. 723.
10. DM, 1721, No. 2.
11. Sp. Arch., I, No. 968; II, No. 330.
12. M-29, Sta. Cruz, Sept. 6, 1734, both sponsors for a wedding.
13. B-29, Sta. Cruz.
14. M-27, S. Juan.
15. Sp. Arch., II, No. 35. A Domínguez de Mendoza might have been the father of these two Sánchez de Iñigo men, the Callados mentioned in 1680; while their mother could well have been one of the adult daughters of Diego López del Castillo.
16. DM, 1696, No. 12; AGN, Mex., Inq., t. 735, f. 275; DM, 1701, No. 4, where she inserts name of "Rodarte."
17. DM, 1697, No. 1.
18. Sp. Arch., I, No. 822.
19. Ibid., II, Nos. 187, 828.
20. Ibid., No. 183a.
21. Bancroft, NMO, 1728.
22. Bur-2, Albuq.
23. B-13, Bern., M. Sec.
24. Sp. Arch., I, No. 864.
25. Ibid., No. 843. Perhaps this Gertrudis was the second wife of old Pedro Durán y Chaves.

José Sánchez and his wife *Teresa Jaramillo*[26] had three known children: *Jacinto II*, who married Efigenia Chaves in 1732;[27] *María Gertrudis*, born on July 20, 1731;[28] and *Juan*,[29] who is in all probability the man of this name who married Barbara Gallegos.[30]

Joaquín Sánchez was thirty years old and widowed of *Manuela Montoya*, who was buried in Santa Fe, when he married *Manuela Francisca Guerrero de la Mora* of Albuquerque, in 1725.[31] His first wife was still living in 1720.[32]

Known children by his second wife were: *María Paula*, born February 2, 1730,[33] who is evidently, but not positively, the one who married Juan Bautista Quintana of Santa Cruz in 1746;[34] and her brother *Francisco*.[35]

Francisco Sánchez and *Josefa de Chaves*[36] had the following children: *Juan Cristóbal*, born September 21, 1726, who married Juana de Chaves, September 24, 1758;[37] *María Barbara*, born December 26, 1730, who married Joaquín Pino in 1763;[38] therefore, presumably, *Teresa*, wife of Mateo José Pino; *Diego Antonio*, who married Ana María Álvarez del Castillo, April 6, 1756;[39] *Marcos*, husband of Margarita Valdés;[40] and *Joaquín*, who married Ana María Padilla in 1769.[41]

---

26. Ibid., II, No. 460.
27. M-3, Albuq., Sept. 28; Sp. Arch., II, No. 460.
28. B-2, Albuq.
29. AGN, Tierras, leg. 426, III, ff. 7-11.
30. B-3, Albuq., bapt. of girl, June 12, 1753.
31. DM, 1725, No. 5.
32. Ibid., 1720, No. 1.
33. B-2, Albuq.
34. M-27, Sta. Cruz. GENEALOGY: **María Paula Sánchez**, José María Quintana, María Josefa Quintana, Desiderio Roybal, Romualdo Roybal, Nicolasa Roybal, Fr. A. Chávez.
35. Sp. Arch., I, No. 864.
36. Ibid., II, No 460.
37. B-2 and M-3, Albuq.
38. Ibid. GENEALOGY: **María Barbara Sánchez**, María Catalina Pino, José Enrique Luna, Toribio Luna, María Encarnación Luna, Eugenio Chávez, Fabián Chávez, Fr. A. Chávez.
39. M-11, Isleta.
40. DM, 1763, in Albuq., no number.
41. Ibid., 1769, loc. cit.

SÁNCHEZ
(Others)

JOSÉ SÁNCHEZ, the son of Lucas and a native of Mexico City, was twenty-six years old when he joined the colonists of 1693. He was tall, with a round face, joined eyebrows, and a somewhat flat nose. His wife, *Josefa Gómez de Ribera*, twenty-one, was the daughter of Alonso, and also born in Mexico City; she had an aquiline face and two moles on the left cheek.[1]

Sánchez and his wife were killed with his "father-in-law," Juan Cortés, at Nambé in the Indian insurrection of 1696.[2] His wife, very likely, was an adopted niece of Juan Cortés, whose wife was María de Ribera. It is not known if they left any children.

* * * * * * * *

ISIDRO SÁNCHEZ BAÑALES was a native of Zacatecas, suspected in 1719 of gambling away certain goods stolen from the Governor's Palace in Santa Fe.[3] In 1725, when he married *Teresa Varela (Jaramillo)* at Albuquerque, he declared that he was twenty-six years old, a native of Zacatecas, and that he had been in New Mexico six years. His parents were Alfonso Sánchez Bañales and María Flores Liscano.[4] But he was back in Santa Fe in 1726, soldiering, when he gave his age as twenty-eight.[5] In 1731 he was tried there for wounding a corporal of the garrison.[6] His nickname was "*El Patrón*."[7] "Don Isidro Sánchez died poor at the age of seventy-three" on April 30, 1770.[8]

His known children were: *José Dionisio*, born February 20, 1729,[9] evidently the man of this name who married María Luisa Padilla; *Bernardo*, April 3, 1734;[10] *Monica*, May 7, 1735; *Alberto*, February 2, 1744; *Manuel de Jesús*, December 28, 1744,[11] who married Antonia González in 1766;[12] and *María Petra*, November 27, 1749.[13]

Dionisio Sánchez and *María Luisa Padilla* were married on June 13, 1758.[14] Their known children were: *Domingo,* who married Juana Aragón;¹⁵ *Juana María,* who married Blas María Montaño in 1788; *Juana Victoria,* married to José Baca in 1799; and *María Antonia,* to Diego Antonio Baca in 1776.¹⁶

The last-named girl was kidnapped with some other people in 1777 by savage Indians at "el Paraje de Santo Tomé." The men were killed, and the women captives were later sold to the French. María Antonia was three months with child; with her was her sister-in-law, Dolores Baca, with a seven-year-old son. After being taken to New Orleans, these women were reportedly ransomed by the Spanish Viceroy. In 1781, Dionisio Sánchez and his wife wrote to the City of Mexico inquiring about their long-lost daughter.¹⁷

* * * * * * * *

IGNACIO SÁNCHEZ VERGARA was a younger brother of Fray Mariano José Sánchez Vergara, and living with his friar-brother at Zuñi in 1790. Ignacio was then twenty-three years old and single.¹⁸ By 1801 he was married to *Juana Vibiana Gabriela de Aragón,* and living at Los Bacas.¹⁹ They had a son, *José Manuel Vicente Ferrer,* born March 4, 1807.²⁰

* * * * * * * *

ANTONIO JOSÉ SÁNCHEZ, nicknamed "Chihuahua" for being a native of that city, was married to *María Gertrudis Alderete.* He died in Belén on February 2, 1810.²¹

* * * * * * * *

Bartolomé Sánchez, a native of Queretaro, who married *Catalina Durán* in 1695, was in all likelihood the same man known as *Garduño.* (See *Garduño.*)

Sánchez de Monroy, or *de Mondragón.* (See *Mondragón,* this section.)

---

1. **Sp. Arch.,** II, No. 54c.
2. **Old Santa Fe,** Vol. III, pp. 332-373.
3. **Sp. Arch.,** II, No. 307.
4. **DM,** 1725, No. 1.
5. Ibid., 1728, No. 3.
6. **Sp. Arch.,** II, No. 363c.
7. **AGN,** Mex., Inq., t. 892, f. 1 et seq.
8. **Bur-2, Albuq.**
9. **B-2, Albuq.**
10. Ibid.
11. The three in **B-57, Isleta.**
12. **DM,** 1766, in Albuq., no number. Here, and also when he enlisted in 1799, Manuel gave his father's name as Isidro Sánchez **Bañares de Tagle** (HSNM, Mil. Papers.)
13. **B-57, Isleta.**
14. **M-11, Isleta.**
15. **B-72, Tomé,** bapt. of son, May 10, 1834.
16. The three in **DM,** in Albuq., no numbers.
17. **MNM, Asuntos,** 198, ff. 19-19v.
18. **Sp. Arch.,** II, No. 1092c.
19. **B-54, Tomé,** sponsors, Jul. 22.
20. **B, Laguna** (in Gallup).
21. **B-54, Tomé,** Bur. Sec.

SANDOVAL

JUAN DE DIOS SANDOVAL MARTÍNEZ and his wife *Juana Hernández,* or *Medina,* joined the 1693 colonists with their eighteen-year-old son, *Miguel.*¹ Juan was the son of Jacinto de Sandoval Martínez and Juana de Estrada, both natives of Mexico City. His Hernández wife died in Santa Fe on March 24, 1695, and on May 12 he married *Gertrudis de Herrera,* widow of José Núñez, at Santa Cruz. Juan was then thirty-seven years of age.² He sold some Santa Cruz land in 1710.³ In 1716 he gave Mexico City as his birthplace, his age as sixty, and Santa Cruz as his residence.⁴ He died on March 12, 1735, at the age of seventy-two. A son, *Antonio,* was born to his second wife, March 6, 1701.⁶

Miguel de Dios Sandoval Martínez gave the City of Mexico as his birthplace, his age as twenty in 1699, and thirty-three in 1709.⁷ He was mentioned as a captain in 1714, and was a member of the Conquistadora Confraternity.⁸

He made his last will in 1755. After naming his parents, he declared that he had been married to *Lucía Gómez* (Robledo) for fifty-eight years and two months; then he named their eight children: *Manuel, Juana* (both dead), *Melchor, Andrés, Antonio, Juan Manuel, Miguel,* and *Felipe* (the last two dead).[9] His widow, a sister-in-law of Ignacio de Roybal, died three years later, when her estate was probated in 1758; here she named some of her children and grandchildren.[10] The first girl, Juana, had been born on July 29, 1700.[11] The only living girl, Melchora, married Alonso Rael de Aguilar in 1729.

Andrés Sandoval married *María Márquez,* December 25, 1729.[12] They had at least two children: *María Ignacia,* August 10, 1751, and *José Miguel,* May 17, 1753.[13]

Antonio Sandoval married *Josefa Chaves,* June 29, 1728.[14] Four children born in Santa Fe were: *Vicente,* April 9, 1752; *José Isidro,* May 22, 1754; *Francisco Matías,* March 5, 1756; and *José Antonio,* December 25, 1757.[15]

Juan Manuel Sandoval married *Josefa Rael de Aguilar,* May 10, 1733.[16] Their known children were: *Juan José Antonio,* July 16, 1750; *Francisco Esteban,* February 22, 1752; *Juan José,* June 30, 1755; and *Antonio José,* July 21, 1758.[17]

Felipe Sandoval married *Teresa Fernández de la Pedrera,* March 29, 1743.[18] They had only one son, *Blas Felipe,*[19] for the father died early, and his widow married Felipe Tafoya in 1750,[20] only seven years after her first marriage. Their son was reared by his cousin and godfather, the Vicar Roybal,[21] and later married a Josefa Baca.[22]

* * * * * * * *

Felipe Rojas de Sandoval was a European Spaniard who came to New Mexico in 1749 or 1750 with some French fur-traders. He had left Spain in 1742, was captured by the British and imprisoned in Jamaica for two years. From there he escaped to Mobile, thence to New Orleans, and from there he joined French trappers in Arkansas who brought him to Santa Fe.[23] On July 13, 1755, he married *María Roybal y Torrado,* widow of José Reaño.[24] They had no children.

---

1. **BNM**, leg. 4, Pt. 1, pp. 790-795.
2. **DM**, 1695, No. 1.
3. **Sp. Arch.**, I, No. 1.
4. **DM**, 1716, No. 13.
5. **Bur-32**, Sta. Cruz.
6. **B-13**, Bern.
7. **DM**, 1699, No. 1; 1709, No. 5.
8. **Sp. Arch.**, I, No. 305; **OLC**, pp. 74-75.
9. Ibid., No. 855.
10. Ibid.
11. **B-13, Bern.**
12. **M-27**, S. Juan.
13. Both in **B, Sta. Fe.**
14. **M-3, Albuq.**
15. All in **B, Sta. Fe.**
16. **M-50**, Sta. Fe.
17. All in **B, Sta. Fe.**
18. **M-50**, Sta. Fe.
19. **Sp. Arch.**, I, No. 995.
20. **M-50**, Sta. Fe.
21. **Sp. Arch.**, I, No. 857.
22. **B**, Sta. Fe, bapt. of son, Juan Manuel, Dec. 24, 1763.
23. Bolton, **Pacific Ocean**, pp. 389-407.
24. **M-50**, Sta. Fe.

SAN JUAN

Miguel de San Juan was born in Guadalupe del Paso, of unknown parentage, and was living in Bernalillo when he married *Isabel Montoya* in 1710.[1] Both were sponsors for the wedding of Antonio Durán y Chaves and Antonia Baca there in 1718.[2] In 1716 Miguel took part in the Moqui campaign of that year.[3] Their daughter, *Margarita de Luna,* married Esteban Durán in 1727.[4]

---

1. **DM**, 1710, No. 9.
2. Ibid., 1718, No. 11.
3. **NMHR**, Vol. VI, No. 2, p. 181.
4. **DM**, 1727, No. 6.

SANTILLANES

JUAN SIMÓN DE SANTILLÁN and his wife, *Barbara Manuela Garicoechea*, were living in the Isleta district as early as 1744 when a son, *Juan José*, was born on April 10.[1] This boy married Juliana González, May 2, 1765.[2]

Another son, *Juan Francisco Loreto*, married María Catalina Aragón, January 2, 1755,[3] and they had a son, Miguel, September 10, 1759.[4] These children used the form "**Santillanes.**"

Juan Santibañes and *María Luisa Ramos* of Abiquiú had two sons: *Joaquín*, March 20, 1741, and *Juan Antonio*, January 20, 1743.[5]

1. B-57, Isleta.
2. M-3, Albuq.
3. Ibid.
4. B-3, Albuq.
5. M-3, Sta. Clara, B. Sec.

SANTISTEBAN

SALVADOR DE SANTISTEBAN was a native of Mexico City, the son of Andrés de Santisteban and Juana de la Concepción. He was sixteen when he married *Polonia Montaño* in Santa Fe, December 20, 1695.[1] In 1710 he gave his age as thirty.[2] He had acquired land on the west bank of the Rio del Norte from Santa Cruz prior to 1714, when he held the rank of *Alférez*.[3] In 1732 he was wounded by accident when a salvo was fired during *Visperas* in the celebration of a feast of Mary in Santa Fe.[4] The wound was not fatal, however, for he and his wife were sponsors the following year.[5]

Two known sons were *Juan* and *José*.

Juan Santisteban was twenty when he married *Juana Cisneros* in 1716.[6] Though married for twenty-four years, they had no children of their own, but reared two adopted ones: *Pedro* and *Juana María*, who married a José de Chaves in Santa Fe in 1756.[7]

José Santisteban married *Josefa Montoya* in 1720; she was the widow of Manuel Silva, who was killed in the Villasur Expedition. José, then twenty-two, was one of the soldiers who survived the massacre.[8]

1. DM, 1695, No. 18; Sp. Arch., II, No. 213.
2. Ibid., 1710, No. 20.
3. Ritch Coll., Box 2, No. 52.
4. Sp. Arch., II, No. 375.
5. M-30, Albuq., Sept. 1, 1733.
6. DM, 1716, No. 2.
7. Sp. Arch., I, No. 856.
8. DM, 1720, No. 4.

SARRACINO

JOSÉ RAFAEL SARRACINO was born in Chihuahua, the son of Mateo Sarracíno and Luisa Bernarda Gutiérrez, both deceased when he married *María Luisa Gutiérrez*, April 10, 1787.[1] In 1790 he gave his age as thirty-eight, and Chihuahua as his birthplace. He was a merchant. His wife was twenty, and they had two sons, three and one years old respectively.[2] José died in September, 1797.[3]

1. M-52, Sta. Fe.
2. Sp. Arch., II, No. 1096a.
3. Bur-49, Sta. Fe.

SAVEDRA

José Salvador Saavedra, the son of Antonio Guillermo Saavedra, deceased, and Rosa López, married *María de la Luz Sedillo* in 1772.[1]

Francisco Saavedra was *Alcalde Mayor* of Laguna in 1821.[2]

Laguna in 1821.[2] It is difficult to say if these were the very first people of this name to come to New Mexico, and their place of origin is not known.

1. **DM**, 1772, in Albuq., no number.
2. **Sp. Arch.**, I, No. 216; II, No. 3081.

SAYAGO
(See *González*)

SEDILLO
(*Cedillo Rico de Rojas*)

PEDRO DE CEDILLO could well have returned to New Mexico with the Reconquest. He was listed as a member of the Conquistadora Confraternity in 1689. His wife, *Isabel López de Gracia*, was alone mentioned as dead in 1692, when a daughter got married; but in 1698 both parents were referred to as deceased when a son got married.

Their known children were: *Isabel*, who married Juan Varela Jaramillo at San Lorenzo del Paso in 1692;[1] *Casilda*, wife of Cristóbal Jaramillo;[2] *Felipa*, married to Francisco Anaya Almazán; and the sons, *Joaquín, Juan,* and *Pedro*. Of this younger Pedro nothing is known except that he was twenty years old in 1694, and worked in the re-building of San Miguel chapel in 1710.[3]

Joaquín Cedillo Rico de Rojas, a native of New Mexico, was twenty-one in 1695 when he married *María Varela* in Santa Fe.[4] They moved down to the Rio Abajo and reared a large family, as follows:

Isabel, born January 13, 1701; *Ana*, August 1, 1702; *Antonio*, October 9, 1704,[5] who married Gregoria González;[6] a second *Isabel*, April 13, 1707; *Domingo Francisco*, August 16, 1709;[7] *Juana*, wife of Carlos López, and then of Francisco García;[8] and *Magdalena*, who married Juan de Dios Martín, and then Antonio Martín in 1734.[9]

Juan Cedillo Rico de Rojas, a native of New Mexico, and twenty-nine years old, married *María de la Concepción Gutiérrez* at Santa Fe in 1698. Both his parents were mentioned as dead.[10] He died prior to 1736, when his widow passed away on October 7, at the age of sixty.[11] A known daughter, *Juana*, married Gregorio Garduño in 1720.[12]

* * * * * * * *

Nicolás Cedillo, a native of Sombrerete, was thirty-eight years of age in 1693.[13] His wife was *Catalina (Jáquez) de Salazar*, also from Sombrerete. Their daughter, *Beatriz*, married Pedro Montes de Oca in 1694.[14] Apparently there were no other children.

1. **DM**, 1692, No. 5.
2. Ibid., 1712, No. 1, mar. of daughter.
3. Ibid., 1694, No. 30; Kubler, pp. 18, 20.
4. Ibid., 1695, No. 16.
5. The three in **B-13, Bern.**
6. **Sp. Arch.**, I, No. 178; **B-2, Albuq.**, bapt. of child, María, Oct. 21, 1731.
7. Both in **B-2, Albuq.**
8. **DM**, 1710, No. 3; **Sp. Arch.**, I, No. 178.
9. Ibid., 1710, No. 7; **B-16, Nambé**, M. Sec.
10. Ibid., 1698, No. 8.
11. **Bur-48, Sta. Fe.**
12. **DM**, 1720, No. 3.
13. Ibid., 1693, No. 10.
14. Ibid., 1694, No. 13; **AASF**, No. 16.

SEGURA

PEDRO DE SEGURA was twenty-two years old in 1694.[1] He was a soldier and a native of Cusiguriachi. His wife was *Simona Bonifacia de Resa*.[2] Pedro was dead in 1728 when a son got married. Two known sons were *Cayetano* and *Tomás*.

Cayetano de Segura was widowed early when *Diega Antonia de la Cruz* died on March 1, 1727.[3] The following year, in April, he married *Francisca Xaviera Lobato*.[4] After her death he married *María de Apodaca*, widow of Lucas Flores, July 25, 1749.[5]

Tomás de Segura married *María Josefa Archuleta* in Santa Fe, August 13, 1730.[6] They had a son, *Simón*, who made his last will in 1764. In it Simón named his wife of eight years' married life, *Margarita Pineda*, and three children: Juana, seven; Julian Cristóbal, five, and Rosa María, one.[7]

1. DM, 1694, No. 33.
2. AGN, Mex., Inq., t. 735, f. 274; t. 758, ff. 468 et seq.
3. Bur-48, Sta. Fe.
4. M-50, Sta. Fe; DM, 1728, No. 6.
5. M-50, Sta. Fe.
6. DM, 1730, no number.
7. Sp. Arch., I, No. 866.

SENA

BERNARDINO DE SENA, a foundling born in the Valley of Mexico, came to New Mexico in 1693 as a boy of nine with his foster-parents, José del Valle and Ana de Ribera. The lad had a round dark face, large eyes, and a thick nose.[1] In 1703 he was still known as Bernardino *del Valle* at Pojoaque where his foster-parents settled.[2] He married *Tomasa Martín González* on February 8, 1705, as "Bernardino de Sena y Valle," when he stated that he had been born in Tezcuco of unknown parentage, and was eighteen years old.[3] However, when he made his last will fifty-three years later, he gave his parents' names as Agustín de Sena and María Ynez de Amparano of Mexico City.[4]

From the time of his marriage until his death, Bernardino lived in Santa Fe, where he acquired considerable property, including the Plaza which now bears his name, and became its most respected citizen.[5] In church matters, he was instrumental in gathering funds for the restoration of San Miguel chapel,[6] was *mayordomo* of the Conquistadora Confraternity through most of his adult life,[7] at the same time serving as handler of money and property for the Franciscans, who mourned the passing of their *Síndico* on November 11, 1765, when he was buried in the ancient chapel of San Miguel.[8] He had asked to be buried in San Miguel, and vested in the Franciscan habit. His first wife, Tomasa Martín González ("*nuestra síndica*," the friars wrote), had been buried in the Conquistadora chapel on February 20, 1727.[9]

Bernardino made his will in July, 1758, but lived to add a codicil on November 10, 1765. In it he declared that he had been married twenty years to Tomasa González, by whom he had only one son, *Tomás Antonio*, who was married to Luisa García. He also mentioned a daughter, *María Francisca*, but it is not clear if she was a real daughter or an adopted one.[10]

His second wife was *Manuela de Roybal*, married to him for twenty-nine years, but without issue. However, they had reared four adopted children: *Santiago, Baltasar, María de los Dolores,* and *José "el Coyote."*[11] His Roybal widow wrote her own will in 1778, and was buried on May 1 of that year in the Conquistadora chapel.[12]

Tomás Antonio de Sena married *María Luisa García de Noriega* in 1723.[13] His profession was that of a blacksmith and armorer,[14] but he also held the post of *Alcalde Mayor* of Galisteo,[15] and continued in his father's footsteps as a pillar of the church.[16] In 1763 he and two others registered a mine of "*N. S. de los Dolores*" south of the hill called "Turquoise."[17]

He and María Luisa had a family of fourteen, according to his last will, the year of which is illegible.[18] These were named as follows: *María Ynez, María Ynez (II), María Yrene, Francisco de Paula, Bernardo, María Rosa, María Ynez de la Encarnación* (all seven dead when the will was made), *Graciana Prudencia, Vicente, Pablo Antonio, José María, Matías David, Francisco,* and *Gertrudis* (these seven living and married).[19]

María Luísa García de Noriega died on July 3, 1767; Tomás de Sena, widower, died on February 11, 1781.[20] Of the girls, *María Ynez de la Encarnación* had married Bartolomé Lobato, October 31, 1749;[21] *Graciana Prudencia* was the wife of Antonio de Ribera.[22]

Bernardo Sena (also called "Bernardino") was reared by his grandfather and namesake.[23] He married *Polonia Casados* on April 10, 1752, and both were sponsors for José Manuel Ribera, child of his sister Graciana Prudencia.[24] He was dead by 1765, leaving only one child, *María*.[25]

Vicente Sena married *María Teresa Vitón*, June 22, 1751.[26] He was also a blacksmith in Santa Fe, when he wounded a soldier in his shop in 1764, and consequently was banished with his family to the Rio Abajo (Bernalillo) area.[27] There a daughter, *Margarita Antonia*, married Tomás de Luna, September 16, 1773.[28] A son, Pablo, was twenty-five when he enlisted as a soldier in 1779.[28a]

Francisco Sena, born December 17, 1750, is very likely the man of this name who married *Manuela Olguín*, April 2, 1771.[29]

Pablo Antonio Sena was also, perhaps, the Pablo Sena who married *María Antonia Esquivel*, July 7, 1772.[30]

---

1. **Sp. Arch.,** II, No. 54c; **BNM,** leg. 4, Pt. 1, pp. 830-834.
2. **AASF,** No. 15.
3. **DM,** 1705, No. 12.
4. **Sp. Arch.,** I, No. 860.
5. **Ibid.,** Nos. 825, 826, 836, 837, 840, 846, 1136.
6. Kubler, pp. 11, 19.
7. **OLC,** pp. 39, 59, 73-77; **El Palacio,** Vol. 54, No. 10, pp. 303-305.
8. **Bur-48,** Sta. Fe; Crespo, par. 294. Church activities are referred to in his will.
9. **Ibid.**
10. **Sp. Arch.,** I, No. 860.
11. **Ibid**
12. **Bur-48,** Sta. Fe; **Sp. Arch.,** I, No. 800.
13. **DM,** 1723, No. 2.
14. **Sp. Arch.,** II, No. 373; **Bancroft, NMO,** 1732 and 1757.
15. **Bancroft, NMO,** 1763; Bolton, **Pacific Ocean,** pp. 389-407.
16. **Twit. Coll.,** Nos. 291, 297; **BNM,** leg. 10, No. 43, **Santa Fe.**
17. **Sp. Arch.,** I, No. 865.
18. Not later than 1767, as his wife is still living.
19. **Twit. Coll.,** No. 291.
20. **Bur-48,** Sta. Fe.
21. **M-50,** Sta. Fe.
22. GENEALOGY: **Graciana Prudencia Sena,** Manuel Ribera, María Guadalupe Ribera, María Dolores Alarid, Romualdo Roybal, Nicolasa Roybal, Fr. A. Chávez.
23. **Sp. Arch.,** II, No. 597.
24. **M-50,** Sta. Fe; **B-62,** Sta. Fe, June 29, 1756.
25. **Sp. Arch.,** loc. cit.
26. **M-50,** Sta. Fe.
27. **Sp. Arch.,** II, No. 579.
28. **M-23,** S. Felipe (Pueblo).
28a. **HSNM,** Mil. Papers.
29. **B-62** and **M-50,** Sta. Fe.
30. **M-50,** Sta. Fe.

SENTENO

Leonisio José Senteno, a native of Queretaro, was the son of José Mateo Senteno and Ignacia Rosalia Dávila. He had been reared by Fray Manuel Vivero in New Spain since the age of eleven, and had come to Albuquerque two years prior to 1761, when he married *Antonia Varela*.[1]

---

1. **DM,** 1761, in Albuq., no number.

SERNA

FELIPE DE LA SERNA and his wife *Isabel Luján* evidently returned with the Reconquest, since they are not mentioned as deceased in the marriages of two children in 1694 and 1698.

Their known children were: *Cristóbal, Gregoria, Antonia,* and, perhaps, *María*, wife of Captain Nicolás García residing at Guadalupe del Paso in 1705.[1] Antonia was married to Matías Madrid,[2] and both were marriage sponsors for Gregoria when she married Lázaro Durán in 1698.[3]

Cristóbal de la Serna married *Josefa Madrid* at Guadalupe del Paso in 1694.[4] He led an expedition against the Navajo as a captain in 1716.[5] In 1748 he applied for a land grant in the valley of Taos.[6] A daughter, *María*, married Nicolás Jacinto Martín at Santa Cruz, December 25, 1712.[7]

1. DM, 1705, No. 8.
2. Relationships, Ibid., 1709, No. 9.
3. Ibid., 1698, No. 10.
4. Ibid., 1694, No. 11.
5. Bancroft, NMO, 1745.
6. Sp. Arch., I, No. 240.
7. DM, 1712, No. 4.

SIERRA

Nicolás Antonio de la Sierra was a European Spaniard, fifty-eight years old in 1768.[1] In 1743, January 24, he had married *Joaquina de Aganza* at Guadalupe del Paso,[2] but by 1766 he was residing in Santa Fe as a merchant.[3]

Francisco Sierra and his wife *Juana Pacheco* were living in the Santa Clara (Chama) area in 1787, when their son, *José Antonio*, married Matilde Vigil.[4] No connection has been found between Francisco and Nicolas Antonio.

1. Sp. Arch., II, No. 640.
2. M, Guadalupe del Paso (Juárez).
3. Sp. Arch., II, No. 619.
4. DM, 1787, no number.

SILVA

ANTONIO DE SILVA, the son of Salvador, was a twenty-three-year-old native of Querétaro who joined the colonists of 1693. He had a round dark face, large eyes, and a sharp nose. His wife, *Gregoria Ruiz*, the daughter of Juan, and born in Mexico City, was twenty-two, with a broad and pockmarked face. Antonio was a blacksmith by trade. They brought a daughter, *Gertrudis*, three years old, born in Mexico City; she had a round face, big eyes, and a small nose.[1]

Antonio first settled in Santa Cruz, where he received a grant of land, and also bought additional property between Santa Cruz and Chimayó.[2] But at the turn of the century he moved down to Bernalillo and thence to Albuquerque, where he died on May 25, 1732. His widow followed on December 8, 1736.[3]

Their known children were as follows: *Gertrudis*, who came with them from New Spain, married Geronimo Jaramillo. *Manuel* married Josefa Montoya.[4] *Francisco* married Gertrudis D. y Chaves. *Felipe*, born May 13, 1704,[5] married Juana Gallegos. *María* was born on August 10, 1706. *Francisca Xaviera*, born on February 2, 1710,[6] married Bernardo Vallejo in 1725.[7] *Micaela* married Antonio Vallejo in 1718.[8] *José* married Rosa Baca, and

Juana became the first wife of Diego Antonio D. y Chaves.⁹

Francisco Silva married *Rosa (Gertrudis) Durán y Chaves* on September 12, 1729.¹⁰ She died on April 17, 1763, at the age of forty-three.¹¹

Their known children were: *Juan Francisco*, born September 10, 1731; *María Barbara*, January 14, 1734; *Juan*, January 6, 1736,¹² who married Ana Lucero in 1769;¹³ *María Agustina*, September 9, 1739,¹⁴ who married Pedro Tafoya;¹⁵ *María Victoria*, January 2, 1749; and *Ana María*, who married Mariano Lucero in 1776.¹⁶

Felipe Silva and *Juana Gallegos* had two known daughters: *María Rosa*, who married Anastacio García in 1762, and *Juana*, who became the wife of Manuel Baca in 1768.¹⁷

José Silva is mentioned in 1727 as the brother-in-law of Antonio Vallejo, husband of Micaela Silva.¹⁸ His wife, *Rosa Baca*, died in this same year on June 9.¹⁹ He was mentioned again years later as a brother of Gertrudis Silva, and as the father (grandfather?) of a María Jaramillo who married Marcos Baca.²⁰ A son of his, *José Manuel*, widowed of *Febronia Baca*, married María Leonarda Salazar at Belén in 1781.²¹

* * * * * * * *

JOSÉ SILVA, a native of Zacatecas, the son of Francisco Silva and Gertrudis Cifuentes, came to New Mexico in the last quarter of the century, and in 1787 married *María Josefa Baca*.²²

---

1. **Sp. Arch.,** II, No. 54c; **BNM,** leg. 4, Pt. 1, pp. 790-795.
2. **Sp. Arch.,** I, Nos. 819, 820.
3. **Bur-2, Albuq.**
4. **DM,** 1717, No. 3.
5. **B-13, Bern.**
6. Both in **B-2, Albuq.**
7. **DM,** 1725, No. 2.
8. Ibid., 1718, No. 7.
9. GENEALOGY: **Juana Silva,** María Guadalupe D. y Chávez, María Isabel Armijo, María Rita Torres, José Chávez, Eugenio Chávez, Fabián Chávez, Fr. A. Chávez.
10. **M-3, Albuq.**
11. **Bur-2, Albuq.**
12. The three in **B-2, Albuq.**
13. **DM,** 1769, in Albuq., no number.
14. GENEALOGY: **Agustina Silva,** Lugarda Tafoya, Pablo Baca, Tomás Baca, Nicanora Baca, Fabián Chávez, Fr. A. Chávez.
15. The three in **B-57, Isleta.**
16. **DM,** 1776, in Albuq., no number.
17. **Ibid.**
18. **Sp. Arch.,** I, No. 82.
19. **Bur-2, Albuq.**
20. **DM,** 1766, in Albuq., no number.
21. **Ibid., 1781, loc. cit.**
22. **Ibid., 1787, loc. cit.**

SISNEROS
(Cisneros)

ANTONIO CISNEROS returned in 1693 with his wife *Josefa Luján* and their family. He was *Alcalde Mayor* of Zuñi in 1706, when he was mortally wounded by Apaches, given the last Sacraments by the Padre, and buried there on August 9.¹ His wife appears to have been at least a half-sister to María Luján (Ruiz Cáceres), wife of her brother-in-law Sebastián Martín.²

Their three children were named in 1727 as follows: *Hermenegildo, Felipe Neri* (sometimes written "*Nereo*"), and *Juana*.³ Felipe was married to María del Castillo in 1728.⁴ Juana had married Juan de Santisteban in 1716.

Other early Cisneros individuals were four Griego brothers and sisters, *Nicolás, Josefa, María,* and *Pedro,* who brought suit against Josefa Luján in 1712 for Griego property on which she lived with four of her own children.⁵ As may be gathered from their respective weddings, they were illegitimates of the Griego family reared in the Cisneros household.

Nicolás Cisneros, parents unknown, mar-

---

1. **Bur-48, Zuñi.**
2. **Sp. Arch.,** I, No. 173.
3. **Ibid.**
4. **Ibid.,** II, No. 355.
5. **Ibid.,** I, No. 301.

ried Casilda Mestas on May 29, 1714,⁶ and died at the age of sixty on January 18, 1752.⁷

Pedro Cisneros, parents unknown, married Juana Mestas, July 7, 1714.⁸

María Cisneros was the wife of Matías Pacheco.⁹

6. **M-24, S. Ild.**
7. **B-16, Nambé,** Bur. Sec.
8. **M-24, S. Ild.**
9. **DM,** 1728, No. 2.

SOLANO

Antonio Solano y Castro married *María Rosa Jirón*, May 20, 1763.¹ But his place of origin is not known.

Andrés Solano, twenty-six years old, lived in Santa Fe in 1790 with his wife *Feliciana Valdés,* who was twenty-one. They had a one-year-old daughter.²

1. **M-50, Sta. Fe.**
2. **Sp. Arch.,** II. No. 1096a.

SUÁREZ

FRANCISCO SUÁREZ CATALÁN, a native of Puerto de Santa María in Spain, came to New Mexico in February, 1771, from Chihuahua, where he had lived for about thirteen years. On June 24 he married *Gertrudis Durán,* daughter of Juan Duran, European, and Barbara Baca.¹ When entering this marriage in the record the Padre made her a "Durán y Chaves"—a patent error.²

The couple resided at Pajarito where a son, *José Ramón,* was born on January 20, 1779.³ A daughter, *María Antonia Rafaela,* married José Miguel Guerrero in 1798.⁴ In these two instances the second name of "Catalán" was not used.

1. **DM,** 1771, no number.
2. **M-11,** Isleta.
3. **B,** Laguna (in Gallup).
4. **DM,** 1798, no number.

SUAZO

LUIS SUAZO was born at Guadalupe del Paso, the natural son of Diego de Padilla while the latter was still a bachelor. Luis was reared in the Padilla home, and was more than twenty-five years old in 1736.¹ He was a widower, but his first wife's name was not given, when he married *Josefa Martín* at El Embudo, October 2, 1734.²

A known son, *Juan Antonio,* was born on June 30, 1735.³

1. **Sp. Arch.,** I, No. 685.
2. **M-27, S. Juan.**
3. **B-27, S. Juan.**

TAFOYA
(Tafoya Altamirano)

JUAN DE TAFOYA ALTAMIRANO and his wife *Felipa Jaguada de Ulloa* very likely did not come north from Mexico City, or, if they did, stayed at Guadalupe del Paso. But three sons of theirs, *Juan, Cristóbal*, and *Antonio*, did come up to New Mexico after the Reconquest.

Juan de Tafoya Altamirano was born at El Real de Talpujagua. Sometime before or after the Reconquest he married *Josefa Pacheco*, widow of José Baca; she died prior to 1707.[1] At this period he was in trouble with the civil authorities, charged with stealing oxen, defrauding his step-daughter, wife of Nicolás Ortiz II, and cheating the Indians.[2] In 1715 he got permission to leave his home at Santa Cruz and visit in Nueva Vizcaya.[3]

He had an illegitimate son, *Cristóbal*, who is most likely the youth of this name, of unknown parentage, who married María Trujillo at Santa Cruz in 1719.[4]

Cristóbal de Tafoya Altamirano, thirty-four years old, left Guadalupe del Paso for New Mexico with his brother Antonio early in 1695. Both were soldiers.[5] He, too, was born at El Real de Talpujagua, but gave his age as twenty-five when he married *Isabel de Herrera* in 1698.[6] The year before he had become involved with some Herrera sisters in Santa Fe, who appear to be a different family from the one into which he married.[7] He also was in escapades with his brother Juan in 1707 and 1711.[8]

In 1718 he made his last will at Santa Cruz, in which he named his parents and birthplace. He declared two legitimate children by Isabel de Herrera: *Juan* and *Antonio*; and also two natural daughters: *Antonia Tafoya Jaramillo*, wife of Sebastián Varela, and *Gertrudis Tafoya Ruiz*. He also had reared a nephew, Cristóbal, a son of his brother Antonio.[9] He was still living in the following year, when he brought suit against Diego Archuleta for beating his wife Isabel.[10]

His two sons married into the Juan González Bas family of Alameda. *Juan*, age twenty-two, married Antonia González in 1716,[11] and *Antonio*, born on May 16, 1700, married her sister Prudencia in 1722.[12]

Antonio de Tafoya Altamirano was twenty-three when he came to Santa Fe in 1695 with his brother Cristóbal. He married *María Luisa Godines*, young widow of Alonso Garcia de Noriega II.[13] Luisa died on September 15, 1747, and Antonio died as a retired *Alférez* on February 17, 1753, "more than eighty years old." At the time of his death he was married to a certain Magdalena ———.[14] On one of his trips north from Guadalupe del Paso, Antonio was entrusted with the dues of the Conquistadora Confraternity sent up to Santa Fe.[15]

A son of Antonio, *Cristóbal*, had been reared in his brother's house, as previously stated. Another, *Felipe*, came to be *Alcalde Mayor* of Santa Fe and Lieutenant General of the Kingdom; he was a charter officer of the Confraternity of Our Lady of Light; in 1728 he had married Margarita (Sayago) González de la Rosa, by whom he had five children, and then Teresa Fernández in 1750, who bore him six more. Felipe made his last will in 1771, and died on May 31 of that year. He had also practiced medicine.[16]

Three daughters of Antonio were mentioned in 1732: *Lugarda*, widow of Juan "Gal-

---

1. Sp. Arch., II, No. 134b; DM, 1708, No. 3.
2. Ibid., Nos. 134b, 171.
3. Ibid., No. 183a.
4. DM, 1708, No. 3; 1719, No. 9.
5. Ibid., 1694, No. 18.
6. Ibid., 1698, No. 6.
7. Sp. Arch., II, Nos. 67, 68.
8. Ibid., II, No. 134b; DM, 1711, No. 7; BNM, leg. 6, No. 11.
9. Sp. Arch., I, No. 938.
10. Ibid., II, No. 298.
11. DM, 1716, No. 19.
12. M-24, S. Ild., B. Sec.; DM, 1722, No. 3.
13. Sp. Arch., I, No. 305.
14. Bur-48, Sta. Fe.
15. OLC, p. 70.
16. M-50, Sta. Fe; Sp. Arch., II, No. 579; ibid., I, No. 995; Bur-48, Sta. Fe; NMHR, Vol. X, No. 3, p. 187.

lego" [Sayago] of Santa Fe, more than thirty years old;[17] *María Rosa*, twenty-five and still single; and *Juana*, twenty-two, married to Agustín Lobato, soldier of Santa Fe.[18] María Rosa is most likely the woman who married Diego Vásquez Borrego.

---

17. If **Pedro Tafoya**, who married Agustina Silva, can be proved to be a son of **Lugarda**, as he seems to be, then a genealogical line would be established as follows: **Lugarda Tafoya**, Pedro Tafoya, María Lugarda Tafoya, Pablo Baca, Tomás Baca, Nicanora Baca, Fabián Chávez, Fr. A. Chávez. Consequently, another line would also be made into the **Godines** family.
18. **AGN, Mex., Inq.,** t. 862, ff. 186-195.

TAMARIS

FRANCISCO TAMARIS, *alias García Carnero*, was a native of El Valle de San Bartolomé who had been soldiering in New Mexico for twenty-three years, so he declared in 1715.[1] He married *Isabel Gutiérrez*, one of the colonists who came in 1693, very possibly at Guadalupe del Paso.[2] They were sponsors together in 1694.[3] In December of 1715, Francisco, at the time a sergeant of the Santa Fe Presidio, was mortally wounded by Alonso Rael de Aguilar. Tamaris' wife and their son, *Felipe*, pardoned Rael at the victim's deathbed request.[4] Besides Felipe, there was a daughter, *Josefa*.[5]

Felipe de Tamaris followed in his father's footsteps as a soldier.[6] He was one of the few survivors of the Villasur Expedition.[7] His wife was *Magdalena Baca*,[8] by whom he had a daughter, *Rosa Teresa*, born on September 8, 1709, and a son, *Pedro*, August 8, 1711,[9] who died as a youth on June 18, 1729.[10]

---

1. Sp. Arch., II, No. 239j.
2. AGN, Mex., Inq., t. 701, ff. 323-9.
3. DM, 1694, Nos. 4, 10.
4. Sp. Arch., II, No. 239j.
5. Ibid., I, No. 936.
6. Ibid.; Bancroft, NMO, 1732.
7. Ibid., No. 13.
8. Ibid., No. 953.
9. Both in M-24, S. Ild.
10. Bur-48, Sta. Fe.

TAPIA

FRANCISCO DE TAPIA, son of Francisco de Tapia and María de Chaves, returned to Santa Fe with the Reconquest, and in 1698 married *María Magdalena Nieto*.[1] He went on the Moqui Campaign of 1716.[2]

Some women of the Tapia family also returned with their husbands, several named "María," so that it is impossible to classify them. One sister of Francisco, *Luisa*, had married Antonio Ramírez de Gamboa at Guadalupe del Paso in 1685.[3] Another, *María*, was the wife of Miguel Gutiérrez of San Luis Potosí.[4] Any of the following Tapias could be Francisco's sons and grandsons.

Tomás Tapia received a land grant in 1742, and was living at Pojoaque in 1751.[5]

Antonio Tapia is mentioned in 1751.[6]

Cristóbal Tapia was a resident of Santa Fe in 1764.[7]

* * * * * * * *

JOSÉ CRISTINO TAPIA was an *Alférez*, only eighteen years old, who came to Santa Fe and enlisted in 1807. He was born at the Presidio of Janos in Nueva Vizcaya, the son of José Tapia and Manuela Garcia.[8] Like José Ramón Bernal, Manuel Telles, and members of the Garcia de Noriega family, he was, apparently, a descendant of seventeenth century New Mexicans returning to his homeland.

---

1. DM, 1698, No. 4.
2. NMHR, Vol. VI, No. 2, p. 181.
3. DM, 1685, No. 1.
4. AGN, Mex., Inq., t. 735, f. 299.
5. Sp. Arch., I, Nos. 962, 241.
6. Ibid., II, No. 508.
7. Ibid., I, No. 989.
8. HSNM, Mil. Papers.

TELLES
(Telles Jirón)

This seventeenth-century family stayed at Guadalupe del Paso, except for some married women who returned with their husbands for the Reconquest of 1693. The name re-appeared at the turn of the eighteenth century in the Rio Abajo and Socorro area, which shows that individuals, descended from this family, eventually moved north. For example:

José Manuel Telles, son of José Luis Telles and Guadalupe Garcia de Noriega, and born in Guadalupe del Paso, came to Santa Fe when eighteen years old and enlisted as a soldier in 1823.[1]

---

1. **HSNM**, Mil. Papers.

TENORIO
(Tenorio de Alba)

MIGUEL TENORIO DE ALBA was a native of Zacatecas, twenty-one or twenty-two years old in Reconquest times.[1] He first settled in the newly-founded town of Santa Cruz in 1696.[2] He was already married in 1708 to *Agustina Romero*,[3] and was a member of the Confraternity of La Conquistadora.[4]

Their children were: *Manuel*, married to Francisca de la Vega y Coca; *Juan*, presumably a son, who married Margarita Coca, October 23, 1728; *Miguel* II, husband of Barbara Tafoya; *Francisca*, who married Cristóbal de Armenta in April, 1735; and *Luisa*, wife of Bartolomé Fernández de la Pedrera, May 8, 1740.[5]

Manuel Tenorio de Alba was a captain and *Alcalde Mayor* of Pecos in 1732.[6] He was mentioned as the son of Miguel Tenorio and husband of *Francisca de la Vega y Coca* in 1758.[7] His wife died on August 6, 1760.[8]

Known children of theirs were: *Teresa*, who enlarged the family name to "Tenorio de Alba y Corona" when she married Joaquín Martínez, October 20, 1749;[9] *Miguel* III;[9a] *Alejandro*, residing in Sonora in 1777; and *Teodora Mariquita*.[10]

His son Alejandro had two sons, Miguel and Manuel, the latter married and residing in Valle de San Buenaventura in New Spain in 1783.[11]

Miguel Tenorio II and *Barbara Tafoya* had the following children: *Joaquina*, April 24, 1748; *Juana Nepomucena*, April 27, 1751; *Salvador de Orta*, March 23, 1757;[12] and *José Miguel*, these two sons enlisting as soldiers in 1779 and 1781, respectively.[12a]

He seems to be the same Miguel Tenorio de Alba y Corona who married *Teodora Fernández de la Pedrera* in 1758.[13] She was the widow of Nicolás Baca of La Cienega, where the Tenorios were after Vega y Coca, Baca, and Romero property.[14] He was already dead in 1794 when Teodora, his widow of a *second* marriage, died on January 26.[15]

---

1. **DM**, 1695, No. 12; 1696, No. 7.
2. **Sp. Arch.**, I, No. 817.
3. **Ibid.**
4. **OLC**, p. 75.
5. All in **B**, Sta. Fe.
6. **Bancroft**, NMO, 1732.
7. **Sp. Arch.**, I, Nos. 440, 652.
8. **Bur-48**, Sta. Fe.
9. **M-50**, Sta. Fe.
9a. Their son Miguel was forty when he enlisted as a soldier in 1771 (**HSNM**, Mil. Papers).
10. These three together in **Sp. Arch.**, I, No. 1003.
11. **Ibid.**
12. All in **B**, Sta. Fe.
13. **M-50**, Sta. Fe.
14. **Sp. Arch.**, I, Nos. 109, 440, 991, 1003.
15. **Bur-48**, Sta. Fe.

Miguel Tenorio III, husband of *Polonia Romero*, was very likely the son of Manuel Tenorio and Francisca de la Vega y Coca; or else he was the other Miguel, a cousin, the son of Alejandro Tenorio. He had a sister, *Ana María*, sixty years old in 1803, who was the mother of José Antonio Alarí,[16] and therefore the second wife of Juan Bautista Alarí. This Miguel died on March 27, 1818.[17]

Manuel Tenorio de Alba y Corona, who married a *Polonia Sandoval*, July 26, 1757,[18] could have been the son of any of the three original brothers.

16. Sp. Arch., II, No. 1661.
17. Bur-51, Castrense.
18. M-50, Sta. Fe.

TERRUS

JOSÉ TERRUS was a native of Vique in Cataluña.[1] He married *Antonia Páez Hurtado* on March 21, 1734.[2] He died on May 25, 1745, and she followed years later, on September 19, 1760.[3] In the will that he drew up in 1745, Terrus named five small children: *Antonio Feliz, Rosa, Teodora, Juan Antonio,* and *Manuel Francisco*.[4]

1. AGN, Mex., Inq., t. 849, f. 55.
2. M-50, Sta. Fe.
3. Bur-48, Sta. Fe.
4. Sp. Arch., I, No. 966.

TOLEDO

Juan José Toledo was dead in 1794 when his son, *Pablo Vicente*, by his wife, *Micaela García*, married María Gertrudis Romero of Tomé, on September 12.[1] The family's origin is not known.

1. B-54, Tomé, M. Sec.

TORRES

CRISTÓBAL DE TORRES, a native of New Mexico, gave his age as thirty in 1698, and forty-four or forty-five in 1710.[1] Hence, he was not the forty-year-old man who passed muster in 1680, but evidently his son. His wife was *Angela de Leyva*, according to his last will and the marriages of their children. He was a soldier, and married, at Guadalupe del Paso in 1698, but by 1710 he was an *Alférez* residing in Albuquerque.[2] But some years later he established himself at Santa Cruz. In 1724 he was given a large grant near the "Old Pueblo" of Chama.[3] He was accused in 1726 of reporting to Juan Páez Hurtado the names of poor people who were trading illegally with non-Pueblo Indians.[4] In this year he made his last will, declaring his wife and the following children: *Diego, Francisca, María, Josefa,* and *Margarita*. The following year, 1727, his widow made her own will in Chama, naming the same children.[5]

Francisca married Felix Lujan and was murdered by him in 1713;[6] *María* married Antonio de Salazar in 1708;[7] *Josefa* was the wife of a certain Martín by whom she had a son, Manuel Martín;[8] and *Margarita* became the wife of Bartolomé Trujillo.[9]

Diego de Torres, son of the late *Cristóbal de Torres*, was numbered among the first settlers of Chama as a village in 1731.[10] He gave his age as thirty-nine in this year as assistant *Alcalde* of Santa Clara.[11] He was already widowed of *Rosa de Varela* when he married again in 1712.[12] Two elder sons of his seem to be the issue of his first marriage: *Salvador*, married to Catalina Naranjo,[13] and his brother *Marcial*, who was married twice, to María Lujan and María Martin, by whom he had several children.[14]

Diego's second wife was a *María Martin* of Santa Cruz, daughter of Alejo Martín and María de la Rocha, the latter a native of Sonora.[15] They had at least eight children: *Francisca Xaviera*, wife of Isidro Trujillo;[16] *Martín*, who was twenty-five when he enlisted as a soldier in 1751;[16a] *Manuel*, who married Tomasa Baca, December 12, 1758;[17] *Juan*, who married Rita Romero, January 14, 1766;[18] *Nicolás*, baptized on December 6, 1731, by Vicar Roybal of Santa Fe,[19] and who married Francisca Padilla in 1763;[20] *Bartolome*, born June 27, 1735; and twins, *Juan José* and *Juana*, June 1, 1738.[21]

Diego was married a third time, to *Rafaela Baca* of the Rio Abajo, who bore him six children and, after his death prior to 1758,[22] became the wife of Baltasar Baca. In her will, in 1804, Rafaela stated that one child died single, two died married, and that her three surviving Torres heirs were: *Lugarda*, *Barbara*, and *Catalina*.[23] Some of these children are found in records as follows: *Juana Catalina Romana*, born August 22, 1744, who married Gregorio Varela, May 6, 1759;[24] *María Josefa de la Luz*, born March 20, 1747; *Lugarda Clementa*, November 30, 1749; *Tomás*, November 2, 1755; and *Antonio Germán*, June 11, 1758,[25] who married Margarita D. y Chaves, August 1, 1782.[26]

Altogether different Torres people of the Rio Abajo district are as follows:

* * * * * * * *

JUAN DE TORRES was a native of Zacatecas and twenty-seven or twenty-eight years old in 1694.[27] He was living in Albuquerque in 1710 when he gave his age as fifty and mentioned his connections in Sombrerete.[28] He appears to be the *Teniente* Juan Torres who was reprimanded by Gov. Valverde for disrespect towards a friar.[29]

* * * * * * * *

SIMÓN DE TORRES, a native of Sombrerete, perhaps related to the preceding man, was thirty years old in 1696.[30] He and his wife, *Juana de Mendoza*, were dead by 1705. An orphan child of theirs, *María de las Nieves*, was thirteen years old in that year.[31]

* * * * * * * *

ANTONIO DE LA TORRE, a native of Jerez, the son of Sebastián de la Torre and Ana del Rio, asked to marry Francisca Montoya in 1694, but was rejected because of an alleged impediment in New Spain.[32] He was staying at San Felipe Pueblo with other suspect bachelors when a morals complaint was made against them.[33]

---

1. **DM**, 1698, No. 3; 1710, Nos. 20, 21.
2. **Ibid.**
3. **Twit. Coll.**, No. 108.
4. **Ocaranza**, p. 188.
5. **Sp. Arch.**, I, No. 948; **Twit. Coll.**, No. 151.
6. **Sp. Arch.**, II, No. 196; here she was called "Gómez de Torres," the original full name.
7. **DM**, 1708, No. 1.
8. **Sp. Arch.**, I, No. 1004.
9. **DM**, 1719, No. 7.
10. **Sp. Arch.**, I, No. 950.
11. **Crespo**, pars. 108-10; **Bancroft NMO**, 1731.
12. **DM**, 1712, No. 3.
13. **Sp. Arch.**, I, No. 643.
14. **Ibid.**, No. 987.
15. **DM**, loc. cit.
16. **Ibid.**, 1727, No. 2.
16a. **HSNM**, Mil. Papers.
17. **M-11**, Isleta.
18. **Ibid.**
19. **B-27**, S. Juan. GENEALOGY: **Nicolás Torres**, Andrés Mariano Torres, María Rita Torres, José Chávez, Eugenio Chávez, Fabián Chávez, Fr. A. Chávez.
20. **DM**, 1763, in Albuq., no number; **Sp. Arch.**, II, No. 592a; Nicolás died on March 11, 1811 (**B-54**, Tomé, Bur. Sec.)
21. These three in **B-27**, S. Juan.
22. Marriage of son Manuel, note 17.
23. **Twit. Coll.**, No. 27.
24. **B-57** and **M-11**, Isleta.
25. All four in **B-57**, Isleta.
26. **M-49**, Isleta.
27. **DM**, 1694, No. 25.
28. **Ibid.**, 1710, No. 20; 1711, No. 1.
29. **Ocaranza**, p. 190.
30. **DM**, 1696, No. 1.
31. **Ibid.**, 1705, No. 6.
32. **Ibid.**, 1694, No. 2.
33. **Crusaders**, p. 245.

TREBOL NAVARRO

FRANCISCO TREBOL NAVARRO, origin not known, came to New Mexico after the middle of the century and on October 9, 1765, married *María Ignacia de la Luz Baca*.¹ While first *Teniente* of the Santa Fe Presidio in 1785 he made his last will, in which he stated that he and his wife were married for twenty years, during which time they had five children. He mentioned a ranch which he still owned at Pajarito.² He and Diego Antonio Baca were *Mayordomos* of the Conquistadora Confraternity in 1773.³

The children named in the will were: *José, Manuela, María Luisa, María Francisca* (dead), and *María Isabel*. Francisco died in Rio Arriba, perhaps during a campaign, and was buried in the military chapel of Santa Fe on June 10, 1785; his widow died on October 25, 1790.⁴ He was referred to simply as "Trebol" in 1769,⁵ and also when he got married.

1. M-11, Isleta.
2. Sp. Arch., I, No. 646.
3. OLC, p. 11.
4. Bur-51, Castrense.
5. AGN, Tierras, 426, III, ff. 7-11.

TRONCOSO

VICENTE TRONCOSO was a native of Mexico City, and thirty-eight years old in 1790, when he was second in command of the Santa Fe garrison. He was a nephew of Governor de Anza. His wife, *María Ignacia Bernal*, was twenty-seven, and they had a six-year-old son and four girls, nine, eight, seven, and two.¹ Troncoso was a very active *Mayordomo* of La Conquistadora in his day.²

Known children of theirs were: *Juan Manuel Andrés*, infant of one year who died on December 13, 1780;³ *Nicolasa*, wife of Juan Esteban Pino; and *Guadalupe*, married to Mariano Peña.⁴

1. Twit. Coll., No. 179; AASF, No. 19.
2. OLC, p. 10.
3. Bur-51, Castrense; mother's maiden name given as "Perea."
4. B-65, Sta. Fe, bapt. of respective children, April 12 and March 18, 1812.

TRUJILLO

JUAN DE TRUJILLO and his wife, *Elvira Sánchez Jiménez*, both natives of the Rio Abajo, returned with the Reconquest.¹ He gave his age as forty in 1695, and forty-seven in 1696, always claiming the Rio Abajo as his place of birth.² Hence, he was in all probability the Juan de Trujillo who passed muster in 1681, and the son of old Francisco Trujillo. At the turn of the century he moved from the Albuquerque area to Pojoaque, where he bought considerable property in 1701 and 1702.³ There he gave his age as sixty-six in 1714.⁴

His two known children were *María*, wife of Juan de Mestas Peralta, and *Antonio*, married to Ana María de Córdoba.

Antonio Trujillo and *Ana María de Córdoba* were married at Pojoaque in 1711, his mother having died by this time.⁵ In 1733 he bought the Sandoval Martínez ranch in Pojoaque.⁶ His wife died on March 26, 1753, "sixty years old more or less." Antonio was buried in the old Mission of Nambé on April 19, 1755.⁷

Their known children were: *Cristóbal,* born July 11, 1717; *José,* September 30, 1719;[8] *Miguel,* October 10, 1712,[9] who seems to be the man of this name who married a María Antonia Archuleta;[10] and *Bernarda,* who married Hilario Archuleta, May 3, 1734.[11]

Other early Trujillos follow, perhaps brothers, cousins, nephews, or even sons of Juan de Trujillo, but impossible to classify because sufficient data are not available.

* * * * * * * *

DIEGO TRUJILLO was married to Catalina Griego in 1701 and 1703 when they were trying to recover her ancestral land in Santa Fe. They had a grown son, *Antonio,* at this time.[12] Diego gave his age as twenty-two or twenty-eight, saying that he had been born in the Rio Abajo country.[13]

* * * * * * * *

BALTASAR TRUJILLO resided at Pojoaque in 1710 when he declared himself to be a native of New Mexico and forty years old.[14] He belonged to the Conquistadora Confraternity.[15] He purchased lands in Taos which he sold back to the original owner around the year 1725.[16]

His known children by his wife *Nicolasa de la Cruz Espinosa* were: *María,* born December 29, 1704; and *Pablo Manuel,* January 31, 1709,[17] who married Francisca Marquez at Pojoaque in September, 1728.[18]

As a "widower of Pojoaque," Baltasar married "*Ynez,* widow of Albuquerque," on May 8, 1728.[19] He and this *Ynez González Bas* were sponsors together in 1739.[20] He died at Pojoaque, June 17, 1740.[21]

* * * * * * * *

JUAN TRUJILLO, a native of Santa Fe, was about forty years old, and a widower, in 1725.[22] His first wife could have been a María López with whom he witnessed a marriage at Guadalupe del Paso in 1692.[23] And he might be the Juan Trujillo married to Ana de Herrera, who bore him a son, *Pedro,* February 24, 1716.[24]

He could also be a brother of José Trujillo, treated next, for in 1693 Juan witnessed the wedding of Catalina Durán, daughter of Antonia Trujillo (his sister?);[25] and when this Catalina married again in 1695, José and his wife Antonia Luján were the witnesses.[26]

JOSÉ TRUJILLO, son of Cristóbal Trujillo and María de Manzanares, natives of New Mexico, married *Antonia Luján* at Santa Fe in 1694.[27] He received a special commendation from Vargas for his service during a Navajo campaign in 1697,[28] receiving other citations, and an appointment as *Alcalde* of Santa Cruz, up to the year 1714.[29] In 1715, as a retired *Alférez* and *Alcalde* of Santa Cruz, he appeared in a land suit in which Capt. Baltasar Trujillo is mentioned together with him.[30] His name is on Inscription Rock, dated July, 1726, with that of Juan Páez Hurtado.[30a]

His known children by Antonia Luján were: *Juan Crisóstomo,* born February 9, 1704;[31] *José,* who married Guadalupe Chirinos in 1716; *Bartolomé,* who married Margarita Torres in 1719;[32] *Margarita,* who became the wife of Cristóbal Tafoya in 1719; and *Isidro,* who married Francisca Xaviera Torres in 1727,[33] two of whose children, María and Santiago, were born in 1739 and 1740.[34]

Jose contracted a second marriage with *Antonia López,* natural daughter of Ana María de Herrera, in 1710.[35] Perhaps he is the José Manuel Trujillo, aged mastersmith and "brother" of Carlos López, who was grievously assaulted by some Valverde men in 1748. *Genízaro* servants of his bearing the Trujillo name were also mentioned.[36]

BARTOLOMÉ TRUJILLO, very likely a brother of the two preceding men, was widowed of *María de Archuleta,* and twenty-three years old in 1693, when he married *Petrona Domínguez,* eighteen, at Ysleta del Paso on February 2.[37]

Cristóbal Trujillo, perhaps another brother, remained with his family at Guadalupe del Paso. (See preceding century.)

* * * * * * * *

PASCUAL TRUJILLO and his wife, *Antonia de Tapia (Durán or Luján)*, were sponsors at Santa Fe in 1694.[38] He was a native of New Mexico, thirty years old in 1700.[39] In 1713, he held the rank of sergeant when he sold some land in Santa Cruz.[40] He was killed by Indians in Nueva Vizcaya sometime after, on a return trip from the City of Mexico; in 1715 his widow asked for a soldiers' insurance he had taken out at the Santa Fe garrison. She was living in Pojoaque.[41]

Their known children were *Juan*, who married María Madrid in 1715,[42] and *Andrés*, who married Juana María Sena, widow of Diego de Anaya, in 1730.[43] Another brother could well have been *Antonio*, who married María Sena, another *criada* of Bernardino de Sena, on April 17 of the same year.[44]

* * * * * * * *

MATEO TRUJILLO was a soldier, native of New Mexico, who gave his age as thirty in 1694, forty in 1704, and fifty-four in 1714.[45] He was too young, apparently, to be the Mateo of the 1680-81 Revolt lists, yet might be the same man. In 1694 he received a grant of land south of Santa Clara Pueblo, and in 1703 bought additional property at Santa Fe while soldiering in Santa Fe; he also sold a Santa Fe house and lot in 1722.[46]

In the Indian Uprising of 1696, a corpse found with those of the martyred Padres at San Ildefonso was thought to be his; however, he reached Santa Fe, shoeless and almost naked, after what was termed a miraculous escape.[47] He belonged to the Conquistadora Confraternity.[48]

Mateo's wife was *María de Tapia*, widow of Alonso Romero, by whom he had a daughter, *Juana*, married to Pedro Montes Vigil. There were also two sons: *Francisco*, father of José and Mariano Trujillo, who made his last will in 1754; and *Agustín*, father of Manuela, Manuel, and Antonio Trujillo.[49]

Lázaro Trujillo was most likely the "Lorenzo" who was recalled almost a century later as a nephew of the preceding Mateo Trujillo.[50] He married *Ynez de Tapia (Lucero, Olguín, or García)* on January 25, 1718.[51] Their known children were: *Miguel Manuel*, born October 1, 1731; *Juana María*, February 14, 1734; *Antonio Alonso*, July 16, 1736;[52] *Juan Antonio*, June 26, 1741;[53] and *Matías*, March 3, 1745, his mother dying at his birth.[54]

In this same year, the following August, a Lázaro Trujillo married *María Márquez de Ayala*;[55] it could have been the same man. Their son, *Mariano*, married María Andrea Lucero in 1797.[56]

---

1. **DM**, 1695, No. 14.
2. *Ibid.*, 1695, No. 19; 1696, No. 12.
3. **Sp. Arch.**, I, Nos. 927, 928.
4. **DM**, 1710, No. 15; 1714, No. 7.
5. *Ibid.*, 1711, No. 2.
6. **Sp. Arch.**, I, No. 1227.
7. Both in **Bur-16**, Nambe.
8. Both in **B-18a**, Nambe.
9. **B-33**, Sta. Cruz.
10. **Bur-16**, Nambe, B. Sec., bapt. of child, April 13, 1738, with Antonio Trujillo and Ana María Córdoba as godparents.
11. *Ibid.*, M. Sec. GENEALOGY: **Bernarda Trujillo**, Julio Archuleta, María Ignacia Archuleta, María Josefa Quintana, Desiderio Roybal, Romualdo Roybal, Nicolasa Roybal, Fr. A. Chávez.
12. **Sp. Arch.**, I, Nos. 294, 926, 929.
13. **DM**, 1694, Nos. 5, 7.
14. *Ibid.*, 1710, No. 15.
15. **OLC**, p. 75.
16. **Ritch Coll.**, Box 2, No. 54; **Sp. Arch.**, I, Nos. 309, 750.
17. Both in **M-24**, S. Ild.
18. **DM**, 1727, No. 1; **Sp. Arch.**, I, No. 513.
19. **M-3**, Albuq.
20. **B-16**, Nambe, April 25.
21. *Ibid.*, Bur. Sec.
22. **DM**, 1694, No. 29; 1695, No. 16.
23. *Ibid.*, 1692, No. 4.
24. **M-24**, S. Ild.
25. **DM**, 1693, No. 5.
26. *Ibid.*, 1695, No. 13.
27. *Ibid.*, 1694, No. 17.
28. **Ritch Coll.**, Box 2, No. 35.
29. *Ibid.*, Nos. 41, 42, 47, 49, 50, 53.
30. **Sp. Arch.**, I, No. 7.
30a. **Mesa, Canyon**, etc., p. 475.
31. **M-24**, S. Ild.
32. **DM**, 1716, No. 13; 1719, No. 7.
33. *Ibid.*, 1719, No. 9; 1727, No. 2, and **M-29**, Sta. Cruz, Mar. 7.
34. **B-27**, S. Juan.
35. **DM**, 1710, No. 12.
36. **Sp. Arch.**, II, No. 498.
37. **DM**, 1693, No. 6, incomplete.
38. *Ibid.*, 1694, No. 3.
39. *Ibid.*, 1699, No. 15; 1700, No. 1.
40. **Sp. Arch.**, I, No. 828.
41. *Ibid.*, II, Nos. 239, 234.
42. **DM**, 1715, No. 6.
43. *Ibid.*, 1730, no number; **M-50**, Sta. Fe.
44. **M-50**, Sta. Fe.
45. **DM**, 1694, No. 15; 1704, No. 6; 1714, No. 1.
46. **Sp. Arch.**, I, Nos. 1339, 930, 1033.
47. **Old Santa Fe**, Vol. III, pp. 332-373.
48. **OLC**, p. 72.
49. **Sp. Arch.**, I, Nos. 1002, 930, 1034; II, No. 273.
50. *Ibid.*, No. 1002.
51. **M-16**, Nambé; **DM**, 1717, No. 5.
52. All in **B-16**, Nambé.
53. **B-24**, S. Ild.
54. **B-16**, Nambé.
55. **M-50**, Sta. Fe.
56. **B-17**, Nambé.

Melchor Trujillo gave his age as nineteen in 1695, stating that he was born in Santa Fe.[57] He was reported killed by the Indians at Jemez in 1696.[58]

Antonio Trujillo was killed by Apaches sometime before 1705. His widow was *Ana Durán*.[59]

* * * * * * * *

NICOLÁS MORENO TRUJILLO, the son of Antonio and a native of Tacuba in the Valley of Mexico, was forty when he joined the colonists of 1693 with his grown family. He was graying, with a large forehead and rather deepset eyes. His wife, *María Ruiz de Aguilera*, the daughter of Nicolás and born in Mexico City, was thirty-four, with big eyes and joined eyebrows.

Their children were: *Gertrudis*, fifteen, married to Miguel de Quintana;[60] *José Damián*, seven, who accompanied another married sister, *Estefania*, and her husband José de Atienza; *José Joaquín*, six, also with the Atienzas; *María de Guadalupe*, thirteen, born in Mexico City, with an aquiline face and dark complexion; *Juana Teresa*, also born in Mexico City, having a round face, a rather flat nose, and a scar on the brow; and *Micaela Antonia*, two, a native of Mexico City, with a broad face, small wide nose, and a high forehead.[61]

One of the single girls, Juana Teresa, married Sebastián Luján in 1705.[62] In this same year their father, tired and disappointed in New Mexico, asked to return to Mexico City, and permission was granted because he had come at his own expense.[63] The three married daughters stayed behind with their husbands, although one of the latter, Luján, tried in vain to go along.

---

57. **DM**, 1695, No. 18.
58. **Old Santa Fe,** loc. cit.
59. **DM**, 1705, No. 7.
60. See **Quintana,** genealogy, note 20.

61. **Sp. Arch.,** II, No. 54c.
62. **DM,** 1705, No. 6.
63. **Sp. Arch.,** II, No. 108.

ULIBARRÍ

JUAN DE ULIBARRÍ and his brother ANTONIO came to New Mexico with the Reconquest. Juan was twenty-four in 1694 when he declared that he had been born in San Luis Potosi.[1] In vouching for Juan's brother Antonio in 1727, Fray Antonio Pérez of San Juan Pueblo deposed that the man's name was *"de los Reyes, here Ulibarrí,"* and that he was a native of San Luis de la Paz in the City of Mexico, the son of José Enríquez de los Reyes and María de Ynojos.[2] Juan was a captain and second in command at the Santa Fe garrison in 1704, and also Procurator in 1706.[3] He "liberated" the Picurís Indians from the Apaches in 1706-07, and brought them back from El Cuartelejo to their Pueblo.[4] His wife at this time was *Juana Hurtado*,[5] by whom he seems to have had a son, *Antonio* (see Note 9 below).

By 1711 he was married to *Francisca de Mizquia*, widow of Bernardo Durán y Chaves, who petitioned the Viceroy to release her husband from detention in Mexico City, where he had been summoned, as she claimed, because of the lies and tricks of the Tafoya brothers.[6] Both Juan and his second wife were dead by 1718.[7] His children, if any, by either wife, are not known. An *Antonio Ulibarrí* was mentioned as his son in 1704,[7a] but this might have been his brother, as discussed further on. Juan's name is found carved on Inscription Rock, dated 1701.[8]

ANTONIO DE ULIBARRÍ is once mentioned as the son of Juan.[9] He could well

---

1. **DM,** 1694, No. 24.
2. **Sp. Arch.,** II, No. 343.
3. **AASF,** No. 15.
4. **AGI, Mex., Aud.,** leg. 561, list-title No. 725; **Ritch Coll.,** Box 2, No. 44.
5. **B-13, Bern.,** 1706.

6. **DM,** 1711, No. 7.
7. **Sp. Arch.,** II, No. 294.
7a. **AASF,** No. 16.
8. **Mesa, Canyon,** etc., p. 473.
9. **AASF,** loc. cit.

have been a much younger half- or step-brother. Antonio was married to *María Durán y Chaves* by 1711.¹⁰ From 1714 on he was *Alcalde* of Laguna, Acoma, and Zuñi, where he destroyed *estufas* by order of Gov. Mogollón. He also took part in important campaigns, like those of 1706 and 1716.¹¹ In 1731 he was *Alcalde Mayor* of Santa Fe, and War Captain, when he testified favorably about the missionaries.¹² He and María de Chaves had no children, but reared a girl, Rosa de Armijo, who was suing him for her adopted mother's inheritance.¹³

Antonio married again, but it is not known what children he had by the second wife. He died on November 2, 1762, more than eighty years old; his wife at this time was *Teresa Rael*.¹⁴

10. **DM**, 1711, No. 1.
11. **Bancroft, NMO**, 1714, 1745; **Sp. Arch.**, II, No. 311.
12. Crespo, pars. 233, 254.
13. **Sp. Arch.**, I, No. 236.
14. **Bur-48, Sta. Fe.**

URBÁN

Juan de Urbán lost his wife, *Micaela de Linares*, on January 3, 1728.¹ Their origin is unknown, and if they had any children, are likely ancestors of people by this name.

However, records abound with Urbán people who are descended from Antonio *Urbán* Montaño. (See *Montaño, Lucas*.)

1. **Bur-48, Sta. Fe.**

URIOSTE

Martín de Urioste, an *Alférez*, appeared with María Gómez Robledo as a wedding witness in 1696.¹ But he is not heard of again, and the name does not appear again until the middle of the century.

Juan de Urioste and *Josefa Vargas* had a son, *Juan*, who was twenty-seven when he enlisted as a soldier in 1771.² He is most likely the following man, while Felix and José could be his brothers.

Juan de Urioste and *María Luz Griego* (*Gil Formosa* or *Giltoméy*) had the following children between 1762 and 1778: *Lorenzo*, September 6, 1762; *Juana Rafaela*, November 4, 1765; *José Miguel*, December 18, 1769; *María Josefa*, March 13, 1773; *Juan Bautista*, June 30, 1775; *María Cristina*, November 13, 1776; *María Magdalena*, July 23, 1778; and *Xavier*, June 5, 1785.³

At the same time, **Felix Urioste** and *Josefa Romero* had these children: *María Barbara*, November 11, 1761; *María Antonia*, May 7, 1766; *Antonio Felix*, June 4, 1773; *María Concepción*, December 12, 1775;⁴ and *José Antonio*, who was nineteen when he enlisted in 1779.⁵

In the same period, **José Urioste** and *Juana Crespín* had the following: *María Juana*, August 3, 1773; *María Encarnación*, March 25, 1776; *María Rosalia*, April, 1777; and *Juana Tomasa*, September 19, 1782.⁶

1. **DM**, 1696, No. 15.
2. **HSNM**, Mil. Papers.
3. All in **B, Sta. Fe.**
4. Ibid.
5. **HSNM, loc. cit.**
6. All in **B, Sta. Fe.**

VALENCIA

Antonio de Valencia, nicknamed "El Tata," lived in Santa Fe in 1704 with his wife, *Luisa Varela Jaramillo*.[1] A soldier, he gave his age as twenty-seven in 1697.[2] A daughter, *Juana*, was the wife of Alonso Rodríguez.[3]

Cristóbal de Valencia died on August 4, 1729.[4]

Antonio de Valencia of Guadalupe del Paso married *Manuela Madrid* in 1710, but it is not clear whether the marriage took place there or in Santa Fe.[5] This is all that was left of a once numerous family.

1. **AASF,** No. 16.
2. **DM,** 1697, No. 8.
3. Ibid., 1705, Nos. 2, 6.
4. **B-16, Nambe,** Bur. Sec.
5. **DM,** 1710, No. 13.

VALENZUELA

Francisco Jurado de Valenzuela, a native of Zacatecas and soldier of Santa Fe, the son of Juan Jurado de Valenzuela and Teresa Cavieles, married *María Leonor Domínguez* in 1694. He gave his age as twenty.[1]

Martín de Valenzuela and his wife were referred to, in passing, as living in Pojoaque in 1703.[2]

Bartolo de Valenzuela, of La Cañada de Cochiti, was in prison in 1762 when his wife, *Barbara Gallegos*, was asking for his release.[3]

Raymundo Valenzuela married *Antonia de Avila* on January 20, 1755.[4]

1. **DM,** 1694, Nos. 10, 13.
2. **AASF,** No. 15.
3. **Bancroft, NMO,** 1762.
4. **M-27, S. Juan.**

VALDES

JOSÉ LUIS VALDÉS was a native of the City of Oviedo in Spain, and thirty years old in 1694.[1] Two years later he was a sergeant at Santa Cruz.[2] His wife was *María Medina de Cabrera*, a native of Mexico City, who came with him in the colony of 1693 with their two children: *José*, four, and *Ana*, one and a half.[3]

José Luis was killed by the Zuñi Indians in the Mission church of Zuñi while he and two other Spanish soldiers were singing an *alabado* after Mass, on Sunday, March 4, 1703.[4]

After arriving in New Mexico, this couple had four more children: *Ignacio Luis, Catalina, Juan Lorenzo*, and *Domingo*. Of the girls, *Ana* married Lázaro Antonio Córdoba in 1710;[5] *Catalina*, nicknamed "La Prieta," was murdered in 1713 by her husband, Miguel Luján. Her mother was still living in this year and gave her age as forty.[6] A *Rosalia*, mentioned below, might have been another daughter.

José Valdés is heard of only once afterwards, as being the natural father of *Francisco Valdés*, whose mother was Josefa de Ontiveros, later the wife of a certain Bustos, or Bustillos. They were all residents of Santa Cruz.

Francisco Valdés, when sixteen, married *Lugarda Martín* at Santa Cruz on October 11,

1723.⁷ They had a girl, *Francisca*, December 12, 1726.⁸ After Lugarda's death, Francisco married *Tomasa de Benavides*, by whom he had three children, two girls who died young, and a son, *Alejandro*, who grew up to marry Manuela Urioste but died without issue prior to 1762.⁹ This Alejandro had had some trouble as a soldier of the Santa Fe garrison in 1759.¹⁰

Old Francisco registered some cattle brands in 1752 as "Francisco Valdés y Bustos."¹¹

Ignacio Luis Valdés was nineteen years old and living in Santa Fe in 1721, when he married *Gertrudis Domínguez*, of unknown parentage.¹²

Juan Lorenzo Valdés married *Josefa de Salazar* at Santa Cruz on May 2, 1729.¹³ With Ignacio and Rosalia Valdés he was sued by Torres people regarding some land in Rio Arriba.¹⁴

This *Rosalía* could well be the Rosa Valdés who acted as a sponsor with her son, Juan Valdés, on January 7, 1739,¹⁵ and was very likely a sister to Juan Lorenzo and the others.

Domingo Valdés married *Ana María Márquez*, grand-daughter of Ana María Pacheco.¹⁶ In 1745 he notarized a declaration stating that his family and that of his wife were all "Spanish and Old Christians." In it he mentioned a daughter, *Angela Francisca*, who was the wife of José Romo de Vera.¹⁷

An *Antonio Valdés*, widowed of *Pascuala del Rio*, married *Manuela Sánchez*, widow of Manuel Montes Vigil, September 23, 1737.¹⁸

* * * * * * * *

Gregorio Valdés, who was High Sheriff, Regent, and Secretary of Government at the time of the Indian Rebellion of 1680, was not a New Mexico colonist. He had a wife, two sons, and a small daughter at the time, but they had left the refugee colony at Guadalupe del Paso by 1681.¹⁹ He probably belonged to the old gubernatorial family of Nueva Vizcaya.

---

1. **DM**, 1694, Nos. 27, 28, 32.
2. **Ibid.**, 1696, No. 14.
3. **BNM**, leg. 4, Pt. 1, pp. 790-95.
4. **Doc. Hist. de Mex.**, p. 183; entered in the burial register by Fr. Yrazábal on June 17, 1709 (**Bur-48, Zuñi**).
5. **DM**, 1710, No. 19; **Sp. Arch.**, II, No. 187.
6. **Sp. Arch.**, loc. cit.
7. **DM**, 1723, No. 6.
8. **B-16, Nambé**.
9. **Sp. Arch.**, I, No. 104.
10. **Ibid.**, II, No. 535.
11. **Twit. Coll.**, No. 133.
12. **DM**, 1721, No. 3.
13. **Ibid.**, 1729, No. 2.
14. **Sp. Arch.**, I, No. 1004.
15. **B-16, Nambé**.
16. **Sp. Arch.**, I, Nos. 717, 1043.
17. **Ibid.**, I, No. 1052; II, No. 464.
18. **M-29, Sta. Cruz**.
19. **Revolt**, I, p. 137; **BNM**, leg. 2, Pt. 3, ff. 267, 271.

VALERIO

José Valerio Martínez and his wife, *Nicolasa del Rosal*, were listed among the colonists of 1693.¹ But it is not known if they actually reached New Mexico. If they did, they could very well be the parents of later Valerio individuals.

Martín Valerio, a native of Sombrerete, was forty-eight years old in 1730, married, and residing in Santa Fe.² He was referred to as "Martín *Fernández* Valerio" at Pojoaque, May 12, 1748.³

Felipe Valerio of Chimayo married *Manuela Mestas* of Pojoaque, on October 1, 1741.⁴ Some of their children were: *María Gertrudis*, March 12, 1745; *Antonia Barbara*, January 18, 1750; and *Tomás Antonio*, February 15, 1754.⁵

Marcelino Valerio and *Luisa Martín* of Abiquiú had a child, *Valentina*, March 3, 1747.⁶

---

1. **BNM**, leg. 4, Pt. 1, pp. 790-95.
2. **DM**, 1730, no number.
3. **B-16, Nambé**.
4. **Ibid.**, M. Sec.
5. **Ibid.**
6. **B-31, Sta. Clara**.

VALLEJO
(Vallejo González)

MANUEL VALLEJO GONZÁLEZ, or GONZÁLEZ VALLEJO, was the son of Juan, born in Acazingo, and thirty-three when he joined the 1693 colonists with his thirty-one-year-old wife, *María López de Arteaga*. He was tall, dark, and bald, with large eyes. With them came a seven-year-old child by Manuel's previous marriage, *Angela Teresa;* she was born in Mexico City, and had a dark complexion, big eyes and forehead, and a thick nose. Her father was a blacksmith by trade.[1]

Manuel's second wife died during childbirth on the journey, at El Puesto de Collosillas, and was buried in the convent church of San Francisco de Santiago in Querétaro.[2] After reaching Santa Fe, Manuel married *Mariana Hurtado,* on November 7, 1694. He gave his age as thirty-four, and his parents, Juan González Vallejo, deceased, and Ana González.[3]

In 1698 he sold his grant at Santa Cruz,[4] and moved to his new wife's country in the Rio Abajo. Two known sons by Mariana were *Antonio,* married to Micaela Silva, and *Lugardo,* to Rosa Romero. *Angela Teresa,* the little girl of Manuel's first marriage and who made the long trip from Mexico City to Santa Fe with her twice-widowed father, became the wife of Miguel Lucero,[5] and later of Matías Romero.[5a]

Antonio Vallejo married *Micaela Silva* in Albuquerque in 1718.[6] She died on December 22, 1726, leaving two daughters, *Matilde* and *Catalina.*[7] He then married *Casilda Jaramillo* in 1727, but died the following year in June at the age of thirty-six.[8] He made his last will in Santa Fe, in which he gave his parents' names, those of his first wife and their two girls, stating that he had no children by the second.[9] Casilda then married Lorenzo Griego in April, 1728.[10]

Lugardo Vallejo was mentioned as Antonio's brother in the latter's will. He married *Rosa Romero,* by whom he had the following family:

Juan, born in 1730; *Ignacio Alberto,* June 9, 1731,[11] who married María Luna in 1756;[12] *Juan Manuel,* March 13, 1733; *Bernardino de Sena,* May 22, 1735;[13] *Gertrudis,* September 18, 1740; *Bernarda de la Luz,* October 3, 1743; and *María Polonia,* February 20, 1746.[14]

Juan Vallejo was married to *Angelina Varela Jaramillo* as early as 1716.[15] He died at the age of fifty on June 4, 1748.[16] His widow, when she died at Fuenclara, June 19, 1762, was called Angelina Jojola.[17] Perhaps Juan was a brother of Antonio and Lugardo, there being no data to link him with them.

* * * * * * * *

Bernardo Vallejo was a natural son of Pedro Durán y Chaves II, bachelor son of old Pedro D. y Chaves,[18] perhaps by a Vallejo girl. Bernardo married *Francisca Silva,* by whom he had several children: *Brigida,* October 11, 1728,[19] who married her second cousin, Toribio Garcia Jurado in 1766;[20] *María Feliciana,* March 5, 1731;[21] *Manuela,* February 8, 1742;[22] and *Luis,* August 28, 1744.[23]

---

1. Sp. Arch., II, No. 54c; BNM, leg. 1, Pt. 1, pp. 790-95.
2. BNM, loc. cit., pp. 830-34; DM, 1694, No. 19.
3. DM, loc. cit.
4. Sp. Arch., I, No. 293.
5. GENEALOGY: **Angela Teresa Vallejo,** Miguel Lucero II, Manuel Lucero, María Manuela Lucero, Tomás Baca, Nicanora Baca, Fabián Chávez, Fr. A. Chávez.
5a. GENEALOGY: **Angela Teresa Vallejo,** Tadéo Romero, María Manuela Romero, Jose Chávez, José Chávez II, Eugenio Chávez, Fabián Chávez, Fr. A. Chávez.
6. DM, 1718, No. 7.
7. Bur-2, Albuq.; Sp. Arch., I, No. 82.
8. M-3, Albuq.; Bur-48, Sta. Fe.
9. Sp. Arch., loc. cit.
10. M-3, Albuq.
11. Both in B-2, Albuq.
12. M-11, Isleta.
13. Both in B-2, Albuq.
14. The three in B-57, Isleta.
15. DM, 1716, No. 1.
16. Bur-2, Albuq.
17. Ibid.
18. DM, 1766, in Albuq., no number.
19. B-2, Albuq.
20. DM, loc. cit.
21. B-2, Albuq.
22. B-57, Isleta.
23. B-2, Albuq.

VALVERDE

DON ANTONIO VALVERDE Y COSÍO, acting Governor of New Mexico from 1717 to 1722, was an uncle of Governor Juan Domingo Bustamante.[1] He commanded the Presidio at Guadalupe del Paso in 1705.[2] In 1719 he led a campaign against the Utes and Cumanches, the journal of which is quite interesting.[3] In 1722 he bought Bustamante's property in Guadalupe del Paso,[4] where he resided until his death on December 15, 1728. He was buried inside the old Mission there.[5]

Valverde was not very popular with the Spanish or the Indian people of New Mexico.[6] He was a member of the Conquistadora Confraternity.[7]

A daughter of his seems to have been a *Doña Juana de Valverde y Cosío*, who was the wife of Juan Antonio Pérez Velarde at Guadalupe del Paso in 1725.[8] The Garcia de Noriega family there also married into the Valverde and Velarde families.[9]

* * * * * * * *

CRISTOBAL VALVERDE, the son of Juan, and born in Mexico City at La Merced, joined the colonists of 1693 when nineteen years old. He was dark, with large eyes, a broad nose, and three moles on the right side of the nose. His wife, *Ynez de Aspeitia*, seventeen, the daughter of Bartolomé, was born in Mexico City at Santa Catalina. She was dark, with big eyes and a sharp nose.

They brought a daughter, *Teresa María*, two years old, also born in Mexico City, who was fair with black hair, eyes, and eyebrows. With them also came Cristobal's fourteen-year-old brother, *Miguel Ruiz,* a native of Mexico City, who had curly hair and large eyes.[10]

Ynez de Aspeitia was godmother to an Indian baptized at Taos in July, 1715.[11]

* * * * * * * *

NICOLÁS VALVERDE was a native of Parral, married and living in New Mexico in 1716, when he gave his age as fifty.[12] He worked as a laborer in the reconstruction of San Miguel Chapel in Santa Fe in 1710.[13] He received initial grants of land on the Chama river immediately after the Reconquest.[14]

Antonio Valverde, living in Chama in 1748, underwent trial with his three sons, *Juan Domingo, Alberto,* and *Pedro* (fourteen), for assaulting a certain José Manuel Trujillo. The three sons were still single.[15] Antonio's wife was *María Antonia Casillas,* who had Pedro on August 28, 1732.[16] Their three boys married as follows:

Juan Domingo married Juana Córdoba at Chama, July 26, 1758.[17]

Alberto married Quiteria Manzanares on January 22, 1755.[18] A son of theirs, Juan Miguel, married María Trinidad Hurtado of Albuquerque in 1779.[19]

Pedro married Micaela Trujillo on April 23, 1754.[20]

---

1. Sp. Arch., II, No. 319.
2. Ritch Coll., Box 2, No. 39.
3. Bancroft, NMO, 1719.
4. Sp. Arch., I, No. 1031.
5. Bur., Guad. del Paso (Juárez).
6. BNM, leg. 6, No. 11; Ocaranza, pp. 183-90.
7. OLC, pp. 73, 77.
8. AGN, Mex., Inq., t. 832, f. 345.
9. Sp. Arch., I, No. 414; II, No. 473.
10. Ibid., II, No. 54c.
11. B-45, Taos.
12. DM, 1716, No. 10.
13. Kubler, p. 19.
14. Sp. Arch., I, Nos. 167, 437, 926.
15. Ibid., II, No. 498.
16. B, Sta. Clara.
17. M, Sta. Clara.
18. Ibid.
19. DM, 1799, in Albuq., no number.
20. M, Sta. Clara.

VARELA
(Varela de Losada)

CRISTÓBAL VARELA, twenty-six years old in 1699, was then living in Bernalillo.[1] He and *Clementa de Ortega* had the following children: *Joaquín,* July 31, 1701; *Antonio,* June 12, 1704;[2] *Salvador,* December 10, 1706; *Marciala,* February 15, 1709; and *Antonia Manuela,* June 12, 1711.[3]

Joaquín Varela married *Juana Garcia* at Albuquerque in 1720.[4] A son, *Juan Esteban,* was born on January 2, 1729.[5] Joaquín died the following year at Guadalupe del Paso.[6]

Salvador Varela married *Maria Antonia Ribera* in 1725.[7] They had a son, *Pedro,* in July, 1726.[8]

* * * * * * * *

JACINTO VARELA was the son of Juan Varela, brother of Luisa Varela who married a Romero (Bartolomé) prior to the Raconquest.[9] His wife was *Valentina González,* by whom he had the following children: *Gregorio,* March 19, 1735, who married Juana Catalina Torres on May 6, 1759;[10] *María Magdalena,* September 4, 1741;[11] *Josefa,* wife of Tomás Montoya;[12] and *Antonio,* who married Gertrudis Pacheco, March 19, 1766.[13]

José Varela, husband of *Juana Rodarte,* died in Santa Fe, February 27, 1733, at the age of eighty. She died on November 30, 1745, more than seventy years old.[14]

Antonio Varela and *Juana de la Cruz* were married on October 1, 1704.[15] They were called Antonio *Jorge* and Juana *Ansures* when two children, *Ana* and *Casilda,* were baptized, August 2, 1705, and February 17, 1707.[16] Then, *Varela* and *Ansures* at the baptism of *Bernarda,* November 1, 1708; and finally *Carvajal* and *Maese* at that of *Sebastián,* February 2, 1711.[17]

It is very possible that some of the *Varela Jaramillo* people also adopted the single appellation of "Varela," though most of them were afterwards known as "Jaramillo."

* * * * * * * *

Manuel Ramos made his last will at Santa Cruz in 1750, stating that he was a native of New Mexico, and had been married to *María de la Encarnación Montoya,* by whom he had four boys and two girls, "all legitimate Varelas." These were: *Antonio, Juan, Marcelino, Sebastián, Petrona,* and *María.*[18]

---

1. **DM**, 1699, No. 8.
2. Both in **B-13, Bern.**
3. All in **B-2, Albuq.**
4. **DM**, 1720, No. 5.
5. **B-2, Albuq.**
6. **Bur., Guad. del Paso** (Juárez).
7. **DM**, 1725, No. 3.
8. **B-2, Albuq.**
9. **DM**, 1777, in Albuq., no number.
10. **B-2, Albuq.; M-11, Isleta.**
11. **B-2, Albuq.**
12. **DM**, loc. cit.
13. **M-3, Albuq.**
14. **Bur-48, Sta. Fe.**
15. **B-13, Bern., M. Sec.**
16. **Ibid., B. Sec.**
17. All in **B-2, Albuq.**
18. **Sp. Arch., I, No. 768.**

VARGAS

Don Diego de Vargas Zapata Luján Ponce de León, the great *Reconquistador* of New Mexico, of an ancient and noble Castilian family, did not leave any descendants in New Mexico. Nor is there any record or hint of natural children here. With him during the Reconquest period were two illegitimate sons, *Don Juan Manuel,* twelve years of age, and *Don Alonso,* eleven, who stayed with their illustrious father until his untimely death in 1704, when he ordered a trusted officer friend and a servant to accompany the youths back to New Spain.¹ For a brief but complete life of the man, see José Manuel Espinosa, *First Expedition of Vargas Into New Mexico*.²

* * * * * * * *

MANUEL FERNÁNDEZ DE VARGAS, and his brother SEBASTIÁN, came to New Mexico with the Reconquest from Guadalajara, their birthplace. They were the sons of Gabriel de Vargas and Juana Fernández, both deceased.³

Manuel de Vargas was a tailor by trade, and nineteen years old when he married *Luisa Pascuala de la Cruz* at San Lorenzo, on January 6, 1695.⁴ She was called *Lucía (Luisa) Ruiz* when their daughter, *Manuela*, married Diego Martín in 1714. By this time her father was dead.⁵ The mother is again mentioned in 1716 as a widow living in Chimayó.⁶

SEBASTIÁN DE VARGAS married *María de Leyva* in 1696. He was twenty-two at the time.⁷ By 1708 he was a captain.⁸ In 1731 he gave his age as fifty-five.⁹ His wife died on July 20, 1742, when he was referred to as a "*Maestro*," and he died "a widower more than eighty years old" on October 19, 1757.¹⁰ He belonged to the Confraternity of La Conquistadora, and was the man who made the iron spikes and nails for the restoration of San Miguel Chapel.¹¹ Several land transfers were made by him in and around Santa Fe between 1710 and 1751.¹²

A *Sebastiana de Vargas,* who married a Marcos Montoya, January 27, 1709,¹³ might have been his daughter. But she could also have been his niece, or even a member of the distinct Vargas Machuca family.

* * * * * * * *

JUAN DE VARGAS MACHUCA was at Guadalupe del Paso in 1681, single and eighteen years of age when he passed muster in that year.¹⁴ His wife was *Ana Olguín*, and a daughter of theirs, *Rosa*, became the wife of Blas Martín in 1705. Both her parents were dead at this time.¹⁵ The following man was in all likelihood Rosa's brother.

Tomás de Vargas Machuca and his wife, *María Benavides*, were sponsors for a child, January 12, 1726.¹⁶ He died a widower on February 3, 1737.¹⁷

Francisco de Vargas, husband of *María Rodríguez,* died on November 21, 1736.¹⁸

* * * * * * * *

Eusebio de Vargas, a captain mentioned as a witness in 1694,¹⁹ was also the leader of a company of Vargas' soldiers in a campaign of that year.²⁰ He is not heard of again. Bancroft thought he might be a brother of the Governor.²¹

---

1. **Sp. Arch.**, I, No. 1027.
2. Also for religious depth, **OLC**, pp. 7-10, 53-5.
3. **DM**, 1694, No. 18; 1696, No. 10.
4. Ibid.
5. Ibid., 1714, No. 4.
6. **Sp. Arch.**, I, No. 260.
7. **DM**, 1696, No. 10.
8. Ibid., 1708, No. 1.
9. **Bancroft, NMO**, 1731.
10. **Bur-48**, Sta. Fe.
11. **OLC**, p. 70; Kubler, p. 5.
12. **Sp. Arch.**, I, Nos. 30, 85, 166, 428, 640, 1033.
13. **M-24**, S. Ild.
14. **Revolt**, II, pp. 44-5, 194.
15. **DM**, 1705, No. 1.
16. **M-29**, Sta. Cruz.
17. **Bur-48**, Sta. Fe.
18. Ibid.
19. **DM**, 1694, No. 25.
20. **NMHR**, Vol. XI, No. 2, p. 184.
21. **Hist. of N. M.**, p. 216.

VASQUEZ

JOSÉ VÁSQUEZ DE LARA, the son of Miguel Vásquez de Lara and Juana de Alcalá, deceased, came as a soldier of the Reconquest. He was born at Nuestra Señora de San Juan, Villa de Los Lagos. On February 3, 1694, he married *Mara Magdalena Baca*.¹ He acted as a notary for the friars in 1700.² A daughter, *María*, married Diego Padilla, widowed of Catalina Gutiérrez, in 1713 at Bernalillo.³

* * * * * * * *

Juan Antonio Vásquez de la Cruz was a native of Tepozotlán, the son of Alonso Vásquez and Ana María. He was seventeen in 1697 when he married *Josefa de la Rosa,* twenty, daughter of Nicolás Arias and Lorenza de la Cruz, all of Zacatecas.⁴

José Vásquez, a maker of *carretas,* twenty years old in 1715, lived at Santa Cruz with his wife, *Francisca de Torres.*⁵

Antonio Vásquez, of unknown parentage, married *Gertrudis Muñiz* at Santa Fe in 1714.⁶

---

1. **DM**, 1694, o. 33.
2. **Ibid.**, 1706, No. 1.
3. **Ibid.**, 1713, No. 1. GENEALOGY: **María Vásquez de Lara,** Francisco Padilla, Francisca Padilla, Mariano Torres, María Rita Torres, Josu Chávez, Eugenio Chávez, Fabián Chavéz, Fr. A. Chávez.
4. **Ibid**, 1697, No. 8.
5. **Sp. Arch.**, II, No. 239c.
6. **DM**, 1714, No. 11.

VEGA

Francisco Blanco de la Vega, fifteen years of age, was among the convicts of 1677. He was a native of Puebla, the son of Andrés, dark, with thick eyebrows and small eyes.¹ He was killed by the Indians at Picuris in 1680.² He might have married and had children in those three years.

Juan de la Vega and *María Madrid,* both natives of New Mexico, were dead by 1716 when their daughter, *Juana,* married Juan de Ledesma in Santa Fe.³

* * * * * * * *

Felipe Vega, twenty, a widower from Guadalajara, married *Dominga de la Concepción* in 1705. They were former slaves of Governor Cuervo.⁴

Fráncisco de la Vega and *Antonia de la Concepción* were wedding witnesses in 1694.⁵

Simon de Vega, daughter of Antonio de Vega and Antonia Hernández of San Luis Potosí, was the wife of a Juan Morones, living in Santa Fe in 1706.⁶ All these people were of low estate.

---

1. **B-H**, III, pp. 317-24.
2. **Revolt**, I, p. 98.
3. **DM**, 1716, No. 12.
4. **Ibid.**, 1705, No. 9.
5. **Ibid.**, 1694, No. 29.
6. **AGN, Mex., Inq.**, t. 735, f. 273.

VEGA y COCA

MIGUEL DE LA VEGA Y COCA, the son of Cristóbal de la Vega and born in the City of Mexico, came to New Mexico with the colonists of 1693. He was sixteen years old, fair-complexioned, with an aquiline face and small eyes. His wife, *Manuela de Medina,* was also sixteen; she was the daughter of Alonso, dark, with big eyes and a rather thick nose.

With them came her mother, Josefa de Cabrera, the widow of Alonso de Medina. She was thirty, a native of Mexico City, having an aquiline face, large eyes, and a small nose.¹ Her other young daughter was the wife of José Luis Valdés.

Miguel's young wife died not long after their arrival, for in 1699, while residing at Santa Cruz, he married *María Montoya.*² From around the years 1727 to 1731 he was *Alcalde Mayor* of Taos and Picurís.³ His second wife died in Santa Fe, where they now resided, on August 22, 1750.⁴ All his known children were girls, perhaps all by his second wife, and each one made a good marriage.

Feliciana (possibly by his first wife) married Don Bernardo de Bustamante y Tagle;⁴ᵃ *Francisca* was the wife of Manuel Tenorio de Alba;⁵ *Apolonia* married Antonio Baca;⁶ *María* became the wife of Manuel Baca;⁷ *Leonarda* married Toribio Alejandro Ortiz in 1735;⁸ *Isabel* was married to Miguel de Alire in 1728;⁹ *Marcelina Antonia* married Manuel Ortiz in 1735;¹⁰ and (presumably) *Margarita*, who was the wife of Juan Tenorio de Alba.¹¹

Juan de Coca and his wife, *Margarita Bustamante*, had a child, *Ynez*, April 21, 1748, for whom Don Bernardo Bustamante and Rosa Bustamante were the godparents.¹² But there is nothing to show if this couple actually belonged to these two families, or were merely servants.

Old Miguel was sometimes referred to simply as "Coca,"¹³ as also some of the daughters when they were married. Juan de Coca could very well be his son, and the progenitor of the Coca family, for the double surname did not survive as such.

1. **Sp. Arch.**, II, No. 54c.
2. **DM**, 1699, No. 1.
3. Crespo, pars. 135, 137.
4. **Bur-48, Sta. Fe.**
4a. GENEALOGY: **Feliciana de la Vega y Cora**, Josefa Bustamante, María Josefa Ortiz, Jose María Alarí, María Dolores Alarid, Romualdo Roybal, Nicolasa Roybal, Fr. A. Chávez.
5. **Sp. Arch.**, I, Nos. 440, 652.
6. Ibid., No. 88.
7. Ibid.
8. M-50, Sta. Fe; Sp. Arch., I, No. 652.
9. Ibid.
10. M-50, Sta. Fe.
11. Ibid.
12. B-62, Sta. Fe.
13. Sp. Arch., I, Nos. 85, 166.

VELARDE

JUAN ANTONIO PÉREZ VELARDE was a native of Muriedas, Valle de Camargo, in Asturias, baptized on April 28, 1702, who was living at Guadalupe del Paso in 1725, when he was appointed High Sheriff of the Holy Office. He was also *Hermano Mayor* of the Third Order of St. Francis. His parents were Francisco Escajedo and María Velarde. His wife was *Doña Juana de Valverde y Cosío*.¹ In his capacity as High Sheriff of the Inquisition, he arrested Francisco Xavier Romero of Santa Cruz as a *"somético"* in 1728.²

Manuel Velarde de Cosío of Guadalupe del Paso was, in all likelihood, a son of Velarde and his Cosío wife. Manuel's wife was *Lugarda Lucero de Godoy*. One of their daughters, *Rosalia*, married José Garcia de Noriega; their daughter, Carmen Garcia de Noriega, married Francisco Ortiz y Bustamante of Santa Fe, and these were the parents of the Rev. Rafael Ortiz.³

* * * * * * * *

Juan Francisco Velarde of Guadalupe del Paso, the son of Francisco Velarde and María Velarde, came to Albuquerque in 1787 and married *Manuela Lopez*, daughter of Miguel Lopez and Manuela de Herrera.⁴ In 1790, he was twenty, and she was twenty-two. They had a son, nine years old, and a daughter who was eight.⁵

* * * * * * * *

Nicolás Velarde and *Leonarda Tenorio* were living at La Soledad in Rio Arriba when a son, *Nicolas Antonio*, was born on April 17, 1779.⁶ Another son, *José Manuel*, was twenty-seven when he enlisted as a soldier in 1781.⁶ᵃ

Joaquín Velarde and *Juana Garcia de Noriega* were living at La Hoya in Rio Arriba. Two children of theirs were *José Rafael*, born December 5, 1779, and *María Luisa*, May 7, 1786.⁷

José Manuel Velarde and his wife, *María Manuela Perea*, lived across the Rio del Norte from La Soledad in the Chama district. A daughter, *María Josefa*, was born there on May 28, 1802; an older daughter, *María An-*

[308]

tonia, acted as a sponsor with her father, June 7, 1804.⁸ They also had a married son, *José Miguel,* whose wife was María Concepción Durán. At the baptism of their child, María Encarnación, March 26, 1804, José Miguel's parents were the sponsors. He and his Perea mother were godparents together in 1805.⁹

1. AGN, Mex., Inq., t. 832, f. 345.
2. Sp. Arch., II, No. 253; Bancroft, NMO, 1728.
3. Twit. Coll., No. 254; HSNM, No. 2828; cf., NMHR, V(XXV, No. 4, pp. 265-295.
4. DM, 1787, in Albuq., no number.
5. Sp. Arch., II, No. 1092b.
6. B-42, S. Juan.
6a. HSNM, Mil. Papers.
7. B-42, S. Juan.
8. B-31, Sta. Clara.
9. Ibid.

VELÁSQUEZ
(*Velasco* and *Velásquez*)

CRISTÓBAL VELASCO came to New Mexico in 1677 as a convict. He was twenty-five, the son of Francisco, and born in Mexico City, Calle de San Francisco; he was tall, fair and freckled, with small deep-set eyes. His sentence was to last six years in military service.¹ When the Indians rebelled in 1680 he was already an *Alférez,* passing muster as a convict, married in New Mexico, with one small child and two female servants.² He ran away from the refugee colony at Guadalupe del Paso in 1692,³ but was caught, or returned voluntarily, to play an important part in the Vargas Reconquest. His wife was *Josefa de Carvajal,* daughter of María Márquez.⁴

By 1693 he was a captain, and working hard for Vargas as a recruiter of colonists in Mexico City, or *Españoles-Mexicanos,* Spanish people from the City and Valley of Mexico. His charges were still in Mexico City on March 21, 1693; they reached Durango on August 19, and Parral on September 1, 1693.⁵ They arrived at Guadalupe del Paso well before the end of the year, but did not arrive in Santa Fe until June 23, 1694,⁶ six months after the battle of Santa Fe. Hence, save for certain individuals who must have joined up as soldiers, these people did not take part in the actual Reconquest of New Mexico. Vargas used a large number of them to found the Villa of Santa Cruz.

Cristóbal Velasco and his family are not heard of again; they very likely went back to New Spain. They perhaps did not even come north with the Mexico City colony, as it was in charge of Fray Francisco Farfán on arrival.

Francisco de Velasco was an eighteen-year-old *Bachiller,* or advanced clerical student, who was sentenced by an ecclesiastical judge to serve two years as a soldier in 1677 (and was thus cut off from further advancement to the priesthood). He was the son of José, and also born in Mexico City at the Calle de San Francisco.⁷ Evidently, he was at least a first cousin of Cristóbal de Velasco. By 1680, Francisco was married, with one little daughter, and acting as a clerk to the *Cabildo* of Santa Fe, when the Indians struck and the colonists fled to Guadalupe del Paso.⁸ Since his term was up, he must have returned to New Spain, for he is not heard of again.

* * * * * * * *

DIEGO DE VELASCO, sometimes referred to by others as "Velásquez," signed his name, "Velasco."⁹ In 1694 he married *María de Tapia,* or *Herrera,* a natural daughter of Ana López. He was born in Guadiana (Durango in New Spain), the son of Lorenzo Velasco and Josefa de Palavis, deceased.¹⁰ He gave his age as thirty-seven in 1705, when he declared that he was a carpenter and a native of Durango.¹¹ Both he and his wife inherited her mother's property in Santa Fe.¹² In 1713 she was referred to as the wife of Velasquez the Lame Carpenter.¹³ He was the

Master Carpenter in charge of the reconstruction of San Miguel Chapel in 1710.[14]

In 1712 Diego killed Miguel de Herrera, who had come to assault him in his own house. Diego referred to his known lameness in denying his guilt, but was found guilty of manslaughter. His sentence, as a Master Carpenter, was to work on the new parish church of Santa Fe, and to build barges for crossing the Rio del Norte at San Felipe and Guadalupe del Paso.[15] Diego was still living in 1746, at Santa Cruz, and still acknowledged as the *"Maestro Carpintero."*[16]

Reference was made during the trial to a son of his whose name was not given. This might have been a second *Diego,* or a *José Inocencio,* both of whom appear to be his sons.

Diego Velasco II married *Ynez de Apodaca* on July 27, 1746.[17] They had a son, *Pedro,* February 27, 1748, and a daughter, *Catalina Antonia,* March 13, 1751.[18] Their mother, a widow, died on May 19, 1751.[19]

Lorenzo Inocencio Velasco, afterwards known as **Velásquez,** practiced the carpenter's trade in the Rio Arriba country; his sister María Antonia was the wife of Juan del Prado, with whom a son of Lorenzo Inocencio tried to escape from military service in 1763.[20] Lorenzo Inocencio himself was accused of encouraging slackers during an Indian campaign in 1757.[21]

He had married *María Mestas* on June 19, 1735.[22] They had a son, *Juan Esteban,* the one who ran away with Prado in 1763.[23] A daughter, *Nicolasa,* married Juan Martín, May 8, 1785.[24]

Juan Esteban Velásquez, son of the above pair, returned home from his evasion of military duty, and proceeded to rear a large family at La Cuchilla in the Santa Clara district. On December 20, 1772, he married *Juana Apodaca,* or *Valverde,* in Santa Fe.[25] They had at least nine children between 1773 and 1790.[26] He died at La Cuchilla on October 8, 1819, at the age of eighty.[27]

He and his wife also reared an orphan or, perhaps, illegitimate Ortiz girl, *María Loreta,* who married Mariano Roybal on June 27, 1781.[28]

Long before the century ended, the *Velasco* surname disappeared, by merging with the Velásquez name of other families.

* * * * * * * *

JOSÉ VELÁSQUEZ CORTÉS, the son of Antonio and a native of Sevilla, was thirty-six years old when he joined the colonists of 1693. He was tall, his broad face pockmarked, and had a wide forehead and deep-set eyes. His wife was *Juana de Caras,* thirty, the daughter of Francisco and a native of Puebla. She was of medium height, with a broad dark face and large eyes.

They had a three-year-old daughter, *María,* born in Guamantla, who had a round face with small eyes and nose.[29] This girl married José de Armijo in 1710, who jointly with José "Blásquez" and Juana de Caras purchased a house and lot by the Santa Fe Plaza.[30]

* * * * * * * *

FRANCISCO VELÁSQUEZ, the son of Nicolás Rodriguez [*sic*] and Andrea de Medina,

---

1. B-H, III, pp. 317-322.
2. **Revolt,** I, pp. 119, 158; II, pp. 53-4, 118-9.
3. **BNM,** leg. 2, Pt. 3, ff. 290-1.
4. **Ibid.**
5. **BNM,** leg. 4, Pt. 1, pp. 790-95, 830-34, is a list carried and amended on occasion by Velasco or Father Farfán. **Sp. Arch.,** II, No. 54c, is an official roster copied in Mexico City in September, 1693, and sent up to Vargas.
6. **Sp. Arch.,** II, No. 55f.
7. B-H, loc. cit.
8. **Revolt,** I, pp. 16, 121, 137.
9. **DM,** 1698, No. 1; **Bancroft, NMO,** 1728.
10. **Ibid.,** 1694, No. 5.
11. **Ibid.,** 1705, No. 9.
12. **Sp. Arch.,** I, No. 160.
13. **AGN, Mex., Inq.,** t. 758, ff. 468 et seq.
14. Kubler, p. 20.
15. **Sp. Arch.,** II, No. 172.
16. **Ibid.,** No. 470.
17. **M-50, Sta. Fe.**
18. Both in **B, Sta. Fe.**
19. **Bur-49, Sta. Fe.**
20. **Bancroft, NMO,** 1763.
21. **AGN, Tierras,** 426, III, ff. 7-11.
22. **Bur-16, Nambé,** M. Sec.
23. **Sp. Arch.,** II, No. 584.
24. **M-33, Sta. Clara.**
25. **M-50, Sta. Fe.**
26. All in **B-31, Sta. Clara.**
27. **Bur-30, Sta. Clara.**
28. **M-33, Sta. Clara.** GENEALOGY: María Loreta Velásquez, Juan Manuel Roybal, Desiderio Roybal, Romualdo Roybal, Nicolasa Roybal, Fr. A. Chavez.
29. **Sp. Arch.,** II, No. 54c; **BNM,** leg. 4, Pt. 1, pp. 790-95.
30. **Ibid.,** I, No. 411.

was a soldier of Santa Fe who married *Felipa Montoya* in 1710.³¹ He next married *Barbara Baca*, widow of Juan Garcia, August 11, 1737.³²

* * * * * * * *

DIEGO VELÁSQUEZ was a native of Sombrerete who came to Santa Fe with his children and wife, *Juana del Rio*, known also as *"Juana la Prieta."*³³ Diego gave his age as twenty-five or twenty-nine, and his origin as Sombrerete, in 1716. He signed his name, "Velásquez."³⁴

The children born in Sombrerete were: *Antonio*, who married Juana Rodríguez in 1705;³⁵ *Diego*, who married Ana María Archuleta the same year;³⁶ *Catalina*, known as *"La Malora,"* and as the daughter of *"La Prieta,"*³⁷ and who married a certain Negrete and then a Morones,³⁸ and was also the natural mother of Juan Antonio de los Rios, *alias* Archuleta;³⁹ and, presumably, *Francisco Velásquez "el Prietito."*⁴⁰

The Velásquez people living in Santa Fe throughout this century can almost with certainty be considered members of the last two families, while those of the north country were "Velascos" originally.

---

31. DM, 1710, No. 4.
32. M-50, Sta. Fe.
33. AGN, loc. cit.
34. DM, 1716, Nos. 9, 12.
35. Ibid., 1705, Nos. 2, 5:
36. Ibid., No. 11.
37. Ibid., No. 6.
38. AGN, loc. cit. Juan Morones de Casares, twenty-eight and a native of Michoacán, was a soldier in Santa Fe in 1696 (DM, 1696, No. 4.).
39. Sp. Arch., II, No. 354. See Archuleta, Juan Antonio.
40. Ibid., I, No. 731.

VIGIL
(Montes Vigil)

FRANCISCO MONTES VIGIL and *María Jiménez de Ancizo* were colonists from Zacatecas. In Santa Fe in 1695, he said that he was a native of El Real de Zacatecas and thirty years old. In 1710 he received a grant of land at Alameda, but sold it two years later.¹

Their known children were: *María*, wife of Martín Romero and mother of Antonio Romero;² *Gertrudis; Elena; Domingo,*³ who married María Estela Márquez;⁴ *Francisco,*⁵ husband of Antonia Jirón and then of Lorenza Medina; *Manuel,*⁶ who married Manuela Sánchez; *Juan*, husband of Ynez López and then of Nicolasa Luján; and, presumably, *Pedro*, who married Juana Trujillo.

Francisco Montes Vigil II and his wife, *Antonia Jirón*, were living at Santa Cruz in 1733, when she accused a man of entering her home at midnight when her husband was away.⁷ On June 28, 1744, widowed of Antonia Jirón *del Castillo*, he married *Lorenza Medina*.⁸

His son, *Francisco III*, when marrying María de Jesús Mestas, May 12, 1748, gave his name as Francisco Montes Vigil *de Santillana*, the son of Francisco Vigil de Santillana and Antonia Jirón del Castillo.⁹ A daughter of Francisco III married Inocencio Martín at Chama in 1776.¹⁰

Manuel Montes Vigil, a soldier of Santa Fe, made his last will in 1733, in which he stated that he had been married to *Manuela Sánchez* for thirteen years. He had a brother named Juan. His four children were: *Josefa, Isabel, Juan Luis,* and *María Antonia.*¹¹

---

1. DM, 1695, Nos. 12, 7; 1696, No. 10; Sp. Arch., I, No. 302.
2. Sp. Arch., I, No. 499.
3. Ibid.
4. Ibid., No. 513.
5. Ibid., No. 499.
6. Ibid., Nos. 499, 1220.
7. Ibid., II, No. 391.
8. M-29, Sta. Cruz.
9. B-16, Nambé, M. Sec.
10. DM, 1776, no number.
11. Sp. Arch., I, No. 1220.

He died on March 21, 1733, at the age of thirty-two,[12] and his widow then married an Antonio Valdés on September 23, 1737.[13]

Juan Montes Vigil, widowed of *Ynez López*, married *Antonia Nicolasa Luján* in Santa Fe, May 16, 1745.[14] He died on May 18, 1762.[15] When he made his last will in this year, he gave his parents' names, stating that he had been married for twenty-nine years to Ynez López, by whom he had three children: *Manuela* (died when eight), *Juan* (died when six), and *Manuel*. He had one daughter, *Manuela de la Luz*, by his second wife.[16] This last son named was the Manuel Vigil who married Gertrudis Armijo of Taos, and settled at her ancestral inheritance of Ranchos de Taos around the year 1776. He later married *Magdalena* Valdéz of Abiquiú, May 8, 1777.[16a]

Pedro Montes Vigil was thirty-three and a resident of Santa Fe in 1717.[17] In 1710 he worked on the restoration of San Miguel Chapel.[18] His wife was *Juana Trujillo*, daughter of Mateo Trujillo.[19] There is no documentary evidence to link him with the preceding men, but apparently he is their brother.

Manuel Gregorio Montes Vigil, who married *Lorenza Fernández Valerio*, April 8, 1742,[20] was perhaps a son of Francisco II and a brother of Francisco III; a Fernández Valerio was the *padrino* for the wedding of Francisco Montes Vigil III and María Mestas in 1748.

---

12. Bur-48, Sta. Fe.
13. M-29, Sta. Cruz.
14. M-50, Sta. Fe.
15. Bur-48, Sta. Fe.
16. Sp. Arch., I, No. 1055.

16a. BNM, leg. 10, No. 43; Taos; Sp. Arch., I, Nos. 48, 240; M-1, Abiquiú.
17. DM, 1717, No. 2.
18. Kubler, pp. 18, 20.
19. Sp. Arch., I, No. 1034; II, No. 273.
20. M-29, Sta. Cruz.

VILLALPANDO

JUAN DE VILLA EL PANDO was a native of La Villa de León, and a soldier of Santa Fe, when he married *Ana María Romero*, June 2, 1694. His parents were Juan de Villa el Pando and Ursula de Olaes.[1] He was dead by 1718, when a son of theirs got married; his widow was known also as *"La Panda."*[2]

Their known children were *Ambrosio, Pablo, Juan Rosalío,* and *Catalina*.[3] The girl became the wife of Antonio Martin of Embudo.[4]

Ambrosio de Villalpando was twenty when he married *María Romero* on October 6, 1718.[5] In 1732 a complaint was made against him for mistreating some Picurís Indians,[6] and in 1735 he was tried for the killing of an Indian, but was found not guilty.[7]

---

1. DM, 1694, No. 2.
2. Ibid., 1718, No. 6; Sp. Arch., I, No. 930; II, No. 296.
3. Sp. Arch., I, No. 1002; II, No. 296.
4. Ibid., I, No. 987.

5. DM, 1718, No. 6.
6. Sp. Arch., II, No. 365.
7. Ibid., No. 404.

VILLANUEVA

VICENTE DE VILLANUEVA, a native of Parral, the son of José Antonio Villanueva and Petra Ibargüen, was twenty-four in 1796, when he enlisted in the Santa Fe garrison.[1] He married *Ana María Alarí* on April 3, 1799.[2] Their known children were: *María Jo-*

---

1. HSNM, Mil. Papers.

2. M-51, Castrense.

sefa, April 21, 1801; *José Domingo de Jesús*, May 14, 1808; *José Vicente de Jesús*, June 3, 1807; and *Juan Nepomuceno*, April 13, 1813.⁴

In 1813 he was *Alcalde Mayor* of Pecos and connected with the newly founded military post of San Miguel del Vado.⁵

3. The three in **B**, Castrense.
4. **B-65**, Sta. Fe.
5. **Sp. Arch.**, I, No. 56; II, No. 2755.

VITÓN

GASPAR VITÓN appears as a name in 1731.¹ He evidently was the husband of *María Diega Garduño*, who had a son, *José Gabriel Garduño*, or *Vitón*.² A daughter of hers was married to Vicente Sena;³ her name was given as *María Teresa Vitón y Gallardo* when a daughter, Margarita Antonia Sena, was married on September 6, 1773.⁴

1. **Sp. Arch.**, I, Nos. 316, 357, 517; **Bancroft, NMO**, 1731.
2. **Ibid.**, Nos. 34, 351.
3. **Ibid.**
4. **M-23**, S. Felipe.

YRIGOYEN

MARTIN YRIGOYEN, a native of Chihuahua, the son of Francisco Yrigoyen and María Luisa de Argüello, was thirty-one years old, and already married, when he enlisted in Santa Fe in 1797.¹ His wife was *Gertrudis de la O*, whom he evidently had married at the Presidio of Guajoquilla.² He either died or returned with his family to New Spain after the turn of the century.

1. **HSNM**, Mil. Papers.
2. **B-66**, Castrense, Aug. 8, 1805. See, **O, José de la**.

YRISARRI

PABLO YRISARRI came to New Mexico in the beginning of the Nineteenth Century and married *Antonia Teresa Romero* on November 1, 1811.¹ She was dead by 1822 when he married *Ana María Ortega*, widow of José Miguel Jaramillo. Pablo was thirty-six at this time.²

Mariano Yrisarri, presumably Pablo's son, married *Juana Otero* on March 26, 1836; she was the daughter of Vicente Otero and Gertrudis Chávez.³

1. **M-4**, Albuq.
2. **DM**, 1822, in Albuq.; no number; **M-4**, Albuq., May 6.
3. **M-11**, Tomé; **DM**, 1836, in Albuq., no number.

YTURRIETA

JOSÉ MARIANO DE LOS DOLORES YTURRIETA acted as a baptismal sponsor with Jacinta Peláez on March 11, 1736, and with María Luisa Baca on March 23, 1736, in Albuquerque.¹ In 1744 he asked for land at Jémez, to no avail.² His wife was very likely a *Juana Teresa Romero*, mother of Pedro Yturrieta of Belen.³

Pedro Yturrieta, just mentioned, married *María Chávez* on May 19, 1751.⁴ She was the daughter of José de Chávez and María Luisa Aragón.⁵ Pedro is mentioned in land questions at Belén in 1756 and 1768,⁶ and also in an assault case.⁷

His known children were: *Petra Vitalia,* who married Bartolo Trujillo in 1776;⁸ *Gaspar,* born February 3, 1759;⁹ and *Manuel,* who married María Barbara Luna.

Manuel Yturrieta, twenty-six, the son of Pedro Yturrieta and María Chávez, both deceased, married *María Barbara,* natural daughter of Antonia Quintana, deceased, on April 27, 1793.¹⁰ He and his wife, Barbara *Luna,* were living at Los Padillas in 1802 with a son, *Pedro.*¹¹ They had a grandchild, María Álvarez del Castillo, who was a sponsor, February 12, 1804.¹²

1. **B-2, Albuq.**
2. **Sp. Arch.,** I, No. 965.
3. Ibid., No. 362; name is here spelled "Yturbieta."
4. **M-4, Albuq.; M-11, Isleta.**
5. **DM,** 1766, in Albuq., no number; complaint by Luisa Aragón against him.
6. **Sp. Arch.,** I, Nos. 113, 362.
7. Ibid., II, No. 612.
8. **DM,** 1776, in Albuq., no number; also preceding **DM,** 1766.
9. **B-14, Cochiti.**
10. **M-54, Tomé,** M. Sec.
11. **AASF,** No. 30.
12. **B-54, Tomé.**

ZAMORA

JUAN DE ZAMORA, most likely the twenty-five-year-old native of New Mexico who passed muster in 1681,¹ was living at Santa Cruz with his wife and three children in 1696.²

1. **Revolt,** II, p. 128.
2. **Sp. Arch.,** I, No. 817.

APPENDIX
OF ADDITIONAL NAMES ON THE
CHARTS AND OTHER
PERSONS

ARCHULETA

JULIO ANTONIO ARCHULETA, son of Hilario Archuleta and Bernarda Trujillo, married *Margarita Lucero*, November 1, 1766. He was dead by 1774, for on March 19 of this year his widow married a Francisco Xavier Quintana.[1] Two known daughters of theirs were *María Manuela*, who married Atanasio de la Cerda on October 14, 1787;[2] and *María Ygnacia*, who became the wife of José María Quintana (q.v.).

* * * * * * * *

The genealogy of the famed COL. DIEGO ARCHULETA, like that of his contemporary, Governor Manuel Armijo, is difficult to trace for lack of immediate data on his parents. According to Twitchell, he was born at Alcalde, March 27, 1814, the son of Juan Andrés Archuleta. Diego had seven children by his wife, *Jesusita Trujillo*.[3] They had a daughter, *Margarita*, who married an Albino Vigil and died at Conejos in 1881.[4] Archuleta's military career is told by Twitchell in his work cited, as well as in an article by Don Diego himself in 1877 for *La Revista Catolica*.[5] He also wrote a defense of the Catholic Faith in 1882 for the same periodical, which printed a brief but poignant obituary when he died in Santa Fe on March 22, 1884.[6]

His father was, to all appearances, the Juan Andrés Archuleta who was the commander of militia in Rio Arriba in 1839.[7]

A similar case is that of another contemporary, the notorious JOSÉ GONZALES, leader of the Rio Arriba insurgents of 1837, who had himself elected Governor of New Mexico during a brief period of terror and bloodshed, and who has been described by all modern writers as a full-blooded Taos Indian.[8] According to the highly intelligent Chacón family of a generation ago, Gonzales was no Indian[9] but even if he had *genízaro* antecedents, he still was not the paint-and-feather Indian in the Governors' Palace which historical and fictional writers have described. Only a tedious and thorough exploration of the relationships mentioned could provide a clue to his true identity and ancestry.

DON ANTONIO JOSÉ MARTÍNEZ, another contemporary maligned in history and fiction, is another case in point. Twitchell wrote that he was the grandson of a General Martínez who came from Chihuahua in the early part of the seventeenth century.[10] But his baptismal and marriage data show Padre Martínez to have belonged to the old Martín Serrano family of New Mexico. He was baptized at Abiquiu on January 20, 1793, the son of Severino Martín and María del Carmen Santisteban. On May 20, 1812, he married María Luz Martín, daughter of Manuel Martín and María Manuela Quintana, and on the same day his sister Juana María married his bride's brother, José Manuel Martín.[11] His subsequent life's story is told by himself and others; a thorough investigation of all persons in it might not only bring out his complete ancestry but also disprove many a calumny.

The bigoted stories about GERTRUDIS BARCELÓ by Josiah Gregg and other pioneer American journalists were thoroughly aired in *El Palacio*.[12]

---

1. Both marriages in **M-25, S. Ild.**
2. **M-33, Sta. Clara.**
3. **The History of the Military Occupation of the Territory of New Mexico** (Denver: 1909).
4. **Revista Catolica**, Vol. VII, No. 12, p. 33.
5. Vol. V, No. 10, pp. 117, 118; other activities and letters in Vol. III, No. 14, pp. 157, 525, 557, 558, 592; No. 34, pp. 398, 406, 408.
6. **Ibid.**, Vol. VIII, No. 30, pp. 356 sqq.
7. See **El Palacio**, Vol. 60, No. 4, p. 159.
8. **Old Santa Fe**, pp. 200, 201.
9. Read, **Historia Ilustrada**, p. 457.
10. Twitchell, **Military Occupation**.
11. **B and M, Abiquiú**; see General José María Chávez, this Appendix, who married another girl of this family.
12. Vol. 57, No. 8, pp. 227-234.

ARMIJO

MANUEL ARMIJO, last Governor of New Mexico under the Mexican flag, is difficult to trace, for lack of a baptismal record and because of conflicting statements printed in the last hundred years. Twitchell wrote that his mother was Barbara Chávez, a sister of Julián Chávez (grandfather of Amado Chávez), and that Manuel had a brother.[1] Coan wrote that Manuel had a sister, *Isidora Armijo*, wife of Jesús María Chávez; their son, David Chávez, married Paz Sánchez, daughter of Desiderio Sánchez and Barbara Chávez, the latter a niece of Governor Armijo.[2] An *Anonymous History of New Mexico,* published in 1907, states that the Governor had a brother, *Juan Armijo,* married to Rosalia Ortega, and that both men were the sons of a Juan Armijo who came from Spain. A son of Juan, and nephew of Manuel, was Juan Cristóbal Armijo, married to a Juana María Chávez.[3]

A good starting point toward solving the problem is the documentary record of this brother Juan:

Juan Armijo and his wife *Rosalia Ortega* were living in the Albuquerque area when two of their children got married in 1830. Their daughter, *Manuela,* married José Chávez, son of Francisco (Xavier) Chávez and (Ana) María (Alvarez) del Castillo on April 11. A week later, April 17, their son, *Juan Cristóbal,* married Juana Chávez, sister of the above-named José Chávez.[4] If Twitchell was correct in saying that the Governor's mother was Barbara Chávez, then this Juan Armijo is in all likelihood the twenty-year-old Juan Armijo, son of Vicente Armijo and Barbara Chávez of Albuquerque, who joined the militia in 1808,[5] and was born around the year 1788. Juan's parents, and the Governor's, would then be the following couple:

VICENTE FERRER ARMIJO, eldest son of Manuel Segundo Durán de Armijo and Francisca Alfonsa Lucero de Godoy, asked to marry *Barbara Chávez,* daughter of Diego Antonio Durán y Chávez and Juana Silva, in 1769.[6] By 1790 they were living at the Plaza de San Antonio in Albuquerque, where he was a stockman and *Teniente,* fifty-five years old; his wife, Barbara *Casilda* Chávez was thirty-five, and they had seven children, not mentioned by name in the census.[7] The couple's difference in ages points to the possibility of Vicente's having been married before, and could very well be the Vicente Armijo who was a son-in-law in 1766 of a José Baca of Albuquerque.[8]

It seems, then, that two of the seven children enumerated were *Juan,* who married Rosalia Ortega, and *Manuel,* who married Trinidad Gabaldón and became famous in his day, if notorious to posterity. Perhaps the rest of the children were girls, *Isidora* among them. It then follows that their mother Barbara was not a sister of Julián Chávez, who had no sister by this name, but his aunt of this name, the sister of his father, Pedro Antonio Chávez. Hence, Julián Chávez and Manuel Armijo were first cousins.

Manuel Armijo gave his parents in 1819 as *Don Vicente Armijo,* deceased, and Doña María *Soledad* Chávez, when he asked to marry *Trinidad Gabaldón,* daughter of José Miguel Gabaldón and María Dolores Ortiz.[9] Here is the crux of the problem. Did the Padre err in writing "Soledad" for "Barbara" or "Casilda," a not unusual case? Or was she his step-mother, perhaps making Manuel and Juan half-brothers?

Manuel Armijo's character as Governor and as a man has been unjustly painted in sources too numerous to mention here. As for his family, he had no children. He reared a girl, Ramona, who married a Luis C. de Baca of Socorro,[10] and whom Armijo mentioned in his last will as "my universal heir

---

1. **Old Santa Fe,** pp. 338, 234.
2. **Hist. of N. M.,** Vol. II, p. 34.
3. Vol. I, pp. 68, 71.
4. Both in M-49, **Isleta.**
5. **HSNM,** Mil. Papers.
6. **DM,** 1769, in Albuq., no number.
7. **Sp. Arch.,** II, No. 1092b.
8. **Ibid.,** I, No. 1231.
9. **DM,** 1819, in Albuq., no number.
10. Twitchell, **loc. cit.**

and daughter, Ramona Armijo." In this will his wife, Trinidad Gabaldón, is mentioned as deceased. Minor bequests are made to Beatriz, a little girl reared by his wife; to three Armijo girls, Cleofas, Albina, and Clara; to Teresa; to Justo Sandoval; and to José Antonio Armijo.[11]

One of these females had married a José Torres of Socorro in 1851 as María Cleofas Armijo, adopted daughter of Manuel Armijo and Trinidad Gabaldón.[12] Perhaps she was a María Rita Cleofas, born on April 11, 1836, to Vicente Armijo and María de Jesús Otero.[13] This Vicente was a first cousin once removed of Manuel Armijo, if all the foregoing tentative genealogy is correct. By this same token, the Governor was a first cousin once removed of Col. Manuel Antonio Chávez, and a double first cousin once removed of José Encarnación Chávez (q.v. in this Appendix).

Manuel Armijo, husband of Trinidad Gabaldón, died at his estate in Lemitar, after receiving all the last Sacraments, and was buried in the church of Socorro on January 20, 1854.[14]

* * * * * * * *

Manuel Antonio Armijo, married to *Soledad Aragón*, was a contemporary of the Governor who might easily be confused because of their similar names and the similarity in sound of their wives' names. The two men were first cousins. This Manuel Antonio was the son of Pablo Antonio Armijo (brother of Vicente Ferrer Armijo) and Josefa Angela Chávez. He enlisted in the militia at the age of twenty-two in 1808,[15] and married Soledad Aragón at Valencia on February 26, 1815.[16]

Their known children were: *Teodoro*, born November 7, 1822;[17] *María Agustina*, May 8, 1825; *José María*, March 24, 1827,[18] who married Josefa Durán of Peña Blanca in 1849;[19] *Marianita*, wife of Mariano Gonzales;[20] *Pablo*, October 23, 1831; *María Librada*, October 2, 1833;[21] *María Leandra*, March 15, 1835;[22] and *Josefa*, wife of José María Montoya.[23]

* * * * * * * *

ANTONIO JOSÉ ARMIJO, son of Manuel Segundo Durán de Armijo and Francisca Alfonsa Lucero de Godoy, married *María Guadalupe Chávez*, daughter of Diego Antonio Chávez and Juana Silva, at Atrisco, June 16, 1774.[24] In 1790 they were living next to his brother, Vicente Ferrer Armijo, married to Guadalupe's sister Barbara Casilda, at the Plaza de San Antonio.[25] Their known children were the following:

Salvador Manuel, born June 9, 1775,[26] who was supposedly ambushed by Apaches at the Baca ranch of La Cienega around the year 1803;[27] *María Isabel*, July 3, 1777, who married Mariano Torres (q.v., this Appendix); *María Ygnacia*, January 18, 1779; and *José Francisco*, October 22, 1780.[28] Five younger children, named as minors in 1803 when their eldest brother was killed, were: *Lucas, Diego, Pedro, José Antonio,* and *Ana María*.[29] This last girl married a José Torres in 1811.[30] One son, José Francisco, is most likely the man of this name who married a Rosalia Mestas on March 19, 1801.[31]

---

11. English Copy of Will A. Kelleher from the original, probated in Socorro Co., Jan. 25, 1873.
12. DM, 1851, no number.
13. B-73, Tomé.
14. Bur., Soccorro.—N. B. Governor Armijo's parents actually were Vicente Armijo and Barbara Chávez. I made the mistake of transcribing "Soledad" for "Barbara" in DM, 1819 (see Note 9), and discovered the error after these pages were printed. The original MS had not been available for checking until now. Fortunately, this simple correction confirms the elaborate deductions made here.
15. HSNM, loc. cit.
16. M-56, Tomé.
17. B-71, Tomé; his godparents were Manuel Chávez and Isidora Armijo.
18. Both ibid.
19. DM, 1849, no number.
20. B-73, Tomé; bapt. of child, Nicolasa, Dec. 6, 1846.
21. Both in B-71, Tomé.
22. B-73, Tomé.
23. Ibid., bapt. of child, José Merced, Dec. 13, 1846.
24. M-3, Albuq.
25. Sp. Arch., II, No. 1092b.
26. B-3, Albuq.
27. Sp. Arch., I, No. 54.
28. The three in B-4, Albuq.
29. Sp. Arch., loc. cit.
30. B-54, Tomé; M. Sec.
31. M-4, Allbuq.; Sp. Arch., II, No. 2657.

BACA

JUAN FRANCISCO BACA, son of Juan Antonio Baca and Petronila García Jurado, married *María de Jesús* (no surname given) on January 2, 1749.[1] On several other occasions her last name is given as *Martín*, or *Martines*. Their known children were as follows:

Lugardo, born April 4, 1751; *Juan Antonio*, April 9, 1756; *Antonia Josefa*, March 13, 1756; *Paulín*, June 29, 1758,[2] who married María Lugarda Tafoya (see next section); and *Juana María*, who became the wife of José Francisco Pino, widower of Barbara Chávez, in 1780.[3] Their mother died sometime after April, 1772, when she acted as a sponsor with her husband.[4]

Juan Francisco next married *María Josefa Pino* on August 7, 1778.[5] They had a daughter, *Juana Lorenza*, who married Miguel Antonio Chávez on March 26, 1795.[6] This girl's mother must have died shortly after her birth, for in 1781 Juan Francisco, widowed of María Josefa Pino, applied to marry Manuela Antonia Sánchez.[7]

Paulín Baca, son of Juan Francisco Baca and María de Jesús Martín, married *María Lugarda Tafoya* at Belén on May 26, 1779.[8] By 1790 they were living in the second Plaza of Belén, when he gave his age as thirty-five, and hers as thirty-one. They had four boys (9-7-5-3) and a girl five months old.[9] Paulín died at Belén on October 12, 1832.[10] The known children were the following:

Pablo, who married María Manuela Lucero (see next section); *Juan*, who married Dolores Luna;[11] *Manuel*, who at twenty enrolled in the militia in 1808, and was then described as having *"pelo güero, ojos garzos, color blanco, sejas güeras, naris rroma y varios lunares en el rostro"*;[12] *José Tomás*, born November 18, 1796, who married Rosalia Lucero in 1819;[13] and *Rafael*, May 5, 1795, who first married Gertrudis García, and then Victoria Alderete on April 6, 1856.[14]

Pablo Baca, son of Paulín Baca and Lugarda Tafoya, married *María Manuela Lucero* in 1803.[15] They had the following known children at Los Bacas:

Rafaela Josefa, born April 21, 1805; *Pedro Sebastián*, January 20, 1808,[16] who married Refugio Serrano;[17] *Ana María Asención*, born May 31, 1810;[18] *María Josefa Lugarda*, June 18, 1813;[19] *Juan José Benigno*, February 15, 1819, who married Altagracia García, December 9, 1845;[20] *María Monica Antonia Francisca de Paula*, May 8, 1823;[21] and *José Tomás*, March 7, 1826,[22] who married Juana García (see next section).

Both parents were dead when their son Benigno appeared as a witness at Belén, October 30, 1845.[23] Sometime after 1860, members of this family joined other Belén families (García, Chávez, etc.) in migrating northeast to the newly-opened territory of present Mora County.

José Tomás Baca, son of Pablo Baca and María Manuela Lucero, married *Juana García* around the middle of the nineteenth century. As with other people mentioned in this Appendix, marriages at Belén for the first half of the century cannot be ascertained because the registers are missing or fragmen-

---

1. M-11, Isleta.
2. All in B-57, Isleta; Paulín's godparents were Domingo de Luna and Josefa Lucero.
3. B-54, Tomé.
4. B-57, Isleta.
5. M-49, Isleta.
6. B-54, Tomé.
7. DM, 1781, no number.
8. M-49, Isleta; DM, 1779, no number.
9. Sp. Arch., II, No. 1092b.
10. B-54, Tomé, Bur. Sec.
11. B-12, Belén, bapt. of child, Leonarda, April 12, 1851.
12. HSNM, Mil. Papers. See María Nicanora Baca, wife of Eugenio Chávez, in this Appendix.
13. B-54, Tomé; DM, 1819, in Albuq., no number.
14. M, Belén; B-54, Tomé.
15. DM, 1803, in Albuq., no number.
16. Both in B-54, Tomé.
17. B-12, Belén, bapt. of child, Jose Marcos, May 6, 1846.
18. B-54, Tomé.
19. B-8, Belén.
20. M-7 and B-8, Belén.
21. B-8, Belén; M, Watrous.
22. B-54, Tomé, rear B sec.
23. DM, 1845, in Belén, no number.

tary; hence the parentage of Juana García cannot be traced.²⁴

Their first recorded child was *Simon (a)*, born at Los Jarales, February 10, 1858, who married Damasio (Sánchez) García, May 19, 1874;²⁵ then *María Nicanora*, January 13, 1861, who married Eugenio Chávez (q.v., this Appendix); and *Felix*, May 23, 1863, who married Manuela Gonzales, February 21, 1898.²⁶ These children had two elder sisters: *Felipa Abelina*, who must have been born around 1850, and *María Gregoria*, her junior by a couple of years. The last-named was left with relatives in Belén when the families of José Tomás and his brother Benigno migrated to virgin territory near present Wagon Mound. The youngest daughter, María Nicanora, young wife of Eugenio Chávez, died at La Ciruela on April 29, 1884. Tomás Baca, husband of Juana García, died there four years later, February 13, 1888,²⁷ the day before death came for Archbishop Lamy in Santa Fe.

Two other known children were *Miguel*, who married Teresa Vargas, November 16, 1879, and *Celsa*, who married Felix García, December 9, 1887.²⁸

---

24. These missing books most likely contained the marriage entries for Col. Manuel A. Chávez and Governor Armijo.
25. **B, Belén.**
26. Both in **B, Belén.** Marriage of Felix in **M, Watrous.** María Nicanora's name was transposed by mistake with that of another girl in the preceding entry, María Victoria Torres.
27. **Bur, Watrous.**
28. Both in **M, Watrous.**

CHÁVEZ

JOSÉ MARIANO CHÁVEZ, son of Cristóbal Chávez and María Josefa Núñez, married *María Manuela Romero*, his second cousin, February 2, 1773.¹ In 1790 they were living in the third Plaza of Los Chávez. His widowed mother, forty-nine, lived with them. He gave his age as thirty-four, and his trade that of a weaver. His wife was twenty-nine, and they had four boys (15-13-8-6) and two girls (14-10).² By 1802 they had moved to the first Plaza of Los Chávez.³ José Mariano died at Belén in May, 1829.⁴

Their known sons were: *José Cristóbal*, born February 20, 1774, who married Agustina Jurado at Tomé;⁵ *Juan José*, who married María Antonia Silva, April 1, 1810, at Belén;⁶ *José Manuel*, born at Los Chávez, March 7, 1794, who married Tomasa Gonzales at Cebolleta, August 17, 1817;⁷ *José Antonio*, who married María de la Luz Salaices;⁸ *José de la Encarnación*, March 25, 1796, at Los Chávez,⁹ who married María Rita Torres (see next section); *Ambrosio*, who married María Ynez Jaramillo at Cebolleta, April 23, 1815;¹⁰ and *José Teodoro*, who married María Josefa Gutiérrez at Cebolleta, April 1, 1818.¹¹

Their known daughters were: *María Gertrudis*, January 11, 1799, who married Juan Antonio Salazar, November 16, 1814, at Cebolleta;¹² *María Barbara*, who married Francisco Antonio Romero at Los Chávez, August 20, 1798, and died May 21, 1831;¹³ and *María Nicolasa*, who married José Andrés Jaramillo at Cebolleta, September 4, 1814.¹⁴

This family of José Mariano Chávez and María Manuela Romero came to be known locally as "Los Chávez Mexicanos,"¹⁵ from the fact that Mariano's mother was an outsider, an *española* of the City of Mexico whom his father had brought to New Mexico as a fourteen-year-old bride.¹⁶ As can be noted in their marriages, some of the children were pioneer settlers of the Cebolleta region, while some children of the son treated next were pioneers of the north Mora country.

José Encarnación Chávez, son of Mariano Chávez and María Manuela Romero, married *María Rita Torres* of Belén. Their wedding date is not known, due to missing registers, but the parents of both are known from the baptisms of their many children. (Fortunately, the Padre at this particular period entered the grandparents in the baptismal books.)

Their known sons were as follows: *José Francisco Sebastián*, born January 20, 1823, at the Plaza de los Trujillos in Belén,[17] who married Encarnación Luna (see next section); *Francisco de Paula*, April 20, 1831,[18] who married María Manuela Padilla, both pioneers of La Ciruela near present Wagon Mound;[19] *Juan Andrés*, February 24, 1833;[20] *José Marcelino*, June 23, 1839,[21] and believed at first to be the "José" who married Encarnación Luna,[22] *José Estanislao*, May 15, 1841;[23] and *José Manuel*, who married Manuela Gallegos at La Cueva in Mora County, October 19, 1866, and then Juana Romero at La Ciruela, November 22, 1868.[24]

Their daughters were: *María de los Santos*, born October 1, 1825;[25] *María Ynez*, January 25, 1835;[26] *María de los Angeles de las Nieves*, August 5, 1836, whose marriage to a José Chávez, a relative, was revalidated at Los Jarales, March 8, 1857;[27] *María Martina*, who married José Rey García, March 14, 1842;[28] and *María Manuela*, January 1, 1844, who married Juan García in 1856.[29]

Their father had died by 1857, when a daughter's marriage was revalidated. The widowed María Rita Torres, with some of her married and single children, joined other families of Belén which moved north to the newly-opened territory which is now eastern Mora County. The date of this migration, from marriage and other data, can be placed at about 1860-1863. They first went to the already settled valley of La Cueva near Mora, where María Rita died at the age of sixty on July 17, 1863. The family then moved east into new country and founded La Ciruela in 1864.[30]

José (Francisco Sebastián) Chávez, son of José Encarnación Chávez and María Rita Torres, married *Encarnación Luna* at Belén on October 3, 1845.[31] The births of three known children are as follows: *Eugenio*, November 16, 1854,[32] who married María Nicanora Baca (see next section); *José Manuel de los Reyes*, January 1, 1858; and *José Tranquilino*, January 9, 1861.[33] Another son, *Remigio*, married Gabina Montoya, October 9, 1880.[33a] The young family moved to the Mora country with María Rita Torres. At La Ciruela, Encarnación Luna died young between the years 1864-1866, the fame of her striking beauty lasting for three generations in the Wagon Mound country. Her young widowed husband married Encarnación Mascareñas at La Ciruela, February 16, 1867.[34] Two known children of this marriage were *Abelina*, who married Jesús María Gallegos, December 10, 1888, and *Filiberto*, born June 10, 1877.[34a]

Eugenio Chávez, son of José Chávez and Encarnación Luna, married *Nicanora Baca* at La Ciruela, January 13, 1877. The witnesses were the groom's uncle and aunt, Francisco Chávez and Manuela Padilla.[35] Their children were: *María Elfida*, November 5, 1877; *Fabián*, January 20, 1879 (see next section); *María Soraida*, April 24, 1881; and *José Demóstenes*, June 18, 1883.[36]

Like her husband's Luna mother, Nicanora

---

1. DM, 1773, No. 4; M-11, Isleta.
2. Sp. Arch., II, No. 1092b.
3. AASF, No. 30.
4. B-54, Tomé, Bur. Sec.
5. B-37, Isleta; B-54, Tomé, M. Sec.; he was dead by Oct. 24, 1841, and she by the end of 1845. (M-7 and B-12, Belén.)
6. B-54, Tomé, M. Sec.
7. B-54, Tomé; M, Laguna, at Gallup; their parents known from bapt. of son, José de Jesús, Aug. 15, 1824 (B-8, Belén).
8. B-8, Belen; bapt. of son, Antonio, Feb. 11, 1824.
9. B-54, Tomé.
10. M, Laguna, at Gallup.
11. Ibid.
12. B-54, Tomé; M, Laguna, at Gallup.
13. B-54, Tomé, M and Bur. Sec.
14. M, Laguna, at Gallup.
15. B-8, Belén, Aug. 15, 1824.
16. DM, 1762, no number; Sp. Arch., II, No. 1092b.
17. B-8, Belen.
18. B-10, Belén.
19. Both sponsors at wedding of Eugenio Chávez (q.v. this Appendix).
20. B-9, Belén; this book (1832-1833) and B-58, Isleta (1829-1842) are fragments of larger books.
21. B-10, Belén.
22. El Palacio, Vol. 55, No. 4, p. 119, note 53.
23. B-11, Belén.
24. M-46, Mora.
25. B-54, Tomé.
26. B-11, Belén.
27. B-11 and M-7, Belén.
28. M-7, Belén.
29. B-12, Belén; M, Tomé.
30. Bur., Mora; La Ciruela, near present Wagon Mound, and long extinct, was 22 years old in 1886 (Rev. Cat., Vol. 12, No. 27, p. 314).
31. M-7, Belén; DM, 1845, no number, has Oct. 25 instead. The groom was 20, and the bride 12.
32. B, Belén.
33. Both, Ibid.
33a. M, Watrous.
34. M-46, Mora.
34a. M and B, Watrous.
35. M, Watrous.
36. All at La Ciruela (B, Watrous).

Baca died young at the age of twenty-four, on April 29, 1884,[37] and likewise left a legend, of possessing unusually blue eyes and blonde hair (see *Baca*, Note 12, this Appendix).

Eugenio then married *Paula Mascareñas* at Santa Clara (now Wagon Mound) on August 3, 1885, by whom he had a large family: *Elías*, May 7, 1886; *María Manuela*, January 1, 1888; *Juan Bautista*, January 26, 1890; *María Encarnación*, October 2, 1892; *Tomás*, May 19, 1894; *María Simona*, February 18, 1896; *María Floripa*, February 16, 1898; *José Eugenio*, March 13, 1900; *Cresencio*, April 9, 1902; *Tomasito*, June 18, 1905; and *Manuela*, March 25, 1908.[38]

Fabián Chávez, son of Eugenio Chávez and Nicanora Baca, married *María Nicolasa Roybal* in Wagon Mound, July 9, 1909, with George and Aurelia King as witnesses.[39] Here they had their first four children: *Manuel Ezequiel*, April 10, 1910 (now *Fray Angélico* in the Franciscan Order); *María Marta*, August 20, 1911; and the twins, *Romualdo Eugenio* and *Nicanora Mónica* (each twin bears both grandparents' names), October 16, 1915.[40] The family then moved to Mora where the following were born: *Dominga Adela*, July 11, 1918; *María Consuelo*, April 9, 1921; and *Francisco Eugenio*, September 4, 1922.[41] The next place of residence was Santa Fe, and the birthplace of *Fabián*, August 31, 1924; *Antonio Esteban*, November 27, 1926; and *José Alfredo Camilo*, July 18, 1931.[42]

* * * * * * * *

FRANCISCO XAVIER CHÁVEZ, son of Pedro Durán y Chávez and Juana Montoya, and who married *Manuela Padilla*, September 29, 1735,[43] had the following known children:

Tomás, December 20, 1737,[44] who married María Josefa Padilla (see next section); *Domingo*, March 28, 1741, who married Agustina Padilla, his second cousin, in 1764, and then María Manuela Aguirre, another second cousin, in 1779;[45] *José Antonio*, April 10, 1746;[46] *María Teresa de Jesús*, born in 1749 and who married her second cousin, Manuel Lucero, in 1763;[47] *María Concepción*, December 22, 1753; and *Miguel Antonio*, September 3, 1756.[48]

Tomás Chávez, son of Francisco Xavier Chávez and Manuela Padilla, married *María Josefa Padilla*, his second cousin and sister-in-law, October 20, 1759.[49] They were living at Los Padillas in 1790, he a stockman fifty-four years old, and his wife, fifty-one. They had five sons (26-25-13-11-?) and two girls (27-17).[50] Their known children's names were:

Francisco Xavier (I), January 10, 1768, who must have died soon after; *Francisco Xavier* (II), April 3, 1769,[51] who married Ana María Alvarez del Castillo (see next section); *Ursula*, wife of Antonio Sandoval;[52] *Geronimo; Agustín; José Antonio;*[53] and *Ramón*, who married Rafaela Sánchez.[54]

Francisco Xavier Chávez, son of Tomás Chávez and María Josefa Padilla, married *Ana María Alvarez del Castillo*, September 14, 1799.[55] They were living at Los Padillas in 1803.[56] He became Governor or *Jefe Politico* of New Mexico, July 5, 1822, upon the establishment of the Mexican Republic, succeeding the last Spanish Governor, Don Facundo Melgares.[57]

His family, according to the records, is as follows: *Mariano José*, December 8, 1808;[58] *José*, who married Manuela Armijo, April

---

37. **Bur, Watrous.**
38. All in **B** and **M, Watrous**. By an error the priest wrote **Tomasita** for the second last child, and also transposed the name of the last child, **Manuela**, with that of a "Dionisia Sinforosa" Martínez, baptized on the same day.
39. **M, Watrous.**
40. All in **B, Watrous.**
41. All in **B, Mora.**
42. All in **B, Santa Fe.** (Cathedral.)
43. **M-11, Isleta.**
44. **B-57, Isleta.**
45. **DM,** 1764 and 1779, in Albuq., no number.
46. **B-57, Isleta.**
47. **B-57, Isleta; DM,** 1763, in Albuq., no number.
48. Both in **B-57, Isleta.**
49. **M-11, Isleta; Sp. Arch.,** I, Nos. 122, 209.
50. **Sp. Arch.,** II, No. 1092b.
51. Both in **B-57, Isleta.**
52. **Sp. Arch.,** I, Nos. 209, 216; II, No. 2620.
53. **Ibid.;** "Antonio José Chávez," wrote Twitchell, was Governor (1823-1831), and a brother of Ursula Chávez, wife of Gov. Antonio Sandoval (**Leading Facts,** II, pp. 25-26, notes).
54. **Sp. Arch.,** I, No. 209.
55. **B-54, Tomé,** M Sec.
56. **AASF,** No. 30.
57. Bancroft, **Hist. of N. M.,** p. 284.
58. **B-54, Tomé;** Twitchell wrote that he married Dolores Perea of Bernalillo and became Governor in 1835 (**op. cit.**).

11, 1830;⁵⁹ *Antonio José,* who married Barbara Armijo,⁶⁰ called "José David" by Twitchell, and who was murdered by Texas outlaws near Chávez Creek in Kansas;⁶¹ *Juana,* who married Juan Cristóbal Armijo, April 17, 1830;⁶² *María Francisca,* who married Antonio José Otero, April 30, 1834; and *Merced,* who married Juan Otero, May 27, 1837.⁶³

Twitchell names another son, *Tomás,* who married a niece of Bishop Zubiría of Durango and became a prominent lawyer in the Mexican Republic, and three more girls: *Dolores,* who married José Leandro Perea of Bernalillo; *Barbara,* married to Juan Gutiérrez of Pajarito; and *Manuela Antonia,* wife of José María Gutiérrez of Bernalillo.⁶⁴ This last girl, as a widow, joined the Sisters of Charity, recently come to New Mexico. After twenty-two years as "Sister Dolores," she died in Santa Fe, April 13, 1887.⁶⁵

* * * * * * * *

PEDRO ANTONIO CHÁVEZ, son of Diego Antonio Chávez and Juana Silva, married *María Catalina Baca* in September, 1772.⁶⁶ He was a stockman, forty years old, residing at Atrisco in 1790; his wife was thirty.⁶⁷ Their place of residence in 1803 was the second Plaza of San Fernando at Los Chávez.⁶⁸ Their children, according to the records, were the following:

María Juliana, March 14, 1774;⁶⁹ *María Gertrudis,* November 11, 1777; *María Toribia,* April 7, 1779; the twins, *Ana Teresa* and *Juana María,* October 23, 1780; *María Gregoria,* November 29, 1781; *Tomás Mauricio,* September 25, 1784;⁷⁰ *Rafael Antonio,* October 20, 1787, who married Polonia García at Cebolleta, December 10, 1830;⁷¹ *María Guadalupe,* December 20, 1800, who married Juan Policarpio Serna at Cebolleta, September 24, 1815;⁷² *Francisca Antonia,* February 15, 1802;⁷³ and *Diego Antonio,* who married Barbara Baca, or Jaramillo, August 11, 1816, at Cebolleta.⁷⁴

A census list of the family at Atrisco in 1802⁷⁵ omits the first three girls, who must have died or were already married, and includes two more boys, *José Julián* and *Ambrosio.* José Julián might well be the firstborn, entered as a girl by mistake in the register of 1774, and who married María Luz García (see next section).

———

Julián Chávez and wife *María Luz García* were living in the Cebolleta country when their son *Pedro* married Asención Chávez on April 13, 1831.⁷⁶ Otherwise they do not appear in the Rio Abajo records, many of which are fragmentary. According to what was told Twitchell, Julián was the son of Pedro Antonio Chávez and Catalina Baca,⁷⁷ and this is substantially proven by the foregoing data. Another son, who became justly famous, was *Manuel Antonio,* whose baptismal record is not extant, but whose parentage was amply testified to by contemporary witnesses who sang his praises as a soldier and Indian fighter, and later as an American officer. According to these sources, he was born at Atrisco on October 18, 1818,⁷⁸ but both date and birthplace seem unlikely. While correct regarding contemporary facts, Lummis and Twitchell are greatly in error when it comes to the more remote ancestry of their hero, as may be seen in the factual record of the family and descendants of Don Fernando Durán y Chávez.

———

Manuel Antonio Chávez, son of Julián Chávez and María Luz García, married *Vicenta Labadie,* a daughter of Lorenzo Labadie according to Twitchell.⁷⁹ No record of this marriage can be found, for reasons given several

---

59. **M-49, Isleta.** Twitchell says he was Governor in 1845, succeeding Gov. Martínez **(op. cit.; Old Santa Fe,** pp. 232, 245).
60. **B-58, Isleta;** bapt. of son José Feliciano Melquiades, Oct. 25, 1841. Their daughter María Felipa Josefa married Felipe, son of José Chávez and Manuela Armijo (bapt. of daughter Margarita, May 11, 1858).
61. **Leading Facts, loc. cit.**
62. **M-49, Isleta.**
63. Both, **ibid.**
64. **Loc. cit.**
65. **Rev. Cat.,** Vol. 13, No. 17, p. 193; No. 18, p. 205.
66. **DM,** 1772, in Albuq., no number.
67. **Sp. Arch.,** II, No. 1092b.
68. **AASF, loc. cit.**
69. **B-3, Albuq.**
70. All in **B-4, Albuq.**
71. **B-4, Albuq.; M, Laguna,** in Gallup.
72. **Ibid.**
73. **B-4, Albuq.**
74. **M, Laguna,** in Gallup.
75. **AASF, loc. cit.**
76. **M, Laguna,** in Gallup.
77. **Old Santa Fe,** pp. 467, 468, 281-284.
78. Twitchell, **loc. cit.,** and **Leading Facts,** II, p. 383, note; C. F. Lummis, **A New Mexico David,** pp. 190-217.
79. **Old Santa Fe, loc. cit.**

times in this Appendix. She was most likely a *María Vicenta*, born at Tomé on October 29, 1829, the daughter of Pablo Labadie and María Rosa de los Reyes Cisneros; this pair had two other known children, José Lorenzo and María Manuela Labadie, born in 1825 and 1827 respectively.[80]

Manuel Antonio and his wife had eight children, among whom were the outstanding citizens, *Amado* and *Irineo*. Their father died at San Mateo in 1889.[81] No matter how poor the documentary data as regards births and marriages, the ancestry of Col. Manuel Antonio Chávez comes out clearly despite some glaring errors by Lummis and Twitchell, who did a great service, nevertheless, in recording his military fame. These writings, and his handsome portrait that used to hang in the Museum at Santa Fe, inspired Walla Cather to paint him masterfully with words in *Death Comes for the Archbishop*.

* * * * * * * *

The ancestry of JOSÉ MARÍA CHÁVEZ, who rose to the rank of Brigadier General in the Army of the United States, is not quite clear, again for lack of documentary data. According to a memory genealogy given to Twitchell, when his descendants let him copy the original will and testament of Don Fernando Durán y Chávez (made in 1707), José María was the son of Francisco Antonio Chávez and Francisca Rosalia Velarde, the grandson of a Tomás *Baca*, and the great-grandson of "Diego Antonio Chávez" and Antonia Baca. This "Diego Antonio" was the son of Don Fernando Durán y Chávez and Lucía Hurtado de Salazar.[82] A careful reading of the old script would have shown them that Don Fernando did not have a son called "Diego Antonio," but his third eldest son was "Antonio" simply. We now know that this Antonio did marry an Antonia Baca, by whom he had a large family, that one son was named "Tomas," and also that the original will and testament of Don Fernando, after the untimely death of his first son, and the later dementia of his second son, had passed into the hands of the third son, Antonio. The following genealogy, then, is quite logical.

TOMÁS CHÁVEZ, son of Antonio Durán y Chávez and Antonia Baca, married Tomasa Padilla on December 3, 1742,[83] and they had the following known children:

María Antonia, November 13, 1743;[84] *Juan José*, February 4, 1745, who married Ana María Baca in September, 1772;[85] *Eugenio Francisco*, January 16, 1749; *Antonio*, December 24, 1752;[86] *Juan Ignacio*, February 1, 1756; *Juan Bautista*, July 14, 1767;[87] and *Victoria Ana* (Antonia?), who married her second cousin, José Baca of Atrisco, in 1784.[88] Either of the sons, Eugenio Francisco or Antonio, could well be the Francisco Antonio who married Francisca Rosalia Velarde.

Francisco Antonio Chávez lived in the Rio Arriba country of his wife, *Francisca Rosalia Velarde*, when their son, *José María del Socorro*, was born on September 27, 1801.[89] Another son, *Mariano Antonio Melquiades*, was born on December 18, 1803.[90] A third, *José Manuel Roque*, married María Dolores Martín, November 21, 1819.[91] The family information given to Twitchell names these three sons as José María, Mariano, and José Manuel, and also, *Teodora, María Manuela, Julián,* and *Josefa,* the latter married to Eusebio Martínez. It also mentions that José María was married to María de Jesús Martínez, daughter of José Manuel Martínez y Serrano, and sister of Dolores Martínez, his brother's wife.

These Martinez people, incidentally, belonged to the old Martín Serrano family of Rio Arriba. The wives of José María and José Manuel were sisters of the short-lived bride of Antonio José Martín, later the fa-

---

80. **B-71** and **B-72, Tomé.**
81. Twitchell, loc. cit.
82. Twit. Coll., No. 204.
83. **M-11, Isleta.**
84. **B-3, Albuq.**
85. **B-57, Isleta;** DM, 1722, no number.
86. Both in **B-3, Albuq.**
87. Both in **B-57, Isleta.**
88. DM, 1784, in Albuq., no number.
89. **B-31, Sta. Clara.**
90. Ibid.
91. **M-1, Abiquiú.**

mous Padre Martínez of Taos. (See *Archuleta* section in this Appendix.)

José María Chávez and his wife *María de Jesús Martín* had their residence in their paternal Abiquiu district. His General's sword, which had belonged to General Santa Ana of Mexico, had been presented to him by a General Oxford of the American Army; in 1920 it was still in the possession of Julián Chávez of La Gallina.[92] Don José María celebrated his hundredth birthday in October, 1901, when the *Revista Catolica* of Las Vegas extolled his rise from a Lieutenant in the Spanish Army to a Colonel in the Mexican, and to a General in the American. He died a year later, on November 22, 1902, at Abiquiu, after receiving the last Sacraments in the full use of his mental faculties.[93]

92. **Twit. Coll.**, loc. cit.
93. **Rev. Cat.**, Vol. 27, No. 42, p. 494; Vol. 28, No. 50, p. 592.

GONZÁLEZ

JUAN DE LOS REYES GONZÁLEZ, according to family recollections, was the son of an Isidora González, sister of a *Pedro González* who had married *Antonia Roybal*, daughter of Mariano Roybal and María Loreta Velásquez. Antonia's brother, Juan Manuel Roybal, adopted and reared Juan de los Reyes. All this happened in the Rio Arriba or Santa Clara Valley. However, the parents of Pedro and Isidora González have not been ascertained so far. Moreover, the parents of Juan de los Reyes, in the baptism of two of his children, are given as Pedro González and Antonia Roybal.

Juan de los Reyes migrated east over the Rockies to the Mora country, evidently with his Roybal relatives, either shortly before or after he had married *María Asención Sánchez*, or *Martín*.

Their known children were baptized at "lo de Mora," the first two by the Padre of Picurís, who attended that district before the parish of Mora was established. These were *José Higinio*, born February 21, 1849,[1] who as a resident later of La Ciruela married María Ygnacia Abeyta on July 5, 1869;[2] and *José Miguel*, born on November 24, 1851, who married Clara Nolán, December 22, 1879.[3] Their younger sister, *María Monica*, was born at La Cueva on August 15, 1856, and baptized on August 25 by the first pastor of Mora.[4] She became the wife of Romualdo Roybal (*q.v.*, this Appendix).

The *Sánchez* and *Martín* people mentioned in the foregoing baptisms are also difficult to trace during this transition period, when families of the north Rio Grande Valley moved directly or in slow stages to the new Mora area through Taos or the Truchas-Picuris route. The priest of Taos or Picuris, traveling hundreds of miles on horseback to visit those areas, could easily have lost some record notes; yet, through known relationships, the identity of an unrecorded person might ultimately be found. For example, *María Asención Sánchez* was first cousin to a Felipe Sánchez, who had migrated to the Mora-Las Vegas area with his wife, Bonifacia Lujan. The latters' children, Pascuala[5] and Patricio[6] Sánchez, regarded Monica González as their second cousin. The eventual discovery of the marriage of Felipe Sánchez' parents, Manuel Sánchez and María Concepción Martín[7] would open new paths, if their parents were fortunately included in the marriage entry.

For **José Gonzales**, insurgent Governor, see *Archuleta* in this Appendix.

1. **B, Picuris.** His paternal grandparents are given as Pedro González and María Antonia Roybal, and the maternal as **Francisco** Martín and María (Nicolasa) Sánchez.
2. **M-46, Mora.**
3. **B, Picuris.** His paternal grandparents are the same as the above, but the maternal are given as **Juan Ignacio** Martín and Nicolasa Sánchez. Miguel's marriage in **M, Watrous.**
4. **B-1, Mora.**
5. Born at Rincon de Tecolote, May 22, 1859 (**ibid.**).
6. Born at Rociada, Feb. 10, 1867 (**ibid.**).
7. Felipe's parents given at bapt. in Tecolote of his daughter **Encarnación**, Feb. 25, 1855 (**B, Las Vegas**).

LUCERO

MARCOS LUCERO DE GODOY, son of Diego Lucero de Godoy and Margarita Baca, married *María Antonia Gómez del Castillo*, October 20, 1749.[1] In 1763 he was living in Ojo Caliente and asking for land near San Ildefonso that had belonged to his wife's grandmother.[2] He died at El Rancho de San Ildefonso on August 15, 1790.[3] His known children were the following:

Margarita Juliana, February 20, 1752,[4] who married Julio Archuleta (q.v. this Appendix), and then Francisco Xavier Quintana, March 19, 1774;[5] *María Andrea*, December 7, 1754, who married Juan Domingo Valdés, and then Mariano Trujillo, January 17, 1797;[6] *José Manuel*, who married María Manuela Sánchez in 1785;[7] *Francisco Miguel*, September 20, 1756; and *María de Jesús*, January 20, 1759,[8] who married José Julián Quintana at Santa Cruz in June, 1772.[9]

* * * * * * * *

MANUEL LUCERO, son of Miguel Lucero II and his first wife Rosa Baca, married his second and third cousin, *Teresa Chávez*, May 20, 1764, at Los Padillas.[10] Their known children were: *María Antonia*, born February 7, 1774; *Vicente*, January 10, 1776;[11] and *Andrés*, who married Tomasa García in May, 1798.[12]

After Teresa's death, Manuel married another second cousin, *Barbara Montoya*, April 27, 1781, at Atrisco.[13] Miguel was dead by 1790 when Barbara, twenty-nine years old and a widow, was living in the Plaza de San Andrés at Los Padillas with her three daughters (10-9-7). By 1803, she was living at the second Plaza de San Fernando at Los Chávez with two daughters, *Josefa* and *Manuela* Lucero.[14] The name of the third daughter is not known. The girl Manuela became the wife of Pablo Baca (q.v., this Appendix).

---

1. M-29, Sta. Cruz.
2. Sp. Arch., I, No. 1351.
3. B-33, Sta. Cruz, Bur. Sec.
4. B-24, S. Ild.
5. M-25, S. Ild.
6. B-24, S. Ild.; B-17, Nambé, M. Sec.
7. M-33, Sta. Clara; DM, 1785, No. 5.
8. Both in B-31, Sta. Clara.
9. DM, 1772, in Albuq., no number.
10. M-11, Isleta; DM, 1763, in Albuq., no number.
11. Both in B-57, Isleta.
12. DM, 1798, in Albuq., no number.
13. M-4, Albuq.; she was the widow of Juan Antonio Baca of Atrisco (DM, 1770, in Albuq., no number).
14. Sp. Arch., II, No. 1092b; AASF, No. 30.

LUNA

JOSÉ TORIBIO LUNA, son of José Enrique Luna and Juana María Gabaldón, was born at the first Plaza of Los Chávez on April 16, 1799.[1] He married *María Manuela Montaño* in the first half of the 1800's, for which the registers are lost, and hence her identity and ancestry are unknown so far (see Manuel Armijo and Manuel Antonio Chávez, this Appendix).

Both parents were dead when their twelve-year-old orphan daughter, *Encarnación*, married José Chávez in Belén, October 3, 1845.[2] Encarnación Luna was a first cousin of Jesús Luna in the following section.

A *José Dolores Luna*, son of Toribio Luna and Manuela Montaño, married María Guadalupe Baca at San Miguel, November 26, 1851.[3] Evidently, he was an orphan brother of Encarnación who had been taken by migrating relatives to San Miguel.

* * * * * * * *

JESÚS LUNA, known to be a first cousin of Encarnación Luna, was the child of any of the other sons (or daughters) of José Enrique Luna and Juana María Gabaldón. (One son, Antonio José Luna, is excepted, for he had a son, also named "Jesus," who is accounted for in the next section.)

On a journey to California, Jesús Luna married *Jesusita Col* at Mission San Luis Obispo, June 3, 1850,[4] and brought her back to New Mexico. Evidently he had driven sheep to the coast on that occasion, perhaps for his uncle Antonio José Luna, who became wealthy out of this trade.[5]

They had a daughter, *Emilia*, who married a Joseph Brown of Canada at Mora, March 8, 1869,[6] and later was the wife of William Nelson King.[7]

* * * * * * * *

ANTONIO JOSÉ LUNA, son of José Enrique Luna and Juana María Gabaldón, was married to *Isabel Baca*, daughter of Juan Cruz Baca and María Luisa Castillo, according to the baptism of a son, *Jesús María y José*, July 9, 1837.[8] This son married Adelaida Luna, September 17, 1858, and years later as a widower married Refugio Sena of Santa Fe, June 28, 1879.[9]

Twitchell wrote that Antonio José was born in 1808 at Los Lunas, and named Jesús María as his eldest son, who became a leading political figure and captain of militia. He also named two other sons who were also civic leaders, *Tranquilino* and *Salomón*, the latter married to Adelaida Otero;[9a] and also two daughters, *Eloisa*, married first to Manuel Basilio Otero and then to Alfred M. Bergere; and *Luz*, wife of José María Romero. There were four other children whom Twitchell does not name.[10]

Don Antonio José Luna, father of the Hon. Tranquilino Luna, delegate to Congress, died on December 20, 1881, at Los Lunas.[11]

---

1. **B-54, Tomé.**
2. **M-7, Belén; DM,** 1845, no number. See Chávez, this Appendix.
3. **M, San Miguel del Vado.**
4. **M-1, Mission San Miguel** (Calif.), p. 56.
5. Twitchell, **Leading Facts,** II, pp. 492-493, notes.
6. **M-46, Mora.**
7. Bapt. of son **George,** June 7, 1879, at Agua Dulce (**B, Ocate**), and marriage of son **Albert,** Oct. 18, 1902 (**M, Watrous**).
8. **B-73, Tomé.**
9. **M, Isleta** and **Sta. Fe.**
9a. Jan. 15, 1882, daughter of Manuel and Ana María Otero (**M-Tomé**).
10. **Loc. cit.,** and **Old Santa Fe,** p. 465.
11. Obituary in **Rev. Cat.,** Vol. VII, No. 52, p. 1.

MONTOYA

MIGUEL MONTOYA, son of Salvador Montoya and Manuela García de la Riva, married *Rosa Baca,* widow of José de Silva, April 9, 1729.[1] She died the following year on April 15, in bearing a daughter, *Gertrudis,* who was baptized on May 15, 1730.[2] This child lived to marry Juan Miguel Alvarez del Castillo.[3]

Miguel then married *Lucía Durán y Chávez* on March 21, 1734.[4] They had the following children: *Miguel,* who married Joaquina Montes Vigil in 1771;[5] *Francisco,* who married Juliana Montes Vigil in 1772 at El Puesto del Cerro Cabezón;[6] *Pedro,* who married Juana Mirabal in 1779;[7] *Juan Cristóbal,* who married Luisa Padilla in 1785;[8] *María de la Luz,* born September 19, 1749; *Juan Manuel,* December 22, 1747; *Antonio Anselmo de la Trinidad,* October 24, 1752; *José Alejandro,* April 26, 1755; and *Barbara,* January 5, 1757,[9] who married her first and second cousin, Juan Antonio Baca of Atrisco, in 1770, and in 1781 became the wife of another second cousin, Manuel Lucero of Los Padillas.[10] One of their daughters, Manuela Lucero, became the wife of Pablo Baca (*q.v.,* this Appendix).

---

1. **M-3, Albuq.**
2. **Bur-2, Albuq.; B-57, Isleta.**
3. **Sp. Arch.,** II, No. 642.
4. **M-3, Albuq.**
5. **DM,** 1771, no number; **Sp. Arch.,** I, No. 571.
6. **DM,** 1772, no number; both parents mentioned as dead.
7. **Ibid.,** 1779, no number.
8. **Ibid.,** 1785, no number.
9. All five in **B-3, Albuq.**
10. **DM,** 1770, 1781, in Albuq., no number.

ORTIZ

JUAN ANTONIO ORTIZ, son of Nicolás Ortiz III and Gertrudis Páez Hurtado, married *María Loreta Ribera*, on December 13, 1755.[1] In 1790 they were living in Santa Fe, he as an *hacendero* fifty-eight years old, while his wife was fifty-two.[2] He made his last will on September 5, 1795, before going out on an Indian campaign as a Lieutenant of Militia. In this will, and hers in 1822, they each name their eight children,[3] although the baptismal records name a ninth, who must have died in early infancy. These children are as follows:

Julián Antonio, born February 19, 1759; *Pedro Antonio*, July 5, 1760; *María Polonia*, February 12, 1762; *María Petrona*, February 4, 1764; *Antonio Matías*, March 4, 1768,[4] who married Francisca Baca, April 11, 1790;[5] *Antonio de Jesús*, February 2, 1770; *Juan Rafael*, October 30, 1774,[6] who married three times and became the father of two priests (see next section); *Gertrudis;* and *Ignacio*, the last two mentioned in the will, and Ignacio becoming the husband of María Luz Silva.[7]

Juan Rafael Ortiz, son of Juan Antonio Ortiz and María Loreta Ribera, married *María Loreta Baca*, August 28, 1796.[8] They had a son, *Juan Felipe*, September 15, 1797,[9] who became a priest and was the Vicar in Santa Fe for the Bishop of Durango when the United States occupied New Mexico in 1846.

Widowed shortly after, Juan Rafael then married *Estéfana Delgado*, April 27, 1801.[10] She bore him the following known children: *María Monica Dolores*, May 5, 1805; *José Manuel Apolinario*, July 25, 1807,[11] who married Ana Durán, April 9, 1824;[12] *José Fernando*, May 20, 1809, who married Estéfana Ortiz, September 8, 1839;[13] and *Francisco Antonio*, January 20, 1812.[14]

The second wife died on February 12, 1814, and Juan Rafael then married *Gertrudis Pino*, widow of Mariano Durán, February 14, 1816.[15] Their known children were: *María Isabel*, November 19, 1816; *Ana María*, January 13, 1818; *Tomás Antonio*, December 29, 1819; *José Justo Damián*, September 27, 1821; *María Josefa*, November 16, 1822, who married Pedro Armendaris (q.v.); *María de la Luz Quirina*, June 4, 1824,[16] who married Miguel Pino, December 31, 1842;[17] *Manuela*, who married a widower, Francisco Tomás C. de Baca, June 10, 1844;[18] and *José Eulogio*, born in Santa Fe and baptized by his eldest half-brother, Don Juan Felipe Ortiz, March 11, 1825.[19]

Jose Eulogio was a young newly-ordained priest in Bishop Lamy's first years in Santa Fe. Because of their great disparity in age, Vicar Juan Felipe and Eulogio were believed to be uncle and nephew.

* * * * * * * *

ANTONIO JOSÉ ORTIZ, son of Nicolás Ortiz III and Gertrudis Páez Hurtado, married *Rosa Bustamante*, December 31, 1754, with his father and step-mother, Josefa Bustamante, as witnesses.[20] In the Santa Fe census of 1790 he is set down as an *hacendero* fifty-six years old; Rosa is fifty-five, and they have a five-year-old grandchild living with them. Next are entered five of their married sons and their families.[21] Antonio José became quite wealthy as a rancher, merchant, and money-lender. Around the turn of the century he rebuilt and enlarged the entire nave and south chapel of the parish

---

1. M-50, Sta. Fe.
2. Sp. Arch., II, 1096a.
3. Copy, Santa Fe Co., R-2, pp. 210-212; R, pp. 212-214.
4. All in B, Sta. Fe.
5. M-52, Sta. Fe.
6. Both in B, Sta. Fe.
7. Ibid., bapt. of their child, April 15, 1811.
8. M-52, Sta. Fe.
9. B, Sta. Fe.
10. M-52, Sta. Fe.
11. Both in B, Sta. Fe.
12. M-53, Sta. Fe.
13. B and M-54, Sta. Fe.
14. B, Sta. Fe.
15. Bur-50 and M-52, Sta. Fe.
16. All in B, Sta. Fe.
17. M-54, Sta. Fe. She died on May 6, 1900, the last surviving sister of Vicar Juan Felipe Ortiz (Rev. Cat., Vol. XXVI, No. 20, p. 229).
18. M-54, Sta. Fe.
19. B, Sta. Fe.
20. M-50, Sta. Fe.
21. Sp. Arch., II, No. 1096a.

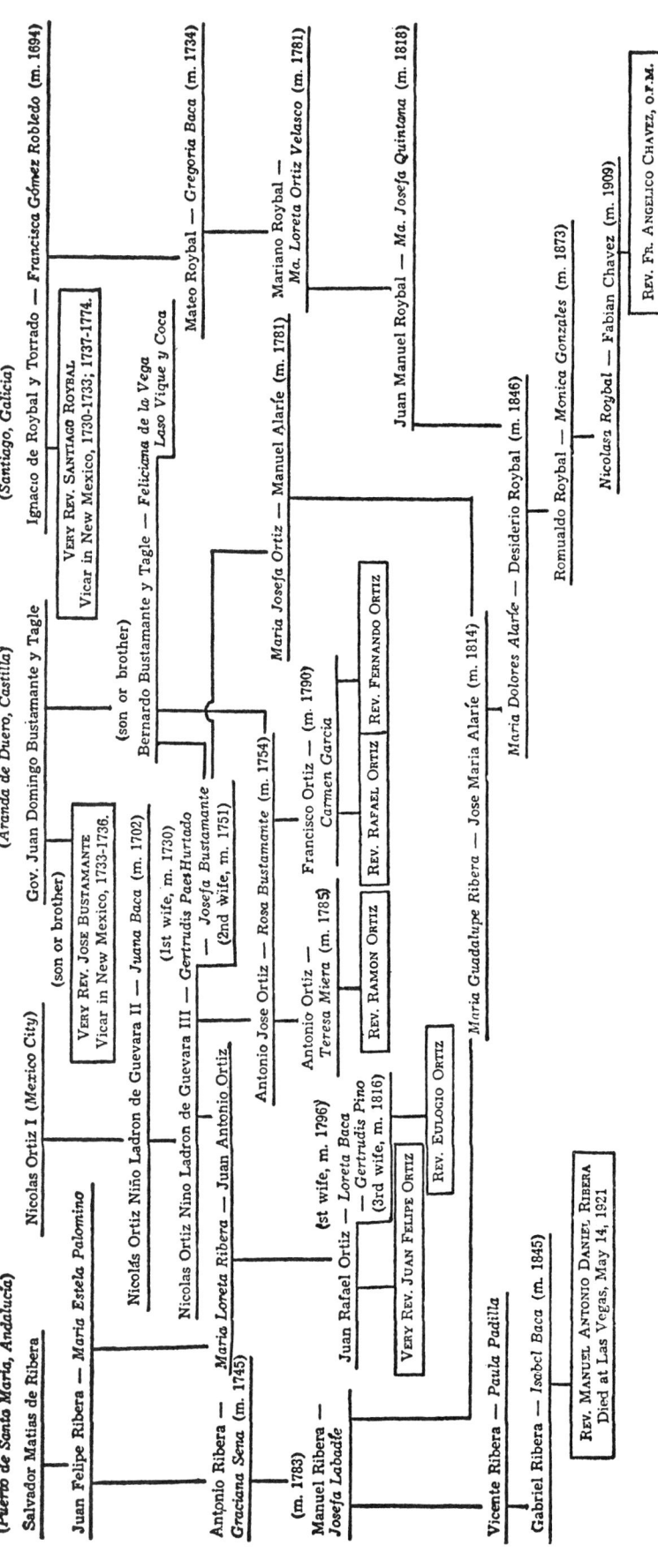

A CLERICAL CHART. — Native clergy in New Mexico were rare in the past. The few shown here, curiously, can be placed in one group formed by the Ribera, Ortiz, Bustamante, and Roybal families. This diagram was originally compiled for an article, "Ramon Ortiz: Priest and Patriot," in the *New Mexico Historical Review*, October, 1950.

church of St. Francis, restoring its old sanctuary and the north chapel of La Conquistadora as well. He likewise rebuilt the sanctuary walls of old San Miguel chapel, and erected the now-famous chapel of Rosario outside the city.[22] He died in August, 1806, and Rosa followed eight years later in the same month, 1814.[23]

Their large family consisted of the following: *María de la Luz,* born on February 16, 1755;[24] *Feliciana Paula,* January 14, 1758, who married José Campos Redondo;[25] *Antonio José,* February 10, 1759, who married María Micaela Baca of Belen;[26] *Antonio de Jesús,* June 22, 1761,[27] who married Teresa Miera (see next section); *María Guadalupe Loreto,* December 17, 1762, who married Juan de Dios Peña;[28] *Ana Gertrudis,* who married a widower, Juan Domingo Baca, November 11, 1782;[29] *José Miguel de Jesús,* March 30, 1764, who married María Isabel Baca of Belen, August 29, 1786;[30] *Pedro Fernando de Jesús,* February 2, 1766, who married a widow, Juliana de la Peña, January 9, 1786;[31] *Isabel,* May 6, 1771; and *Francisco Matías,* February 24, 1772,[32] who married María del Carmen García de Noriega (see two sections below).

Antonio de Jesús Ortiz, son of Antonio José Ortiz and Rosa Bustamante, married *Teresa Miera y Pacheco,* June 20, 1785.[33] In 1783 he had enlisted at the Santa Fe Presidio, giving his age as twenty-one.[34] On April 27, 1837, he drew up his last will, in which he named his parents, his wife, and their eleven children. He also deeded an Oratory of the Ortiz family in Santa Fe to his brother Francisco.[35] The children of this family were as follows:

Francisco de Paula, February 8, 1790, who married Martina de Arce, April 13, 1809;[36] *José Ramón,* who was a priest already in 1837, when his father made his last will; greatly venerated by all and sundry, Don Ramón Ortiz died at Guadalupe del Paso (Juárez) after a long and historically colorful life;[37] *María Barbara,* wife of José de Jesús Sánchez; the twins, *Miguel* and *Manuel,* June 5, 1795, who died in infancy;[38] *Ana María del Rosario,* September 4, 1799;[39] *María del Refugio,* April 30, 1805; *María Josefa,* March 18, 1810,[40] who married Manuel Doroteo Pino, November 15, 1826;[41] *Ana María,* who became the wife of Fernando Delgado, and then of José Antonio Vizcarra, April 14, 1824; *Juana María* and *Ana Teresa,* both of whom died in infancy.[42]

Francisco Matías Ortiz, son of Antonio José Ortiz and Rosa Bustamante, married *María del Carmen García de Noriega,* April 6, 1790; she was a daughter of José García de Noriega, member of this New Mexico family's branch in Guadalupe del Paso since 1680, and of his wife Rosalia Velarde.[43] Their known children were the following:

The twins, *José Rafael* and *Fernando Miguel,* born May 23, 1797,[44] both of whom became priests, but not simultaneously, as Rafael's investigation for *"limpieza de sangre"* does not mention Fernando;[45] *María Guadalupe,* December 12, 1799; *María Josefa Dolores,* March 13, 1801; *Antonio José de Jesús,* June 14, 1804,[46] who married Francisca de la Peña, October 4, 1825;[47] *José Manuel Julio,* April 13, 1806; *José Manuel de la Trinidad,* May 22, 1807; *José Marcos,* April 25, 1809; and *José Isidro Francisco,* May 15, 1810.[48]

The two priests, Rafael and Fernando Ortiz, were active in the parishes of New Mexico when Bishop Lamy arrived in 1851.

* * * * * * * *

---

22. OLC, pp. 43-44.
23. Bur-50, Sta. Fe.
24. B, Sta. Fe. See Olona and Pino.
25. B, Sta. Fe; Sp. Arch., I, No. 666; HSNM, Ortiz Roll.
26. B, Sta. Fe; M-49, Isleta; Sp. Arch., II, 1092b.
27. B, Sta. Fe.
28. Ibid.; HSNM, loc. cit.
29. M-50, Sta. Fe; HSNM, loc. cit.
30. M-49, Isleta; B, Sta. Fe; Sp. Arch., II, 1096a.
31. B, Sta. Fe; M-51, Castrense; Sp. Arch., loc. cit.
32. Both in B, Sta. Fe.
33. M-51, Castrense; Sp. Arch., loc. cit.
34. HSNM, Mil. Papers.
35. HSNM, Ortiz Roll.
36. B-65, Sta. Fe; M-51, Castrense.
37. For his full life, and drastic corrections of family legends and genealogies, see NMHR, Vol. XXV, No. 4, pp. 265-295.
38. B-13, Nambe; HSNM, loc. cit.
39. B-23, Poj.
40. Both in B-65, Sta. Fe.
41. M-53, Sta. Fe.
42. M-51, Castrense; HSNM, loc. cit.
43. M-52, Sta. Fe; HSNM, No. 2829; Twit. Coll., No. 254.
44. B-65, Sta. Fe.
45. See preceding Note 43.
46. All in B-65, Sta. Fe.
47. M-53, Sta. Fe.
48. All in B-65, Sta. Fe.

Santiago Baca y Ortiz of Santa Fe, a cleric of first tonsure at Durango in 1813, was a grandson of Antonio José Ortiz and Rosa Bustamante.[49] He was, therefore, the *Santiago*, son of Juan Domingo Baca and Ana Gertrudis Ortiz born on January 1, 1790.[50] Apparently, he did not finish his seminary studies towards the priesthood, and remained in the Mexican Republic. For he sounds very much like the "Santiago Baca Ortiz" who in 1825 brought the first printing press up to Durango from Mexico City, and who also might well have been the father of Jesús María Baca, a printer brought from Durango to New Mexico by Padre Martínez of Taos.[51]

A priest who was Vicar in Santa Fe in 1818, **Don Juan Bautista Guevara**, has been confused with the Ortiz family because of associations of affinity, and also because Nicolas Ortiz II had appended "Niño Ladrón de Guevara" to the Ortiz name. This Vicar belonged to a distinct family, *Ladrón de Guevara*, of Guadalupe del Paso, or possibly of Chihuahua and Durango originally. A sister of his, Barbara, married a García de Noriega at Guadalupe del Paso, and their son José García de Noriega was the father of María del Carmen Garcia, who married Francisco Matías Ortiz in Santa Fe.

Hence, the Vicar Ladrón de Guevara was a granduncle of these Santa Fe Ortizes, but through the García side, not the Ortiz.[52]

Another Vicar in Santa Fe in the early part of the nineteenth century was **Don Juan Rafael Rascón**,[53] who has been made an Ortiz in a similar fashion. His family, like the other Vicar's, could have been the prominent Rascón family of Guadalupe del Paso, or from other points in the diocese of Durango. Related to him, to all appearances, were a Francisco Rascón, alderman of Santa Fe;[54] and José María Rascón, married to a Doña Josefa ———, whose daughter María Juana married Nicolás Pino, February 16, 1842.[55]

A Doña *Francisca Rascon* and Don Guadalupe Miranda, both "familiars of His Lordship" (the Vicar?), were married on January 28, 1830.[56]

49. **Twit. Coll.**, No. 168.
50. **B-65, Sta. Fe.**
51. **NMHR**, Vol. 12, pp. 6-7.
52. See preceding Note 43; **Sp. Arch.**, II, No. 2752.
53. **NMHR**, Vol. III, pp. 150, 161, 337-338.
54. **Sp. Arch.**, I, No. 905.
55. **M-54, Sta. Fe.**
56. **M-53, Sta. Fe.**

PADILLA

FRANCISCO PADILLA, son of Diego de Padilla and María Vásquez Baca, married *Isabel Baca* on March 13, 1732, with his parents as witnesses.[1]

Their known children were: *Agustina*, born August 28, 1734;[2] *Juan Domingo*, February 8, 1739; *María Josefa*, who married Tomás Chávez;[3] *Francisca*, December 8, 1742,[4] who married Nicolás Torres, in October, 1763 (see *Torres*, this Appendix); and *Agustina Lucía*, December 5, 1744, who married her second and third cousin, Juan Domingo Chávez, in 1764.[5]

1. **M-11, Isleta.**
2. **B-57, Isleta.**
3. **Sp. Arch.**, I, No. 122.
4. **B-57, Isleta.**
5. Ibid.; DM, 1764, in Albuq., no number.

QUINTANA

JOSÉ MARÍA QUINTANA, son of Juan Bautista Quintana and María Paula Sánchez, married *María Ygnacia Archuleta* (q.v., in this Appendix). They had a very large family, their known children being the following:

José Miguel, born May 19, 1786; *Juana Manuela*, October 16, 1788;¹ *María Antonia de la Luz*, February 22, 1791; *María Josefa*, March 16, 1793, who married Juan Manuel Roybal (*q.v.* in this Appendix); the twins, *María Juliana Romula* and *María Anastasia Claudia*, February 17, 1795; *José Mariano de Jesús*,² who married María Dolores Luján in 1834;³ *Antonio José*, June 10, 1799; *José Pablo*, January 25, 1802,⁴ who married María Dolores Archuleta, August 28, 1825;⁵ *José Miguel*, March 15, 1804; *José Francisco*, March 20, 1808,⁶ who married Altagracia Tafoya;⁷ *María Margarita*, August 12, 1810; and *José Vicente*, September 12, 1813.⁸

1. Both in **B-23, Nambé, Poj.**
2. All in **B-25, S. Ild.**
3. DM, 1834, in Santa Cruz, no number.
4. Both in **B-25, S. Ild.**
5. DM, 1825, no number.
6. Both in **B-25, S. Ild.**
7. **B-23, Nambé, Poj.**; bapt. of child, Nov. 2, 1837.
8. Both in **B-25, S. Ild.**

RIBERA

MANUEL ANTONIO JOSÉ RIBERA, son of Antonio de Ribera and Graciana Prudencia Sena, married *Josefa Labadía* on June 29, 1783, in the Military Chapel of Our Lady of Light in Santa Fe.¹ Both he and his wife were very active members of the combined Confraternities of the Blessed Sacrament and of La Conquistadora; they did not pay dues because they played for the processions and Masses.² What they played is not known. (There was a family legend about the statue of La Conquistadora bowing and smiling when he was singing before it.) While in charge of troops at the military post of San Miguel del Vado, he reported rumors of an American invading party in October, 1819.³ Their known children were the following:

Vicente José, born January 22, 1785, who married María Paula Padilla;⁴ when he enlisted as a soldier in 1808, he was described as a native of Santa Fe, twenty years old, "*pelo, zeja, y barba rojas, ojos pardos, color blanco rosado, cara aguileña y naríz regular*";⁵ *María Trinidad*, September 30, 1789;⁶ *María Micaela*, September 8, 1782;⁷ *María Guadalupe*, November 1, 1797,⁸ who married José María Alarí (*q.v.*); *María Juana*, who died on March 8, 1808;⁹ and *José Guadalupe*, who married María de los Angeles Padilla at San Miguel, June 27, 1813.¹⁰ There was also an adopted son, *José Antonio* (Ortiz?), who married a María Rosa Ribera in 1795.¹¹

Vicente José Ribera, son of Manuel José Ribera and Josefa Labadía, and his wife, *Paula Padilla*, had a son, *Gabriel*, who married Isabel Baca at San Miguel, December 28, 1845.¹² Another son, *Jesús*, died in Antonchico, December 22, 1904, at the age of eighty-one.¹³

Gabriel Ribera and *Isabel Baca* were the parents of the Rev. *Manuel Antonio Daniel Ribera*, who preached his first sermon on September 29, 1886, Feast of St. Michael, at the church of San Miguel where he had been baptized.¹⁴ Greatly revered all his life, he died at Las Vegas on May 14, 1921. His mother died on April 6, 1904.¹⁵

Other known children of Gabriel Ribera were: *María de los Angeles*, born on October 3, 1849, who married Frederic Desmarais in San Miguel, June 22, 1867;¹⁶ *Lamberto*, married to Veneranda López; *Paula*, wife of Prudencio López;¹⁷ *José Lino*; and *Francisco*, married to Escolastica López.¹⁸

1. **M-51, Castrense.**
2. **AASF,** Bk. LXXIX.
3. Sp. Arch., II, No. 2850.
4. **B-65,** Sta. Fe. See Note 12 below.
5. **HSNM,** Mil. Papers.
6. **B-42,** S. Juan.
7. Ibid., date perhaps should be 1792.
8. **B-65,** Sta. Fe.
9. **Bur-50,** Sta. Fe.
10. **M, San Miguel del Vado.**
11. **M-52,** Sta. Fe.
12. **M, San Miguel del Vado**; place called Ribera named after this family.
13. **Rev. Cat.,** Vol. XXI, No. 1, p. 1.
14. Ibid., Vol. XII, No. 41, p. 481.
15. Ibid., Vol. XXXI, No. 16, p. 181.
16. Ibid., Vol. XII, No. 39, p. 457.
17. Ibid., Vol. XIII, No. 30, p. 348.
18. Ibid., Vol. XXXI, No. 16, p. 181; Vol. XXVI, No. 2, p. 12.

ROYBAL

MARIANO ROYBAL and *María Loreta Velásquez* were married at La Cuchilla on June 27, 1781.[1] His wife's surname is omitted in the marriage entry, and in the baptisms of some children, while in others it appears several times as Ortiz, then as Velarde or Valverde, but most often as Velásquez, the name of the family which had reared her. María Loreta Ortiz, widow of Mariano Roybal, died on May 26, 1845, leaving seven surviving children. Of their very large family, the sons are as follows:

Juan de Dios, born May 9, 1789; *Juan Manuel,* January 16, 1787, who married María Josefa Quintana (see next section); *Rafael Vicente,* August 7, 1791,[3] who married Anastasia Quintana;[4] *José Juan,* February 16, 1798, who married María Juliana Quintana;[5] and *José de Jesús,* June 1, 1800, who married Margarita Durán.[5a]

Their known daughters were: *María Manuela,* May 21, 1783;[6] *Teodora,* April 1, 1785, who married Pedro Martín, April 14, 1804;[7] *Juana Barbara,* April 23, 1793;[8] and *María Antonia,* October 25, 1795,[9] who married Pedro González (q.v., this Appendix).

Juan Manuel Roybal, son of Mariano Roybal, deceased, and María Loreta Velásquez, married *María Josefa Quintana,* May 13, 1818, at El Rancho de San Ildefonso.[10] Sometime after 1851, the family moved to the newly-settled Mora valley and its environs, where Juan Manuel died on April 8, 1858.[11]

Their known sons were as follows: *José Desiderio,* born February 11, 1821, who married María Dolores Alarid (see next section); the twins, *José Monico* and *José Fernando,* May 20, 1830;[12] and *José Candelario,* February 5, 1837.[13]

Their known daughters were: *Ignacia,* who married Jesús Trinidad Sandoval on November 7, 1836; *María de Jesús,* who married José Dolores Coca, November 6, 1843;[14] *María Guadalupe,* born August 15, 1825; *María Dolores,* January 9, 1828; and *Ana María,* October 21, 1832.[15]

Desiderio Roybal, son of Juan Manuel Roybal and María Josefa Quintana, married *María Dolores Alarid* of Santa Fe at El Rancho, February 16, 1846.[16] According to their children's baptisms and marriages, they were living at Buena Vista east of Mora in 1853, at La Cebolla in 1861-1867, and at Los Fuertecitos by 1885.

Their known children were: *Romualdo Abad,* born at Jacona on April 6, 1849, who married María Monica González (see next section); *José Teodoro,* April 1, 1851,[17] who married Juana Valdes in 1876, and then Eugenia Velásquez at La Cebolla, January 26, 1885;[18] *José Ignacio,* born at Buena Vista, August 1, 1853;[19] *María Albina,* November 27, 1854, who married José María Martín, November 11, 1867;[20] *María Trinidad,* born at Jacona, February 4, 1847;[21] the infants, *María Rita* and *Francisco,* buried at La Cueva in 1861 and 1864;[22] and *Fructuosa,* who married Sacramento Baca, February 10, 1879.[22a]

Romualdo Roybal, son of Desiderio Roybal and María Dolores Alarid, married *María Monica González* on February 20, 1873. His family was living at Los Fuertecitos, and the

---

1. B-24, S. Ild.; M-33, Sta. Clara.
2. Bur-22, Poj.
3. The three in B-31, Sta. Clara.
4. B-25, S. Ild., bapt. of two children, Aug. 28, 1821, and Sept. 5, 1824.
5. B-31, Sta. Clara; M-25, S. Ild.; three brothers married three sisters.
5a. B-31, Sta. Clara; bapt. of child, Aug. 14, 1836 (B-23, Poj.).
6. B-31, Sta. Clara.
7. B-23, Nambé, Poj.; M-25, S. Ild.
8. B-25, S. Ild.
9. B-31, Sta. Clara.
10. M-28, S. Ild.
11. Bur-14, Mora.
12. All in B-25, S. Ild.
13. B-23, Nambé.
14. Both in M-25, S. Ild.
15. All three in B-25, S. Ild.
16. M-25, S. Ild.
17. Both in B, Sta. Cruz.
18. M, Mora.
19. B-1, Las Vegas. He married Francisca Montoya (bapt. of children, 1883, 1885), and then Epimenia Bueno, May 19, 1906 (B, Las Vegas; M, Watrous).
20. Ibid., M. Mora.
21. B, Sta. Cruz.
22. Bur, Mora.
22a. M-Watrous.

bride's at La Ciruelita.²³ They later resided at the new town of Santa Clara, later named "Wagon Mound," and also had a ranch at the nearby Cañada de Tata Vegué.

Their known children were: *Andres*, November 23, 1873; *Eva*, November 3, 1877, who married José Donato Herrera, October 3, 1892, and then Ricardo Martínez, January 20, 1901; *Aurelia*, July 23, 1882, who married George M. King, November 4, 1899; *Nicolasa*, born at La Cañada de Tata Vegué, November 29, 1884, who married Fabián Chávez (q.v.); *Victoria*, March 6, 1888, who married Agustin A. Sosaya, August 12, 1909; *Tranquilino*, April 13, 1891, who married Tena Lewis; and *Romualdo*, born December 15, 1895.²⁴

---

23. **M-46, Mora.**
24. All at Wagon Mound (**B** and **M, Watrous**).

TORRES

NICOLÁS TORRES, son of Diego de Torres and María Martín Serrano de Salazar of Rio Arriba, married *Francisca Padilla* of Rio Abajo in October, 1763.¹ In 1790 they were living at Belén, he being fifty-eight, and she forty-four. They had five sons (25-23-16-14-6) and two girls (10-8).² In 1767 Nicolás brought suit against his step-mother, Rafaela Baca, widow of Diego de Torres.³ In 1803 he and Francisca had their residence at the Plaza de los Trujillos of Belen; three of their children living in the same place were Agustín, Josefa, and Mariano with his wife María Isabel Armijo.⁴ Nicolás died on March 11, 1811.⁵

Their known children were: *Andrés Mariano*, who married María Isabel Armijo (see next section); *Agustín; Josefa; Manuela*, married to Pedro Tafoya; and *Lorenzo*,⁶ who married Juana Nepomucena Ruiz in 1802.⁷

Andrés Mariano Torres, son of Nicolás Torres and Francisca Padilla, married *María Isabel Armijo* on August 8, 1794.⁸ As already mentioned, they lived at the Plaza de los Trujillos in 1803; in 1806, Mariano was the guardian of the persons and property of his wife's four minor brethren, following the tragic death of their eldest brother, Salvador Armijo.⁹

Their known children were: *Tomasa*, born at San Antonio de los Trujillos in December, 1797; *Juan Nepomuceno Urbano*, May, 1800; *María Rita Altagracia*, July 19, 1802,¹⁰ who married José Encarnación Chávez (q.v., this Appendix); *Mariano de Altagracia Fabián*, January, 1805, who might be the child "José Mariano" who died in July, 1807;¹¹ *María Gregoria*, May, 1807; and *Juan*, who married Lorenza Baca, May 13, 1815.¹³

Their mother died at Belén on July 22, 1808, and Mariano then married a *María Isabel Baca* in the following year, February 9, 1809.¹⁴ A Mariano Torres of Belen, who was killed by Apaches with thirteen other men on the road from El Paso, February 12, 1810, was most likely this man.¹⁵

---

1. **DM**, 1763, in Albuq., no number.
2. **Sp. Arch.**, II, No. 1092b.
3. **Ibid.**, No. 592a.
4. **AASF**, No. 30.
5. **B-54, Tomé**, Bur. Sec.
6. **AASF, loc. cit.**
7. **DM**, 1802, in Albuq., no number.
8. **M-4, Albuq.; DM**, 1794, no number
9. **AASF, loc. cit.; Sp. Arch.**, I, No. 54; II, No. 1927; **B-54, Tomé**, f. 36v.
10. All in **B-54, Tomé**.
11. **Ibid.**, B and Bur Sec.
12. **Ibid.**, B Sec.
13. **Ibid.**, M. Sec.
14. **Ibid.**, Bur and second M Sec.
15. **HSNM**, Autographs.

ADDENDA
TO ORIGINAL 1954 EDITION

ADDENDA TO THE 1954 EDITION

In the Introduction to my book on the original families of New Mexico,[1] I pointed out that the facts listed there were comprehensive but far from complete. Since publication I have discovered further items, even some new names, chiefly during my work of cataloguing the Archives of the Archdiocese of Santa Fe. These nuggets of information are culled from documents that had been grossly misfiled or which lay scattered among unclassified pages and scraps. As they always supplement the material in my book, the latter will be designated as NMF when frequently referred to. And to avoid a prolixity of footnotes, this work and the several sources in the church archives will be noted in parentheses in the text: *New Mexico Families* (NMF, page); *Diligencias Matrimoniales* (DM, year, number); *General* (Gen., year, number); and Baptismal, Marriage, Burial registers (B, M, *Bur.*, name). Other occasional sources will have a footnote.

---

1. Fray Angélico Chávez, *Origins of New Mexico Families in the Spanish Colonial Period, 1598-1821* (Santa Fe, Historical Society of New Mexico, 1954; reissue 1975, William Gannon, Publisher, Santa Fe), 354 pp., illustrated. $7.50.

ABEYTA

DIEGO DE ABEYTA (NMF, 119) was a native of Durango, the natural son of Diego de Ribera and Juana de Beitia, also of Durango. He was sixteen and a soldier of Santa Fe in 1696 when he asked to marry Juana de Torres, recent widow of Felix de Aragón (DM, 1696, no. 21). This marriage did not take place, for she apparently married Miguel de Ayala sometime later (DM, 1698, no. 19). Diego finally married *Catalina Leal*, 28, natural daughter of María de la Concepción, native of New Mexico. Here Diego gave Durango as his birthplace, his age as 18, and said that he was the natural son of "Ana de Abeyta" (DM, 1698, no. 22).

Their daughter, *Juana*, widow of José Antonio Fernández, married Antonio de Armenta in 1725, with *Antonio Abeyta* and wife standing as witnesses. Old Diego was dead by this time (DM, 1725, no. 10). Hence another daughter was *Manuela Abeyta*, sister-in-law of Antonio de Armenta.[2]

---

2. *Spanish Archives of New Mexico*, vol. II, no. 437.

ABREU

SANTIAGO ABREU II was killed by the Chimayó insurgents in 1837, and in September the insurgent Governor, José Gonzales, ordered an inventory made of his estate. *Josefa Baca* is there mentioned as his widow.[3] Of their children mentioned in NMF, p. 120, *José* married María Piedad Salazar, daughter of Pablo Salazar and Juliana Otero (DM, 1839), and *Soledad* became the wife of Esquipula Caballero on August 2 of the same year (M-54, Santa Fe).

Marcelino Abreu and his wife *Brigida Olona*

(NMF, 120) have other children besides *María Justa*. *Juan de Jesús* married María Luz Chávez, November 2, 1856 (M-*Tomé*); *María Veneranda* became the wife of Juan de Jesús Chávez (DM, 1842); and *Maximo* married María Gallegos, October 7, 1856 (M-*Tomé*).

The origin and exact time of arrival in New Mexico of the original Santiago Abreu (NMF, 120) are unknown as yet. From his wife's name and other connections we can suppose with almost complete certainty that he came with two other soldiers of the period, José de la O and Martín Yrigoyen (NMF, 244, 313) from the Presidio of Guajoquilla in Nueva Vizcaya.

---
3. Huntington Library, *Ritch Collection*, Box 4, no. 164.

AGUILA

MIGUEL GERONIMO DEL AGUILA, included under "Aguilar" in NMF, evidently did not reach New Mexico with his family, or else he returned soon after the Reconquest to El Paso, for there his daughter *Josefa*, 24, married a Juan Maese in 1711. Her father was still living, but "Gerónimo de Florido" was dead by this time (DM, 1711, no. 12).

AGUILAR

MIGUEL DE AGUILAR was a native of Toluca, 20, and residing in Santa Cruz when he married Gracia Bautista de Olivas, also 20 and a native of Sombrerete (DM, 1697, no. 10). This is a new item, not found in NMF, and it explains the presence of several Aguilar families in the Rio Arriba district after the Reconquest.

ALEJABU

ISIDRO ALEJABU was living in the Santa Clara district with his wife *Juana Luján* in 1791, when their daughter *Teresa* married a Manuel Antonio Bachicha on September 21 (M-33, *Santa Clara*). Their son *Agustín* married María de Jesús Martín on February 27, 1797 (*ibid.*), and Isidro himself, widowed of Juana Luján, married a *Francisca Herrera* on September 29, 1791 (*ibid.*).

Agustín Alejabu had a son *Antonio* who married María Dolores Mestas on July 28, 1862 (M-34, *Santa Clara*).

ANAYA

JOAQUIN DE ANAYA of Santa Fe (NMF, 125), widowed of Margarita Ortega, married *Josefa Martín* of Santa Cruz on August 12, 1719 (DM, 1719, no. 23).

ANCIZO

People of this name in NMF (125) were all females, the wives of new colonists from Zacatecas, but there was a MARCOS DE ANCIZO, 20, and living in Santa Fe in 1699, the son of Marcos de Ancizo and Petrona Quintana of Guanajuato. He married *Isabel de Perea*, 30, a native of New Mexico of unknown parentage, on September 7 (DM, 1699, no. 12).

ANGELES

NICOLÁS DE LOS ANGELES, 29, born in Guadalajara, was a slave of Governor Valverde. On July 25, 1718, in Santa Fe, he married *Francisca Enríquez*, native of New Mexico and freed slave of the same master (DM, 1718, no. 25).

ANSURES

GABRIEL DE ANSURES (NMF, 126) was dead by 1709 when his widow *Felipa Villavicencio*, daughter of Domingo Villavicencio and Margarita Lechuga, married Antonio Martín (DM, 1709, no. 24).

Bartolomé Ansures (NMF, 126) and his wife *María de la Cruz* were both dead when a daughter, *Juana*, married Antonio Varela in 1704 (DM, 1704, no. 8).

In 1708 at Albuquerque a widowed Apache by the name of Agustín Muñiz Baca married *Teresa Ansures*, daughter of "*Viejo Ansures el arriero*" and Catalina (DM, 1708, no. 13).

ANZA

DON FRANCISCO DE ANZA, brother of the Lord Governor, died on June 10, 1785, after making his last will and testament before his famous brother (*Bur.*, 51, *Castrense*).

APODACA

JOSÉ GONZÁLEZ DE APODACA, 36, son of Diego de Apodaca and Sebastiana de Gracia, did not bring his wife *Isabel Gutiérrez* back to New Mexico in 1693 (as stated in NMF, 126) because she had died at El Paso in May of that year. On June 3, he married *Francisca Durán*, widow of Antonio Gómez (DM, 1693, no. 21). This was his third wife. Besides *Juan Esteban* and *Juan Antonio*, by Isabel Gutiérrez, there was an elder son, *Francisco*, by his first wife, Antonia Martín. This Francisco was twenty and living at Santa Cruz in 1692 when he married María López de Luna of Rio Abajo, October 5 (DM, 1692, no. 9).

Juan Antonio de Apodaca (NMF, 126), son of José de Apodaca and Isabel Gutiérrez, was 28 in 1710 when he married *María Durán*, 30, on January 2 (DM, 1709, no. 25). At Santa Cruz they had a daughter, *María*, May 12, 1711, and a son, *Marcos*, May 6, 1713 (*Gen.*, 1710, no. 7). This Marcos and his wife Monica Valverde appear in NMF on page 127.

Ventura de Apodaca (NMF, 127) was an uncle of María Montaño y Apodaca (DM, 1694, no. 40).

Cristóbal de Apodaca (NMF, 127) and his wife *Regina Peralta*, both dead by 1709, had a daughter, *Cayetana*, who married Antonio Rodríguez (DM, 1709, no. 15). There was also an *Antonia*, daughter of Cristóbal de Apodaca and "Melchora de los Reyes," both deceased, who married Domingo Gómez (DM, 1714, no. 19).

Sebastián de Apodaca (NMF, 127), 20, a native of New Mexico who did not know who his parents were, married *Juana Hernández*, also a native of New Mexico (DM, 1707, no. 13).

Francisco de Apodaca married *María Josefa de Moraga* in 1718, but their parents were not given (DM, 1718, no. 31).

ARAGON

IGNACIO DE ARAGÓN (NMF, 127, 128), a native of Mexico City and the son of Juan de Aragón and Mencia de las Ruelas Galindo, widowed of Sebastiana Ortiz, married *Luisa Baca* of Bernalillo in April, 1708. My guess that she was the daughter of Cristóbal Baca, now deceased, and Ana Moreno de Lara proved correct (DM, 1708, no. 10).

Felix de Aragón (NMF, 128), native of Durango, was a soldier at Santa Fe when he was shot, evidently an execution, and buried in the cemetery "of the old parish church" in 1696 (DM, 1696, no. 21). See *Abeyta* and *Ayala*.

Juan de Aragón, a native of New Mexico who was 33 in 1697 (DM, 1697, no. 20), and 40 as a resident of Santa Cruz (DM, 1703, no. 7), died at the age of "80" on August 13, 1729 (*Bur.*, 48, Santa Fe). He could have belonged to the 17th-century López de Aragon family (NMF, 54). Likewise, a *José Aragón*, native of New Mexico and resident of El Paso, who there married *Juliana Gamboa* on February 26, 1696. He was 22, and his parents were Antonio Luján and Ana de Aragón, both deceased natives of New Mexico (DM, 1696, no. 18). José's mother was very likely the woman who had married Francisco Campusano during the 1680 exile at El Paso.

ARCE

ANTONIO DE ARCE and *Soledad Olguín* had a daughter named *María Luciana Verónica* and not "Maria Luisa Verónica" as erroneously stated in NMF, 128. This girl married Ignacio Ortiz of Santa Fe, June 25, 1815 (M-Santa Fe).

José María de Arce (NMF, 128) was an *Alférez* of the Santa Fe Presidio when he had a natural daughter, *María Josefa*, by María Angela Romero, a Taos Indian widow, May 1, 1809 (B-38, *Taos*). As second *Teniente* of Santa Fe he returned to Chihuahua to marry Doña Justa Pastor de Uranga, February 24, 1818 (M-51, *Castrense*).

ARCHIBEQUE

JUAN DE ARCHIBEQUE'S first nuptial investigation to marry *Antonia Gutiérrez* was first noticed by Bandelier, and mentioned as lost in NMF, 129. It has now been found, however. An original petition had been made on April 3, 1696, but matters were held pending until the death of the bride's first husband was ascertained. This petition of November, 1697, states that the bride's first husband, Tomás de Hita (or Sánchez de Ytta), had been actually murdered at a rancho near El Real de Zacatecas, by a mulatto "because of jealousies regarding his wife." Juan was 25 at the time, a native of France soldiering in Santa Fe. *Antonia Gutiérrez*, 26, was a native of Tezcuco who had come to New Mexico with the Miguel García (de la Riba) family of Mexico City, following her husband's murder. She is referred to as *La Vermeja*, the "Redhead" (DM, 1697, no. 13). Also found is the missing part of the incomplete investigation of Archibeque's second marriage with *Manuela de Roybal* in 1709, as mentioned in NMF, 129. It also gives the same family background related in NMF, 129.

ARCHULETA

A daughter of old JUAN DE ARCHULETA and *María Luján* of the 17th century (NMF, 6), by the name of *María*, married Bartolomé Trujillo in 1682 (DM, 1682, no. 9).

JUAN DE ARCHULETA and *Isabel González* (NMF, 131, 132) had other children who married as follows. *Diego*, 22, married Josefa González, 20, on May 8, 1714 (DM, 1714, no. 16); *María* became the wife of Miguel Martín in 1706 (DM, 1706, no. 6); and *Luis* married María Martín in 1718. Mentioned in NMF as very likely their son, Luis was the son of Juan and Isabel (DM, 1718, no. 12).

Agustín de Archuleta and *María de la Cruz* (NMF, 132) remained at El Paso. One daughter, *Micaela*, married Pedro Fresqui at Socorro del Paso in 1712 (DM, 1712, no. 7), while a son, *Juan José*, widowed of a María Ramos, came to New Mexico and married a María de la Cruz, 15, of unknown parentage (DM, 1713, no. 3).

ARMENTA

LUIS and ANTONIO DE ARMENTA (NMF, 135) were the sons of *Salvador Manuel de Armenta* and María Luján, or Maese. Their father was dead by 1718. Luis was 25 in this year and a soldier in Santa Fe when he married *Brigida Brito*, sister-in-law of Antonio

Olguín (DM, 1718, nos. 10, 32). Antonio was also a Santa Fe soldier when he married *Juana Abeyta*, widow of José Antonio Fernández (DM, 1725, no. 10). But where their father originated cannot be ascertained. He could well have been a certain soldier of the Reconquest often referred to simply as *Salvador Manuel*, a native of the "Pueblo de Fistla" in the bishopric of Puebla, who was 28 in 1696 (DM, 1696, no. 25).

ARMIJO

VICENTE DURÁN DE ARMIJO (NMF, 136) used his full baptismal name "Vicente Ferrer" in 1703 when he married *María Apodaca*, whose full Christian name was here given as "María Magdalena," natural daughter of Juana de Apodaca. Both gave their age as 21 (DM, 1703, no. 8).

José de Armijo (NMF, 136) was 26 in 1710 when he married *María Manuela Blásquez*, or *Velásquez*, on June 10 (DM, 1710, nos. 14, 24). The bride's parents were not too happy about the marriage. She was already dead when a daughter, *Manuela*, was in trouble in 1725; this girl, at 16, married a widower, Cayetano Moya, in 1727 (*Gen.*, 1725, no. 1; DM, 1727, no. 10).

ARRATIA

FELIPE DE ARRATIA (NMF, 139) was not a pre-Revolt New Mexican, but a native of Valle de San Bartolomé (DM, 1707, no. 11; 1718, no. 12).

ARTEAGA

Different from the MANUEL DE ARTEAGA (NMF, 138) was an *Andrés de Arteaga*, married and living in Santa Fe in 1696 (DM, 1696, nos. 6, 17). He was a native of Sombrerete, the son of Antonio de Arteaga and María de la Cruz, both dead by 1712 when, widowed of *Juana Rodríguez*, he married *Francisca de Villavicencio* at El Paso (DM, 1712, no. 6).

ATENCIO

JOSÉ DE VALMAÑA Y ATIENZA and his wife *Micaela Rodríguez de la Rosa* were residing at Puebla in 1693 when they intended to come to New Mexico. They had a son, *Manuel*, 6 years old. This was José's testimony before his cousin, *Juan de Atienza*, 25 (DM, 1693, no. 18). However, it seems as though this pair did not start out for New Mexico.

JOSÉ DE ATIENZA and *Gertrudis Sevillano* (NMF, 139) were married in the Cathedral of

Mexico City prior to 1680 (DM, 1693, no. 26). Their son *Juan* seems to be the same man who took the preceding testimony from his cousin; he was tried for concubinage with Felipa Martín, wife of Agustín Salazar (*Gen.*, 1704, no. 2). Their other son, *José*, gave his age as 28 and Mexico City as his birthplace in 1709 (DM, 1709, no. 24); he and his wife *Estefánia Trujillo* had a daughter *Francisca* at Santa Cruz, July 26, 1712 (*Gen.*, 1710, no. 7), and a boy *Juan*, September 6, 1714 (*ibid.*). A *Pedro Atencio* of Santa Cruz, 51 years of age, and who said he was their son also, married *Isabel*, 30, a squaw of the Aa Nation belonging to *Francisco Atencio* (DM, 1707, no. 5).

AVALOS

The AVALOS family stayed at El Paso instead of returning to New Mexico with the Reconquest (NMF, 8).

Antonio de Avalos and *Petronila Hidalgo*, both natives of New Mexico, were married in 1690; Antonio had a sister, *Antonia* (DM, 1690, nos. 3, 5). *Pedro de Avalos* and his wife *Francisca de Torres* were still alive and residing at El Paso in 1696 (DM, 1696, no. 33), but two years later, unless it is a different man, he was married to *Juana de Herrera* (DM, 1698, no. 24). *Leonardo de Avalos* and his wife *Francisca de Valencia* had a son, *Salvador*, who married Lugarda Torres in 1718 (DM, 1718, nos. 12, 29).

A descendant of these people was *Juan José de Avalos*, native of El Paso, who married María Rodríguez in Santa Fe, February 4, 1782 (M-51, *Castrense*).

AVILA

MIGUEL DE AVILA, an orphan, married *Felipa de Ayala* in the parish of La Vera Cruz in Mexico City on August 10, 1691. She was a native of Cuyoacán, the daughter of Agustín de Ayala and Agustina Sánchez (DM, 1693, no. 16). But it is not known if they set out for New Mexico.

PEDRO DE AVILA, soldier of Santa Fe, married *María (Rosa) de Apodaca (Montaño)*, August 31, 1694 (DM, 1694, no. 38). He was a native of Sombrerete, 25 in 1696, and living in Rio Arriba when, widowed of María Rosa Montaño, he married *Manuela Fresqui*, 24, of unknown parentage, June 9, 1709 (DM, 1696, no. 6; 1709, no. 17). Hence he could not have been the Pedro de Aguilera of Mexico City, a possibility surmised in NMF, 140.

At San Lorenzo del Paso at this time a Juan Moro married *Antonia*, reared in the wagontrains, the child of *Pedro de Avila* and Petrona de Lara (DM, 1698, no. 24). Evidently this was a different family.

AYALA

MIGUEL DE AYALA, 20, was a native of Zacatecas living in Santa Fe, the son of Francisco de Ayala and Margarita Martín, both deceased. He asked to marry Juana de Torres,

24, native of La Villa de León, the daughter of Blas Navarro and Matiana de Torres, and also widow of Felix de Aragón (DM, 1698, no. 19). Hence Ayala was not possibly a son of Angela González as stated in NMF, 140.

Francisco de Ayala, husband of *Angela González* (NMF, 140), was killed during the fiestas of Villa de Jerez in 1694. Juan Páez Hurtado wrote to Governor Vargas asking him to notify the widow, September 21, 1694 (DM, 1697, no. 13).

An *Ignacio Miguel de Ayala* married *Juana de la Encarnación*, 30, widow of Simón de Torres, on December 4, 1699 (DM, 1699, no. 13a). Perhaps he is the same man as Miguel de Ayala above, who perhaps failed to marry Aragón's widow, as did Diego de Abeyta before him.

BACA

IGNACIO BACA (NMF, 10, 141) was still active as a *Sargento Mayor* in October, 1690 (DM, 1690, nos. 2, 7), but died within the next two years and was buried in the church at San Lorenzo del Paso; his widow, *Juana de Anaya Almazán*, married Juan de la Cruz y Olivas on February 17, 1693 (DM, 1693, no. 22). Of the children mentioned in NMF, 11, 141, *Magdalena* married Felipe Tamaris in 1707 (DM, 1707, no. 6), while another girl, *Antonia*, married Miguel de Valencia at Guadalupe del Paso (DM, 1707, no. 9), where she must have been left with relatives when her mother returned to New Mexico in 1693.

JOSÉ BACA (NMF, 10, 141), son of Cristóbal Baca and Ana Moreno de Lara, was 18 when he married *Josefa Pérez Pacheco*, 16, on November 19, 1684 (DM, 1684, no. 1). His sister *Luisa* married Ignacio de Aragón in 1708 (DM, 1708, no. 10).

Their brother MANUEL BACA (NMF, 10, 141) and wife *María de Salazar* returned to New Mexico with a big family. Besides the daughters mentioned, there was *Bernarda*, 17, who married Antonio Montoya at Bernalillo in 1707 (DM, 1707, no. 7). The sons *Diego Manuel* and *Cristóbal* (NMF, 141, 142) married two sisters, María and Polonia de la Vega y Coca of Santa Fe, on the same day, August 14, 1719 (DM, 1719, no. 12).

BACHICHA

Bachicha people were living in the Rio Arriba villages in the second half of the eighteenth century. MANUEL ANTONIO BACHICHA, son of Salvador Bachicha and María Mestas, deceased, married María Teresa Alejabu, September 8, 1790 (M-33, *Santa Clara*).

His brother *Pedro Bachicha* and wife Carmel Atencio had a son, *José Arcadio*, Feb. 16, 1834 (B-49, *Taos*). Certain indications lead one to suspect that this family stems from Juan Bautista Duran, alias *Bachicha* (NMF, 171).

BARRIOS

JUAN ANTONIO BARRIOS (NMF, 146) was a native of Casas Grandes (DM, 1696, no. 28).

BECERRA

TOMÁS ANTONIO BECERRA, the son of Don Antonio Becerra and Nicolasa Obando, married *María Luz Archuleta* at Taos, August 8, 1815 (M-37, *Taos*). A son of theirs, *Jesús María José Roque*, was baptized on August 23, 1829 (B-10, *Belén*).

BELMONTES

ANTONIO BELMONTES, resident of Trampas, the son of Miguel Belmontes and María Luisa Rodríguez, of El Real de Santa Rosa in New Spain, married *María Ynez Martín*, daughter of Eusebio Martín and María Antonio Armijo, February 7, 1796 (M-21, *Picuris*).

BENAVIDES

JUAN ESTEBAN BENAVIDES and wife María de Diezmos (NMF, 147) were natives of La Villa de Nombre de Dios and residents of Santa Fe in 1696 when their daughter *María*, born in Durango, married Diego González Bas (DM, 1696, no. 19).

Francisco Xavier (Benavides), no parents given, was a soldier of Santa Fe; at 18, widowed of *Josefa Tamaris*, he married *Jacinta Romero*, 14, of Albuquerque, in 1708 (DM, 1708, no. 8).

BERNAL

FRANCISCO BERNAL (NMF, 148) gave his age as 60 in 1689 (DM, 1689, no. 4). *Antonio Bernal* and his wife *Rosa María* were sponsors together as early as 1714 (DM, 1714, no. 20). They had two daughters at Santa Cruz, *Gertrudis*, February 20, 1713, and *Polonia*, October 23, 1715 (Gen., 1710, no. 7).

BETANZOS

DIEGO DE BETANZOS (NMF, 148) had married *María Luisa de Selorga* of Mexico City, daughter of Francisco Munar and Damiana de Selorga, perhaps before the colony reached New Mexico. He was killed by the rebel Tanos at San Cristóbal on June 4, 1696, and in the same year his widow married Francisco de la Mora (DM, 1696, no. 25). It almost seems as though Diego de Betanzos is the same man as *Diego de Salas* in NMF, 278, 279. The statement that Diego de Salas, Luisa de Senorga's husband, was tried for bigamy (NMF, 238) is an inadvertent mistake.

BLEA

CARLOS DÍAZ BLEA and *Pascuala de Herrera* had, besides their two sons (NMF, 149), three known daughters. *Micaela*, at 21, married Melcher Rodríguez in 1717; *Manuela* married a widower, Lazaro Durán, in 1724; and *María Rosalia* became the wife of Juan Jiménez in 1728 (DM, 1717, no. 15; 1724, no. 2; 1728, no. 10).

BRITO

JUAN DE LEON BRITO (NMF, 149, 150), Mexican Indian and "*poblador*" of Analco in Santa Fe, and his wife, *María de los Reyes Granillo*, had another daughter, *Brigida*, who married Luis de Armenta in 1718 (DM, 1718, nos. 10, 32).

Juan Brito, 27, son of Antonio Brito, deceased, and Magdalena Gómez, married *Antonia Martín*, 17, of unknown parentage, in Santa Fe, January 6, 1717 (DM, 1716, no. 30). Juan was undoubtedly a brother of *Pedro Brito* in NMF, 50.

Another *Juan Brito*, native of El Paso and of unknown parentage, came to Santa Fe and married *María Gerónima*, 18, also of unknown parentage. The investigation states that there was a large number of soldiers and other men from El Paso in Santa Fe at this time (DM, 1714, no. 14).

At El Paso, *Antonia Brito*, daughter of *Francisco Brito*, deceased, and Micaela Francisca de la Cruz, married Cayetano Maese (DM, 1714, no. 22).

BRUSELAS

JUAN DE BRUSELAS was a resident of San Lorenzo del Paso in 1697 (DM, 1697, no. 5).

BRUSIAGA

DON ANTONIO DE BRUSIAGA, deceased, lived in Santa Fe during Governor Bustamante's term.[4] When he died in Santa Fe, September 5, 1729, the Padre wrote "Don Antonio de Gruciaga," 56, and *soltero*, either single or a widower (*Bur.*, 48, *Santa Fe*).

---

4. Bancroft Library, *New Mexico Originals*, 1731.

BUENO

DON FRANCISCO BUENO DE BOHÓRQUEZ was *Alcalde Mayor* of Santa Fe in 1724 and other years of Governor Bustamante's term. He was a former aide of Governors Bustamante and Valverde.[5] There is no known connection as yet between him and Bueno families later found in the Rio Arriba district.

---

5. *Ibid.*; Fernando Ocaranza, *Establecimientos Franciscanos, etc.* (Mexico, 1934), pp. 136, 139.

CADENA

FRANCISCO DE LA CADENA (NMF, 154) was also referred to as Francisco Cadena *Ynojos* in 1727, then married to *Leonor Montaño*. In 1680 he had been taken captive as a lad by the Picuris Indians together with a María La Mozonga and her son Francisco Rendón (DM, 1727, no. 12).

CALLES

ANDRÉS CALLES, a native of Chihuahua, and widowed of *María Josefa Calves*, married *Ana Josefa Sandoval* in Santa Fe, September 22, 1816 (M-52, *Santa Fe*). A son by his previous wife, *Manuel*, married María Rosalía Baldonado in 1834 (DM, 1834).

CANDELARIA

FELIX (FELICIANO) DE LA CANDELARIA (NMF, 155, 156) sold his San Clemente inheritance to Captain Bernabé Baca, who later sold it to Nicolás de Chavez in 1746 (*Gen.*, 1746, no. 2). He had a sister, *Rosa de Manzanares*, who married Alonso García in 1707, having two children by him already (DM, 1707, no. 12). Felix gave his age as 25 in 1701 at Bernalillo, and 48 in 1716 at Albuquerque (DM, 1701, no. 9; 1716, no. 14).

FRANCISCO CANDELARIA (NMF, 156) and his wife *Francisca Montoya* had the daughter *Isabel* there mentioned, and she married Juan Maese in 1720 (DM, 1720, no. 9); also a son *Juan* who married a Juana de la Candelaria of unknown parentage in 1717 (DM, 1717, no. 7). Another *Juan*, whose full name was *Juan Antonio*, and who married Manuela Varela on May 30, 1728, was also another son of theirs (DM, 1728, no. 12). This turns out to be the "Juan Candelaria" who penned a faulty descriptive history of New Mexico in 1777.[6]

Ventura Candelaria (NMF, 156) was still another son of Francisco Candelaria and

Francisca Montoya, as discovered from his marriage to *Petrona Efigenia García* in 1719 (DM, 1719, no. 15). Therefore, Ventura was a nephew of Felix and son of Francisco, and not their brother, and he was a brother of the now famous author Juan.

---

6. *New Mexico Historical Review*, "Noticias of Juan Candelaria," vol. 4, no. 3, pp. 274-297. Candelaria himself gives the date 1777 in his closing line, while Editor Bloom says 1776 in the opening footnote. Giving his age as 84 in the title, and 26 in 1720 (NMF, 156), he could not have been born in 1692 as he claims on the title (under the current mistaken impression that the Vargas colonists came in 1692), but most likely in the early part of 1694, since the colonists came in December 1693.

CAPITÁN

A JUAN CAPITÁN, 20, and a native of Mexico City, was in Santa Fe in 1694 (DM, 1694, no. 35a).

CÁRDENAS

Besides the Cárdenas family in NMF, 156, there was a LUCAS DE CÁRDENAS, 27, living in Santa Fe after its capture in December, 1693 (DM, 1693, no. 22).

Paula, child of an *Antonio de Cárdenas* and *Pascuala López*, was born on January 29, 1736 (*Gen.*, 1736, no. 2).

CARRILLO

MIGUEL CARRILLO (NMF, 157) was actually a native of Villa de Jerez. He named his parents as Agustín Carrillo and Margarita Rodarte when he married *María de Mondragón*, December 26, 1693 (DM, 1693, no. 24). They had several children, the eldest of whom was the girl *Juana* in NMF, and who falsely accused her father of rape (*Gen.*, 1712, no. 5).

CARVAJAL

ANTONIO DE CARVAJAL, resident of El Paso, and widowed of *Catalina del Rio*, there married *Micaela Francisca de la Cruz* (DM, 1714, no. 10).

Lorenzo de Carvajal (NMF, 157) and his wife *Sebastiana Fresqui* were "*indios vestidos*" of New Mexico, whose son *Antonio*, living in Bernalillo, married Juana Maese, 18, a native of Isleta of unknown parentage, July 25, 1705 (DM, 1705, no. 21). Another son, *Baltasar*, residing in Albuquerque, married María Durán, born in Zacatecas, the natural daughter of Catalina Durán, February 5, 1715 (DM, 1715, no. 16).

CASADOS

FRANCISCO LORENZO DE CASADOS (NMF, 157) was married to *Ana Pacheco*, who was dead in 1716 when their son *Francisco José*, 23, married María de Archibeque on October 28 (DM, 1716, no. 23).

CASTRILLÓN

In 1707 the ALFÉREZ, DON ANTONIO CASTRILLÓN, 27, had been in Santa Fe two years (DM, 1707, no. 6).

CASTRO

CRISTÓBAL DE CASTRO, native of Zacatecas, the son of Miguel de Castro and Juana Guerrero, married *Bernarda de Gamboa*, of unknown parentage, at Santa Cruz, May 19, 1705 (DM, 1705, no. 16).

JOAQUÍN DE CASTRO, born in the province of Sonora, came to Santa Fe and married *Juana González* on February 10, 1782 (M-51, *Castrense*).

CHAFALOTE

JOSÉ ANTONIO CHAFALOTE and his wife *Soledad Suazo* of Taos had a son *José Pablo*, June 1, 1780. Then there was a *Domingo Chafalote*, or *Caigua* (Kiowa), married to *Victoria Delgado*. These had a daughter *Juana*, April 8, 1804, and a son *Juan Antonio*, June 9, 1805 (all in B-38, *Taos*).

CHAVEZ

A DON JUAN DE CHAVES who married *Doña María Rosa de San Juan*, or *Luna* (Cf. NMF, 283), at Bernalillo on December 8, 1727 (DM, 1727, no. 15), could well have been the eldest son of Bernardo Durán y Chaves and Francisca Mizquia (NMF, 161). For he later resided at Guadalupe del Paso, home of his wife's and mother's folks (Cf. *Mizuia*, NMF, 74, 75).

FRANCISCO DURÁN Y CHAVES (NMF, 162, 163), fourth son of Don Fernando, was about 20 when he married *Doña Juana*, 14, "of unknown parentage," May 18, 1713. He was from Atrisco and she from Bernalillo, and they were second cousins (DM, 1713, no. 4).

LUIS DURÁN Y CHAVES (NMF, 163), fifth son of Don Fernando, married *Leonor Montaño* on June 13, 1707. They were second and third cousins (DM, 1707, no. 4).

Among the "Other Chávez" folks in NMF, 164, *Juan de Aparicio Chaves* is mentioned. He was a Pánana (Pawnee), 19, of unknown parentage, living in Atrisco in 1722 when he asked to marry *María Antonia de la Rosa* of Santa Fe, also known as "*La Prieta*" (DM, 1722, no. 6).

CHURA

JUAN AGUSTÍN CHURA, Indian of Guadalupe del Paso, and widowed of *Felipa Candelaria*, married *Victoria Candelaria, india de Belén*, in 1768 (DM, 1768).

CONDE

SANTIAGO CONDE and *María Antonia Lobato* had a girl *Juana*, July 11, 1808 (B-38, *Taos*).

CONTRERAS

JOSÉ DE CONTRERAS (NMF, 165) and his wife *María de Valencia* were living in El Paso when their daughter *Juana*, born in Santa Fe, married Diego Madrid at El Paso in 1711 (DM, 1711, no. 5).

Simón de Contreras of Zacatecas (last par., NMF, 165) was living in Bernalillo in 1708 (DM, 1708, no. 10).

CÓRDOBA

ANTONIO DE CÓRDOBA and wife *Eugenia de Herrera* (NMF, 165) had another son, *Tomás*, who was 20 in 1716 when he married *Francisca de Torres* of Bernalillo on June 16 (DM, 1716, no. 24).

CORTÉS

JOSÉ CORTÉS DEL CASTILLO (NMF, 166) and *María de Carvajal* brought a son *Dionisio* who on September 27, 1718, when 23, married Josefa Martín (DM, 1718, no. 15). Another son, *Juan Antonio*, was 26 in 1720 when he married Juana de Mata Espinosa of Santa Cruz (DM, 1720, no. 10). There was also another daughter, *Ynez*, who was 20 in 1718 when she married Francisco Jurado (DM, 1718, no. 24).

CRUZ

JOSÉ DE LA CRUZ and his wife *Josefa de la Cruz*, natives of Mexico City, were living in New Mexico in 1696 when their daughter *Isabel*, widow of Juan de Ribera, married Juan de Guido (DM, 1696, no. 17).

Agustín de la Cruz, born in New Mexico, the son of Mateo de la Cruz and Catalina de Gracia, both dead, married *Manuela Zamora* at Albuquerque in 1723 (DM, 1723, no. 12), while the bride of José Manuel Reinoso in 1720 was *Elena de la Cruz*, native of Santa Fe, and daughter of *Agustín* de la Cruz and María de la O (DM, 1720, no. 11). There might be some connection between these "Agustíns" and the one in NMF, 167.

CUBERO

In 1767, LORENZO CUBERO, Piro Indian of Senecú del Paso, widowed of *María Agreda*, also a Piro, married *María Manuela Peralta* of San Agustín de Isleta (DM, 1767).

CUSA

MANUEL CUSA Y LISONDA and his wife *Anamaría González* had a daughter, *Antonia Micaela*, who married Juan Miguel Roybal on February 27, 1813 (M-25, *San Ildefonso*).

DOMÍNGUEZ

JUAN DOMÍNGUEZ DE MENDOZA (NMF, pp. 25-26) had for his wife *Doña Isabel Durán de Chávez y Bohórquez*, 42 in 1683, who was the mother of *María Domínguez de Mendoza*, 21, and also mother-in-law of Diego de Hinojos (DM, 1683, no. 3). She was, therefore, a sister of Don Fernando (I) and Don Pedro Durán y Chávez (NMF, p. 19). But since her daughter María was married to Diego Lucero de Godoy, there was another who was the wife of Hinojos.

FRANCISCO DOMÍNGUEZ DE MENDOZA and his wife *Juana de Valencia* had a son, *Carlos*, who was a native of New Mexico and 20 years old when he married Juana de Ribera, 18, a native of Mexico City, in Santa Fe, Sept. 17, 1699 (DM, 1699, no. 13). Francisco was very likely the fourth son of Tomé Domínguez de Mendoza II (NMF, p. 26) and now residing in Nueva Vizcaya.

JOSÉ DOMÍNGUEZ (NMF, pp. 27, 169, 170), father of *María Domínguez*, wife of Dimas Jirón, was also the natural father of *Juan Antonio Domínguez*, who married Catalina Maese (NMF, p. 170). José was rumored to be the father of other individuals; he escorted Governor Treviño back to New Spain prior to the 1680 Rebellion (DM, 1727, no. 12).

DURÁN

SALVADOR DURÁN and wife *Ana Márquez* (NMF, p. 170) had two other daughters: *Gregoria*, who married Antonio de Lara at El Paso, in 1701 (DM, 1701, no. 7), and *María*, 30, when she married Juan Antonio Apodaca in 1709 (DM, 1709, no. 25).

LAZARO DURÁN (NMF, p. 171), widowed of *María de Cárdenas*, married *Manuela Blea* in Santa Fe, May 18, 1724 (DM, 1724, no. 2).

LUIS DURÁN (NMF, p. 171) was a native of New Mexico and the son of Luis Durán, deceased, and Ana de Archuleta, and 22 when he married *María Ramírez de Salazar*, a native of New Mexico of unknown parentage, in Santa Fe, Oct. 27, 1697 (DM, 1697, no. 16). They had a son, *Nicolás*, who married Ana Sedillo in 1728 (DM, 1728, no. 9); his mother also used the name "Romero."

If not this same man, there was another *Nicolás Durán* who married Ana Carrillo at Isleta in New Mexico (DM, 1720, no. 15).

MIGUEL DURÁN, a soldier of Santa Fe of unknown parentage, had been born in New Spain at the Hacienda of Don Luis de Sabala; he married *María Rincón* (DM, 1708, nos. 7, 11).

ENRÍQUEZ

DON MANUEL ENRÍQUEZ, Alcalde of Taos (*ca.* 1720), was profiteering in trade with the Plains Indians to the detriment of the poor settlers.[7]

---
7. Ocaranza, p. 186.

ERRONIZ

ISIDRO ERRONIZ, whose origin is not known, married *María Teresa Sena*, April 17, 1784 (M-52, *Santa Fe*).

ESCALABIS

DIEGO DE ESCALABIS was a resident of Santa Fe in 1717 (DM, 1717, no. 9).

ESPINOSA

NICOLÁS DE ESPINOSA (NMF, p. 172) was related to a José López of Santa Cruz (DM, 1697, no. 5a). He and his wife *Josefa de la Cruz* had a daughter, *Juana de Mata*, who married José Antonio Cortés in 1720 (DM, 1720, no. 10).

ESQUIVEL

VENTURA DE ESQUIVEL (NMF, p. 173) gave his parents as Antonio de Caraña and María de Esquivel when he married *Rosa Bernardina Lucero de Godoy* in Santa Fe, May 3, 1702. He was 22, and she was 16. He was also a *criado* or aide of the Governor, and a brother to ANTONIO DE ESQUIVEL. Ventura had been sued previously by a Juana Lujan, 16, who had a child by him (DM, 1702, no. 5).

José Esquivel (NMF, p. 173) was living in Santa Cruz in 1707, when he gave his age as 54 (DM, 1707, no. 5).

FAJARDO

ALONSO FAJARDO and *Magdalena Luján*, both natives of New Mexico, had a son, *Cayetano*, who married María Ledesma in Santa Fe, June 29, 1706 (DM, 1706, no. 4). Most likely they belonged to the Fajardo group in NMF, p. 174.

FERNÁNDEZ

JUAN FERNÁNDEZ DE ATIENZA (NMF, p. 175) and *Teresa Fernández* were married in the Cathedral of Mexico City, Feb. 2, 1688 (DM, 1693, no. 13).

BERNARDINO FERNÁNDEZ (NMF, p. 175), a native of Sombrerete, gave his parents as Juan de Santiago and Melchora de los Reyes, when he married *Ynez González* in Santa Fe, Nov. 10, 1694. He was then 23 years old (DM, 1694, no. 39). But when he married again, he named his parents as Juan Fernández de Vela y Gutiérrez and Melchora de los Reyes Ledesma y Angulo, both deceased. His second wife was *Antonia Martín*, 16, while Bernardino was 45.

They were married on March 19, 1718 (DM, 1718, no. 14). The previous year he had tried to marry a Gertrudis Sánchez de Otón, but the marriage was turned down by the authorities on moral grounds; this time Bernardino gave his father's name as Juan Fernández de Santiago Vela-Gutiérrez (DM, 1717, no. 10). Bernardino had a son, *José Antonio*, by his first wife (*ibid.*), and this seems to be the man who married Juana Abeyta (see Armenta, DM, 1725, no. 10). The two children in the second paragraph of NMF, *loc. cit.*, belonged to the distinct Fernández Valerio family and should go under "Valerio."

ALONSO FERNÁNDEZ, who follows Bernardino in NMF, was indeed his brother. He and his wife *Catalina Martín de Salazar* had a daughter, *María*, who married Juan José de Sandoval Martínez (DM, 1720, no. 14).

FLORES

LUCAS FLORES and *María Ramos* (NMF, p. 176) had another son, *Juan Antonio*, who married Antonia Martín (DM, 1723, no. 14), and a daughter, *Juana*, who had married Blas Lobato II in 1702 (DM, 1702, no. 4a). Lucas gave his age as 40 in 1710 when he said that he had been born in Santa María de la Parra (DM, 1710, no. 11).

FRÉSQUEZ

JOSE FRESQUI and *María de Herrera* had their daughter *Gertrudis* (NMF, p. 177) baptized at Santa Cruz on Feb. 8, 1711, and also a son, *José*, on Feb. 12 (*Gen.*, 1710, no. 7).

PEDRO FRESQUI and *Micaela de Archuleta* were married at Socorro del Paso, the bride's birthplace, in 1712. He was a native of the Rio Abajo (DM, 1712, no. 7).

At El Paso in 1681, *Juan de la Cruz Fresco*, a native of New Mexico and son of Diego Fresco, Jumano Indian, and Beatriz Varela, Apache, married *María León*, natural daughter of Luisa Garcia of Isleta (DM, 1681, no. 10).

GABALDÓN

MARÍA GERTRUDIS CHÁVEZ, wife of *Miguel Gabaldón* (NMF, p. 178), was not a child of Diego Antonio Chávez as tentatively indicated with a dotted line in the Chávez chart (*ibid.*, p. 18), but the daughter of Antonio de Chávez and Barbara Padilla, according to a matrimonial tree made in 1833 (DM, 1833, no. 1).

GAITÁN

The second marriage of JOSÉ GAITÁN with the widow *Gerónima de la Cruz*, 24, took place on June 29, 1697. He was 34 and a native of San Luis Potosí, while she was a native of Los Lagos near Zacatecas (DM, 1697, no. 6).

GALLEGOS

JOSÉ GALLEGOS, who married *María Silva* in 1721, was actually the son of the *Sargento* Antonio Gallegos and Rosa Montoya (NMF, p. 179). He was from Bernalillo and the bride from Albuquerque (DM, 1721, no. 9).

GALVES

JUAN JOSE GALVES, or *Galvis*, and *María Ynez Martínez* had a son, *Felix*, who married Guadalupe Vigil and had a daughter, María Luz, Feb. 4, 1846 (B-52, *Taos*).

Diego Galves and *Manuela Montoya* had a son *Clemente* who married Ana María Ortega in 1783 (M-33, *S. Clara*). A *Salvador Galves* of Chama married Bernarda Torres on Nov. 5, 1781 (*ibid.*). What relation these people bore to each other is hard to say. Nor can they be traced to JOSÉ CALVES (NMF, p. 155), who evidently had no sons.

GARCÍA DE NORIEGA

An error regarding the identity of JUAN GARCÍA DE NORIEGA must be pointed out here. In NMF, pp. 34, 181, he is identified with a Juan García of Zacatecas, husband of Margarita Márquez, and therefore given two successive wives. However, this other "Juan Garcia" was a soldier of Conchos, and his wife Margarita, a native of New Mexico, was dead when their daughter, Ana María, 19, married Miguel de Herrera (DM, 1790, nos. 1, 16). This man could well have been a younger brother of Alonso Garcia I.

JUAN GARCÍA DE NORIEGA was a native of New Mexico, the son of the *Maese de Campo* Alonso García and Teresa Varela, settlers of New Mexico who were residing at Guadalupe del Paso when Juan married his first and only wife, *Doña Francisca Sánchez de Yñigo* (no parents given!), on May 4, 1681 (DM, 1681, no. 7). His known children at El Paso, where this family stayed instead of returning to New Mexico with the Reconquest, are the ones listed in NMF, plus another daughter, *María Magdalena*, who married José Telles Jirón (DM, 1711, no. 16).

ALONSO GARCÍA DE NORIEGA II and his family are as listed in NMF, p. 181. There is no record of the marriage of one son, *Alonso III;* but he seems to be the "Alonso Garcia" who married Rosa de Manzanares, sister of Felix de la Candelaria, at Albuquerque, Oct. 7, 1707 (DM, 1707, no. 12). But this is by no means certain, for this Alonso had a brother in Albuquerque (*Gen.*, 1746, no. 2) who cannot, so far, be connected with Alonso II.

JUAN GARCÍA DE NORIEGA, "*El Cojo*" (NMF, p. 182), did not know who his parents were when at 26 he married *María de la Vega Carpio*, 16, on May 17, 1705 (DM, 1705, no. 15). He lived all his life in Santa Fe, and gave his age as 46 in 1727 (DM, 1727, no. 12).

FRANCISCO GARCÍA DE NORIEGA (NMF, p. 182) married *María de Ribera* when he was 20, on Oct. 27, 1697. He was the natural son of Nicolasa Varela by Lázaro García (DM, 1697, no. 17)—in all likelihood the son of old

Alonso who was killed by the rebel Indians in 1680 (NMF, p. 34). Their son, *Lázaro*, first married Nicolasa López in 1720 (DM, 1720, no. 12) and then Francisca Varela in 1728 (DM, 1728, no. 7). Their daughter, *Francisca*, born in 1705, married Salvador Márquez, Nov. 8, 1725, and another, *Petrona Efigenia*, became the wife of Ventura Candelaria in 1719 (DM, 1725, no. 8; 1719, no. 15).

GARCÍA (OTHERS)

CRISTOBAL GARCÍA and *Isabel Romero* (NMF, p. 181) were married on Nov. 6, 1702. He was 16, and the bride was 20 (DM, 1702, no. 4, now complete).

NICOLÁS GARCÍA of El Paso was a native of New Mexico and 23 in 1693 (DM, 1693, no. 21). A captain, he, by his wife *María de la Serna*, had a daughter, *Lorenza*, who married Antonio Sambrano (DM, 1705, no. 8). In 1714, *Antonia*, daughter of Captain Nicolás García and Margarita de Otón (second wife?), married Gregorio Ortega of El Paso (DM, 1714, no. 12).

Also at El Paso, *Nicolás García*, of unknown parentage and a native of Santa Fe, widowed of *Antonia Montoya*, married *Lucía Antonia Durán*, likewise of unknown parentage, Jan. 20, 1709 (DM, 1708, nos. 4, 5).

MIGUEL GARCÍA DE LA RIBA and *Micaela Velasco* (NMF, p. 183) were married in the parish church of Santa Catalina Mártir in Mexico City, sometime between the years 1662-1667 (DM, 1693, no. 29).

Florencio García de Lira was also known as García *Marujo* (DM, 1718, no. 25).

GILTOMEY

JOSÉ MANUEL GILTOMEY (NMF, p. 186) was the son of Don Juan Manuel de Giltomey and Doña Antonia Flores de Valdés, both deceased, evidently a Spanish official family in the Philippines, where José Manuel was born, in the Province of "Albay." He was 31 in 1696 when he married *Isabel Bautista Olivas*, 22, a native of Sombrerete and a widow of Salvador de Esparza, who had died there (DM, 1696, no. 30). Their daughter *Rosalía* first married Miguel de la Mora Pineda in 1718 (DM, 1718, no. 21); Juan Manuel Varela must have been a subsequent husband of hers.

GÓMEZ

ANTONIO GÓMEZ was killed in the "battle of Zia" and was buried in the ruined house of Juan Domínguez, five years prior to 1693, when his widow, *Francisca Durán*, married José de Apodaca (DM, 1693, no. 21). Their daughter *Ana María* married Antonio Martín at El Paso (DM, 1700, no. 2).

A *Francisco Gómez*, son of Antonio Gómez and Sebastiana Tadeo, both deceased, married *Francisca Archuleta* at El Paso (DM, 1710, no. 4).

LAUREANO GÓMEZ, who was killed by the Indians at Cochití in 1696 (NMF, p. 188), and his wife *Josefa de la Cruz* were both from the city of Zacatecas. Their son *Domingo*, 17, born in New Mexico, married Antonia Apodaca, 17, on July 8, 1714 (DM, 1714, no. 19); he was living in Santa Cruz in 1722 when he married *Apolonia Martín*, now giving his father's birthplace as Sombrerete (DM, 1722, no. 5). Old Laureano, 30 in 1696, had given his birthplace as Guanajuato (DM, 1696, nos. 12, 13). A *Miguel Laureano* and his wife Ana María Fajardo of Santa Cruz had a child, María, Sept. 21, 1759 (*Gen.*, 1758, no. 2).

JOSÉ BERNARDO GÓMEZ, a native of Real de Sacualpa and resident of Santa Cruz, the son of Antonio Gómez and Petrona de Arellano, married *Lugarda Valerio Fernández* on May 21, 1726 (DM, 1726, no. 4).

GÓMEZ ROBLEDO

Lucía, a native of Santa Fe and daughter of ANDRÉS GÓMEZ ROBLEDO, deceased, and Doña Juana Ortiz, married Miguel de Sandoval Martínez in 1697, after such strong opposition from her family that she had to be placed in a "neutral home" (of Diego Arias de Quirós) in order to state her own mind (DM, 1697, no. 11). All of Lucía's sisters had married various soldiers whom Governor Vargas had recruited in Spain, while her intended was a colonist from Mexico City, and this evidently was the cause of their objections.

GÓNGORA

JUAN DE GÓNGORA and *Petronila de la Cueva* (NMF, p. 188) were married in the Cathedral of Mexico City on June 16, 1672 (DM, 1693, no. 11). Their youngest son, *Juan José*, born in Mexico City, went from Santa Fe to live at El Paso, where he married Lucía de Perea in 1718. She was the natural daughter of the widow of Antonio de Avalos. The groom gave his father's name as Juan *de Maestre Góngora* (DM, 1718, no. 30). His elder brother, *Cristóbal*, was also living at El Paso by 1714 (DM, 1714, no. 22).

GONZÁLEZ (BERNAL, BAS)

The large and important family of *González Bernal*, or *Bas* (NMF, pp. 40, 41, 189, 190), takes clearer shape with a few newly discovered items.

JUAN GONZÁLEZ BERNAL of the seventeenth century, whose wife was *Apolonia Varela*, from all indications turns out to be a son of the original Sebastián González who married Isabel Bernal of the Juan Griego family. Of the daughters of Juan there mentioned, *Melchora* and *Antonia*, the latter was the wife of Apolinar Martín Serrano (DM, 1692, no. 6). Two known sons were *Juan II*, who married Nicolasa Zaldívar Jorge, and *Sebastián*, husband of Lucía Ortiz. Their mother appears to be the same Apolonia Varela whose marriage to Juan

Bautista Zaragoza was annulled in 1641, a *cause célèbre* of the period.[8]

JUAN GONZÁLEZ BERNAL (II) must have acquired his wife outside New Mexico proper, as Zaldívar Jorge is an unusual name, or else she had reached back some generations to an ancestral name, as sometimes happened in this century. A young woman, *Inez*, living in Santa Fe with her grandmother Apolonia Varela, and who had a brother *Juan*, silversmith (DM, 1694, no. 40), was to all appearances their daughter. Her brother would then be Juan González Bernal III, or as he and his brother and sisters later called themselves, "González Bas." Brother to this Juan III was *Diego*, who married María de Benavides.

JUAN GONZÁLEZ BAS I (the same Juan González Bernal III of the pre-Revolt period) returned in the Vargas Reconquest with his wife, *María López del Castillo*, to settle in the Alameda district (NMF, p. 189). Among their children there enumerated, *Inez*, born in 1703, married Cristóbal (or Juan Antonio) Varela Jaramillo in 1718, and then Baltasar Trujillo in 1728 (DM, 1718, no. 16; 1728, no. 11).

DIEGO GONZÁLEZ BAS married *María de Benavides* (NMF, p. 190) on April 30, 1696, when he was 23 and she was 14. His brother Juan and wife María López were the witnesses (DM, 1696, no. 19). Their daughter, *Teodora*, married Antonio García in 1718 (DM, 1718, no. 18).

The "Antonio Torivio González" described in NMF, p. 38, was not the González de Escalante individual who stayed at El Paso, but a different man who returned to Santa Fe, where he was both soldier and wagon-train driver in 1694, when he was supposed to have married the first Ynez González Bernal (DM, 1694, no. 40).

---

8. AGN, *Mex., Inq.*, t. 571, exp. 8, f. 230.

GONZÁLEZ (OTHERS)

DOMINGO GONZÁLEZ, "el Gallego," who had died well before 1680 (NMF, p. 38), and *Francisca Martín Barba* had a son *Pedro* who married Josefa Cisneros in 1681 at San Pedro de Alcántara (DM, 1681, no. 6). This is the "Pedro" and "Domingo" described among the refugees of 1680 and 1681 (NMF, p. 39).

ANDRES GONZÁLEZ of Zacatecas and *Francisca de Gambo* (NMF, p. 191) also had a daughter, *Josefa*, who was 20 in 1714 when she married Diego Archuleta of Santa Cruz (DM, 1714, no. 16).

PEDRO GONZÁLEZ and *Francisca Izquierdo*, who volunteered to join the colonists of 1693, were married in the Cathedral of Mexico City on May 18, 1688 (DM, 1693, no. 12a).

Francisco González, 22, a native of San Miguel el Grande, was at El Paso in 1699 (DM, 1699, no. 14).

FRANCISCO (GONZÁLEZ) DE LA ROSA (NMF, p. 191) and *Antonia de la Cerda* were married in the Cathedral of Mexico City on July 14, 1678 (DM, 1693, no. 28).

GRIEGO

JUAN GRIEGO (NMF, p. 192), widowed in Albuquerque of *Antonia Varela*, married *Juliana Saiz* of Santa Fe in 1716 at Albuquerque. A sister of his, Josefa, had married a José Romero in 1699. Both were the children of the *Alférez* Blas Griego, deceased, and Ynez Romero of El Paso, the latter still living at San Lorenzo del Paso (DM, 1716, no. 26; 1699, no. 15). Their father Blas was an uncle of Josefa Pacheco, bride of José Baca, and 30 years old in 1684 (DM, 1684, no. 1).

AGUSTÍN GRIEGO (NMF, pp. 42, 192) was the son of a seventeenth-century Captain Agustín (?) Griego and Francisca Montoya, both living at the Presidio of San José when the young Agustín, 22, married *Josefa Durán*, 19, on Nov. 6, 1682 (DM, 1682, no. 10). Of their known children, *Lorenzo* (NMF, p. 192) married Sebastiana Serna on May 5, 1715 (DM, 1715, no. 14), by whom he had a son, Francisco Xavier, Nov. 10, 1721 (*Gen.*, 1721, no. 5), and next he married Casilda Jaramillo, widow, on April 24, 1728 (DM, 1728, no. 8). Another son of Agustín and Josefa Durán was *José*, who married Ana María Ortiz on July 17, 1718 (DM, 1718, no. 17). Josefa Durán had been living in concubinage with the famed Roque de Madrid for 23 years, and had two grown sons by him, when she was tried in 1700 (*Gen.*, 1700, no. 1). Her husband Agustín was dead by this time, and she actually married Madrid 15 years later.

The *Ana Griego Montoya* (NMF, p. 47), who was the wife of Pedro Hidalgo, was in all likelihood a sister of Agustín Griego.

NICOLÁS GRIEGO (NMF, p. 42) and *Antonia Martín* had a daughter *Catalina*, who, after the death of her first husband Diego Trujillo, married Melchor de Herrera in 1708 (DM, 1707, no. 11; 1708, no. 12).

GUIDO

JUAN DE GUIDO (EJIDO?), born in Zacatecas, was the son of Juan de Bonifacio and María González, natives of Guanajuato. In Santa Fe he married *Isabel de los Reyes Cruz*, widow of a Juan de Ribera who had died in Zacatecas (DM, 1696, no. 17).

GUILLÉN

PEDRO GUILLÉN (NMF, p. 193) was the brother or half brother of a Josefa de Mendoza, daughter of Tomás de la Mora and Gerónimo *Guillén*, natives of New Mexico. Josefa was the first wife of a Marcos Montoya and she died at El Paso in 1708. Pedro was a survivor of the fatal Villasur Expedition of 1720 (DM, 1727, no. 12).

GUTIÉRREZ

ROQUE GUTIÉRREZ and *María de Tapia* (NMF, pp. 44, 194) had the children there listed and also the *Juan Roque* mentioned as a possible son.

JUAN ROQUE GUTIÉRREZ, 19, had asked to marry a María García in 1690, but contrary suit was brought by *Antonia Martín*, whom he married on Feb. 18, 1692 (DM, 1690, no. 4). He was a brother-in-law of José de Apodaca and a cousin of Pedro Luján (*ibid.*). In 1696 he was stationed at the El Paso Presidio (DM, 1696, no. 18).

FELIPE GUTIÉRREZ and *Isabel de Salazar* (NMF, p. 44) returned with the Reconquest; in 1696 he testified that he was 36 and a native of the Rio Abajo (DM, 1693, no. 24; 1696, no. 6). They had two known sons: *Antonio* and *Bartolomé*. Antonio (NMF, p. 194), 20, living in Bernalillo, married Gregoria Góngora on Nov. 4, 1702 (DM, 1702, nos. 6, 7). Bartolomé, 20, married Nicolasa Montoya in 1708; they had a soldier son, Bartolomé II, who died during an expedition to Sonora (HSNM, Mil. Papers).

MIGUEL GUTIÉRREZ (NMF, p. 195) of San Luis Potosi was the son of Juan Gutiérrez and María Martínez, both deceased, when he married *María de Tapia* in Santa Fe, Dec. 18, 1693 (DM, 1693, no. 25).

HERNÁNDEZ

NICOLÁS DE LA TRINIDAD HERNÁNDEZ and *Petrona Gómez* (NMF, p. 195) had a daughter, *Juana*, who married Sebastián de Apodaca (DM, 1707, no. 13).

JOSÉ ANTONIO HERNÁNDEZ, 22, a native of Sombrerete living in Santa Fe, was the son of Tomás Hernández and Antonia Pascuala, Creoles of Quatlitlan. He married *Isabel María*, widow of Martín Caxua of Tesuque who was killed at El Alto de Cuma on the road to Tesuque (DM, 1697, no. 12; 1698, no. 22).

HERRERA

MIGUEL DE HERRERA, son of Captain Juan de Herrera and Ana López, both deceased (NMF, p. 196), married *María Ana García* (DM, 1690, no. 6). Their son, *Miguel II*, 19, married Antonia Trujillo, 14, at Santa Cruz on April 26, 1716 (DM, 1716, no. 28). Their daughter *María*, born at El Paso, had married Diego Trujillo at Santa Cruz in 1790 (DM, 1790, no. 21). Another son, *José*, by Miguel's second wife, *Antonia (Archuleta)*, was born at Santa Cruz on April 25, 1712 (*Gen.*, 1710, no. 7).

ANTONIO DE HERRERA (NMF, p. 46), who stayed at El Paso, was still a soldier there in 1696 and 43 years old (DM, 1696, no. 22).

MELCHOR JAIMES DE HERRERA (NMF, p. 196), widowed of *Angela González*, married *Catalina Griego*, widow of Diego Trujillo; after her death he was married a third time, to *Josefa Luján*, widow of Matías Martín, Jan. 3, 1717 (DM, 1707, no. 11; 1708, no. 12; 1716, no. 22). In 1714 his daughter *María*, by the first wife, married Antonio Martín (DM, 1714, no. 20).

TOMÁS DE HERRERA SANDOVAL and *Pascuala de la Concepción* were married in the city of Salvatierra, May 7, 1684 (DM, 1685, no. 2).

HIDALGO

PEDRO HIDALGO (NMF, pp. 47, 48) and *Ana Montoya Griego* had three other known sons, besides *Alfonso* who married at El Paso. *Nicolás*, born in Santa Fe, married *María de la Serna;* his parents, natives of Santa Fe, were still living at San Lorenzo del Paso (DM, 1696, no. 33). *Cristóbal*, born in Santa Fe and residing at San Lorenzo, there married Petrona de Herrera in 1701, his father being mentioned as dead (DM, 1701, no. 8). *Francisco*, 18, a soldier of El Paso, married Gregoria Varela, 10 years his senior (DM, 1701, no. 8; 1706, no. 3).

HINOJOS

DIEGO DE HINOJOS (NMF, p. 49) was a cousin of Antonio Jorge II and son-in-law of Doña Ysabel Durán de Chávez y Bohórquez (DM, 1683, no. 3).

Nicolás Ruiz de Hinojos, 42, was living at El Paso in 1695 (DM, 1695, no. 17).

JARAMILLO NEGRETE

ROQUE JARAMILLO NEGRETE (NMF, p. 199) and *Petrona de Cárdenas* were living at Santa Cruz when these three children were born: *Sebastián*, Feb. 18, 1711; *Manuela*, Sept. 24, 1712; *María*, May 14, 1714 (*Gen.*, 1710, no. 7).

JARAMILLO (VARELA)

LUISA VARELA (NMF, p. 110), who married the Adjutant Bartolomé Romero de Pedraza in 1681, and then Antonio Feliz Valencia in 1696, was actually the daughter of Pedro Varela Jaramillo and Lucía Madrid (DM, 1681, no. 8; 1696, no. 29).

CRISTÓBAL VARELA JARAMILLO and Casilda Sedillo (NMF, p. 198) had these other children besides the three there listed: *Cristóbal*, who married Ynez González Bas in Albuquerque in 1718; *Casilda*, who became the wife of Antonio Vallejo and then of Lorenzo Griego in 1728; and *Rosa*, wife of Francisco Lucero and then of Diego de Torres in 1711 (DM, 1718, no. 16; 1728, no. 8; 1711, no. 15).

PEDRO VARELA, son of Juan Varela Jaramillo (NMF, p. 199), married Juana González Bas on June 4, 1716 (DM, 1716, no. 31).

JIMÉNEZ

JOSÉ JIMÉNEZ, driver for the wagon-trains, married *María Hernández* of Santa Fe on Oct. 12, 1680, at El Paso (DM, 1680, no. 2).

JUAN JIMÉNEZ, a native of San Juan del Rio, the son of José Jiménez and Antonia Rodríguez, deceased, married *María Rosalía Blea* on Mar. 6, 1728 (DM, 1728, no. 10).

JIRÓN

GERTRUDIS JIRÓN DE TEJEDA (NMF, p. 200), a native of Mexico City and 4 years old in 1693, and daughter of the colonists Diego Jirón de Tejeda and María de Leyva, or Mendoza, married *Manuel Antonio de las Rosas* in 1723 (DM, 1723, no. 16).

TOMÁS JIRÓN DE TEJEDA (NMF, p. 200) married off his son *Dimas* to a María Domíguez, in order to forestall her marrying Francisco Rendón, according to a testimony of 1727 (DM, 1727, no. 12). A daughter, *María*, 5 years old in 1693, married Francisco García de Noriega, born at El Paso, in 1710 (DM, 1710, no. 3). The eldest son, *Nicolás*, who had come from Mexico City with his wife Josefa de Sedano, was taken to court by her for mistreatment and other charges (Gen., 1711, no. 5).

The first-mentioned son, DIMAS JIRÓN DE TEJEDA, was practicing medicine in 1728 (*Gen.*, 1728, no. 4). Some of his descendants, to distinguish themselves from those of his brother or his uncle, began using the appellation "Dimas Jirón," and by the middle of the nineteenth century some descendants in the Cochití-Majada area had shortened the surname to DIMAS. Hence, this is the origin of this surname, and not what was supposed in NMF, p. 168. A similar case is that of some descendants of Urbán Montaño, in the very same area and period, who shortened their surname to "Urbán" (NMF, p. 300).

JOLLANCA

BONIFACIO JOLLANCA, or *Joyanca*, were heirs of Feliciano Candelaria of Albuquerque (Gen., 1746, no. 2), but the name's origin remains unknown (NMF, p. 201).

JORGE

ANTONIO JORGE DE VERA II (NMF, p. 51), son of Captain Antonio Jorge and Gertrudis Baca, both deceased, was 29 in 1683 when he asked to marry Josefa García de Noriega (DM, 1683, no. 3); certain impediments were brought up, and the marriage evidently did not take place, for the girl married Alonso Rael de Aguilar not long afterward. Antonio took part in a battle at Zía around the year 1687 (DM, 1693, no. 21).

JUALA

MANUEL JUALA and *María Lucero* of Angeles near San Juan had a son, *José*, April 23, 1786 (B, *S. Juan*).

JURADO

FRANCISCO JURADO DE GRACIA and *Lucía Varela* (NMF, p. 52) had two other known daughters: *María Magdalena*, 14, born at La Toma below El Paso, who married Toribio Benito Sánchez in 1697; and *Juana*, who became the wife of Domingo de Mizquia in 1705 (DM, 1697, no. 9; 1705, no. 18).

FRANCISCO JURADO of El Paso was the son of Miguel Jurado, a native of Sombrerete, and Antonia Lucero, deceased, of New Mexico. He was 16 in 1718 when he married *Ynez Cortés* of Chimayó, 20, on June 15 (DM, 1718, no. 24).

Francisco Jurado, born in the city of Zacatecas, was living in Santa Fe in 1696 when he said that he was 20 years old (DM, 1696, no. 25).

LALANDA

JUAN BAUTISTA LALANDA, a Frenchman and single, the son of Bautista Lalanda and Margarita Lestrada of Louisiana, and both deceased, married *María Rita Abeyta*, widow of Antonio José Martín, on Oct. 18, 1807 (M-37, *Taos*). Witnesses to this marriage were José Yarbé and Pedro Vial (*ibid.*). On Oct. 15, 1812, he married *Isabel Casados*, although he is not mentioned as a widower, and his parents are given as Don Juan Bautista Lalanda and Doña Margarita "Alameda" (*ibid.*). The second wife must have died soon after, for records of his children by an *Apolonia Lucero* begin in 1814. His burial entry, Feb. 8, 1821, states that the Frenchman Don Juan Bautista Lalanda was the husband in second (?) nuptials of Apolonia Lucero (B-38, *Taos*, burial section). It is possible that one of the two former marriages could have been found null.

Recorded children are the following: One child by Rita Abeyta, *Josefa*, born Dec. 25, 1808, married an Ignacio González, by whom she had several recorded children between 1829 and 1841 (B-38, B-47, B-51, *Taos*). There are none by Isabel Casados. By Apolonia Lucero there are: *Tomás Benito*, Jan. 1, 1814, who married María Margarita Martínez, Nov. 4, 1839 (B-38; M-37, *Taos*); *Dolores*, April 9, 1816, who married Gervasio Nolán, Aug. 5, 1828 (B-38; M-39, *Taos*); *María Guadalupe*, Feb. 6, 1821 (B-38, *Taos*); and *Rita*, who married Luis Lamoré, according to the birth of a son in 1834 (B-49, *Taos*). On July 20, 1819, was baptized *María Soledad*, a 13-year-old Gentile Indian ransomed and adopted by Lalanda (B-38, *Taos*), and who went under his surname thereafter.

LARA

MIGUEL DE LARA (NMF, p. 204) was a native of Valle de Estapa and 42 years old when residing in Santa Fe in 1696 (DM, 1696, no. 28).

DAMIÁN DE LARA was the son of Juan de Lara and Antonia Márquez, deceased, both natives of New Mexico. Damián himself, however, was born in Mexico City and traveled with the wagon-trains. Widowed of *Teresa Rodríguez*, he then married a *Francisca*, a New Mexican of unknown parentage, the widow of Juan el Zapatero, Feb. 15, 1682 (DM, 1682, no. 11).

ANTONIO DE LARA, 36, was a soldier of the El Paso Presidio, the son of Francisco de Lara and Isabel Martín; he married *Gregoria Durán* on May 14, 1701 (DM, 1701, no. 7).

LEAL

DIEGO ANTONIO LEAL, 23, the son of Juan and a native of the city of Sevilla, was one of the convicts brought to New Mexico in 1677 (B-11, pp. 317-324). But he seems to have left before the 1680 Rebellion, for the name does not appear among the refugees of that year or the returning colonists of 1693.

NICOLÁS LEAL was living in the Chimayó area in 1752 (*Sp. Arch.*, vol. I, no. 358). On Aug. 5, 1755, *Juan Domingo* was born to Nicolás Leal and Ambrosia Martín (B-34, *Santa Cruz*). Juan Domingo Leal and his wife Verónica Cortés were living at Taos when their daughters Lorenza and Dolores were born, Aug. 17, 1777, and Dec. 6, 1783 (B-22, *Picurís*). *Agustín Leal*, presumably a brother of Juan Domingo, married Verónica Aragón on Nov. 7, 1773 (M-26, *Picurís*).

LEDESMA

LUIS LEDESMA and *María Martín de la Paz* were given as the parents of *María Ledesma*, a native of New Mexico, when she married Cayetano Fajardo (DM, 1706, no. 4).

LEYVA

PEDRO DE LEYVA II (NMF, pp. 53, 205) gave his age as 53 in 1693 (DM, 1693, no. 22). Two other known daughters by his wife *María de Nava*, or *Sedillo*, were *Antonia*, who married Felipe Pacheco in 1701, and *María Magdalena*, who married Francisco de Vargas, May 14, 1714 (DM, 1701, no. 6; 1714, no. 13).

FRANCISCO DE LEYVA, the 1693 colonist and miner who ran away before the colony reached New Mexico (NMF, p. 54), must have been caught, for he was in Santa Fe in 1691, residing with Pedro Sandoval and Rosa de Contreras, when he said that he was an *azoguero* and 50 years old (*Gen.*, 1694, no. 5).

LIRA

GABRIEL DE LIRA gave his age as 40 in 1694 when, widowed of *Petrona Ramírez*, he married *Teresa Varela*. His parents were Francisco de Lira and Ana María (DM, 1694, no. 7). Teresa Varela was dead by 1698 when he asked to marry María de la Vega, widow of Juan de Zamora; this time Gabriel said he was 50, a native of Querétaro, and a soldier of Santa Fe (DM, 1698, no. 20). Whether this third marriage took place is not known, or else he had a fourth wife, for in 1717 at El Paso an Agustín Márquez married *Francisca de Piña*, daughter of José de Piña and Juana de San Antonio, and widow of Gabriel de Lira (DM, 1717, no. 8).

FABIÁN DE LIRA, 50 and married, was a soldier of Santa Fe in 1699 (DM, 1699, no. 11). He and his wife *María Teresa* had a son *Lázaro*, born in Santa Fe, who in 1714 married Antonia Luján at Socorro del Paso (DM, 1714, no. 8). It is quite possible that Fabián and Gabriel were one and the same man.

LOBATO

BLAS LOBATO (NMF, p. 206), born at El Real de Sombrerete, the son of Blas Lobato and Magdalena Cárdenas, was soldiering in Santa Fe in 1702 when he married *Juana Flores* on Mar. 14 (DM, 1702, no. 4a). Another known child of theirs was *Manuela*, April 20, 1713 (Gen., 1710, no. 7).

MATÍAS LOBATO (NMF, p. 206) gave his age as 25 in 1693, stating that he had known a certain man from San Luis Potosí all his life (DM, 1693, no. 25).

Juan Lobato of Santa Fe was sued in 1725 for heartbalm by María Manuela Armijo, daughter of José de Armijo and María Velásquez (Gen., 1725, no. 1).

LÓPEZ

Old *Juan Luis* (NMF, p. 62), who was 80 in 1689, was married to ISABEL LÓPEZ DEL CASTILLO, daughter of ESTEBAN LÓPEZ, native of Mexico City, and María de las Nieves, native of New Mexico (DM, 1689, no. 1). This might provide a key to the definite origin of the seventeenth-century *López* (unclassified) and *López de Gracia families*, and even the *López del Castillo* group (NMF, pp. 55, 56, 58).

NICOLÁS LÓPEZ, killed in 1680 at Santo Domingo (NMF, p. 207), and *Ana Luján* also had a daughter, *Ana María*, who married Juan Cristóbal Losada in 1695 (DM, 1695, no. 5).

CARLOS LÓPEZ (NMF, p. 207) gave his age as 19 in 1697, and the Rio Abajo as his birthplace (DM, 1697, no. 17). His daughter *Nicolasa*, by his first wife, was asked for by Lázaro García of Albuquerque in 1720 (DM, 1720, no. 12).

LUIS LÓPEZ (NMF, p. 207) and his wife *Ana Bernal* led a stormy marital life (Gen., 1703, no. 5). Their daughter *Micaela Antonia* became the wife of Francisco Mascareñas (DM, 1718, no. 23).

PEDRO LÓPEZ GALLARDO (NMF, p. 208) was born in Querétaro, the son of Pedro López and Antonia Gallardo, a native of Mexico City. On May 30, 1694, young Pedro married *Sebastiana Martín* (DM, 1694, no. 35). They had a son, *Gerónimo*, at Santa Cruz, Nov. 12, 1711 (*Gen.*, 1710, no. 7).

ALFONSO LÓPEZ DE SALAZAR was the husband of *Luisa Gómez de Arellano*, a woman who was murdered in 1704 by Francisco Rodríguez Callero (NMF, p. 269). Alfonso is also mentioned as dead in 1721 when their son *Manuel*, 17, married Francisca de la Vega y Coca as Manuel "Tenorio de Alba" (DM, 1721, no. 5). A daughter, *Inez*, became the wife of Juan Montes Vigil in 1733 (DM, 1733, no. 1).

LOSADA

JUAN CRISTÓBAL LOSADA, 25, born in the city of Córdoba, the son of Pablo de Losada and María de la Concepción, was soldiering in Santa Fe in 1695 when he married *Ana María López* on Jan. 27 (DM, 1695, no. 5).

LUCERO

FRANCISCO LUCERÓ DE GODOY and *Josefa Sambrano* (NMF, pp. 60, 61, 209, 210) had two other daughters: *Juana*, 17, who married José Montiel in Santa Fe, June 10, 1696, and *Antonia Gregoria*, who married Andrés Montoya, Jan. 24, 1698; their mother was already dead (DM, 1696, no. 28; 1698, no. 21).

JUAN DE DIOS LUCERO DE GODOY and *María Varela* (NMF, p. 61), who remained at El Paso in 1693, also had a daughter, *Micaela*, who there married José Valdés (DM, 1711, no. 17).

JUAN LUCERO DE GODOY (NMF, p. 209) was the son of Antonio Lucero and Antonia Varela, both dead, when at 25 he married *Isabel López (Luján)* in Santa Fe, May 7, 1703 (DM, 1703, no. 9).

JUAN LUCERO DE GODOY (NMF, p. 209) and his third wife, *Isabel Hurtado*, had a son *Luis* who married María Romero at Albuquerque in 1719 (DM, 1719, no. 17).

NICOLÁS LUCERO (NMF, 209) and *María Montoya* had two other sons: *Juan*, born in Bernalillo, who was 23 when he married María López Olguín, 15, born at El Paso, in Santa Fe on Mar. 6, 1696 (DM, 1696, nos. 24, 32); here the mother's name is given as "de Vera" instead of Montoya, which makes her a daughter or granddaughter of Diego de Montoya and María Ortiz de Vera, or Baca (see NMF, p. 77). *Miguel* was the other son, as we definitely learn from his marriage to Angela Teresa Vallejo in 1700 at Bernalillo, where he was stationed as a soldier (DM, 1700, nos. 3, 4).

LUERA

FELIPE LUERA (NMF, p. 212) and *Francisca Chávez* had a son, *Martín*, whose wife, María Dolores Moya, had a child, José Luciano, Dec. 30, 1820 (B, *Acoma*).

This family is not to be confused with that of FRANCISCO LOBERA (NMF, p. 207), a native of Durango, son of Pablo Licoechea Lobera and María Antonia Díaz, who married *María Reyes Gutiérrez* of San José de las Huertas near Bernalillo, Mar. 10, 1766 (M-23, S. *Felipe*).

LUIS

JUAN LUIS (LUJÁN) (see NMF, p. 62), was married to *Isabel López del Castillo*, child of Esteban López and María de las Nieves. He was 80 in 1689, when he gave his parents as Captain Juan Luis and María Luján (DM, 1689, no. 1). Children of theirs, for sure, were *Pedro Luján*, who married Francisca Martín (López) de Salazar, and *Ana María*, who married Juan Olguín in 1682 and gave her father's full name as "Juan Luis Luján" (DM, 1689, no. 4; 1682, no. 8).

LUJÁN

MIGUEL LUJÁN (NMF, pp. 64, 213), who was the brother-in-law of Juan Ruiz Cáceres, was married to *Elena Ruiz Cáceres*; both were dead by Jan. 1, 1695, when their daughter *Josefa* married Antonio Cisneros (DM, 1694, no. 6). They also had a son, *Cristóbal*, who was 18 when he married Micaela Martín Serrano in Santa Fe, April 11, 1696 (DM, 1696, no. 20). Another daughter, *María*, had married Sebastián Martín Serrano in 1691, when 17, on Sept. 24 (DM, 1691, no. 4a), when she gave her parents' names as Miguel Luján and Elena Ruiz. However, in her last will and testament María named as her legitimate parents *Don Fernando Durán y Chávez* and the same Elena Ruiz Cáceres (NMF, 223, 224), which misled me into concluding that this woman was the wife of Chávez massacred with her family at Taos in 1680 (NMF, pp. 21, 22). However, it is evident that Elena Ruiz Cáceres escaped to El Paso in 1680 with her husband Miguel Luján. Then one has to conclude that María Luján was an adulterous daughter of Elena Ruis Cáceres and one of the two Don Fernandos! Since the Lujáns were Rio Arriba folks, the finger of suspicion points to the Don Fernando of Taos, who there lost his family and did not return to New Mexico with the Reconquest. And it is significant that María's wedding sponsors at El Paso in 1691 were the other Don Fernando Durán y Chávez and wife Lucía Hurtado, Don Fernando swearing that he knew both bride and groom from their birth.

MATÍAS LUJÁN and *Francisca Romero* (NMF, pp. 63, 213), besides the daughter *María* who at 18 married the widower Pedro Sánchez in 1698 (DM, 1698, no. 23), had another son, *Juan*, 30 in 1716 when he married María Trujillo, 12, on Jan. 13, 1717 (DM, 1716, no. 29).

There was another *Matías Lujan* (NMF, p. 213) who in 1702 was living in Santa Cruz with his wife *Francisca de Salazar*. They had a daughter, *Juana*, 16, who had a child by Ventura Esquivel. This Juana was a first cousin of an Ana Luján, 45, also of a Felipa Manzanares and of Salvador Olguín, and a cousin of Simón Martín (DM, 1702, no. 5).

DOMINGO LUJÁN and *Juana Domínquez* had several children (NMF, p. 212), one of whom, *Josefa*, married Matías Martín of Santa Cruz when she was 14 (DM, 1698, no. 22); after her husband's death she became the wife of the widower Melchor de Herrera, Jan. 3, 1717 (DM, 1716, no. 22).

At Socorro del Paso, *Francisco Luján*, son of Agustín Luján and María Cisneros, deceased, married *Antonia Pacheco*, 14, of unknown parentage (DM, 1714, no. 17). At El Paso also, *Micaela*, daughter of a *Domingo Luján* and *Antonia de Avalos*, both deceased, married Cayetano Padilla (DM, 1710, no. 22).

PEDRO LUJÁN married *Francisca Martín de Salazar* in 1689 when he was 20 and she 14; he was the son of Captain Juan Luis (see preceding section) and Isabel López, natives of New Mexico. Pedro was a soldier of the El Paso Presidio at the time (DM, 1698, no. 4). Their daughter *Isabel* was 15 when she married Juan Lucero de Godoy in 1703 (DM, 1703, no. 9).

JUAN LUJÁN, 56, husband of *María Martín*, and a soldier of Santa Fe in 1727, was a nephew of Captain José Domínguez (DM, 1727, no. 12).

LUNA

DIEGO DE LUNA (NMF, pp. 65, 214) had *Elvira García* for a wife, according to the marriage of their daughter *María*, 15, to Francisco González de Apodaca, Oct. 5, 1692 (DM, 1692, no. 9). Diego had given his age as 19 in 1654 (NMF, p. 65), 46 in 1681, with Isleta jurisdiction as his birthplace, and 48 in 1685 (DM, 1681, no. 8; 1685, no. 3), hence he was born around the year 1635.

ANTONIO DE LUNA of Bernalillo (NMF, p. 214) said he was of unknown parentage when he married Doña Jacinta Peláez of Albuquerque in 1718. Yet he knew that she was his second and third cousin (DM, 1718, no. 19), hence he was an illegitimate of the related Chávez, Luna, and San Juan families of the period.

VICENTE DE LUNA, son of Domingo de Luna (NMF, p. 214), was to marry María Bárbara Chávez, daughter of Francisco de Chávez, this girl being his second and third cousin. He finally did marry *Victoria Chávez*, daughter of Vicente de Chávez, who was supposedly Bárbara's first cousin, but judged to be no relation of his because her father Vicente allegedly was not a real son of Nicolás.

JOSÉ ENRIQUE LUNA and *Juana María Gabaldón* had another de Chávez, brother of Bárbara's father Francisco (*Gen.*, 1774, no. 2), daughter, *Rosalía*, who married Francisco Sánchez in 1833 (DM, 1833, no. 1).

MADRID

JUAN DE MADRID (NMF, p. 66) was actually the son of Francisco de Madrid and Juana Ruiz, both dead by 1691 when Juan, 49 years old and 4 years widowed of *Ana López Olguín*, married *María Martín Barba*, 22, on May 6. He was related to her in the third degree of affinity, and she was a first cousin of his first wife (*María Martín*) (DM, 1691, no. 5). Hence, this was his fourth wife. As noted in NMF, this family stayed at El Paso.

One daughter by Ana Olguín, *Juana*, was 16 when she there married Juan Valencia in 1689, and another by Micaela Martín, *María*, 19, became the wife of Alonso Cisneros in 1690 (DM, 1689, no. 6; 1690, no. 2).

PEDRO DE MADRID and *Yumar Varela Jaramillo* (NMF, pp. 66, 67) also had a son, *Diego*, living at El Paso in 1711 when he married Juana de Contreras, born in Santa Fe but also living in El Paso, on Dec. 9 (DM, 1711, no. 18). Another daughter of theirs, *María Magdalena*, 19, married Miguel de Zaragoza at San Lorenzo (DM, 1690, no. 7).

LORENZO DE MADRID (NMF, pp. 66, 216) married *Juana Domínquez* in 1707 (DM, 1707, no. 3).

ROQUE DE MADRID (NMF, pp. 66, 216) gave his age as 60 in 1715 when he married *Josefa Durán*, 50, the widow of Agustín Griego, on Feb. 20 at Santa Cruz. Roque had been widowed of *Juana de Arvid*, and he gave his parents' names as Francisco de Madrid and Sebastiana Ruiz Cáceres (DM, 1715, no. 10). Cf. GRIEGO, Agustín, for Roque's long concubinage with his wife. A daughter by Josefa Durán, *Antonia*, married Cristóbal Martín in 1720 (DM, 1720, no. 8).

A son of Roque by his first wife, "Juana de Arbí y Gamboa," was *Pedro Madrid* (NMF, p. 216), who at 20 married *Isabel Serna*, 16, on Jan. 16, 1689 (DM, 1689, no. 5). This pair had a son, *Bernardo*, 22 and a resident of Santa Cruz when he married Gertrudis Martín of Pojoaque, July 7, 1714 (DM, 1714, no. 18).

Also a son of Roque by "Juana de Arvides" was *Matías Madrid* (NMF, p. 217), who was 20 when he married *Antonia Serna* at El Paso, Feb. 12, 1696 (DM, 1696, no. 22).

MAESE

ALONSO MAESE and *Catalina Montaño* (NMF, p. 68) had other children: *Miguel, Juan,* and *Cayetano*. Alonso had given his age as 40 in 1682, 55 in 1695, 60 in 1690 and 1692, when he also gave his full name as Alonso *López* Maese (DM, 1682, no. 10; 1695, no. 17; 1690, no. 2; 1692, no. 6). He stayed at El Paso, where he gave his age as 70 in 1705 (DM, 1705, no. 18).

Miguel Maese (NMF, p. 217) married *María Varela*, or *Perea de Losada*, on June 15, 1693 (DM, 1693, no. 20). Their daughter *Catalina* married Francisco Rendón in 1727 (DM, 1727, no. 12).

Juan Maese was 21, and his mother dead, when as a soldier at El Paso he married *Josefa del Aguila* in 1711 (DM, 1711, no. 12).

Cayetano Maese, also soldiering at El Paso, said both his parents were dead when he married *Antonia Brito* on July 17, 1714 (DM, 1714, no. 22).

Juan Maese, a different man from the one mentioned already, married *Isabel Candelaria* of Albuquerque on Jan. 30, 1720. He was 25 and a native of San Lorenzo, the son of Juan Maese and Estéfana González de Calín, both residing at San Lorenzo del Paso (DM, 1720, no. 9). His sister *María* had married Juan de Varela at San Lorenzo in 1709 (DM, 1709, no. 3).

Cristóbal Maese (NMF, p. 217) was dead by 1717 when his widow, *Gertrudis Sánchez*, was tried and sentenced for philandering (DM, 1717, nos. 10, 11).

MARCELINO

CRISTÓBAL MARCELINO (Cf. LADRÓN DE GUEVARA in NMF, p. 202) was a native of Osuna in Andalucía and 19 years old in 1695 (DM, 1695, no. 5). He and *Juana de Góngora* at El Paso had a daughter, *Bartola*, who married Manuel de la Peña in 1717, when her father's full name was given as "Marcelino Ladrón de Guevara" (DM, 1717, no. 3). Hence the supposition in NMF proved correct.

MARMOLEJO

An ANTONIO MARMOLEJO married *Teodora Archuleta* on July 1, 1763 (M-50, *Santa Fe*). They had a son, Antonio Rafael, Jan. 22, 1764 (B-53, *Santa Fe*).

MÁRQUEZ

FRANCISCO MÁRQUEZ (NMF, p. 70) was married to *Ynez López de Gracia*. Their son *Nicolás*, born in the Salinas of New Mexico, married María López Olguín on Oct. 26, 1681 (DM, 1681, no. 9).

MATEO MÁRQUEZ, 22 in 1702 when he was to have married a Juana Luján (DM, 1702, no. 5), married *Agustina Romero* in that year. He was dead by 1719, and his widow had married Miguel Tenorio de Alba, when their daughter *Ana María*, 16, married Domingo Valdés (DM, 1719, no. 10).

FRANCISCO MÁRQUEZ (NMF, p. 220) and his wife *Estela Luján* had a daughter, *Rosa Isabel*, 15, who married Cristóbal Varela de Losada at El Paso, Oct. 10, 1694 (DM, 1694, no. 34a).

Diego Márquez II, the son of Diego Márquez and Juana Martín (NMF, p. 221), was born at Santa Cruz, Nov. 25, 1710 (*Gen.*, 1710, no. 7).

At El Paso, *María*, 13, daughter of *Francisco Márquez* and *Antonia Varela*, both deceased, married Nicolás Montoya in 1710 (DM, 1710, no. 23).

Also at El Paso, *Agustín Márquez*, 17, born at El Real de Talpujagua of Lucas Márquez, now deceased, and Andrea de Espinosa, married *Francisca de Piña* of Querétaro, widow of Gabriel de Lara (DM, 1717, no. 8).

DIEGO MÁRQUEZ DE AYALA (NMF, p. 221) and *María de Palacios Bolívar* had two daughters, *María* and *Juana*. The first was 17 when she married Lázaro Trujillo in 1715, and the other 21 when she became the wife of José Naranjo in 1719 (DM, 1715, no. 12; 1719, no. 16).

MARTÍN BARBA

ESTEBAN BARBA, Captain (NMF, p. 71), and his wife, *María Lujan*, were both mentioned as dead in 1692 when their daughter *María* married Diego Martín Serrano. This girl was also a niece of Alonso López Maese (DM, 1692, no. 6).

DOMINGO MARTÍN BARBA (NMF, p. 71) had been married to *Sebastiana Varela de Mondragón*. He was dead when their daughter *María*, 22, married the widower Captain Juan de Madrid in 1691. The girl was a cousin of Ana López Olguín, Madrid's first wife (DM, 1691, no. 5).

MARTÍN SERRANO

The ponderous MARTÍN SERRANO relationships in NMF (pp. 71-73, 222-226) will have to be revised, drastically in a few instances, due to new data which clarify some errors rising out of similarity in names.

LUIS MARTÍN SERRANO II, husband of *Antonia de Miranda* (NMF, pp. 73, 222), gave his age as 50 in 1681 and 60 in 1689 (DM, 1681, no. 6; 1689, no. 5). Some children by this wife were *Antonio*, *Hernando*, *Francisco*, *Cristóbal*, and *María*, who were suing the children by a second wife in 1711 at Santa Cruz (*Gen.*, 1711, no. 6). Another daughter was *Antonia*, who had married Juan Roque Gutiérrez on

Feb. 18, 1692 (DM, 1690, no. 4). María, widowed of Antonio Luján, married Domingo de Herrera in 1683 (DM, 1683, no. 1).

Luis' second wife was *Melchora de los Reyes* (*González?*), by whom he had a daughter, *Polonia*, who married Domingo Laureano (Gómez) in 1722 (DM, 1722, no. 5), and a son, *Diego*, who married Josefa de Torres in 1716, by whom he had a son, Nicolás, Nov. 3, 1721 (DM, 1716, no. 21; *Gen.*, 1721, no. 5). Children of this second marriage mentioned in the 1711 suit were *Rosa* and *Catalina* (*loc. cit.*). Rosa was the wife of Nicolás López, while Catalina married Alonso Fernández in 1695 (DM, 1695, no. 19). A son, *Manuel*, married María Josefa de la Candelaria Montaño in Santa Fe, Aug. 25, 1730 (DM, 1730, no. 3).

DOMINGO MARTÍN SERRANO (NMF, p. 222) was not a son, but a brother, of Luis. The sons of Luis listed above married as follows:

ANTONIO MARTÍN SERRANO, as in NMF, p. 222.

HERNANDO MARTÍN SERRANO married *María Montaño*, widow of Juan de Moraga, in 1685. He was 24, a native of La Cañada, while she was a native of the Salinas district, and both had been reared together (DM, 1685, no. 3). They had a son, *Antonio*, born in Chimayó, who was forbidden to marry a Gertrudis Sánchez in 1717 because of serious impediments (DM, 1717, no. 11). There was also a daughter, *Pascuala*, who married Diego Durán on Dec. 29, 1694 (DM, 1694, no. 29).

This particular Hernando is maddeningly and easily confused with his uncle HERNÁN MARTÍN SERRANO (NMF, p. 224), whose first wife was certainly not María Montaño; yet, was he the same man who married Catalina Griego and then Josefa de la Asención González?

DOMINGO MARTÍN SERRANO, brother of Luis II, had these other children by *Josefa de Herrera*, besides those mentioned in NMF, p. 222: *Sebastiana*, who married Pedro López in 1694; *Josefa*, who married Joaquín de Anaya in 1709; and *Miguel*, who married María Archuleta in 1703 (DM, 1694, no. 35; 1709, no. 23; 1703, no. 6). On May 4, 1725, Domingo married a *Juana Bautista* of unknown parentage (DM, 1725, no. 11). The Miguel Martín married to María de Archuleta (NMF, p. 225) belonged to this family.

CRISTÓBAL MARTÍN and *Antonia de Moraga* had these other children besides the ones in NMF, p. 224: *Simón*, who married Petrona Domínguez in 1705; *Antonio de Jesús*, who married Ana María Domínguez in 1717; and *Josefa*, who became the wife of Dionisio Cortés (DM, 1705, no. 17; 1717, no. 12; 1718, no. 15). Another son, *Cristóbal* II, who married María Montoya in 1698, was married a second time to Juliana Maese (DM, 1728, no. 13). The senior Cristóbal was not a son of María Montaño as stated in NMF, p. 224, but her son-in-law, she being the mother of his wife Antonia by a first husband, Juan de Moraga.

PEDRO MARTÍN SERRANO and *Juana de Argüello* (NMF, p. 222) had these other children: *Francisca*, who married Pedro Luján in 1689, and *Micaela*, wife of Cristóbal Luján [Juan Olguín?] and then of Agustín Trujillo (DM, 1689, no. 4; 1696, nos. 20, 27). The son, *Antonio*, took a third wife, Felipa de Villavicencio, in 1709 (DM, 1709, no. 24).

ANTONIO MARTÍN SERRANO (NMF, p. 223) had these two other children by his first wife *Ana María Gómez*: *María* and *Antonia*, who in 1718 married Luis de Archuleta and Bernardino Fernández, respectively (DM, 1718, nos. 12, 14).

SEBASTIÁN MARTÍN SERRANO'S wife, *María Luján* (NMF, pp. 223, 224), had a daughter *Rosa* who married the widower Felipe Pacheco in 1709 (DM, 1709, no. 16). The origin of María Luján (Ruiz Cáceres of Chávez) has been discussed under "Miguel Luján," this list *supra*.

APOLINAR MARTÍN SERRANO of the seventeenth century (NMF, p. 73) had been married to *Antonio González Bernal*, or *Bas*. Their son *Diego*, born in Santa Fe, was 17 when he married María Martín Barba, July 27, 1692 (DM, 1692, no. 6).

MARUNGO

GERÓNIMO MARUNGO, native of Ciudad de Durango, was in Santa Fe in 1694 and 1696 when he gave his age as 21 (DM, 1694, no. 5; 1696, no. 21).

MASCAREÑAS

FRANCISCO MASCAREÑAS (NMF, p. 228), the son of José de Mascareñas and María de Acosta, was a resident of Santa Fe and 22 years old when he married *Antonia López* of Santa Cruz, Nov. 15, 1718 (DM, 1718, no. 23).

MATA

BALTASAR DE MATA, who married *Isabel de Chávez* on Jan. 14, 1705 (NMF, p. 228), was a native of Spain, the son of Pedro de Mata and Isabel Martínez, both deceased (DM, 1704, no. 10).

María de Mata, 19, who married Juan Antonio Ramos in Santa Fe, May 4, 1699, was a native of Zacatecas, the daughter of Miguel de Mata and Felipa Pérez (DM, 1699, no. 11).

MEDINA

DIEGO DE MEDINA and *María Zapata Jirón* (NMF, p. 228) had these other children: *Isidro*, who married Catalina Martín in 1717; and the girls *Antonia* and *Juana*, who in 1718 married Juan Luis Martín and Antonio Montoya, respectively (DM, 1717, no. 16; 1718, nos. 20, 22).

A man who gave his name as *Juan de Medina Ortiz*, 34, a native of Mexico City and resident of Santa Cruz (DM, 1703, no. 6), was most likely the JUAN DE MEDINA married to Juana Márquez (NMF, pp. 228, 229).

MENA

At Isleta in 1678, a JOSÉ DE MENA, native of Puebla and son of Francisco de Mena and Nicolasa de Ontiveros, married *Polonia de Tapia* (DM, 1678, no. 1). The Padre was Fray Francisco de Ayeta, and this is the oldest ecclesiastical document found in N. M. to date.

MENDIZÁBAL

DOMINGO MENDIZÁBAL, 21, was a soldier of Santa Fe when he married *Ana María Brusuelas*, 15, of unknown parentage, on Aug. 4, 1717. He was a native of the Valley of Oposura in Sonora, the son of Pedro de Mendizábal and María de Espinosa (DM, 1717, no. 9).

MIRANDA

MATÍAS DE MIRANDA (NMF, p. 232) was 38 and a resident of Albuquerque when he married *Catalina Durán y Chávez* in 1711, and was actually a brother of Fray Antonio de Miranda of Acoma (DM, 1711, no. 10).

MIZQUIA

DOMINGO DE MIZQUIA (NMF, p. 75), only son of Captain Lázaro de Mizquia and María Lucero de Godoy, was soldiering at El Paso when he married *Juana Jurado* there on Oct. 5, 1705 (DM, 1705, no. 18). This explains why the name did not survive in New Mexico proper, and is most likely the origin of the surnames "Misquis" and "Mísquez" in northern Mexico.

MOLINA

SIMÓN DE MOLINA MOSQUERA (NMF, p. 232) married *Micaela Medina* in the parish church of Santa Cruz in Mexico City, Aug. 31, 1666. He was the son of Don Tomás de Molina and Nicolasa de Castro, while the bride's parents were Cristobal Carvallo and Ana Romero (DM, 1693, no. 12). Simón gave his age as 44, and Mexico City as his birthplace, in 1694 (DM, 1694, no. 39).

MONDRAGÓN

JUAN ALONSO MONDRAGÓN, or MONROY (NMF, p. 233), was the son of Sebastián de Mondragón, or Monroy, deceased, and María Bernal, both natives of New Mexico, and living at Santa Cruz when he married *Sebastiana Trujillo* on Nov. 28, 1703. He was 24 and the bride was 23 (DM, 1703, no. 7). The birthdate of their daughter *Juana* is given as Feb. 20, 1711, in a different register (*Gen.*, 1710, no. 7); another daughter, *Feliciana*, married Juan

Antonio Martín in 1725 at the age of 24 (DM, 1725, no. 9).

Old *Sebastiana de Mondragón* (NMF, p. 233) was also the grandmother of a Margarita Martín, child of Francisco Martín, for whose custody she was fighting in 1704 (*Gen.*, 1704, no. 3). And she could very well have been the Sebastiana *Varela* de Mondragón, widow of Domingo Martín Barba, whose daughter *María* married Juan de Madrid in 1691 (DM, 1691, no. 5).

MONTAÑO

LUCAS MONTAÑO (NMF, p. 76) was a captain of the Salinas district in the middle of the seventeenth century, and his wife was the *Sebastiana López de Gracia* mentioned on the same page; hence her three daughters there mentioned were his also. Both parents were dead by 1685 when their daughter *María*, native of the Salinas and widow of Juan de Moraga, married Hernando Martín (DM, 1685, no. 3).

SEBASTIÁN MONTAÑO (NMF, p. 76), most probably Lucas' son, was dead by 1690; he was believed to be the father of a *mestizo, José Montaño*, 18, who married Isabel Naranjo on June 26, 1690. This José had been born in the house of José González de Apodaca, and he deposed that he had been told who his mother was (Juana, a Pira of Tabirá) and that Sebastián Montaño was merely his foster father (DM, 1690, no. 5).

MONTIEL

JOSÉ DE MONTIEL (NMF, p. 235) was 24 in 1696, and a soldier of El Paso, when he married *Juana Lucero de Godoy*, 16, in Santa Fe, on June 10. Born at Real de Talpujagua, he was the son of Gregorio Montiel and Francisca González de Aragón (DM, 1696, no. 28).

MONTOYA

ANTONIO DE MONTOYA (NMF, pp. 78, 235, 236) was the son of Diego de Montoya and Doña María de Vera (DM, 1689, no. 1); this is the couple in NMF, p. 77, through whom practically all of the New Mexico Montoyas descend from the original colonist of this name. Of the children by Antonio's first wife, *María Hurtado*, a daughter, *Nicolasa*, married Bartolomé Gutiérrez (DM, 1708, no. 6). The grandson Miguel Ortiz mentioned in María Hurtado's testament (NMF, p. 235) indicates that one of the remaining three daughters, *Angela, Antonia*, or *Manuela*, had married a son of Nicolás Ortiz I.

ANDRÉS MONTOYA and *Antonia Lucero* (NMF, p. 236) were married in Santa Fe, Jan. 24, 1698, when he was 20 and the bride was 16 (DM, 1698, no. 21). Their daughter *Manuela* married Joaquín Sánchez at Santa Fe in 1719, while at Bernalillo their sons *Andrés* and *José* married Ana Baca and Juana Quintana in 1723 and 1729, respectively (DM, 1719, no. 14; 1723, no. 13; 1729, no. 5). The senior Andrés was related to Ana María de Almazán, living at Pecos, and to her brother Francisco Rendón (DM, 1727, no. 12).

DIEGO MONTOYA (NMF, pp. 78, 236) was in all probability a brother of Antonio Montoya *supra*, and therefore the son of Diego de Montoya and María de Vera. Among his children by *Josefa de Hinojos*, there was another son, *Marcial*, residing in Bernalillo when he married Doña María ---, of unknown parentage, June 24, 1717 (DM, 1717, no. 17).

The wife of *Miguel Montoya*, son of Salvador Montoya, given as *Rosa Baca* in the Albuquerque marriage register (NMF, p. 236), is given as Rosa *de Luna* in the DM, and her parents as unknown (DM, 1729, no. 6).

Antonio Montoya (NMF, p. 236) gave his age as 18 when he was betrothed to *Bernarda Baca*, 17, at Bernalillo, May 6, 1707 (DM, 1707, no. 7).

FELIPE DE MONTOYA (NMF, pp. 78, 238) was also most likely a son of Diego de Montoya and María de Vera, and brother of Antonio and Diego. Besides his two children noted in NMF, there was another son, *Antonio*, residing at Chimayó, who married Juana Medina of Santa Fe, Nov. 30, 1718 (DM, 1718, no. 20).

Besides the foregoing main Montoya family, there are some odd ones who are unidentifiable for being illegitimates:

Onofre Montoya, no parents given, married *Ana Martín* of unknown parentage in 1694 (DM, 1694, no. 6). A daughter, *Felipa*, married Francisca Blásquez, or Rodríguez, in 1710; and a son, *Cristóbal*, 22, married Juana de Dios Gutiérrez, or Argüello, 15, of Zacatecas, the natural daughter of Juana Gutiérrez, Feb. 24, 1716 (DM, 1710, no. 14; *Bur.*, 48, Santa Fe, Feb. 23, 1727; DM, 1716, nos. 16, 20).

Marcos Montoya, a native of Los Ranchos de Valencia at Guadalupe del Paso, was first married to *Josefa de Mendoza*, sister (or half sister) of Pedro Guillén, who was the son of a Tomás de la Mora and Gerónima Guillén, both New Mexico natives. After Josefa died at El Paso in 1708, Marcos came to New Mexico and the next year married *Sebastiana de Vargas Machuca* at San Ildefonso, Jan. 27, 1709 (DM, 1709, no. 18; M-24, *S. Ild.*). He next married *María Rosa Baca*, daughter of Simón Baca and Magdalena Martín (DM, 1726, nos. 1, 6).

Another *Marcos Montoya*, of unknown parentage, was 19 years old in 1718 when he married *María Antonia de la Cruz* in Santa Fe, Mar. 1 (DM, 1718, no. 4).

Manuel Montoya of El Paso, also of unknown parentage, married *Juana Sánchez* of Bernalillo, Jan. 7, 1704 (DM, 1704, no. 19).

At El Paso, the soldier *Nicolás Montoya*, 22, no parents given, married *María Márquez*, Feb. 9, 1710 (DM, 1710, no. 23).

MORA

A pre-1680 man of this name was TOMÁS DE LA MORA, who through *Gerónima Guillén* was the father of Pedro Guillén, very likely a natural child (DM, 1709, no. 18).

FRANCISCO DE LA MORA is indeed the same man known as Francisco *Guerrero* de la Mora (NMF, p. 238), who married *María Luisa de Selorga* at Santa Cruz, Aug. 29, 1696. He was 30, a soldier of Santa Fe, and a native of Xacona, Villa de Zamora, in New Spain, the natural son of Juan de la Mora and Mariana Guerrero. The bride was the young widow of Francisco de Betanzos, *q.v.* Witnesses were Antonio Sayago and María de la Mora (DM, 1696, nos. 25, 30).

MORAGA

JUAN DE MORAGA, the eldest individual of this name (NMF, p. 79), had been married to *María Montaño* of the Salinas district and died in Santa Fe in 1680 or some years before. His widow married Hernando Martín Serrano in 1685 (DM, 1685, no. 3).

Lázaro Moraga (NMF, p. 79) was 50 years old and a resident of Senecú del Paso in 1710 (DM, 1710, no. 22).

MORO

JUAN MORO, of unknown parentage, was a Tigua of Isleta who married *Juana Pacheco* at Guadalupe del Paso, Jan. 25, 1683. His first wife, *Isabel*, had been buried in the Isleta church three years before (DM, 1683, nos. 2, 4).

Juan Tomás Moro of Isleta del Paso, the son of Juan Moro and María Ana, deceased, married *Antonia de Lara y Avila*, May 25, 1698, at El Real de San Lorenzo. She was a *criolla de los carros*, the daughter of Pedro de Avila and Petrona de Lara (DM, 1698, no. 24).

MORONES DE CASARES

JUAN MORONES DE CASARES (NMF, footnote, p. 311) was a native of Pátzcuaro, and 28 when soldiering in Santa Fe, when he married *Simona Bejar*, widow of Mateo Negrete, July 2, 1697. She was a native of Zacatecas, daughter of Antonio de Bejar and Antonia Hernández (DM, 1697, nos. 14, 20). See NMF, p. 311, for the girl "Catalina Velásquez," widow of Negrete who married Morones; if not the original scribe's mistake, it means that she used two distinct names.

MOYA

ANTONIO DE MOYA (NMF, p. 240) and *Francisca Antonia de Morales* were married in the Cathedral of Mexico City, Aug. 26, 1691 (DM, 1693, no. 15). Later on the wife used the surname *Eguijosa* or *Guijosa*. Another son of theirs was *Cayetano José* who was 16 in 1721 when he married Gertrudis Sánchez, widow of Cristóbal Maese. His father had already died, and his mother was married to Andrés de la Paz (NM, 1721, no. 7). Cayetano was married a second time, to Manuela Armijo of Santa Fe (DM, 1727, no. 10). Another son, *Pedro Antonio*, had died at Taos prior to 1717, when his widow, Ana María Domínguez, 18, married Antonio de Jesús Martín (DM, 1717, no. 12).

NALDAS

A DESIDERIO NALDAS married *María Agueda Valencia* in Santa Fe, June 22, 1817 (M-52, *Santa Fe*).

NARANJO

PASCUAI NARANJO and *María Romero* (NMF, p. 80) had another son, *Fabián*, 27, who married a Tegua of New Mexico, Micaela de la Cruz, at El Paso (DM, 1711, no. 13); also a daughter, *Isabel*, 18, who became the wife of José Montano (DM, 1690, no. 5).

In 1694 Don Juan Páez Hurtado had written to Governor Vargas, requesting him not to give away the Rancho de las Huertas, since the owner, his "*compadre Naranjo*," was coming up to N. M. to claim it (DM, 1697, no. 13). This man was most likely *José López Naranjo* (NMF, p. 211), husband of *Catalina Luján*; their son *José Antonio*, 21, married *Juana Márquez*, 21, May 15, 1719 (DM, 1719, no. 16).

NAVARRO

JOSE RAFAEL NAVARRO, 40, and his wife *Juana de la Cruz Muñoz*, 28, were living with their family at La Joya, San Juan district, in 1816. Their children were: *María Paula*, 6; *José Manuel*, 3; and *Manuel Antonio*, 1 (*Gen.*, 1816, no. 16). This ancestor of the northern N. M. Navarros was most likely descended from the El Paso family in NMF, p. 212.

According to the baptism of a child, María Catarina, May 1, 1851, a *Manuel Navarro* married Dolores Romero (B-51, *Taos*). Evidently this was the third child "Manuel Antonio" *supra*. A *José Manuel Navarro*, evidently the second child of José Rafael, acted as a sponsor with Soledad Sandoval, April 14, 1811 (B-51, *Taos*).

NEGRETE

MATEO NEGRETE was a native of Zacatecas and 25 years old in 1696 (DM, 1696, no. 17). He died in Santa Fe that same year, and his widow, *Simona Hernández Bejar*, n. of Zacatecas also, married Juan Morones de Casares *supra* (DM, 1697, no. 14). Not to be confused with the contemporary Jaramillo Negrete family.

NIETO

JUAN NIETO, the son of Miguel Nieto and Gertrudis Durán, residents of San Juan del Rio, came to Santa Fe and in 1723 married an Apache, *Juana Francisca* (DM, 1723, no. 11). From the names of both his parents one can assume that they were pre-1680 New Mexicans.

NORIEGA

MIGUEL DE NORIEGA, Captain, and 37 in 1661, was a resident of Mexico City who came to N. M. in the escort of 1658 as secretary to Governor Mendizábal. He was a native of San Vicente de la Barquera in the Mountains of Burgos and had a wife in Mexico City (AGN, *Mex. Inq.*, t. 594, f. 16; *ibid.*, t. 52, pp. 52-53; *ibid.*, t. 587, p. 392; AGI, *Contad.*, leg. 719). Apparently there is no connection here with the García de Noriega family.

OCAÑA

JUAN BAUTISTA OCANA and *María Cruz Telles* had resided in Santa Fe, and were dead by 1814, when their son *Pedro Antonio* married María Manuela Espinosa of Pojoaque, Nov. 7, 1814 (M-22, *Pojoaque*).

Ramón Ocaña, son of Francisco Ocaña and Bárbara Gutiérrez, married *María Serafina Coriz (Cortés?)* in the military chapel at Santa Fe, Dec. 27, 1828 (M-51, *Castrense*). This was possibly a related family of the preceding from Guadalupe del Paso.

José Ocaña married *María Josefa Blea* on May 18, 1821 (M-52, *Santa Fe*). He could have been the son of either Juan Bautista or Francisco Ocaña.

OLGUÍN

CRISTOBAL OLQUÍN (NMF, p. 81) was recalled in 1696 as a bastard son of Juan López Olguín (DM, 1696, nos. 21, 26). Besides *Salvador*, he and his wife *Melchora de Carvajal* had another son, *Cristóbal II*, who was 27 when he married Ana María de Cobos, natural daughter of Agustina de Carvajal, Jan. 28, 1683 (DM, 1683, no. 4). All parents were dead by this time.

Salvador Olguín, the elder son *supra*, and his wife *Magdalena Fresqui* (NMF, p. 82) had two daughters, *Ana* and *María*, who in 1681 married Juan de Vargas Machuca and Nicolás Márquez, respectively (DM, 1681, nos. 5, 9). Their son *Juan* (NMF, p. 234) and his wife María Lujan were married when he was 22 and she 20, May 30, 1682 (DM, 1682, no. 8): these had two sons, Salvador and Antonio, who married Lucía Nieto and María Magdalena Brito de León, respectively (DM, 1705, no. 14;

1710, no. 11). This Juan was married a second time, to *Juana Martín de Salazar*, and their daughter *María* married Juan Lucero in Santa Fe, Mar. 6, 1696 (DM, 1696, nos. 24, 32).

TOMAS OLGUÍN, parents as yet not ascertained, was a soldier who in 1692 saw the bones of Antonio Gómez, killed at Zia five years previously, disinterred and brought to El Paso (DM, 1693, no. 21). He could be the *Tomás Olguín* once married to Ursula Gómez, whose daughter Francisca married Francisco Gamos at El Paso in 1714 (DM, 1714, no. 9). A Juan Olguín, son of Tomás Olguín and María de la Cruz, deceased, who married Tomasa Rodríguez in Santa Fe, might have been a son by a different wife (DM, 1715, no. 2).

OLIVAS

JUAN BAUTISTA DE OLIVAS (NMF, p. 245) and his wife *Magdalena Juárez y Portanto* had two other daughters, *Isabel* and *Gracia*, who married José Manuel Giltomey and Miguel de Aguilar, respectively (DM, 1696, no. 30; 1697, no. 10).

JUAN DE LA CRUZ Y OLIVAS, 22, a native of the city of Durango, married *Juana de Anaya Almazán*, 30, the widow of Ignacio Baca, on Feb. 17, 1693, at El Real de San Lorenzo, in whose church Baca had been buried the previous year. Juan was the son of Pedro de Olivas de la Rueda and Magdalena de Abeyta, both natives of Durango (DM, 1693, no. 22). Hence he could have been a first cousin to another Durango colonist, Diego de Abeyta. It is not known if he had any children to pass on the Olivas name, for his wife was massacred with some of her Baca children in 1696 (NMF, pp. 11, 141).

OLONA

MIGUEL DE OLONA (NMF, p. 246) was married a second time, to *María Margarita Espinosa* of Santa Cruz, Aug. 27, 1798 (M-33, *Santa Cruz*). Two known sons were *Francisco* and *Antonio José* (see data below).

Miguel Olona II, eldest son by the first wife, María Luz Ortiz, married *Bárbara Sánchez* of the Rio Abajo. One daughter, *María Luz*, married José Chávez in 1839, while another, *Brigida*, widow of Marcelino Abreu, married Felipe Valles in 1840 (DM, 1839; 1840).

Francisco Olona went to live with the Plains Indians and had two sons by an "*india del norte*." These were *José*, 7 years old when baptized on Aug. 26, 1836; and *Pedro Ignacio*, 6 years old when baptized on Dec. 26, 1838 (B-19, B-51, *Taos*). Francisco later returned to Taos and married *Rafaela Madrid*, by whom he had a daughter, *María Refugio*, July 4, 1842 (B-51, *Taos*).

Antonio José Olona married *Teodora Páiz*, by whom he had a daughter, *Antonia María*, Feb. 9, 1843 (B-51, *Taos*).

ORCASITAS

DON JOSÉ DE ORCASITAS was Alcalde of Santa Cruz in 1732 (*Bancroft Lib.*, NMO, 1732, ff. 19-20). Some of his *criados* were baptized on June 27, 1738 (B-24, *S. Ild.*).

ORTEGA

TIBURCIO DE ORTEGA (NMF, pp. 82, 246) was married to *Margarita Otón*. Their son *Pablo* married Teresa de Trujillo at Guadalupe del Paso, May 6, 1717 (DM, 1717, no. 14). Because of the late date, and the fact that he is not mentioned as a widower, he cannot be the Pablo de Ortega of 1680 (NMF, pp. 82, 83), but very likely is a nephew. A *Gregorio* de Ortega, who married Antonia García at El Paso in 1714, might have belonged to Tiburcio's family (DM, 1714, no. 12).

GERONIMO DE ORTEGA (NMF, p. 246), who married *Sebastiana de la Cruz* [or *de Jesús González*], of unknown parentage, July 15, 1715, was a native of Zacatecas soldiering in Santa Fe. His parents were María de Mares and Simón de Ortega, who had died in Santa Fe "*apeloteado con habito de Misericordia*" (DM, 1715, no. 13).

Dionisio de Ortega, a native of Mexico City, was a soldier at Guadalupe del Paso in 1692 (DM, 1692, nos. 7, 8).

JUAN CRISTOBAL ORTEGA, resident of the Albuquerque area in 1809, was referred to as "*el Poblano del Río Abajo*" (Gen., 1809, no. 1), and thus was evidently a native of Puebla. He was headman of the Plaza de San Antonio de los Poblanos, Albuquerque, and his wife was *María Gertrudis García* (Gen., 1802, no. 30).

ORTIZ

NICOLAS ORTIZ I, a native of Mexico City who arrived in Santa Fe in 1694 with his wife *Mariana Coronado* and their several children (NMF, p. 247), was one of the original settlers of Santa Cruz de la Cañada and a sergeant of the militia there in 1696 (Gen., 1700, no. 5). There a daughter, *Josefa*, 16, married a Gregorio Vicente de Piérola, Jan. 16, 1697 (DM, 1696, no. 31), who must have taken her back to New Spain, for neither of them are heard of again, nor does the Piérola name survive. Another daughter, *Juana*, acted as sponsor with her father at Santa Cruz, Nov. 25, 1711 (Gen., 1711, no. 7). One son, *Luis*, was still soldiering in Santa Fe in 1717 (DM, 1717, no. 16).

A different Ortiz was *Gregorio Andrés Ortiz*, native of San José del Parral, of unknown parentage, who came to Albuquerque and there married *Rosa Hurtado*, of like estate, Oct. 30, 1727 (DM, 1727, no. 17).

PACHECO

FELIPE PACHECO (NMF, p. 253) was a son of Juan Pérez Pacheco and Antonia de Arratia (same section), both of whom were dead when Felipe married *Antonia de Leyva*, Jan. 16, 1702 (DM, 1701, no. 6). Hence Felipe, and perhaps Matías Pacheco also, was a brother of Josefa Pacheco in that same section. Felipe was a sergeant and 35 years old in 1709, when he took a second wife, *Rosa Martín* of Santa Cruz (DM, 1709, no. 16).

FRANCISCO PACHECO, 20 and a native of Puebla, was in Santa Fe in 1694 (DM, 1694, no. 38).

JOSE PACHECO, a native of Puebla de los Angeles, married *Francisca Chacón* at Soledad on April 24, 1732 (M-27, San Juan).

PADILLA

JOSE DE PADILLA and *María López* (NMF, pp. 84, 253) had two other sons: *Juan Antonio*, who married María del Río at El Paso, Sept. 23, 1697; and *Cayetano*, who married Micaela Luján at El Paso, May 21, 1710 (DM, 1697, no. 15; 1710, no. 22).

JUAN PADILLA, who married *Margarita Martín* on Feb. 24, 1721, gave his name as *Juan Manuel* Padilla. Unfortunately, the document is fragmentary, so that his parents cannot be ascertained (DM, 1721, no. 8).

JUAN PABLO PADILLA, a native of El Paso del Norte, the son of Juan Nepomuceno Padilla and María Carmen Vanegas, came to the Trampas country and there married *María Reyes Aragón*, June 21, 1789 (M-21, *Picurís*). Evidently he belonged to the members of the original Padilla family, which stayed at El Paso.

PÁEZ HURTADO

DON JUAN PAEZ HURTADO (NMF, p. 254) had another child by his first wife, *Pascuala López*. She was *Rosa María*, born in El Real de Talpujagua, and still residing at El Paso in 1699 when she married a widower, Captain Alonso del Río (DM, 1699, no. 10).

PAZ

ANDRES JACOME DE LA PAZ (NMF, pp. 151, 152) was a native of Mexico City, 40 years old in 1702 and still residing in N. M. (DM, 1702, no. 5).

At El Paso in October, 1680, there was a *Juan Paz*, an Indian of Puebla and driver of the wagon-trains. And in June, 1692, the Governor's Secretary of War was the *Alférez, Juan de Paz* (DM, 1680, no. 2; *Gen.*, 1692, no. 3).

PEÑA

BALTASAR DE LA PENA and *Lucía Gutiérrez* had a son, *Manuel*, who was a soldier of the Janos Presidio when he married Doña Bartola Marcelino Ladrón de Guevara at El Paso in 1717 (DM, 1717, no. 13).

PEREA

FRANCISCO GARCIA DE PEREA (NMF, p. 257), a native of the Río Abajo and of unknown parentage, was soldiering in Santa Fe in 1707 when he married *María Romero*, or *Varela*, of Albuquerque (DM, 1707, no. 8).

ESTEBAN DE PEREA (NMF, p. 257) was married to *Francisca García*. Besides *Jacinto*, they had another son, *Antonio*, who as "Antonio García," son of "Esteban García de Perea," deceased, and Francisca García, married Teodora González in Santa Fe, Sept. 26, 1718 (DM, 1718, no. 18). The recurrence of certain names in the Perea family indicates some very possible connection with the López de Gracia family of the seventeenth century.

PÉREZ

In 1693, a CRISTÓBAL PÉREZ was a soldier at El Presidio del Gallo staying at El Paso. He was a native of El Valle de Tlaltenango (DM, 1693, no. 9).

In 1701, another *Cristóbal Pérez*, 23, from El Puerto de Panamá, was living in Santa Fe (DM, 1701, no. 5).

PERIS

DON MANUEL PERIS, husband of *Doña Josefa Orrantia*, and First *Teniente* of El Presidio de San Buenaventura, was buried at Taos, Oct. 21, 1819 (B-38, *Taos*, burial section).

PIÉROLA

GREGORIO VICENTE DE PIEROLA, 20, a native of Pachuca, the son of Juan Vicente de Piérola, native of Navarra, and of Doña Josefa García de la Vega, native of Pachuca, was a soldier of Santa Fe in 1697 when he married *Josefa Ortiz*, Jan. 16 (DM, 1696, no. 31).

PINEDA

JUAN DE LA MORA PINEDA and *Clara de Chávez* had a son, *Miguel*, who married María Manuela Giltomey on Feb. 14, 1718 (DM, 1718, no. 21).

QUINTANA

JOSE DE QUINTANA and *Antonia Luján* had a daughter *Juana* (NMF, p. 262) who married José Montoya in 1729 (DM, 1729, no. 5).

RAEL

ALONSO RAEL DE AGUILAR and *Josefa García de Noriega* had several children as shown in NMF, p. 263. A daughter, *Francisca*, married Feliz Sánchez in 1723 (DM, 1723, no. 15). One son, *Eusebio*, 24 in 1718 and an *Alférez Real Reformado*, applied to marry Doña Isabel de Chávez; however, the document is incomplete and it is not known if the marriage took place (DM, 1718, no. 11a). This Isabel had married Jacinto Peláez in 1700, and then Baltasar de Mata in 1705 (Cf. NMF, pp. 161, 228, 256). Another son, *Juan*, was 21 in 1720 when he married Manuela de Sandoval Martínez (DM, 1723, no. 15).

RAMÍREZ

ALONZO RAMIREZ, with the Leyva party at El Paso when the Indians rebelled in 1680 (NMF, p. 90), was a native of New Mexico residing at Ysleta del Paso shortly after the rebellion, and there gave his full name as Alonso Ramírez *de Salazar* (DM, 1680, no. 3).

JOSE DE RAMIREZ SANTIBANES, residing in El Paso in 1718, was a native of Querétaro, the son of Nicolás Ramírez and Pascuala Hernández, both deceased. There he married *María Martín Barba*, a native of Santa Fe, the daughter of Marcos Antonio Pulinares and María Martín Barba (DM, 1718, no. 27).

RAMOS

JUAN ANTONIO RAMOS (NMF, p. 264) was 23 and a resident of Santa Fe in 1699 when he lost his wife *Catalina Jirón* and then married *María Mata*, 19, on May 4 (DM, 1699, no. 11). He gave his parents as Felís Ramos and Sebastiana Núñez (*ibid.*). His second wife was most likely the María *Canseco* who died in 1715.

NICOLAS RAMOS (NMF, p. 264) was a native of Spain, while his wife, *Ana Manríquez de Reinoso*, was born in Zacatecas. They had another daughter, *Josefa*, who married Antonio Velásquez in 1715 (DM, 1715, no. 11).

REINOSO

JOSE MANUEL REINOSO, a slave of Governor Valverde, was the natural son of Don Antonio Reinoso and María de la Encarnación, slave of Doña Merencia de Reinoso. He came up to New Mexico with his master and married *Elena de la Cruz*, native of Santa Fe, on Feb. 6, 1720 (DM, 1720, no. 11).

RENDÓN

FRANCISCO RENDON (NMF, p. 265) was proficient in the Indian languages because he was reared as a captive child in the Indian Pueblos between 1680 and 1692. He was the natural son of María Madrid (alias "*la Mozonga*") and had a sister, Ana María de Almazán, living at Pecos Pueblo in 1727. Francisco and his mother were taken captive by the Picurís Indians in 1680 and were liberated by the Vargas forces at San Juan in 1692. Subsequently, Francisco assumed the name *Rendón*, in memory of Fray Matías Rendón, the 1680 martyr of Picurís. After the Reconquest of 1693, Francisco and other boys attended a little school in Santa Fe conducted by Fray Antonio de Azebedo, his mother being the Padre's cook at the time. By 1727 Francisco had lost his first wife, *Petrona Gómez*, and was soldiering in Santa Fe when he married *Catalina Maese* on Feb. 2, 1727 (DM, 1727, no. 12).

La Mozonga, his mother, was a mulatto slave of Francisco Xavier at the time of her captivity in 1680 and was then believed dead in Picurís together with a certain Francisco Blanco de la Vega (Revolt I, p. 98). According to the same source, she had three small daughters besides Francisco when rescued in 1692 and placed in the care of Francisco de Almazán, which explains the surname of daughter Ana María at Pecos in 1727. The mother was once married to a Juan de la Vega (who could be the Francisco de la Vega of 1680), and she was also the mother of *Juana "la Mozonga"* who married Juan de Ledesma (NMF, p. 307). The Rendón descendants went back to live in the Picurís (Embudo or Dixon) area, some of the next generation moving down to Santa Fe and thence to San Miguel del Vado at the turn of the century.

RIBAS

JUAN MARCOS RIBAS, a native of San José del Parral, and son of Nicolás Ribas and Micaela Trujillo, was first married to *María Valenzuela*. In 1762 he married *María Alberta González* of Albuquerque (DM, 1762, no. 32).

RIBERA

JUAN FELIPE DE RIBERA (NMF, p. 267), 21, born in Zacatecas, the son of the Adjutant Salvador Matías de Ribera and Juana de Sosa Canela, married *Doña María Rendón Palomino*, 15, on March 24, 1715 (DM, 1715, no. 15).

JUAN DE RIBERA and his wife *Luisa de Ocanto*, or *Otón* (NMF, pp. 91, 92), had a daughter *María* who at 17 married Francisco García in 1697 (DM, 1697, no. 17).

RINCÓN

ANTONIO RINCON and *Antonia de Valenzuela* (NMF, p. 268) were married in the Cathedral of Mexico City a few years before 1680, according to a certificate issued on April 15, 1693 (DM, 1693, no. 3). Their daughter *María* married Miguel Durán in 1708, her father being dead by this time (DM, 1708, nos. 7, 11).

José Rincón, a native of El Paso, was most likely a descendant of this family. He and his wife, *Francisca Moreno*, were living in Sabinal when their son *José Francisco* was born, July 21, 1833 (B-9, *Belén*).

RÍO

ALONSO DEL RIO, Captain (NMF, p. 92), was a native of Santa Fe, the son of Captain Diego del Río and María Madrid, both dead before the 1680 Revolt. Alonso lost his wife, *María González*, at San Lorenzo del Paso in 1696. Three years later he married a young girl, *Rosa María López*, 14, a daughter of Don Juan Páez Hurtado by his first wife, Pascuala López (DM, 1699, no. 10).

JUAN DEL RIO (NMF, p. 92) and *Ana Moraga* had another daughter, *María*, who at 18 married Juan Antonio Padilla at El Real de San Lorenzo. Juan gave his age as 50 in 1691 (DM, 1697, no. 15; 1695, no. 17).

DOMINGO DEL RIO (NMF, p. 93) and *Juana Luján* were both dead by 1695 when their son *Diego*, 25, married Isabel Romero at Senecú del Paso on Aug. 31 (DM, 1695, no. 17).

RODARTE

BALTASAR RODARTE (NMF, p. 268) was a native of Sombrerete who gave his age as 21 in 1696 and 23 in 1699. He came to N. M. as a soldier (DM, 1696, no. 30; 1697, no. 10; 1699, no. 11).

RODRÍGUEZ

ALONSO RODRIGUEZ VARELA (NMF, p. 268) and *Juana de Valencia* had a son, *Carlos*, who was 20 in 1696 when he married María de la Encarnación, 17, of unknown parentage, in Santa Fe (DM, 1696, no. 23). Their other son, *Antonio*, married Cayetana Apodaca in Santa Fe, Oct. 10, 1709 (DM, 1709, no. 15).

JOSE RODRIGUEZ (NMF, pp. 268, 269) and *María de Samano*, or *López Conejo*, celebrated the wedding of their son *José* to Gertrudis de Tapia in 1726 (DM, 1726, no. 5; 1710, nos. 14, 24).

FRANCISCO RODRIGUEZ CALERO was still at El Paso in 1711 in the capacity of armorer (DM, 1711, no. 16).

LORENZO RODRIGUEZ of Zacatecas was 19 in 1696 when he married *Teresa García*, 15, of El Paso, at Santa Fe, Mar. 6 (DM, 1696, no. 6).

AGUSTIN RODRIGUEZ was 28 to 30 years old in 1696-1697, and gave his birthplace as Sombrerete as well as Zacatecas. His wife's name is also given here as *Nicolasa Ortiz Leonarda*, and his trade that of a caster of metals (DM, 1696, no. 30; 1697, nos. 10, 14).

NICOLAS RODRIGUEZ and *Catalina Mondragón* were living in Santa Cruz when they had these three children: *María*, Feb. 8,

1711; *Francisco Xavier*, Oct. 20, 1712; and *María Efigenia*, Nov. 22, 1714 (*Gen.*, 1710, no. 7).

SEBASTIAN RODRIGUEZ, the Negro drummer (NMF, p. 270), married *Isabel Olguín*, widow of Captain Francisco Madrid, dead 2 years, on June 4, 1692 (DM, 1692, no. 7). In 1689 Governor Reneros de Posado impeded the wedding out of spite because of the Negro's insolence after the Governor's term was over. Governor Vargas pushed the marriage to a happy solution, even writing to Reneros de Posada to retract a false impediment he had proposed (*ibid.; Gen.*, 1689, no. 1; 1691, no. 1; 1692, no. 2).

Sebastián next tried to marry a María de la Cruz, Indian servant of Luis Granillo, but finally married *Juana de la Cruz (Apodaca, Arzate, Maese)*. Their son Melchor was 20 in 1717, and both his parents dead, when he married Micaela Díaz Blea, 21, in Santa Fe, Oct. 4 (DM, 1717, no. 15). Clara de Villaroel (NMF, p. 270) must have been Melchor's second or third wife.

There was another Negro in Santa Fe in 1697, by the name of *Francisco Rico*, 26, a native of the Congo (DM, 1697, no. 12), but nothing else is known about him.

ROJAS

PEDRO DE ROJAS LISCANO, a native of Sombrerete, was a soldier in Santa Fe in 1697. His parents were José de Rojas and Teresa de los Reyes. In 1694 he had given his age as 18, and 24 in 1704 when he married *Melchora Fresqui*, 25, of the Rio Abajo and unknown parentage (DM, 1694, no. 39; 1697, no. 20; 1704, no. 15). He was the same Pedro de Rojas who worked on the restoration of San Miguel Chapel in 1710 (NMF, p. 285), but not, as suggested there, a possible son of Pedro de Cedillo Rico de Rojas.

ROMERO

BARTOLOME ROMERO DE PEDRAZA (NMF, pp. 97, 98) was the son of Captain Matías Romero and Isabel de Pedraza, both mentioned as deceased when he was residing as Adjutant at San Pedro de Alcantara in 1681, when he married *Doña Lucía* (or Luisa) *Varela Jaramillo* (DM, 1681, no. 8). Besides *Matías* and *Juana*, mentioned in NMF, of whose parentage now there is no doubt, they had two other daughters: *María*, who married Francisco García Perea in 1707; and *Antonia*, who became the wife of Sebastián Varela in 1711 (DM, 1707, no. 8; 1711, no. 14). Bartolomé died in Santa Fe shortly after the Reconquest, "three years ago," when his widow married Antonio Felix Valencia on May 17, 1696 (DM, 1696, no. 29).

FRANCISCO ROMERO DE PEDRAZA (NMF, pp. 98, 271) was a brother of Bartolomé. In 1689 he gave his age as 55, saying he was a son of Matías Romero and Isabel de Pedraza and married to *Francisca Ramírez [de Salazar]*, a native of New Mexico. In previous and subsequent years he gave his age so consistently that we can say with some certainty that he was born in 1634-1635. He was an uncle of Lucía Gómez Robledo, daughter of Andrés Gómez Robledo (DM, 1697, no. 11).

SALVADOR ROMERO (NMF, pp. 98, 272) returned with the Reconquest to settle eventually in Chimayó with his wife María López. There a daughter, *Agustina*, 20, married Miguel Tenorio de Alba in 1705 (DM, 1705, no. 20).

JUAN ROMERO (NMF, p. 98) said he was 24 in 1682 (DM, 1682, nos. 8, 10). He appears to be the Juan Romero married to *Pascuala Vásquez*. Their daughter *María*, 22, married Ambrosio Villalpando in 1718, when Juan is mentioned as dead (DM, 1718, no. 6). Juan's widow had married Agustín Sáiz in 1710 (DM, 1710, no. 25).

A *José Romero* of unknown parentage was a soldier in Santa Fe in 1699 when he married *Josefa Griego* (DM, 1699, no. 15).

BALTASAR ROMERO (NMF, pp. 271, 272) and *Francisca de Góngora* had a daughter, *María*, who married Luis Lucero in 1719 (DM, 1719, no. 17).

In 1714, at El Paso, *Francisca*, daughter of Baltasar Romero de Pedraza, deceased, and Josefa de Herrera, married Luis de Valencia (DM, 1714, no. 15); hence this must have been a different Baltasar.

At Albuquerque, in 1708, *Jacinta*, 14, daughter of Baltasar Romero and Francisca Montoya, deceased, married Francisco Xavier Benavides (DM, 1708, no. 8). This, again, was a third Baltasar, very possibly a son of Felipe Romero and Jacinta de Guadalajara.

BERNARDO ROMERO, 16, who married *María de Córdoba* at Santa Cruz, Aug. 8, 1727 (DM, 1727, no. 16), was in all likelihood the son of Francisco Xavier Romero of Mexico City (NMF, p. 273). Bernardo was born on Oct. 19, 1710, and had a daughter *Antonia*, Jan. 15, 1736, as noted in some fragments of baptisms (*Gen.*, 1710, no. 7; 1736, no. 2).

ROSAS

MANUEL ANTONIO DE ROSAS, 17, a New Mexican of unknown parentage, was living in Santa Cruz when he married Gertrudis Jirón, 30, on Sept. 20, 1723 (DM, 1723, no. 16). Probably a bastard member of the Gonzáles de la Rosa family, he was very likely the Manuel de la Rosa living in Rio Arriba in 1751 (NMF, p. 191).

RUIZ

ANDRES RUIZ, 31 and married, was a native of Janos Presidio and residing in Santa Fe in 1723 (DM, 1723, no. 15).

SEBASTIAN ROIS, 22, married *María de la O*, 24, at El Paso, Nov. 5, 1699 (DM, 1699, no. 14).

RUIZ DE ESPARZA

JOSE TEODORA RUIZ DE ESPARZA and *María Josefa Angulo* resided at San Miguel del Vado in 1812 when a daughter, *Manuela Juana Francisca*, was born there, July 12 (B-20, *Pecos*). Another daughter, most likely, was *Antonia* Ruiz Esparza, who married Manuel Alarí at San Miguel in 1830 (NMF, p. 123).

SÁEZ

AGUSTIN SAEZ, 35, a native New Mexican, the son of Ambrosio Sáez and María Rodríguez, applied to marry *Pascuala Vásquez*, 25, the widow of Juan Romero, in 1710 (DM, 1710, no. 25). Hence, Pascuala was not the same woman as *Antonia Márquez*, his second wife (NMF, p. 278), but was actually his third wife. His daughter, *Juliana*, by Antonia Márquez, married Juan Griego in 1716 (DM, 1716, no. 26).

SALAZAR

AGUSTIN DE SALAZAR and *Felipa de Gamboa* (NMF, p. 279) had another son, *Miguel*, who married María Trujillo, 17, of Santa Fe, on Feb. 4, 1721. His parents were still alive and residing in Santa Cruz (DM, 1721, no. 6). Felipa de Gamboa had been involved in a public scandal with Juan de Atienza in 1704 (*Gen.*, 1704, no. 2).

Antonio de Salazar, their other son (NMF, p. 279), and *María de Torres* had these known children at Santa Cruz: *Juan Antonio*, Sept. 23, 1714; and *Nicolás*, Sept. 17, 1721 (*Gen.*, 1710, no. 7).

Nicolás Salazar and *Lucía de Torres* had a child, *Nicolasa*, Sept. 28, 1721; her godparents were the preceding couple (*ibid.*). Hence, in all likelihood, this Nicolás was another son of Agustín who had married his brother Antonio's sister-in-law.

SAMBRANO

SALVADOR SAMBRANO, a native of Mexico City, married *Antonia Andrea Armijo* in Santa Fe, Sept. 3, 1748 (M-50, *Santa Fe*). He might have been related to Fray Manuel Zambrano, who was stationed in Santa Fe at this time.

SÁNCHEZ

JOSE SANCHEZ, a native of Mexico City, the son of Lucas (NMF, p. 281), was most likely the son of that Lucas Sánchez, deceased, and María de Ribera, both natives of Mexico City, who were the parents of a Juana de Ribera who married Carlos Domínguez de Mendoza in Santa Fe, Sept. 17, 1699 (DM, 1699, no. 13). Hence, José must have been closely related to his own wife, *María de Ribera*.

PEDRO SANCHEZ DE INIGO (NMF, pp. 279, 280), natural son of Juana López, was first married to *Leonor Baca*, who was killed in the 1696 Indian Revolt at San Ildefonso. He was a soldier of Santa Fe in 1698, and 25 years old, when he there married *María Luján*, 18 (DM, 1698, no. 23).

His son *Pedro*, by Leonor Baca, deceased, married Micaela Quintana at Santa Cruz on Jan. 20, 1718 (DM, 1718, no. 26).

JACINTO SANCHEZ DE INIGO (NMF, p.

28) and his mother Juana López were sponsors together in 1692 (DM, 1692, no. 9). Two children by his first wife, *Juana* and *Joaquín*, married Manuel Montoya and Manuela Montoya in 1704 and 1719, respectively (DM, 1704, no. 9; 1719, no. 14). *María*, a daughter by his second wife, was born at Santa Cruz, May 7, 1713 (*Gen.*, 1710, no. 7).

FELIPE SANCHEZ, native New Mexican, was 20 in 1699 (DM, 1699, no. 12). His wife was *Olaya Otón*, who was dead by 1721 when their daughter *Gertrudis*, widow of Cristóbal Maese, married Cayetano José Moya (DM, 1721, no. 7). Felipe could well have been a third natural son of Juana López.

TORIBIO BENITO SANCHEZ was a Spaniard from the Mountains of Burgos, 33 in 1697 when he married *María Magdalena Jurado*, 13-14, at El Paso on April 28. His parents were Toribio Benito Sánchez, native of El Lugar de San Miguel, Villa de la Vega, in Castilla la Vieja, and his wife María de Polanco (DM, 1697, no. 9). Toribio still resided at Socorro del Paso in 1710, when he gave his age as 50 (DM, 1701, no. 8; 1705, no. 18; 1710, no. 22). But he and Magdalena had a son, *Felix*, born at El Paso, who was residing in Santa Fe in 1723, when he married Francisca Rael de Aguilar on Feb. 6 (DM, 1723, no. 15). This is a brand new addition to the diverse Sánchez list in NMF.

SANDOVAL

JUAN DE DIOS SANDOVAL MARTINEZ (NMF, p. 282) married his first wife, *Juana Hernández*, in the parish church of Santa Catalina Mártir in Mexico City sometime after 1672 (DM, 1693, no. 14). Their son *Miguel* de Dios married Lucía Gómez Robledo in Santa Fe, Oct. 28, 1697 (DM, 1697, no. 11).

Another son could have been a *Pedro de Sandoval*, born in the Valley of Toluca, and 20 years old in 1698 when he was soldiering in Santa Fe (DM, 1698, no. 6). The soldier of this name who was brought to trial in 1694 for mistreatment of his wife, Rosa de Contreras, might have been this same man (*Gen.*, 1694, no. 5). And he might also be the *Pedro Martínez* in NMF, p. 227.

Old Juan de Dios next married *Gertrudis de Herrera*, by whom he had *Antonio*, who married Josefa Villalpando at Santa Cruz in 1722 (DM, 1722, no. 8); *Juan José*, who married María Fernández in 1720 (DM, 1720, no. 14); *Miguel*, born at Santa Cruz, Oct. 1, 1713; and *Feliciano Antonio*, July 31, 1715 (*Gen.*, 1710, no. 7).

ANTONIO SANDOVAL and Josefa Villalpando had a son, *Antonio Mateo*, born at Santa Cruz, Sept. 24, 1721 (*Gen.*, 1710, no. 7).

MIGUEL DE DIOS SANDOVAL MARTINEZ and *Lucía Gómez Robledo* had a difficult time getting married in 1697 because her mother and relations strongly objected. All the other Gómez Robledo girls had married Spaniards brought by Vargas from Spain, while Miguel belonged to the Creole colonists from Mexico City. They did get married, finally. Among their many children in NMF, pp. 282, 283, *Manuela* married Juan Rael de Aguilar in 1720 (DM, 1720, no. 7). When another daughter, *Melchora*, was to become the second wife of Alonso Rael de Aguilar II, an impediment was brought up, but her mother testified that this girl was an adulterous child of hers by another man (*Gen.*, 1728, no. 4).

FELIPE ROJAS DE SANDOVAL, the Spanish adventurer mentioned last in NMF, p. 283, was born in the city of Puerto de Santa María. He sailed from Cádiz to America in 1742. The date of arrival in Santa Fe was Mar. 1, 1750 (*Gen.*, 1746, no. 1).

SANTIAGO

In 1623 JUAN PÉREZ DE SANTIAGO was paid for a trip to New Mexico (AGI, *Contad.*, leg. 725), and a *Diego de Santiago* was living in Santa Fe in 1632 with his wife *Felipa* (AGN, *Mex., Inq.*, t. 304, f. 188).

Francisco de Santiago Pérez, the son of Luis Pérez and Melchora de los Reyes, natives of Querétaro, was a widower who married *Catalina Durán* at El Paso in 1693. The following year they were sponsors together (DM, 1693, nos. 5, 20; 1694, no. 7).

JOSE DE SANTIAGO, 24, the son of Don Luis de Santiago and Doña María Carrillo of San José del Parral, and a soldier of the Presidio of San Francisco de Conchos, married *Doña Catalina de Esparza*, or *Montoya*, 25, at El Paso, Feb. 27, 1693 (DM, 1693, no. 9).

Julián de Santiago married *Francisca de la Vega* in 1694 (DM, 1694, no. 35a).

SANTISTEBAN

ANTONIO DE SANTISTEBAN, son of the Adjutant Salvador de Santisteban and Polonia Montaño (NMF, p. 284), married *Francisca Fernández Valerio* of Santa Cruz, Sept. 11, 1728 (DM, 1728, no. 14).

SAYAGO

DIEGO SAYAGO was married to *Teresa Domínguez de Mendoza*, who was dead by 1728 when their daughter *Margarita* married Felipe Tafoya (DM, 1728, no. 16). He was, no doubt, the Diego de *Arroyo* who came from Mexico City in 1694 with his mother and stepfather, Antonio Sayago (NMF, p. 191). The name soon disappeared, becoming confused with "Gallegos," or in some cases reverting to "Arroyo" (Cf. NMF, pp. 191, 291, 292).

SEDILLO

JOAQUIN SEDILLO and *María Varela* had a daughter *Ana* (NMF, p. 285) who married Nicolás Durán in 1728 (DM, 1728, no. 9). A son, *Domingo Francisco*, born in 1709, was most likely the Domingo Sedillo of Alameda who married Micaela Gonzáles, and had a girl, María Dolores, born April 7, 1736 (*Gen.*, 1736, no. 1).

SENA

BERNARDINO DE SENA (NMF, p. 285) declared himself a native of Mexico (Valley), and widower of *Tomasa González*, when he married *Doña Manuela Roybal*, widow of Captain Juan de Archibeque, May 25, 1727 (DM, 1727, no. 11).

SERNA

FELIPE DE LA SERNA and *Isabel Luján* (NMF, pp. 103, 288) married off some of their children as follows: *Isabel* to Pedro Madrid in 1689; *María* to Nicolás Hidalgo; and *Antonia* to Matías Madrid, all at El Paso (DM, 1689, no. 5; 1696, nos. 22, 33).

SERVÉ

JOSE SERVE, the son of José *Exarvé* (Charvet?) and Luisa or Lucía "Santana" or "Satania," married *María Isabel Casados* at Taos on Sept. 20, 1810, by whom he had two known daughters: *Juana Gertrudis*, born May 15, 1814; and *María Luz*, who married Juan Bautista Yarat on Sept. 30, 1826, both the parents being dead by this time (M-37 and B-38, *Taos*). This was most likely the man of the same name who was married to *Teodora Lobato* (1818-1822) when two other daughters were born: *Ana María de Jesús*, Nov. 25, 1818, and *María Guadalupe*, Jan. 22, 1822 (B-38, *Taos*). Ana María married Victor Sánchez, by whom she had two known sons, Juan Narciso, Jan. 1, 1834, and Juan Nepomuceno, May 19, 1840 (B-49 and B-51, *Taos*).

JOSE MANUEL SERVE was also the son of José Exarvé and *María Luisa* "Antonia," the latter also designated simply as a woman "*de la nación del Norte*" (Plains Indian?). José Manuel married *Dominga Coca* of Taos, where they had the following children: *Polonia*, wife of Pablo Salazar (baptism of child Juan Bautista, April 14, 1840, in B-51, *Taos*); *María Ludovina*, Nov. 24, 1822; *María Altagracia*, Oct. 5, 1825; *José María*, Jan. 25, 1828; *María Rufina*, --------, 1831; *María Antonia*, June 13, 1834; and *José Antonio*, June 13, 1840 (all in B-38, 47, 48, 49, 51, *Taos*).

LUIS SERVE, a third son of José Exarvé and wife, married *Juliana Aguilar* at Taos in 1814. Their son *José* married Anastasia Bueno, who bore him a son, José Luis, May 11, 1845 (M-37 and B-52, *Taos*).

This was undoubtedly a French name, like "*Charvet*," which the Spanish Padres first wrote phonetically as "*Exarvé*," and which later became "*Servé*," written less often as "*Sarbé*." Much later, when more Frenchmen came, and the French clergy after 1850, it was interpreted as "Charrette." The three brothers Servé were evidently the sons of a Frenchman or French-Canadian by a Northern or Plains squaw, and reached Taos a generation before the French-Canadian trappers arrived in force.

At Santa Fe, a *Francisco* SERVIN married *Lugarda Moya*, Nov. 8, 1819 (M-52, *Santa Fe*). Following the death of this wife, Lugarda "Montoya," and while a soldier in Santa Fe, he had to ask the Governor's permission to marry *María Deluvina Hurtado* of San Miguel del Vado, which he did on Mar. 13, 1836 (*Gen.*, 1836, no. 3). Was he another Servé brother or a totally different individual?

SILVA

FRANCISCO DE SILVA and *Gregoria Ruiz* had a daughter *María*, born in 1706 (NMF, p. 288), who married José Gallegos in 1721 (DM, 1721, no. 9). The son *Francisco* married "Rosa" de Chávez in 1729, according to the Albuquerque marriage book, but the nuptial investigation carries her correct name, "Gertrudis" (DM, 1729, no. 4).

SISNEROS

BARTOLOME CISNEROS and *Ana Gutiérrez de Salazar* (NMF, p. 104) had a son *Alonso*, 19, who married María Madrid on Oct. 8, 1690; another, *Antonio*, 42, who married Josefa (Juana?) Luján on Jan. 1, 1695; and a daughter, *Josefa*, who became the wife of Pedro González in 1681 (DM, 1690, no. 2; 1694, no. 36; 1681, no. 6). Captain Bartolomé was mentioned as dead in 1681.

ANTONIO CISNEROS and Juana (Josefa?) Luján had the three children given in NMF, pp. 104, 289. Of these, *Hermenegildo*, 22, married María de Medina y Valdés, of unknown parentage, in Santa Fe, Feb. 11, 1721 (DM, 1721, no. 4).

SORIA

DON FELIPE DE SORIA, 22, a native of Ciudad de Pátzcuaro, was in Santa Fe in 1696, and residing in Santa Cruz the following year (DM, 1696, no. 25; 1697, no. 10).

SUBIRÁN

DON JOSE SUBIRAN married *Doña Rafaela de la O* in Santa Fe, Jan. 6, 1806 (M-52, *Santa Fe*).

TAFOYA

ANTONIO TAFOYA and *María Luisa Godines* were 18 and 17, respectively, when they were married on April 28, 1697; both their parents are given as in NMF, p. 291 (DM, 1697, no. 19).

TAGLE

DON JOSÉ DE TAGLE VILLEGAS was Captain of the Santa Fe Presidio in 1719 (Bancroft, NMO, 1719).

TAMARIS

FELIPE TAMARIS and *Magdalena Baca* were married in Santa Fe in 1707 (DM, 1707, no. 6); both parents given as in NMF, p. 292.

TAPIA

PEDRO DE TAPIA and *María de Salazar* had a daughter, *Polonia*, who married José de Mena in 1678 (DM, 1678, no. 1).

FRANCISCO DE TAPIA and *Magdalena Nieto* (NMF, p. 292) had a daughter, *Gertrudis*, who married José Rodríguez in 1726 (DM, 1726, no. 5).

NICOLAS ANTONIO DE TAPIA married *Pascuala Vásquez* in Santa Fe, April 14, 1723 (DM, 1723, no. 18).

TELLES

RAFAEL TELLES JIRON and *Mariana (Montoya) de Esparza* (NMF, p. 106) were living at San Lorenzo del Paso in 1711 when their son *José* married *María Magdalena García de Noriega* (DM, 1711, no. 16). Their daughter *Catalina*, 25, had married José de Santiago in 1693 (DM, 1693, no. 9).

TENORIO

MIGUEL TENORIO DE ALBA (NMF, p. 293), a native of the city of Zacatecas, was a captain in 1705, 30 years old, when he married *Agustina Romero*, 20, the widow of Mateo Márquez. His parents were Juan Tenorio de Alba and Josefa López Sandoval, deceased (DM, 1705, no. 20). In 1697 Miguel had stated that he was a blacksmith by trade (DM, 1697, no. 14). Besides those in NMF, two other sons were *Cayetano*, born at Santa Cruz, Feb. 8, 1711, and *Estanislao*, May 17, 1713 (*Gen.*, 1710, no. 7).

JOSE TENORIO, most probably a close relative of Miguel, was also a native of Cuidad Zacatecas, and 24 years old in 1722 when he married *María Vigil*, 34, in Santa Fe, on Feb. 9. His parents were Nicolás Tenorio and María de Errada (DM, 1722, no. 7).

MANUEL TENORIO DE ALBA, 17, who married *Francisca de la Vega y Coca*, July 13, 1721 (DM, 1721, no. 5; NMF, p. 293), was not a real son of Miguel Tenorio de Alba but of Alfonso López and Luisa Gómez de Arrellano, both deceased (*ibid.*). The boy's mother, Luisa, was murdered by Francisco Rodríguez Calero in 1704 (NMF, p. 269), and evidently Tenorio had reared him from babyhood and given him his name.

TORRES

CRISTOBAL DE TORRES and *Angela de Leyva* (NMF, pp. 107, 294) married off some of their children as follows: *María* to Antonio Salazar in 1708; *Diego*, 22, to Rosa Varela in 1711; and *Josefa*, 22, to Diego Martín in 1716 (DM, 1708, no. 9; 1711, no. 15; 1716, no. 21). Diego's eldest son, *Marcial* (NMF, p. 295), married his second wife, María Martín, at Santa Bárbara, Sept. 8, 1749 (M-26, *Picurís*).

JUAN DE TORRES (NMF, p. 295), a native of the Mines of Sombrerete, requested a belated nuptial blessing for his wife, *María de Ontiveros*, Sept. 4, 1693 (DM, 1693, no. 23).

MATEO DE TORRES, 23, a resident of Bernalillo, married *Isabel González*, Nov. 1, 1701; however, his parents are not given (DM, 1701, no. 9). A daughter, *Francisca*, married Tomás Córdoba in Bernalillo in 1716 (DM, 1716, no. 24). Another daughter, *Lugarda*, born in Santa Fe, married Salvador Avalos in El Paso in 1718 (DM, 1718, no. 29).

TRUJILLO

JUAN DE TRUJILLO, husband of *Elvira Sánchez Jiménez* (NMF, pp. 108, 296), gave his birthplace as the jurisdiction of Isleta in New Mexico, and his age variously as 40 in 1692 and 1696, again in 1696 as 45, and 43 in 1697 (DM, 1680, no. 2; 1692, no. 9; 1696, nos. 20, 29; 1697, no. 17). Besides *Antonio*, who married Ana María Córdoba, there was another son, *Baltasar*, who married Nicolasa Espinosa, and then Ynez González Bas.

BALTASAR DE TRUJILLO (NMF, p. 297) was the son of the preceding couple, as we learn from his second marriage to *Ynes González Bas* at Albuquerque, May 18, 1728; his parents were dead as well as his first wife, *Nicolasa de Espinosa* (DM, 1728, no. 11). A daughter by this first wife was *María*, who at 12 married Juan Luján, Jan. 13, 1717 (DM, 1717, no. 29).

CRISTOBAL DE TRUJILLO II (NMF, p. 108) and *Micaela de Archuleta* had another daughter, *Teresa*, who married Pablo Ortega at El Paso in 1717 (DM, 1717, no. 14). Their son, *Diego*, born at El Paso, had married María Herrera at Santa Cruz in 1709 (DM, 1709, no. 21).

BARTOLOME DE TRUJILLO (NMF, pp. 108, 297) was actually a son of Cristóbal Trujillo I and María de Sandoval (Manzanares), as we learn from both of his marriages, to *María de Archuleta* in 1682 and to *Petronila Domínguez* in 1693. The latter married Simón Martín after Bartolomé's death (DM, 1682, no. 9;

1693, no. 6; 1705, no. 17). *Sebastiana*, a daughter by his first wife, married Juan Alonso Mondragón in 1703 (DM, 1703, no. 7).

JOSE DE TRUJILLO, also a son of the first Cristóbal and his Sandoval wife (NMF, p. 297), had a daughter, *Antonia* (by his first wife), who married Miguel de Herrera in 1716 (DM, 1716, no. 28). Another, *Teodora*, by his first wife, was born at Santa Cruz on Feb. 16, 1713 (*Gen.*, 1710, no. 7).

JUAN TRUJILLO of Pojoaque and his wife *Ana de Herrera* (NMF, p. 297) had a son *Juan* who married Gregoria Chirinos, daughter of Juan Manuel Chirinos (Martínez) and María Navarro, in Santa Fe, Oct. 6, 1722 (DM, 1722, no. 9).

DIEGO TRUJILLO and *Catalina Griego* (NMF, p. 297) had a son *Antonio* at Santa Cruz who married *María Márquez de Ayala*, 17, in Santa Fe, Jan. 7, 1716 (DM, 1715, no. 12).

PASCUAL TRUJILLO and *Antonia Durán* (NMF, p. 298) had a daughter *María* who married Miguel de Salazar in 1721 (DM, 1721, no. 6).

MATEO TRUJILLO (NMF, p. 298) and *María de Tapia* had a son *Agustín* who married Micaela Martín of Santa Cruz, widow of Cristóbal Olguín, in 1696; the boy had been born in the Rio Abajo but was a soldier of Santa Fe at this time (DM, 1696, no. 27).

VALDÉS

JOSE VALDES, born in Mexico City, son of the late José Luis Valdés and María de Cabrera, was a soldier at El Paso when he married *Micaela Lucero de Godoy* on Oct. 5, 1711 (DM, 1711, no. 17). He is mentioned as the natural father of Francisco Valdés y Bustos of Santa Cruz (NMF, p. 301). Not heard of again in New Mexico, he evidently settled definitely in El Paso.

DOMINGO VALDES, José's younger brother (NMF, 302), was 23 in 1719, and residing in Santa Fe, when he married *Ana María Márquez* of Santa Fe (DM, 1719, no. 10).

VALENCIA

JUAN DE VALENCIA, the son of Francisco de Valencia and María Millán, had been married to *Juana Martín*, who died at Ysleta del Paso in 1688. The following years, Captain Juan, at the age of 40, married *Juana Madrid*, 16, on June 9 (DM, 1689, no. 6). Besides the children by his first wife listed in NMF, there was a son, *Miguel*, 27, who in 1707 married Antonia Baca Almazán at Socorro del Paso (DM, 1707, no. 9). The girl *Jacinta*, who married Andrés Ruis in 1717, was a daughter by the second wife.

LUIS DE VALENCIA, no parents given, was a soldier of El Paso who there married *Francisca Romero de Pedraza* in 1714 (DM, 1714, no. 15).

ANTONIO FELIX VALENCIA (NMF, p. 301), of unknown parentage, was a native of the Province of Sonora, 34 years old, and a soldier of Santa Fe when he married *Luisa Varela*, 30, widow of Bartolomé Romero, May 13, 1696 (DM, 1696, no. 29).

VALENZUELA

MARTIN DE VALENZUELA (NMF, p. 301) was the son of Cristóbal de Valenzuela and Manuela de la Cruz, both deceased and natives of the city of Zacatecas. Martín was 38 when he married *María de Aragón*, 19, at Santa Cruz, Sept. 8, 1714 (DM, 1714, no. 21). He had come as a Reconquest soldier, at 26, in 1693 (DM, 1693, no. 24). A daughter, *María Magdalena*, was born at Santa Cruz, November 22, 1714 (*Gen.*, 1710, no. 7).

CRISTOBAL TOMAS DE VALENZUELA, a resident of Bernalillo, was the son of Martín de Valenzuela and Ynez de la Rosa, natives of the city of Zacatecas (apparently the preceding Martín and a first wife). On Feb. 5, 1716, he married *Josefa Montoya*, 16, bastard daughter of Captain Diego Montoya (DM, 1716, no. 25).

VALERIO

MARTIN FERNANDEZ VALERIO (NMF, p. 302) must have been a lad of 12 or so when he came from Sombrerete in 1694. Shortly after the Reconquest he attended a small school for boys conducted by Father Azebedo (DM, 1727, no. 12; cf. *Rendón*, Francisco). His wife was *María Montoya*, and known children were *Lugarda*, who married José Bernardo Gómez in 1726, and *Francisca*, who married Antonio Santisteban at Santa Cruz in 1728 (DM, 1726, no. 4; 1728, no. 14).

ANTONIO MARCELINO FERNANDEZ VALERIO, who married *Luisa Martín* at Santa Cruz, June 24, 1742, was most likely a son of the preceding couple, as also *Lorenza Fernández Valerio*, who married Manuel Gregorio Montes Vigil, April 8, 1742 (M-29, *Santa Cruz*).

VALLE

JOSE DEL VALLE and his wife *Ana de Ribera* were among the Mexico City colonists who arrived in Santa Fe in June, 1694. He was a native of Seville, 38, the son of Juan, able-bodied, having an aquiline face, and large eyes and nose. His wife was a native of Tezcuco, 28, able-bodied, with a broad face, large eyes, and a mole on the left side of her nose (*Sp. Arch.*, vol. II, no. 54c). Another list simply names "Don José del Valle with his wife and a boy" (BNM, leg. 4, pt. 1, pp. 830-834). This last was an adopted foundling, *Bernardino del Valle*, who became Bernardino de SENA (NMF, p. 286). In 1695 José del Valle gave his age as 40 and Seville as his birthplace (DM, 1695, no. 5).

VALVERDE

ASENCIO VALVERDE, 40, was in Bernalillo in 1707; he and his wife *María de Ledesma* [?] had a daughter, *Gregoria*, who married Cristóbal de la Vega in 1712 (DM, 1707, no. 7; 1712, no. 5).

VARELA

DIEGO VARELA DE LOSADA and *Maria Ana Fresqui*, a family that stayed at El Paso (NMF, p. 111), had these other children: *Cristóbal*, 18, who married Rosa Isabel Márquez at El Paso, Oct. 10, 1694; and *Gregoria*, 28, who became the wife of Francisco Hidalgo of El Paso in 1706 (DM, 1694, no. 34a; 1706, no. 3).

Cristóbal Varela and *Rosa Márquez* had a son *Juan*, 18, who married Catalina Telles, 15, of unknown parentage, at El Paso in 1716 (DM, 1716, no. 27).

ANTONIO VARELA, no parents given, was married in 1704 to *Juana de la Cruz*, daughter of Bartolomé Ansures and María de la Cruz, both deceased (DM, 1704, no. 8); hence the use of both names in NMF, p. 305.

Teresa Varela (wife of Alonso García de Noriego) and *Alfonsa Varela* (wife of Juan de Perea) were sisters (DM, 1683, no. 3).

VARGAS

JUAN DE VARGAS MACHUCA (NMF, p. 306) was a native of Jalapa, the son of Diego de Vargas Machuca and Sebastiana Medina Baca. On Oct. 26, 1681, he married *Ana López Olguín* (DM, 1681, no. 5). *Sebastiana*, 21, who married Marcos Montoya, widower, at San Ildefonso on Jan. 27, 1709, was their daughter (DM, 1709, no. 18) and not of the Fernández de Vargas family.

TOMAS DE VARGAS MACHUCA and *María Benavides* (NMF, p. 306) had a son, *Antonio*, Nov. 18, 1721 (*Gen.*, 1721, no. 5).

MANUEL FERNANDEZ DE VARGAS and *Luisa Ruiz Brito* (NMF, p. 306) had a son *Francisco*, 20, who married María Magdalena Leyva, 22, at Santa Fe, May 11, 1711 (DM, 1711, no. 13).

VÁSQUEZ

TOMAS VASQUEZ and *Angela Brito* had a daughter *Pascuala*, 25, widow of Juan Romero, who married Agustín Sáez in 1710 (DM, 1710, no. 25).

JOSE VASQUEZ, of unknown parentage (NMF, p. 307), was a native New Mexican residing in Santa Fe when he married *Francisca Martín* (Torres), also of unknown parentage, at Santa Cruz, Nov. 11, 1709 (DM, 1709, no. 20).

VEGA

FRANCISCO DE LA VEGA CARPIO and his wife *Antonia de la Trinidad Fajardo* were natives of Nueva Vizcaya. Their daughter *María*, 18, married Juan García in 1705, and their son *Cristóbal* married Gregoria Valverde in 1712 (DM, 1705, no. 15; 1712, no. 5).

VELÁSQUEZ

ANTONIO VELASQUEZ was a native of Sombrerete, the son of Diego Velásquez and Juana de los Ríos (NMF, p. 311); he was 27 and a soldier of Santa Fe when he married *Josefa Ramos*, 25, on Aug. 25, 1715 (DM, 1715, no. 11).

VIGIL

FRANCISCO MONTES VIGIL and *María Jiménez de Ancizo* (NMF, p. 311) had a daughter *María*, 31, who married José Tenorio at Santa Fe in 1722. Francisco was assistant Captain of the Presidio at this time (DM, 1722, no. 7). He had a slave by the name of Juan Eugenio Capetillo (DM, 1718, no. 25).

JUAN MONTES VIGIL, son of the preceding couple, was 21 when he married *Ynez López de Salazar*, 22, in 1731 (DM, 1731, no. 1).

VILLALPANDO

JUAN DE VILLALPANDO and *Ana María Romero* (NMF, p. 312) had a daughter, *Josefa*, who married Antonio Sandoval of Santa Cruz in 1722 (DM, 1722, no. 8).

VILLASEÑOR

JOSE RAFAEL VILLASENOR, the son of Benito Villaseñor and Simona Muzos, married *Margarita Olguín*, daughter of José Antonio Olguín and María Doroteo García, on Mar. 9, 1811 (M-21, *Picurís*).

YBÁÑEZ

JOSE MIGUEL YBANEZ married *María Micaela del Castillo* in Santa Fe, Oct. 9, 1791 (M-52, *Santa Fe*).

YRISARRI

PABLO YRISARRI, European, married *María Manuela Rael* at Alameda some years prior to 1780 (M-17, *Sandía:* exact date lost from my notes). She died on June 18, 1780, and he must have remarried soon after, for he himself died as the husband of *Barbara Coleta Martínez* at Alameda, April 7, 1782 (Bur., 46, *Sandia*).

PABLO YRISARRI II, presumably the son of the preceding man, contracted the two marriages in 1811 and 1820 as related in NMF, p. 313.

MARIANO YRISARRI (*ibid.*), who married *Juana Otero* in 1836, was actually the son of the junior Pablo and his first wife, Antonia Teresa Romero (DM, 1836, no. 1).

ZAMORA

JUAN DE ZAMORA (NMF, p. 311) gave his age as 26 in 1693 (DM, 1693, no. 25). He was presumed killed at Cochití in the Indian Revolt of 1696, with Laureano Gómez: the latter's body was found but not Zamora's. His widow, *María de la Vega*, married Gabriel de Lira in 1698 (DM, 1698, no. 20).

ZARAGOZA

MIGUEL DE ZARAGOZA was the son of Juan Bautista Zaragoza and María Gonzalez, both deceased "natives of New Mexico" of pre-1680 Revolt times. (See González Bernal *supra*.) Miguel was a widower residing in Namiquipa in 1690 when he came to El Paso and married María Magdalena Madrid, 19, on April 10 (DM, 1690, no. 7).

ZÁRATE

MIGUEL DE ZARATE, 30, was a native of Zacatecas residing at Santa Cruz in 1697-1698 (DM, 1697, no. 10; 1698, no. 19).

NEW NAMES IN NEW MEXICO, 1820–1850

In cleaning up one's research files and notes, a person sometimes discovers a body of related facts that helps to throw some light on local history. Often certain details prove invaluable to others doing research. While examining the pre-1850 mission registers and related papers in the Santa Fe archdiocesan archives with the purpose of compiling a general catalogue,[1] I jotted down baptismal and marriage data on new family names appearing among the older New Mexico families between 1820 and 1850. It was almost a mechanical act of curiosity, having previously gathered and published whatever I could find about New Mexico family origins from 1598 to 1820.[2]

These newcomers to New Mexico arrived in the Mexican Period, 1820-1846, and in the four American years preceding the erection of Santa Fe as a diocese in 1850. (Mission and parish registers after 1850 are not in Santa Fe but in their respective parishes.) The addition of new names during this thirty-year period is amazing, once the scattered notes are brought together. No less astounding is their variety, for new Spanish or Mexican surnames are exceeded by the number of French-Canadian, U.S. American, and some North European aggregations. The goodly number of Americans in New Mexico prior to the arrival of Kearny's Army in 1846 is of itself significant, and these consist only of those who came in contact with the Church through baptism or marriage. There must have been more who, because of marital impediments or other reasons, took common-law wives and thus went unrecorded.

Another revelation is the fact that Taos with its environments was the very center of this new migration. Next comes Santa Fe, but a far second, while the Rio Abajo south of the Capital has relatively few accretions. Some of the few new names at modern Socorro (founded ca. 1815) point to their origin in Guadalupe del Paso or other places in northern Mexico. The Taos concentration of immigrants also highlights the energetic activities of *Cura* Don Antonio José Martínez who, through much of this period, also covered the extensive Picurís and Mora areas. The converts he made were not always with matrimony in view, and he records these baptisms as having been preceded by thorough instruction in the Faith. His entries, and those of other Spanish-Mexican priests in other parishes, are marred only by the bad and difficult spelling of what were, to them, totally strange names and places of origin. Nor could they receive assistance in this matter from the subjects in question — Americans and French-Canadians who were illiterate for the most part.

Some of these individuals passed on to California, alone or with New Mexico families they had acquired. I point to some at random in Bancroft's lists of California pioneers.[3] To avoid cluttering the text with reference footnotes, I hereby place the sources in parentheses; these references are to the numbered baptismal (B) and marriage (M) registers of the Archives of the Archdiocese of Santa Fe (AASF); others are to *Diligencias Matrimoniales* (DM) in these same archives. Some back references are to my *New Mexico Families* (NMF) work.

---

1. Fray Angélico Chávez, *Archives of the Archdiocese of Santa Fe*. Published in 1957 by the Academy of American Franciscan History, Washington, D.C. For reasons of space, this volume does not contain the detailed material in this article.

2. Fray Angélico Chávez, *Origins of New Mexico Families in the Spanish Colonial Period, 1598-1821* (Santa Fe, Historical Society of New Mexico, 1954). In my further filing and cataloguing of archdiocesan archives I uncovered misplaced papers and fragments that contributed further data to this Spanish Colonial Period, including some early French-Canadian names prior to 1820, like *Lalanda* and *Servé*. These lists have been published serially in EL PALACIO, of the Museum of New Mexico in Santa Fe, beginning with vol. 62, no. 11.

3. H. H. Bancroft, *Works*, vols. XIX and XX (San Francisco, 1886).

ABILUCIA. *Vicente Abilucia*, widowed of *Nepomucena Romero*, married *María Altagracia Romero* at Socorro, Aug. 19, 1849. His place of origin is not given. (M-58, *Socorro*.)

ACEBES. *Andrés Acebes* and his wife *Soledad Chávez* lived in the Río Abajo area where a daughter, *María Rafaela Estefana*, was baptized on Nov. 30, 1854. Andrés was the son of Guadalupe Acebes and Vibiana Estrada, both of Chihuahua. (B, *Isleta*.)

AGILES. *Juan A'giles* (sic), no parents given, married *María Teodora García* at Socorro, Jan. 27, 1854. (M-58, *Socorro*.) Perhaps it is a mispronunciation and misspelling of "Aviles."

AGUILAR. *José Aguilar*, a native of Chihuahua, the son of Ciriaco Aguilar and Dionisia Mendoza, married *Apolonia Leyva* in Santa Fe, Mar. 27, 1847. (M-55, *Santa Fe*.)

ALDÁS. *Paulín Aldás* and wife *Tomasa Sena* were living in Albuquerque when their children, *María Luz* and *Mariano de Jesús*, were baptized, May 27, 1846, and Nov. 21, 1848, respectively. Father's origin not given. (B-10, *Albuq*.) The name suggests a possible derivation from Captain Martín de Aldai, in northern Mexico during Reconquest times.

A *José Patrocinio Aldás*, son of Paulín Aldás and María Dolores Martínez, was first married to *Margarita Valdez*, then married *Octaviana Muñiz* on July 29, 1872. He was then residing at La Cueva in Río Arriba County, and could possibly be the son of the original Paulín Aldás by a second wife. (M, *El Rito*.)

ALEXANDER. *David Alejandro* (Alexander), of the United States of North America, the son of Samuel Alejandro and Marta de Fulerton (Martha Fullerton), married *Guadalupe Valencia* in Santa Fe, Aug. 7, 1842. (M-54, *Santa Fe*.) Bancroft mentions a David W. Alexander, Irish trader from New Mexico at San Bernardino and Los Angeles; but his wife there was a daughter of Manuel Requena. (*Op. cit.*)

For *Cyrus Alexander*, see Gordon *infra*.

ALFARO. *Guadalupe Alfaro*, residing at Alameda, married *Paula García* in 1837. His parents were José María Alfaro and María Luz Mata, residents of Mexico City. (DM, 1837.) Three known children were: *Juan Pablo*, Jan. 28, 1841; *Ana María*, July 29, 1842; and *Victor Modesto*, June 22, 1844. (B-8 and B-9, *Albuq*.) Here the mother's name is given as "Dolores" for the first and last child, and as "Paula" for the middle one.

ALLEN. *José Manuel Alen*, a native of Canada and 31 years old, was baptized at Taos on May 18, 1828. His parents were Justo Alen (Hughes Allen?) and Careh (Cary?) --------. (B-47, *Taos*.)

Gabriel Allen, a native of the United States of North America, married *María Refugio Sánchez* in Santa Fe, Mar. 31, 1843. His parents were -------- Allen and Ana Richas (Richards?). (M-54, *Santa Fe*.)

ALMANSA. *Feliz Almansa*, a native of the province of San Antonio Bejar, married *María Lorenza Baca* in Santa Fe, Feb. 24, 1824. His parents were Eulogio Almansa and Josefa Franco. (M-53, *Santa Fe*.) Their son *Francisco* married *Narcisa Vigil*, who had a child, *Bernabé*, at Las Vegas, June 11, 1856. (B, *Las Vegas*.)

ALVARADO. *Rafael Alvarado*, the son of Apolinario Alvarado and María Francisca Moreno, married *María Guadalupe Baca* at Socorro, Jan. 6, 1825. His place of origin is not given. (M-57, *Socorro*.)

ALVAREZ. *Agapito Alvarez* and wife *Juana García*, natives of Plaza Tabalopa, were living in Albuquerque when their son *Anselmo* was baptized, April 22, 1846. The couple's parents were Vicente Alvarez and Victoria Sánchez, Pablo García and Antonia Martínez, respectively. (B-10, *Albuq*.)

AMBRULE. *Luis Ambrule*, a Frenchman and native of St. Louis, married *Marcelina Casados* at Taos, Aug. 14, 1824. His parents were Francisco Ambrues and María Maglen. (B-38, *Taos*, M section.)

ANDRADA. *José Alberto Pablo de Andrada* married *María Gertrudis Barranca* in Taos, Mar. 31, 1833. (M-39, *Taos*.) Their place of origin is not given. Two children of theirs were baptized in Taos, *Atanasio* in 1834 and *María Dolores* in 1837. Here the grandparents are given as José Manuel de Jesús de Andrada and María Olalla Trinidad Caba, Juan Barranca and Josefa (or Ana María) Durán, respectively. (B-49 and B-51, *Taos*.)

ANDRES, ANDREWS. *George Andrés*, a native of Pennsylvania, 26 years old, and the son of Abraham Andrés (Andrews?) and Luciana Aleri (Lucy Ann Ellery?), was baptized at Taos, Oct. 29, 1828. (B-47, *Taos*.) On Mar. 3, 1829, he married *María Luz Hurtado*. Here his mother's name is given as Luciana Rechi (Lucy Ann Ritchie?). (M-39, *Taos*.)

ANGNEY. *William Angney*, of the United States of America, the son of R. and C. Angney, married *Isabel Conklin* in Santa Fe, Feb. 11, 1849. (M-55, *Santa Fe*.)

ANONYMOUS. *Juan Manuel*, 26 years of age and a native of New Jersey, was baptized in Santa Fe in 1826. (AASF, 1826, no. 4.)

José Tomás, an "American Adult" living in Pojoaque, was baptized on Sept. 28, 1825. He was a native of Philadelphia and 29 years old. (B-25, *San Ildefonso*.)

José Benito, an "American Adult" and native of the "City of Quintoque" (Kentucky), was baptized at San Miguel on April 3, 1835. (B-1, *San Miguel del Vado*.)

Julián "el Americano," native of the United States of America, married *María Francisca Toledo* at San Miguel, Nov. 28, 1848. (M-2, *San Miguel del Vado*.)

ANTAYA. *Isidro Antaya*, a stranger and native of St. Louis, received permission to marry *Teodora Romero*, widow of José Francisco Sandoval, of Taos, July 17, 1829. (AASF, *Patentes*, LXX.) The marriage took place at Taos on July 29. Here his parents are given as Pedro Antaya and Catarina Pelquié. (M-39, *Taos*.)

ARCENÓ. *Miguel Arcenó*, a Frenchman of Canada, married *María Encarnación*, widow of José Manuel Romero of Taos, Aug. 15, 1825. (B-38, *Taos*, M section.) The baptisms of their children contain a confusing variety of names, as follows. *María Alvina*, child of Miguel Arcenó and Rita Sánchez, May 26, 1829; paternal grandparents, Luis Arcenó and Maria Alvina Laví. (B-47, *Taos*.) *María Rosa*, child of Miguel *Arronó* and Rita Sánchez, Aug. 8, 1829 (delayed baptisms of twin, or adopted child?); paternal grandparents, Luis *Arronó* and María Alvina ------------. (*Ibid*.) *Luis de la Asención*, son of Miguel *Arromó* and *Mariana* Sánchez, June 1, 1832; paternal grandparents, Luis Arromó and María Alvina "de Canadá." (B-48, *Taos*.) On Jan. 31, 1825, Miguel *Arcenón* and Rita Sánchez had stood as godparents for a bastard Pawnee child belonging to Antonio Ledoux. (B-38, *Taos*.)

ARCHUNDI. *José María Archundi*, 28 years old and single, married *María Manuela Chávez* at Tomé, Oct. 24, 1825. His parents were José Francisco Archundi and María Marcelina Cambrán (Sambrán?). No place of origin given. (B-54, *Tomé*.)

ARMENDARIS. *José Antonio Armendaris* married *María Manuela Laguna*, widow of Pedro Cariago (*see* Carriaga *infra*), at Socorro, May, 1839. His parents were Pedro Armendaris and María de Jesús Quesada. No place of origin given. (M-57, *Socorro*.) Most likely a scion of the Pedro de Armendaris family of Chihuahua and of the original grantee of the Valverde grant near Socorro. *See* NMF, p. 135.

ARRIETA. Antonio Romero and his wife *Ana María Arrieta*, daughter of Ramón Arrieta and Dolores Maes (Mier?), had a son, José Miguel, baptized at Taos, Oct. 2, 1829. Mother's place of origin not given. (B-47, *Taos*.)

A *Rufina Arrieta*, adult and a native of El Paso, died in Santa Fe, Feb. 16, 1781. (*Bur.*, 51, *Castrense*.) She was evidently a soldier's wife.

AVILA. *Francisco Avila*, a native of Durango and the son of Tomás Avila and Guadalupe Montes, married *María Josefa Vigil* at Santa Cruz, June 21, 1821. (M-32, *Santa Cruz*.)

José Miguel Avila, a native of Guadalajara and 7 years in New Mexico, married *María Lugarda Montoya* in Albuquerque, July 30, 1827. (M-5, *Albuq.*)

BACHLET. *José Bachlet*, a native of Germany, married *María Refugio Martínez* at Taos, Aug. 28, 1848. His parents were Francisco Xavier Bachlet (Balket, Baclay?) and María Catarina Jacobina. (M-41, *Taos*.)

BALDISÁN. *José Antonio Baldisán*, the son of Francisco Baldisán and Ana María Prudencio, married *Juana Gertrudis Maes* at San Miguel, Nov. 24, 1848. (M, *San Miguel del Vado*.) At the baptism of their first child, *Francisco Antonio*, Oct. 22, 1849, the name is spelled *Balisán*, and the grandmother's surname is rendered *Provencio*. For a second child, *Epigmenia*, Mar. 25, 1851, the family name is spelled *Valdisán*. (Both in B-54, *Taos*.)

BALLANT. *Juan Santiago José Ballant*, the son of Francisco Ballant and María Teresa "Gutiérrez," married *María Candelaria Cortés* at Taos, Jan. 25, 1836. (M-40, *Taos*.) Place of origin not given. At the baptism of one child, *María Teresa*, Oct. 23, 1839, the surname is spelled "Ballán," and the paternal grandmother is María Teresa Gotier (Gautheir). The date of baptism of another child, *José Cicilio*, is illegible. Here the surname is spelled "Bayá." (Both in B-51, *Taos*.)

BALY. *Alejandro Baly*, a native of St. Louis, married *Carmen Seballes* in Santa Fe, Oct. 17, 1845. His parents were Charles Valy (Valley, Bailey?) and Angilio de Lord (Ann Julia Lord?). (M-55, *Santa Fe*.)

BAÑUELOS. *Eugenio Bañuelos* and wife *Juana Montaño* were residents of Belén, where two children were born. He was the son of Gabriel "Vañuelos" and Teresa Avila, but his place of origin is not given. A daughter, *María Concepción*, was baptized on Dec. 8, 1826, and a son, *José Tiburcio*, on April 14, 1829. (Both in B-10, *Belén*). Ten years later the family name is rendered CAÑUELOS in the baptism of *María Marcelina*, Nov. 9, 1835, child of Eugenio Cañuelas and Ana María García (second wife?); paternal grandparents are Gabriel Cañuelas and Teresa Avalos. (B-11, *Belén*.)

BARCELÓ. This family furnished enough material for an article, which was published in EL PALACIO, vol. 57, no. 8, and which dealt mainly with the origin and character of the famed Gertrudis Barceló. Her only known brother was *Trinidad Barceló*, who was married to *María Dolores Griego*. These had a daughter, *María Filomena*, baptized at Taos, July 7, 1831. (B-48, *Taos*.) Although the Barceló family was originally established in the Tomé district, Trinidad in later years followed political and educational pursuits in the north Río Arriba country, hence possibly the reason for his famed sister being thought a native of Taos.

An *Antonio Barceló*, the son of Antonio Barceló and Josefa Lafuente, was living in Las Vegas with his wife, *Juana Sánchez*, when their son *Zenobio* was baptized, Oct. 30, 1854. (B, *Las Vegas*.) He evidently did not belong to the preceding family yet could be somehow related and from the same place of origin.

BARRANCA. *Juan Barranca* and wife *Josefa Durán* were residents of Taos, but their place of origin is not known. Their daughter *Gertrudis* had a natural child, Ana María, Sept. 17, 1829 (B-47, *Taos*), and later married Pablo Andrada, *q.v. supra*.

BARRIOS. *José Gumercindo Barrios*, a native of the province of Sonora, married *Rafaela Carvajal* of Albuquerque in 1826. IIe was the son of Francisco Barrios and Juana María Arias. (DM, 1826.) The same surname existed in New Mexico prior to the 1680 Indian Revolt but seems to have been corrupted to "Varos" and "Baros." *See* NMF, pp. 11, 146.

BAULÓN. *Rafael Baulón* of Sabinal, the natural son of María Manuela Baulón, married *María Josefa Jirón* at Belén, Jan. 1, 1842. Place of origin not given. (DM, 1841; M-7, *Belén*.)

BEAUBIEN. *Carlos Hipólito Beaubien*, the son of Pablo Beaubien and María Luisa Durocher, married *Marie Paula Lobato* at Taos, Sept. 11, 1827. Place of origin not given. (M-39, *Taos*.) Their known children were: *José Narciso*, Oct. 30, 1827 (B-47, *Taos*); *María de la Luz*, June 28, 1829, who married Lucien Maxwell, Mar. 27, 1842 (B-47 and M-40, *Taos*); *Pablo*, who married Rebeca Abreú, natural daughter of Soledad Abreú, in Santa Fe, Aug. 6, 1870 (M, *Santa Fe*); *María Leonor Dolores*, Mar. 31, 1833 (B-49, *Taos*); *María Teodora*, Jan. 31, 1835 (*ibid.*); *Juana*, July 8, 1838; *Juan Lucas*, July 6, 1840; a second *María Teodora*, May 8, 1842; *María Petra*, July 2, 1844 (all in B-51, *Taos*); and *Juan Cristóbal*, Aug. 24, 1848 (B-53, *Taos*). Curiously, the mother's name is left out in the last baptism. On Sept. 7, 1839, was baptized Juan Manuel, a Ute slave (*famulo*) of Carlos Beaubien. (B-51, *Taos*.)

Juan Bautista Beaubien, a native of Canada and resident of San Antonio del Río Colorado, married *María Arcaria Espinosa* at Taos, Oct. 2, 1849. He was the son of Antonio Beaubien and Teresa Parant. (M-41, *Taos*.) Their known children were: *María Simona*, Nov. 7, 1850 (B-54, *Taos*); *José Nerio*, Aug. 28, 1854; *Juan Bautista*, Mar. 20, 1857; and *Charles Frederick*, Feb. 5, 1860 (all in B-1, *Arroyo Hondo*).

BECERRA. See EL PALACIO, *loc. cit.*

BECKWITH. *José Enriques Beckwith*, from the United States of America, the son of Ricardo Beckwith, married *Refugio Rascón* in Santa Fe, Dec. 22, 1849. (M-55, *Santa Fe*.)

BEIDLER. *Juan Beidler*, 27 years old and a native of Pennsylvania, the son of Jacob Beidler and Magdalena Tauque (Tauch?), was baptized on Jan. 1, 1832. (B-48, *Taos*.)

BELIZ. *José Demetrio, Beliz*, 26 years old and a native of "Senequii" (Senecu del Paso?), married *María Bartola Silva* at Belén, Oct. 2, 1843. His parents were Manuel Beliz and Guadalupe Páiz. (DM, 1843; M-7, *Belén*.)

BENT. *María Soledad*, natural child of *Guadalupe Bente*, was baptized at Taos, Mar. 24, 1845. The mother was a squaw ransomed from the "Indians of the North" and a servant of Carlos Bent. The godparents were *Elfego Bent* and Romualda Luna. (B-51, *Taos*.)

BERGAND. *Luis Bergand (Bergaud?)*, a native of St. Louis living in Arroyo Seco, received permission to marry *María Paula Sánchez* of Taos, Aug. 22, 1830. (AASF, *Patentes*, LXX.)

BERTOL. *Alejandro Bertol* and wife *Carmen Sisneros* had a child, *María Donaciana*, baptized at Taos, Feb. 21, 1842. His parents are given as Juan Bautista Bertol and María Basilia Segundo. Place of origin not given. (B-51, *Taos*.)

BLACK. *Julián (William) Blax* married *Juana María Chávez* at Socorro, Jan. 12, 1851. No other data given. (M-58, *Socorro*.) On June 27, 1861, *María Ana Blak*, daughter of Julián Blak and Marcelina Salas (first wife?), married Teofilo Chávez of Valencia in Santa Fe. (M, *Santa Fe*.) It is to be noted that the old Padres consistently rendered "William" as "Julián."

BLANCHARD. *Antonio Blanchard* married *Gertrudis Trujillo* at Taos, July 12, 1826. (M-38, *Taos*.) They had these known children: *José Francisco*, April 6, 1831, and *María Vibiana*, June 23, 1833, when the surname is spelled "Brachal." In the first baptism the father is designated as a Frenchman; in the second he is mentioned as the son of Bautista Brachal and Vibiana Motray. (B-48 and B-49, *Taos*.) Another child was *Susana*, who had two illegitimate children: Desiderio, Feb. 12, 1851, and Juan Antonio, June 17, 1852 (B-54, *Taos*); she then married Francisco Antonio Lafebre,

June 6, 1853, when her surname is spelled "Brashal." (M-41, *Taos*.) Another son, *Bartolo*, married *María Rosa Gutiérrez*, Feb. 21, 1842, when the surname is "Branchal." (M-40, *Taos*.) Still another son, *Antonio Domingo*, married *María Paula Sandoval*, Nov. 2, 1848, when the name is "Brashal" (M-41, *Taos*); then as "Blanchard" he married *María Asención Chávez*, widow of Rafael Sáiz of Ocate, Feb. 7, 1867. (M-46, *Mora*.)

Old Antonio "Brashall" himself, a native of Canada and widowed of Gertrudis Trujillo, married *María Rosalía Silva* in Taos, Mar. 4, 1850. (M-41, *Taos*.)

BLANCO. *Enrique Blanco (Blanc)*, vagrant stranger, received permission to marry *María Guadalupe López* of Taos, Feb. 16, 1832. (AASF, *Patentes*, LXX.) They had a son, *Francisco Antonio*, Jan. 13, 1845; here the father's name is "Alarid" Blanco, the son of Francisco Blanco and Amable Colorada. (B-52, *Taos*.) These grandparents were very likely a French-Canadian and a northern squaw.

Guillermo Blanco (Blanc) was a native of "Nueva Costa de Canadá" (Nova Scotia?), the son of Augustín Blanco and Margarita Rubinson (Robinson). He married *María Albina Vigil* of Taos, Nov. 27, 1844. (M-40, *Taos*.) They had a son, *José Antonio*, Sept. 21, 1845, when the same paternal grandparents are given. (B-52, *Taos*.)

BLANE. *José Manuel de Blan* was living at Santa Barbara (Peñasco) when he married *Cristerna Martín*, Feb. 25, 1828. (M-21, *Picurís*.) They had a son, *José Crisanto*, at Lo de Mora, Oct. 25, 1853, when the surname is spelled "Blane." (B, *Las Vegas*.) A daughter, *Rafaela*, married Andrés Menedú at Mora, Feb. 13, 1866, when the name is "Blay" and "Blan." (M-46, *Mora*.) Another daughter, *Manuela*, married Domingo Leal at Mora, Dec. 19, 1868 (*ibid*.).

BLUMTER. *Carlos Bernardo Teodoro Daniel Blumter*, a native of Prussia, married *María Feliciana Quintana* in Santa Fe, Feb. 3, 1849. His parents were Daniel Blumter and Juana Peters. (M-55, *Santa Fe*.)

BOCANEGRA. *José Antonio Bocanegra*, 45 years old and a native of Querétaro, married *Juana María Cordoba*, widow of Juan Francisco Herrera, May 16, 1809. His parents were José Bocanegra and Dominga Antonia Monares (?). (M-21, *Picurís*.) This pre-1820 item belongs in NMF.

BOGGS. *José Tomás Boggs*, 37 years old and a native of the United States of America, the son of Andrés Boggs and Elena Hopkins (?), was baptized at Taos, April 3, 1827. (B-48, *Taos*.)

Tomás Bogs, single, a native of Missouri, married *María Romualda Luna* of Taos, May 22, 1846. His parents were Lilborn Bogs and Maria Pantalu (?) Boon. (M-41, *Taos*.) They had a son, *Carlos Adolfo*, Oct. 2, 1848; for the paternal grandparents' names is the undecipherable phrase, "Yum Paeteha" (?). (B-53, *Taos*.)

BOLÍVAR. *Don Atanasio de Bolívar* is mentioned, Dec. 29, 1805, as having a ranch in the Pecos Valley. (*Bur*., 9, *Galisteo-Pecos*.) On Aug. 13, 1809, he received permission to marry *Doña Petra Bustamante*. He was a native of Villa de Vilvao (Bilbao) in the province of Santander. (AASF, *Patentes*, LXX.) The pre-1820 item should be in NMF.

BONNY. *Enriques Boné* and *Francisca Varela* had a daughter, *María Rufina*, Jan. 9, 1844. His parents are given as Francisco Boné and María Luz Vin. (B-51, *Taos*.)

Santiago Boné (Bonney) and *María Juana Mascareñas* were living at La Junta de los Rios (Watrous) when an adult servant or slave of theirs (*famulo*) was baptized on Feb. 13, 1845. (B-52, *Taos*.)

Ramón Bonny, son of Santiago Bonny and María Vibiana Martín, married *Concepción Padilla*, Nov. 21, 1875. (M-46, *Mora*.)

BORDEAUX. *Victor Bordéo, Bardaux,* or *Vordaux,* a native of France and settler in the United States, married *Rafaela González* at Socorro, May 6, 1849. His parents were Pedro Bordaux and Angelica Gelin. (DM, 1849; M-58, *Socorro.*)

BRANCH. *José de Jesús Branch,* 30 years of age and a native of Virginia, the son of Pedro Branch and María Escort (Scott), was baptized at Taos, June 8, 1828. (B-47, *Taos.*) On Jan. 14, 1829, he married *María Paula Luna.* (M-39, *Taos.*) Their known children were: *José Ricardo* and *José Alejandra* (twins evidently), baptized on Dec. 4, 1830 (1829?) and Jan. 9, 1831 (1830?), respectively. (B-47 and B-48, *Taos.*) Ricardo married María Francisca Trujillo of Taos, May 10, 1852. (M-41, *Taos.*) Then there were: *Vital,* May 2, 1833; *María Luisa,* June 4, 1835; *Elfego,* Jan. 22, 1837 (all in B-49, *Taos*); a second *Alejandro,* April 3, 1839; and *José de Jesús,* Oct. 22, 1840 (both in B-51, *Taos*).

On April 24, 1838, were baptized two Ute children, María Ignacia (12) and José Antonio (4), belonging to this family; likewise, in 1840, the lad José Francisco (7), ransomed from the Paiutes. (All in B-51, *Taos.*) In all these entries the family name is variously spelled "Branch, Branche, Branchi," while Branch's own mother appears as "Marta Scott, Matiana Escorte, Mades Scott, Matea Escot and Escor."

BRESEDA. *José Espiridión Breseda,* a native of Monterrey, and rescued from Indian captivity, married *Vibiana Ulibarrí* at San Miguel in 1843. His parents were Ramón Breseda and Juana García. (M, *San Miguel del Vado.*)

BRISOL. *Juan Olivia Brisol* was a Frenchman living in Taos in April, 1826. (AASF, *Accounts,* LXVI.) He married *María Teodora Romero,* July 27, 1826. (*Ibid.,* LXVII; B-38, *Taos.*) Compare with Sanserman *infra.*

BRISON. See Sanserman *infra.*

BRITAN. *Tomás Britan* (Burton?) and *Guadalupe Esquivel* had a daughter, *Dorotea,* who married Juan B. Carter in Santa Fe, Dec. 15, 1845. (M-55, *Santa Fe.*) Bancroft mentions a Lewis T. Burton, a Tennessean from New Mexico with the Wolfskill party in California in 1831. (*Op. cit.*)

BROWN. *Francisco Broune,* a native of St. Louis, requested to marry *María Rosalía González* of Vallecito in Jémez, Feb. 15, 1851. His parents were George Broune and María Dewitt. (DM, 1851.) Known children were: *José Ynés,* Feb. 21, 1854 (B, *Jémez*), who married Antonia González of Las Vegas, Sept. 26, 1881 (M, *Las Vegas*); *Florencia,* confirmed on June 16, 1855 (B, *Jémez*), who married Manuel Sozalla at Las Vegas, May 9, 1881 (M, *Las Vegas*); *María Estefana de los Reyes,* Jan. 6, 1859 (B, *Jémez*); *Prudencia,* who married Jacinto Sedillo, Feb. 2, 1885; and *Jacinta,* who married Luis Ulibarrí, Sept. 3, 1888 (both in M, *Las Vegas*).

BUJANDA. *Miguel Bujanda,* a native of Oposura in Sonora, married *Simona Lucero* of Albuquerque, Sept. 15, 1840. His parents were Dolores Bujanda and Josefa García. (DM, 1840; M-4, *Albuq.*)

BUSALET. Burial at Taos, June 30, 1824, of *Esteban BuenSalet* (corrected "Busalet"), bastard son of Francisco Buen Salet and an Indian servant in St. Louis. (B-38, *Taos.*)

CAMPBELL. *Ricardo Cambel* married *María Rosa Grijalva* at Taos, Sept. 25, 1828. (M-39, *Taos.*) He and Esteban Luis Lé (*see* Lee *infra*), both Presbyterians, had requested Catholic baptism in June, 1826; both men were natives of St. Louis. (AASF, *Accounts,* LXVI.) In the baptisms of two Campbell children, the father's parents are given as Juan Cambel and Nazarena Shircuy or Shiraig. The known children were as follows: *María Peregrina,* Nov., 1828 (B-47, *Taos*), who became the wife of Simón Delgado (*see* marriage of brother Manuel *infra*); *José Julián Ricardo,* Aug. 11, 1831 (B-48, *Taos*), who married Antonia Constante in Santa Fe, Jan. 7, 1859 (M, *Santa Fe*); *María Petra,* Mar. 10, 1833 (B-49, *Taos*), who married José Peregrino Peres in 1847 (B-55, *Santa Fe*); *José*, Jan. 1, 1835 (B-49, *Taos*); *Gertrudis*, who married William Henry Lent (Kent?), Aug. 19, 1860 (M, *Santa Fe*); *María de la Paz*, who married Manuel Nevares in 1846 (M-55, *Santa Fe*); and *Manuel*, who married Josefa Delgado in Sept., 1868, with a dispensation (M, *Santa Fe*).

CANO. Two women of this name in Santa Fe had come from military posts in northern Mexico with their families or husbands. *Doña Guadalupe Cano*, a native of Real de Cosihuiriachic, came with her husband, Don Rafael Marioni; after his death she received permission to marry Rafael López, a Santa Fe soldier, Dec. 16, 1830. (AASF, *Patentes*, LXX.) *María Ignacia Cano*, daughter of Ignacio Cano and Ana María del Pilar Quiroa, married Franklin Read, Oct. 28, 1849. (M-55, *Santa Fe*.)

CANTÚN. *José Felipe Cantún*, living in the Santa Cruz valley, married *María Francisca Martínez*, Nov. 10, 1852. He was the son of Toribio Cantún and Guadalupe Benavides. No place of origin mentioned. (M-33a, *Santa Cruz*.) He next married *María Refugio Salazar*, Jan. 19, 1863. (M-45, *San Ildefonso*.)

CAÑUELAS. *See* Bañuelos *supra*.

CAQUINDÓ. *Juan Caquindó*, 24 years old and a native of Quintoque (Kentucky), the son of Santiago Caquindó and María Espier (Spear?), was baptized at Taos, Mar. 3, 1831. (B-48, *Taos*.) Juan Kaquindó and a Quirina Lodú were godparents together at Mora, Feb. 12, 1845. (B-52, *Taos*.) He was referred to as a convert when buried at Lo de Mora, Oct. 18, 1845. (Bur., 21, *Picurís*.)

CARBONÓ. *Luis Carbonó (Carboneau?)* and María Rosalía Ordens were godparents together at Mora, Aug. 12, 1845. (B-52, *Taos*.)

CÁRDENAS. *Quirino Cárdenas*, a soldier of the Company of Carrizal in Santa Fe, married *Concepción Torres*, Dec. 15, 1844. His parents were José Cárdenas and Vicenta Salinas. (M-54, *Santa Fe*.)

CARIEL. *See* Larié *infra*.

CARREJO. *Juan José Carrejo*, a native of the state of Chihuahua, married *María Tomasa Trujillo* in Santa Fe, Dec. 26, 1834. His parents were Juan José Carrejo and Guadalupe Tafoya. (M-53, *Santa Fe*.)

CARRIAGA. *Pedro Carriaga*, "an adult and outlander," died at Tomé, Oct. 1, 1838. "Wife unknown." (Bur., 54, *Tomé*.) We know that his wife was *Manuela Laguna*, from the marriage of their son Desiderio to Dolores Baca at Socorro, June 8, 1851. (M-58, *Socorro*.) In 1839 Manuela Laguna married Pedro Armendaris, *q.v. supra*.

CARSON. *Cristóbal Corson*, 32 years old and a native of Missouri, the son of Linsey Corson and Rebeca Roberson, was baptized at Taos, Jan. 28, 1843, with Luis Lee and María Cruz Padilla as godparents. "In this region since the age of 14—acted as a hunter in the region to the North; baptized by Anabaptists, whose errors he abjured." (B-51, *Taos*.) On Feb. 6, 1843, he married *María Josefa Jaramillo*, a native of Santa Cruz, with George Bente and María Cruz Padilla as sponsors. The same parents are given (mother's name spelled "Roverzon"), with Missouri as his place of origin. (M-40, *Taos*.) Known children: *Carlos Adolfo*, May 6, 1850, his father absent at the time (B-53, *Taos*); and *Julián*, Oct. 6, 1852 (B-54, *Taos*).

CARTER. *Juan Bautista Carter*, of the United States of America, married *Dorotea Britan* in Santa Fe, Dec. 15, 1845. His parents were Roberto Carter and Liano (Lee Anna?) Davis. (M-55, *Santa Fe*.) Their daughter *Francisca* married Bartolomé Varela, Oct. 3, 1864. (M, *Santa Fe*.)

CEBADA. *José María Cebada*, a widower of Tomé, asked to marry *María Serafina Varela* in 1840. No place of origin given. (DM, 1840.)

CELIS. *Gregorio Celis*, a soldier of the Company of San Elizario in Santa Fe, married *María Juana Rael*, April 12, 1845. His parents were Julián Celis and Josefa Tafoya. (M-54, *Santa Fe*.) He was evidently a member of the Rubín de Celis family of El Paso.

CHALIFÚ. *Pedro Chalifú*, stranger, widower of Victoria Carsot, married *María Dolores Apodaca* at Taos, Dec. 29, 1829. (M-39, *Taos*.) He was designated as a native of Canada and the widower of Victoria Curzot, when granted permission to marry the Apodaca woman of Taos, Dec. 6, 1829. (AASF, *Patentes*, LXX.) Their known children were: *Juan de Jesús*, July 10, 1831, when the paternal grandparents are given as Pedro Chalifú and María Veltrán; and *José Pablo*, Dec. 8, 1832, when the same grandparents are written down as José Chalifú and María Angul. In both baptisms the mother's surname is "Carrillo" instead of "Apodaca." (B-41, *Taos*.) Bancroft mentions a certain Charlefoux, a Canadian from New Mexico who went to California in 1837-40, with a company of Shawnees, trappers, traders, and horse thieves. (*Op. cit.*)

CHAMBERS. On Jan. 12, 1831, *Samuel Chambres* and María Petra Valle were godparents in Taos for a Partué child. (B-48, *Taos*.)

CHANGLE. *Tomás Changle (Chandler?)*, a native of Quintoque (Kentucky), married *Juliana López*, widow of Ramón Cárdenas and a native of Santa Rosalía de Chihuahua, June 3, 1849. His parents were Juan Changle and Urinea (Irene?) ----------. (M-55, *Santa Fe*.)

CHARETTE. *Pedro Sharete* and wife *Ignacia Miera* had a son, *Juan Luis*, Aug. 26, 1828, when the paternal grandparents are given as Pedro Sarete and Margarita Lovó. (B-47, *Taos*.) This son married Candelaria Martínez at Taos, Feb. 3, 1851. (M-41, *Taos*.) Another son, *Jesús María Charette*, married María Manuela Martínez at Cimarrón, Jan. 10, 1872. (M-46, *Mora*.) A daughter, *Romualda Charette*, married Henry Schultz in Santa Fe, Mar. 3, 1868. (M, *Santa Fe*.)

CHARRET or CHARVET. *See* Servé in EL PALACIO, *loc. cit.*

CHAUBELÓN. *Juan Chaubelón*, the son of Juan Chaubelón and María Blé, married *María Vibiana Martínez* at Taos, July 23, 1827. (M-39, *Taos*.) Three known children were: *José Antonio*, April 24, 1828 (B-47, *Taos*), who married Gabriela Gallegos, Mar. 10, 1866 (M-46, *Mora*); *Juan Bautista*, Feb. 14, 1830, who married María Francisca Salas, Nov. 25, 1850 (B-47 and M-41, *Taos*); and *José Manuel*, June 18, 1833, when his father's mother is designated as "Ana María de Francia." (B-49, *Taos*.) In the 1866 marriage entry the family name is spelled "Choplot."

CHAVARRÍA. *Don Manuel Chavarría* was a Mexican official residing in the Bernalillo area in the years following Mexico's independence. He and a Petra Felipa Crespín acted as godparents for a Peña Blanca child, Jan. 6, 1826. (M-35, *Santa Ana*.)

CHILAGE. *José Chilage*, son of Román Chilage and María Antonia Montoya, married *María Gerónima Martín*, Feb. 20, 1837. (M-22, *Pojoaque*.) This might be a local Indian name. Likewise, CHIRINA: *Pedro Chirina*, the son of Antonio or Asencio Chirina and Agustina Gemes or Gemé, was married to *Rosalía Silva*. Two known children were *María Quirina*, Feb., 1830, and *José Eugenio*, Mar. 22, 1838. (B-47 and B-51, *Taos*.)

CHUNT. *Catarina*, French, infant daughter of *Francisco* and *Isabel Chunt*, was buried on Dec. 13, 1823. She had been baptized on Sept. 23, when her parents are given as Francisco "Lut" and Isabel Escoyens. (B-38, *Taos*.)

CISNEROS. *Alcario Cisneros*, a soldier of the Company of Chihuahua in Santa Fe, married *María Eduvigen Sarracino*, Mar. 29, 1845. His parents were Pantaleón Cisneros and Fabiana García. (M-54, *Santa Fe*.)

CLARK. *Elías Clarque*, a native of Ireland and son of Santiago Clarke and María Siquerine (?), married *María Marta Lucero*, April 26, 1850. (M-29, *San Juan*.)

CONKLIN. *Santiago Concle*, stranger, the son of Santiago Concle and María Baltivin (Baldwin?), married *Juana Ortiz* of Santa Fe, Jan. 23, 1829, a dispensation from affinity having been granted. (M-53, *Santa Fe*.) Known children married as follows: *María Trinidad* to Julián Tully, Jan. 5, 1848; *Isabel* to William Angney in 1849 — and evidently later to Oliver B. Hovey (marriages of Clara and Santiago Hovey in 1880, 1886); *Josefa* to Clemente Ortiz, Oct. 25, 1861; and *Carlos* (surname first spelled "Conklin") to Josefa Valencia, June 11, 1859. (All in M, *Santa Fe*.)

CONN. *Francisco Conn*, 30 years old and a native of Quintoque (Kentucky), the son of Samuel Conn, Presbyterian, and María Isabel Ris (Reece?), was baptized at Taos, Jan. 26, 1834. (B-49, *Taos*.)

CONNELLY. *Enrique Conel* was married to *Dolores Perea* of the Río Abajo, by whom he had these known children: *María Victoriana*, Dec. 15, 1849; and *Julián*, 1855, at Los Pinos, and name now spelled "Connelly" (both in B, *Isleta*). The girl married John F. Viven of Albany, N.Y., in 1866 (M, *Santa Fe*), while another son, *Henry*, married Eufelia Romero at Los Lunas, Feb. 1, 1879. (M, *Isleta*.)

CONOLE. *Pedro Conole* (*Concle* or *Conklin*, or *Connelly?*) and wife *María Reyes Durán* were living in Taos when their daughter *María Ignacia* was baptized, Feb. 7, 1827. The paternal grandparents were Mateo Conole and Rosalía Sánchez. (B-47, *Taos*.)

CONSTANTE. *Andrés Constant*, of the United States of America, married *Ramona Sandoval* in Santa Fe, Mar. 19, 1840. (M-54, *Santa Fe*.) When their daughter *Antonia* married Ricardo Campbell in 1859, her mother's name was given as Juana Sandoval.

Luis Constante, from St. Louis, the son of Luis Constante and Magdalena Salltes (?), married *Francisco Sandoval* in Santa Fe, April 7, 1847. (M-55, *Santa Fe*.) Perhaps he was a younger brother or relative of Andrés.

COPA. *Juan Manuel Copa*, the son of Julián Copa and Isabel Rico, married *María Josefa Varela* at Taos, May 1, 1828. (M-39, *Taos*.) Two children of theirs were *Juana María*, May 18, 1828 (B-47, *Taos*), and *José Celedón*, Aug. 28, 1830, when his mother's name is given as "Mat" instead of "Rico." (B-48, *Taos*.)

CORTES. *José María Cortés*, a native of Mexico City but living in Santa Fe since childhood, married *Apolonia Lobata*, May 8, 1823. (M-53, *Santa Fe*.)

A *Juan Cristóbal Cortés del Rey* was living in Taos in 1801, when he petitioned the bishop to build the church in the Plaza de Nuestra Señora de Guadalupe. (AASF, *Patentes*, XV.) This pre-1820 item should be in NMF.

COY. *Pedro Andrés Coy*, stranger, married *Marcelina Roybal* in Santa Fe, Dec. 16, 1832. No other data given. (M-53, *Santa Fe*.)

CRUÉ. *José Marcial Crué* (*Joseph Marshall Grey?*), 34 years old, and a native of "Glen in the United States of America," was baptized when very ill at the *vinatería* of Don Blas Trujillo in the Cañon del Río de Don Fernando near Taos. His parents were Julián Crué and María Silveria Naen. (B-51, *Taos*.)

DAVID. *José David*, 26 years old and a native of Pennsylvania, the son of Jacob David and Nancy Nima (Niemer, Niemeyer?), was baptized at Taos, June 19, 1831. (B-48, *Taos*.)

DAVIS. *Julián Devis*, "de la Independencia de los E.U." (Independence, Mo., or Republic of the U.S.?), married *Refugio Rodríguez* in Santa Fe, Nov. 5, 1849. His parents were Andrés Devis and María Fled (?). (M-55, *Santa Fe*.)

DAY. *Benjamin Day*, a native of Quintoque (Kentucky), married *María Polonia Trujillo* of Taos, June 2, 1851. His parents were José and Sarah Day. (M-41, *Taos*.) There was a daughter, *María Leonor*, Oct. 22, 1848, when her father's name is given as "Benito," and her grandmother's as "Serafina" instead of "Sarah." (B-53, *Taos*.) Bancroft has a Benjamin Day, American hatter at Monterey in 1834-46, who was perhaps one of Young's trappers from New Mexico. (*Op. cit.*)

DECLUET. *Julio Decluet*, a native of New Orleans, received permission to marry *Dolores Trujillo* of Taos, June 19, 1829. (AASF, *Patentes*, LXX.) Mentioned together with four other Frenchmen who wished to marry Taos women is a *Francisco Le-Clair*, June 5, 1826, asking to marry a Dolores Trujillo (*ibid.*, *Accounts*, LXVI). In any case, Julio Decluet, the son of Caballero (Chevalier) Decluet and Francisca Vilse, did marry Dolores Trujillo, July 2, 1829. (M-39, *Taos*.) Two known children were: *José Polonio*, Feb. 10, 1830, when the father's name is given as "Francisco Yul" (Jules) without "Decluet" (B-47, *Taos*); and *María Petra*, May 3, 1832, when the father's name is "Francisco Julio," son of Caballero de Clued and María Francisca Vilze. (B-48, *Taos*.)

DELORA. *Pascual de la Hora, de la Ora*, or *Delora*, and wife *María Josefa Arias* were residents of Santa Fe for many years, but their place of origin is not given. A son, *José Demetrio*, born in Santa Fe, married María Isidora Trujillo at Taos, Sept. 7, 1841. (M-40, *Taos*.) Another son, *Miguel*, had married María Ignacia Martín in Santa Fe, April 11, 1824 (M-53, *Santa Fe*), and these had a son, Mariano, who married María Rosa Luján, Mar. 13, 1848. (M-55, *Santa Fe*.)

DENER. *Cristino Dener* (Christian Dehner?), a native of Kambogen in Germany, married *Soledad Gómez* at Taos, June 20, 1842. His parents were Auron (Aaron) Denera and Ana Margarita Denera. (M-40, *Taos*.) Known children were: *María Teodora*, April 2, 1843, whose paternal grandparents are given as Sanson (Samson) Dener and Margarita Ganson (B-51, *Taos*); *María Benigna*, Sept. 2, 1844 (B-52, *Taos*); *María Margarita*, May 22, 1846 (*ibid.*); and a second *María Teodora*, Sept. 11, 1850 (B-54, *Taos*). In these two entries the paternal grandparents are given as Tanson Denier and Margarita Demes, Auron Deme and Margarita Nimes. The second Teodora married José María Mestas of Agua Negra, Jan. 7, 1864. (M-46, *Mora*.)

An *Antonio de la Cruz Deanero*, the son of Leonisio Deanero and Juana Catalina López, married María Vidal Solán, Oct. 3, 1864. (*Ibid.*)

DEPEW. *Nicolás DePew*, a native of New York State, married *María Dolores Trujillo* at Taos, Dec. 30, 1850. His parents were Nicolás and Jessica DePew. (M-41, *Taos*.) Known children were: *María Catarina*, July 18, 1852, when the name is spelled "Lipiú" (B-54, *Taos*); and *María Eulogia*, named spelled "Dipiú," who married Juan de Jesús Salazar in 1873. (M-46, *Mora*.)

DESMARAIS. *Miguel Desmarais*, merchant, and a native of Canada, married *María Deluvina Vigil*, Jan. 24, 1848. His parents were Miguel Desmarais and María Luisa Chiconil. (M-41, *Taos*.) Known children were: *Luisa*, who married José Miguel Bernard, Jan. 1, 1865; *Paula*, who married Rafael Romero, June 27, 1871; and *Emma*, who married A. A. Senecal, May 1, 1881. (All in M, *Las Vegas*.)

DESPOR. *Francisco Despor*, a native of Canada, married *María Ynés Chávez* at Taos *in articulo mortis*. They already had two children. His parents were Juan Felix Despor and María Rombor. (M-39, *Taos*.) Their son *Francisco* married María Rafaela Madrid, April 3, 1848. (M-41, *Taos*.)

DEVENS. *José Martín Devens*, 27 years old and a native of Kentucky, the son of Agustín Devens and María Haliday, was baptized at Taos, Oct. 29, 1828. (B-47, *Taos*.)

DIAZ. *Longino Díaz*, son of Antonio Díaz and Dolores Romero, was a native of El Paso living in Belén with his wife *María Lázara*

Castrillo, when their daughter *María Ignacia Dolores* was baptized, Aug. 7, 1831. (B-10, *Belén*.)

Ermenegildo Díaz and wife *María Cruz Guerra* were also living in Belén when their daughter *María Estefana* was baptized, Dec. 28, 1835. The father was the son of Juan Francisco Díaz and Juliana Granillo; the mother's parents were Luz Guerra and Rita Ferán. (B-11, *Belén*.) These two *Díaz* families were probably closely related.

DORENCE. *Luis Dorence*, a native of Plamonte in France, married *María Juana Sandoval* in Santa Fe, July 6, 1850. His parents were Carlos Luis Dorence and Luisa Zarceur (?). (M-55, *Santa Fe*.)

DOYLE. *José Dayle*, a native of St. Louis residing at San Carlos de Napeste, married *María de la Cruz Suazo*, Oct. 14, 1844. His parents were Alejandro Dayle and Ana María Evans. (M-40, *Taos*.) Known children were: *Francisca Teresa*, Dec. 30, 1852, parents' surnames given as "Doly" and "Saíz"; *Florencia*, Nov. 8, 1855, parents' surnames given as "Doll" and "Suazo"; and *Alejandro*, May 27, 1858, parents' surnames given as "Doyle" and "Suazo." (All in B, *Las Vegas*.)

DUQUE. *Amado Duque*, a native of France, married *María Elena Mendoza* at San Miguel, Aug. 15, 1848. No other data given. (M-2, *San Miguel del Vado*.) See Amado Lamoris *infra*.

DURO. *Juan Duro*, a native of Chihuahua, married *Trinidad Ortega* in Santa Fe, Jan. 15, 1848. His parents were *José Duro* and -------- Serrano. (M-55, *Santa Fe*.)

ENELET. *George Enelet*, a stranger from "North America," married *Encarnación Mondragón* at Taos, Dec. 9, 1843. His parents were Pedro Enelet and María Benavides. (M-40, *Taos*.)

ERON. *Luis Antonio Eron (Erin, Aaron?)*, 25 years old and a native of Quintoque (Kentucky), the son of Tomás Eron and Rute Pen (Ruth Penn or Payne?), was baptized at Taos, Feb. 12, 1832. (B-48, *Taos*.)

ESCALANTE. *Juan Marcelino Escalante* married *María Polonia Cruz* at Taos, Nov. 1, 1832. No other data given. (M-39, *Taos*.) A son, *José Marcos*, was baptized on April 27, 1834, when the paternal grandparents are given as Jorge Escalante and Maxima García. (B-49, *Taos*.)

Tiburcio Escalante, a native of Villa de la Concepción, state of Chihuahua, asked to marry *María Manuela Chávez* of Albuquerque in 1846. He was the son of Pablo Escalante and Cirila Hernández. (DM, 1846.)

ESCOBAR. *Loreto Escobar*, vagrant, received permission to marry *Altagracia Trujillo* of Santa Fe, July 14, 1832. No other data given. (AASF, *Patentes*, LXX.)

ESPALÍN. *José Espalín* and wife *María Varela* lived in Taos where a daughter, *María Soledad*, was baptized on Jan. 13, 1825. The paternal grandparents were José Espalín and María Nieves Robles of El Paso del Norte. (B-38, *Taos*.)

FALEN. *Ricardo Falen (Phalen?)* and *Isabel Roberto (Roberts?)* were a foreign couple at Taos in 1842, when their child *Santiago (James)* was baptized on Nov. 10. Paternal grandparents were Santiago Falen and Margarita Bouven (Bowen?); the maternal were Hilario Roberto and Helene Clere (Cleary?). (B-51, *Taos*.) These people were probably on their way to California.

FARÍN. *Rosalío Farín* of El Paso married *María Nicolasa Peralta* at Socorro, Feb. 14, 1836. He was the son of Encarnación Farín and María Angeles Estrada. (M-57, *Socorro*.)

José Onofre Farín married *María Concepción Sáiz* at Socorro, Nov. 2, 1843 (*ibid.*). No other data given; probably a brother of the first man.

FERGUSON. *José María Paca (Parker?)*, the son of Joshua C. Ferguson and Lucindy Fey, from "Brasuri" (Missouri?) in North America, married *Manuela Lucero* in Santa Fe, Sept. 26, 1848. (M-55, *Santa Fe.*)

FISHER. *Noverto Ficha (Norbert or Robert Fisher)*, 24 years old and a native of Virginia, the son of Gillelmo Ficha and Nancy Bahan, was baptized in Taos, June 23, 1831. (B-48, *Taos.*) He married *Romualda López* on May 8, 1842; here his mother's surname is spelled "Vahan" (Vaughn?). (M-40, *Taos.*) Their known children were: *Antonio George*, May 30, 1844, when paternal grandparents are given as "Julián Ficha" and "María Ynés Nance" (B-51, *Taos*); *José Melquiades*, Sept. 4, 1845, when the above are given as "David Ficha" and "María Isabel Mosuet" (B-52, *Taos*); *Alejandro*, July 26, 1847; *María Preciliana*, Sept. 6, 1848; and *Noverto*, June 4, 1850; in these three entries the paternal grandparents are given as "William Ficher" and "Nancy Candley." (All in B-53, *Taos.*)

FLORES. *Toribio Flores*, a native of Chihuahua, the son of Esteban Flores and Dolores Arrola, married *María del Espíritu Santo Trujillo*, Jan. 10, 1843. (M-28, *San Juan.*)

FOLES. *Francisco Foles (Fowles, Foley?)*, 24 years old and a native of Quintoque (Kentucky), the son of Benjamin Foles and Sara Nolan, was baptized at Taos, Jan. 1, 1832. (B-48, *Taos.*)

A *Simón Foles* of Taos had a seven-year-old Ute slave (*famula*) who was baptized María Soledad, Sept. 21, 1843. (B-51, *Taos.*)

FORNIER. *Luis Fornier*, a native of France, married *Juana María Ortiz* at Toas, Mar. 20, 1843. His parents were Agustín Fornier and María Adelaida Forcoú. (M-40, *Taos.*) A daughter, *María Adelina*, was baptized on Dec. 16, 1843, when the paternal grandparents are given as "Fornié" and "Farcó." (B-51, *Taos.*)

FOUM. *Carlos Foum*, from Mesuri (Missouri), the son of Etharem Foum (Ethan Frome!) and Rebeca Foum, was baptized at Taos, Mar. 6, 1845. His godparents were José Pley and wife Benigna Lee. (B-52, *Taos.*) He married *María Antonia Montaño* in Taos, April 7, 1845. Here his parents are given as "Etheren" and "Rebeca Foun." (M-40, *Taos.*) They had a daughter, *Juana María*, May 9, 1848, when the paternal grandparents are given as "Charles" and "Mary Fown." (B-53, *Taos.*)

FRAMEL. *José Julian (William) Framel*, 20 years old and a native of Missouri, the son of Felipe and Anah Tramel, was baptized at Taos, Aug. 30, 1828. (B-47, *Taos.*) As a stranger from Missouri he received permission to marry *María Rufina Córdoba* of Taos, July 10, 1829. (AASF, *Patentes*, LXX.) The marriage took place on July 26, when his parents are given as Felipe and Ana Framel. (M-39, *Taos.*) They had a son, *José Julián*, Mar. 29, 1832, when the father is mentioned as dead, and the paternal grandparents are given as Felipe Framel and María "Yont" (Young?). (B-48, *Taos.*)

FRANCO. *Pilar Franco*, a soldier of the Company of San Elizario in Santa Fe, married *María Petra de la O*, Jan. 11, 1845. He was the son of Juan Franco and María Verdugo. (M-54, *Santa Fe.*)

FUCHS. *José María Fucus (Fuchs?)*, from the United States of America, the son of Richard and Nensi (Nancy) Fucus, married *María Eleuteria Ortiz* of Santa Fe, Mar. 18, 1849. (M-55, *Santa Fe.*)

FUENTES. *Ramón Fuentes* married *Juana María Gonzáles* at Socorro, Oct. 2, 1843. No other data given for the groom; the bride was the daughter of Epifanio González and María Rita Reyes, or Teyes (Telles?). (M-47, *Socorro.*) Two infant daughters who died at Lemitar were *María Demetria*, Jan. 6, 1847, and *María Francisca*, Dec. 9, 1848. (*Bur.*, 56, *Socorro.*) Ramón Fuentes migrated northeast and at San Hilario, widowed of Juana María González by 1875, he married *María de Jesús Armijo*, the widow of Cipriano Colombia. (M, *Watrous.*)

Juan José Fuentes, widowed of *María Anas-*

tasia *Hernández*, married *Rita Baca*, widow of Mariano Trujillo, at Socorro, Mar. 4, 1852. (M-58, *Socorro*.) He could have been the father, or most likely a brother, of Ramón Fuentes.

José Manuel Fuentes of Socorro lost his wife, *María Nieves Márquez*, April 18, 1839. He himself died on Oct. 31, 1841. (*Bur.*, 55, *Socorro*.) These might well have been the parents of the two preceding men. And this family could derive from the De La Fuente families in NMF, p. 30, which settled in Nueva Vizcaya (northern Mexico) even before the Revolt of 1680.

FURCAT. *Francisco Furcat*, the son of Francisco Furcat and María Dufent, married *Antonia Josefa Tafoya*, Aug. 19, 1828. (M-39, *Taos*.) Known children were: *María Ignacia*, Jan. 23, 1830, when the father's surname is "Furcata" and the mother's is "Luna" (B-47, *Taos*); *María Dolores*, April 14, 1832, when the paternal godparents are given as "José Furcate" and "Margarita Dores" (B-48, *Taos*); and *María Ynéz*, who had a natural child, María Polonia, April 12, 1845. (B-52, *Taos*.) Ynés and Ignacia could be one and the same girl.

GALIS. *Francisco Galis*, "European," was a resident of San Miguel with his wife, *María Soledad Montoya*. They had a daughter, *María Francisca*, Jan. 1, 1833, when the paternal grandparents are given as Lorenzo Galis and Isabel Mariño. (B-1, *San Miguel del Vado*.)

GANSAL. *Carlos Gansal* and wife *Bartola Romero* had a son, *José Antonio*, Mar. 17, 1827, when the paternal grandparents are given as Pedro Gansal and Aniceta García. (B-47, *Taos*.)

GARCÍA. *Don Isidro García*, a native of Villa de L. Cebrián (?) de Marote in Spain, received permission to marry *Doña Marcelina Bustamente* in Santa Fe, Jan. 15, 1832. (AASF, *Patentes*, LXX.)

José Calistro García, a native of Monterrey and the son of José María García and María Magdalena de la Mora, married *María Antonia Archibeque* in Santa Fe, Feb. 21, 1845. (M-54, *Santa Fe*.)

Don Manuel García, a native of Córdoba in Spain, and the son of Manuel García and Rafaela Mestanza, married *María José Gabriela Abeyta* of Santa Fe, Aug. 15, 1845. (M-55, *Santa Fe*.)

GARZA. *José Juan Luciano de la Garza*, a native of Presidio del Río Grande, province of Coahuila, and four years a resident in San Miguel, married *María del Carmen García*, Mar. 10, 1825. (M-10, *Galisteo-Pecos*.)

Florencio de la Garza married *Juana Silva* in Santa Fe, Nov. 11, 1832. No other data given. (M-53, *Santa Fe*.)

GAUTIER. *Julián Gautier*, from the United States of America, the son of Francisco Gautier and Charlotte Dupont, married *Magdalena Baca* in Santa Fe, Dec. 12, 1836. (M-54, *Santa Fe*.)

GEMENTO. *José Agapito Gemento* and wife *María Josefa Tapia* of Albuquerque had a son, *Manuel Antonio*, Oct. 25, 1849, when the paternal grandparents are given as Juan Gemento and Victoria Jaramillo. (B-10, *Albuq.*)

GILBERT. *Don Alberto Gilbert*, a native of the United States, asked to marry *Doña Ana María Chávez* of Belén in 1827. (DM, 1827.) However, the woman he actually married on April 1, 1827, was *Doña María Rita Ortiz*. No other data given, except for groom's second name "Vicente." (M-7, *Belén*.) A known son was *José Manuel Apolonio*, baptized on April 10, 1829, when the surname is spelled "Guilbert," and the mother's name is given as Rita Esquipula Ortiz. (B-10, *Belén*.) This José Manuel married María Francisca Castillo, and at the baptism of their child, José de la Merced, the paternal surname is spelled "Gilver," while the grandmother's is "Torres" instead of "Ortiz" or "Chávez." (B-12, *Belén*.) Bancroft mentions an Albert Gilbert who went to buy cattle in California in 1830, and was in trouble with the local authorities, then went to Honolulu on the *Volunteer* in 1832. (*Op. cit.*)

GILLEFOR. *Pablo Gillefor*, or *Gillesjar (Gilford?)*, the son of Josefa Valdés, married *María Rosario del Carmen Sandoval* in Santa Fe, Jan. 10, 1850. No other data given. (M-55, *Santa Fe.*)

GIRENS. *Santiago Girens*, of the United States of America, the son of George Girens and Francisca Yandy, married *Petra Gutiérrez* in Santa Fe, May 6, 1842. (M-54, *Santa Fe.*)

GOLD. *George Guldes*, a native of Scotland, and the son of José and Isabel Gold, married *María Estefana Montoya* at Taos, and their children were legitimized, Mar. 17, 1850. (M-41, *Taos.*) These were: *María Facunda*, who married Vidal Pacheco at Guadalupita, May 27, 1867, when the surname is spelled "Gull" (M-46, *Mora*); *María Elisa*, who married Jacques Wischart, Feb. 23, 1874, with a *David Gold* as witness (*ibid.*); *Pedro José*, June 11, 1848 (B-53, *Taos*); *José Guillermo Guales (Wallace?)*, Feb. 7, 1850, when the father's name is written "Choches Gull" (*ibid.*); and *María Guadalupe*, Feb. 7, 1851 (B-54, *Taos*).

GONZÁLEZ. *José Cosme González*, the son of José Antonio González and María Matiana González, natives of Chihuahua, married *María Altagracia Sánchez* at Santa Clara, Sept. 23, 1844. (AASF, 1844, no. 7.)

GORDON. *Julián (William) Gordon* of Taos, an "Anglo-American," received permission to marry, June, 1826. (AASF, *Accounts*, LXVI.) He married *Juana María Lucero*, June 27, 1826. (B-38, *Taos*, M section.) Their children were: *José Tomás*, April 29, 1827 (B-47, *Taos*); *Juan de Jesús*, Sept. 6, 1829 (*ibid.*); *María Isabel*, Aug. 27, 1831 (B-48, *Taos*); *Julián*, Sept. 27, 1833 (B-49, *Taos*); *Manuel*, Dec. 5, 1835 (*ibid.*); and *José Ricardo*, Nov. 29, 1840 (B-51, *Taos*). In all these baptisms the paternal grandparents are given as "Juan Gon" or "Gort" and "Isabel Art" or "Toren." The parents' residence was at San Francisco del Rancho, now Ranchos de Taos. Bancroft wrote that Wm. Gordon, a native of Ohio and a Mexican citizen of New Mexico, had married María Lucero, and in 1841 went to California with the Rowland-Workman party. There his wife died in 1844; her sister was the wife of Cyrus Alexander. One daughter, *Sarah*, married a man called Ingraham, while *Isabel* married Nathan Coombs. (*Op. cit.*)

GREEN. *Carlos de Jesús Green*, 18 years old and a native of "Carolina in North America," the son of Julián (Wm.) Green and Sara Holcomb, was baptized at Taos, Aug. 20, 1831. (B-48, *Taos.*)

GREGAN. *José Manuel Grem (Graham?)*, a stranger in Taos, received permission to marry *Soledad Lobato*, July 12, 1830. (AASF, *Patentes*, LXX.) According to the baptism of a daughter, *María Ignacia*, Aug. 2, 1845, his parents were Antonio *Gregan* and María Bul or Biel. (B-52, *Taos.*) In 1847, José Manuel *Gregam* was ordered not to trespass in a certain *vinatería* (winery, saloon?) at Taos. (AASF, 1847, no. 3.) A Manuel *Gregoin* who sold some goods to J. Robidoux, May 6, 1827, seems to be the same man. (AASF, 1827, no. 7.)

GRIJALVA. *Marcelino Grijalva* and wife *María Petra del Valle* of Taos had a daughter, *María Rosa*, who married Richard Campbell in 1828, and another, *Gertrudis*, who was the wife of Francisco Miera (baptism of son Jacobo Luis, Dec. 12, 1831, B-48, *Taos*). The origin of this family is not given.

Juan José Grijalva, son of José Francisco Grijalva and Gertrudis Burruela (Brusuela?), asked to marry *Juliana Griego* of Albuquerque in 1840. No other data given. (DM, 1840.)

GRILLETE. *Antonio Grillete*, a native of Canada, the son of Louis Grillete and Margarita Bertano, married *María Victoria López* in Santa Fe, April 25, 1836. (M-54, *Santa Fe.*) Yet, when he was married a second time at Las Vegas, to *Leogarda López*, Mar. 25, 1854, his surname is spelled "Guitts" (Witts?). (M, *Las Vegas.*) Children by Victoria López were: *Luis Jose*, May 2, 1840, when the name is spelled

"Villete," and the grandmother's is "Montaño" for "Bertano" (B-51, *Taos*); *José Guadalupe*, Dec. 14, 1842, when the name is "Grillette," but the grandmother's is "Montoya" (*ibid.*); this son married Cesaria Martín at Mora, Aug. 20, 1863, when the surname is spelled "Dieta" but corrected "Guillet" on the margin (M-46, *Mora*); *María Piedad*, May 7, 1845, with the paternal grandmother's name as "Borto" (B-52, *Taos*); and *María Dolores*, Nov. 13, 1850, at Mora, when the family name is spelled "Dillete" (B-54, *Taos*); this last girl, as "Grillet," married John Isaac Buster at Mora, Feb. 17, 1864. (M-46, *Mora*.)

GRIÑE. *Don José Griñe*, a native of Canada, the son of Juan Bautista Griñe and María Luisa Sarvé (?), married *María Manuela Sánchez* of Taos, Aug. 20, 1823. (B-38, *Taos*, M section.) Their son, *Antonio José*, was baptized on Jan. 20, 1828, when the paternal grandmother's name is spelled "Serví." (B-47, *Taos*.) This son married Josefa Olguín (baptism of daughter María Matilde at Las Vegas, April 3, 1855, when the surname is spelled "Grenier"). (B, *Las Vegas*.) Another son was *Manuel*, born in Santa Fe, who first married María Antonia Sandoval, and then María de la Cruz Medina of Taos, Oct. 16, 1848 (M-41, *Taos*); a daughter by the Sandoval wife was María Antonia, Feb. 19, 1837 (B-49, *Taos*).

Don José was most likely the father of the following two half-breed Griñe individuals, having brought them along to Taos when he married Manuela Sánchez.

Miguel Griñe married *María de Jesús Montoya* at Taos, Dec. 6, 1830, his first name erroneously entered as "Manuel." (M-39, *Taos*.) They had a large family: *Juana María*, Oct. 4, 1831 (B-48, *Taos*); *Juan José*, Mar. 7, 1834 (B-49, *Taos*); *José Pablo*, Jan. 27, 1836 (*ibid.*); *María Candelaria*, April 19, 1838 (B-51, *Taos*); *María Soledad*, May 13, 1840 (*ibid.*), who married Tomás Espinosa at Cimarrón when the family was living at Agua Negra, Sept. 9, 1867 (M-46, *Mora*); *José Francisco*, April 14, 1842 (B-51, *Taos*), who married Rufina Medina, Sept. 9, 1867 (B-46, *Mora*); *María Refugio del Pilar*, Nov. 5, 1844 (B-52, *Taos*); *Antonio David*, Aug. 27, 1851 (B-54, *Taos*); and *María Tiburcia*, April 19, 1855 (B, *Las Vegas*). In 1844, a *María Justa Griñé* acted as godparent with Juan de Dios Aguilar (B-51, *Taos*); she might have been another daughter, or else a child of the next family listed. In all these many baptisms the paternal grandfather is José Griñé or Grenier, and the grandmother is designated as a "wild Indian" or "an Indian from the North," and once as an "*India Pánana*" (Pawnee squaw).

Manuel Griñé was also a son of José Griñé and of an Indian squaw from the "Northern Nation," according to the baptism of one known daughter, *María Alejandra*, June 27, 1844, by his wife *Antonia Lucero*. (B-51, *Taos*.) Manuel and his sister-in-law, María de Jesus Montoya, stood as sponsors, May 8, 1844. (*Ibid.*)

GRUY. *Julián Gruy* (Wm. Gray?), the son of Julián and Magdalena Gruy, married *María Prudencia González*, Feb. 12, 1854. (M-41, *Taos*.) He might have been the father of Marcial Crué *supra*.

GUARÁ. *Carlos Guará*, among four other Frenchmen, applied to marry a woman of Taos, June 5, 1826, his choice being *María Suazo*. (AASF, *Accounts*, LXVI.) The other Frenchmen were Carlos Vicent, Francisco Le-Clair, Pedro Rey, and José Roture. Guará and María Suazo were married on Sept. 30, 1826, his parents being given as Juan Bautista Guará and María Margarita Sapró. (B-38, *Taos*.) Their known children were: *Juan del Carmen*, Dec. 8, 1827 (B-47, *Taos*); *María Dolores de la Paz*, Mar. 10, 1830 (*ibid.*); *Juana Rosalía*, May 1, 1832 (B-48, *Taos*); *José Encarnación*, May 2, 1834 (B-49, *Taos*); and *María Rafaela*, April 26, 1837 (*ibid.*). In these baptisms the paternal grandmother's name is variously spelled "Everó, Sapró, Shapró." The eldest son, Juan, was first married to Manuela Martínez, and then to María Luz Madrid, Sept. 7, 1855 (M-41, *Taos*); Juan's son by his first wife was Buenaventura, July 14, 1850, when the surname is spelled "Wará." (B-54, *Taos*.)

GUERECA. *José Agapito Guereque*, a native of San Juan del Río, married *Refugio Martín* at San Miguel, April 7, 1825. (M-10, *Galisteo-Pecos*.) One son, *José Melitón*, died on June 14, 1826. (*Bur.*, 9, *Galisteo-Pecos*.) Another son, *Antonio "Vuereque,"* married Anastasia García, Oct. 1, 1845. (M-55, *Santa Fe*.)

Antonio Guereca, or *Gureña*, soldier, the son of Francisco Guereña and María Chávez, married *Altagracia Tenorio* in 1841. (M-54, *Santa Fe*.)

GUERRERO. *Teodoro Guerrero*, son of Jose Antonio Guerrero and Dolores Escobedo, was married to *Estansláa Medina* and living in Taos where they had a son, *José Rafael*, May 2, 1825. (B-38, *Taos*.)

GUI. *Enrique Gui*, widowed of *Toribia Gilmor*, married *María Refugio Ortiz* at Socorro, Jan. 19, 1851. (M-58, *Socorro*.)

HAMILTON. *Santiago H. Hamilton*, 31 years old and a native of Tenesi (Tennessee), the son of Ruben and Isabel Hamilton, was baptized in Taos, Oct. 29, 1850. (B-54, *Taos*.) He married *María Josefa Archuleta*, Nov. 11, 1850. (M-41, *Taos*.)

HAMMONS. *José Tomás Hammons*, 23 years old and a native of Quintoque (Kentucky), the son of Carlos Hammons and Rachel Johnson, was baptized in Taos, Sept. 2, 1832. (B-48, *Taos*.) He married *María del Carmen Cisneros*, Sept. 30, 1833; here his mother's name is given as "Jacson." (M-40, *Taos*.) A son, *Carlos*, was born in 1834; here the surname is spelled "Jamnes." (B-49, *Taos*.)

HARAISTER. *Antonio Haraister (Harvester?)*, 22 years old and a native of Tenecía (Tennessee), the son of Generico (Hendrick) and Leran (?) Haraister, was baptized in Taos, June 28, 1831. (B-48, *Taos*.)

HARRISON. *Carlos Harrison*, of the United States of America, married *María Luz Martínez* of Santa Fe, Jan. 20, 1850. His parents were John Harrison and Ruth Britten. (M-55, *Santa Fe*.)

HENERO. *Don Juan Henero (Henry?)*, a Catholic in Santa Fe and a native of the United States of North America, stood as godfather for Martín de la Mora (Moore?), a deathbed convert, Aug. 24, 1823. (*Bur.*, 52, *Santa Fe*.)

HIDALGO. Cresencio Luna of Belén married *Antonina Ydalgo*, daughter of Don Victoriano Ydalgo, officer of the Presidio of San Elizario, and María Josefa Ronquillo, June 17, 1833. (M-7, *Belén*.)

Eutimio Hidalgo, a soldier of the Company of San Elizario in Santa Fe, married *Juana María Pacheco*, Mar. 5, 1845. His parents were Victoriano Hidalgo and Tomasa Montes. (M-54, *Santa Fe*.) Evidently Eutemio was a half brother of Antonina *supra*. These people, too, seem to be descendants of the pre-1680 New Mexico Hidalgos that stayed at Guadalupe del Paso.

HIGGINS. *Juan Higgins*, 25 years old and a native of Ireland, a former resident of the United States, and the son of Juan Higgins and Isabel McDonald, was baptized in Taos, May 29, 1831. (B-48, *Taos*.) Bancroft records a John Higgins, Irish trapper from New Mexico, who went to California in 1830 with Young's party. (*Op. cit.*)

HINOJOS. *Pedro Hinojos*, a native of the state of Chihuahua, married *Antonia Castro* of Santa Fe, daughter of Narciso Castro and Juliana García, Oct. 24, 1846. His parents were Manuel Hinojos and María Rosa Betancú. (M-55, *Santa Fe*.)

HUBBELL. *Santiago Jobelt* and wife *Juliana Gutiérrez* were Rio Abajo residents, where they had a son, *Santiago Francisco*, Oct. 13, 1850. Father's parents or place of origin not given. (B, *Isleta*.) A daughter, *Luisa*, married John Warning Thomas in 1878; here the surname is spelled "Hubbell." (M, *Isleta*.)

HUM. *Charles Hum (Hume?)*, a native of "the Kingdom of Portugal," married *María Quirina Tafoya* of Taos, Oct. 11, 1847. His parents were José Francisco Hum and María Catarina de Jesús. (M-41, *Taos*.)

HUNT. *Santiago Hunt*, a native of New York, married *María Sandoval* in Santa Fe, Sept. 28, 1848. His parents were Humphrey and Mary Hunt. (M-55, *Santa Fe*.) A marriage of the same man and "Ana María" Sandoval is recorded in Feb., 1858. (M, *Santa Fe*.) It is either a second marriage with another Sandoval woman or else a revalidation of the first.

IMPERIAL. *José de Jesús Imperial*, the son of Ignacio Imperial and Josefa Valenzuela, married *María Isidora Chávez* of Albuquerque, Dec. 4, 1832. No other data given. (DM, 1832; M-4, *Albuq*.)

JACKSON. *Santiago Yaquison*, 28 years old, the son of Juan Yaquison (Jackson) and María Mequentaya (McIntyre?), "natives of Europe and subjects of the State of England" (*sic*), was baptized at Taos, Jan. 28, 1831. (B-48, *Taos*.)

JIMÉNEZ. *Antonio Jiménez*, a native of Andalucia, asked to marry *Manuela Carrillo*, widow of José Antonio Salazar, at Albuquerque in 1824. (DM, 1824.)

Juan Nepomuceno Jiménez, the son of José Jiménez and Juana Benita Vélez, of San Antonio de Bejar, married *María Asención García*, Dec. 31, 1827. (M-22, *Pojoaque*.)

JOHNSON. *Antonio Johnson*, of St. Louis, the son of José and Asfrose (?) Johnson, married *María Cruz Lobato*, July 3, 1850. (M-55, *Santa Fe*.) Their son *Francisco* married Luz Aragón, Feb. 28, 1881. (M, *Las Vegas*.)

JOSÉ. *Juan Senón José (Joseph? Hosey?)*, the son of Pedro José and Mariana Willse, was baptized at Taos, June 27, 1847. Paternal grandparents are given as Pedro and María José, but the entry does not indicate if the subject was a child or an adult. (B-53, *Taos*.)

KENNEDY. *Tomás Kenedy*, vagrant from overseas, received permission to marry *Doña Luz Basán* of Pajarito, June 23, 1832. (AASF, *Patentes*, LXX.)

KING. *José King*, the son of Santiago King and María Maid or Maiu (?), "American Protestants," was baptized in Albuquerque, Jan. 24, 1850. (B-10, *Albuq*.) The entry does not indicate if the subject was a child or an adult.

KIRCHHOFF. *Francisco Kirchhoff*, a native of Prussia (Russia?), the son of Robert Kirchhoff and Guillerme Betcanvor (?), married *Trinidad Sena*, Mar. 30, 1847. (M-55, *Santa Fe*.)

LACAMBE. *José Rosario Lacambe*, the son of Juan Nepomuceno Lacambe and María Angel, married *Juana María Romero*, Jan. 31, 1844. (M-54, *Santa Fe*.) The "L" often appears to be an "S," hence possibly "Sacambe."

LACHONÉ. *Luis Lachoné*, a native of "San Luis de Misipi" (Mississippi), married *Dolores García*, April 26, 1841. His parents were Santiago Lachoné and Elena Varon. (M-40, *Taos*.) His García widow later married Cristino Velten, Oct. 8, 1855. (M-41, *Taos*.) Known Lachoné children were: *Felipe Santiago*, May 24, 1842 (B-51, *Taos*); *María Elena*, Feb. 3, 1845 (B-52, *Taos*); *Luis Felipe*, July 21, 1847 (B-53, *Taos*); *Manuel Antonio*, May 6, 1850 (*ibid.*); and *María Porfiria*, Jan. 9, 1853 (B-54, *Taos*). The mother's surname is García for the first child and Martín or Martínez for the rest. The paternal grandmother's name is variously given as "Bisonete, Bisonent, Van, Basor."

LACOME. On May 10, 1852, *Agustín Lacoma* and his brother, Frenchmen, sold a 3-year-old Paiute boy, whose godparents at baptism were Juan Bautista Lacoma (the brother?) and Dolores Alarid. (B-1, *Arroyo Hondo*.) *Agustín Lacome* married *María Rosa Arrellano* in 1855. (M-42, *Taos*.) Their known children were: *José Eulogio*, Mar. 16, 1856; *Gabriel Agustín*, Feb. 2, 1858; and *Silvestre Agustín*, Aug. 28, 1859. (All in B-1, *Arroyo Hondo*.)

LACROIX. *José Julián Lacrois*, the son of Juan Bautista Lacrois and María Gree, both "French by nationality," was baptized at Taos, Sept. 6, 1842. Paternal grandparents were José de la Cruz Lacrois and María Suñe (Sunier?); the maternal, José Mariano Gree and María Rosar. (B-51, *Taos*.)

Juan Bautista La Croix and *María Salazar* had two known sons: *José Manuel*, Dec. 24, 1845, when the surname is spelled "Lacrue," with paternal grandparents Juan Bautista Lacrue and Aniceta Furni (?), and maternal, Francisco Salazar and María Angre (?); and *John Baptist Lacroix*, who, widowed of Eleuteria Apodaca, married María Manuela Lobato at Mora in 1873; his Salazar mother is mentioned as dead at this time. (M-46, *Mora*.)

LAFAR. *José Benito Lafar* and *María Guadalupe Montoya* had a son, *José Casimiro*, Mar. 4, 1830. Paternal grandparents were Bautista Lafar and María Furg. (B-47, *Taos*.)

LAFEBVRE. *Manuel Lafebre*, the son of Agustín Lafebre and María Feliciana Bayancur, married *María Teodora López*, Dec. 1, 1827 (M-39, *Taos*). Known children of this large family were: *María Dolores*, June 29, 1828 (B-47, *Taos*), who married Richard Wooton, Mar. 6, 1848 (M-41, *Taos*); *José Vicente*, April 7, 1830 (B-47, *Taos*); *Francisco Antonio*, April 3, 1831 (B-48, *Taos*), who married María Susana Blanchard, June 5, 1853 (M-41, *Taos*); *María Francisca Guillerma*, Mar. 12, 1833 (B-49, *Taos*), who married Carlos Guillermo Starkweather (Charles Williams), Nov. 30, 1850 (M-41, *Taos*); *María Pacifica*, Feb. 6, 1834(5) (B-49, *Taos*); *María de la Luz*, May 22, 1835 (B-51, *Taos*), who married Cresencio Naranjo, and then Charles Fraker at Ocate, June 19, 1867 (M-46, *Mora*); *María Leonor*, who married Gilbert Hamon, Feb. 6, 1867 (*ibid.*); *María Teodora*, July 16, 1848 (B-53, *Taos*); *Manuel Carlos*, April 23, 1850 (*ibid.*); and *José Manuel*, Oct. 20, 1851 (B-54, *Taos*).

LAFORÉ. *Francisco Laforé*, the son of Francisco Laforé and María Feliciana Camvel (?), married *María Dolores Armenta*, July 25, 1828. (M-39, *Taos*.) Their known children were: *José Antonio*, April 12, 1829 (B-47, *Taos*), who as a resident of San Antonio del Río Colorado married Martina Pacheco, Dec. 9, 1848 (M-41, *Taos*); *Juan Crisóstomo*, Feb. 28, 1831 (B-47, *Taos*); and *María Isabel*, July 31, 1835 (B-49, *Taos*).

LALANDA. See EL PALACIO, *loc. cit.*

LAMELAS or LAMEDA. *Domingo Lamelas* married *María Encarnación Sánchez*, Aug. 28, 1830; no other data given. (M-39, *Taos*.) Known children were: *Celestino*, June 12, 1833 (B-49, *Taos*); *José Gregorio*, May 10, 1835 (*ibid.*); and *María Polonia*, April 19, 1840 (B-50, *Taos*). Paternal grandparents were Juan Lamelas and Rosalía Boruna or Trejo.

These grandparents evidently were living in Taos also. There a daughter, *Gabriela*, a native of the state of Chihuahua, married José María Sánchez, May 18, 1844 (M-40, *Taos*). Another daughter, *María Concepción*, was married to José Antonio Sánchez; their child, María Rufina, was baptized on June 4, 1838, and here the maternal grandmother's name is given as "Grajas" instead of Trejo. (B-51, *Taos*.) Therefore, Gabriela and Concepción (though perhaps one and the same person) were sisters to Domingo Lamelas, and all from the state of Chihuahua.

LAMORÉ. *Luis Lamoré*, stranger, married *María Rita Lucero* (Lalanda), Mar. 10, 1833 (M-39, *Taos*). Their son *Luis* was baptized on Aug. 24, 1834, when the paternal grandparents are given as Pedro Lamoré and Lucía Baré, and the maternal as Bautista Lalanda and Polonia Lucero. (B-49, *Taos*.)

LAMORÍ. *Amador Lamorí*, Frenchman, a native of Canada, married *María Rafaela Baca*, Nov. 8, 1825 (B-38, *Taos*, M section). On Sept. 30, 1826, "Amador Amable" and Rafaela Baca were witnesses for J. B. Yarat and María Luz Servé (*ibid.*). Known children were: *Juan Antonio*, April 3, 1827 (B-48, *Taos*); *María*

Dolores, April 18, 1828, when the paternal grandparents are given as Alejandro Lamorí and María Tura or Fura (B-47, *Taos*); and *Francisco*, Jan. 11, 1832, when the father's name is given as "Amable la Mori" (B-48, *Taos*). The elder son married Francisca Mestas, May 14, 1854 (M-41, *Taos*).

On Oct. 8, 1832, *"Amable la Menon,"* widower, married *María Guadalupe Martín* (M-39, *Taos*). And at San Miguel, May 26, 1848, was baptized *María Josefa*, child of "the Frenchman Amado Lamoris" (mother's name omitted). (B-4, *San Miguel del Vado*.) See Lecliet *infra*.

LANFORT or LANGLORE. *Julián Langlore*, 41 years old, a native of Virginia, and the son of Juan Langlore and Sarah Fulton, was baptized at Taos, Mar. 25, 1832 (B-48, *Taos*). As Julián "Langoré" he had married *María Juana Vigil*, Mar. 15, 1832 (M-39, *Taos*). As Julián "Lagrore" he had received permission for this marriage from the Vicar in Santa Fe, April 7, when he is designated as a stranger and native of Virginia (AASF, *Patentes*, LXX). Known children were: *María Encarnación*, Feb. 12, 1836 (B-49, *Taos*); and *José Santiago*, July 29, 1838, when the surname is spelled "Lanfor." (B-51, *Taos*). As Santiago "Lanfort" this son married María Asención Quintana at Mora, Oct. 6, 1867 (M-46, *Mora*). On Dec. 6, 1837, Padre Martínez baptized and then buried an Ignacio Rain (Hain, Wain?), stranger, who died from razor wounds inflicted by Julián Lanfor. (*Bur.*, 40, *Taos*.)

LANGRUE. *Pedro Langrue*, the son of Pedro Langrue and Margarita Manyon, married *Ana María Tafoya*, Dec. 27, 1828 (M-39, *Taos*). Known children were: *José Rafael*, May 11, 1830 (B-38, *Taos*); and *José de la Cruz*, May 5, 1833 (B-49, *Taos*). In these baptisms the paternal grandmother's surname is given as "Maryon" and "Guile."

LARIÉ or CARIEL. *Anastasio Larié*, Frenchman, and widower of a first marriage, married *María Guadalupe Córdoba*, Aug. 14, 1824.

His parents were Bautista Larié and María Giné or Girez (?), natives of Canada. (B-38, *Taos*, M section.) Known children of this marriage were: *María Barbara*, Dec. 5, 1824, when the surname is rendered "Cariel" (B-38, *Taos*); and *Vibiana*, wife of Juan Andrés Arellano (baptism of child María Dorotéa, May 29, 1842, when the grandparents' names are given as "Eustaquio Cariel" and "Esquipula García," B-51, *Taos*).

Anastasio Cariel, widowed of María de "Esquipula" Córdoba, next married *María Luisa Gutiérrez*, or *Ortiz*, May 15, 1827 (M-39, *Taos*), and then *María Isabel Roybal*, Sept. 9, 1829 (*ibid.*).

LAVÉ. *Pedro Lavé*, the son of Miguel Lavé and María Rosalía Lansarya (?), married *María Asención Martínez*, Jan. 7, 1829 (M-39, *Taos*). Known children were: *José Manuel*, who married María del Refugio Apodaca, June 24, 1850 (M-41, *Taos*); *José Miguel*, Aug. 24, 1833 (B-49, *Taos*), who married María Rita Trujillo, Feb. 4, 1856 (M-41, *Taos*), and then María Leonarda Madrid at Las Animas, Dec. 18, 1864 (M-46, *Mora*); *María Dolores*, Mar. 5, 1837 (B-49, *Taos*); *José Antonio*, Jan. 30, 1840 (B-51, *Taos*); and *José Rafael*, Oct. 17, 1841 (*ibid.*). In the two earlier baptisms Pedro Lavé's parents are given as "Miguel Labé" and "María Rosa Bansan," and as "José Labé" and "Claudia *francesa*."

LE-CLAIR. See Decluet *supra*.

LECLIET. *Juan Amador Lecliet*, natural son of Amable Lecliet and a squaw of "the northern Nation," was baptized at Taos, Oct. 24, 1832. The paternal grandparents were Francisco Lecliet and María Epró. (B-48, *Taos*.) There seems to be some connection here with Amador or Amable Lamorí *supra*.

LEDESMO. *Facundo Ledesmo*, a native of La Villa del Paso, the son of Domingo Ledesmo and Andrea Vargas, married *María Ignacia García*, June 27, 1842 (M-40, *Taos*). Their son, *Juan del Carmel*, was born at El Río Colorado,

July 24, 1843 (B-51, *Taos*). The father was evidently descended from the pre-1680 *Ledesma* family that stayed at Guadalupe del Paso.

LEDOUX. *Antonio Ledoux* and *Polonia Lucero* had these children: *Pedro Celestino*, May 25, 1825 (B-38, *Taos*); *José Victor*, Mar. 23, 1828 (B-47, *Taos*); *María Quirina de los Angeles*, April 27, 1830 (*ibid.*); and *María Dolores*, April 19, 1835 (*ibid.*). Antonio also had a bastard son, *Antonio*, by a Pawnee squaw, who was baptized on Jan. 31, 1825, when 7 years old (B-38, *Taos*). The surname is variously spelled "Ledú, Lidú, Lodú," and the paternal grandparents are given as Antonio Ledú and Magdalena Lucíe. Antonio Lodú and Polonia Lucero acted as godparents at Mora, Feb. 11, 1845 (B-52, *Taos*).

José Ledú, presumably José Victor, acted as godparent at Mora with Rita Lalanda, April 13, 1844 (*ibid.*). He had a son, David, at Mora, Feb. 22, 1853, by Refugio García, when the surname is hispanicized "Ledud" (B-54, *Taos*). If the same man, and married a second time, he had a daughter, Juana, also at Mora, July 1, 1855, by Juana Luján; here the surname is spelled "Ledoux." (B, *Las Vegas*.) But one of these Josephs could be a first cousin (José Celedón or José Julián in the next paragraph). The girl Quirina *supra* acted as godparent at Mora with Juan Kaquindo, Feb. 12, 1845 (B-52, *Taos*).

Abrán Ledoux was a brother of Antonio Ledoux. His known children by *Magdalena Trujillo* were: *José Julián*, April 12, 1827, when the paternal grandparents are given as Antonio Ledú and Magdalena de la A(merica?) (B-47, *Taos*); *José Celedón*, Mar. 5, 1830 (*ibid.*); *María Tiburcia*, May 19, 1832 (B-48, *Taos*); *Felipe de Jesús*, 1835 (B-49, *Taos*), who married María Luz Trujillo in 1855 (M-41, *Taos*); *María Asunción*, Aug. 12, 1839 (B-51, *Taos*); and *María Teófila*, Aug. 2, 1842 (*ibid.*). In these other baptisms the paternal grandmother is Magdalena Lucia or Lucie.

LEE. *Esteban Luis Lé* and Ricardo Campbell, both Presbyterians, requested Catholic baptism in June, 1826. Both were natives of St. Louis, Mo. (AASF, *Accounts*, LXVI, LXVII.) Esteban Luis *Lee* married *María Luz Tafoya*, Jan. 23, 1829 (M-39, *Taos*). A known child was *María Benigna*, April 15, 1830 (B-47, *Taos*), who married José Pley, June 10, 1844 (M-40, *Taos*). Lee had a native slave (*famulo*), José Rafael, 12 years old when baptized on May 30, 1840 (B-51, *Taos*). There was also a José Antonio Lee, a ransomed Navajo, who was married to Margarita Trujillo, and had a son, José Irineo Esquipula, July 22, 1846 (B-52, *Taos*).

José Elías Lee, 45 years old and a native of St. Louis who came to Taos in the November of the preceding year, the son of Juan and Mariana Lee, was baptized on Jan. 22, 1847 (B-52, *Taos*).

LEITENSDORFER. *Juan Eugenio Leitensdorfes*, a native of St. Louis, married *Soledad Abreú*, widow of the *Teniente* Esquipula Caballero, Dec. 6, 1845. His parents were Juan Eugenio Leitensdorfes and Gfresena (Euphrosena?) Gamache (?). (M-55, *Santa Fe*.)

LERMA. *Juan Nepomuceno Lerma*, a native of the state of Chihuahua, and son of Crisanto Lerma and Dolores Sosa, married *Antonia Padilla*, Oct. 24, 1846 (M-55, *Santa Fe*).

Antonio Lerma, a native of Chihuahua, the son of María Dolores Lerma, married *Ana María Rodríguez*, Nov. 2, 1847 (*ibid.*).

LEROUX. *Antonio Lerous*, a native of "North America," married *Juana Catalina Vigil*, Nov. 4, 1833. His parents were Antonio Lerous and Elena José. (M-40, *Taos*.) In the baptisms of several children this grandmother's name is given variously as "Elena José," or "Lagoien" or "Lagoré," and once as "Isabel Jacques." These children were: *María Paula*, Sept. 24, 1834 (B-49, *Taos*); *Luis*, June 23, 1836 (*ibid.*); *Juan de Jesús*, Sept. 7, 1838 (B-51, *Taos*); *María Elena*, Oct. 31, 1840 (*ibid.*); *María Deluvina*, May 3, 1842 (*ibid.*); *José David*, May 29, 1844 (*ibid.*); *María Teresa*, June 6, 1847 (B-53, *Taos*); and *María Carolina*, June 12, 1849 (*ibid.*). In these baptisms the family name is variously spelled Leroux, Ledú, Lorous, Loreus, Loud, and Lodud.

María Asención Leroux, widow of Antonio Vigil who married Francisco Argüello at Guadalupita, Nov. 14, 1863 (M-46, *Mora*), might have been another daughter. *Barbarita Leroux*, who married Dolphus Malone, July 6, 1864, was the daughter of Antonio Leroux and María Francisca Romero (*ibid.*), hence probably a child from a second marriage.

LEVI. *Simón Levi* and *Candelaria Chávez* had a son, *José Manuel*, Dec. 31, 1835 (B-49, *Taos*).

LEYBA. *José Inocente Leyba*, a native of Chihuahua, married *María Altagracia Rael*, widow of Antonio Chávez, Feb. 3, 1850. His parents were Juan Antonio Leyba and María Nieves Escansa. (M-55, *Santa Fe*.) The groom was evidently a descendant of pre-1680 Leyvas of New Mexico who settled in what is now northern Mexico.

LÍAS. *José Clemente Lías*, the son of Gabriel Lías and Juana Alcalá, married *María Marcelina Chávez* of Tomé, Mar. 23, 1835. Place of origin not known. (DM, 1835; M-56, *Tomé*.) This surname came to be misspelled "Elías."

LIMITE. *María* and *Felicitas*, French, the children of *Luis* and *María Limite*, were baptized in Taos, July 29, 1823 (B-38, *Taos*).

LOLLA CABALLERO. *Don Jesús Lolla Caballero*, a native of the Department of Durango, married *Antonia Tenorio*, a widow of Santa Fe, Jan. 27, 1845. His parents were José Antonio Lolla Caballero and María Antonia Lolla y Díaz. (M-54, *Santa Fe*.)

LONG. *George Lony (Long)*, a stranger, married *Juana María Herrera*, Mar. 9, 1840 (M-40, *Taos*). He had been previously baptized on Jan. 1, as "Jorge, formerly Oracio" (Horace), 34 years old and a native of the "City of Kintoque," the son of Benjamin Lony and Sara Evern (B-51, *Taos*). Known children were: *Julián Sóstenes*, Dec. 6, 1840 (*ibid.*); *Carlos*, June 4, 1842 (*ibid.*); *María Guadalupe*, Nov. 3, 1843, when her father's name is given as "Jorge Vult" (*ibid.*); *Jorge*, June 13, 1846 (B-52, *Taos*); and *José Manuel de la Luz*, Jan., 1852, when the father's name is "Choches Long" (B-54, *Taos*). In the other baptisms the family name is spelled "Lon," while Sara Evern appears also as "Eden" and "Veden."

LONTÉ. *Agustín Gerónimo Lonté* married *María Luz Trujillo*, Jan. 7, 1829. His parents were Gerónimo Lonté and Magdalena Rea (?). (M-39, *Taos*.) Their known children were: *José Felis*, Nov. 21, 1829 (B-47, *Taos*), who married María Antonia Mestas at La Cueva as "José Felix Lonten," June 23, 1867 (M-46, *Mora*); *María Rosa*, Aug. 31, 1832 (B-48, *Taos*), who had a natural child, Norberto Samuel, June 17, 1852 (B-54, *Taos*), and had acted as godparent with a Guillermo Kaerne, Feb. 24, 1849 (B-53, *Taos*); and *María Leduvina*, Nov. 10, 1834 (B-49, *Taos*). In these baptisms the family name is given as "Lonté, Lontin, Lonten," while the Rea grandmother is also given as "Rei" and "de los Reyes."

LÓPEZ. *Dámaso López*, "el Español," and *Seferina del Carmen Esparza* had a son at San Miguel, *José Francisco Julián*, Feb. 27, 1844 (B, *San Miguel del Vado*).

Francisco López, a soldier of the Company of San Elizario, married *Dolores Ferrales* in Santa Fe, Mar. 11, 1845. He was a son of Faustino López and Catarina Esquivel, while his bride, a native of Chihuahua, was the daughter of the *Teniente* Don Francisco Ferrales and Juana Aragón. (M-54, *Santa Fe*.)

LOREN. *Francisco Felipe de Jesús Loren*, 56 years old and a native of "the state of Bordeo belonging to France," the son of Juan and María Loren, was baptized on Feb. 12, 1832. (B-48, *Taos*.)

LUEBANO. *Felipe Luebano* and *María Carmel Chávez* were living at Ranchos de Taos, where these two children were born: *María Dolores*,

April 14, 1851; and *Manuel Antonio*, July 16, 1853. Paternal grandparents were Juan, or Justo, Luebano and Mariquita Martínez. (B-54, *Taos*.)

LUN. *Viví de Lun (Lune?)* and *María Micaela García* had a son, *Antonio José*, May 26, 1848 (B-4, *San Miguel del Vado*).

LUNA. *José Nieves Luna*, a native of the state of Chihuahua, the son of Pablo Luna and Juana Gutiérrez, married *Jacinta Sarracino*, Feb. 14, 1849 (M-55, *Santa Fe*.) He was evidently a descendant of pre-1680 Luna and Gutiérrez families that stayed at Guadalupe del Paso.

LUT. See Chunt *supra*.

MADARIAGA. *Juan José Madariaga*, a native of Chihuahua, asked to marry *María Tomasa Sedilla* of Tomé in 1829. His parents were Justo Pastor Madariaga and María del Refugio Serrano (DM, 1829). One known child was *María Refugio Fortunata*, Oct. 17, 1830 (B-72, *Tomé*).

MADRID. *Ramón Madrid*, a native of La Villa del Paso residing at Sabinal, married *María Candelaria Trujillo*, Feb. 9, 1845. His parents were Juan Francisco Madrid and Valentina Ortega. (M-7, *Belén*.) He was evidently a descendant of Madrid and Ortega families of pre-1680 New Mexico who stayed at Guadalupe del Paso.

MAGEN. *Hilaria Magen*, daughter of *Juan Rosalio Magen* and *Juana Medrán*, had a natural child, María Manuela, Jan. 2, 1845 (B-52, *Taos*).

MAIQUE. *Miguel Maique (Mackay?)*, 29 years old and a native of Missouri, the son of Patricio Maique and Ranchel Conquen (Rachel Conklin?), was baptized on May 11, 1831 (B-48, *Taos*).

MANTA. *José Manta*, son of Juan Manta and Josefa Brachal (Blanchard), had a natural son, *José Francisco*, by María de Jesús Romero, Oct. 22, 1845 (*ibid.*).

MAQUE. *Agustín Maque (Mack, Mackay, McCoy?)*, of the United States of America, married *Dolores Lucero*, Oct. 30, 1850 (M-55, *Santa Fe*).

MARIONI. *Don Rafael Marioni* and *Doña Guadalupe Cano de los Ríos* had these two sons who married in New Mexico: *Jesús*, to Ana Ribera, Jan. 25, 1836 (M-54, *Santa Fe*); and *Mariano*, to [name misplaced], Mar. 12, 1842 (M, *San Miguel del Vado*). Their widowed mother married Rafael Lopez, Dec. 16, 1830 (M-53, *Santa Fe*). A daughter might have been *Doña María Concepción Marioni*, a native of Real de Cosiquiriachic, who married Don Melquiades A. Ortega (*infra*) in Santa Fe.

MARS. *Juan Mars (Marsh?)*, a native of Marilan (Maryland) in the United States, the son of Guillermo Mars and Ana María Alvin, married *Ana María Jirón*, May 9, 1836 (M-54, *Santa Fe*).

MASON. *José Alejandra Mason*, 26 years old and a native of Pennsylvania, the son of Juan Mason and Anna Quigler, was baptized at Taos, June 29, 1829 (B-47, *Taos*). On Sept. 2 of that year he had received permission to marry *María Luz Lobato* of Taos, and the marriage took place on Oct. 19. (AASF, *Patentes*, LXX; M-39, *Taos*.)

MAXWELL. *Luciano Marsuell*, a native of the "Villa de Karcaria (?) in the United States," married *María Luz Beaubien*, Mar. 27, 1842. His parents were D. Hueche (Hugh H.) Marsuell and María Odilia Manard. (M-40, *Taos*.) Known children were: *Pedro Minar*, May 4, 1848, when the paternal grandparents are given as Alejandro and Lamenor (?) Maxwell (B-53, *Taos*); *María Sofía*, June 25, 1849 (*ibid.*); *María Guadalupe*, Dec. 16, 1850, when the paternal grandparents are Hugh H. Maxwell and Odile Marshall (*ibid.*); and *María Emilia*, Oct. 10, 1852 (*ibid.*).

MAYEN. *Felipe de Mayen (Mayer?)*, a native of Germany and the son of Patricio de Mayen and Margarita Rorfe (?), married *Antonia Ortiz*, Dec. 11, 1849 (M-55, *Santa Fe*).

MEGINES. *José Megines (McGinnis?)*, a French (?) stranger, was buried in Santa Fe, Sept. 1, 1833, after Vicar Ortiz made sure from his papers that he was a Catholic. (*Bur.*, 52, *Santa Fe.*)

MELGARES. *Pablo Melgares*, a soldier, married *Guadalupe Trujillo* in Santa Fe, May 2, 1820 (M-52, *Santa Fe*).

Pascual Melgares, of unknown parentage, married *Facunda Márquez*, May 12, 1834 (M-53, *Santa Fe*).

Luis Melgares, stranger, and *María Paula Sánchez* had a son, *Diego Antonio*, May 3, 1832 (B-48, *Taos*).

MENAR. *José Menar (Menard?)* and *Guadalupe Madrid* had a child, *María Benita*, Mar. 23, 1835. The paternal grandparents were Juan Menar and María Braquel. (B-49, *Taos*.)

MENDOZA. *Xavier Mendoza*, a native of El Río Grande and rescued from Indian captivity, married *María Guadalupe García* at San Miguel, June 16, 1830. His parents were José Quirino Mendoza and María Tomasa Savedra. (M, *San Miguel del Vado*.) In the baptism of a child, *Francisca Antonia*, April 28, 1833, the mother's name is Gómez instead of García, while the paternal grandmother's is Saucedo instead of Savedra. (B-1, *San Miguel del Vado*.)

MERINO. *José Concepción Merino* and *María de Jesús Córdoba* had a son at Trampas de Taos, *Juan Lorenzo Severino*, Feb. 21, 1825. The paternal grandparents were Pascual Merino and Teresa Espinosa. (B-38, *Taos*.)

METCALF. *Carlos Metcaf (Metcalf)*, 30 years old, a hunter and native of New York, the son of Tomás Metcaf and Juana Pearsana (Pearson?), was baptized at Taos, Aug. 15, 1845. Carlos Beaubien and Paula Lobato were his godparents. (B-52, *Taos*.) He married *María Luz Trujillo*, Oct. 13, 1845 (M-40, *Taos*).

MEXILLAS. *Juan Mexillas*, a native of Barrio de Torreón, and husband of *María Carmen Chávez*, was buried from the military chapel in Santa Fe, June 15, 1821 (*Bur.*, 51, *Castrense*).

MIRANDA. A dispensation from banns was granted for the marriage of *Don Guadalupe Miranda*, a native of El Paso and lay Notary of Vicar Rascón's Visitation, and *Doña María Francisca Rascón*, a native of El Real de Cosiguiriachic, Jan. 28, 1830 (AASF, *Patentes*, LXX). But the marriage did not take place, at least its solemnization, until June 28, when the parties are designated as *"familiares de S. Sa."* (of the Vicar's household). (M-53, *Santa Fe.*)

MITOTE. *Francisco Mitote (Metot?)*, 58 years old and a Frenchman of Canada, married *María Josefa*, a squaw of the "Widehead" tribe (*Cabezas Anchas*) that neighbored on the Utes, June 4, 1828. They had cohabited for 18 years already and had four children (M-39, *Taos*). In the baptismal entry of a post-marriage child, *María Isabel*, Mar. 21, 1830, the father's full name is given as José Zan. (Chanon) Mitote, the son of José Francisco Mitote and María Josefa Fransue (?), while the mother, María Josefa, is designated as a Shoshone squaw (B-47, *Taos*). In the baptism of a second child, *José Manuel*, Oct. 6, 1832, the father is called José Shanán (Chanon), Frenchman, and the unnamed mother is designated as a Flathead squaw (*Cabeza Aplastada*) of the Western Nation (B-48, *Taos*).

Juan Pedro Metote, the son of Francisco Metote and María Josefa "Nolán," seems to be a brother or half brother of Francisco Mitote *supra*, unless "Nolán" was the adopted French name of the squaw, María Josefa. Thus Juan Pedro would be one of the children born before their marriage. He married *María Manuela Herrera*, Feb. 28, 1836 (M-40, *Taos*). They had a son, *José Encarnación*, Dec. 14, 1839 (B-51, *Taos*).

Juan Bautista Mitote and *María González* were also Taos residents. Two known children were: *Pedro Nicanor*, June 21, 1840 (B-51, *Taos*); and *Juan Nepomuceno*, May 20, 1843 (*ibid.*). In the first baptism, the unnamed paternal grandparents are referred to as belonging to "the Gentile Nation." Hence, Juan Bautista was most likely another premarital son of Chanon Mitote and María Josefa.

MOGOMBRE. *Alejandro Mogombre (Montgomery?)*, the son of Alejandro Mogombre and María Emite (Mitty? Smith?), and *Juana María Lucero* had a son, *José Guadalupe*, Dec. 12, 1844 (B-52, *Taos*).

MOLINA. *Victoriano Molina*, a stranger and vagrant, received permission to marry *María Dolores Romero* of Taos, Dec. 13, 1831 (AASF, *Patentes*, LXX).

MONTES. *Basilio Montes*, a soldier of the Company of San Elizario in Santa Fe, married *María del Rosario Espinosa*, Mar. 6, 1845. His parents were Ramón Montes and María Carmen Durán (M-54, *Santa Fé*).

MOORE. *Martín Jesús de la Mora (Moore, Delmore?)*, an "Anglo-American" 40 years old and single, was baptized on his deathbed. He was a native of Buome Canture (Boone, Kentucky?), the son of Samuel and Paula de la Mora (*Bur.*, 52, *Santa Fé*).

MORAGA. *Santiago Moraga*, a native of La Villa del Paso residing in Belén, married *María Altagracia Espinosa*, also a native of El Paso, May 25, 1846. His parents were Pablo Moraga and Guadalupe García; the bride's are not given (M-7, *Belén*). Evidently a descendant of pre-1680 New Mexico families that stayed at Guadalupe del Paso.

MORER. *Lucas Morer* and *Manuela Lucero* had a child, *María Teresina*, Aug. 2, 1849. The paternal grandparents were Daniel Morer and Luisa Marshal (B-53, *Taos*).

MORGAN. *José David Morgan*, 19 years old and a native of Pennsylvania, the son of Moris Morgan and Susana Estentes (Stanton?), was baptized at Taos, Jan. 1, 1832 (B-48, *Taos*).

MORILLOS. *Pedro Morillos*, the son of Vicente Morillos and Guadalupe Barreras, married *Isabel González* of Albuquerque, Nov. 4, 1845 (M-5, *Albuq.*).

MULFEY. *Tomás Mulfey*, or *Mulfely (Murphy?)*, a native of New York, married *Encarnación de los Dolores Tenorio*, Feb. 22, 1847. His parents were Juan and Nancy Mulfey (M-55, *Santa Fé*).

MUÑOZ. *Cornelio Muñoz*, a native of San Elizario del Paso, and the son of Rafael Muñoz and Josefa Alvarado, married *Petrona Armijo*, Oct. 11, 1848 (M-55, *Santa Fe*).

NARVÁEZ. *Don Santiago Narváez* and *Doña Juliana Montoya* of Belén had a son, *Juan José Ramón*, June 24, 1823. The paternal grandparents were Guadalupe Narváez and Benita Rosas y Delgado (B-3, *Belén*). Probably a Guadalupe del Paso family.

NASH. *Pedro Nash*, a native of Chose (Jersey?) in the United States, the son of Daniel Nash and Anemelter (Annie Mae?) Ringham, or Kingham, was baptized at Taos in 1836 (B-49, *Taos*).

NAVARRETE. *José Rafael Navarrete*, a native of El Paso, married *María Ignacia Montoya* of Santa Cruz in 1829. His parents were Juan José Navarrete and María Juana Delgado (M-32, *Santa Cruz*). They had a daughter, *María Dolores*, Dec. 7, 1834 (M-49, *Taos*), who married Guillermo H. J. Baullat (?), May 3, 1852 (M-41, *Taos*).

NEVARES. *Manuel Nevares* of El Paso, the son of Miguel Nevares and Benita Varela, married *María de la Paz Campbell* of Santa Fe in 1846 (M-55, *Santa Fe*). Evidently a descendant of pre-1680 New Mexico families that stayed at Guadalupe del Paso.

NEWMAN. *Juan Rafael Numen*, stranger, married *María Altagracia Esquivel* of Santa Fe, Nov. 7, 1832. Their son, *José Newman*, married María Encarnación García at San Miguel, Jan. 24, 1870 (M, *San Miguel del Vado*). Probably a daughter of Juan Rafael was a *Gertrudis Newman* who married Jules Jeanneret, or Genneret, in 1855 (M-55, *Santa Fe*).

NOLÁN. *Gervasio Nolán (Nolin)*, the son of Francisco Nolán and María Angela Coplatrur (?), married *María Dolores Lalanda*, Aug. 5, 1828 (M-39, *Taos*). Known children were: *Juan Bautista*, May 30, 1830 (B-47, *Taos*); *María Dolores*, April 8, 1832 (B-48, *Taos*); *Fernando*, June 1, 1835 (B-49, *Taos*), who as "Fernandes" first married Juliana Abeyta of Wagon Mound, and then Agapita Ortiz, a widow of Santa Fe, Aug. 10, 1893 (M, *Santa Fe*); *Juan Eugenio*, Nov. 15, 1837 (B-48a, *Taos*); and *Antonio Venceslao*, Sept. 4, 1841 (B-8, *Albuq.*). In these entries the paternal grandmother's name is given as "Angelica Couture, Angelina Coplahur, Angelica Cutiur." Godmother for the last child was *Doña Yrinéa Nolán*, probably an older daughter. María Manuela, a 4-year-old Ute slave of Nolán's, was baptized on Jan. 15, 1832 (B-48, *Taos*).

OCANES. María Antonia, June 1, 1842, child of José Calisto Borrego and María Reyes Cháves (?), had for maternal grandparents *Santiago Ocanes (Ocaña?)* and Juana Hurtado (B-51, *Taos*).

OCHOA. *José Ochoa*, a native of El Pitique or Pitigue (?), the son of Xavier Ochoa and Josefa Espinosa, married *Ynéz Garduño* of Santa Fe, Feb. 12, 1838 (M-54, *Santa Fe*).

O'CONNOR. *Patricio* and *Nensi (Nancy) Ocaner* had these two children baptized at Taos, both designated as "French": *Isabel*, Sept. 23, 1823, and *María Juliana de Jesús*, Feb. 13, 1824 (B-38, *Taos*).

O'NEIL, O'REILLY. *Antonio Jorge*, 29 years old and a native of England belonging to the United States (New England?), the son of Goschua Orial, or Onial (Joshua O'Reilly or O'Neil?), and María Isabel Palín (?), was baptized at Taos, Feb. 12, 1832 (B-48, *Taos*).

ORNELAS. *Andrés Ornelas* and *Francisca Gallegos* had the following family: *Juan Andrés*, Nov. 30, 1831 (B-22, *Picurís*); *José de Jesús*, Nov. 10, 1833 (*ibid.*); *Juan Antonio*, July 15, 1838 (B-51, *Taos*); *Juan José*, Mar. 11, 1844 (?) (*ibid.*); and *María Guadalupe*, who married José Ignacio Alcón at Lo de Mora, Nov. 15, 1853; here her deceased mother's name is given as Gurulé instead of Gallegos. (M-41, *Taos*.) In the baptismal entries the paternal grandparents are given as José Arnel, or Ornelas, and María Gertrudis Valenzuela, or Vizcarra.

ORRANTIA. *José Julián Orrantia*, a native of Chihuahua, asked to marry *Catalina Chávez* of Albuquerque in 1826. His parents were Miguel Orrantia and María Cristina de la Luz Lavora (DM, 1826).

ORTEGA. *Don Melquiades A. Ortega*, a native of La Villa del Paso and resident of Santa Fe, received permission to marry *Doña María Concepción Marioni*, a native of Real de Cosiquiriachic, Oct. 26, 1830 (AASF, *Patentes*, LXX).

ORTIBI. *Carlos Ortibi*, a native of St. Louis, the son of Francisco Ortibi and Serafina Teyta (Sarah Tate?), married *María Serafina Avila* at Taos, Nov. 28, 1842 (M-40, *Taos*). Their known children were: *María Francisca*, Sept. 17, 1843, when the paternal grandparents are given as José Ortibi and María Minimo (?) (B-51, *Taos*); *María Manuela*, June 13, 1846 (B-52, *Taos*); and *José Manuel*, who married Guadalupe Gallegos, Dec. 27, 1854 (M-42, *Taos, Arroyo Hondo*).

Tomás Ortibi, son of Bartolomé Ortibi and Serafina Tishman (same Teyta woman *supra*?), was married to *Pascuala Bernal*. They had a son, *Juan de Jesús*, Oct. 18, 1846 (B-52, *Taos*). Ten years later the surname is given as Tomás

Tobin or *Tobens*, if the same man, and married to Pascuala Bernal. Two Tobin children were: *Juan Nepomuceno*, April 26, 1858, and *María Serafina*, Sept. 4, 1860 (B-1, *Arroyo Hondo*).

PARSONS. *Columbia Parson* and *Paula Aragón* had a child, *María Dionisia*, Sept. 7, 1853. Paternal grandparents were Haron (Aaron?) and Jane Parsons (B-54, *Taos*).

PARTUÉ. The marriage of *Tomás Partué* and *María Guadalupe*, of the "Western Nation," was revalidated at Taos, Dec. 22, 1830 (M-39, *Taos*). A son, *Juan Miguel*, was baptized on Jan. 12, 1831, when the mother is designated as an Indian squaw of the "Western Nation." The paternal grandparents are given as Luis Partué and Cecilia Canayta (B-48, *Taos*).

PATTERSON. *Manuel Antonio*, 21 years old and a native of Missouri, the son of Tomás and Pales (Alice?) Patteon or Pariuchon (Patterson?), was baptized at Taos, Jan. 1, 1832 (B-48, *Taos*).

PEQUET. *Francisco Antonio Pequet*, the son of Solis Pequet, deceased, and María Refugio Martín, married *Deluvina Gutiérrez*, April 8, 1864 (M-42, *Taos*).

José Paquete and *María Refugio Mares* had a son, *José Lucas*, May 1, 1849. The paternal grandparents were Rafael and Catarina Paquete (B-53, *Taos*).

PERES. *José Peregrino Peres*, or *Peri*, a native of the United States of America, married *Petra Campbell*, Nov. 26, 1847 (M-55, *Santa Fe*).

PÉREZ. *Demetrio Pérez*, the son of Albino Pérez [Mexican Governor], deceased, and Trinidad Trujillo, married *María Dolores Newman* in 1861, after a dispensation of 4th degree consanguinity (M, *Santa Fé*).

PERIBÚ. *Antonio Abán Peribúr* and *Pascuala Chávez* had a son, *José Antonio*, Feb. 24, 1852. The paternal grandparents were Andrés Peribú and María Gladjellez (?) (B-54, *Taos*).

PLEY. *José Pley*, a native of the city of Cádiz, married *María Benigna Lee*, June 10, 1844. His parents were Francisco Pley and Josefa Bosedie, or Rosedie. (M-40, *Taos*.)

POBA. *Cristóbal Poba*, a widower of North America, married *María Barbara Aragón*, Sept. 28, 1823 (B-38, *Taos*, M section).

POPE. *Julián Pope*, 26 years old and a native of Quintoque (Kentucky), the son of Juan Pope and María Paula Vance, was baptized at Taos, Jan. 28, 1831 (B-48, *Taos*). He married *María Juliana Salazar*, Dec. 8, 1834, when his mother's name is given as Margarita Bera (M-40, *Taos*). For some reason a second wedding ceremony took place in Santa Fe, July 11, 1835 (M-53, *Santa Fe*).

PORRAS. *Juan Porras* married *María Juana Romero*, July 9, 1832 (M-39, *Taos*). At the baptism of their son, *José Julián*, the paternal grandparents are given as José Porras and Rita Gallardo (B-48, *Taos*).

PORTELANCE. *José Portelanse*, stranger, married *María Josefa Torres*, Dec. 17, 1832 (M-39, *Taos*). Two known children were *María Soledad*, Jan. 27, 1840, when the paternal grandparents are given as Santiago Protelance and María Genoveva Bre (B-51, *Taos*); and *María Luisa*, Dec. 3, 1843 (*ibid.*).

PORTER. *Carlos Porter*, a native of Ireland and the son of Tomás and Nancy (?) Porter, married *Lucinda Bibar (Weaver)* in Santa Fe, Dec. 23, 1849 (M-55, *Santa Fe*).

PORTUGUÉ. *Pedro Portugé*, the son of Francisco and Guadalupe Portugé, and his wife *Mariana Portugé* had twins, *Francisco Antonio* and *María Luz*, Oct. 16, 1846. The mother's parents were not verified "because they were strangers" (B-52, *Taos*). For what may be the same couple, *see* Yerris *infra*.

PROVENCIO. *Nepomuceno Provencio*, a resident of El Paso, the son of Romualdo Provencio, deceased, and Gertrudis Boruda, married *María Soledad Sánchez* of Albuquerque, July 25, 1836 (M-5, *Albuq.*).

Francisco Prudencio, the son of Feliz Prudencio and Jacinta Martín, married *Manuela Pineda* in Santa Fe, Oct. 25, 1827 (M-53, *Santa Fe*). This name is probably a corruption of "Provencio."

QUENEL. *Pedro Quenel* married *María Ignacia Trujillo*, July 26, 1832 (M-39, *Taos*). Known children were: *José Dolores*, 1833 (B-49, *Taos*); *María Virginia*, April 19, 1837 (*ibid.*); and *María Candelaria*, Feb. 3, 1842 (B-51, *Taos*). Most likely another daughter was *María Ignacia Quenel* who married Juan Cristóbal Leftruk, April 10, 1853 (M-41, *Taos*). In the first baptismal entry the father is designated as Pedro Quinel "of America." In the other two the surname is given as "Gueneco" and "Caneco."

QUIFLE. *Julián Antonio Quifle* (?), an adult native of the United States of North America, was baptized at San Miguel, Feb. 18, 1842 (B-2, *San Miguel del Vado*). See "Julián el Americano" in Anonymous *supra*.

QUINTANA. *Don Teodosio Quintana*, a native of Villa de León and later resident of Chihuahua, married Josefa Alarid, widow of Ignacio Salazar, in Santa Fe, Jan. 6, 1826. His parents were Miguel Quintana and María Loreto Sandoval (M-53, *Santa Fé*).

QUINTO. *Carlos Quinto (Kent?)*, 25 years old and a native of Quintoc (Kentucky), the son of Santiago Quinto and Sera (Sarah) Young, was baptized at Taos, Oct. 29, 1828 (B-47, *Taos*). He married *Juana María Gallegos*, Mar. 3, 1829, with Julián Gon (Gordon) and Juana María Lucero as witnesses (M-39, *Taos*). Two known children were *Juan Bautista*, Jan. 14, 1832 (B-47, *Taos*), and *Carlos*, who married Encarnación Naranjo at Mora, Dec. 17, 1867 (M-46, *Mora*). In this wedding entry the father is mentioned as deceased, while the mother's name is given as Antonia instead of Juana María.

QUIRÓS. *Luis Quirós*, a soldier of the Company of Chihuahua in Santa Fe, married *Josefa Gallegos*, Mar. 28, 1845. His parents were Regino Quirós and Trinidad Salmeras (M-54, *Santa Fé*).

RAMÍREZ. *José María Ramírez*, of the province of Cuaguila, a captive of the Comanche since childhood, married *María Manuela --- ------* at San Miguel, Dec. 27, 1848 (M-2, *San Miguel del Vado*).

RAMOS. *José de la Cruz Ramos*, descended from the Apache tribe, married *Ana María Pacheco*, Feb. 21, 1842 (M-40, *Taos*).

RANGEL. *Narciso Rangel*, 28 years old and a native of San Luis Potosí, married *Rafaela Tapia* of Los Padillas, July 14, 1846. His parents were Paulín Rangel and Rita Tapia (M-49, *Isleta*).

READ. *Francisco Rian (Franklin?) y Perigo*, from the United States of America, the son of Larkin Bran (?) y Perigo and Edith Mecez (Mathis, Matthews?) Perigo, married *María Ignacia Cano* in Santa Fé, Oct. 28, 1849 (M-55, *Santa Fé*). A son of theirs, *Benjamin*, married Asención Silva, Jan. 22, 1877, and then her sister, Magdalena Silva, July 7, 1879 (M, *Santa Fe*). Another son, *Alejandro*, of Tierra Amarilla, married Perfecta Madrid, Jan. 12, 1875 (M, *El Rito*). In the sons' marriage entries the surname is given as "Read."

RED. *Juan de Jesús Red (Reed, Reid?)*, 24 years old and a native of the "City of Missouri," the son of Samuel Red and Isabel Fevel or Ferel (Farrell?), was baptized at Taos, Sept. 18, 1840 (B-51, *Taos*). He married *María Nieves Rolem*, Sept. 21, 1840 (M-40, *Taos*).

REGALADO. *Pedro Regalado*, son of Julián Regalado and Rita García, married *Manuela Atencio* of Belén, April 14, 1828 (DM, 1827; M-7, *Belén*).

REY. *Pedro Rey*, with four other Frenchmen in Taos, applied to marry, June 5, 1826. His intended was *María Luz Sarbed* (Servé). (AASF, *Accounts*, LXVI.) See Guará and Yarat, *supra et infra*.

RINCÓN. *José Rincón* and *Francisca Moreno* of El Paso had a son at Belén, *José Francisco*, July 21, 1833 (B-9, *Belén*).

RIVAS. *José Francisco Rivas*, a native of Pueblo de Chubisca, married *María Eugenia Tafoya* at Taos, Oct. 11, 1847. His parents were José Francisco Rivas and Guadalupe Gutiérrez (M-41, *Taos*).

ROBINSON. *Santiago Robinson*, a native of the United States, married *María Severiana Rael* of Los Gabaldones, Jan. 22, 1851 (M-7, *Belén*).

ROBLEDO. *Don Dámaso Robledo*, a native of Santander, married *Prudencia Ortiz* of Santa Fe, July 13, 1840. His parents were Eusebio Robledo and Gabina Ocaris. (M-54, *Santa Fe*.) They had a son, *José Candido Esquipulas Eusebio*, Dec. 29, 1843 (B-2, *San Miguel del Vado*).

Francisco de Paula Robledo was Dámaso's brother, as we learn from the baptism of his son, *José George*, April 23, 1842. The wife and mother was *Manuela Jaramillo;* the paternal grandparents are Eusebio Robledo and Gabina Ocaris (*ibid.*). A daughter, *Gabina*, became the wife of Carlos Eckart of Saxony, Feb. 12, 1866 (M, *Santa Fe*).

ROBLERO CALDERÓN. *Ramón Roblero Calderón*, widowed of his first wife, *Petra López*, married *María Ignacia Romero* of Santa Fe, Sept. 30, 1844 (M-54, *Santa Fe*).

ROBLES. *José Cecilio Roble*, a native of the city of Guadalajara, parish of El Sagrario, married *María Dolores Baca* of Santa Fe, Nov. 16, 1845. His parents were Manuel Roble and Dorotéa López (M-55, *Santa Fé*). He next married *Juana Sena*, Oct. 3, 1863, when his parents are given as Manuel Roblero and Dorotéa López de Nava (M, *Santa Fe*).

José María Robles was a brother of José Cecilio. A native of Guadalajara and son of the same parents, he asked to marry *María de Jesús Baca* of the Río Abajo in 1848 (DM, 1848).

RODRIGUEZ. *Juan Crisóstomo Rodríguez*, from the province of Bejar, married *Lucía Benavides* of the Río Abajo, Oct. 11, 1824. His parents were José Balio (Basilio?) Rodríguez and Paula Cruz (M-49, *Isleta*).

ROLES. *Tomás Roles (Rawlis, Rollins, Rowland?)*, "from the United States of America," married *Tomasa Trujillo* of Santa Fe, Feb. 21, 1843. His parents were Norberto Roles and María Macley (?) (M-54, *Santa Fé*). *María Luz Rolenes*, daughter of Tomás Rolenes [mother's name omitted], married Antonio Vigil, Oct. 1, 1848 (M-55, *Santa Fe*).

Juan Rolis, a native of Pennsylvania, married *María Encarnación Martín* at Taos, Oct. 27, 1825 (B-48, *Taos*). Their known children were: *José Manuel*, May 28, 1825 (?) (B-38, *Taos*); *María Nieves*, Aug. 10, 1828 (B-47, *Taos*), who married Juan de Jesús Red, Sept. 21, 1840 (M-40, *Taos*); *María Rosalía*, June 13, 1830 (B-47, *Taos*); *Juan Bautista*, Feb. 13, 1832 (B-48, *Taos*); *María Rita*, June 12, 1833 (B-49, *Taos*); *José Tomás*, Dec. 5, 1834 (*ibid.*); *José Julián*, Oct. 19, 1838 (B-51, *Taos*); and *María Refugio*, Aug. 3, 1841 (*ibid.*). The father is here given variously as "Roles, Role, Roland, Rouland." The paternal grandfather is "Juan Rolen, Roles, Roberto, Bojante, Santiago Role, Norverto Rouland, Tomás Roles, Ruperto Rolis." The paternal grandmother is "María Roles, Metrol Mecol (?), Manuela Mecoy, Ysidora Micoi, María Quintoquiel, María Rolis." In the 1825 baptism the father is designated as a native of Canada. Perhaps he was a brother or half brother of the preceding Tomás Roles. The surname is spelled "Rolan" when Juan and his wife acted as sponsors at Lo de Mora, Nov. 5, 1836 (B-49, *Taos*). Were these the leaders of the famed Rowland party that went to California?

ROMO DE BIBAR. *Manuel Romo de Bibar*, a native of Sonora, the son of Francisco Romo de Bibar and Teresa Martínez, married *Doña Jesús Trujillo* of Santa Fe, July 5, 1828 (M-53, *Santa Fe*).

RONQUILLO. *Ramón Ronquillo*, widowed of *Eulalia ----------*, parish of San Lorenzo de Picurís, married *Sebastiana Páez*, Feb. 14, 1841 (M-40, *Taos*).

ROTURE. *José Roture*, one of four Frenchmen in Taos who applied to marry, June 5, 1826, had as his intended *María Luisa Vigil* (AASF, *Accounts*, LXVI). See Carlos Guará supra. However, he married *María Josefa González* of Taos, June 26, 1826 (B-38, *Taos*, M section). Known children were *María Dolores*, April 5, 1827, when the paternal grandparents are given as Pedro Rotura and "María America" (B-47, *Taos*); and *José Francisco*, April 13, 1828, the paternal grandparents being Pedro Rutura and Josefa Lacar (*ibid.*).

RUBIDOUX. *Francisco Rubidoux*, Frenchman, had a natural daughter, *María Juana*, Jan. 30, 1826, by Luisa Romero of Taos (B-38, *Taos*).

RUBÍN. *José Francisco Rubín*, 25 years old and a native of Nueva Ullorca (New York), the son of Santiago Rubín and María Tomasa Bruce, was baptized at Taos, April 5, 1828 (B-47, *Taos*). He married *María de Jesús Gallegos*, August 30, 1828 (M-39, *Taos*).

Andrés Rubín, a stranger 65 years old, died at Taos five minutes after he was baptized on his deathbed, June 7, 1831 (B-48, *Taos*).

RUSSELL. *Luis Rossell* and *María Doloritas Aragón* of La Cebolla had a daughter, *María*, who married José Ramón Aragón, Nov. 23, 1863. "Ruysell" is written on the margin (M-46, *Mora*).

SABLET. *José Miguel Sablet*, a native of Quintoc (Kentucky), the son of Felipe Sablet and Isabel Suise or Guisle (Wesley?), was baptized at Taos, June 8, 1828 (B-47, *Taos*).

SALALLANDIA. *José Reyes Salallandia*, a native of El Paso, asked to marry *Juana Nepomucena Sisneros* of Albuquerque in 1829. His parents were Anastasio Salallandia and Dorotéa Provencio (DM, 1829).

SALINAS. *Guillermo Salinas*, a native of Villa de Candela, province of Coahuila, married *Juana Gertrudis Sandoval*, Nov. 22, 1825. His parents were Juan José Salinas and Josefa Ramírez (M-53, *Santa Fe*).

José Agapito Salinas, a native of San Pedro Alcantara in Monterrey, married *María Josefa Gabriela Frésquez* in 1830. His parents were José María Salinas and María Isabel Ramos (M-22, *Pojoaque*).

SAMBRANO. *José Francisco Apolonio Sambrano*, a native of El Paso, married *María Margarita Pacheco*, Feb. 19, 1828. His parents were Gregorio Sambrano and María Yrene Grijalva (M-32, *Santa Cruz*).

Albino Sambrano, a soldier of the Company of San Elizario in Santa Fe, widowed of Cresencia Grageda, married *María Luisa Romero*, Dec. 25, 1844 (M-45, *Santa Fe*). Evidently both Sambrano men were descendants of pre-1680 New Mexico families that stayed at Guadalupe del Paso.

SÁNCHEZ. *Mariano Sánchez*, a native of Querétaro residing throughout the state of Chihuahua for three years, and thirteen months in Santa Fe, married *Rosario Sandoval* of Santa Fe in 1825. His parents were Ignacio Sánchez and Marcelina Cubillos (M-53, *Santa Fe*).

SAN MARTÍN. *José Manuel San Martín* was married to *María Manuela Chávez de Perea* and resided in the Bernalillo-Jémez area. Both acted as wedding sponsors, Dec. 14, 1818, and Jan. 5, 1819 (M-17, *Jémez*). Known children were *José Diego Victoriano*, Nov. 8, 1819 (*ibid.*, B section); and *José Felix Esquipulas*, Nov. 20, 1820 (*ibid.*). According to the latter baptisms, José Manuel San Martín was the son of Catarina Tafoya and an unknown father. On Sept. 11, 1820, at San Ysidro, was baptized José Concepción, the natural son of a grandson of Manuel San Martín "El Ynvalido" and of a *coyota* of his household (*ibid.*). This surname most likely continued as "Martínez."

SANSERMAN. *Bautista Brison*, a Frenchman of Canada, the son of Alexo Brison and María Luisa Chabon, married *María Manuela Mondragón* at Taos, Aug. 14, 1824 (B-38, *Taos*, M section). Known children were: *José Francisco*, Mar. 14, 1825, when "Brisol" is the surname (*ibid.*); *José Francisco Eugenio*, Oct. 7, 1827, when the father is designated as "Sanserman" and a native of France (B-47, *Taos*); *Juan Bautista*, Aug. 22, 1832, when the father is called "Luis Sanserman" and the paternal grandparents are given as Luis Sanserman y Brisol and Ana María Sabot (M-48, *Taos*); *José Antonio*, Feb. 17, 1835, when the paternal grandparents are given as José Sanserman and Teresa Lobato (B-49, *Taos*); *María Pacífica*, May 6, 1839, when these same grandparents are given as José Brigido Sanserman and Luisa Sarete (B-51, *Taos*); and *María Donaciana*, May 27, 1841, when the same are given as José Grisal and María Lobato (*ibid.*). One of the two elder sons, José Francisco, married María de Jesús Rodarte, Feb. 17, 1845, when the surname is "Brichal" (M-40, *Taos*).

SANTETE. *Juan Santete*, a native of Bordeaux, received permission to marry *María Tiburcia Trujillo*, June 19, 1829 (AASF, *Patentes*, LXX). They were married at Taos, July 2, 1829. His parents were Juan Santete and María Baruet (M-39, *Taos*). Known children were: *José Gabriel*, Mar. 19, 1830 (B-47, *Taos*), who married María de la Cruz Valdez, June 23, 1851 (M-41, *Taos*); *Juan de Jesús*, Aug. 26, 1832 (B-48, *Taos*); *José Francisco*, Nov. 27, 1835 (B-49, *Taos*); *Pedro Eugenio*, Mar. 18, 1839 (B-51, *Taos*); and *María Leonor*, Sept. 6, 1841 (*ibid.*). In these baptisms the paternal grandfather is given as Juan, or Bautista, or Juan Formé de Santete; the grandmother is given as María Busut or Borue, Margarita Donay, and once as "Ortiz" (?).

SAUNIER. *Victor Suñé*, a native of France, widowed of Micaela Sisneros, married *Marie Seferino Sena* at San Miguel, May 17, 1848 (M-2, *San Miguel del Vado*). As Victor Saunier he later married *Ana María Córdoba*, widow of Ramón Aragón, at Las Vegas, April 13, 1853 (M, *Las Vegas*).

SCOLLY. *Juan Escolly (Scolly?)*, a native of Ireland, the son of Patricio Escolly and Igura (?) Bradis (Brady?), married *Juana López* in Santa Fe, Mar. 30, 1843 (M-54, *Santa Fe*).

SEBALLES. *Francisco Seballes*, the son of Juan Seballes and Luisa Carreras, natives of the state of Sonora and San Luis Potosí, married *Dolores García* in Santa Fe, Feb. 25, 1835 (M-53, *Santa Fe*). Their daughter, *Leonides*, residing at Pecos, married Juan Luis Rougemont, Feb. 6, 1865 (M, *Santa Fe*).

SEIJAS. *Pedro Faustino Seifar or Seijas (?)*, widowed of *María Manuela Ylesi*, applied to marry *Juana María Chávez* of the Río Abajo in 1818 (DM, 1818).

SERVÉ. See EL PALACIO, vol. 64, nos. 5, 6.

SERVÍN. *Francisco Servín* (a Spanish, not French, surname) married *Lugarda Moya (Montoya?)* in Santa Fe, Nov. 8, 1819 (M-52, *Santa Fe*). Widowed of Lugarda Montoya (Moya?), and as a soldier of Santa Fe, he asked the Governor for permission to contract marriage with *María Deluvina Hurtado* of San Miguel del Vado, Mar. 13, 1836 (AASF, 1836, no. 3).

SHULL. *Francisco Shull (Schul?)* was married to *María Dolores Trujillo* at Taos. Two known children were *Apolonio*, who married María Francisca Silva, Mar. 11, 1850 (M-41, *Taos*), and had a daughter, María de Jesús de Talpa, Aug. 25, 1852 (B-54, *Taos*); and *María Petra*, who had a natural son, Toribio, Mar. 5, 1851 (*ibid.*).

SIMPSON. *George Simpson*, a native of St. Louis and residing at San Carlos de Napeste, married *Ana María Suazo*, Oct. 14, 1844. His parents were Robert Simpson and María Bricia (Breece?) (M-40, *Taos*). Three known children were: *María Isabel*, Oct. 13, 1844 (B-52, *Taos*); *José Alejandro*, at Lo de Mora, Oct. 29, 1853, when the paternal grandparents are given as Norbert and Mary Grace Sampson (B, *Las Vegas*); and *José Noverto*, of San Antonio de Mora (Cleveland), who married *María Josefa García*, June 8, 1868 (M-46, *Mora*).

SIOTE. *Francisco Siotte*, stranger, received permission to marry, Sept. 1826 (AASF, *Accounts*, LXVI). He married *María Soledad González* and they were living at Santa Barbara where a son, *José Francisco*, was baptized on Aug. 8, 1833, when the paternal grandparents are given as Pedro Siote and Santana ---------- (B-22, *Picurís*). This son married Agapita Leyva, who bore a son, Juan, at Mora, Feb. 14, 1854 (B, *Las Vegas*).

SKINNER. *Don Guillermo C. Esquine* (Wm. C. Skinner?), a sort of lawyer, was involved in parish difficulties at Belén, August, 1847 (AASF, *Patentes*, LXXI).

Josefa Margarita Esquiner, daughter of Santiago Esquiner and adopted daughter of Soledad Abreu, married Cipriano Lara of Chihuahua, Jan. 19, 1863 (M, *Santa Fe*).

SMITH. *José Francisco Esmite* (Smith), 27 years old and a native of Quintoc (Kentucky), the son of Cristóbal Esmite and Mariana Lont, was baptized at Taos, Feb. 8, 1828 (B-47, *Taos*).

Antonio Esmite, of the United States of America, the son of Emil Esmite and María Piure (?), married *Juana Ortiz* of Santa Fe in 1836 (M-54, *Santa Fe*).

SOLIS. *Julián Solis*, 27 years old, the son of Esteban Solis and María Arellano, married *Juana Griego* at Pajarito, Feb. 11, 1846 (M-49, *Isleta*).

SOMOSA. *Filomeno Somosa*, a native of Valladolid, the son of Raymundo Somosa and Cornelia Naredo, married *Dolores Guerrero* in Santa Fe, Jan. 4, 1849 (M-55, *Santa Fe*).

SOTO. *José Dolores Soto*, a native of the city of Aguas Calientes, married *María de Jesús Montoya*, Dec. 2, 1840. His parents were José Urbano Soto and María Paulina Martínez (M-54, *Santa Fe*).

Marie Victoria Sota, or *Sosa*, a native of El Paso and stepdaughter of Ramón Tenorio of Taos, was granted permission to marry Miguel Antonio Lucero of Jémez, Mar., 1831 (AASF, *Patentes*, LXX).

SPAULDING. *David Spaulding*, a native of Velmonte (Vermont) in the United States of America, married *María Gerónima García* at Taos, Mar. 20, 1842. His parents were Samson Spaulding and María Temperance Nott (M-40, *Taos*). A daughter, *María Rosario*, was baptized on Dec. 23, 1842, when the grandfather's name is given as Simon instead of Samson (B-51, *Taos*).

STANLEY. *Eliseo Stanley*, a citizen of the United States of North America, filed suit against the priest of Albuquerque, June 17, 1829, on a debt owed him since December of the previous year (AASF, 1830, no. 19). Another suit, same subject, was filed by *Augusto Storrs*, or *Storn*, for his countryman, *Ricardo Rowess*. Still another was filed by *Richard Stowers* (same man as Rowess?) and Luis Roubidoux (*ibid.*).

SUÁREZ MONTERO. *Antonio Montero*, a native of Oporto in Portugal, married *María Francisca Vigil*, Aug. 9, 1841. His parents were José Soarez Montero and Ana María Manuela Montero (M-40, *Taos*). Permission for the overseas groom to marry had been granted on July 25 (AASF, *Patentes*, C-1). Known children were *María Paula*, Feb. 6, 1843 (B-51, *Taos*), and *Antonio*, May 25, 1845 (B-52, *Taos*). In these two entries the surname is given as Suares Montero.

SUPAUME. *José Santos Supaume* and *José Suñé* (*see* Saunier), strangers and vagrants at

Taos, were granted permission by the Santa Fe Vicar to contract marriage, July 2, 1831 (AASF, *Patentes*, LXX). Supaume, widower of María Luisa Bergad, married *María Josefa Bernal*, July 20, 1831 (M-39, *Taos*).

SUR. *Francisco Sur*, Frenchman, had a natural son, *Juan Nepomuceno*, in 1825, by María de Jesús Martínez (B-38, *Taos*).

TABACO. *Matías Tabaco* and *Martina Luján* had a son, *Hilario*, married to María Carmel Trujillo and living at Ranchos de Taos; these had a child, Josefa, April 15, 1829 (B-47, *Taos*). These were *genízaro* Indians, perhaps.

TAICOGUETE. *Nazario Taicoguete* and *Margarita* ---------- had a child, *Francisco*, of French nationality, who was buried at Taos, Dec. 16, 1823 (B-38, *Taos*).

TASACARRA. *Ignacio Tasacarra*, of French nationality, the son of José Tasacarra, was buried at Taos, June 2, 1824 (B-38, *Taos*).

TAUSLE. *Juan José Tausle*, or *Taush* (?), married *Trinidad Abrego* in Santa Fe, Jan. 9, 1849 (M-55, *Santa Fe*).

TAYLOR. *Diques (Dick, Richard) Julián (Wm.) Tichutepe*, stranger, the natural son of María Isabel Tichutepe, married *María Esquipulas Sandoval*, Dec. 12, 1831 (M-39, *Taos*). As Julián Tichutepe, vagrant and stranger, he had received permission from the Santa Fe Vicar, Nov. 29, to marry this woman (AASF, *Patentes*, LXX). In his son and grandchildren the name changes to *Taylor*, and one wonders if Tichutepe (Tissue-tape?) had been kidding the Padre with a false and ridiculous name.

Antonio Rodrigo Telar (Taylor), the son of Ricardo Telar and María Esquipula Sandoval, both deceased, married *María Ignacia Lucero* of Taos, Feb. 27, 1852 (M-42, *Taos*). Known children of theirs were: *María Susana*, May 26, 1855 (B-1, *Arroyo Hondo*); *María Francisca*, Nov. 20, 1856 (*ibid.*); and *José Lino*, Sept. 25, 1858 (*ibid.*). "Taylor" is the spelling in all these baptisms.

TEDESCHI. *Roque Tedeschi*, a native of Italy, the son of Juan Bautista Tedeschi and María Ana Arabatania (?), married *María Ignacia Larrañaga*, Sept. 15, 1842 (M-54, *Santa Fe*). Their son, *José Gabriel*, married Petra Salas of Santa Fe, May 30, 1866, when the surname is spelled "Tudeschi" (M, *Santa Fe*).

THORPE. *Juan Antonio Tharp*, 32 years old and a native of North America, the son of Aron Tharp (Aaron Thorpe?) and María Eduares (Edwards?), was baptized at Taos, Aug. 3, 1828 (B-47, *Taos*).

TICHUTEPE. See Taylor *supra*.

TOBINS, TOBEN. See Ortibi *supra*.

TREVIÑO. *José Villervo (Viterbo?) de Treviño*, a native of Villa de San Andrés de Nava, and residing at Abiquiú, asked to marry *María Antonia Alvina Apodaca* of Cañón de Jémez in 1826. His parents were Canuto Treviño, deceased, and María Josefa de la Garza (DM, 1826).

TRIDEAU. *Juan Bautista Trideau*, an "Anglo-American" in Taos, was granted permission by the Santa Fe Vicar, June, 1826, for contracting marriage (AASF, *Accounts*, LXVI). He married *María Guadalupe Córdoba* in Taos, July 19, 1826 (B-38, *Taos*). Known children were: *María Magdalena*, July 3, 1827, when the grandfather is given as Bautista Tridú of Missouri (B-47, *Taos*); *María Martina*, Mar. 16, 1829, when the paternal grandparents are given as Bautista Truidú and Magdalena de Francia (*ibid.*); *Lorenzo Urbán*, May 29, 1831, when the same grandparents are given as Lorenzo Truidú and Magdalena Reyes (B-48, *Taos*); and *María Jacinta*, Feb. 27, 1833 (B-49, *Taos*).

The son, Lorenzo, living at Ojo Caliente, married María Dolores Durán, Sept. 2, 1856 (M-34, *Santa Clara*). He seems to be the same

Lorenzo Urbán Trida, son of Juan Bautista Trida and Guadalupe Córdoba, who married María Manuela Lucero at Servilleta in 1874 (M, *El Rito*).

TULLY. *Julián Tully*, of the United States of America, the son of Luis B. and Asah Tully, married *Trinidad Concle (Conklin)*, Jan. 5, 1848 (M-55, *Santa Fe*).

URIBES. *Jesús Uribes*, 28 years old and from Chihuahua, the son of Crisóstomo Uribes and Josefa Alfaro, married *Casilda Chávez* of Belén, Jan. 17, 1847 (DM, 1847; M-7, *Belén*).

URRUTIA. *Francisco Urrutia*, son of José Antonio Urrutia and María Ignacia Palacios, married *Dolores Armijo* of Albuquerque, Dec. 7, 1847 (M-5, *Albuq.*).

URTIAGA. *Valentín Hurtiaga*, 26 years old, the son of Santiago Hurtiaga and Juana Escajeda, asked to marry *Josefa Chávez* of the Río Abajo in 1845 (DM, 1845).

VALENCIA. *Tomás Valencia* of Taos, a native of the state of Sonora and a resident for many years in Hermosillo, received permission to marry, April 24, 1835; but the bride is not mentioned (AASF, *Patentes*, LXXVI).

VALLES. *José Antonio Valles* married *María Carmen Maes*, June 4, 1832. [Source lost.]

Felipe Valles, son of Pedro Valles and Piedad Balderrain, married *Brigida Olona*, a widow of Tomé, Oct. 29, 1840 (DM, 1840; M-56, *Tomé*).

VAUGHN. *Henry Vaughn*, 26 years old and a native of the state of Arcansas (Arkansas), the son of Julián and Lucia Vaughn, was baptized at Taos, Dec. 24, 1842 (B-51, *Taos*). He married *María Francisca Varela*, Jan. 9, 1843 (M-40, *Taos*).

VELID. *Francisco Velid* of Taos, the son of José Velid and María Josefa Pacheco, married *María Ignacia Vigil* of Santa Cruz, Oct. 3, 1847 (M-33a, *Santa Cruz*).

VIAL. *Don Pedro Bial*, Frenchman, after receiving the last Sacraments and completing his last testament, died in Santa Fe, Oct. 8, 1814 (*Bur.*, 51, *Castrense*).

VIAN. *Marcos Vian* and *Catarina Pando* had a daughter, *Magdalena*, who had a natural son, José Antonio, May 27, 1827 (B-47, *Taos*).

VICENT. *Carlos Vicent* applied with four other Frenchmen in Taos for permission to marry. His intended was *Bartola Romero*. (AASF, *Accounts*, LXVI.) See Guará supra. The marriage took place, July 26, 1826 (B-38, *Taos*, M section).

VILLAOSCURA. *Mariano Villaoscura* of Santa Cruz married *Dolores Luna*, Mar. 7, 1830 (M-33, *Santa Clara*).

VISONET. *José Visonet*, the son of Luis Visonet and María Buquiet, married *María Juliana Aguilar* of Taos, May 29, 1828 (M-39, *Taos*). They had a daughter, *María Peregrina*, July 22, 1832, when the paternal grandparents are given as Juan Bisonete and María Lan (B-48, *Taos*).

VIZCARRA. *Juan Vizcarra*, from Rael de San Antonio de Cuencame, widowed of Doña Micaela Toro, married *Dolores Campos Redondo* in Santa Fe, Oct. 21, 1824 (M-53, *Santa Fe*).

Don José Antonio Vizcarra, "special *Teniente Coronel* for Arms in this Province," married *Doña Ana María Ortiz* in Santa Fe, April 14, 1824. His parents were Don Juan José Vizcarra and Doña Gertrudis Alvarado, residents of Real del Cuencame in the province of Durango (M-51, *Santa Fe*).

VUELSE. *Pedro Vuelse (Welsh?)*, of the United States, and wife, *Ana María Tafoya*, had a daughter, *María Francisca*, July 30, 1835 (B-49, *Taos*).

WALDO. *José David Waldo*, 28 years old and a native of Virginia, the son of Jedediah Waldo and María Panter (?), was baptized at Taos, June 6, 1831 (B-48, *Taos*).

His brother, *Lorenzo Waldo*, 18 years old and a native of Virginia, the son of Jedediah Waldo and María *Porter*, was baptized at Taos, Oct. 13, 1831 (*ibid.*).

WASHINGTON. *Luis Washington*, of the United States of America, the son of Luis Washington and María Vuol (?), married *Marcelina Salas* in Santa Fe, Jan. 7, 1836 (M-54, *Santa Fe*).

WATROUS. *Don Samuel Worres (Watrous)* was living at La Junta de los Ríos where Juan Nepomuceno, a little Indian bought by him, was baptized on April 30, 1854 (B, *Las Vegas*). His wife was *Tomasa Crespín*, according to the baptism of *Samuel Beaumon*, child of Samuel Loatrom (?) and Tomasa Crespín, Feb. 15, 1855 (*ibid.*). A daughter, *Manuela Worres*, married to Julián (Wm.) Tipton, had a daughter, Susana, July 24, 1852, and then another, Susan, at Junta de los Ríos, Mar. 29, 1854 (*ibid.*).

WEAVER. *Paulín de Jesús Guivar (Weaver)*, 29 years old and a native of Tennessee, the son of Benito Guivar and Cecilia Guamaca (?), was baptized at Taos, Aug. 26, 1832 (B-48, *Taos*). He married *María Dolores Martín*, Sept. 10, 1832 (M-39, *Taos*). Known children were: *José Benito Jorge*, April 28, 1833, when the paternal grandparents are given as José Benito Guivar and María Yeles (B-49, *Taos*); *María Guadalupe*, Jan. 21, 1835 (*ibid.*); and *Lucinda*, who married Carlos Porter in Santa Fe, Dec. 23, 1849, when the name is "Bibar," and is further corrected as "Weaver" (M-55, *Santa Fe*).

WILLIAMS. *Carlos Guillermo*, a native of the state of New York, the son of Asa and Mary Starkweather, married *María Guillerma Lafebre*, Nov. 30, 1850 (M-41, *Taos*). Two known children were: *Margarita*, Feb. 16, 1852, when the paternal grandparents are given as Oca and Mary Williams (B-54, *Taos*); and *María*, July 22, 1853, when the surname is spelled "Wianes" (*ibid.*). The family was residing at Ocate when Mary married James May in October, 1866, and Margaret married Henry Blattman in 1868 (M-46, *Mora*).

Julián Ysau Willicicio (?) (Wm. Esau Williams?), 30 years old and a native of Pennsylvania, the son of Ebneser Dillicicio (?) and Unis (Eunice) Gardoerro (?), was baptized at Taos, June 23, 1831 (B-48, *Taos*).

WITT. *María Sedat (Sadie?)*, child of *Julián Guit* (Wm. Witt?), Methodist, and of Rosa Ana Flandel or Handel, Catholic, was baptized on Nov. 17, 1849. Only the paternal grandparents are given: Tomás Guit and Luz Eslec (Lucy Eastlake?). (B-10, *Albuq.*)

WOLFSKILL. *José Guillermo Volesquil*, 32 years old and a native of St. Louis, the son of José Volesquil and Sarah Reid, was baptized at Taos, Mar. 21, 1830 (B-47, *Taos*). Evidently the leader of the famed Wolfskill party to California.

WOOTON. *Richard Wooden (Wooten)*, a native of Virginia, the son of David Wooden and María Francisca Brin (Breen or Green), married *María Dolores Lafebre*, Mar. 6, 1848 (M-41, *Taos*). Known children were *Eligia*, Feb. 24, 1849, when the paternal grandmother's name is Grén (Green?) (B-53, *Taos*); *Richeur* (Richard), July 28, 1850 (B-54, *Taos*); and *María Dolores*, May 30, 1842 (*ibid.*).

WORKMAN. *José Julián Workman*, 26 years old, the son of Tomás Workman and "María de ladin Cook," natives of England belonging to the United States of North America (New England?), was baptized at Taos, June 4, 1828 (B-47, *Taos*). He seems to be the Julián Guaqueman who acted as sponsor on Sept. 18, 1840 (B-51, *Taos*).

YARAT. *Juan Bautista Yarat*, stranger, the son of Francisco Yarat and María Margarita Evaro, married *María Luz Servé*, Sept. 30, 1826 (M-38, *Taos*). See Pedro Rey *supra*. Known children were *José Francisco*, Dec. 14, 1828 (B-47, *Taos*); *José de Jesús*, July 11, 1831 (B-

48, *Taos*); and *María Asención*, May 18, 1833 (B-49, *Taos*). In all these baptisms the paternal grandmother's surname is given as Evero.

YERRIS. *Pedro José Yerris (Jeris, Teris?)*, 37 years old, a merchant, and native of the "City of Portugal," the son of Francisco Teris and Juana Gaula, married *Mariana Verques* in Taos, Jan. 10, 1850. The bride was 20, his servant for 6 years, the daughter of Pedro and Netee Verques, and a native of the state of Morel (Maryland?) in the United States. Their children, not named, were legitimized. A deathbed marriage, apparently (M-41, *Taos*). See Portugué *supra*.

YLISE. *Severiano Ylise* and wife *Juana Montaño* lived in the Tomé-Belén area. Known children were: *José Marcos*, Oct. 22, 1826 (B-10, *Belén*); *José Pablo*, Jan. 25, 1831 (*ibid.*); and *José Lino de la Merced*, Sept. 25, 1828 (*ibid.*). Here the surname is spelled "Elicio" and the paternal grandparents are given as Pablo Elicio and María Valencia. One son, Lino Ylise, married María Quirina Gonzáles, Nov. 24, 1851, but "Luis" is written for "Lino" in one entry (DM, 1851; M-54, *Tomé*), and also at the baptism of a son, José Camilo, Feb. 12, 1853 (B, *Tomé*). A *María Manuela Ylise*, who had been married to Pedro Fausto Seifar or Seijas prior to 1818, might have been Severiano's sister.

YON. *Joaquín Yon* (Young?), 35 years old and a native of Tennessee, the son of Carlos Yon and María Rebeca Uiliquines (Wilkins?), was baptized at Taos, May 11, 1831 (B-48, *Taos*).

YUYE. *Luis Yuye* (Jules?), an adult of French nationality, the son of Bautista Yuye, was buried in Taos, Feb. 18, 1824 (B-38, *Taos*).

ZEPEDA. *Juan Zepeda* of Coahuila, the son of Juan Manuel Zepeda and María Juana Rivas, married *María Isabel Herrera*, Dec. 13, 1830 (M-33, *Santa Clara*).

BIBLIOGRAPHY

I. MANUSCRIPT SOURCES

AASF — *Archives of the Archdiocese of Santa Fe.* These are a few odd documents, numbered from 1 to 30, but not every number filled.

AGI. — *Archivo General de Indias, Sevilla:* 1. *Audiencia;* 2. *Escribania de Camara;* 3. *Guadalajara;* 4. *Patronato.* All these are photo copies, bound and numbered according to general title and *legajo* number, in the Coronado Library of the University of New Mexico. *Patronato, legajo* 244, quoted, from Library of Congress. 5. *Contaduria:* transcript copies loaned by Dean France V. Scholes.

AGN. — *Archivo General de la Nacion, Mexico:* 1. *Inquisicion;* 2. *Tierras: Civil;* 3. *Provincias Internas;* 4. *Historia.* Photo copies in the Coronado Library of the University of New Mexico. Some *Inquisicion* references by page, instead of *foja,* are to transcript copies owned by Dean Scholes, to be found also in Library of Congress and Ayer Collection.

AYER COLL. — *Spanish American MSS,* in the Edward A. Ayer Collection, Newberry Library, Chicago.

BANCROFT, NMO, SWO. — (*New Mexico Originals, Southwest Originals,* with year of document.) Manuscripts collected by H. H. Bancroft, and now in the Bancroft Library, University of California, Berkeley. They are described in *New Mexico Historical Review,* Vol. XXV, No. 3, pp. 248-252. — Also, *Libros de Entradas y Recepciones,* etc., three manuscript volumes in *Mexican MSS* section, Nos. 216, 217, 218.

B, BUR., M. — *Baptismal, Burial,* and *Marriage* Books (with or without number) and Mission of origin. E. g., B-27, S. Juan; Bur-48, Sta. Fe; M-11, Isleta. Extant volumes collected from the missions and parishes in 1934 and now in the Archives of the Archdiocese of Santa Fe, each tagged and numbered by L. B. Bloom. (Some fell into private hands decades ago and may still exist. The first Baptismal, Burial, and Marriage Books of Santa Fe, from 1694 to about 1726, were long ago lost or pilfered. The first Baptismal Book of Albuquerque had an early section (1711-1726) removed even before being bound in its ancient rawhide cover. Some volumes of other places are incomplete because of deterioration and poor care.) — Three late eighteenth-century volumes of *Laguna-Acoma* are at the cathedral parish of Gallup. — *Guadalupe del Paso* registers quoted are at the Old Mission in Ciudad Juárez, Mexico. References to the First Marriage Book of Guadalupe del Paso, now lost, are from the "Bandelier Notes" in the Peabody Museum, Cambridge. — Some Roybal baptisms, as noted, are from the parish files of Santo Tomás, Caldas de Reyes, Galicia, Spain.

BNM. — *Biblioteca Nacional de Mexico.* Photo copies, bound and designated according to general title, etc., in the Coronado Library of the University of New Mexico.

DM. — *Diligencias Matrimoniales,* year, with or without number. Nuptial investigations and testimonies, some fragmentary, in the Archives of the Archdiocese of Santa Fe. I numbered the ones from 1680 to 1729. The rest remain unnumbered, but sorted as to years. Others, duly noted as such, are in the parish files of Belén, Santa Cruz, and San Felipe in Albuquerque, neither numbered nor sorted.

HSNM. — *Historical Society of New Mexico.* Assorted manuscripts in the Archive of the Museum of New Mexico, including Military Papers of enlistments.

MNM. — *Museo Nacional de Mexico: Asuntos.* Bound photo copies in the Coronado Library of the University of New Mexico.

RITCH COLL. — *Ritch Collection* in the Huntington Library, San Marino. The oldest ones are manuscripts taken from the Spanish Archives of the Palace of the Governors by Territorial ex-Secretary W. G. Ritch. These are described in *New Mexico Historical Review,* Vol. XXV, No. 3, pp. 245-248.

ORTIZ TRIAL, *Criminal Contra Nicolas Ortiz,* etc., 1642, Archivo del Parral, transcript of F. V. Scholes.

SP. ARCH., I *and* II. — *Spanish Archives of New Mexico,* Vols. I and II, indexed and described by Ralph E. Twitchell, Cedar Rapids, 1914.

(*Note*: His transcriptions of words and proper names, plus comments, often misleading.) Contents of Vol. I are wills and land-transfers from the Palace of the Governors, and now in the vault of the United States Land Office in Santa Fe. Those of Vol. II, judicial and military documents, are still at the Palace, in the vault of the Museum of New Mexico.

TWIT. COLL. — Old manuscripts and fragments collected by Twitchell, presumably after he had indexed the Spanish Archives. These are in the vault of the Museum of New Mexico.

II. BOOKS AND MONOGRAPHS

BANCROFT, HUBERT HOWE, *History of New Mexico and Arizona,* San Francisco, 1889.

BANDELIER, ADOLPH F., *The Gilded Man,* New York, 1893.

B-H, III. — Bandelier-Hackett, *Historical Documents relating to New Mexico, Nueva Viscaya, and Approaches thereto, to 1773.* Collected by F. A. and F. R. Bandelier, and edited by Charles Wilson Hackett, Washington, 1937.

BENAVIDES, FRAY ALONSO DE, *Memorial on New Mexico, 1630,* translated by Mrs. E. E. Ayer, Chicago, 1916. — *Fray Alonso de Benavides' Revised Memorial of 1634,* edited by F. W. Hodge, G. P. Hammond, and Agapito Rey, Albuquerque, 1945.

BOLTON, HERBERT EUGENE, with Morse H. Stephens, *The Pacific Ocean in History,* New York, 1917.

CARROLL, H. B., and J. V. HAGGARD, *Three New Mexico Chronicles,* Albuquerque, 1942.

CEJADOR Y FRAUCA, JULIO, *Historia de la Lengua y Literatura Castellana,* T. III, Madrid, 1930.

CH. AND STATE. — SCHOLES, FRANCE V., *Church and State in New Mexico, 1610-1650,* Santa Fe, 1937.

CRESPO, DON BENITO, *Memorial Ajustado que de Orden del Consejo Supremo de Indias se ha Hecho del Pleyto Que Siguio . . . Don Benito Crespo, Obispo que fue de Durango, etc.,* Mexico, 1738.

CRUSADERS. — ESPINOSA, J. MANUEL, *Crusaders of the Rio Grande,* Chicago, 1942.

DOC. HIST. DE MEX. — *Documentos para la historia de Mexico,* Tercia Seria, T. IV, Mexico, 1856.

DOC. INED. — *Coleccion de documentos ineditos relativos al descubrimiento, conquista y organizacion de las antiguas posesiones espanolas de America y Oceania,* T. XVI, Madrid, 1864-1884.

FIRST EXPEDITION. — ESPINOSA, J. MANUEL, *First Expedition of Vargas Into New Mexico, 1692,* Albuquerque, 1940.

HEWETT, EDGAR L., and REGINALD G. FISHER, *Mission Monuments of New Mexico,* Albuquerque, 1943.

HODGE, F. W., and THEODORE H. LEWIS, *Spanish Explorations in the Southern United States,* New York, 1907.

KUBLER, GEORGE, *The Rebuilding of San Miguel at Santa Fe, 1710,* Colorado Springs, 1937.

LEADING FACTS. — TWITCHELL, RALPH E., *Leading Facts of New Mexican History,* Vol. II, Cedar Rapids, 1912.

LUMMIS, CHARLES F., *A New Mexico David,* New York, 1905. — *Mesa, Canyon, and Pueblo,* New York, 1938.

OCARANZA, FERNANDO, *Establecimientos Franciscanos en el Misterioso Reino del Nuevo Mexico,* Mexico, 1934.

OLC. — CHAVEZ, FRAY ANGELICO, *Our Lady of the Conquest,* Santa Fe, 1948.

OLD SANTA FE. — TWITCHELL, RALPH E., *Old Santa Fe,* Santa Fe, 1925.

ONATE. — HAMMOND, GEORGE P., *Don Juan de Onate and the Founding of New Mexico,* Santa Fe, 1927.

READ, BENJAMIN M., *Illustrated History of New Mexico,* Santa Fe, 1912; *Historia Ilustrada de Nuevo Mexico,* Santa Fe, 1911.

REVOLT, I AND II. — HACKETT, CHARLES WILSON, *Revolt of the Pueblo Indians of New Mexico and Otermin's Attempted Reconquest, 1680-1682,* Vols. I and II, Albuquerque, 1942.

SANTAREN, EULOGIO MONTERO, *Monografia Historico-Descriptiva de la Ciudad de Llerena,* Badajoz, 1900 (?).

TROUBL. TIMES. — SCHOLES, FRANCE V., *Troublous Times in New Mexico, 1659-1670,* Santa Fe, 1942.

TAMARON, DON PEDRO DE, *Visita de Durango, 1760,* Bancroft Library, Mexican MSS., No. 162.

THOMAS, ALFRED B., *Forgotten Frontiers,* Norman, 1932.

VETANCURT, FRAY AGUSTIN DE, *Menologio Franciscano de los Varones mas senalados,* Mexico, 1697.

VILLAGRA, GASPAR PEREZ DE, *History of New Mexico,* Alcala, 1610, translated by Gilberto Espinosa, Los Angeles, 1933.

III. PERIODICALS

Art and Archaeology, Archaeological Institute of America, Washington, D. C.

Colorado Magazine, HENRY FOLMER, "The Mallet Expedition of 1739 through Nebraska, Kansas, and Colorado to Santa Fe," Vol. XVI, No. 5.

El Palacio, FRAY ANGELICO CHAVEZ: "The Archibeque Story," Vol. 54, No. 8; "El Vicario Don Santiago Roybal," Vol. 55, No. 8; "Don Fernando Durán de Chavez," Vol. 55, No. 4; "Journey's End for a Pilgrim Lady," Vol. 56, No. 4; "DeVargas' Negro Drummer," Vol. 56, No. 5; "La Conquistadora is a Paisana," Vol. 57, No. 10; "San José de Chama and its Author," Vol. 60, No. 4.

Ferias y Fiestas de Llerena, 1947. Annual Fair Program, Llerena, Badajoz.

New Mexico Folklore Record, FRAY ANGELICO CHAVEZ, "The Mad Poet of Santa Cruz," Vol. III.

New Mexico Historical Review, "*Noticias* que da Juan Candelaria, etc.," Vol. IV, No. 3. — LANSING, B. BLOOM edits Twitchell article, "A Campaign Against the Moqui Pueblos," Vol. VI, No. 2; "The Vargas Encomienda," Vol. XIV, No. 4; "Amado Chaves," Vol. VI, No. 1. — HERBERT E. BOLTON, "Escalante in Dixie and the Arizona Strip," Vol. III, No. 1. — FRAY ANGELICO CHAVEZ, annotations and genealogical chart to "Ramon Ortiz: Priest and Patriot," Vol. XXV, No. 4; "Some Original New Mexico Documents in California Libraries," Vol. XXV, No. 3. — HENRI FOLMER, "Contraband Trade Between Louisiana and New Mexico in the Eighteenth Century," Vol. XVI, No. 3.

New Mexico Quarterly, FRAY ANGELICO CHAVEZ, "A Romeo and Juliet Story in Early New Mexico," Vol. XX, No. 4.

Old Santa Fe, RALPH E. TWITCHELL, "The Pueblo Revolt of 1696," Vol. III, No. 12.

Revista Catolica, originally published at Las Vegas, N. M., now at El Paso, Texas. News items, Vols. III-XXXI.